Eastern Caribbean

Glenda Bendure
Ned Friary

Eastern Caribbean

2nd edition

Published by
Lonely Planet Publications
Head Office: PO Box 617, Hawthorn, Vic 3122, Australia
Branches: 150 Linden St, Oakland, CA 94607, USA
              10a Spring Place, London NW5 3BH, UK
              1 rue du Dahomey, 75011 Paris, France

Printed by
The Bookmaker International Ltd
Printed in China

Photographs by

Glenda Bendure	Kevin Schafer
Ned Friary	Tony Wheeler

Front cover: Richard Elliott, Tony Stone Images

First Published
1994

This Edition
September 1998

Although the authors and publisher have tried to make the information as accurate as possible, they accept no responsibility for any loss, injury or inconvenience sustained by any person using this book.

National Library of Australia Cataloguing in Publication Data

Bendure, Glenda.
    Eastern Caribbean.

    2nd ed.
    Includes index.
    ISBN 0 86442 422 1.

    1. Antilles, Lesser – Guidebooks. 2. Caribbean Area –
    Description and travel. I. Friary, Ned. II. Title.

    917.2904

Glenda Bendure & Ned Friary

Glenda grew up in California's Mojave Desert and first traveled overseas as a high school AFS exchange student to India.

Ned grew up near Boston, studied social thought and political economy at the University of Massachusetts in Amherst and upon graduating headed west.

They met in Santa Cruz, California, where Glenda was completing her university studies. In 1978, with Lonely Planet's first book, *Across Asia on the Cheap*, in hand, they took the overland trail across southern Europe, through Iran and Afghanistan, and on to trains in India and treks in Nepal. The next six years were spent exploring Asia and the Pacific, with a home base in Japan, where Ned taught English and Glenda edited a monthly magazine.

They now live on Cape Cod in Massachusetts – at least when they're not on the road.

Ned and Glenda have a particular fondness for islands and tropical climates. In addition to this *Eastern Caribbean* guide, they are also the authors of Lonely Planet's guidebooks to Hawaii, Micronesia, Bermuda and Denmark, and they write the Norway and Denmark chapters of Lonely Planet's *Scandinavian & Baltic Europe on a shoestring*.

From the Authors

A hearty thanks to the various island tourist offices and their representatives in the USA, especially those of Barbados, Grenada, St Lucia and the Netherlands Antilles. Thanks also to the many friends and travelers who shared insights and experiences with us along the way.

A special thanks to Elizabeth Subin, executive director of the Anguilla National Trust; Michelle Henry, director of the Museum of Antigua & Barbuda; Gillian Cooper of the Environmental Awareness Group in Antigua; Québec journalist Andrée-Paule Mignot; and Grenadian Peace Corps director Gwen Pelletier.

From the Publisher

Working with Lonely Planet's US office, Valerie Haynes Perry edited this 2nd edition of *Eastern Caribbean*. Jacqueline Volin escorted the book through production, with help from Kate Hoffman. Rini Keagy, Deborah Rodgers, Cyndy Johnsen, Patrick

Huerta, Margaret Livingston and Hayden Foell drew the maps, with guidance from Alex Guilbert. Rini designed the book, with a hand from Scott Summers. Hayden designed the cover and he, Rini, Tamsin Wilson and Lisa Summers created the illustrations.

Thanks
Thanks also to those travelers who wrote in with information: Tina Abbey, Juliet Allan & Mark Boon, Neal Ashcroft, MA Beevers, James Bell, Larry & Annette Bell, Pierre-Yves & Sarianna Benain, Susann Elmquist Bentsen, Ruth Ann & Gerry Bieker, Steve Brookwell, Andrew DR Brown, William Brymer, Ernest Carwithen & Elsa Coudon, Jean Chapple, Todd Clark, Maurice Conroy, Gabrielle Dijon, Matthias Dürbeck, Thomas Dyvik, Josef Ebener, Wolfram Engelhardt, Alexander Etterich, Tara Farley, Jesse Ferris, Ray Frank, Magnus Fredrikson, Barb Garii, Suzanne Gondouin, Peter Granquist, Alenka Grealish, Mary Hancock, Al Herbert, Rich Holmes, Art Horrox, C & A Hutchinson, Susanne Kästle, June Knack, Pia Hesse Kovstrup, Marion Dale Lage, Kurt Lehmann, Harriet Lewis, Raj Lucas, Karen Mancey-Barratt, Harry Manzinger, Wolfgang Mayr, Denise & Malcolm McDonough, Fiona Meadley, Jens Meincke, Glen Menzies, Lynn Miller, Anne Miller, David S Miller & Barbara A Kelly, John C Nason, Ian Nicholson, Mariko Obokata, Jan-Åke Olsson, Darcy Perkins, GB Poppelwell, Julianne Power, David Reeder & Joni Kyle, John Reesky, John Reid, Sarah Reid, Jo Robinson, Su Roper, Susanne Runde, Johnnie H Russell, Udo J Sabock, Susie Sailly, Volker Sauer, Günther Schäfer, Andi Scheef, Paul Simonite, Rilke Slatt, Barry Smiler, Jay Stewart, Jan Stieber, Jonna Toft, Karen Vaughan, Wendy A Walsh, Janine Watson, Paul & Sarah Westcar, Keith Worby, Rolf Wrelf, Chandi Wyant, Robert Youker, Mary Young, Natalie Zacek

Warning & Request
Things change – prices go up, schedules change, good places go bad and bad places go bankrupt – nothing stays the same. So, if you find things better or worse, recently opened or long since closed, please tell us and help make the next edition even more accurate and useful.

We value all of the feedback we receive from travelers. A small team reads and acknowledges every letter, postcard and email, and ensures that every morsel of information finds its way to the appropriate authors, editors and publishers. All readers who write to us will find their names in the next edition of the appropriate guide and will also receive a free subscription to our quarterly newsletter, *Planet Talk*. The very best contributions will be rewarded with a free Lonely Planet guide.

Excerpts from your correspondence may appear in new editions of this guide, in *Planet Talk* or in the Postcards section of our website – so please let us know if you don't want your letter published or your name acknowledged.

Contents

Map Legend

BOUNDARIES

— · — · — · — · — International Boundary

— · · — · · — · · — Provincial Boundary

AREA FEATURES

Park

NATIONAL PARK — National Park

National Forest, Watershed Area

HYDROGRAPHIC FEATURES

Water
Reef
Coastline
Beach
Swamp
River, Waterfall
Mangrove, Spring

ROUTES

Freeway

Primary Road

Secondary Road

Tertiary Road

Dirt Road

Trail

Ferry Route

Railway, Train Station

SYMBOLS

✪ **NATIONAL CAPITAL**	✈ Airfield	🅿 Gas Station	)(Pass
◉ **Administrative Center**	✈ Airport	⌂ Golf Course	⋒ Picnic Area
● **City**	∴ Archaeological Site, Ruins	⊙ Hospital, Clinic	★ Police Station
● City, Small	⑤ Bank, ATM	❶ Information	▭ Pool
● Town	⌂ Baseball Stadium	🛆 Lighthouse	▭ Post Office
	🏖 Beach	☀ Lookout	☒ Shipwreck
○ Point of Interest	⊥ Buddhist Temple	🛒 Mine	❖ Shopping Mall
	◕ Bus Station, Bus Stop	▮ Monument	♭ Snorkeling
■ Hotel, B&B	⊟ Cathedral	▲ Mountain	🏛 Stately Home
⛺ Campground	⌒ Cave	⌂ Museum	⚓ Surfing
⛺ RV Park	✝ Church	✔ Music, Live	☎ Telephone
⌂ Shelter, Refugio	☒ Dive Site	⌂ Observatory	▣ Tomb, Mausoleum
▾ Restaurant	◑ Embassy, Consulate	← One-Way Street	🚶 Trailhead
▮ Bar (Place to Drink)	⨾ Foot Bridge	▲ Park	⚘ Winery
☕ Cafe	❖ Garden	🅿 Parking	🐘 Zoo

Note: Not all symbols displayed above appear in this book.

Introduction

Collectively, the islands of the Eastern Caribbean fit all of the tropical images: they have powdery white sands, clear turquoise waters, lush jungle rainforests, balmy weather and an unhurried pace.

Taken individually, however, the islands vary widely. Some places are picture-perfect coral islands, nearly flat and fringed with palm-lined beaches, while other islands are high and mountainous with a terrain dominated by waterfalls and steaming volcanoes.

Culturally, the islands are a hybrid – largely of African, English and French heritage but with a notable measure of Dutch and East Indian influences as well. Politically, the islands make up eight independent nations, two British colonies, two French *départements* and an affiliated state of the Netherlands.

From Anguilla in the north to Trinidad in the south, these islands make a 600-mile-long sweep that forms the eastern boundary of the Caribbean. Although it's certainly possible – with an open schedule and a fair bit of time – to island hop from one end of the Eastern Caribbean to the other, most visitors opt for a smaller slice.

Certainly if you're looking for specific activities or ambiance, you'll need to select destinations accordingly. In Martinique, you can have croissants and espresso at a sidewalk café and shop for French fashions in trendy boutiques. In Trinidad don't expect to find croissants – the bakeries sell Indian curry rotis and English meat pies – and instead of boutiques you can pass an afternoon visiting back-street *mas camps* (workshops), where artisans design and sell elaborate Carnival costumes.

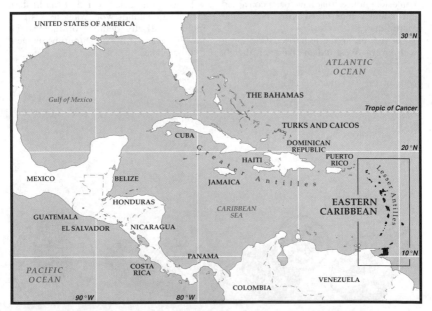

Divers can find a good variety of underwater attractions off most islands, including lesser known spots such as Saba, Dominica and Tobago, which offer pristine dive sites with abundant marine life.

Many of the islands have splendid beaches, but particularly notable as beach destinations are St Martin, Anguilla, St Barts, Antigua, Barbados and some of the smaller Grenadine islands.

For hikers, Dominica and Guadeloupe are special places with extensive tracks leading to unspoiled rainforests, steamy craters and towering waterfalls. If you're a birder, Trinidad and Tobago offer the greatest variety of bird life in the Caribbean, and both have small rainforest retreats catering to naturalists.

For colonial history buffs, there are notable fort ruins at Brimstone Hill on St Kitts, Pigeon Island on St Lucia and Fort Shirley and Nelson's Dockyard on Antigua. To absorb even more colonial character, you can stay in former soldiers' quarters at Nelson's Dockyard or in old sugar plantation estate houses that have been converted into country inns on St Kitts, Nevis and Martinique.

For a look at the unhurried Caribbean with a rural West Indian character, there's Scottish-influenced Carriacou, the Dutch island of St Eustatius and the sleepy French island of Marie-Galante. On Saba you can easily imagine yourself to be in an Alpine village, while St Barts has much the feel of a Mediterranean isle. Other off-the-beaten-path charmers include Tobago, Bequia and Terre-de-Haut.

If you don't want to budget much money for traveling around, but want to see a number of islands, a few destinations can become a multi-island combination without much effort or cost. From Guadeloupe, high-speed ferries run day trippers to the nearby islands of Terre-de-Haut, Marie-Galante and La Désirade, and from both St Vincent and Grenada there are mail boats to the nearby Grenadine islands. From St Martin, there are frequent boats to Anguilla and St Barts, and it's but a 15-minute flight to Saba or St Eustatius.

Part of the charm of the Eastern Caribbean lies in its diversity and the opportunity to experience a variety of cultures and environments in a single trip. This book will help you decide which of the Eastern Caribbean islands you want to visit. It includes all the details for inter-island travel – whether it's by ship, private yacht or prop plane.

Facts about the Eastern Caribbean

HISTORY

The Caribbean islands were originally inhabited by Amerindians who migrated from the American mainland.

For the most part, early European explorers were intent on ridding the islands of their native inhabitants and in the end enslaved, killed or exiled the majority of Amerindians in the Caribbean.

The Europeans recorded precious little about these societies and the native islanders had no written languages of their own. Much of what is now known about their cultures comes from archaeological explorations; the discovery of stone tools, shellwork, pottery shards and petroglyphs is the main means for piecing together the history of the pre-Columbian period.

Not all islands in the Eastern Caribbean were populated by the same peoples at the same time. Archaeological research is still ongoing in the region; dates of migration are debated and occasionally revised by new discoveries.

Ciboneys

The first people to arrive in the Eastern Caribbean were wandering Stone Age hunters and gatherers from the Archaic (pre-pottery) Period. Usually called Ciboneys, or Siboneys, they may have been present on some islands as early as 4000 BC. Their existence is mainly known through carbon dating of midden piles, crude stone axes and scraping tools.

Arawaks

The Arawak Period in the Eastern Caribbean is generally thought to have begun about 2000 years ago, near the beginning of the Christian era.

The Arawaks were not a single tribe, but rather a group of South American tribes that all spoke the Arawak language and shared cultural similarities. They were a gentle, peaceful people who fished, hunted and farmed. They grew tobacco, cotton, corn, sweet potatoes and pineapples. Their main crop was cassava, also called manioc or yuca, from whose tuberous roots comes cassareep, a bitter juice used as a preservative, and tapioca, a nutritious starch the Arawaks used to make cassava bread, their main food staple.

The Arawaks were very artistic. Women made pottery of red clay that was often engraved, painted with white designs or decorated with figurines called *adornos*.

The society was well organized. Villages consisted of a grouping of round dwellings, each of which housed several families. Like the native people of the American mainland, the Arawaks had bronze-colored skin and long black hair. They wore little or no clothing.

In the religion of the Arawaks, Yocahu, or Jocahu, was the God of Creation, also known as 'The Giver of Cassava.' The Arawaks carved anthropomorphic objects of stone or shell, called *zemis*, which they kept near places of worship.

It is believed that there were no Arawaks remaining in the Eastern Caribbean at the end of the 15th century when Europeans appeared on the scene.

There were, however, Arawak-speaking people living in the northern Caribbean in regions the Caribs had not yet conquered. One tribe of Arawaks, the Taino, were the people who Columbus first encountered and documented. It is from the Taino that much of the early knowledge of the Arawak culture was obtained.

Caribs

Sometime around 1200 AD the Caribs, a group of warring tribes from South America, invaded the Eastern Caribbean and migrated in a northerly direction through the islands. They drove off or killed all of the Arawak men, reputedly eating the flesh of some of their victims (the word 'cannibal' is derived from 'caribal' or 'Carib'). Some of the Arawak women were spared to be slaves for Carib men and for a while these women kept some remnants of the Arawak culture alive.

The Caribs did not farm much, but instead obtained most of their food from hunting and gathering. They were not as sophisticated or artistic as the Arawaks and their pottery was of an inferior quality. They were, however, ferocious defenders of their land and on many islands managed to keep the Europeans at bay for more than a century.

Christopher Columbus

The first European to explore the Caribbean was Christopher Columbus, who reached the islands in 1492 while looking for a westward route to Asia. Over the course of a decade, Columbus made four voyages to the New World, opening the region to exploitation and colonization. In his first voyage, which took him to the Caribbean's northerly islands, he left a party of soldiers on Hispaniola, establishing Spain's first settlement in the Americas.

On September 25, 1493, just six months after returning to Portugal from his initial voyage, Columbus set sail with a flotilla of 17 ships. He took a more southerly course this time, hoping to find new territory on his way back to Hispaniola. It was during this second voyage that he 'discovered' most of the islands of the Eastern Caribbean. The first island was sighted on November 3, 1493, a Sunday, and was thus christened Dominica. From Dominica, he sailed north, landing at Marie-Galante, an island he named after his ship, the 'gallant' *Santa Maria*. He next touched land on Guadeloupe's Basse-Terre and then sailed northwest up the chain, sighting and naming the islands of Montserrat, Antigua, Redonda, Nevis, St Kitts, St Eustatius and Saba, before heading to the Virgin Islands and points west.

On Columbus' third voyage, in 1498, he sailed farther south still, making his first landfall at Trinidad. From there he sailed west along the coast of Venezuela and sighted Tobago and Grenada before he headed north once again to Hispaniola.

Despite the significance of his journeys, Columbus never fully realized that what he had discovered was indeed a new world and not islands off the coast of east Asia. It is as a consequence of his geographic disorientation that the native peoples of the Americas are still known as 'Indians.'

Colonialism

The Spanish explorers, in pursuit of gold, concentrated their attention on the larger islands of the northern Caribbean and on the American mainland, paying scant notice to the smaller islands that comprise the Eastern Caribbean. They did, however, settle on Trinidad, conveniently just off the coast of mineral-rich Venezuela.

A flurry of colonial activity was set off in 1623, when the English became the first Europeans to establish a permanent settlement in the Eastern Caribbean (with the exception of Trinidad), founding a colony on the island of St Kitts. In 1625 Captain John Powell landed a party of settlers on Barbados, and other British colonies were soon established on Nevis, Antigua and Montserrat. In the 1630s the French settled

Christopher Columbus

Martinique and Guadeloupe and the Dutch settled Saba, St Eustatius and St Martin.

The Dutch, French and English all laid claims and counter-claims throughout the Eastern Caribbean. In some instances, such as on St Martin and St Kitts, different colonial powers established settlements on opposite sides of the same island. Sometimes the European powers coexisted peacefully, especially when jointly battling the native Caribs, but more often than not they were involved in a tug-of-war, each of them trying to gain control of the other's colonies. Over the next two centuries most islands of the Eastern Caribbean changed hands so many times that they developed societies with an almost hybrid culture, most commonly a British-French mix.

Sugar Cane Plantations

The Dutch were largely concerned with establishing military and trade stations on the islands that they held. The French and British, on the other hand, saw the primary value of their Caribbean possessions in terms of agricultural production and quickly went about clearing the forests and planting crops. The original fields were largely in tobacco, cotton and indigo, but by the mid-1600s sugar had proven itself the most profitable crop and larger islands like Barbados and Martinique were heavily planted in sugar cane.

Unlike tobacco, which was cultivated in small plots, sugar production was large-scale and labor-intensive. Sugar cane must be crushed almost immediately after cutting or it will spoil, and as the mills that crushed the cane were expensive to build and operate, the plantations needed to be large enough to justify the expense.

To meet the increased demand for labor the planters began to import great numbers of slaves from Africa. By the end of the 17th century the islands had a firmly established plantation society comprised of a minority of free whites and a majority of black slaves. (See the sidebar on the following page.)

On the British islands many of the plantations were owned by absentee planters, who returned to England leaving the plantation operation in the hands of managers. The absentee owners were among the wealthiest members of British society and had a powerful influence in enacting protectionist legislation that guaranteed British markets for their sugar. There were similar parallels in the French West Indies.

By the early 1800s, sugar's heyday had passed. Merchants who were tired of the interruption of supplies during the military skirmishes between the British and the French began to replace Caribbean cane with European-grown beet sugar. As the market for Caribbean sugar waned, so too did the influence of the planters. At the same time the abolitionist movement was gaining momentum.

In 1807 British legislation abolished the slave trade, although planters were allowed to keep the slaves they already had until 1833. On the French islands emancipation was enacted in 1848.

Even after its decline, sugar cane continued to be grown on most islands and played a formative role in the shaping of island society. As blacks left the plantations, indentured servants, mostly from India, were brought in to replace them. Sizable East Indian minorities were established on Trinidad, Martinique and Guadeloupe, and their culture has become an integral part of these islands' identity.

The 20th Century

During the world depression of the 1930s most of the Caribbean was torn by high unemployment, labor unrest and civil strife. On many islands a concerted labor movement developed with demands for both economic and political independence. The British responded by enacting the first meaningful measures of internal self-government, the French by incorporating the islands more thoroughly with mainland France and the Dutch by allowing heightened domestic rule under association with the Netherlands.

The British Islands In the post-WWII period Britain moved to divest itself of its

...very in the Caribbean

...e Atlantic slave trade stands as one of the most abhorrent social injustices in history, ...ith a scale so overwhelming that it virtually depopulated vast tracts of western Africa. From the slave trade origins, starting with Portuguese and Spanish colonists in the 1500s, to the final outlawing of New World slavery on Cuba in 1886, an estimated 10 million enslaved African people were brought to the Americas. In addition, countless millions died in the process of being captured or during the long trans-Atlantic crossing.

The Caribbean islands accounted for more than a third of all slave importations – nearly four million people in all. The British and French West Indies each imported an estimated 1.6 million enslaved blacks, while the Dutch-held islands accounted for about 500,000. In contrast, the USA imported an estimated 400,000 slaves.

Snatched from their homelands, these captive people were brought to the New World for one reason only – to provide a cheap labor source – and they were treated as property by those who purchased them.

So much money was involved in the trafficking of captive African people that nations laid claim to the slave trade itself. The Treaty of Utrecht, signed in 1713, for example, gave England the sole right to provide slaves to the Spanish colonies. When the Spanish tried to rescind the treaty in 1739, England declared war on Spain to defend its dominance in the West Indies slave trade.

For the British it was a lucrative triangular route. Ships set sail from English ports with trinkets and muskets to barter for slaves in Africa. Once the slaves were delivered to the New World, the ships were loaded with sugar, molasses and rum for the journey back to England.

Slavery was a brutally inhumane institution. West Africans, who were captured from their villages in sweeping raids by rival tribes, were marched like cattle to the coast where they were sold to European slave traders. The slaves were then crowded shoulder to shoulder into the sweltering holds of cargo ships – some perished from dehydration and suffocation, others from their first contact with Western diseases. It took about two months to complete the wretched middle passage from West Africa to the Caribbean. If at least 90% of the 'cargo' made it alive, it was considered a good crossing, although much higher mortality rates were commonplace.

Upon arrival in the Caribbean the slaves were marched to an auction block, exhibited and sold to the highest bidder. On the British and Dutch islands, families were deliberately broken up and slaves were denied any rights under the law. On the French islands, the *Code Noire*, rather feebly enacted in 1685, forbade the separation of families and gave slaves legal protection from hideous abuses like mutilation and murder, although this same code also prescribed floggings and other degrading penalties for slaves who did not obey their masters.

Despite the dehumanizing conditions of plantation society, Africans uprooted from their homelands managed to maintain elements of their native culture. On the French islands, where the slaves were readily converted to Christianity, they held onto traditional African beliefs as well, and over time merged the Christian and African religions into their own unique spiritual practices. Voodoo, for example, uses the names of both African deities and Catholic saints in its ceremonies.

Slaves were forced to learn the language of the plantation owners, but they blended their own use of it into a hybrid Creole language that was liberally spiced with African terms. To this day, islanders throughout the Eastern Caribbean still slip into Creole when chatting among themselves. Much of West Indian music takes its roots from a spirit of rebellion that prevailed during the slavery period – most prominent is calypso, a sharp, rap-like music that was developed by slaves poking fun at their unsuspecting masters. ■

Top Left: Mountain apples (Ned Friary)
Middle Left: Royal poinciana tree (Ned Friary)
Bottom Left: Hibiscus (Ned Friary)
Bottom Middle: Coconuts (Ned Friary)

Top Right: From top to bottom, cocoa, nutmeg, mace (Ned Friary)
Middle Right: Black-eyed Susan (Ned Friary)
Bottom Right: Pride of Barbados (Ned Friary)

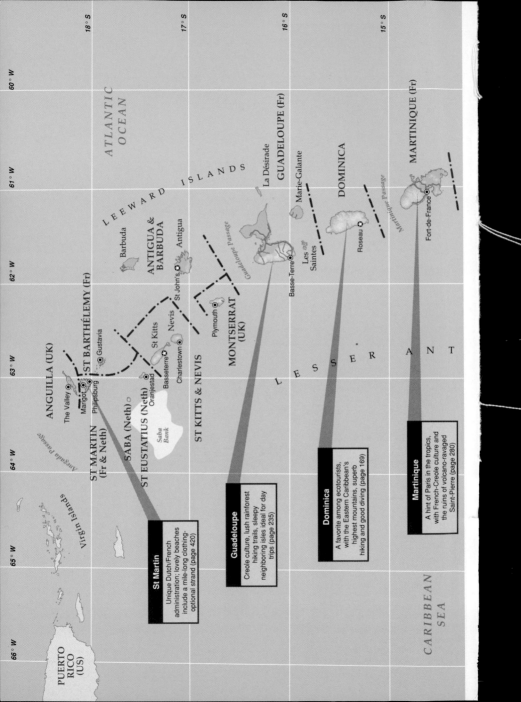

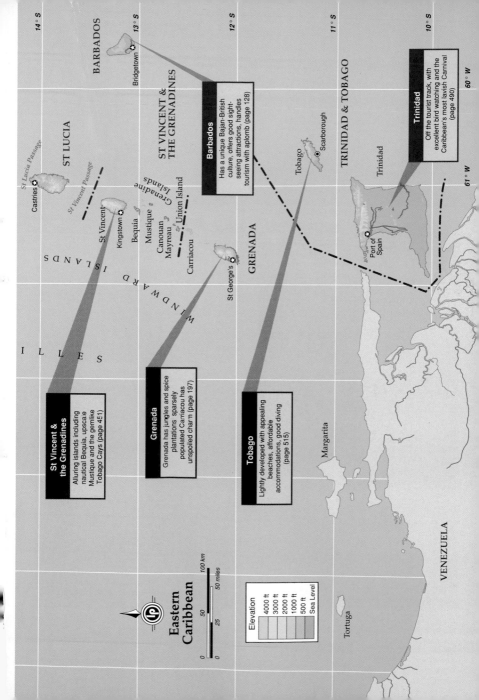

Eastern Caribbean

Elevation
4000 ft
3000 ft
2000 ft
1000 ft
500 ft
Sea Level

0 25 50 100 km
0 50 miles

St Vincent & the Grenadines
Alluring islands including nautical Bequia, upscale Mustique and the gemlike Tobago Cays (page 451)

Grenada
Grenada has jungles and spice plantations, sparsely populated Carriacou has unspoiled charm (page 197)

Tobago
Lightly developed with appealing beaches, affordable accommodations, good diving (page 515)

Barbados
Has a unique Bajan-British culture, offers good sight-seeing attractions, handles tourism with aplomb (page 128)

Trinidad
Off the tourist track, with excellent bird watching and the Caribbean's most lavish Carnival (page 490)

ANTILLES

WINDWARD ISLANDS

ST LUCIA
Castries
St Lucia Passage

St Vincent Passage

ST VINCENT & THE GRENADINES
St Vincent
Kingstown
Bequia
Mustique
Canouan
Mayreau
Union Island
Grenadine Islands
Carriacou

GRENADA
St George's

Tobago
Scarborough

TRINIDAD & TOBAGO
Trinidad
Port of Spain

BARBADOS
Bridgetown

VENEZUELA

Margarita

Tortuga

10° S
11° S
12° S
13° S
14° S

60° W
61° W

Top Left: Black-bellied whistling duck, Trinidad
(Ned Friary)
Bottom Left: Green monkey at Barbados Wildlife
Reserve (Ned Friary)

Top Right: Blue-crowned motmot, Tobago
(Ned Friary)
Bottom Right: Scarlet ibis, Caroni Bird Sanctuary,
Trinidad (Ned Friary)

Caribbean colonies by attempting to create a single federated state that would incorporate all of the British-held Caribbean. One advantage of the federation was that it was expected to provide a mechanism for decolonizing smaller islands that the British felt would otherwise be too small to stand as separate entities.

After a decade of negotiation, Britain convinced its Caribbean colonies – the British Windward and Leeward islands, Jamaica, Barbados and Trinidad – to join together as the West Indies Federation. The new association came into effect in 1958, with the intent that the federation work out the intricacies of self-government during a four-year probationary period before the islands emerged as a single new independent nation in 1962.

Although the West Indies Federation represented dozens of islands scattered across some 2000 miles of ocean, the British established Trinidad, at the southernmost end of the chain, to be the governing 'center' of the federation.

For centuries the islanders had related to each other via their British administrators and the political and economic intercourse between the islands had been quite limited. In the end, the lack of a united identity amongst the islands, coupled with each island's desire for autonomy, proved much stronger than any perceived advantage in union.

Jamaica was the first to develop a rift with the new association and opted to leave the federation in 1961. Trinidad itself soon followed suit. Both islands felt they were large enough, and rich enough in resources, to stand on their own. They were also wary of getting stuck in a position where they would have to subsidize the federation's smaller islands, which had a history of being heavily dependant upon British aid. Thus in 1962, Jamaica and Trinidad became independent nations. The concept of a smaller federation limped along for a few more years, but after Barbados broke rank and became an independent nation in 1966, the British were forced to go back to the drawing board.

The remaining islands continued to splinter. Dominica and St Lucia gained independence as single-island nations. Antigua, St Vincent, Grenada and St Kitts were each linked with smaller neighboring islands to form new nations.

Anguilla, which was linked with St Kitts and Nevis, rebelled three months after the new state's inauguration in 1967 and negotiated with the British to be reinstated as a Crown Colony. Montserrat also refused to be dispensed with so readily by the British and was allowed to continue as a Crown Colony.

During the same period, Barbuda made a bid to secede from its union with Antigua, but with barely 1000 inhabitants its independence movement failed.

The islands linked to both St Vincent and Grenada also initially grumbled, but have managed to work out their differences well enough to maintain their unions.

In the federation of St Kitts & Nevis, which already forms the smallest nation in the Western Hemisphere, a secessionist movement is currently brewing on Nevis.

The French Islands In the French West Indies the policy has been one of assimilation rather than independence. Since 1946 Guadeloupe (whose administration includes St Barts and the French side of St Martin) and Martinique have been separate, if somewhat hesitant, departments of France, with representation in the Senate and National Assembly in Paris.

Separatist sentiments have long existed in the French islands, particularly on Guadeloupe, although the reliance upon economic aid from France has tempered the movement in recent years. Still, many islanders think it's but a matter of time before the islands achieve some measure of greater internal autonomy.

The Dutch Islands The Dutch, like the British, also hoped to create a single federation of all their Caribbean possessions – Curaçao, Aruba, Bonaire, St Martin, St Eustatius and Saba – collectively known as the Netherlands Antilles. In 1954 a charter

	Main Languages Spoken	Official Currency	Population	Sq Miles	People per Sq Mile
ANGUILLA	English	Eastern Caribbean Dollar	9000	60	150
ANTIGUA & BARBUDA	English	Eastern Caribbean Dollar	66,200	108	613
BARBADOS	English	Barbados Dollar	265,000	166	1596
DOMINICA	English	Eastern Caribbean Dollar	71,000	290	243
GRENADA	English	Eastern Caribbean Dollar	97,600	133	734
GUADELOUPE	French	French Franc	367,600	629	584
MARTINIQUE	French	French Franc	400,000	417	959
MONTSERRAT	English	Eastern Caribbean Dollar	4000	41	98
SABA	English/ Dutch	Netherlands Antilles Guilder	1200	5	240
ST BARTS	French	French Franc	5000	8	625
ST EUSTATIUS	English/ Dutch	Netherlands Antilles Guilder	2100	8	263
ST KITTS & NEVIS	English	Eastern Caribbean Dollar	45,000	68	662
ST LUCIA	English	Eastern Caribbean Dollar	150,000	238	631
ST MARTIN	English/ Dutch	Netherlands Antilles Guilder/ French Franc	77,000	34	2265
ST VINCENT & THE GRENADINES	English	Eastern Caribbean Dollar	112,000	150	747
TRINIDAD & TOBAGO	English	Trinidad & Tobago Dollar	1,265,000	1980	639

Political Status	Geography	Highlights
UK Dependency	Relatively flat dry, sandy	Beautiful beaches; popular with wealthy travelers
Independent	Both islands are largely dry and scrubby	Antigua has a wealth of colonial ruins; Barbuda has the largest frigatebird colony in the Caribbean
Independent	Low hills in the interior, white-sand beaches along the coast	A leading tourist destination with good-value accommodations, British flavor, plantation-era homes
Independent	Ruggedly mountainous with rainforests and waterfalls	An ecotourist destination with good hiking and diving and the Eastern Caribbean's highest mountains
Independent	High mountainous islands with deeply indented coastlines	Renowned for its nutmeg and other spices; a scenic capital town and harbor and relaxed outer islands
Overseas Department of France	Two main adjoining islands and several offshore islands; largely mountainous	Creole culture, expansive national park, the region's highest waterfalls, an active volcano
Overseas Department of France	Mountainous interior topped by 4524-foot Mount Pelée	A cosmopolitan capital, predominantly French ambiance; ruins of Saint-Pierre, destroyed by Pelée's 1902 eruption
UK Dependency	Central mountains, with a volcano that's been erupting since 1995	A once delightful rural island that's been depopulated by volcanic eruptions
Part of the Netherlands Antilles	Small but disproportionately high and mountainous	Quaint alpine-like character, good hiking and diving
Part of Guadaloupe	Hilly terrain with deeply indented bays	Fashionable destination with nice white-sand beaches and a distinctly French flavor
Part of the Netherlands Antilles	Largely dry island dominated by an extinct crater	Peaceful one-town island with an intriguing history and colonial-period buildings
Independent	Both islands are high with central volcanic peaks	Both islands are rural and quiet and offer accommodations in plantation-era homes
Independent	Mountainous rainforested interior, bubbling sulphur springs	Scenic landscapes, niches for budget travelers and resort vacationers
North side is part of Guadeloupe; south side is part of Netherlands Antilles	Hilly interior; shoreline dotted with bays, coves and salt ponds	Lovely beaches; unique dual-nation status; duty-free shopping; good, reasonably priced French food
Independent	St Vincent is mountainous; the Grenadines are a mix of hilly islands and sandy cays	A multi-island nation; the scenic Grenadines are a haven for yachters and offer good sailing, diving and snorkeling
Independent	Both islands have mountain ranges, rainforests and lowlands	Both islands have abundant bird life; low-keyed Tobago has nice beaches and affordable prices; Trinidad has the Caribbean's top Carnival

was enacted that made these six islands an autonomous part of the Netherlands, with its central administration in the southerly island of Curaçao. Under the charter, island affairs were largely administered by elected officials, although the Dutch continued to hold the purse strings and maintained other controls. The islands were expected to develop the mechanisms for self rule and move gradually, as a unit, towards full independence from the Netherlands.

The islands, however, have not looked favorably towards the concept of union as a single nation. In the late 1970s Aruba moved to secede from the federation and in 1986 became a single island state. The remaining five islands have also grown weary of the concept of independence as a single federation; St Martin politics have centered as much upon independence from its union with Curaçao as independence from the Netherlands.

GEOGRAPHY & GEOLOGY

Geographically, the islands in this book make up the easternmost slice of the Caribbean, or West Indies. Included are all of the Leeward Islands (from Anguilla to Dominica) and the Windward Islands (from Martinique to Grenada) plus Barbados, Trinidad and Tobago. All the islands except Trinidad and Tobago are part of the Lesser Antilles.

Geologically, most of the Eastern Caribbean is part of a double arc of islands running north to south. The islands on the inner arc, which extends from Saba to Grenada, are volcanic in origin. While most of the volcanic activity has long ceased, there are still steaming craters, bubbling hot water springs and pungent sulphur vents on some of the higher islands, and during the past century there have been major eruptions from Mt Pelée (1902) in Martinique and the Soufrière volcano (1979) in St Vincent.

In 1995 the Soufrière Hills volcano on Montserrat awoke from a 400-year sleep and blasted through its dome, beginning an ongoing eruption that has buried the capital of the island and left much of Montserrat uninhabited.

The outer arc of islands, which extend from Anguilla to Barbados, are not volcanic, but rather are of marine origin, comprised of uplifted coral limestone built upon a base of rock.

Trinidad and Tobago are geologically unique, having broken off from the South American continent. Trinidad's southern plains were created by deposits from Venezuela's Orinoco River and its Northern Range is an extension of the Andes.

CLIMATE

The entire Eastern Caribbean lies in the tropics. Consequently, the islands have near-equable temperatures year round and only slight seasonable variations in the number of hours of daylight. Although it's hot and humid most of the time, tradewinds blowing from the northeast temper the humidity; they are prevalent most of the year, but are strongest from January to April.

The rainiest time of the year is generally May through November. On low-lying islands rainfall is relatively light. On the high, mountainous islands the precipitation varies greatly with location: rainfall is much heavier on the windward (northeast) sides of the islands and in the interiors, and lighter on the leeward sides.

ECOLOGY & ENVIRONMENT

When Columbus first set eyes on the islands of the Eastern Caribbean they were thickly covered with forest. European colonizers, however, quickly set about uprooting the trees, replacing them with crops such as indigo, coffee and sugar.

While the early colonists concentrated on the more arable lowland areas, a second wave of deforestation has occurred in the past century. Once modern advances in shipping made bananas a viable export crop, the interior rainforest began to be carved away to make room for banana plantations.

Some islands, such as St Martin and Antigua, have only token tracts of woodlands remaining, while other islands, like Guadeloupe, Martinique and Dominica,

Hurricanes

The hurricane season in the Caribbean, like that of the eastern USA, is from June to November, with most activity occurring in August and September. Hurricanes can also appear outside the official season but are much less frequent then. While the annual average is only about five hurricanes per year, their frequency can vary greatly from year to year.

Even more important is the intensity. 'Big Ones' – hurricanes that wallop head-on with winds of more than 125 mph – have torn into a number of Eastern Caribbean islands in past decades. The most recent was Hurricane Luis in September 1995, which smashed Antigua and St Martin with enough force to cause an estimated US$1.5 billion in damages.

Hurricanes are defined as storms that originate in the tropics and have winds in excess of 74 mph. Those that hit the Caribbean form off the coast of Africa and whip in an westerly direction across the Atlantic. The winds of these hurricanes revolve in a counterclockwise direction around a center of lower barometric pressure, picking up energy from warm waters and moisture as they approach the Caribbean. When wind speeds are under 40 mph it's called a tropical depression, and when winds are between 40 and 74 mph it's a tropical storm.

If you are caught by an approaching hurricane stay calm and follow local warnings. Hotels are typically of concrete and steel construction capable of withstanding strong winds with minimal damage. However, in low-lying areas ocean swells can also pose a hazard – if you have an oceanfront room it's a wise precaution to relocate to a unit farther inland. Most hurricane injuries are the result of flying debris, so don't be tempted to venture outside in the midst of a storm. ■

have set aside sizable portions of the interior rainforest as national reserves.

For many island governments it's a constant struggle between trying to preserve what remains and resisting influences from overseas developers. On St Lucia, for example, an exclusive resort was recently built smack between the Pitons, the two coastal mountains that have long stood as the very symbol of that island's unspoiled natural character. The development crushed a move by islanders to have the land set aside as a new national park. At the same time, however, three sizable inland tracts of rainforest were set aside as forest reserves, thus giving those areas protection from encroaching development and creeping banana plantations.

In many ways the St Lucia situation represents the potential positive and negative effects of tourism. Upscale resort projects often vie for some of the more environmentally sensitive niches and in the process debase the 'unspoiled nature' that they are attempting to market. On the other hand, the rise in ecotourism and the recognition that nature reserves attract hikers, bird watchers and other visitors sensitive to the environment, has helped contribute to preservation efforts. Indeed some places, such as Dominica and Saba, primarily target ecotourists, emphasizing hiking and diving in newly set aside forest and marine preserves.

Travelers can make a positive contribution by exhibiting a healthy respect for the environment, treading lightly and supporting environmentally friendly businesses. When hiking, stick to established paths. When shopping, avoid buying products containing coral, bird feathers or turtle shells. Give thought to the impact businesses have on the native environment and culture and do what you can to help local communities benefit from the money you spend. Consider staying in locally managed hotels and guesthouses, hiring hiking guides from nearby villages, buying island-made handicrafts and patronizing family-owned restaurants.

For more on ecotourism, see the Organized Tours section in the Getting There & Away chapter.

Lost Species

Dramatic changes to the ecology of the Eastern Caribbean occurred with the arrival of European settlers, who introduced exotic creatures to the islands, some by accident, others by design. Rats, nesting in crevices in the holds of ships, sailed to the islands with the first colonists. Plantation managers, irritated by the damage the rats caused to their sugar crops, introduced the Burmese mongoose in an attempt to control the rats. But the mongooses, which do their hunting during the day, turned out to be ill suited for the task of preying on the nocturnal rats. Instead, they developed an appetite for lizards, eggs and the chicks of native ground-nesting birds.

Having evolved with limited competition and few native predators, the islands' indigenous species have generally fared poorly against more aggressive introduced fauna. Uncounted species have become extinct since the colonial era. Parrots, for example, which were once common to rainforests throughout the Eastern Caribbean, now survive on only five islands and

---

Environmental Groups

Although the environmental movement is not as active in the Eastern Caribbean as the need warrants, there are some noteworthy efforts being made.

Environment Tobago This is a grassroots organization led by ornithologist David Rooks. It is dedicated to protecting wetlands and other environmentally sensitive coastal areas on the island of Tobago. For information: Environment Tobago, PO Box 403, Scarborough, Tobago, Trinidad & Tobago.

Environmental Awareness Group EAG has its roots in Antigua's Historical and Archaeological Society and has grown into a broad-based organization that's challenging a government plan to build a massive resort development on Antigua's ecologically sensitive northeast islands. For information on their struggles: EAG, Long & Market Sts, PO Box 103, St John's, Antigua; eag@candw.ag.

RARE Center for Tropical Conservation RARE works to preserve threatened habitats and ecosystems throughout the tropics. In the Eastern Caribbean, they've been active in protecting the endangered St Lucia parrot. For information: RARE Center for Tropical Conservation, 1616 Walnut St, Suite 911, Philadelphia, PA 19103 USA.

Wider Caribbean Sea Turtle Conservation Network WIDECAST is at the forefront of protecting endangered sea turtles. Efforts include supporting environmental legislation, implementing education programs and sponsoring watches on beaches where turtles nest. For information: WIDECAST, 17218 Libertad Drive, San Diego, CA 92127 USA.

World Wildlife Fund WWF sponsors programs throughout the Caribbean as diverse as aiding in the development of the Saba Marine Park to funding brochures that educate people about the illegal trade in wildlife products. For information: World Wildlife Fund, 1250 24th St NW, Washington DC 20037 USA.

all of the remaining species are endangered, some with populations of just a few hundred birds.

The foraging animals introduced by colonists, particularly goats, which continue to roam freely on many islands, have had a similarly devastating effect on native flora. Their grazing has undermined fragile native ecosystems and spelled extinction for many island plants. Erosion, deforestation and competition from thousands of introduced plants have taken a tremendous toll. In all, an estimated half of the native flora on the islands of the Eastern Caribbean has become extinct or endangered.

Fortunately, conservation efforts ranging from recent attempts at controlling the goat populations in the Grenadines to concentrated efforts to bring the remaining Eastern Caribbean parrots back from the brink of extinction are showing promise.

FLORA & FAUNA

The flora and fauna of the Eastern Caribbean varies with each island's topography and rainfall.

The low islands tend to support a largely scrub vegetation and are pocketed with salt ponds that provide habitat for shorebirds and seabirds. The mountainous islands have far more diverse ecosystems that include lush interior rainforests of tall trees, ferns, climbing vines and a variety of colorful forest birds.

Additionally, location is a major determining factor in the types and variations of native flora and fauna. As a general rule, the more isolated an island is from its nearest neighbor and the farther it is from a continental land mass, the more restrictive its plant and animal life.

On isolated Barbados, for instance, indigenous mammals are largely limited to a handful of bat species, while on Trinidad, which lies just a couple of miles off the coast of Venezuela, there are a hundred types of mammals replicating those found on the nearby South American mainland.

Correspondingly, Trinidad and Tobago have the greatest diversity of bird life amongst the Eastern Caribbean islands.

More than 400 species of birds are found on these two islands, which is greater than the total found on all the other Eastern Caribbean islands combined. Among the many varieties of colorful birds nesting on Trinidad and Tobago are scarlet ibises, blue-crowned motmots, chestnut woodpeckers, palm tanagers, channel-billed toucans and white-bearded manakins.

For comparison, only 28 bird species nest on Barbados and they tend to be more common birds such as doves, blackbirds, cattle egrets, herons and finches.

Plant life also reaches its greatest diversity on Trinidad and Tobago, which provide a habitat for more than 700 orchid species and 1600 other types of flowering plants. As you continue north up the Eastern Caribbean chain, and away from the South American continent, the diversity of plants markedly decreases.

More information on flora and fauna can be found under the individual island chapters.

Plants

Because the Eastern Caribbean's climate ranges from dry desert conditions to lush tropical rainforests, you'll find it embraces a wide variety of vegetation. There are wetlands with mangrove swamps; dry scrubland areas with Turk's-head and prickly pear cacti; and rainforests with bamboo groves and thick-trunked gommier (gum) trees.

Some trees are common to coastal areas throughout the Eastern Caribbean. The ubiquitous coconut palm thrives in coral sands and produces about 75 coconuts a year. Another easily identifiable coastal tree is the pandanus, or screw pine, which has spiny leaves, fruit that resembles pineapples and a trunk that's anchored with multiple prop roots. The sea grape, which grows in sand, is also distinctive with fruit that hangs in grape-like bunches and round green leaves.

Three of the most common flowering trees found throughout the region are: the umbrella-shaped flamboyant, or poinciana tree, which has gorgeous scarlet blossoms from late May through the summer; the frangipani, or plumeria, which boasts fragrant waxy pink or white flowers in winter and spring; and the African tulip tree, which has large orange blossoms that flower year-round but are most abundant in spring.

A common coastal plant is the beach morning glory, which has pink flowers and is found on the sand just above the wrack line. The flower of the beach morning glory blooms for only a day, as do the colorful blossoms of thousands of varieties of hibiscus that are planted in gardens throughout the Eastern Caribbean.

Other bright tropical Caribbean flowers include blood-red anthuriums, brilliant orange birds of paradise, colorful bougainvilleas, red ginger, torch ginger and various heliconias with bright orange and red bracts. There are also hundreds of varieties of orchids.

On dry islands where goats are a particular problem, oleander bushes, which have pink or white flowers, are often the main vegetation, as their leaves are toxic to foraging animals.

Birds

The Eastern Caribbean hosts a variety of both resident and migrant birds. Although the diversity of bird life varies greatly between islands some species are spotted throughout the Eastern Caribbean. These include the brown pelican, which can readily be seen feeding along the shoreline from St Kitts to Tobago; the magnificent frigatebird, an aerial pirate that nests on a limited number of islands but hunts throughout the chain; the cattle egret, a stark white bird common in open fields; and the bananaquit, a friendly little yellow-bellied nectar feeder that's nicknamed the 'sugar bird.' Other widely dispersed birds include the brown booby, spotted sandpiper, royal tern, Zenaida dove, Antillean crested hummingbird, tropical mockingbird and Lesser Antillean bullfinch.

Native parrots make their home in the mountainous rainforests of Dominica, St Lucia, St Vincent, Trinidad and Tobago.

In terms of bird watching, Trinidad & Tobago is the Caribbean's premier site, offering splendid birding that includes huge flocks of roosting scarlet ibises, bands of squawking parrots and hundreds of other colorful tropical birds. The country has a number of bird sanctuaries, including the Asa Wright Centre, a frequent destination of Audubon Society tours.

Mammals

With the exception of Trinidad, the variety of mammals in the Eastern Caribbean is quite limited and consists predominantly of introduced species. The main native mammals found on the more remote islands are bat species.

Early Amerindian settlers are thought to have introduced agoutis, small rabbitlike rodents, and opossums, which are known in the Caribbean as manicous. Europeans introduced half a dozen species of rats; the ferretlike mongoose, which on many islands is now the most commonly sighted nondomesticated animal; and the green monkey, which was brought from Africa in the 17th century. The monkeys occupy remote areas on the islands of Barbados, Grenada, St Kitts and Nevis; they tend to be shy, but sightings of them, particularly on St Kitts' southwest peninsula, are not uncommon.

Marine mammals found in the waters of the Eastern Caribbean include numerous species of whales and dolphins. Most plentiful amongst the whales are pilot whales, which grow to 23 feet, travel in large pods and have an overall black appearance; because of their color and the fact that they are still hunted for meat they are called 'black fish' by islanders.

Also relatively common are sperm whales. This species can grow as long as 69 feet, has a head that comprises nearly one-third of its body and feeds on squid. Less frequent but spotted seasonally are humpback whales, which reach lengths of 45 feet, have distinctive long white flippers and are renowned for enthralling whale watchers with their arching dives, lobtailing and breaching.

Among the dolphins are spinner dolphins, a slender-beaked, slim and grayish dolphin that grows to seven feet, swims in large herds and is seen year round, and bottlenosed dolphins, which reach 12 feet, have dark gray backs and a reputation for coming within touching distance of divers.

Amphibians & Reptiles

A variety of frogs and toads exist in the Eastern Caribbean. Visitors are likely to take notice of one of the smallest of them, the tree frog, which is common throughout the region and creates a symphony that can be almost deafening at night. At the other end of the scale is the crapaud, a large forest frog that is found in Dominica and Montserrat; it's also called the mountain chicken for the taste of its legs, considered a delicacy.

Lizards, such as the Jamaican anole, which puffs out a showy orange throat sac as a territorial warning to encroachers, are common throughout the islands. In all, there are more than two dozen species of lizards, from the common gecko that hangs around the windows of houses snatching pesky mosquitoes to colorful ground lizards that are specific to just one island. The iguana, a large arboreal lizard with stout legs, is indigenous to the Caribbean but is now prevalent on only a handful of islands. Despite the fierce-looking crest of spines that runs from its neck to tail, the iguana has a strictly herbivorous diet.

There are several snakes in the islands. Most, like the Barbadian grass snake *Liophis perfuscus* and the St Lucian kouwes snake, have a limited range and are harmless. Boa constrictors, found on Trinidad and St Lucia, are nonvenomous and pose little threat to people. The fer de lance snake, however, which is found in brushy areas on St Lucia, Martinique and Trinidad, is a highly venomous snake whose bite can be fatal. (For information on snake bites see the Health section in the Facts for the Visitor chapter.)

Sea Turtles Sea turtles are large air-breathing reptiles that inhabit tropical seas but must come ashore to lay eggs. Found in the Caribbean are hawksbill turtles, loggerhead turtles, green turtles, and mighty leatherbacks that can weigh up to a half-ton. All are endangered. Depending on the species, sea turtles take 15 to 50 years to reach their reproductive age. The females dig a shallow pit and lay their eggs in sand just above the high tide line; they nest only once every two to four years, laying about 100 Ping-Pong-ball-size eggs. The hatchlings emerge from their nests, usually at night, about 60 days later.

Predators such as birds take a heavy toll on the hatchlings, but the greatest threat to sea turtles comes from human beings. Shoreline development disturbs their nesting sites; artificial lights lure inland the hatchlings that would otherwise make a beeline to the sea; and improperly discarded trash, such as floating plastic bags that are confused for jellyfish and swallowed, present life-threatening hazards. Despite international bans prohibiting the trade of sea turtles, they are widely hunted in the Caribbean. Jewelry made from the glossy hawksbill shell is still found in markets and turtle meat is sold on a number of islands.

GOVERNMENT & POLITICS

Most of those Eastern Caribbean islands that were formerly administered by the British are now independent democracies with a parliamentarian form of government and a Commonwealth affiliation. Two of the islands, Montserrat and Anguilla, continue by their own request as British colonies.

The French islands have been incorporated into the French fold as overseas departments of France, with a status on par with that of the 96 departments that comprise mainland France.

Saba, St Eustatius and the Dutch side of St Martin are part of the Netherlands Antilles, a union that also includes the southern Caribbean islands of Curaçao and Bonaire. The Netherlands Antilles is a parliamentary democracy that's linked to the Netherlands and administered by a governor who is appointed by the Queen.

For more information see the end of the earlier History section as well as individual island chapters.

ECONOMY

The economies of many Eastern Caribbean islands are still heavily dependent upon the West, either for direct financial assistance or to provide favorable markets for island products.

On many islands agriculture remains the most important sector of the economy. Much of the arable land on some islands, such as Barbados and St Kitts, is still planted in sugar cane, while bananas are the major export crop on high, rainy islands like Dominica, St Vincent and St Lucia.

Because of historic European ties to the Caribbean, the European Union (EU) has maintained a trade policy favoring the import of Caribbean-grown bananas over cheaper Central American ones. That situation is now in jeopardy. Although the USA is not a banana exporter, in 1997 the Clinton administration filed suit with the World Trade Organization (WTO) to force the EU to abandon trade policies that give the edge to Caribbean bananas. The WTO's preliminary ruling was in agreement with the US' position.

While this news was given scant attention in the US press, the European media blasted it as a payoff to the agribusiness giant Chiquita Brands, a dominant player in the Central American banana trade and a major donor to US political campaigns. Although it's still under appeal, the WTO ruling poses a potentially heavy blow to the economies of the Caribbean's banana-producing islands. Much of the banana production in the Eastern Caribbean is on a family-farm scale, so the impact would be widespread.

In part because of depressed world markets for the Caribbean's agricultural products, tourism has become an increasingly important industry for most of the islands.

Trinidad, the most resource-rich island in the Eastern Caribbean, has oil, asphalt and other petroleum-based industries. Elsewhere in the region, with the exception of rum distilleries and a few small garment and electronics-assembly factories, there's very little industry. What industry exists doesn't pay well. For example, the prevailing wage on St Lucia for an electronics assembler or a sewing machine operator is about US$1 an hour. In the French Caribbean wages are significantly higher but the per-capita GNP is only about half of what prevails on the French mainland, and unemployment hovers around 25%.

Most trade is with the USA and Europe. In part due to their lengthy colonial history, the Eastern Caribbean islands do not trade extensively among themselves and customs barriers between islands have thus far frustrated the development of strong regional markets. Although they are outside of the North Atlantic Free Trade Agreement (NAFTA), the Caribbean nations have been, without success, petitioning for the same duty-free commercial relationship with the United States that Mexico and Canada have under the NAFTA provision.

POPULATION & PEOPLE

The population of the Eastern Caribbean is nearly three million, of which Trinidad accounts for more than a third.

Population densities vary greatly. One of the world's most densely populated countries is Barbados, which has 265,000 people and a population density of 238 people per sq mile. Some of the smaller islands, including St Barts, Saba and St Eustatius, have fewer than 5000 people.

With some islands, like Grenada, there are more native islanders living abroad than at home. Most overseas West Indians live in the UK, USA or France.

With the Eastern Caribbean taken as a whole, the vast majority of islanders are of African ancestry. This varies between islands, however. There are also sizable numbers of people of European and East Indian ancestry, as well as many of mixed ethnicities and smaller numbers from the Middle East, Asia and the Americas.

Although the native Caribs were almost completely wiped out by early colonists, about 3000 Caribs still live on the east side of Dominica and there are smaller Carib populations on St Vincent and Trinidad.

EDUCATION

All the islands of the Eastern Caribbean have compulsory education for children, though the number of years varies. Most educational systems are modeled on either the French, British or Dutch systems.

The University of the West Indies, the largest university in the English Caribbean, has campuses in Trinidad and Barbados. On the French islands, the Université des Antilles-Guyane has campuses in Guadeloupe and Martinique.

Barbados has a literacy rate of 99%, the same as Australia and the USA. Literacy rates on other islands range from about 78% in St Lucia to 96% in Trinidad & Tobago.

ARTS
Literature

The Eastern Caribbean has produced a number of notable literary figures. The most widely acclaimed contemporary writer is St Lucia-born poet and playwright Derek Walcott, who won the 1992 Nobel Prize in Literature after publishing his epic poem, *Omeros* (1990), which explores themes of exile and spiritual travel.

Another widely recognized regional author is VS Naipaul of Trinidad, who projects a sense of the Caribbean's multi-ethnic culture through the eyes of individuals struggling to make sense of their existence. His classic work, *A House for Mr Biswas* (1961), creates a vivid portrait of life as an East Indian in Trinidad.

Similar sensibilities surface in *The Castle of My Skin* (1954) by acclaimed Barbadian author George Lamming, who presents a vivid image of coming to age as a black in colonial Barbados.

Dominica's most celebrated author, Jean Rhys, was born in Roseau in 1890. Although she moved to England at age 16, much of her work draws upon her childhood experiences in the West Indies. Rhys touched upon her life in Dominica in *Voyage in the Dark* (1934) and in her autobiography *Smile Please* (1979). Her most

famous work, *Wide Sargasso Sea*, a novel set in Jamaica, was made into a film in 1993.

Jamaica Kincaid, another widely read Caribbean author, has penned numerous novels and essays including *A Small Place* (1988), which gives a scathing account of the negative effects of tourism on Antigua. Other internationally recognized works include her novel *Annie John* (1983), which recounts growing up in Antigua, and *At the Bottom of the River* (1985), a collection of short stories.

The leading contemporary novelist in the French West Indies is Guadeloupe native Maryse Condé. Two of her best-selling novels have been translated into English. The epic *Tree of Life* (1992), centers around the life of a Guadeloupean family, their roots and the identity of Guadeloupean society itself. Condé's latest novel, *Crossing the Mangrove* (1995), is an enjoyable tale that reveals nuances of rural Guadeloupean relationships as it unravels the life, and untimely death, of a controversial villager.

The most renowned poet of the French West Indies was Guadeloupe's Saint-John

Derek Walcott

Perse, who won the Nobel Prize for Literature in 1960 for the evocative imagery of his poetry. One of his classic works, *Anabase* (1925), was translated into English by TS Eliot.

Martinique has produced two notable contemporary poets, Aimé Césaire and Édouard Glissant, both of whom write about the struggles of blacks seeking their cultural identity under the burden of colonial influences. Césaire, a poet and political figure, was a force behind the Black Pride movement known as *négritude* that emerged as a philosophical and literary movement in the 1930s. His works have been translated into English under the title *The Collected Poetry of Aimé Césaire* (1983). Édouard Glissant's *Le Quatrième Siècle* (1962) and *Malemort* (1975) examine contemporary West Indian life against the backdrop of slavery.

Visual Arts

The most celebrated artist to have worked in the Eastern Caribbean was Paul Gauguin, who lived on Martinique for five months in 1887.

While the modern-day Eastern Caribbean has not produced world-renowned artists, numerous native artists and expatriates paint, draw and sculpt, displaying and selling their works in island gift shops and galleries. Most Caribbean art draws upon the island environment for influence – watercolors of rainforest scenes, tropical flowers and schoolchildren are common themes.

Also ubiquitous are the distinctive folk-art paintings made in Haiti and sold throughout the Eastern Caribbean; among the items are carved and brightly painted images of tropical fish and crowded buses.

Niches of the Eastern Caribbean have their own specialized crafts. On the island of Bequia in St Vincent, boat building, both full-scale and models, has long been an island art form. Although the hand-hewn lumber vessels that were once built along the Bequian shore have fallen victim to competition from steel-hulled boats, Bequia's shipbuilding heritage lives on through local artisans who now make a

living building wooden scale models of traditional schooners and Bequian whaling boats. The model boats are crafted to exact proportions, painted in traditional colors and outfitted with sails and rigging. Popular with collectors, the finest can cost several thousand dollars.

On the island of Saba the craft most closely identified with island life is Spanish work, or Saba lace, a drawn threadwork first introduced from South America in the 19th century. The lace-like embroidery work is high quality, but unlike the Bequian ship models, the market for the lace is so limited that the craft is a dying art practiced only by an aging group of craftswomen.

The Carib Indians of Dominica still maintain their traditional crafts including the making of dugout canoes and the weaving of quality baskets, for which they use native fibers and traditional Carib designs. The baskets are made for both domestic use and for sale to visitors. In adapting to new markets the weavers also use traditional fibers to make woven placemats, hats and pocketbooks.

Architecture

West Indian architecture is a blending of European tradition and tropical design. When European settlers moved to the islands they tended to build cities in grid patterns, with houses in orderly rows. Many in-town buildings are substantial two-story structures of stone and wood. Houses are often painted in bright colors such as turquoise, lime, pink and yellow. Peaked corrugated iron roofs that turn a rusty red add a distinctive element, as does frilly architecture such as gingerbread trim, veranda latticework and wooden shutters.

Music

The Caribbean has a rich musical heritage. Most of the music has its roots in African folk music and drumming, with some Spanish, French and English/Irish influences as well.

In the Eastern Caribbean, reggae and calypso are the two types of music heard most often, their catchy, singable tunes blasted in minibuses and emanating from restaurants and beachside bars. Those visiting Trinidad in the months leading up to Carnival should be sure to visit Port of Spain's panyards and calypso tents where steel pan bands practice their music in preparation for the Caribbean's grandest festival.

Calypso Calypso originated in Trinidad in the 18th century as satirical songs sung in French patois by slaves working on the plantations. Many of the songs mirrored their discontent and mocked their colonial masters, while in other songs the singers would try to top each other in a battle of verbal insults. The lyrics of early calypso songs were usually ad-libbed.

Contemporary calypso is nearly always sung in English and composed, choreographed and rehearsed in advance. Most popular are songs of biting social commentary, political satire or sexual innuendoes, usually laden with double entendres and local nuances. In most cases the melodies and rhythms of calypso are well established and it is mainly the lyrics that change from song to song.

Calypso and Carnival were linked almost from the beginning. Calypso competitions continue to be a major part of Carnival festivities, with each singer trying to best the others for a prize and the title of king.

Trinidad's long-standing king of calypso is the Mighty Sparrow. Other major Trinidadian calypso artists include Cro Cro, Shadow, Pretender, Lord Kitchener, David Rudder and Winston 'Gypsy' Peters.

Relatively new crossover sounds include rapso, a combination of rap and calypso, and chutney, a blend of calypso and East Indian music. One recommendable crossover album is David Rudder's *Wrapped in Plain Brown Paper*, an interesting mix of calypso, rapso, soca and chutney tunes wrapped in social commentary.

Soca Blend soul with calypso and you've got soca, a dance music with bold rhythms, heavy on the bass sounds. Soca was created in the mid-1970s by Ras Shorty I of Trinidad. Other top soca stars include Arrow from Montserrat and SuperBlue from Trinidad.

Steel Pan The steel drum, also called pan, is a uniquely Trinidadian invention. It has its origins in the 1940s when aspiring musicians took discarded oil drums and hammered out the steel bottoms, tuning different sections to specific pitches. Steel pan drummers play together in bands, practicing in outdoor panyards and performing at Carnival during pan competitions. The distinctive, melodious sounds of the steel pan are found throughout the Caribbean, but are synonymous with Trinidad. Pan jazz, a fusion of jazz and steel pan music, has become increasingly popular.

Ska The predecessor to reggae is ska, which evolved in Jamaica in the 1950s as a blend of calypso, rhythm and blues and African-Jamaican folk music. It has pop-style lyrics, jazzy horn riffs and a shuffling tempo.

Reggae Born in Jamaica and derived from a blend of ska, blues, calypso and rock, reggae is characterized by lyrics of social protest and a danceable syncopated rhythm. Popularized by the late Bob Marley, reggae's cheerful infectious beat dominates the music scene throughout the Eastern Caribbean. While walking along the beach or catching a local bus, you're almost certain to hear someone blasting now-classic tunes such as 'No Woman, No Cry' and 'Rastaman Vibration.'

Zouk Created in the French West Indies, zouk draws on the *biguine*, an Afro-French dance music with a bolero rhythm, the swing music of Haitian *compas*, bebop-like *cadence* and other French Caribbean folk forms. It has a Carnival-like rhythm with a hot dance beat. In recent years it has taken Paris by storm and is now as popular in Europe as it is in the Caribbean. The popular Martinique zouk band Kassav has moved to Paris and has made a number of top-selling recordings including the English-language album *Shades of Black*.

SOCIETY & CONDUCT
Traditional Culture
Because the Eastern Caribbean is so diverse, there are many variations in local customs and lifestyles. The French West Indies are essentially provincial outposts of France, with French language, customs and cuisine predominating. Some of these islands, like St Barts and Terre-de-Haut (off Guadeloupe), retain a character that approximates that of rural France, while others, such as Guadeloupe and Martinique, have a more dominant French Creole culture that incorporates African and West Indian influences.

On the islands with a British past, cultural influences largely represent a mix of African and British heritage. The latter predominates in institutional ways, including the form of government, education and the legal framework of the islands. African influences remain strong in music, dance and family life.

Throughout the Caribbean, there tend to be clear divisions of labor along gender lines: most of the hundreds of vendors in the marketplace are women, most of the taxi and minibus drivers are men.

Cricket is the region's most popular sport and a number of world-class cricket players have hailed from the Eastern Caribbean. Soccer is also very popular, especially on the French islands.

Most islanders dress neatly. Women's clothing is conservative and rather old-fashioned on some islands, smartly chic on others. Many women vendors in the marketplaces wear matronly dresses and tie up their hair in kerchiefs, while women who work in offices are apt to wear high heels, frosted lipsticks and the latest fashions. Generally, the smaller and more rural the island, the more casual the dress.

Dos & Don'ts
Keep in mind that the tropical climate slows things down and most islanders take life at an easy-going pace, so don't expect things to run like clockwork. Whether you're changing money, having a meal or catching a flight at the airport – always allow more time than you would back home.

Throughout the Caribbean, neatness in dress and politeness in attitude goes a long way. As a rule, bathing suits, very short shorts and other skimpy clothing should not be worn in town or other non-beach areas – this holds true even on the French islands where topless bathing is de rigueur on the beach.

Always start with 'Good day' or 'Bonjour' before launching into a conversation or abruptly asking questions. Many people, including those in the marketplaces, do not like to be photographed; ask first, and respect the wishes of those who refuse.

RELIGION
Roman Catholicism is the dominant religion in the French islands, Protestantism on most of the English and Dutch islands.

There are also African-Christian traditions. Rastafarianism, a Jamaica-based belief system dating from the late 1920s, has followers throughout the Eastern Caribbean. It looks to Africa as the promised land to which all believers will some day return, and to Haile Selassie, the late emperor of Ethiopia, as the Messiah. The name is derived from the emperor's pre-coronation name, Prince (Ras) Tafari.

Rastafarians are drawn to Ethiopia because of its biblical significance and believe that they are the reincarnations of the Old Testament prophets, exiled from their homelands because of the transgressions of their descendants. They embrace many Black Pride issues, let their hair grow in long rope-like dreadlocks and believe that the smoking of ganja (marijuana) holds sacramental value.

Rastafarianism has played an important role in the development of Jamaican ska and reggae music, whose rhythm is influenced by the Rastafarian akete drum. In addition to cutting social commentary, many popular reggae songs have lyrics of praise to Ras Tafari.

Some islanders believe in *obeah*, which is not a religion per se but embodies a type of black magic used to cast spells on one's enemy. Similar to Haitian voodoo practices, obeah uses conjurations, sorcery and magical rituals to align supernatural forces. Despite centuries of repression by Christian forces the practice of obeah continues to some extent on most Eastern Caribbean islands, although often in secret.

Hinduism or Islam is the faith of about 30% of the population of Trinidad; these Eastern religions also have followings on other islands (such as Guadeloupe) where there are sizable minorities of East Indians.

LANGUAGE

English is the main language spoken on all the islands in the Eastern Caribbean except for the French West Indies (Guadeloupe, Martinique, St Barts and the French side of St Martin), where French is the primary language.

English speakers can travel throughout the Eastern Caribbean without major problems. The difficulty of getting around the French West Indies for those travelers who do not speak French is generally exaggerated. Although many people outside the hotel and tourism industry don't speak English, as long as you have an English-French dictionary and phrasebook, a measure of patience and a sense of humor you should be able to get by.

Dutch is spoken on Saba, St Eustatius and Dutch St Maarten (the south side of St Martin), and is the official language of gov-

---

Common Colloquialisms

Here are some popular colloquialisms heard in the Eastern Caribbean:

boy, girl – commonly used by islanders when casually addressing adults as well as children

fire a grog, fire one – drink rum

go so, swing so – used in giving directions (be sure to watch the hand movements at the same time!)

limin' (also lime, lime about) – to laze about, hang with friends and pass the time with small talk

natty – dreadlocks, also called *natty dread*

no problem – all-purpose response to any request

one time – immediately, right away

roots – communal experience, or coming from the people

study – take time to consider, think about

wine – sensuous dance movement winding the hips, essential to Carnival dancing

workin' up – dancing in general

---

ernment on those islands. However, for most practical purposes Dutch is a secondary language after English.

French Creole and patois are also common on many Eastern Caribbean islands and often are the first language spoken at home. In addition, Hindi is spoken among family members on islands with sizable East Indian populations, most notably on Trinidad.

Facts for the Visitor

PLANNING

When to Go

The busiest time for travel in the Eastern Caribbean is from mid-December to mid-April. Although this period does have drier and slightly cooler weather, the principal variable in making it the high season is the weather *elsewhere*, as the bulk of Caribbean tourists are 'snow birds' escaping colder weather in North America and Europe.

You can enjoy steeply discounted 'summer' hotel prices by visiting the islands in the low season, from mid-April to mid-December. In addition, most airfares to the Caribbean are cheaper during this period, the beaches are less crowded, tourist areas have a more relaxed pace and last-minute bookings for cars, flights and hotels are seldom a problem.

On the minus side, the tradewinds aren't as prevalent in summer, so the chance of encountering oppressively muggy weather is higher. Summer is also the hurricane season, albeit the odds of encountering a hurricane on any particular island aren't much higher than they would be along the east coast of the USA.

November and early December can be a pleasant time to visit. Many hotels have taken a late-summer break to spruce up, so their rooms are at their pre-season finest, the crowds are just beginning to show and the prices are still low.

Maps

Island tourist offices typically provide free tourist maps that will suffice for most visitor needs. Travelers who intend to explore an island thoroughly may want something more detailed.

On the former British islands, British Ordnance Survey maps are generally the best maps available. They show topography, the location of colonial ruins and the like, although they're not always up to date. On the French islands the Institut Géographique

National (IGN) maps are very detailed and they are updated frequently. Both types of maps can be bought at bookstores in the Eastern Caribbean.

In addition, Ordnance Survey and IGN maps can be obtained by mail-order from:

France
    Espace IGN, 107 rue La Boétie, 75008 Paris (☎ 01 43 98 85 00)
UK
    Ordnance Survey International, Romsey Rd, Maybush, Southampton SO9 4DH, England (☎ 0703 79 2000, fax 0703 79 2404)
    Stanfords, 12-14 Long Acre, London WC2E 9LP (☎ 0171-836-1321, fax 0171 836-0189)
USA
    Map Link, 25 E Mason St, Santa Barbara, CA 93101 (☎ 805-965-4402, 800-627-7768; fax 805-962-0884)

For information on marine charts, see the Yachting section in the Getting Around chapter.

What to Bring

Traveling light, a good policy anywhere, is easy in the tropics as heavy jackets and bulky clothing are totally unnecessary.

Ideal clothes are made of cotton (which breathes best in hot humid weather), are loose fitting and don't need to be tucked in, and can be hand washed in a sink and hung up to dry without wrinkling.

Dress in the Eastern Caribbean is casual. Sportswear, including shorts and neat T-shirts, is fine during the day in most places. For dinner at nice restaurants, a cotton dress for women and lightweight slacks for men are usually sufficient. Only a few top-end restaurants expect men to wear a tie and jacket. One long-sleeved shirt, lightweight cotton jacket or windbreaker might be useful against indoor air-conditioning and outside insects. You'll probably spend most of your time in sandals, but bring footwear with good traction if you're planning on hiking.

A flashlight is good to have on hand for the occasional power blackout and to walk in some areas at night. Bird watchers should bring along binoculars. A Swiss Army knife is always worth its weight in gold. If you plan to do a lot of snorkeling, you'll save money by bringing your own snorkeling gear. You might want to consider a passport pouch or money belt to wear around your neck or waist.

Zip-lock plastic sandwich bags in a couple of sizes are indispensable for keeping things dry. You can use them to protect your film and camera equipment, seal up airline tickets and passports, and keep wet bathing suits away from the rest of your luggage.

A one-cup immersion heater, usually available for a few dollars from hardware or department stores, and a durable lightweight cup can come in handy. Not only can you boil water and make coffee and tea in your room but you can use it to make up a quick meal if you carry a few packets of instant oatmeal, soup, noodles or the like.

Medical supplies and toiletries are available in most places, though on the smaller islands the selection may be limited. See the Health section for some suggestions on medical-related items to bring.

Those who don't speak French and are planning to visit Martinique, Guadeloupe or St Barts should take along an English-French dictionary and phrasebook.

SUGGESTED ITINERARIES

Since the Eastern Caribbean encompasses a wide variety of destinations, whatever itinerary you plan will depend on your specific interests and the time you have available.

No two people are likely to agree on which island has the best beaches, but low-lying coral islands like Anguilla can lay claim to the most dazzling sands. If your interest is in hiking, the high islands, such as Dominica, offer the greatest variety of trails and terrain.

Should you want to crash the grandest party in the Caribbean, then Trinidad's colorful Carnival is the place to go – if you prefer a more cozy experience, then many of the smaller islands, including neighboring Tobago, throw good Carnival celebrations of their own.

Someone looking at a one-week vacation may well opt to spend their time on just one island or select a destination such as Guadeloupe or St Martin, which allows easy access for day trips to nearby islands. With a couple of weeks or more, travelers can begin to do some serious island hopping. LIAT, the main inter-island air carrier, offers a tempting 21-day air pass that allows unlimited travel throughout the region, letting you select from all the major islands and a number of the smaller ones as well.

Yachters likewise have a wide variety of islands to choose from. Some of the most popular sailing is found in the Grenadines, where there are protected waters and a plethora of idyllic little isles and cays. Charter operations from Antigua to Grenada make it easy to arrange your own bareboat cruise and you can even rent the boat just one way, picking up the yacht at one end of the chain and dropping it off at the other. See the Yacht section in the Getting Around chapter for more information.

VISAS & DOCUMENTS

Bring your passport or other identifying documents required to enter all the islands you intend to visit. Passport and visa requirements vary from island to island; specific information is given in the individual island chapters.

Note that upon arrival at many islands, the immigration officer will ask how long you're staying and stamp that exact number of days in your passport or on your entry card. Give yourself plenty of leeway, so if you stay longer than originally planned you won't need to make a trip to immigration or the police station for an extension. Another question commonly asked by the immigration officer is where you will be staying; it's a good idea to have a hotel in mind, although it doesn't seem to matter where you actually end up staying.

One more thing to keep in mind as you travel throughout the region is that many islands require visitors to be in possession of either an onward or roundtrip ticket. As part of this policy, LIAT and other regional airlines often won't allow you to board a flight to an island unless you're in possession of an onward ticket out of that island.

Driver's Licenses

You'll need your home driver's license in order to rent a car. On most of the former British islands, you'll need to purchase a local license when you rent a car, but that's done simply by showing your home license and dishing out the appropriate fee. If you're going to St Lucia, having an International Driving Permit (IDP) will save you the price of a local license there, but on the other islands there's no benefit in having an IDP in addition to your home license.

Other Documents

Divers should bring their certification cards. Those who are members of a National Trust in one of the Commonwealth countries should bring their membership card to gain free or discounted entry to Barbados' National Trust sites. If you have a student or youth card, bring it along, though discounts in the Caribbean are very limited.

An International Health Certificate is required only if you're coming from a country where yellow fever is a problem.

CUSTOMS

All islands in the Eastern Caribbean allow tourists to bring in a reasonable amount of personal items duty free, as well as an allowance of liquor and tobacco. For more details, see the individual island chapters.

Spear guns are prohibited in the waters around many islands; divers interested in spear-fishing should make advance inquiries. Most non-French islands prohibit firearms; yachters who have guns on board should declare them on entry. Some islands are free of rabies and have strict rules on the importation of animals; this is mainly of interest to sailors who might not be allowed to bring their pets onto land.

MONEY
Costs

Overall, the Eastern Caribbean is a fairly expensive region and you'll need a tidy sum to explore it thoroughly. Still, costs can vary greatly depending upon which islands you visit, the type of accommodations you choose and how you travel.

Accommodations will generally be the heftiest part of a traveler's budget in the Eastern Caribbean. On islands such as Barbados, which has a good range of low and mid-priced accommodations, expenses for a conventional hotel room or apartment can be quite reasonable, whereas on pricier islands like Antigua it could easily cost twice as much for a comparable room. Of course the type of accommodations will also dictate cost – daily expenses can vary from US$25 at a cheap guesthouse to US$1000 at an exclusive resort.

Food is relatively expensive, in part because much of it is imported – prices are generally a good 50% higher than in the USA or Canada.

Transport costs vary greatly. Car rentals generally cost between US$30 and US$70 a day depending upon the island. There are public buses on the more developed islands, which provide a very cheap alternative for getting around.

For inter-island travel, there are some reasonably priced ferries, mostly in the Grenadines and around the French islands. Air travel between islands can be expensive, but there are numerous deals floating around, including airpasses with LIAT (the main regional airline) that can take you from one end of the Caribbean to the other for as little as US$249. See the Getting Around chapter for details.

There are also some little nagging costs that can add up quickly, particularly if you're island-hopping. On most of the English-speaking islands car renters are required to buy a temporary local driver's license, which ranges from US$10 to US$15; most islands have airport departure taxes, commonly from US$10 to US$15; and many add tax and service charges (up to 25%) on top of quoted hotel rates and sometimes onto restaurant bills as well.

If you're buying air tickets in the Caribbean, try to buy them on a tax-free island, such as St Martin, as many Eastern Caribbean islands add 5% to 20% sales or value-added tax (VAT) to ticket sales.

ATMs

Automatic teller machines (ATMs) can be found on major islands throughout the region. For those who want to withdraw money from a bank account back home, ATM cards from the two main networks – Cirrus and Plus – are accepted at many ATMs, including all of those operated by the Royal Bank of Canada.

Credit Cards

Major credit cards are widely, though not universally, accepted throughout the Eastern Caribbean. The most commonly accepted cards are Visa and MasterCard, followed by the American Express charge card. Note that on some islands, hotels may add a surcharge if you're using a credit card, so you might want to inquire in advance.

Currencies & Exchange Rates

There are five official island currencies in the Eastern Caribbean, which can make things a bit confusing if you're jumping back and forth between islands. Fortunately, the US dollar (US$) can also be used outright on virtually all the islands and is by far the most handy currency to carry. Indeed, many Eastern Caribbean islands quote hotel prices and car rentals in US dollars. However, for most transactions you'll be better off exchanging your money into the local currency. British sterling (UK£) and Canadian dollars (C$) can also be readily exchanged at banks but are not commonly accepted by businesses.

Eastern Caribbean Dollar The Eastern Caribbean dollar (EC$) is the official currency of Anguilla, Antigua & Barbuda, Dominica, Grenada, Montserrat, St Kitts &

Nevis, St Lucia and St Vincent & the Grenadines. One dollar is worth 100 cents. Coins are in 1, 2, 5, 10 and 25 cents and EC$1 denominations. Bank notes are in 5, 10, 20, 50 and 100 dollar denominations.

The EC$ is pegged to the US$ at a rate of US$1=EC$2.70. The exchange rate given by banks (on islands where the EC$ is the official currency) is US$1= EC$2.6882 for traveler's checks and US$1=EC$2.67 for cash. If you have left-over EC dollars, you can sell them back at the rate of EC$2.7169=US$1.

When exchanging UK£ or C$ against EC$ there's a greater variation between buying and selling rates than there is for the US$. The margin between buying and selling is about 2% for sterling and nearly 5% for Canadian dollars. Other foreign currencies are generally treated as an oddity and exchanged at below market rates or slapped with hefty surcharges.

Major currencies fluctuate against the EC$ in accordance with their value against the US$ on world markets. As we go to print, the current rate of exchange for the EC$ is:

Australia	A$1	=	1.94EC
Canada	C$1	=	1.93EC
Germany	DM1	=	1.51EC
UK	UK£1	=	4.32EC
US	US$1	=	2.70EC

French Franc The French franc (F) is the official currency of Martinique, Guadeloupe, St Barts and the French side of St Martin. One franc is worth 100 centimes. French coins come in denominations of 5, 10 and 20 centimes and 1/2, 1, 2, 5 and 10 francs. Bank notes are issued in denominations of 20, 50, 100, 200 and 500 francs.

The French franc fluctuates daily with other currencies according to world markets. As we go to print, the current rate of exchange is:

Australia	A$1	=	4.31F
Canada	C$1	=	4.30F
Germany	DM1	=	3.36F
UK	UK£1	=	9.56F
US	US$1	=	5.98F

Netherlands Antilles Guilder The Netherlands Antilles guilder or florin (commonly written NAf at banks and Fls in stores) is the official currency of Saba, St Eustatius and Dutch St Maarten.

The Netherlands Antilles guilder, which differs from the guilder used in the Netherlands, has coins in denominations of 1, 5, 10, 25 and 50 cents as well as 1 and 2½ guilders; bank notes are in 5, 10, 25, 50, 100, 250 and 500 guilders. NAf 10.50 is spoken '10 guilders 50.'

Islanders on the Dutch islands commonly carry both guilders and US dollars; businesses accept and give change in either. As there's no advantage to paying in guilders (and there's a small loss when exchanging money), most visitors simply use US dollars.

The NAf is pegged to the US dollar. The exchange rate for cash is US$1=NAf 1.77, for traveler's checks, US$1=NAf 1.79.

Other major currencies fluctuate in accordance with their value with the US dollar in world markets. As we go to print, the current rate of exchange is:

Australia	A$1	=	1.28NAf
Canada	C$1	=	1.27NAf
Germany	DM1	=	1.00NAf
UK	UK£1	=	2.83NAf
US	US$1	=	1.77NAf

Barbados Dollar The Barbados dollar (B$) is the official currency of Barbados. Details are in the Barbados chapter.

Trinidad & Tobago Dollar The Trinidad & Tobago dollar (TT$) is the official currency of that two-island nation. Details are in the Trinidad & Tobago chapter.

Tipping & Bargaining

The tipping situation varies. On some islands it's automatically added to your restaurant bill as a service charge, while on other islands you're expected to add a tip of about 10% to the bill.

Expect to do a bit of gentle bargaining in market places when purchasing produce and souvenirs, though in some situations the asking price will be the final price. When shopping in stores prices are generally fixed. However, if you doing any specialized shopping, such as for duty-free electronics on St Martin – you may be able to negotiate a better deal by letting the salesperson know you've seen the same product at a lower price in a nearby shop.

POST & COMMUNICATIONS
Post

Delivery time for airmail sent from the Eastern Caribbean varies greatly. From the French islands it generally takes about a week to European destinations and 10 days to the USA, while from some of the smaller independent nations, like St Vincent & the Grenadines, overseas mail can easily take two to three weeks from the postmark date.

Hotels and other businesses on the smaller islands often have no street address or post office box; when no address is given in this book, you can address correspondence by simply following the hotel name with the town, country and 'West Indies.'

You can receive mail by having it sent care of poste restante or general delivery to the general post office (GPO) on each island you're visiting.

Specific information on island post offices, including hours and postage rates, is given in the individual island chapters.

Telephone

Overall, the telephone systems work relatively well throughout the Eastern Caribbean. You can make both local and long distance calls from virtually all public phones. Most islands have two types of public telephones: coin phones that accept local currency and card phones for which you can use pre-paid phonecards.

Phonecards Public card phones are very popular in the Eastern Caribbean. They operate on plastic phonecards the size of a credit card, which are inserted into the phone. Each phonecard has an original value and the cost of each call is deducted automatically as you talk. You can use your phonecard for multiple calls until the initial value of the card runs out.

The card phones are convenient if you make long-distance calls or a lot of local calls, as you don't have to keep pumping in coins. However, on those few islands (mainly the French West Indies) where coin phones have been virtually eliminated, the card phone concept can be a real pain when you want to make just one quick call but are forced to find a phonecard vendor and pay for a card you won't fully utilize!

There's little advantage in buying phone-cards in the larger denominations, as the per-unit cost is virtually the same on all cards. In addition, phonecards occasionally fail before their value expires.

Calling Cards Foreign calling cards can be used in the Eastern Caribbean. Overseas visitors can make reverse charged calls through AT&T's USA Direct, MCI World Phone, Sprint's Global One and British Telecom. On most islands you can reach AT&T by dialing 1-800-872-2881, MCI by dialing 1-800-888-8000, Sprint by dialing

1-800-277-7468 or 1-800-785-5648 and British Telecom by dialing 1-800-342-5284; on the Dutch islands prefix these 800 numbers with 011 instead of the initial 1.

As an example of costs, on a call to North America, AT&T charges an initial fee of US$5 if you're calling collect or US$2.50 if you're using an AT&T calling card. The charges then range from US$1.55 to US$2 for the first minute, and US$1.35 to US$1.43 for each additional minute, depending on which island you're calling from. Rates are the same regardless of the hour or day of the week.

French Islands When calling from one French West Indies island to another, or from France to the French West Indies, it's a long-distance domestic call and you need to dial the island code (0596 for Martinique or 0590 for the other French West Indies) + the six-digit local number.

When calling to the French West Indies from other countries, dial the access code of the country you're calling from + the island code + the six-digit local number.

French phonecards, called *télécartes*, are sold in 50-unit and 120-unit measures, which cost 37F and 89F, respectively. One unit is valid for a few minutes on a local call; 7 seconds to nearby non-French Caribbean islands; 3.6 seconds to distant non-French Caribbean islands, the USA or Canada; 3 seconds to most European countries; and 2 seconds to Australia. Calls between any two French West Indies islands are substantially cheaper than calls to non-French Caribbean islands.

Dutch Islands The Netherlands Antilles islands of Saba, St Eustatius and the Dutch side of St Martin have a country code of 599. To call these islands from overseas, dial the access code of the country you're calling from + 599 + 3 for St Eustatius, 4 for Saba or 5 for Dutch St Martin + the five-digit local number.

Antelecom, the Dutch telephone company, sells Netherlands Antilles phonecards for US$9.85 (17.35 Fls) for 60 units and US$16.75 (Fls 29.60) for 120 units.

New Area Codes

Until recently, all the English-speaking islands of the Caribbean shared the same 809 area code. In 1997 each island was given its own specific area code and the old 809 code is now headed for the dust bin. If you come across any numbers on brochures that still show the 809 area code, simply replace 809 with the new code for the island you're calling and the connection should ring through fine.

The new area codes are:

264	Anguilla
268	Antigua & Barbuda
246	Barbados
767	Dominica
473	Grenada
664	Montserrat
869	St Kitts & Nevis
758	St Lucia
784	St Vincent & the Grenadines
868	Trinidad & Tobago

English Islands The English-speaking islands of Anguilla, Antigua & Barbuda, Barbados, Dominica, Grenada, Montserrat, St Kitts & Nevis, St Lucia, St Vincent & the Grenadines and Trinidad & Tobago have a similar telephone system, which on most islands is under the umbrella of the Cable & Wireless Company.

When direct dialing to these islands from North America, dial 1 + area code + the seven-digit local number. When calling these islands from outside North America, dial the access code of the country you're calling from + area code + the seven-digit local number.

Rates for long-distance calls from these islands are similar but not identical. The typical cost for one minute's phone time varies from EC$1.20 to EC$2 to nearby islands and from EC$2.50 to EC$3.75 to more far-flung Caribbean islands, while calls to the Americas average EC$5 a minute, to Europe EC$7, to the rest of the world EC$9. These rates are during the daytime period. In general, rates average about 25% cheaper in the evening from 6 pm until 6 am and all day on Sunday and public holidays.

Caribbean Phone Cards, which can be used on all these islands (as well as the British Virgin Islands, the Cayman Islands and the Turks & Caicos Islands), are sold in amounts of EC$10, EC$20 and EC$40. You can use multiple phonecards on the same phone call. Shortly before a phonecard's time runs out, a buzzer goes off; if you then push the star button, on the bottom left side, the old card comes out and you can insert a second card without losing your connection.

Fax
You can send faxes from the telephone company offices listed in the individual island chapters. In addition most hotels will provide fax service for customers, though you may want to inquire about the fee in advance as it can vary from nominal to exorbitant.

Email
Email services are still quite limited in the Eastern Caribbean but a handful of Internet cafés have recently emerged and more are likely to follow. On some islands, such as Dominica, Internet service is available at the phone company's central office, while on others, notably the Dutch islands, public libraries have recently come online.

For those traveling with a laptop, a few of the more modern hotels have separate lines for modem hookup but this is still relatively unique; if you'll need a modem hookup always inquire before booking.

BOOKS
Information on bookstores and books specific to individual islands are found in those island chapters. The following are books that relate to more than one island.

Lonely Planet
If you plan to island-hop outside the Eastern Caribbean, then Lonely Planet has two other Caribbean island guidebooks – *Jamaica* and *Cuba* – jammed full of all the nitty-gritty details you'll need to explore those destinations. If Miami is your gateway to the Caribbean and you're considering a stopover, Lonely Planet's *Miami* city guide and *Florida* guide are also invaluable resources. For those visiting the French West Indies, Lonely Planet has a handy French-language phrasebook full of useful phrases.

History & Culture
From Columbus to Castro by Eric Williams is an authoritative history book of the West Indies, written by the late prime minister of Trinidad & Tobago. It covers the period from the first European contact to the late 1960s and gives a good grasp of the dynamics of colonialism that shaped this region.

A Short History of the West Indies by JH Parry & Philip Sherlock provides a historical overview of the West Indies, from colonial times through the post-independent struggles experienced by the islands in the mid-1980s.

Seeds of Change, edited by Herman J Viola & Carolyn Margolis, is one of many books that appeared around the time of the Columbus Quincentennial. Like most of the others, it chronicles Columbus' four journeys and their impact on Caribbean history.

Wild Majesty: Encounters with Caribs from Columbus to the Present Day, edited by Peter Hulme & Neil L Whitehead, is an anthology of writings about the Carib people, from the time of the first European contact, through the colonial period when the Caribs were annihilated on many islands, and up to the present day.

Literature

Green Cane and Juicy Flotsam: Short Stories by Caribbean Women, edited by Carmen Esteves & Lizabeth Paravisini-Gebert, pulls together short works by Caribbean women writers, including stories by Maryse Condé and Jeanne Hyvrad about the French Caribbean and by Jean Rhys and Jamaica Kincaid about the English Caribbean.

The Heinemann Book of Caribbean Poetry, edited by Ian McDonald & Stewart Brown, is a collection of works by English-speaking Caribbean poets, including Derek Walcott, Olive Senior, Edward Kamau Brathwaite and others.

The Traveller's Tree by Patrick Leigh Fermor, originally published in 1950, is a classic among Caribbean travel journals. This intriguing account of Fermor's jaunt through the Lesser Antilles, Haiti, Jamaica and Cuba gives vivid descriptions of the people and places visited.

For other literary works by Eastern Caribbean authors, see Literature under the Arts section in the earlier Facts about the Region chapter.

Natural History

The Nature of the Islands by Virginia Barlow is the best overall guide to the flora and fauna of the Eastern Caribbean. This well-written book is easy to use, with descriptions of plants and animals accompanied by 40 color photos and 140 drawings.

Peterson's Field Guide to Birds of the West Indies by James Bond is a revision of *Birds of the West Indies*, the classic guide to the region's bird life. This comprehensive book has detailed descriptions of each bird, including information on habitat, voice and range, all accompanied by illustrations.

Birds of the Eastern Caribbean by Peter Evans covers birds sighted in the Eastern Caribbean islands. It has general introductory sections, species-by-species accounts and checklists. There are color photos of some birds, illustrations of others.

Lonely Planet's Pisces Books, which explore the best diving and snorkeling sites in a region, make great companions for those planning to dip into the underwater world. Two fine Pisces Books covering the Eastern Caribbean area are *St Maarten, Saba & St Eustatius* by Jerry Schnabel and Susan Swygert and *Best Caribbean Diving* by Suzanne and Stuart Cummings.

Other Pisces Books that can enrich a vacation to the Eastern Caribbean include *Snorkeling...Here's How* by Bob French, *Shooting Underwater Video* by Steve Rosenberg and John Ratteree and the detailed *Caribbean Reef Ecology* by William Alevizon.

Diving Guide to the Eastern Caribbean by Martha Gilkes provides information on the reefs, wrecks and popular diving sites of the region, with a chapter on Caribbean marine life.

Other good references for divers and snorkelers are *Peterson Field Guide to Coral Reefs* by Eugene Kaplan and *Fishes of the Caribbean* by Ian Took. Both have detailed information on marine ecosystems and individual species.

Cruising Guides

There are a number of cruising guides to the Eastern Caribbean for yachters. The most widely used are those published by Cruising Guide Publications: *Sailors Guide to the Windward Islands*, *Cruising Guide to the Leeward Islands* and *Cruising Guide to Trinidad and Tobago, Venezuela and Bonaire*, all three written by Chris Doyle. Updated every couple of years, these books are thoroughly researched and packed with information from navigational approaches and entry regulations to where to pick up provisions and marine supplies.

Another well-regarded guide is *Street's Cruising Guide to the Eastern Caribbean* by Donald M Street Jr.

Those new to sailing might want to read *Deck with a View: Vacation Sailing in the Caribbean* by Dale Ware & Dustine Davidson. It covers basic topics such as determining whether you have the personality to sail with a group, suggests sailing itineraries, details various yachting options and lists charter rental companies.

Resources

Macmillan Caribbean, a division of the Macmillan Press, publishes a range of books about the Caribbean. To order books or obtain a catalog contact Macmillan Caribbean (☎ 0256 29 242, fax 0256 20 109), Houndmills, Basingstoke, Hampshire RG21 2XS, England.

Cruising Guide Publications (☎ 813-733-5322, 800-330-9542; fax 813-734-8179), PO Box 1017, Dunedin, FL 34697 USA, sells its own cruising guides as well as numerous other books about the Caribbean, and will send out a catalog on request.

West Indies Books Unlimited (☎ 813-954-8601), PO Box 2315, Sarasota, FL 34230 USA, sells Caribbean-related fiction and nonfiction and specializes in hard-to-find and out-of-print books.

ONLINE SERVICES

A growing number of the Eastern Caribbean's hotels, businesses and tourist offices are going online. A list of the websites for places mentioned throughout this book can be found in the Internet Resources appendix at the back of the book.

Here are good starting points for surfing the net:

Lonely Planet
    This award-winning website will help with practical information wherever your travels lead you. (http://www.lonelyplanet.com)

CPSCaribNet
    This site covers numerous Caribbean islands, with information on accommodations, things to see and do, yachting and various other topics. (http://www.cpscaribnet.com)

Interknowledge
    This site also covers a wide range of Caribbean destinations. (http://www.inter-knowledge.com)

NEWSPAPERS

Most Eastern Caribbean islands have their own newspapers – some published daily, others weekly – and these are well worth reading to gain insights into the local politics and culture. Foreign newspapers, such as the *International Herald-Tribune* and *USA Today*, are usually available as well and can be found at newspaper stands, bookstores and top-end hotels.

Caribbean Week (Caribbean Communications, Lefferts Place, River Rd, St Michael, Barbados) is the most substantial weekly newspaper in the English-speaking Caribbean. It covers island news, politics, business, sports and cultural activities for the entire Caribbean region. Written in Barbados and printed in Florida, the newspaper is as widely circulated to islanders living abroad as it is to islanders within the Caribbean. Subscriptions cost US$30 for one year.

MAGAZINES

Caribbean Travel & Life (PO Box 420732, Palm Coast, FL 32142 USA) is a four-color monthly magazine covering travel in the Caribbean region. It has feature articles on specific destinations and regular columns on new resorts, food, shopping, etc.

The Caribbean Writer (UVI, RR2, PO Box 10000, Kingshill, St Croix, USVI 00850), an annual literary anthology published by the University of the Virgin Islands, includes works by writers who were either born in the Caribbean or use the Caribbean as a theme.

RADIO & TV

Most islands have their own radio stations, which is a great way to tune in to the latest calypso, reggae, soca and steel band music. Local radio stations are also a good source of regional news and occasionally offer up interesting glimpses of island life – such as the somber reading of obituaries accompanied by appropriately maudlin music.

There's some kind of TV on almost every island, often relayed by satellite or cable. Not all hotels (not even all top-end hotels) offer TVs in the rooms.

PHOTOGRAPHY & VIDEO
Film & Equipment
Print film is available on the main islands, but it's often harder to find slide film. There are same-day photo processing centers on the French islands and in heavily touristed areas on other large islands.

In terms of camera equipment, it's wise to bring everything you'll need from home. The availability of camera gear varies from island to island. Although on the larger French islands you can generally find a fair range of cameras and accessories, on most other islands camera shops are few in number and poorly stocked. In virtually all cases, expect to pay more than you would at home for both film and gear.

Photography
The high air temperatures in the tropics, coupled with high humidity, greatly accelerate the deterioration of film, so the sooner you have exposed film developed, the better the results. If you're just in the Caribbean for a week or two it's no problem to wait until you get home, but if you're traveling for a long time consider making other arrangements. One way to avoid carting film around is to bring prepaid processing mailers with you to send off along the way. We do this with our slide film and have never lost anything in the mail, although we post it from the larger islands in the expectation that the mail will be speedier.

Don't leave your camera in direct sunshine any longer than necessary. A locked car can heat up like an oven in just a few minutes, damaging the film.

Sand and water are intense reflectors and in bright light they'll often leave foreground subjects shadowy. You can try compensating by adjusting your f-stop or attaching a polarizing filter, or both, but the most effective technique is to take photos in the gentler light of early morning and late afternoon.

Video
It's best to bring everything you'll expect to need with you on the trip, as video tapes and gear can be hard to find and prices will be high.

Photographing People
It's a common courtesy to ask permission before taking photos of people. Occasionally those who have their pictures taken without permission will become quite upset and may demand money. As a general rule, children like to pose, but adults are much more reluctant to have their pictures taken. You should always respect people's wishes. One good approach in markets is to buy something from the person whose photo you wish to take.

TIME
All islands in the Eastern Caribbean are on Atlantic Time, four hours behind Greenwich Mean Time. Daylight-saving time is not observed.

Thus, when it is noon in the Eastern Caribbean (and not daylight-saving time elsewhere) the time in other parts of the world is: 11 am in Jamaica, New York and Montreal, 8 am in Los Angeles and Vancouver, 4 pm in London, 5 pm in Paris, 2 am in Sydney and 4 am in Auckland.

In summer, when North America and Europe go on daylight-saving time, it is the same time in New York and Montreal as it is in the Eastern Caribbean; Britain is five hours ahead, rather than four; France is six hours ahead, rather than five.

ELECTRICITY
The electric current varies in the Eastern Caribbean.

In the French islands the current is 220 volts, 50/60 cycles, and a rounded two-pronged plug is used, the same type as in mainland France.

In the Dutch islands the current is 110 volts, 60 cycles, and a flat two-pronged plug is used, the same type as in the USA.

The former British West Indies are a mixed lot – a few use 110 volts, but most use 220 volts.

Whatever the current, you can still bring along small appliances as long as you have an adapter. Most hotel bathrooms have a dual voltage outlet for electrical shavers and some hotels can provide adapters for other items.

WEIGHTS & MEASURES

Some Eastern Caribbean islands use the metric system, while others use the imperial system.

On islands that use the metric system, such as those of the French West Indies, distances and elevations are posted in meters and kilometers, while on the former British islands they're posted in feet and miles.

In each of the island chapters throughout this book, we use the system of measurement that is prevalent on that particular island. That makes it easier to use this book in conjunction with local road signs, directions and maps. As roads and sights on many islands are often poorly marked (or not marked at all), this will also make it possible for those exploring by car or motorcycle to follow directions given in this book using their vehicle odometer, which will read in miles on islands using the imperial system and in kilometers on islands using the metric system.

Should you need to use a conversion table, there's a handy one on the back inside cover of this book.

LAUNDRY

Some of the islands have coin laundries, others have drop-off services for nearly the same price. On a few of the smaller islands however, the only option is to send out laundry at a hotel. For convenience and to control your budget, it's a good idea to bring a little laundry soap and plan on doing some hand washing.

HEALTH

In general, the Eastern Caribbean is a fairly healthy place to visit. Still, infections, sunburn, diarrhea and intestinal parasites all warrant precautions.

If you're coming from a cold, dry climate to the heat and humidity of the Caribbean you may find yourself easily fatigued and more susceptible to minor ailments. Acclimatize yourself by slowing down your pace for the first few days.

Predeparture Preparations

Health Insurance A travel insurance policy to cover theft, loss and medical problems is a wise idea. There are a wide variety of policies and your travel agent will have recommendations. Check the fine print, as some policies exclude 'dangerous activities' such as scuba diving, motorcycling and even trekking.

Give serious consideration to a policy that covers emergency flights. Many islands in the Eastern Caribbean are not prepared to handle complicated medical problems, so for something serious a flight home may be the best option. In addition, some of the smaller islands have very limited or no medical facilities and medivac (medical evacuation) to a larger island (or Miami) is commonplace.

Medical Kit A small first-aid kit is a sensible thing to carry. A basic kit should have things like aspirin or Panadol for pain or fever; an antihistamine (such as Benadryl) for use as a decongestant, to relieve the itch from insect bites or to help prevent motion sickness; an antiseptic and antibiotic ointment for cuts and scratches; calamine lotion to ease the irritation from bites and stings; Band-Aids and bandages; scissors, tweezers, insect repellent and sun block.

Bring adequate supplies of any prescription medicine or contraceptive pills you are already taking.

Immunizations No immunizations are required to enter any of the islands in the Eastern Caribbean, with one exception:

travelers who have been in any country in the past six months where yellow fever is endemic are required to have a vaccination certificate showing immunization against yellow fever. The disease in endemic in many South American and African countries between 15° north and 15° south of the equator. All vaccinations should be recorded on an International Health Certificate, which is available from your physician or government health department.

Basic Rules

Care in what you eat and drink is the most important health rule; stomach upsets are the most likely travel health problem, but the majority of these upsets will be relatively minor. Don't become paranoid, as trying the local food is part of the experience of travel after all.

Water Water quality varies from island to island. It's safe to drink from the tap in most places, but if you don't know that for certain, always assume the worst.

In general the higher islands, which have abundant supplies of fresh water from the interior rainforests, have excellent drinking water. Some of the more developed low islands, such as St Martin, have desalination plants that provide potable, but not necessarily tasty, drinking water. The less developed low islands almost invariably get their water from rain catchment and as a rule their waters should be treated before drinking as the water can vary greatly in bacteria counts and purity.

Bottled water is available just about everywhere; coconut water, soft drinks and beer are other alternatives. Tea or coffee should also be OK, since the water should have been boiled.

Water Purification The simplest way of purifying water is to boil it thoroughly. Technically, this means boiling for 10 minutes, something that happens very rarely!

Simple filtering will not remove all dangerous organisms, so if you cannot boil water it should be treated chemically.

Everyday Health

A normal body temperature is 98.6°F or 37°C; more than 2°C higher is a 'high' fever. A normal adult pulse rate is 60 to 80 per minute (children 80 to 100, babies 100 to 140). You should know how to take a temperature and a pulse rate. As a general rule the pulse increases about 20 beats per minute for each °C rise in fever.

Respiration (breathing) rate is also an indicator of illness. Count the number of breaths per minute: between 12 and 20 is normal for adults and older children (up to 30 for younger children, 40 for babies). People with a high fever or serious respiratory illness (like pneumonia) breathe more quickly than normal. More than 40 shallow breaths a minute usually means pneumonia.

You can avoid many health problems by taking care of yourself. When the water is suspect, clean your teeth with purified water rather than straight from the tap. Avoid climatic extremes: keep out of the sun when it's hot and avoid freezing blasts from air-con vents.

Dress sensibly: you can get dangerous cuts by walking barefoot over coral. Avoid insect bites by covering bare skin when insects are around, by screening windows or beds or by using insect repellents. Seek local advice: if you're told the water is unsafe because of jellyfish or bilharzia, don't go in. In situations where there is no information, discretion is the better part of valor. ∎

Chlorine tablets will kill many but not all pathogens. Iodine is very effective in purifying water and is available in tablet form, but follow the directions carefully and remember that too much iodine can be harmful. Stores that specialize in camping gear sell both kinds of tablets.

If you can't find tablets, tincture of iodine (2%) can be used. Four drops of tincture of iodine per liter or quart of clear water is the recommended dosage; the treated water should be left to stand for 30 minutes before drinking. Iodine loses its effectiveness if exposed to air or damp so keep it in a tightly sealed container. Flavored powder will disguise the taste of treated water and is a good idea if you are traveling with children.

Food Food in the Eastern Caribbean is usually sanitarily prepared. Thoroughly cooked food is safest but not if it has been left to cool or if it has been reheated. Take great care with fish or shellfish (including that in fancy buffets) and avoid undercooked meat. If a place looks clean and well run and if the vendor also looks clean and healthy, then the food is probably safe. In general, places that are packed with travelers or locals will be fine, while empty restaurants are questionable.

Nutrition Make sure your diet is well balanced and you get enough protein. Eat plenty of fruit; there's always some fruit that's plentiful and cheap – bananas, papayas and coconuts are good common sources of vitamins.

Because the Caribbean has a hot climate, make sure you drink enough – don't rely on feeling thirsty to indicate when you should drink. Not needing to urinate or very dark yellow urine is a danger sign. Always carry a water bottle with you on long trips, or if you're doing any hiking. Excessive sweating can lead to loss of salt and therefore muscle cramping. Salt tablets are not a good idea as a preventative, but in places where salt is not used much adding salt to food can help.

Medical Care

Hospital locations and emergency numbers are given in each island chapter and certainly if you have a major ailment you shouldn't hesitate to use them. For less serious ailments, the front desk of your hotel or guesthouse can usually recommend a doctor, as can many tourist offices.

Climatic & Geographical Considerations

Sunburn Sunburn is a definite concern in the Eastern Caribbean because the islands are in the tropics where fewer of the sun's rays are blocked by the atmosphere. Don't be fooled by what appears to be a hazy overcast day, as the rays still get through. The most severe sun is between 10 am and 2 pm. Fair-skinned people can get first and second-degree burns in the hot Caribbean sun, so particularly in the first few days meter out your time in the sun carefully.

Sunscreen with an SPF (sun protection factor) of at least 15 is recommended if you're not already tanned; if you're going into the water use one that's water resistant. A hat is a good idea for added protection. You'll not only be protecting against sunburn but also against potential skin cancer and premature aging of the skin. Calamine lotion is good for mild sunburn.

Good sunglasses will help protect your eyes from potentially damaging sunlight. Makes sure they're treated to absorb ultraviolet radiation – if not, they'll actually do more harm than good by dilating your pupils and making it easier for ultraviolet light to damage the retina.

Prickly Heat Prickly heat is an itchy rash caused by excessive perspiration trapped under the skin. It usually strikes people who have just arrived in a hot climate and whose pores have not yet opened sufficiently to cope with greater sweating. Keeping cool by bathing often or resorting to air-conditioning may help until you acclimatize.

Heat Exhaustion Dehydration or salt deficiency can cause heat exhaustion. Take time to acclimatize to high temperatures and make sure you get sufficient liquids. Salt deficiency is characterized by fatigue, lethargy, headaches, giddiness and muscle cramps and in this case salt tablets may help. Vomiting or diarrhea can deplete your liquid and salt levels.

Heat Stroke This serious, sometimes fatal, condition can occur if the body's heat-regulating mechanism breaks down and the body temperature rises to dangerous levels. Long, continuous periods of exposure to high temperatures can leave you vulnerable to heat stroke. You should avoid excessive alcohol or strenuous activity when you first arrive in a hot climate.

The symptoms are feeling unwell, not sweating very much or at all and a high body temperature. Where sweating has ceased the skin becomes flushed and red. Severe, throbbing headaches and lack of coordination will also occur, and the sufferer may be confused or aggressive. Eventually the victim will become delirious or convulse. Hospitalization is essential, but meanwhile get patients out of the sun, remove their clothing, cover them with a wet sheet or towel and then fan continually.

Fungal Infections The same climate that produces lush tropical forests also promotes a prolific growth of skin fungi and bacteria. Hot weather fungal infections are most likely to occur on the scalp, between the toes (athlete's foot), in the groin (jock itch) and on the body (ringworm).

To prevent fungal infections, it's essential to keep your skin cool and allow air to circulate. Choose cotton clothing rather than artificial fibers, and sandals rather than shoes.

If you do get an infection, wash the infected area daily with a disinfectant or medicated soap and water, and rinse and dry well. Apply an antifungal powder like Tinaderm. Try to expose the infected area to air or sunlight as much as possible and wash all towels and underwear in hot water as well as changing them often.

Motion Sickness Eating lightly before and during a trip will reduce the chances of motion sickness. If you are prone to motion sickness try to find a place that minimizes disturbance – near the wing on aircraft, close to midships on boats, near the center on buses. Fresh air usually helps; reading or cigarette smoke doesn't. Commercial anti-motion-sickness preparations, which can cause drowsiness, have to be taken before the trip commences; when you're feeling sick it's too late. Ginger is a natural preventative and is available in capsule form.

Diseases of Poor Sanitation
Diarrhea A change of water, food or climate can all cause the runs; diarrhea caused by contaminated food or water is more serious. Despite all your precautions you may still have a bout of mild travelers' diarrhea but a few rushed toilet trips with no other symptoms is not indicative of a serious problem.

Dehydration is the main danger with any diarrhea, particularly for children, so fluid replenishment is the number one treatment. Weak black tea or bottled water are good choices. Coconuts, which are readily available on many islands, are not only a good source of uncontaminated water but they're also an excellent rehydration drink, full of vitamins and minerals.

With severe diarrhea a rehydrating solution is necessary to replace minerals and salts. You should stick to a bland diet as you recover.

Lomotil or Imodium can be used to bring relief from the symptoms, although they do not cure the problem. Only use these drugs if absolutely necessary – for example, if you *must* travel. For children Imodium is preferable. Do not use these drugs if the patient has a high fever or is severely dehydrated.

Dysentery This serious illness is caused by contaminated food or water and is characterized by severe diarrhea, often with blood or mucus in the stool. There are two kinds of dysentery. Bacillary dysentery is characterized by a high fever and rapid onset; headache, vomiting and stomach pains are also symptoms. It generally does not last longer than a week, but it is highly contagious.

Amoebic dysentery is often more gradual in the onset of symptoms, with cramping abdominal pain and vomiting less likely; fever may not be present. It is not a self-limiting disease: it will persist until treated and can recur and cause long-term health problems.

A stool test is necessary to diagnose which kind of dysentery you have, so you should seek medical help immediately.

Hepatitis Hepatitis A is the more common form of this disease and is spread by contaminated food or water. Protection is through the vaccine Havrix or the short-lasting antibody gammaglobulin.

The symptoms are fever, chills, headache, fatigue, feelings of weakness and aches and pains, followed by loss of appetite, nausea, vomiting, abdominal pain, dark urine, light-colored feces and jaundiced skin; the whites of the eyes may also turn yellow. In some cases there may just be a feeling of being unwell or tired, accompanied by loss of appetite, aches and pains and the jaundiced effect.

You should seek medical advice, but in general there is not much you can do apart from resting, drinking lots of fluids, eating lightly and avoiding fatty foods. People who have had hepatitis must forego alcohol for six months after the illness, as hepatitis attacks the liver and it needs that amount of time to recover.

Diseases Spread by Animals & People

Bilharzia Bilharzia, also called schistosomiasis, is endemic in Guadeloupe, Martinique and St Lucia and may occur sporadically on other islands, such as Antigua.

Bilharzia is carried in water by minute worms. The larvae infect certain varieties of freshwater snails found in rivers, streams and lakes. The worms multiply and are eventually discharged into the water surrounding the snails.

The worms attach themselves to your intestines or bladder, where they produce large numbers of eggs. The worm enters through the skin, and the first symptom may be a tingling and sometimes a light rash around the area where it entered. Weeks later, when the worm is busy producing eggs, a high fever may develop. A general feeling of being unwell may be the first symptom; once the disease is established abdominal pain and blood in the urine are other signs.

The main method of preventing the disease is to avoid swimming or bathing in freshwater where bilharzia is present. If you do get wet, dry off quickly and dry your clothes as well. Seek medical attention if you have been exposed to the disease and tell the doctor of your suspicions, as bilharzia in the early stages can be confused with malaria or typhoid.

Leptospirosis Visitors should be aware of leptospirosis, a bacterial disease found in some freshwater streams and ponds. The disease is transmitted from animals such as rats and mongoose.

Humans most often pick up the disease by swimming or wading in freshwater contaminated by animal urine. Leptospirosos enters the body through the nose, eyes, mouth or cuts in the skin. Symptoms, which resemble the flu, can occur within two to 20 days after exposure and may include fever, chills, sweating, headaches, muscle pains, vomiting and diarrhea. More severe symptoms include blood in the urine and jaundice. Symptoms may last from a few days to several weeks and in rare cases can result in death.

As a precaution, avoid swimming and wading in freshwater, especially if you have open cuts.

Dengue Fever There is no malaria in the Eastern Caribbean, but mosquito-spread dengue fever is endemic to most of the region.

There is no prophylactic available for this disease; the main preventative measure is to avoid mosquito bites. Consider using mosquito repellents on exposed areas, burning mosquito coils or using a mosquito net.

A sudden onset of fever, headaches and severe joint and muscle pains are the first signs before a rash starts on the trunk of the body and spreads to the limbs and face. After a further few days, the fever will subside and recovery will begin. Serious complications are not common.

HIV/AIDS HIV, the Human Immunodeficiency Virus, may develop into AIDS, Acquired Immune Deficiency Syndrome. Any exposure to blood, blood products or bodily fluids may put the individual at risk.

Apart from sexual abstinence, the most effective preventative is always to practice safe sex using condoms. It is impossible to detect the HIV-positive status of an otherwise healthy-looking person without a blood test.

HIV/AIDS can also be spread through infected blood transfusions or by dirty needles – vaccinations, acupuncture, tattooing and ear-piercing can potentially be as dangerous as intravenous drug use if the equipment is not clean.

Cuts, Bites & Stings

Cuts & Scratches Skin punctures can easily become infected in hot climates and may be difficult to heal. Treat any cut with an antiseptic solution. Where possible avoid bandages and Band-Aids, which can keep wounds wet. Coral cuts are notoriously slow to heal, as the coral injects a weak venom into the wound. Avoid coral cuts by wearing shoes when walking on reefs, and clean any cut thoroughly.

Snakes The poisonous fer-de-lance snake is present in Martinique, St Lucia and Trinidad. It's a very deadly snake as it has an anticoagulating agent in its venom. However, bites are not that common.

To minimize your chances of being bitten wear boots, socks and long trousers when walking through undergrowth where snakes may be present and don't put your hands into holes and crevices.

Snake bites do not cause instantaneous death and antivenins are usually available but it's important to get the victim to the hospital as quickly as possible. Keep the victim calm and still, wrap the bitten limb tightly, as you would for a sprained ankle, and then attach a splint to immobilize it. Tourniquets and sucking out the poison are now comprehensively discredited. If the snake has been killed bring it along for identification; if it's still alive, do not approach it if there is even a remote possibility of being bitten again.

Jellyfish Jellyfish make only periodic appearances in most places that they're found and local advice is the best way of avoiding contact with these sea creatures and their stinging tentacles. Stings from most jellyfish are painful. Dousing in vinegar will deactivate any stingers that have not 'fired.' Calamine lotion, antihistamines and analgesics may reduce the reaction and relieve the pain.

Women's Health

Poor diet, lowered resistance through the use of antibiotics for stomach upsets and even contraceptive pills can lead to vaginal infections when traveling in hot climates. Keeping the genital area clean and wearing skirts or loose-fitting trousers and cotton underwear will help to prevent infections.

Yeast infections, characterized by a rash, itch and discharge, can be treated with a vinegar or even lemon-juice douche or with yogurt. Nystatin suppositories are the usual medical prescription.

Trichomonas is a more serious infection; symptoms are a discharge and a burning sensation when urinating. Male sexual partners must also be treated. If a vinegar-water douche is not effective, medical attention should be sought. Metronidazole (Flagyl) is the prescribed drug.

If you're pregnant, take note that most miscarriages occur during the first three months of pregnancy, so this is the most risky time to travel. The last three months should also be spent within reasonable distance of good medical care.

Women travelers often find that their periods become irregular or even cease while they're on the road. Remember that a missed period in these circumstances does not necessarily indicate pregnancy. There are health or family planning clinics on most islands where you can seek advice and have a urine test to determine whether you are pregnant or not.

TOILETS

The concept of public toilets is not one that has widely taken root in the Eastern Caribbean, and toilet facilities are the exception rather than the rule at beaches and most other public places.

WOMEN TRAVELERS

Although the situation varies between islands, women traveling alone should take safety precautions. As a general rule, single women travelers will be more comfortable on the Dutch and French islands than on the former British islands. On some islands, such as Antigua and Grenada, men can act quite aggressive toward unaccompanied women; catcalls and very forward come-ons are not uncommon. Avoid walking alone after dark, heading off into the wilderness on your own, hitching or picking up male hitchhikers. Dress as modestly as possible and try not to get into any situations where you're isolated and vulnerable.

The *Handbook for Women Travelers* by Maggie & Gemma Ross, *The Traveling Woman* by Dean Kaye and *Travel Alone & Love It* by Sharon Wingler are three books filled with advice and handy tips for women travelers.

GAY & LESBIAN TRAVELERS

Taken as a whole, the Eastern Caribbean is not a particularly gay-friendly destination and on many of the islands an element of homophobia and macho-ism is prevalent.

Still, there are some niches for gay travelers. Saba is a gay-friendly little island, albeit there's not a lot happening. Barbados has a gay guesthouse and is more gay-tolerant than other former British islands. The French islands are reasonably tolerant as well.

The situation for gay men and lesbians is a low-profile one on all the islands and public hand-holding, kissing and other outward signs of affection are not commonplace. Discretion is advised.

The following organizations can recommend travel agents, tour companies and cruises that book gay-friendly travel:

Gay & Lesbian Travel Services Network
2300 Market St No 142, San Francisco, CA 94114 USA (☎ 415-552-5140, fax 415-552-5104, gaytvlinfo@aol.com)
International Gay & Lesbian Travel Association
4331 N Federal Hwy, Suite 304, Fort Lauderdale, FL 33308 USA (☎ 954-776-2626, fax 954-776-3303, iglta@aol.com)

Australia Gay & Lesbian Travel Association,
4 Baker St, St Kilda, Victoria 3182
(☎ 61-3-9525-4040, fax 61-3-9534-3224)

Ferrari Publications (☎ 602-863-2408, fax 602-439-3952), PO Box 37887, Phoenix, AZ 85069 USA, has several travel guides for gay men and lesbians, including *Spartacus International Gay Guide*. Another resource is *Odysseus: The International Gay Travel Planner* (☎ 516-944-5330, fax 516-944-7540), PO Box 1548, Port Washington, New York, NY 11050 USA.

DISABLED TRAVELERS

Travel in the Eastern Caribbean is not particularly easy for those with physical disabilities. Overall, there is little or no consciousness of the need for curb cuts, jetways or other easy access onto planes, wheelchair lifts on buses, or rental vehicles for the disabled.

Visitors with special needs should inquire directly to prospective hotels for information on their facilities. The larger, more modern resorts are most apt to have the greatest accessibility with elevators, wider doorways and the like.

While land travel presents obstacles, cruises are often a good handicapped-accessible travel option in the Caribbean. For more information, see the Cruises section in the following Getting There & Away chapter of this book.

Physically challenged travelers might also want to get in touch with national support organizations in their home country. These groups commonly have general information and tips on travel and are able to supply a list of travel agents specializing in tours for the disabled. Here are some resources:

Society for the Advancement of Travel for the Handicapped, 347 Fifth Ave No 610, New York, NY 10016 USA (☎ 212-447-7284, fax 212-725-8253). Publishes a quarterly magazine for US$13 annually and has various free information sheets on travel for the disabled.
Royal Association for Disability & Rehabilitation, 12 City Forum, 250 City Rd, London EC1V 8AF UK (☎ 0171-250-3222). Provides general information on overseas travel.

The Wheelchair Traveler, 23 Ball Hill Rd, Milford, NH USA 03055 (☎ 603-673-4539). Publishes a newsletter for travelers.

Access to Travel, PO Box 43, Delmar, NY 02054 USA (☎ 518-439-4146, fax 518-439-9004). A quarterly magazine geared specifically to physically challenged travelers; the cost is US$16 annually.

SENIOR TRAVELERS
The Eastern Caribbean makes a good destination for senior travelers, but the slew of 'senior discounts' that are prevalent in North America and Europe are rare in the Caribbean.

Still, some organizations in your home country may offer discounted tour packages, car rentals etc to seniors. In the USA, the nonprofit American Association of Retired Persons (AARP) is a good source for travel bargains. For information on joining this advocacy group for Americans 50 years and older, contact AARP (☎ 800-227-7737), 601 E St NW, Washington DC 20049 USA.

For information on Elderhostel study vacations, see the Organized Tours section in the Getting There & Away chapter.

TRAVEL WITH CHILDREN
The Eastern Caribbean can make a good destination for families with children. Some of the more popular family destinations are Barbados, St Martin and Guadeloupe.

Successful travel with young children requires planning and effort. Try not to overdo things; even for adults, packing too much into the time available can cause problems. Include children in the trip planning; if they've helped to work out where you will be going, they will be much more interested when they get there.

For those vacationing with children, Lonely Planet's *Travel with Children* by Maureen Wheeler has lots of valuable tips and interesting anecdotal stories.

DANGERS & ANNOYANCES
Pesky Creatures
You can expect to find mosquitoes and sand flies throughout the region, both of which can be quite voracious, so consider bringing insect repellent. In addition, a few of the islands have chiggers and centipedes. For information on poisonous snakes, which are found on Martinique, St Lucia and Trinidad, see the Health section in this chapter.

Manchineel Trees
All visitors should learn to identify manchineel trees, which grow on beaches throughout the Eastern Caribbean. The fruit of the manchineel, which looks a like small green apple, is very poisonous, and the milky sap given off by the fruit and leaves can cause severe skin blisters, similar to the reaction caused by poison oak. If the sap is rubbed in your eyes, it can result in temporary blindness. Never take shelter under the trees during a rainstorm, as the sap can be washed off the tree and onto anyone sitting below.

Manchineel trees can be quite sizable, growing as high as 40 feet with widely spreading branches. The leaves are green, shiny and elliptic in shape. On some of the more visited beaches, trees will be marked with red paint or warning signs. Manchineel is called *mancenilla* on the French islands and *anjenelle* in Trinidad and Tobago.

Crime
In terms of individual safety and crime, the situation is quite varied in the Eastern Caribbean. For instance, it's hard to imagine a more tranquil area than Saba, where most people don't even have locks on their doors, whereas walking the streets of Port of Spain in Trinidad after dark can certainly be a risky venture. Consequently the precautions you should take depend on which island you're visiting. For a better grasp of the situation, see the individual island chapters.

BUSINESS HOURS
On most islands, business offices are open from 8 or 9 am to 4 or 5 pm Monday to Friday. Shops and stores are typically open from around 9 am to 5 or 6 pm on weekdays and until noon on Saturday. However, there is variation between islands.

Never on Sunday

On our first trip to the Caribbean, we asked a shopkeeper in Grenada about her hours of business: 'We're open daily,' she told us. 'Every day?' we asked. '*Every* day of the week,' she emphasized. 'Even on Sundays?' we asked. 'Oh no – never on *Sundays!*' she answered.

And so we came to realize that in most of the Eastern Caribbean the word 'daily' – whether spoken, written in ads or posted on storefront signs – quite often means 'every day but Sunday.' ■

For specifics on business hours, as well as a listing of public holidays and cultural events, see Facts for the Visitor in each island chapter. Keep in mind that banks on many islands are only open to noon on the day preceding a public holiday.

PUBLIC HOLIDAYS & SPECIAL EVENTS

Specific information on public holidays and special events, which vary throughout the region, is found in the Facts for the Visitor section of the individual island chapters.

One event, Carnival, stands unique as the major festival throughout the Eastern Caribbean. As elsewhere, it has traditionally been a pre-Lenten celebration – a period of merriment before the abstinence and fasting that many Christians, particularly Catholics, observe during Lent.

On Trinidad and on all of the French-influenced islands, Carnival remains a strictly pre-Lenten celebration, while on many of the British-influenced islands, Carnival celebrations are held at other times during the year.

The changing of Carnival dates has been largely the result of practical considerations – smaller islands simply couldn't compete with larger islands, particularly Trinidad, which attract the finest performers and the lion's share of visitors. As a result, visitors to the Eastern Caribbean can now find Carnival celebrations on one island or another throughout the year.

Carnival festivities usually include contests and performances by calypso singers and steel bands; the election of a Carnival 'king' and 'queen'; street dancing, called jump-ups; costume and dance competitions; and a parade with floats, music and masquerading revelers.

For more information on Carnival celebrations, see the individual island chapters.

ACTIVITIES

For those who get bored just hanging out on a beach, there are a slew of activities available throughout the Eastern Caribbean. Diving and sailing are two of the most popular but there are also plenty of opportunities for snorkeling, windsurfing, hiking, horseback riding, golf and tennis.

Diving

There's good year-round diving throughout the Eastern Caribbean. As a general rule, the calmer leeward shores of the islands have the best diving conditions.

Most of the Eastern Caribbean has good visibility, with average water temperatures ranging from 75°F to 85°F.

The marine life around the islands is superb. Hundreds of colorful fish species live in Caribbean waters, including common tropicals like reef-chomping parrotfish. In addition, divers often encounter stingrays, octopus, lobster, moray eels, sea turtles, spinner dolphins and large schools of barracuda.

Caribbean waters harbor all sorts of colorful sponges and both soft and hard corals, including wavering gorgonian fans and gem-like black coral. One creature common to the Caribbean that bears caution is the brownish-yellow fire coral, which is actually an encrusting hydroid colony that can provide a nasty sting to those who brush against it.

Underwater scenery in the Eastern Caribbean includes sea caves, canyons, pinnacles and vertical walls. Having a long maritime history, the Caribbean also has its share of sunken ships.

Most of the islands of the Eastern Caribbean have good diving opportunities and numerous dive shops. Complete gear can be rented and prices are quite competitive between shops.

If you want to experience diving for the first time, some of the dive operations offer a short beginners course for nondivers; commonly dubbed a 'resort course,' it includes brief instructions, followed by a shallow beach or boat dive. The cost generally ranges from US$75 to US$100, depending upon the operation and whether a boat is used.

For those who want to jump into the sport wholeheartedly, a number of dive shops also offer full open-water certification courses. The cost generally hovers around US$400, equipment included, and the entire course usually takes the better part of a week.

Generally, no two divers agree on the best sites for diving but among the places in vogue these days in the Eastern Caribbean are Saba, Dominica, Tobago and the Grenadines. More information on diving, including lists of dive operations, can be found in the individual island chapters. See also Dive Tours in the Getting There & Away chapter.

Snorkeling

Donning a mask and snorkel allows you to turn the beach into an underwater aquarium. There are numerous sites throughout the Eastern Caribbean that offer splendid coral gardens and varied and abundant reef fish. The nearshore waters harbor lots of colorful tropical fish, including many varieties of wrasses, damselfish, sergeant majors, blue tangs, goatfish, butterfly fish, large rainbow-colored parrotfish, angelfish, odd-shaped filefish and ballooning pufferfish, just to list a few.

Some travelers cart along their own mask, snorkel and fins but if you prefer to travel light they can be rented at many dive shops at reasonable prices. Snorkel sets can also be rented from water sports huts on some of the busier beaches, though rates tend to be higher. More information on snorkeling can be found in the individual island chapters.

Windsurfing

The popularity of windsurfing, or sailboarding, varies widely in the Eastern Caribbean. The main venues, and the most readily available rentals, are largely found on the French islands. However, there are favorable tradewinds and good water conditions throughout the region, so if by chance you travel with your own equipment, the range of possibilities is greater. Generally, winds are most constant during the summer months.

Windsurfing gear can easily be rented at the main windsurfing beaches in Guadeloupe, St Barts, Martinique, St Martin and Barbados, and on some of these islands there are also hotels that cater to windsurfers. In addition, many standard 1st-class hotels on Guadeloupe and Martinique have water sports huts that provide free use of windsurfing gear to their guests – a situation that can make for a reasonably economical windsurfing vacation.

Although the sport is not as widely popular in most of the English-speaking Caribbean, Antigua and the Grenadine island of Bequia each have a windsurfing school and gear rentals. Windsurfing is also catching on in Tobago and St Lucia and there are a couple of places on those islands where gear can now be rented.

More information on windsurfing can be found in the individual island chapters.

Surfing

The Eastern Caribbean is not a particularly hot spot for board surfers. The exception is isolated Barbados, which is situated farther out into the open Atlantic than other Eastern Caribbean islands and is thus exposed to unimpeded Atlantic swells.

In late summer, swells generated by tropical storms off the African coast begin to race toward Barbados, producing the Caribbean's highest waves and finest surfing conditions. The most reliable time for catching good, high, surfable waves is September, October and November. Bathsheba, on Barbados' east coast, is the center of activity, attracting wave action from the north, south and east.

Surfing is also possible at times in Guadeloupe, Tobago and St Martin. For more information see the relevant island chapters and the Surfing Tours section in the Getting There & Away chapter.

Fishing

There's reasonably good deep-sea fishing in the Eastern Caribbean, with marlin, tuna, wahoo and barracuda among the prime catches. Charter fishing boat rentals are available on a number of islands, but rates tend to be high. Expect that a half-day of fishing for four people will run about US$350. Charter boats are usually individually owned and consequently the list of available skippers tends to fluctuate; local tourist offices and activity desks can provide the latest information on availability.

Sailing

The Eastern Caribbean is a first-rate sailing destination. If you just want to spend a few hours out on the water, water sports huts at resort hotels rent Sunfish or other small sailboats that can be used for nearshore exploring. Should you want to take an island-hopping day excursion by sailboat, or join a sunset sail, there are cruises available on most islands. For information on getting about by skippering your own bareboat yacht (or hiring a yacht with a skipper) see the Yachting section in the Getting Around chapter.

Hiking

The hiking situation in the Eastern Caribbean varies significantly between islands. On many of the smaller low-lying islands there are few, if any, established trails, but as cars are also few in number the dirt roads that connect villages can make for good walking.

If you want to get off into the woods the higher rainforested islands offer the best opportunities. On lofty Dominica you can hike to a variety of waterfalls, take an easy rainforest loop trail through a parrot sanctuary or hire a guide for an arduous trek to an eerie volcanic valley with a boiling lake. On Guadeloupe and Martinique there are also established rainforest hikes that take in scenic waterfalls and smoldering volcanoes. St Lucia has recently opened trails into its new nature preserves so rainforest hiking is becoming a viable option on that island as well.

Small but steep Saba has some good easy-access hiking, including a trail through a cloud forest to the island's highest point, and a lightly trod network of footpaths that served to connect Saba's villages before the introduction of paved roads and cars just a few decades ago.

For more detailed information on hiking see the individual island chapters.

Hiking Precautions Some rainforest hiking trails take you into steep, narrow valleys with gullies that require stream crossings. The capital rule here is that if the water begins to rise it's not safe to cross, as a flash flood may be imminent. Instead, head for higher ground and wait it out.

Another potential danger on trails is falling rocks. Be wary of swimming directly under high waterfalls, as rocks can be dislodged from the top. Often a waterfall will have a second pool farther downstream that's safer.

Island trails are not a good place to be caught unprepared in the dark. It's wise to carry a flashlight when you're hiking, just in case. And of course if you're heading off into the wilderness you should always have a compass.

Long pants will protect your legs from sharp saw grass on overgrown sections of trails. Sturdy footwear with good traction is advisable on most hikes.

Horseback Riding

Horseback riding can be a fun way to explore a place. On about half of the larger Eastern Caribbean islands there are guided horseback rides. Some of the rides head out across quiet valleys, others go along remote beaches, and a few combine both in a single outing. Specific information on horseback riding can be found in the individual island chapters.

Golf & Tennis

While golf is not nearly as popular in the Eastern Caribbean as it is on more northerly locales such as Bermuda and Jamaica, most of the heavily touristed islands of the Eastern Caribbean have at least one golf course. The top-rated golf course in the region is the new 18-hole championship course designed by Robert Trent Jones II at the Four Seasons Resort on Nevis. Tennis courts are available at many of the larger resorts throughout the Eastern Caribbean. For more information see the individual island chapters.

WORK

The Eastern Caribbean has high unemployment rates and low wages, as well as strict immigration policies aimed at preventing foreign visitors from taking up work.

Generally the best bet for working is to crew up with a boat. As boat hands aren't usually working on any one island in particular, the work situation is more flexible and it's easier to avoid hassles with immigration. Marinas are a good place to look for jobs on yachts; check the bulletin board notices, strike up conversations with skippers or ask around at the nearest bar – most marinas have a watering hole where sailors hang out.

ACCOMMODATIONS

There are a wide range of accommodations available in the Eastern Caribbean, from inexpensive guesthouses and good-value efficiency apartments to luxury villa resorts. However, not all islands have rooms in all price categories – and a few have no low-end accommodations at all. Accommodations options are detailed in each island chapter.

In this book we use the phrase 'in summer' to refer to the low season and 'in winter' to refer to the high season. At the vast majority of hotels, summer rates are in effect from April 15 to December 14, winter rates from December 15 to April 14. Perhaps 10% of the hotels in the Eastern Caribbean make some minor deviations from these dates, usually with the addition of a mid-range rate in the spring and autumn and/or with higher rates for a few weeks at the end of December and the beginning of January.

Many hotels close for a month or so in late summer, usually around September. If business doesn't look promising, some of the smaller hotels and guesthouses might even close down for the entire summer.

'Private bath' in this book means that the room has its own toilet and shower – it does not necessarily mean that it has a bathtub, and in most cases it will not.

When you're looking for a hotel keep in mind that new hotels, especially 1st-class hotels, often have enticing rates for the first couple of years until they build up a clientele. Conversely, some of the busier older hotels are not good value but have simply built up name recognition over the years.

Camping is very limited in the Eastern Caribbean – the only established camping is at a handful of small, private campgrounds on Guadeloupe and Martinique.

At the national park in Grenada, camping is officially allowed but there are no facilities; other than that, there are no established campgrounds in the English-speaking Eastern Caribbean and freelance camping is either illegal or discouraged.

Reservation Systems

Reservations at some hotels and guesthouses can be made through overseas booking agencies. Those that operate on a single island are listed under that island. The following reservation services book many places on multiple islands – as it may be easier and cheaper to inquire about many hotels in a single call, you might want to try them first.

International Travel & Resorts
    ITR, the largest single reservation system operating throughout the Caribbean, books numerous hotels in the moderate and upper ranges. ITR will send out individual hotel brochures on request, as well as an annual directory.
    The reservation number is ☎ 800-223-9815 in the USA, Canada, Puerto Rico and the US Virgin Islands or ☎ 212-476-9444, fax 212-476-9476 from anywhere in the world.
Resinter
    Resinter books all Marine, Mercure, Novotel and Sofitel hotel chains, which together account for nearly a third of the hotel rooms on Martinique and Guadeloupe, as well as a few places on St Martin, St Barts and St Lucia.
    Resinter's reservation numbers are ☎ 800-221-4542 in the USA and Canada, ☎ O1 60 77 90 90 in France, ☎ 0171-724-1000 in the UK, ☎ 6196-48 3800 in Germany, ☎ 02 29 51 07 01 in Italy, ☎ 155-80 22 in Switzerland, ☎ 800 185 95 in Denmark and ☎ 020 793 153 in Sweden.
WIMCO
    The West Indies Management Company, or WIMCO (☎ 401-849-8012, fax 401-847-6290), PO Box 1461, Newport, RI 02840 USA, specializes in renting exclusive villa properties. Its extensive listings include villas on Mustique, St Martin, St Barts, Nevis and Barbados.
    Toll-free reservation numbers are ☎ 800-932-3222 in the USA, ☎ 0-800 89 8318 in the UK, ☎ 0 800 90 16 20 in France and ☎ 01 30 81 57 30 in Germany.

FOOD
Foods in the Eastern Caribbean reflect the mix of cultures. Throughout the region you'll find West Indian food – predominantly local root crops, vegetables, fresh seafood and goat – prepared with African and Western influences. Also prevalent on most islands is Creole food, a spicy mix of French and West Indian flavors. On the French islands, pâtisseries, crêpe shops and

Tropical Fruits
Many Eastern Caribbean islands have a variety of tropical fruits that can be found in the marketplace. Some of the more widespread ones are as follows:

breadfruit – a large, round, green fruit; this Caribbean staple is comparable to potatoes in its carbohydrate content and is prepared in much the same way
guava – a round, yellow fruit that's about 2½ inches in diameter, it has a moist, pink, seedy flesh, all of which is edible. Guavas can be a little tart but tend to sweeten as they ripen. They're a good source of vitamin C and niacin
mango – big old mango trees are abundant in the Caribbean, with juicy oblong fruits that are about three inches in diameter and five inches long. The fruits start out green but take on deeper colors as they ripen, usually reddening to an apricot color. Mango is sweet and a good source of vitamins A and C; it's mainly a summer fruit
papaya – usually called paw paw in the Eastern Caribbean, this sweet orange fruit, which is harvested year round, is a good source of calcium and vitamins A and C
passionfruit – a vine with beautiful flowers which grow into small, round fruits; the thick skin of the fruit is generally purple or yellow and wrinkles as it ripens. The pulp inside is juicy, seedy and slightly tart
pineapple – there are a variety of pineapples found throughout the Caribbean; the small ones known as black pineapples are among the sweetest
plantain – a starchy fruit of the banana family that usually is fried or grilled like a vegetable
soursop – a large green fruit with a pulpy texture that's slightly acidic and is often made into a vitamin-rich drink
starfruit – also called carambola, this translucent yellow-green fruit has five ribs like the points of a star; it has a crisp, juicy pulp and can be eaten without being peeled
tamarind – the pod of a large tropical tree of the legume family; the juicy, acidic pulp of the tamarind seeds is used in beverages

sidewalk cafés are nearly as prevalent as they would be in a Paris suburb.

East Indian, British, North American and continental foods can be found in varying degrees throughout the region. Barbados has plenty of places selling English-style fish & chips, on St Eustatius you can enjoy a Dutch smorgasbord breakfast of deli meats and cheeses, while moderately priced pizza and Italian food can be found throughout the region.

A few chain restaurants like KFC are common on the bigger islands but the quintessential fast food in the region remains a West Indian creation – the roti. It's comprised of a curried filling, most commonly potatoes and chicken, that's placed inside a tortilla-like wrapping and eaten much like a burrito. It's cheap and as filling as a good-sized sandwich.

Public markets are the place to go for fresh local fruit and vegetables – that's

---

Common Dishes of the Eastern Caribbean

accras – Creole-style cod or vegetable fritters

bake – a sandwich made with fried bread and usually filled with shark or other fish

blaff – a seafood preparation poached in a spicy broth

bul jol – roasted breadfruit and salt fish made with tomatoes and onions

callaloo soup – the quintessential Eastern Caribbean soup, made with dasheen leaves and often with coconut milk; it resembles a creamy spinach soup

christophene – also known as chayote, a common Caribbean vegetable shaped like a large pear; it can be eaten raw in salads, used in soup or cooked like a squash

colombo – a spicy, East Indian-influenced dish that resembles curry

conch – also called *lambi*, the chewy meat of a large gastropod, it's common throughout the Caribbean and is often prepared in a spicy Creole sauce

conkies – a mixture of cornmeal, coconut, pumpkin, sweet potatoes, raisins and spice, steamed in a plantain leaf

cou-cou – a creamy cornmeal and okra mash, commonly served with salt fish

crabes farcis – spicy stuffed land crabs

cutter – a salt-bread roll used to make meat and fish sandwiches, or the name of such a sandwich

dasheen – a type of taro; the leaves are known as callaloo and cooked much like spinach or turnip leaves, and the starchy tuberous root is boiled and eaten like a potato

dolphin – a common type of white-meat fish, also called mahimahi; no relation to the marine mammal

flying fish – a gray-meat fish named for its ability to skim above the water; particularly plentiful in Barbados

goat water – a spicy goat meat stew often flavored with cloves and rum

jambalaya – a Creole dish usually consisting of rice cooked with ham, chicken or shellfish, spices, tomatoes, onions and peppers

johnnycake – a cornflour griddle cake

jug-jug – a mixture of Guinea cornmeal, green peas and salted meat

mahimahi – see dolphin

mauby – a bittersweet drink made from the bark of the mauby tree, sweetened with sugar and spices

mountain chicken – the legs of the *crapaud*, a type of frog

oil down – a mix of breadfruit, pork, callaloo and coconut milk

pepperpot – a spicy stew made with various meats, accompanied by peppers and cassareep

pigeon peas – the brown, pea-like seeds of a tropical shrub which are cooked like peas and served mixed with rice

roti – a curry filling, commonly potatoes and chicken, rolled inside a tortilla-like flat bread

souse – a dish made out of a pickled pig's head and belly, spices and a few vegetables, commonly served with a pig-blood sausage called pudding

where it's at its freshest and you're contributing 100% of your money to the local economy by buying it direct from the farmer. On larger islands, the capital city has a produce market that's open every day but Sunday. On other islands public markets are commonly held only a couple of days a week. Saturday is invariably the biggest and liveliest market day everywhere.

DRINKS
Nonalcoholic Drinks
An island favorite among nonalcoholic drinks is the drinking coconut, which makes a nice option to a sugar-laden soft drink and can be purchased inexpensively from street vendors in many places. Another nutritious local drink is sorrel, a lightly tart, bright-red drink rich in Vitamin C that's made from the flowers of the sorrel plant.

Bottled water is available at stores throughout the Eastern Caribbean. Water is safe to drink from the tap on many but not all islands; see the individual island chapters for details.

Alcoholic Drinks
With their histories so tightly tied to sugar cane, it's only natural that rum remains the

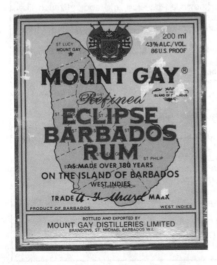

most common alcoholic beverage throughout the Eastern Caribbean. Most larger islands produce their own rum. Some like Martinique and Guadeloupe use freshly harvested sugar cane, while others like Grenada import molasses to produce their rum. There are scores of labels, from internationally recognized favorites like the Barbadian-produced Mount Gay to small obscure distilleries producing solely for local consumption. Rum is invariably cheap throughout the islands.

Certainly the most popular beer in the Eastern Caribbean is Carib, first brewed in Trinidad in 1951 and now brewed in St Kitts and Grenada as well. You'll see advertisements all around the region proclaiming 'In This Country a Beer is a Carib.' In and around the Dutch islands, Heineken is the beer of choice.

ENTERTAINMENT
Whether you'd prefer to club-hop on Barbados or soak up the steel-pan rhythm at Trinidadian mas camps, the Eastern Caribbean has enough musical and cultural offerings to ensure that you won't be at a loss for things to do after the sun goes down. More information is given in individual island chapters.

SPECTATOR SPORTS
On the English-speaking islands, cricket is by far the leading spectator sport. During cricket season, those who aren't at the match are generally glued to the radio broadcast. On some islands, the main cricket season is April through September, but on others, such as Barbados, cricket is played throughout the year.

Second in popularity is football (it's called soccer in the USA), which is played throughout the Caribbean, with the main season in winter.

Horse racing is a popular spectator sport on a couple of the larger islands.

THINGS TO BUY
St Martin is the most popular island for duty-free shopping, but virtually any island

Things Not to Buy

Sea turtle shells make beautiful jewelry – too beautiful, in fact, for the welfare of the turtles, which are endangered worldwide. Buying any turtle products increases the demand for hunting the turtles. Turtle shell jewelry, as well as sea turtle taxidermy and food products, are prohibited entry into the USA, Canada, Australia and most other countries.

Travelers should also avoid products that contain tropical feathers as many of the most colorful Caribbean birds, such as parrots and the scarlet ibis, are endangered – even people who unwittingly bring home feathers from protected species are subject to steep fines.

The importation of black coral is likewise banned in more than 100 countries. The purchase of other corals, which are often taken live from their fragile reef ecosystems and sold in chunks or made into jewelry, should also give pause to the environmentally conscious. ■

that has large cruise ship facilities will have at least a few generic duty-free shops selling liquor, perfumes, jewelry and some designer clothing.

You'll find lots of wood carvings from Bali, colorfully painted ceramic buses and market scenes made in Colombia and folk paintings from Haiti – some quite nice, but not made in the Eastern Caribbean.

Quality crafts that *are* made in the Eastern Caribbean include dolls in native Creole costumes, natural-fiber basketwork and stylish cotton clothing. Caribelle Batik makes good quality batik clothing, as well as wall hangings with Caribbean scenes, which are for sale on several islands. Locally grown spices make nice lightweight souvenirs. And of course there's rum.

Getting There & Away

This section contains an overview of the transportation options for getting to the Eastern Caribbean from countries outside the region. More specific information, including airfares, can be found in the Getting There & Away section of each island chapter.

Information on LIAT and other regional airlines flying within the Eastern Caribbean, and information on boat services between Eastern Caribbean islands, is in the Getting Around chapter.

The phone numbers listed in this section are the reservation numbers from the countries indicated.

AIR
USA

There are more flights from the USA to the Eastern Caribbean than from any other part of the world.

American Airlines (☎ 800-433-7300) is the main US carrier into the region. American has direct flights from the US to a few of the larger Eastern Caribbean islands, although to most destinations travelers must first fly to San Juan, Puerto Rico, and then change planes, continuing on American's inter-island carrier American Eagle. Overall, American's inter-island schedule coordinates closely with its flights between the US mainland and San Juan, making for convenient connections.

Continental Airlines (☎ 800-525-0280), the only other US carrier offering flights to the Eastern Caribbean, operates flights from New York City to St Martin and Antigua.

The Trinidad-based airline BWIA (☎ 800-538-2942) has a fairly extensive schedule from both Miami and New York to the larger non-French islands of the Eastern Caribbean.

Air France (☎ 800-237-2747) has a twice-weekly flight from Miami to Guadeloupe and Martinique.

Canada

Air Canada (☎ 800-776-3000) has direct flights from Toronto to Barbados, Antigua and Trinidad.

From Toronto the carrier BWIA (☎ 800-538-2942) also flies to Barbados, Antigua and Trinidad.

UK

British Airways (☎ 0181-897-4000) operates flights from London to Antigua, St Lucia, Barbados, Grenada and Trinidad.

BWIA (☎ 0171-745-1100) has flights from London to Antigua, Barbados, St Lucia and Trinidad.

Europe

Paris is the main European gateway to the Eastern Caribbean. Air France (☎ 0 802 802 802) flies from Paris to Martinique, Guadeloupe, St Martin and Antigua.

Air Liberté (☎ 0 803 09 09 09), Nouvelles Frontières (☎ 01 41 41 58 58) and Air Outre Mer, or AOM (☎ 01 49 79 12 34), fly from Paris to Martinique and Guadeloupe.

KLM (☎ 20 47 47 747) operates twice-weekly flights from Amsterdam to St Martin.

South America

There are connections between South America and the Eastern Caribbean with LIAT, Aeropostal, Air France and Air Guadeloupe.

Australia

The main routing and cheapest fares from Australia to the Eastern Caribbean are via the USA. Qantas' roundtrip fare from Melbourne or Sydney to Los Angeles ranges from A$1599 in the low season to A$2059 in the high season. For example, excursion fares from Los Angeles to Barbados start at about A$800 roundtrip, and to Martinique, A$900 roundtrip.

Air Travel Glossary

Apex Apex ('advance purchase excursion') A discounted ticket that must be paid for in advance. There are penalties if you wish to change it.

Baggage Allowance For international travelers, it's usually one 20 kg item to go in the hold, plus one item of hand luggage. Most US airlines allow passengers to check in two bags, each weighing up to 70 pounds, and carry on a lighter third piece.

Bucket Shop An unbonded travel agency specializing in discounted airline tickets.

Bumped Just because you have a confirmed seat doesn't mean you're going to get on the plane (see Overbooking).

Check In Airlines ask you to check in a certain time ahead of the flight departure (commonly two hours on international flights). If you fail to check in on time and the flight is overbooked the airline can cancel your booking and give your seat to somebody else.

Full Fares Airlines traditionally offer tickets that are 1st class (coded F), business class (coded J) and economy class (coded Y). These days there are so many promotional and discounted fares available from the regular economy class that few passengers pay full economy fare.

Lost Tickets If you lose your ticket an airline will sometimes treat it like a bank would treat a traveler's check and issue you another one, though there may be a lengthy waiting period and a reissuance fee. Legally, however, an airline is entitled to treat a ticket like cash and if you lose it then it's gone forever. Take good care of your tickets.

No Shows No shows are passengers who fail to show up for their flight, sometimes because of unexpected delays, sometimes because they made more than one booking and didn't bother to cancel the one they didn't want. Full-fare passengers who fail to turn up are often entitled to travel on a later flight. The rest of us are usually penalized.

Open Jaws A roundtrip ticket where you fly out to one place but return from another. If available, this can save you backtracking to your arrival point.

Overbooking Airlines hate to have empty seats, and because every flight has some passengers who fail to show up, airlines often book more passengers than they have seats. Usually the excess passengers balance out those who fail to show up but occasionally somebody gets bumped. If this happens guess who it is most likely to be? The passengers who check in late.

Reconfirmation With some airlines it's necessary to reconfirm your reservation at least 72 hours prior to the departure of an onward or return flight. If you don't do this, in some cases an airline could delete your name from the passenger list, causing you to lose your seat.

Restrictions Discounted tickets often have various restrictions on them – advance purchase is the most usual one. Others are restrictions on the minimum and maximum period you must be away, such as a minimum of three days or a maximum of 30 days.

Standby A discounted ticket where you fly only if there is a seat free at the last moment.

Tickets Out An entry requirement for many Caribbean countries is that you have an onward or roundtrip ticket – in other words, a ticket out of the country. If you're not sure what you intend to do next, the easiest solution is to buy the cheapest onward ticket to a neighboring country or a ticket from a reliable airline that can later be refunded if you do not use it.

Transferred Tickets Airline tickets cannot be transferred from one person to another. Travelers sometimes try to sell the return half of their ticket, but officials can ask you to prove that you are the person named on the ticket. On international flights tickets are usually compared with passports, and even on domestic flights identification is commonly required for security purposes.

Travel Agencies Travel agencies vary widely. Full-service agencies handle everything from tours and tickets to hotel bookings, but if all you want is a ticket at the lowest possible price, then you may be better off with an agency specializing in discounted tickets.

Charters

Charter flights from the USA, Canada, the UK and Europe offer another option for getting to the islands. Fares are often cheaper than on regularly scheduled commercial airlines, but you usually have to go and come back on a specific flight, commonly with a week-long stay, and you'll probably have no flexibility in extending your stay.

In the high season, charters often operate with such frequency that they carry more passengers to some islands than the scheduled airlines.

Although charter companies do most of their business booking package tours that include both hotel and air, they commonly find themselves with a few empty seats on planes that they've chartered. Some companies will then sell these empty seats for bargain prices a week or two prior to departure.

In the USA you can sometimes find these seats advertised in the travel pages of larger Sunday newspapers, such as the *New York Times* and the *Boston Globe*. Travel agents who specialize in discount travel can also be helpful.

FREIGHTERS

While passenger-carrying freighters have become a thing of the past in much of the world, there are still a couple of interesting freighter options for getting to the Caribbean. One is the M/V *Amazing Grace*, a 257-foot 'workhorse' ship that once carried supplies to English lighthouse keepers and now sails the length of the Caribbean servicing Windjammers' fleet of tall ships. The other is CGM, which operates modern cargo ships that carry goods from France to the French West Indies, returning home with bananas from Martinique and Guadeloupe.

Amazing Grace

The Windjammers' supply ship, the *Amazing Grace*, departs from West Palm Beach, Florida, once a month. Because it's not allowed to pick up passengers at US ports, southbound passengers board at Freeport,

Bahamas. Northbound passengers can embark at the turnaround point of Port of Spain, Trinidad. In all, the ship makes about 20 stops over the 26-day roundtrip voyage, making it an excellent way to see a wide swath of Caribbean islands. Ports of call can include Antigua, Bequia, Dominica, Grenada, Les Saintes, Palm Island, Statia, St Barts, St Kitts, Nevis, St Lucia, St Martin and Tobago.

To take the voyage one way – a 13-day trip – fares range from US$1075 for a berth with a washbasin to US$1300 for a top-deck berth with private bath. All meals are included, as is wine with dinner. Roundtrip fares are double. A US$100 premium is charged from November through May, and there's a 20% discount in the hurricane-prone months of August and September. Singles can either share a cabin or pay 175% of the double rate for their own cabin. Although the ship carries 94 passengers, services are streamlined; there's a bar and TV room, but no pool, laundry room or doctor on board. Optional shore excursions are reasonably priced from US$10 to US$25. Reservations can be made through Windjammer Barefoot Cruises, PO Box 120, Miami Beach, FL 33119 USA (☎ 305-672-6453, 800-327-2601).

CGM

The Compagnie Générale Maritime (CGM) sails nearly weekly between mainland France and the French West Indies, stopping in both Guadeloupe and Martinique. The CGM vessels, which are modern cargo ships that carry bananas and limes to France, have a dozen comfortable passenger cabins, a TV room and a swimming pool. French meals with wine are included in the tariff, which is approximately US$1100 (one way) for the 10-day voyage, with reduced fares offered to travelers age 26 and under. As cabin space is very limited, the boat commonly books up far in advance.

Passage can be booked in Guadeloupe through Transat Antilles Voyages (☎ 0590 83 04 43), Quai Lefevre, Pointe-à-Pitre; in Martinique through CGM (☎ 0596 71 34 23), 8 Boulevard du Général-de-Gaulle,

Fort-de-France; or in Paris through either CGM (☎ 01 46 25 70 00) or Sotramat Voyages (☎ 01 49 24 24 73), 12 Rue Godot-de-Moroy, 75009 Paris, France.

CRUISES

More than two million cruise ship passengers sail the Caribbean annually, making the Caribbean the world's largest cruise ship destination. The ships average four to five ports of call each, adding up to a whopping 10 million 'passenger visits' throughout the region.

The most visited ports in the Eastern Caribbean are St Martin, with 500,000 passenger arrivals, Barbados and Martinique, each with 400,000 passenger arrivals, followed by Antigua, Guadeloupe, Grenada, St Lucia, Dominica, St Kitts, St Vincent & the Grenadines and Trinidad & Tobago.

The typical cruise ship holiday is the ultimate package tour. Other than the effort involved in selecting a cruise, it requires minimal planning – just pay and show up – and for many people this is a large part of the appeal.

Some cruise lines put more emphasis on the thrill of cruising around the seas on a floating resort than they do on visiting any actual destination. If 'being there' is more important than 'getting there,' travelers will need to choose a cruise accordingly.

For the most part, the smaller 'unconventional' ships put greater emphasis on the local aspects of their cruises, both in terms of the time spent on land and the degree of interaction with islanders and their environment. While the majority of mainstream cruises take in fine scenery along the way, the time spent on the islands is generally quite limited and the opportunities to experience a sense of island life are more restricted.

Still, the fact that most cruise ships call on many islands in a short time can be useful in providing an overview for those who plan to come back to the region later but haven't decided which islands to visit.

Because travel in the Eastern Caribbean can be expensive and because cruises cover rooms, meals, entertainment and transportation in one all-inclusive price, cruises can also be comparatively economical. All cruises will cost more than budget-end independent travel, but the least expensive cruises will not necessarily cost more than a conventional air/hotel package tour or a privately booked vacation at a resort hotel.

Cost

Cruise lines do not divide passengers into class categories, but rather provide the same meals and amenities for all passengers on each ship.

Virtually all cruises are offered at a range of rates, however, depending mainly on the size, type and location of the cabin. Bottom-end cabins might well be uncomfortably cramped and poorly located, while top-end cabins are often spacious, luxurious suites. Price also depends on the season and dates of the cruise, the number of people in each cabin, transportation options between your home and the departure point and, of course, which cruise you choose. In addition, discounts off the brochure rates are commonplace.

Standard rates are quoted per person, based on double occupancy. A third and fourth person in the same cabin is usually given a heavily discounted rate.

Provisions vary widely for single travelers who occupy a double cabin; a few cruise lines allow this at no extra charge, while most charge from 110% to 200% of the standard rate. Some cruise lines offer single cabins and some have a singles share program in which they attempt to match up compatible (same-sex) cabin mates to share the double cabins.

Some cruise lines provide free or discounted airfare to and from the port of embarkation in their quoted rates (or will provide a rebate if you make your own transportation arrangements), while others do not.

Most cruises to the Eastern Caribbean end up costing around US$125 to US$350 per person per day, including airfare from a major US gateway city.

Meals, which are typically frequent and elaborate, are included in the cruise price.

Alcoholic drinks are usually not included and are comparable in price to those in bars back home.

Guided land tours are almost always offered at each port of call, generally for about US$35 to US$100 each. If you opt to see the sights yourself, you'll need to budget for taxis, admission fees, etc.

Entertainment shows and most on-board activities are included in the cruise price but personal services such as hairstyling and laundry usually cost extra as do most shore-side activities, such as diving or windsurfing.

Some cruise lines include tipping in the quoted price. Most do not, however, and usually suggest that each passenger tip, per day, US$3 to the cabin steward, US$3 to the dining room waiter and US$1.50 to the table attendant, given in a lump sum on the last night of the cruise. For cocktail waiters, a 15% tip is sometimes included in the drink price and if not is generally given on the spot.

Port charges and government taxes typically add on about US$100 per cruise. Be sure to check the fine print about deposits, cancellation and refund policies and travel insurance.

Discounts

When all is said and done, very few cruises are sold at the brochure rates.

Just a few years ago the cheapest rates were those obtained at the last minute – essentially stand-by rates for whatever cabins had not been booked – but a concerted effort by the cruise lines to reverse this trend has been largely successful. These days, the general rule is the earlier the booking the greater the discount (and, of course, the better the cabin selection).

Some cruise lines offer an across-the-board discount of around 25% to those who book at least 90 days in advance, while others discount up to 40% for even earlier bookings and then lower the discount rate as the sailing date gets closer.

Still, cruise lines want to sail full, so if there are leftover seats at the end, there will be discounts available.

And then there are promotions: some cruise lines offer a 50% discount for the second person on designated sailings, offer free cabin upgrades if certain qualifications are met, run two-for-one specials in selected markets, offer discounts to senior citizens etc.

Booking a Cruise

A good travel agent should be able to work through the maze, providing comparisons on cruise lines, itineraries, facilities, rates and discounts. Be aware that the industry has also attracted the occasional fly-by-night company that advertises heavily, then takes the money and runs, so be sure you're dealing with a reputable agent.

Those travel agents most knowledgeable about cruises are apt to belong to Cruise Lines International Association (CLIA), an organization of cruise lines that works in affiliation with about 20,000 North American travel agencies. You might also want to find a travel agent who subscribes to the *Official Cruise Guide*, which is a good source of information on cruise lines, listing schedules and facilities for virtually all ships.

Your local travel agent may be able to provide all the help you need. If not, there are numerous travel agents who specialize only in cruises and are therefore generally up to speed on the latest promotional deals and other discounts. In the USA, a few of those that book widely in the Eastern Caribbean are:

Cruise Outlet, 1890 Dixwell Ave,
    Hamden, CT 06514
        (☎ 203-288-1884, 800-775-1884)
Cruises Inc, 5000 Campuswood Drive,
    East Syracuse, NY 13057
        (☎ 315-463-9695, 800-854-0500)
Cruise Time, 9864 Main St,
    Fairfax, VA 20130
        (☎ 703-352-1261, 800-627-6131)
White Travel Service, 127 Park Rd,
    West Hartford, CT 06119
        (☎ 203-233-2648, 800-547-4790)
World Wide Cruises, 8059 W McNab Rd,
    Fort Lauderdale, FL 33321
        (☎ 954-720-9000, 800-882-9000)

For travelers with physical limitations, Flying Wheels Travel (☎ 507-451-5005, 800-535-6790; thq@ll.net), PO Box 382, Owatonna, MN 55060 USA, specializes in booking handicapped-accessible Caribbean cruises.

Choosing a Cruise

In addition to finding a cruise that fits your budget, here are some other things to consider:

Schedule Most cruises last between one and two weeks, though there are a few that are shorter or longer.

Caribbean cruises are most popular and thus most expensive during the northern hemisphere's midwinter (with the peak time being the Christmas/New Year holidays) and least crowded in autumn, with spring and summer in between.

Departure Point Most cruises that take in destinations in the Eastern Caribbean depart from Miami or Fort Lauderdale, Florida; San Juan, Puerto Rico; St Thomas, US Virgin Islands; or from within the Eastern Caribbean itself.

The cost and ease of getting to the departure point should be considered when choosing a cruise. Also important is your interest in the port and nearby islands if you plan to extend your holiday either before or after the cruise.

Itinerary Consider which islands you want to visit. The largest cruise ships generally stop only at islands with substantial port facilities, such as St Martin, Antigua, Guadeloupe, Martinique, Dominica, St Lucia and Grenada, while some of the smaller 'unconventional' ships are able to take in less visited islands like Saba, St Barts and the Grenadines.

Ship Type & Facilities The conventional cruise ship is indeed a floating resort, some holding a good 2500 passengers, with multiple swimming pools, Las Vegas-type entertainment, casinos and nightclubs.

Smaller ships, which might have between 50 and 250 passengers, will have less lavish entertainment but are more personal and can pull into smaller ports, marinas and snorkeling coves.

There is a huge variety in style. Some cruise lines appeal to active vacationers who enjoy water sports, hiking and exploration. Some lines feature luxury boats with a sophisticated ambiance and prices to match. Some don't accept young children. Others are more middle-class oriented, welcoming young families, retired seniors, singles and couples alike, with activities for all ages and interests. Likewise, dress codes, meal quality and types of shore excursions vary.

Some ships can accommodate special diets with advance notice. Many ships are handicapped-accessible, although details such as the measurement of bathroom clearance for wheelchairs should be checked carefully, as problems with cabins for the disabled are not uncommon. In general, the newer ships are more accessible, with fewer barriers, larger cabins situated near elevators and wider doorways and halls.

Again, a good travel agent can help match cruises to each customer's interests.

Cabin Outside cabins are best and least claustrophobic, as you get a view. The higher decks are preferable, as are of course the largest and fanciest cabins, and prices will correspond accordingly. Although modern cruise ships have stabilizers to prevent roll, if you're prone to motion sickness you might want to get a cabin in the center of the ship which is more stable and rocks less in bad weather.

The inside cabins (with no portholes) on the lowest decks are the least desirable, but also the cheapest. Bottom-end cabins sometimes have bunk-style beds and minuscule bathrooms and they can be uncomfortably cramped. Avoid the cabins nearest the engine room, as they may be noisy.

Sanitation All cruise ships that arrive in US ports – which includes the majority that sail the Caribbean – are subject to unannounced US sanitation inspections. The inspectors rate ships in four categories: potable water supply; food preparation and holding; potential contamination of food; and general cleanliness, storage and repair.

A summary sheet that lists ships, the latest date of inspection and their ratings is published weekly and may be obtained free by writing to: Chief, Vessel Sanitation Program, National Center for Environmental Health, 1015 North American Way, Room 107, Miami, FL 33132 USA.

Environmental Sensitivity Not all cruise ships have equally clean environmental records and this should be taken into account when choosing a cruise vacation. When you book a cruise ship, consider asking the travel agent whether the cruise line company has been cited for violating marine pollution laws.

While on your cruise, be inquisitive about the ship's recycling program and how waste is being handled and disposed – it will help raise the level of environmental consciousness. If you do sight any violations, report them to the Center for Marine

Conservation (see the following section) and to your travel agent back home, so the information can be used by travelers who come after you.

Environmental Considerations The US Coast Guard is responsible for tracking down ships that illegally dump wastes at sea within the USA's 200-mile Exclusive Economic Zone. Efforts are concentrated on cruise ships, which tend to carry more garbage than other vessels.

The Center for Marine Conservation (CMC), a nonprofit organization dedicated to the conservation of marine wildlife, has become the unofficial repository of information on cruise line dumping cases. CMC compiles information on violators but as it doesn't have the capacity to have staff on board cruise ships, it relies almost solely upon cruise passengers to report pollution violations.

The center will send anyone planning to go on a cruise (or who is otherwise interested) a packet that includes information about the problem, a list of cruise lines that have been implicated in illegal dumping and a form for reporting unlawful dumpings.

MARPOL Annex V

Marine pollution is a serious issue in the Caribbean and cruise ships dumping rubbish overboard have traditionally been a major part of the problem. Annex V of MARPOL 73/78, an international treaty resulting from the 1973 International Convention for the Prevention of Pollution from Ships, makes it illegal to dump plastics anywhere at sea and also places near-shore restrictions on the disposal of other solid waste. Some garbage can still be dumped, as long as it's disposed of at least 3 miles offshore; bottles and cans cannot be dumped within 12 miles of land.

Despite the limits of the treaty, which went into effect in 1988, most countries have paid little heed to enforcing the regulations. Indeed, only a handful of Caribbean countries have ratified the treaty and thus some cruise ships have continued to randomly dump garbage in Caribbean waters.

On the other hand, the USA, from whose waters most Caribbean cruise ships depart, has cracked down hard on violators within its 200-mile Exclusive Economic Zone.

In 1993 the cruise ship industry got a wake-up call when the *Regal Princess* of Princess Cruises received the maximum fine of US$500,000 for dumping 20 plastic bags full of garbage off the Florida Keys. The successful prosecution was the consequence of a cruise passenger's videotaping of the dumping.

Princess Cruises, incidentally, has since initiated stringent environmental guidelines. In 1996, it received the American Society of Travel Agents/Smithsonian Magazine Environmental Award for its proactive stance on pollution prevention, becoming the first cruise line to win the award. ■

In addition, the US government provides a monetary incentive for passengers to assist with enforcement. If a citizen provides information leading to fines, the court may award that person up to one-half of the fine, which can be as much as US$250,000!

The information packets are available by writing to the Center for Marine Conservation (☎ 757-496-0920), 1432 N Great Neck Rd, Suite 103, Virginia Beach, VA 23454 USA. Include US$5 for postage and handling.

Other Considerations Cruise ship passengers who show interest in the local culture and put money directly into the hands of small merchants are more appreciated by islanders than those who stay wrapped in the cocoon of organized land tours or see nothing beyond the duty-free shops.

While the cruise line's optional land tours are conveniently packaged to take in many of the island's sightseeing highlights, they also move quickly and tend to shield visitors from interaction with the local people. In addition, a fair percentage of the money paid for these tours stays with the cruise line organizers rather than going into the local economy.

On some islands you might want to take a closer look at a smaller area rather than trying to breeze around the whole island on a tour. It can be a fun alternative to wander the streets of the main town, poke into little shops, eat at local restaurants and buy souvenirs from street vendors and small businesses where you can chat with the owners. Buy local rums in small shops instead of on board ship – you might even save money in the process.

Cruise Ship Lines

Most travel agents have stacks of cruise ship brochures available for the taking. Brochures can also be obtained by contacting the cruise lines directly.

The following cruise lines sail to one or more of the islands of the Eastern Caribbean. In some cases, not all ports of call listed are visited on a single cruise. While only Eastern Caribbean ports of call are listed, other parts of the Caribbean might also be visited during the same cruise.

The 800 phone numbers are toll-free from the USA and sometimes from Canada.

Conventional Cruises Contact details and ports of call of conventional cruise lines are as follows:

American Canadian Caribbean Line,
PO Box 368, Warren, RI 02885 USA
(☎ 800-556-7450, 401-247-0955)
Ships sail from San Juan and Trinidad. Ports of call are mostly at the northern and southern extremities of the chain.

Carnival Cruise Lines, Carnival Place,
3655 NW 87 Ave, Miami, FL 33178 USA
(☎ 800- 327-2058, 305-599-2600)
Ships depart from Miami and San Juan. Ports of call include St Martin, Dominica, Grenada, Barbados, Martinique and St Lucia.

Celebrity Cruises, 5201 Blue Lagoon Dr, Miami, FL 33166 USA (☎ 800-437-6677, 305-262-6677)
Ships depart from San Juan and Fort Lauderdale. Ports of call include Grenada, St Lucia, St Martin, Antigua, Barbados and Martinique.

Cunard Line, 555 Fifth Ave, New York, NY 10017 USA (☎ 800-528-6273, 212-880-7500)
This line operates mainly in Europe but has some sailings from Miami that call upon Grenada, Barbados, St Lucia and Dominica.

Holland America Line, 300 Elliott Ave West, Seattle, WA 98119 USA (☎ 800-426-0327, 206-281-3535)
Ships depart from Fort Lauderdale and Tampa. Ports of call include Barbados, Trinidad, Dominica, Martinique, St Kitts, St Lucia and St Martin.

Norwegian Cruise Line, 7665 Corporate Center Dr, Miami, FL 33126 USA (☎ 800-327-7030, 305-436-4008)
Ships depart from Miami and San Juan. Ports of call include Antigua, St Kitts, Barbados, Dominica, St Lucia and St Martin.

Premier Cruises, 901 S America Way, Miami, FL 33132 USA (☎ 800-990-7770, 305-358-5122)
Ships depart from Santo Domingo and call at Barbados, Grenada, St Lucia, Martinique, Guadeloupe, St Martin and Dominica.

Princess Cruises, 10100 Santa Monica Blvd, Los Angeles, CA 90067 USA (☎ 800-568-3262, 310-553-1770)

Ships depart from Fort Lauderdale and San Juan. Ports of call include Barbados, Dominica, Guadeloupe, Martinique and St Martin.

Royal Caribbean Cruise Line, 1050 Caribbean Way, Miami, FL 33132 USA (☎ 800-327-6700, 305-539-6000)

Ships depart from Miami and San Juan. Ports of call include St Martin, Barbados, Antigua and Martinique.

Royal Olympic Cruises, 1 Rockefeller Plaza, New York, NY 10020 USA (☎ 212-397-6400; in the USA: 800-872-6400; in Canada: 800-368-3888)

Ships depart from Fort Lauderdale and Galveston, Texas. Ports of call include Antigua, Barbados, Bequia, St Vincent, Grenada, Tobago and Trinidad, the latter also in conjunction with an Amazon River cruise.

Seabourn Cruise Line, 55 Francisco St, San Francisco, CA 94133 USA (☎ 800-929-9595, 415-391-7444)

Ships depart from Fort Lauderdale and St Thomas. Ports of call include St Martin, Antigua and St Barts.

Unconventional Cruises In addition to the cruises listed here, see the Yacht section in the Getting Around chapter for information on cruising the Caribbean by yacht; and Dive Tours in the Organized Tours section later in this chapter for information on live-aboard dive boats.

Clipper Cruise Line, 7711 Bonhomme Ave, St Louis, MO 63105 USA (☎ 800-325-0010, 314-727-2929)

While it's a conventional cruise ship, the *Yorktown Clipper* carries only 138 passengers and has a shallow draft, enabling it to navigate secluded waterways. One tour departs from Grenada and visits Anguilla, Antigua, Bequia, Dominica, Les Saintes, Saba, St Eustatius, St Kitts, St Lucia and Union Island. Another departs from Curaçao and includes Tobago and Trinidad en route to a tour of Venezuela's Orinoco River.

Club Med, 40 West 57th St, New York, NY 10019 USA (☎ 800-453-7447, 602-948-9190)

The 617-foot *Club Med I* has computerized sails and a high-tech design, holds 386 passengers and operates much like any other all-inclusive Club Med resort, except that it's at sea. Departs from Martinique. The itinerary varies but ports of call include Marie-Galante, St Kitts, Nevis, St Martin, Dominica, Les Saintes, St Barts and Antigua.

Sea Cloud is booked through Cruise Company of Greenwich, PO Box 866, Norwalk, CT 06856 USA (☎ 800-825-0826, 203-852-0941)

This four-masted 360-foot tall ship has luxury accommodations and departs from Antigua. Ports of call include Bequia, Palm Island, Grenada, Carriacou, St Kitts, Nevis, St Lucia, Martinique, Dominica, Barbuda, St Barts, Anguilla and St Martin.

Star Clippers, 4101 Salzedo Ave, Coral Gables, FL 33146 USA (☎ 800-442-0551, 305-442-0550)

These modern four-masted clipper ships have tall ship designs and carry 180 passengers. They depart from Antigua and Barbados. Ports of call include St Martin, Dominica, Les Saintes, Martinique, St Barts, St Kitts, St Lucia, St Vincent, Bequia, Union Island and the Tobago Cays.

Tall Ship Adventures, 1389 South Havana St, Aurora, CO 80012 USA (☎ 800-662-0090, 303-755-7983)

The *Sir Francis Drake*, a 165-foot three-masted schooner, is a vintage tall ship built in 1917. Cruises are mostly around the Virgin Islands, but during the summer they relocate in the Southern Caribbean, sailing out of St Lucia on one-week cruises. The boat holds 30 passengers.

Windjammer Barefoot Cruises, PO Box 120, Miami Beach, FL 33119 USA (☎ 800-327-2601, 305-672-6453)

The fleet consists of a restored 282-foot four-masted stay-sail rigged schooner and other tall sailing ships, carrying from 65 to 128 passengers. They tend to attract a younger, more active and budget-minded crowd. Some cruises are geared for singles only. Boats depart from Freeport, Antigua, Grenada and St Martin. Ports of call include Anguilla, Dominica, Les Saintes, Saba, St Barts, St Eustatius, St Kitts, Nevis, St Lucia, Bequia, Canouan, Mayreau, Union Island, Palm Island, the Tobago Cays, Carriacou, Trinidad and Tobago.

Windstar Cruises, 300 Elliott Ave West, Seattle, WA 98119 USA (☎ 800-258-7245, 206-281-3535)

These luxury four-masted 440-foot boats have high-tech, computer-operated sails and take 148 passengers. They depart from Barbados. Ports of call include Nevis, St Martin, St Barts, Guadeloupe, Bequia, Tobago, Grenada, Tobago Cays, Martinique and St Lucia.

ORGANIZED TOURS

There are scores of conventional package tours to the Eastern Caribbean available from the USA, Canada and Europe. Most are a week in duration, though they sometimes can be extended. If you are going to the Caribbean for just a short vacation, package tours can be quite economical, as the cost to book the same flight and hotel separately on your own is typically much higher.

Particularly in the USA package tours are highly competitive, with week-long tours that include hotel and airfare from the US east coast for as little as US$600. The ads found in the travel sections of big-city Sunday newspapers are a good source of information. Package tours represent a substantial part of the bookings for most travel agents, who can usually pile you high with tour brochures.

Bargain hunters can sometimes find some good last-minute deals as consolidators that book out a block of hotel rooms and airplane seats often have to pay for them whether they're full or not – it's to their advantage to let them go cheaply (even below cost) a week or two prior to the flight. If you're flexible enough to book a discounted package on relatively short notice, let your travel agent know so he or she can keep you posted.

Ecotourism

An elevated concern for the environment and a healthy desire to minimize the adverse affects of tourism has spurred the growth of tour organizers who promote themselves as environmentally friendly. 'Ecotourism' and 'green tourism' are now becoming trendy terms in the Eastern Caribbean. Some of those using the terms, such as groups affiliated with nonprofit nature and conservation societies, are genuinely promoting travel that contributes to environmental and cultural preservation. On the other hand, some tour operators in the more traditional tourism industry appear to be using ecotourism buzzwords primarily as a marketing opportunity.

Before booking a trip, it's a good idea to take a close look at any tour operator that claims to offer environmentally friendly travel and ask what they base their claims on. Two organizations that can provide general guidelines are the Center for Responsible Tourism, PO Box 827, San Anselmo, CA 94979 USA, which publishes a 'code of ethics for travelers,' and the National Audubon Society, 700 Broadway, New York, NY 10003 USA, which publishes a 'travel ethic for environmentally responsible travel.'

Tourism can indeed have a positive impact on host communities. Diving fees in Saba, for instance, help support the Saba Marine Park and are used to install floating buoys that eliminate the need for boats to drop anchor on fragile reefs. On islands such as Dominica, Guadeloupe, Martinique and St Lucia, recognition that the remaining rainforests are a positive asset for both islanders and visitors has contributed to the setting aside of sizable parks and preserves.

In addition to the tours that follow in this section, you'll find information on nature preserve and bird sanctuary outings, rainforest accommodations, and ecologically minded tour guides in individual island chapters throughout this book.

Birding & Natural History Tours

The National Audubon Society (☎ 212-979-3066, fax 212-353-0190), 700 Broadway, New York, NY 10003 USA, offers tours with a natural history orientation, led by Audubon staff members. Most of the society's Caribbean tours are aboard regularly scheduled cruises, such as an eight-day sail through the Leeward and Windward islands (from US$1950) and a 12-day bird watcher's trip to Trinidad, Tobago and Venezuela (from US$3140); both are aboard Clipper Cruise Line's 138-passenger *Yorktown Clipper*. Prices do not include airfares.

Caligo Ventures (☎ 800-426-7781, 914-273-6333; info@caligo.com), 156 Bedford Rd, Armonk, NY 10504 USA, runs frequent birding tours to Trinidad and Tobago, with stays at the *Asa Wright Nature Centre* in Trinidad and *Blue Waters Inn* on Tobago. One-week tours of Tobago cost US$925 in the low season and US$1155 in the high season, based on double occupancy and including airfare from Miami; add US$50 for flights from New York. Eleven-day tours that combine Trinidad and Tobago cost US$1595 in the low season, US$1975 in the high season, including airfare from either Miami or New York.

Natural History Travel of the Massachusetts Audubon Society (☎ 800-289-9504, 617-259-9500; fax 617-259-1040; nhtravel @massaudubon.ort), 208 S Great Rd, Lincoln, MA 01773 USA, offers an ornithologist-led, 10-day bird watching tour to Trinidad and Tobago each winter. Accommodations are at the *Asa Wright Nature Centre* in Trinidad and the *Blue Waters Inn* on Tobago. The cost of US$1995 includes outings, meals and accommodations based on double occupancy, but not airfare.

The Smithsonian Institution (☎ 202-357-4700, fax 202-633-9250), 1100 Jefferson Drive SW, Washington DC 20560 USA, leads natural history tours and cruises that sometimes include islands at the southern end of the Eastern Caribbean. Costs vary depending upon the type and length of the outing.

Volunteer & Educational Programs

Caribbean Volunteer Expeditions (☎ 607-962-7846), PO Box 388, Corning, NY 14830 USA, sends volunteers to work at historic sites in conjunction with local national trusts, historical societies and other preservation groups. One ongoing project includes surveying the more than 100 windmill ruins in Antigua. Other projects are conducted on St Vincent, Barbados, St Lucia, Grenada and Nevis. Fees typically range from US$300 to US$800 per week, including accommodations, food and land transportation, but not airfare.

Elderhostel (☎ 617-426-8056), 75 Federal St, Boston, MA 02110 USA, is a nonprofit organization offering educational programs for those aged 55 or older. The organization has its origins in the youth hostels of Europe and the folk schools of Scandinavia. It has a few courses in the Caribbean, such as a two-week Caribbean Cultural Awareness program in St Vincent & the Grenadines that includes lectures by professors from the University of the West Indies on topics ranging from the Rastafarian movement to folklore, flora and fauna field trips, and sailing in the Grenadines. The cost for the two weeks is US$1764, including accommodations, meals and classes but excluding airfare.

Earthwatch (☎ 800-776-0188, 617-926-8200; fax 617-926-8532; info@earth-watch.org), PO Box 9104, Watertown, MA 02272 USA, sends volunteers to work on scientific and conservation projects worldwide. Recent Caribbean projects have included excavating St Kitts' Brimstone Hill Fortress for evidence of slave life and studying the effects of global warming on Trinidad. Rates for two-week courses generally hover around US$1700, including meals and accommodations but not airfare.

Dive Tours

PADI Travel Network (☎ 714-662-3821, fax 714-540-2983), 1251 East Dyer Rd 100, Santa Ana, CA 92705 USA, has dive package tours at a number of Eastern Caribbean destinations including Dominica, Saba, Bequia and Anse Chastanet in St Lucia. Rates per person based on double occupancy for a week-long hotel/dive package start in the high season at US$605 in Bequia, US$741 in Dominica, US$845 in Saba and US$2199 in St Lucia. Airfare is not included. Arrangements can be made through any PADI dive center worldwide, or in the USA by calling ☎ 800-729-7234.

Explorer Ventures (☎ 307-235-0683, 800-322-3577; fax 307-235-0686), PO Box 310, Mills, WY 82644 USA, books the M/V *Caribbean Explorer*, a 16-passenger live-aboard dive boat. One-week tours depart from St Martin on Saturday, take in two days of diving on St Kitts and four days of diving on Saba, before returning to St Martin. The cost of US$1195 per person, based on double occupancy, includes on-board accommodations, meals, five dives daily and the use of tanks, weights and belts. Airfare is not included.

World Dive Adventures (☎ 954-433-3483, 800-934-3483; fax 954-434-4282), 10400 Griffin Rd, Suite 109, Fort Lauderdale, FL 33328 USA, has dive tours to Dominica for around US$900 that include seven nights' accommodations, two dives a day, breakfasts and dinners. This company also arranges tours to Saba, St Eustatius, St Vincent and Tobago and can book the aforementioned M/V *Caribbean Explorer*.

Scuba Voyages (☎ 909-371-1831, 800-544-7631; fax 909-279-0478, scubavoy @ix.netcom.com), 595 Fairbanks St, Corona, CA 91719 USA and Landfall Productions (☎ 510-794-1599, 800-525-3833; lndfall@aol.com), 39675 Cedar Blvd, Suite 2958, Newark, CA 94560 USA also book room/dive packages at multiple locations in the Eastern Caribbean.

In addition, most dive shops listed in this book can arrange package tours that include accommodations and diving fees, so if you're interested in a specific island consider contacting the dive shops directly.

Surfing Tours

Surfing package tours to Barbados are offered by Surf Express (☎ 407-779-2124, fax 407-779-0652), 568 Hwy A1A, Satellite Beach, FL 32937 USA. The summer-season per-person cost for a one-week tour, including airfare from Miami, starts at US$540 based on triple occupancy in a small efficiency cottage or US$652 based on double occupancy at the Edgewater Inn. From New York, add US$30. Reasonably priced two-week packages are also available.

Clothing-Optional Tours

A handful of US tour companies cater to those looking for a holiday *au naturel*. The most common destinations are Orient Beach on St Martin and Hawksbill Beach Resort on Antigua. There are also clothing-optional cruises on Windjammer and Star Clipper tall ships.

Bare Necessities, 1802 West 6th St, Austin, TX 78703 USA (☎ 512-499-0405, 800-743-0405; fax 512-469-0179)

Go Classy Tours, 2676 W Lake Rd, Palm Harbor, FL 34684 USA (☎ 813-786-8145, 800-725-2779; fax 813-784-4284)

Travel Au Naturel, 35246 US 19 N, Suite 112, Palm Harbor, FL 34684 USA (☎ 813-948-2007, 800-728-0185; fax 813-948-2832)

WARNING

The information in this chapter is particularly vulnerable to change: prices for international travel are volatile, routes are introduced and canceled, schedules change, special deals come and go, and rules and visa requirements are amended.

Airlines and governments seem to take a perverse pleasure in making price structures and regulations as complicated as possible. You should check directly with the airline or a travel agent to make sure you understand how a fare (and any ticket you may buy) works. In addition, the travel industry is highly competitive and there are many lurks and perks.

The upshot of this is that you should get opinions, quotes and advice from as many airlines and travel agents as possible before you part with your hard-earned cash. The details given in this chapter should be regarded as pointers and are not a substitute for your own careful, up-to-date research.

Getting Around

AIR

LIAT is the Caribbean's main inter-island carrier, connecting a total of 24 destinations from Puerto Rico to Caracas, most of which fall within the Eastern Caribbean. The airline has nearly 150 flights each day, which accounts for roughly half of all inter-island flights in the region.

BWIA, the Trinidad-based airline, flies between some of the larger islands of the Eastern Caribbean but is predominantly an international carrier and has a far more limited inter-island schedule than LIAT.

Other airlines cover only a segment of the Eastern Caribbean. Winair services the islands around St Martin, from Anguilla to St Kitts. Airlines of Carriacou is a puddle jumper connecting the Grenadine islands between St Vincent and Grenada. In the French West Indies, Air Guadeloupe and Air Martinique are the main carriers, but there are also a handful of small commuter airlines – such as Air St Martin and Air St Barts – that fly between a couple of islands on scheduled flights.

Specific airfare and schedule information is in each individual island chapter. Like everything else, these are subject to change and it's certainly a wise idea to pick up the latest printed schedules from airline counters as soon as you arrive in the islands.

LIAT

LIAT, formerly Leeward Islands Air Transport, is owned by the governments of a dozen Caribbean islands and is home-based in Antigua.

In addition to straightforward one-way and excursion tickets, LIAT offers a varied but confusing array of discounted fares and passes. As any extensive travel in the Caribbean is almost certain to involve flights on LIAT, you can save yourself a great deal of money by figuring out the various options in advance and deciding which one best suits your itinerary.

LIAT offers a range of roundtrip excursion fares, including the standard type valid for either 21 or 30 days that allows one or two en-route stopovers and costs an average of 50% more than a one-way ticket. These excursion tickets are available on most LIAT routes and can be purchased either before or after you arrive in the Caribbean – they generally have no advance purchase requirements and are fully refundable.

In addition, LIAT offers some deeply discounted one-day and seven-day excursion tickets on selected routes; these tickets are often cheaper than the price of a one-way ticket. Some one-day and seven-day tickets can only be purchased on the island where they originate and getting information on these tickets outside the islands is difficult. Essentially, short-stay tickets are marketed to local residents as an affordable opportunity to go to a neighboring island for a shopping spree or short vacation. However, you don't need to be a Caribbean resident to buy them.

LIAT also has senior citizen fares and youth fares that normally cut as much as 50% off the regular fares; airpasses are not discounted.

LIAT's reservation number in the USA is: ☎ 800-468-0482 or 268-462-0700, fax 268-462-2682. In the UK, Carib Jet (☎ 0181-571-7553, fax 0181-571-6807) handles LIAT bookings. In France LIAT can be booked through Air France and in Germany through Lufthansa.

Unlimited One-Way Fares Many of LIAT's long distance one-way fares allow unlimited en-route stopovers and have virtually no restrictions. They are valid for a year and you can change your flight dates or have the ticket rewritten to delete or add islands without additional fees. These tickets can be a bargain if you're traveling to and from the Caribbean on an open-jaw ticket – such as flying into Trinidad and out of St Martin. As an example, LIAT's one-way fare between Trinidad and St Martin costs US$306 and allows en-route stopovers on Tobago, Grenada, Carriacou, St Vincent, St Lucia, Martinique, Dominica, Guadeloupe, Antigua, Nevis and St Kitts.

Airpasses The following LIAT airpasses can be an excellent deal for anyone interested in doing some serious island hopping.

The king of the airpasses is the LIAT Caribbean Super Explorer, which costs US$449 and is valid for 30 days of travel to any or all of the 24 destinations served by LIAT. You can only visit each destination once, although you can go through an airport any number of times as required for onward connections.

There's no advance purchase requirement. Passes can be purchased at home (but not in Venezuela) before your trip or after you arrive in the Caribbean. You must decide your itinerary at the time of purchase, and any subsequent changes are subject to a US$35 surcharge. Tickets must be purchased at least seven days in advance or within 48 hours of making reservations, whichever comes first. Once you start to use the pass, the remainder of the pass coupons cannot be refunded or used as payment toward another ticket.

The LIAT Explorer is a good airpass if you just want to visit a few islands, especially if they're far flung. This pass allows you to visit any three islands in LIAT's network, costs US$249 and is valid for 21 days. The ticket must be purchased before you arrive in the Caribbean and must begin and end on the same island. Once ticketed, no changes are allowed.

The LIAT Airpass is sold only in Europe and in the UK in conjunction with a transatlantic ticket. Coupons for a minimum of three destinations and a maximum of six destinations can be purchased for travel throughout LIAT's Caribbean network, with the exception of Venezuela. Coupons cost US$80 per destination and the airpass is valid for 21 days from the start of the first flight. Once ticketed, no changes are allowed.

Whenever It Arrives

Those acronym-named airlines that fly around the Caribbean bear the brunt of many jokes from islanders.

BWIA is mocked as 'But Will It Arrive?' LIAT is said to stand for 'Luggage in Another Terminal' or 'Leave Island Any Time' and WIA (Winair) becomes 'Whenever It Arrives.'

Despite this good-natured ribbing, during scores of flights we have never lost luggage and all the airlines have gotten us where we wanted to go. Well, there is one oddity – flights often leave a good 20 minutes *early* with no advance warning! ■

BWIA

BWIA has a 'butterfly' fare for US$449 that's valid for 30 days and allows travelers to visit all of its Caribbean destinations. All travel is on widebody aircraft, as each inter-Caribbean flight is a leg of an international flight. Consequently, BWIA has a much more limited Caribbean network than LIAT. Currently BWIA serves Barbados, Antigua, Grenada, St Lucia, St Martin, Trinidad, Jamaica and Guyana only. On this 30-day pass, the itinerary must be set in advance and there's a US$20 charge to make changes. Each destination can be visited only once, other than for connecting flights.

BWIA's reservation numbers are ☎ 800-538-2942 in the USA and Canada, ☎ 0171-745-1100 in the UK.

BUS

There's inexpensive bus service on most islands, although the word 'bus' has different meanings in different places. Some islands have full-sized buses, while on others a bus is simply a pick-up truck with wooden benches in the back.

Perhaps the most common type of bus is the Toyota minivan, the sort that accommodates a family of six elsewhere. However, in the Eastern Caribbean these minivans have four or five rows of seats, as well as jump seats in the aisle that fold down as the rows fill. As more and more people get on, the bus becomes an uninterrupted mass of humanity – children move onto their parents' laps, schoolkids share seats, people squeeze together and everyone generally accepts the crowding with good nature. Whenever someone gets off the back of a crowded minivan, it takes on the element of a human Rubik's Cube, with the jump seats folding up and down and everyone shuffling places; on some buses there's actually a 'conductor' to direct the seating.

Buses are often the primary means of commuting to work or school and thus are most frequent in the mornings and from mid to late afternoon. There's generally good bus service on Saturday as well, as it's the big market day. On Sunday, bus service on many islands virtually grinds to a halt.

TAXI
Taxis are available on virtually all of the populated islands, with the exception of a few that don't have roads! Details are in the individual island chapters.

CAR & MOTORCYCLE
Road Rules
On islands that were formerly British, driving is on the left-hand side of the road and on the French and Dutch islands it is on the right-hand side.

On the French islands, note that there's a rather confusing *priorité à droite* rule in which any car approaching an intersection from a road to your right has the right-of-way; you must slow down or stop to let them pass.

Rental
Car rentals are available on all islands, with the exception of a few very small ones. On most islands there are affiliates of one or more of the international chains like Hertz, Avis, Budget and National/Europcar.

You can often get a better deal by booking a car before you go. Even on islands such as Martinique and Guadeloupe, where the advance booking price is often the same as the walk-in price, reservations are a good idea. Without one, you may arrive at the airport and find the cheaper

cars all sold out – a situation that's not uncommon in winter.

Island car rental agents frequently affiliate and disaffiliate with international chains, particularly on the smaller islands, so even if there's not an affiliate listed in the island's car rental section it's worth checking the latest status with the international firms mentioned above.

On many islands you need to be 25 years old to rent a car, and some car rental companies will not rent to drivers over 70.

BICYCLE
Although the popularity of cycling in the Eastern Caribbean is limited, some of the islands have bicycles for rent and details on renting bicycles are noted in those island chapters. Cyclists should ride on the same side of the road as car traffic.

HITCHHIKING
Hitchhiking is common among islanders on several islands, though the practice among foreign visitors, particularly outside the French islands, is not very common.

Hitchhiking is never an entirely safe practice in any country in the world, and Lonely Planet does not recommend it. Travelers who decide to hitchhike should understand that they are taking a potentially serious risk. People who do choose to hitchhike will be safer if they travel in pairs and let a friend or acquaintance know where they are planning to go.

BOAT
Ferry
There are daily, or near-daily, ferry services between St Martin and Anguilla; St Kitts and Nevis; St Vincent and Bequia; Grenada and Carriacou; and Trinidad and Tobago; as well as from the main part of Guadeloupe to the outlying islands of Terre-de-Haut, Marie-Galante and La Désirade.

In the Grenadines, a thrice-weekly ferry connects St Vincent and Bequia with Mayreau, Canouan and Union Island. There's a catamaran service between St Martin and Saba several days a week that's geared for day tours from St Martin. Catamarans also

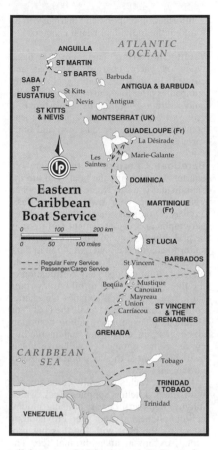

ANGUILLA
ATLANTIC OCEAN
ST MARTIN
ST BARTS   Barbuda
SABA
ST EUSTATIUS   St Kitts   ANTIGUA & BARBUDA
Nevis   Antigua
ST KITTS & NEVIS   MONTSERRAT (UK)
GUADELOUPE (Fr)
La Désirade
Les Saintes   Marie-Galante
DOMINICA

Eastern Caribbean Boat Service

0   100   200 km
0   50   100 miles

MARTINIQUE (Fr)

– – – Regular Ferry Service
– – – Passenger/Cargo Service

ST LUCIA

St Vincent   BARBADOS

Bequia   Mustique
Canouan
Mayreau
Union   ST VINCENT
Carriacou   & THE GRENADINES

GRENADA

CARIBBEAN SEA
Tobago
TRINIDAD & TOBAGO
Trinidad
VENEZUELA

sail between St Martin and St Barts for day trips.

High-speed catamaran ferries connect the islands of Guadeloupe, Dominica, Martinique and St Lucia several days a week.

Details on all these boats are in the relevant individual island chapters.

Windward Lines Limited

Windward Lines Limited operates the 180-foot passenger/cargo boat M/V *Windward* between St Lucia (Castries), Barbados (Bridgetown), St Vincent (Kingstown), Trinidad (Port of Spain) and Venezuela (Guiria one week, Margarita Island the

next). As it's primarily a cargo boat, it lays over at each port for several hours to unload, giving passengers time to do a little on-shore exploring. The boat usually alternates its southbound itinerary every other week and it occasionally runs an odd week with an altered schedule adjusted to holidays or heavier cargo pickups.

On the usual southbound schedule, arrival and departure times are as follows:

Week One
Departs St Lucia	9 am (Sun)
Arrives Barbados	7 pm (Sun)
Departs Barbados	10 pm (Sun)
Arrives St Vincent	7 am (Mon)
Departs St Vincent	4 pm (Mon)
Arrives Trinidad	8 am (Tue)
Departs Trinidad	6 pm (Tue)
Arrives Margarita, Venezuela	6:30 am (Wed)

Week Two
Departs St Lucia	7 pm (Sun)
Arrives Barbados	6 am (Mon)
Departs Barbados	8:30 am (Mon)
Arrives St Vincent	4 pm (Mon)
Departs St Vincent	8 pm (Mon)
Arrives Trinidad	10 am (Tue)
Departs Trinidad	5 pm (Tue)
Arrives Margarita, Venezuela	9:30 am (Wed)

On the northbound schedule, sailing times are as follows:

Departs Venezuela	6 pm (if Margarita; Wed) 11 pm (if Guiria; Wed)
Arrives Trinidad	7 am (Thur)
Departs Trinidad	5 pm (Thur)
Arrives St Vincent	7:30 am (Fri)
Departs St Vincent	10 am (Fri)
Arrives Barbados	7 pm (Fri)
Departs Barbados	10:30 pm (Fri)
Arrives St Lucia	8 am (Sat)

One-way/roundtrip fares from Trinidad are US$62/95 to St Lucia, US$60/90 to Barbados or St Vincent, US$40/60 to Guiria and US$50/70 to Margarita. Other one-way/roundtrip fares are US$39/60 between St Lucia and Barbados, US$46/71 between St Vincent and Barbados, US$106/148 between Venezuela and Barbados and US$114/158 between Venezuela and St Lucia.

Cabins are available from US$10 per berth per night, based on double occupancy, though it's wise to book them ahead of time.

There's a restaurant and a duty-free shop on board. Check-in is one hour before the scheduled departure time.

Those planning to take the boat should contact one of the following booking agents and request copies of the latest schedule, which is printed calendar-form a couple of months in advance.

Barbados
Windward Agencies, 7 James Fort, Hincks St, Bridgetown
(☎ 246-431-0449, fax 246-431-0452)
St Lucia
Toucan Travel, Rodney Bay Marina, PO Box 1114, Castries
(☎ 758-452-9963, fax 758-452-9806)
St Vincent
Perry's Customs & Shipping Agency, Sharpe St, PO Box 247, Kingstown
(☎ 784-457-2920, fax 784-456-2619)
Trinidad
Global Steamship Agencies, Mariners Club, Wrightson Rd, Port of Spain
(☎ 868-624-2279, fax 868-627-5091)
Venezuela
Acosta Asociados, Calle Bolivar 31, Guiria
(☎ 58-948-1679, fax 58-948-1112)

Yacht

The Caribbean is one of the world's prime yachting locales, offering diversity, warm weather and fine scenery. The many small islands grouped closely together are not only fun to explore but also form a barrier against the raging Atlantic Ocean, providing relatively calm sailing waters in the Caribbean Sea.

In the Eastern Caribbean, the major yachting bases are in St Martin, Antigua, Guadeloupe, Martinique, St Lucia, St Vincent and Grenada.

It's easiest to sail down-island, from north to south, as on the reverse boats must beat back into the wind. Because of this, several yacht charter companies allow sailors to take the boats in just one direction, later arranging for its own crew to bring the boats back to home base.

Information on ports and marinas can be found in the individual island chapters.

Yacht Chartering There are two basic types of yacht charters: bareboat and crewed. In addition, some yacht charter companies offer live-aboard sailing courses, land/sail tours, flotilla sails (consisting of a group of bareboats accompanied by a lead boat with an experienced crew) and other variations.

Bareboat Charters With a bareboat charter you rent just the boat. You are the captain and you sail where you want, when you want, on your own (more or less, anyway – you must stay within designated geographical areas and night sailing may be prohibited). You must be an experienced sailor to charter the boat. Although in most cases you won't need proof of having completed a sailing course, any certification or the like, you will need to fill out a written sailing resume which satisfies the charter company that you can handle the boat. You should have experience sailing a similar-sized boat, in anchoring and in reading charts. Some companies will give you a trial check-out at the dock before allowing you to sail away.

Bareboat yachts generally come stocked with linen, kitchen supplies, fuel, water, dinghy, outboard, charts, cruising guides, cellular phone and other gear. Provisioning (stocking the boat with food) is not provided, except at an additional fee. The charter company can provide a licensed skipper (generally costing from US$125 to US$150 a day) or a cook (about US$100 a day) if you don't want to do all the work yourself (this is sometimes called a semi-bareboat charter), but you still maintain responsibility for the boat. You'll have to pay a security deposit and should check the fine print in regards to refunds, insurance and cancellation penalties.

Crewed Charter With a crewed charter, the yacht comes with a captain, crew, cook and provisions. You don't have to know how to sail, or anything else about boats.

You can either make your own detailed itinerary or provide a vague idea of the kind of places you'd like to visit and let the captain decide where to anchor.

Cost Rates vary greatly. The better established companies generally charge more than small, little-known operators, and large ritzy yachts of course cost more than smaller, less luxurious boats. These days, many yachts are equipped with amenities such as TV, video, CD player, ice-maker, snorkeling equipment etc on board – more toys add to the cost.

Although a whole book could be written just comparing prices, the following gives a sense of mid-range costs. The Moorings, which is one of the larger companies, has a fleet containing a dozen different types of yachts that vary in size, amenities and price. At the low end is a 33-foot *Beneteau Oceanis 321,* which rents at a weekly bareboat charter rate of US$1785 in spring, US$1400 in summer, US$1300 in fall and US$2380 in winter. The boat holds four passengers comfortably, five in a squeeze. Nearer the top end is a 44-foot *Beneteau Oceanis 440* that holds eight or nine passengers and costs approximately double that rate.

With the Moorings, fully crewed yacht charters can be arranged at a *per-person* rate that in the low season begins at around US$1600 per week and in winter begins at around US$2220 per week, each based on four passengers on a 50-foot sloop.

Yacht Charter Companies The following charter companies offer both bareboat and crewed yacht charters in the Eastern Caribbean. Listings begin with the yacht charter company's US or European office, followed by the island addresses where the charter boats are based.

Catamaran Charters
    141 Alton Rd, Miami Beach,
    FL 33139 USA
    (☎ 305-538-9446, 800-262-0308;
    fax 305-538-1556)
    Marigot, St Martin
    (☎ 0590 87 02 82, fax 0590 87 01 55)

Marina Bas du Fort, Guadeloupe
    (☎ 0590 90 71 89, fax 0590 90 72 93)
The Moorings, 19345 US Hwy 19 N,
    4th Floor, Clearwater, FL 34624 USA
    (☎ 813-535-1446, 800-535-7289;
    fax 813-530-9747; yacht@moorings.com)
Port de Plaisance du Marin, Martinique
    (☎ 0596 74 75 39)
Marigot Bay, St Lucia (☎ 758-453-4357)
Secret Harbour, St George's, Grenada
    (☎ 473-444-4924)
Bas du Fort Marina, Point-à-Pitre,
    Guadeloupe (☎ 0590 90 81 81)
Captain Oliver's Marina, Oyster Pond,
    St Martin (☎ 0590 87 32 55)

Nautor's Swan Charters
    40 Mary St, Newport, RI 02840 USA
    (☎ 401-848-7181, 800-356-7926;
    fax 401-846-7349)
    Port Hamble Marina, Satchell Lane,
    Hamble, Southampton, SO3 5QD, England
    (☎ 01703 454 880, fax 01703 455 547)
    BP 5253, Grand Case, 97072 St Martin
    (☎ 0590 87 35 48, fax 0590 87 35 50)

Star Voyage
    5 rue Lincoln, 75008 Paris, France
    (☎ 01 42 56 15 62)
    Pointe du Bout Marina,
    Trois-Ilets, Martinique
    (☎ 0596 66 00 72, fax 0596 66 02 11)
    Marina du Marin, Martinique
    (☎ 0596 74 70 92)

Sun Yacht/Stardust Charters
    PO Box 737, Camden, ME 04838 USA
    (☎ 207-236-9611, 800-772-3500;
    fax 207-236-3972, sunyacht@midcoast.com)
    Captain Oliver's Marina, Oyster Pond,
    St Martin (☎ 0590 87 30 49)
    English Harbour, Antigua
    (☎ 268-460-2615, fax 268-460-2616)
    Blue Lagoon, Gosier, Guadeloupe
    (☎ 0590 90 92 02, fax 0590 90 97 99)
    Pointe du Plaisance, Marina du Marin,
    Martinique (☎ 0596 74 98 17)
    Clifton, Union Island, St Vincent &
    the Grenadines (☎ /fax 784-458-8581)

Sunsail
    Annapolis Landing Marina,
    980 Awald Rd, Suite 302,
    Annapolis, MD 21403 USA
    (☎ 410-280-2553, 800-327-2276;
    fax 410-280-2406)

The Port House, Port Solent,
Portsmouth, Hampshire PO6 4TH, UK
(☎ 01705 222 222, fax 0175 219 827)

Marina Bas du Fort, Guadeloupe
(☎ 0590 90 82 80)

Marigot, St Martin
(☎ 0590 87 83 41)

Rodney Bay Marina, St Lucia
(☎ 758-452-8648)

Marina du Marin, Martinique
(☎ 0596 74 77 61)

Trade Wind
  PO Box 1186, Court Circle,
  Gloucester, VA 23061 USA
  (☎ 804-694-0881, 800-825-7245;
  fax 804-693-7245)

  Marina Bas du Fort, Guadeloupe
  (☎ 0590 90 76 77)

  Box 2158, Blue Lagoon, St Vincent
  (☎ 784-456-9736, fax 784-456-9737)

Charter Brokers For those who don't want
to be bothered shopping around, charter
yacht brokers can help. Brokers work on
commission, like travel agents, with no
charge to the customer – you tell them your
budget and requirements and they help
make a match.

A few of the better known charter yacht
brokers in the USA are:

Ed Hamilton & Co, 28 Nielson Lane,
  N Whitefield, ME 04353
  (☎ 207-549-7855, 800-621-7855;
  fax 207-549-7822)

Lynn Jachney Charters,
  PO Box 302, Marblehead, MA 01945
  (☎ 800-223-2050, fax 781-639-0216)

Nicholson Yacht Charters,
  29 Sherman St, Cambridge, MA 02138
  (☎ 617-661-0555, 800-662-6066;
  fax 617-661-0554)

Russell Yacht Charters, 404 Hulls Hwy,
  Suite 108, Southport, CT 06490
  (☎ 203-255-2783, 800-635-8895;
  fax 203-255-3426)

Other Sailing Options Another option is
to book a tour package aboard a yacht,
much the same as you would book a traditional cruise. The schedule, itinerary and

price will already be fixed and you will sail
with a few other passengers who have
booked the same yacht. A number of yacht
charter companies provide this service.

If you just want to work in a couple of
days of sailing after you arrive in the Caribbean, you may be able to find something on
the spot. On many islands, small one-boat
operators advertise trips to neighboring
islands; look for flyers, ask at local tour
companies or check with the island's tourist
offices.

For sails on tall ships, windjammers and
the like, see Unconventional Cruises in the
Cruises section of the Getting There &
Away chapter.

Hitching a Ride on a Yacht In major
yachting centers such as St Lucia, Antigua
and Bequia, it's sometimes possible to hitch
a ride between islands with yachters. With
luck you might find someone just looking
for company; however, most yachters will
expect you to either help share expenses or
provide crew work in exchange for a ride.
Marinas have general notice boards, and
these sometimes have a posting or two by
yachters looking for crew or passengers. If
you don't find anything promising on the
boards, you can add a notice of your own. It
should include where you want to go; what
you're willing to do in exchange for passage, such as cooking and cleaning; the
date; and where you can be contacted.

In addition to the notice boards, there's
always a bar or restaurant, usually at or

near the marinas, that's a favorite haunt for sailors and thus a ready place to make contacts.

Resources Cruising guides to the Eastern Caribbean are listed under Books in the Facts for the Visitor chapter.

To navigate through the islands of the Eastern Caribbean, yachters will need either Imray yachting charts, US Defense Mapping Agency charts or British Admiralty charts. They are available throughout the islands, especially at boating supply shops at marinas and in some bookstores. They can also be ordered in advance from Bluewater Books & Charts (☎ 954-763-6533, 800-942-2583), 1481 SE 17th St Causeway, Fort Lauderdale, FL 33316 USA.

There are various sailing magazines published worldwide. The following have articles and tips for sailors, ads for yacht charter companies and charter brokers and sometimes a few classified ads for crew positions:

Cruising World, PO Box 3045,
    Harlan, Iowa 51537 USA
    (☎ 401-847-1588, 800-727-8473)

Sail, PO Box 56397, Boulder, CO 80322 USA
    (☎ 617-720-8600, 800-745-7245)

Yachting, 2 Park Ave, New York, NY 10016
    USA (☎ 212-779-5000, 800-999-0869)

Anguilla

Anguilla's main appeal to visitors is its beautiful beaches – long, uncrowded stretches of powdery white coral sands and clear aquamarine waters.

Although it's just a few miles across the channel from bustling St Martin, Anguilla retains the laid-back character of a sleepy backwater. The island is small and lightly populated, the islanders friendly and easy going.

Anguilla, which had almost no visitor facilities just a decade ago, made a decision in the 1980s to develop tourism with a slant towards luxury hotels and villas. It

has since become one of the trendier top-end destinations in the Eastern Caribbean.

Although attention goes to the exclusive resorts that are scattered along some of the island's finest beaches, there are also a number of small and locally owned guest houses and apartments that make Anguilla accessible to vacationers on a more moderate budget.

The interior of Anguilla is flat, dry and scrubby, pockmarked with salt ponds and devoid of dramatic scenery. Anguilla's main attraction certainly lies in its fringing beaches, but there are also some offshore coral-encrusted islets that offer good opportunities for swimming, snorkeling and diving.

Inexpensive ferries shuttle between Anguilla and St Martin, making Anguilla easy to visit as a day trip.

HIGHLIGHTS

- Shoal Bay East, one of the finest beaches in the Eastern Caribbean
- Sandy Ground, with its casual beach bar and old salt works
- Sandy Island and Prickly Pear Cays, for snorkeling and picnic outings
- Anguilla's luxury hotels, worth a look even if you're not staying

Facts about Anguilla

HISTORY

The first Amerindians settled on Anguilla about 3500 years ago. Archaeological finds indicate that the island was a regional center for the Arawak Indians, who had sizable villages at Sandy Ground, Meads Bay, Rendezvous Bay and Island Harbour.

The Carib Indians, who eventually overpowered the Arawaks, called the island Malliouhana. Early Spanish explorers named the island Anguilla, which means 'eel,' apparently because of its elongated shape.

The British established the first permanent European colony on Anguilla in 1650 and despite a few invasion attempts by the French it has remained a Crown Colony ever since. While arid conditions thwarted attempts to develop large plantations, the island did become an exporter of tobacco, cotton and salt. In the early

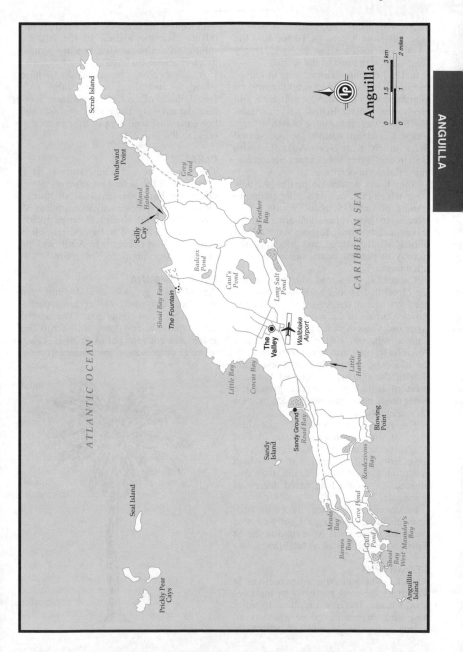

1800s Anguilla's population began to taper off from a peak of 10,500 and the island slid into a slow decline, largely forgotten by the rest of the world.

In 1967 Britain, in an attempt to loosen its colonial ties, lumped Anguilla into an alignment with the islands of St Kitts and Nevis, the nearest British dependencies. The intent was for the three islands to form a new Caribbean nation, the Associated State of St Kitts-Nevis-Anguilla, with Britain continuing to hold the reins on foreign affairs and defense.

Anguillians wanted no part of the new state, which they viewed as subjugation to a more powerful St Kitts. Within a few months, the Anguillians had armed themselves and revolted, forcing the St Kitts police off the island and blocking the runway to prevent a 'reinvasion' by Kittitian forces.

The British, concerned with the potential for bloodshed should St Kitts attempt to use force against the Anguillians, stationed Royal Marines in the waters off Anguilla. After two years of failed attempts to negotiate a solution, British forces invaded Anguilla in 1969. But rather than resisting, the islanders, content that some resolution was in the making, welcomed the first wave of British paratroopers, giving the event the bizarre aura of an Independence Day celebration.

The Anguillians eventually got their way: Britain agreed to drop the idea of Anguillian union with St Kitts and to continue British administration of the island according to a modified colonial status that granted Anguilla a heightened degree of home rule.

Incidentally, throughout the entire two-year rebellion, including the early days of the revolt when shots were fired at the St Kitts police, there were no fatalities.

GEOGRAPHY

Anguilla, which lies five miles north of St Martin, is the most northerly of the Leeward Islands. The island is about 16 miles long and three miles wide and has an indented shoreline punctuated generously with white-sand beaches. The terrain is relatively flat; the highest of the island's rolling hills, Crocus Hill, reaches a mere 213 feet above sea level.

A number of unpopulated offshore islands – including Scrub Island, Dog Island, Prickly Pear Cays and distant Sombrero Island – are also part of Anguilla and bring the total land area of the territory to 60 sq miles.

CLIMATE

The average annual temperature is 81°F (27°C), with the hottest weather occurring during the hurricane season from June to October. The average annual rainfall is 35 inches (890 mm), though it varies greatly from year to year. The lightest rainfall is generally from February to April, and the heaviest from August to November.

FLORA & FAUNA

Anguilla's vegetation is a dryland type that's been degraded by overgrazing, particularly from free-ranging goats. The vegetation is sparse and predominantly scrub. Sea grape and coconut palms grow in beach areas, as do poisonous manchineel trees.

Although most are migratory, in all about 80 species of birds are found on Anguilla. Two colorful year-round residents that visitors might spot are the black and yellow bananaquit and the green Antillean crested hummingbird. The island's numerous salt ponds are top birding areas, attracting egrets, herons, stilts, yellowlegs and white-cheeked pintail ducks. Anguilla's national bird is the commonly seen turtle dove.

GOVERNMENT & POLITICS
As a result of its revolt from St Kitts, Anguilla remains a British dependency. Under the Anguilla constitution, which came into effect in 1982, Britain is represented by a governor appointed by the Queen. The governor presides over an appointed Executive Council and an elected House of Assembly.

ECONOMY
Many Anguillians still make a living from catching lobsters and fish, though since the 1980s there has been a dramatic shift in the economy towards the tourism industry. Anguilla gets about 120,000 tourists annually of which 80,000 are day visitors.

POPULATION & PEOPLE
The population is approximately 9000. The majority of islanders are of African descent, though there's a bit of an admixture of Irish blood, particularly among people on the eastern end of the island.

SOCIETY & CONDUCT
Anguilla has a typical West Indian culture with a blend of British and African influences. Because of the dry and barren nature of the island, the small population on Anguilla has traditionally struggled to make ends meet and has looked towards the sea, in the form of fishing and boatbuilding, for its livelihood. One consequence of this seafaring heritage is a penchant for boat racing.

Dos & Don'ts
Dress is casual and simple cotton clothing is suitable attire for any occasion. In the more upscale restaurants, men will want to wear long pants, but ties and jackets are not necessary. To avoid offense, swimwear should be restricted to the beach.

RELIGION
There are Anglican, Methodist, Roman Catholic, Seventh Day Adventist, Baptist, Jehovah's Witness and Church of God churches on Anguilla.

LANGUAGE
English is the official language, spoken with a distinctive lilt.

Facts for the Visitor

ORIENTATION
The airport is in The Valley, the capital of Anguilla, which is right in the center of the island. The ferry terminal is four miles west of The Valley in the small village of Blowing Point.

From The Valley a single road leads to the west end of the island and two main roads head to the east end. All other island roads, including the spur roads that lead to the beaches, branch off from these central arteries.

Maps
The main map to the island is *Road Map Anguilla*, published annually by Cartographers Limited and distributed free by the tourist office and island businesses.

TOURIST OFFICES
Local Tourist Offices
The main tourist office (☎ 497-2759, fax 497-2710, atbtour@candw.com.ai), on Wallblake Rd in The Valley, is open from 8 am to 5 pm Monday to Friday. There's also a year-round tourist information booth at the Blowing Point ferry terminal.

When requesting information by mail, write to: Anguilla Tourist Board, PO Box 1388, The Valley, Anguilla, British West Indies.

ANGUILLA

Tourist Offices Abroad

Tourist information can be obtained from these overseas agencies:

Germany
>Anguilla Tourist Board,
>c/o Sergat Deutschland, Feldstrasse 26,
>64319 Pfungstadt
>(☎ 6157-87816, fax 6157-87719)

Italy
>Anguilla Tourist Board,
>c/o B & DP srl, Piattari 2, 20122 Milano
>(☎ 2-89516917, fax 2-8460841)

UK
>Anguilla Tourist Board,
>c/o Windotel, 3 Epirus Rd,
>London SW6 7UJ
>(☎ 0171-937-7725, fax 0171-938-4793)

USA
>Anguilla Tourist Information,
>1208 Washington Drive,
>Centerport, NY 11721
>(☎ 800-553-4939, fax 516-425-0903)

VISAS & DOCUMENTS

US and Canadian citizens can enter Anguilla with proof of citizenship in the form of a birth certificate with a raised seal accompanied by an official photo ID such as a driver's license. Citizens of most other nations require passports.

CUSTOMS

A carton of cigarettes and a bottle of liquor may be brought in duty free.

MONEY

The Eastern Caribbean dollar (EC$) is the official currency. Generally hotels, car rental agents and restaurants list prices in US dollars, while grocers and local shops mark prices in EC dollars, but you can readily use either currency and most places give a fair rate of exchange.

Barclays Bank and Scotiabank, both in The Valley, are open from 8 am to 2 pm (Scotiabank to 3 pm) Monday to Thursday, 8 am to 5 pm on Friday.

Visa, MasterCard and American Express cards are accepted at many (but not all) hotels on Anguilla, as well as moderate to high-end restaurants.

A 15% service charge is added to most restaurant bills and no further tipping is necessary. An 8% government tax and a 10% service charge is added onto hotel bills.

POST & COMMUNICATIONS
Post

Anguilla's post office is in The Valley and is open from 8 am to 3:30 pm Monday to Friday.

If you want to send mail to Anguilla, simply follow the business name with the post office box or the village/beach and 'Anguilla, British West Indies.'

The cost to mail a postcard is EC$0.35 to North, South and Central America, and EC$0.45 to Europe; letters (per half-ounce) cost EC$0.80 to the Americas, EC$1 to Europe.

Telephone

Both coin and card phones are common around the island. You can also make calls, as well as send faxes and telegrams, at the Cable & Wireless office in The Valley, which is open from 8 am to 5 pm weekdays, 9 am to 1 pm on Saturday.

Phonecards are sold at the Cable & Wireless office, the airport and numerous shops. When calling Anguilla from overseas, dial the area code 264 before the seven-digit local number.

The area code for Anguilla is 264.

NEWSPAPERS & MAGAZINES

The island's little weekly newspaper, *The Light*, comes out on Monday and covers local news and events.

The tourism guide called *What We Do in Anguilla* has visitor information, restaurant listings and lots of ads. *Anguilla Life* magazine, published three times a year, features articles on everything from archaeology to cultural events and island happenings. Both can be picked up free at the tourist office and some hotels.

RADIO & TV
The local government-run radio station is Radio Anguilla at 1505 AM and 95.5 FM. Anguilla has cable TV, with local programming on Channel 3.

ELECTRICITY
Electricity is 110 volts, 60 cycles, and a plug with two flat prongs is used, the same as in the USA.

WEIGHTS & MEASURES
Anguilla uses the imperial system. Speed limit signs are in miles as are most car odometers.

HEALTH
The island's 36-bed hospital (☎ 497-2551) is in The Valley. See the introductory Facts for the Visitor chapter for information on travel health.

DANGERS & ANNOYANCES
Anguilla has very little crime, and no unusual safety precautions are necessary.

EMERGENCIES
For police, fire or ambulance emergencies call ☎ 911.

BUSINESS HOURS
Business hours are generally 8 am to noon and 1 to 4 pm weekdays.

PUBLIC HOLIDAYS & SPECIAL EVENTS
Public holidays observed in Anguilla are:

New Year's Day	January 1
Good Friday	late March/early April
Easter Monday	late March/early April
Labour Day	May 1
Whit Monday	eighth Monday after Easter
Anguilla Day	May 30
Queen's Birthday	June 11
August Monday (*Emancipation Day*)	first Monday in August
August Thursday	first Thursday in August
Constitution Day	August 6
Separation Day	December 19
Christmas Day	December 25
Boxing Day	December 26

Note that holidays falling on the weekend are often taken on the following Monday.

Anguilla's main festival is its Carnival, which starts on the weekend preceding August Monday and continues until the following weekend. Events includes boat races, costumed parades, a beauty pageant, calypso competitions, music and dancing.

ACTIVITIES
Beaches & Swimming
Anguilla has lots of lovely white-sand beaches and you never have to go far to find one. Sandy Ground has calm turquoise waters, as do the glorious sweeps at Shoal Bay East and Rendezvous Bay. Other top beaches worth a visit include Meads Bay and Shoal Bay West. Top honors in The Valley area go to Crocus Bay, a quiet beach with good swimming and snorkeling.

Diving & Snorkeling
Anguilla has clear water and good reef formations. In addition, since the mid-1980s a number of ships have been deliberately sunk to create new dive sites; they lie on sandy bottoms in depths of 35 to 75 feet and attract numerous fish.

Offshore islands popular for diving include Prickly Pear Cays, which has caverns, ledges, barracudas and nurse sharks; Dog Island, a drift dive along a rock face with good marine life; and Sandy Island, which has soft corals and sea fans.

The Dive Shop (☎ 497-2020, fax 497-5125), PO Box 247, is at Sandy Ground. One-tank boat dives cost US$45, two-tank dives cost US$80 and night dives cost US$55, the latter requiring a minimum of four people. Resort courses are offered for US$100, PADI open-water certification courses for US$450 and open-water referral courses for US$250. Snorkel sets rent for US$10 a day.

Anguillian Divers (☎ 497-4750, fax 497-4636, axadiver@candw.com.ai), at Island Harbour, dives on the east end of Anguilla and has comparable rates.

Shoal Bay East, Sandy Island, Little Bay and Prickly Pear Cays are popular snorkeling spots. For more information see Organized Tours in the Getting Around section.

Horseback Riding
El Rancho Del Blues (☎ 497-6164), on the road to Blowing Point, offers beach and trail rides for US$25 for one hour, US$45 for two hours.

ACCOMMODATIONS
Anguilla has a reputation for being an expensive destination and for the most part accommodations are pricey.

Although visiting Anguilla can be a challenge for budget travelers, there are a few places on the island with simple rooms for around US$50. The middle range varies widely, beginning with apartments for US$75 and moving up to small beachside hotels with US$200 rooms. At the top end there are fine luxury hotels, with prices generally beginning around US$400.

In the summer many top-end and mid-range hotels drop prices substantially, while some places close down entirely if bookings are slack.

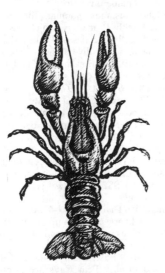

Crayfish

Despite their high prices, even many mid-range hotels lack TV and air-con. The latter is especially noteworthy for summer travelers, as many spots on the island (Sandy Ground is one place in particular) have periods of dead air when nights can be unbearably muggy.

FOOD
Lobster (common spiny lobster) and crayfish (spotted spiny lobster) are two locally caught Anguillian specialties. The crayfish, while smaller than the lobster, are reasonably sized creatures that have sweet moist meat and are commonly served three to an order.

Although a few traditional staples, such as corn and pigeon peas, are still grown on Anguilla, most food is imported and prices are higher there than they are on neighboring islands.

DRINKS
Tap water comes from rainwater catchment systems and thus should be boiled before drinking. Bottled water is readily available in grocery stores.

ENTERTAINMENT
One of the more happening places is Johnno's Beach Bar at Sandy Ground, which has live music and dancing from 8 pm on Saturday, with a US$5 cover charge.

Johnno's Beach Bar, Uncle Ernie's at Shoal Bay East and Scilly Cay, just off Island Harbour, all have live music on Sunday afternoon.

La Sirena hotel at Meads Bay has a dinner show featuring the Mayoumba Folkloric Theatre, who perform Anguillian folk songs and dance at 7:30 pm Thursday.

Several of the larger hotels and restaurants have steel drum bands, guitarists or other live music a few nights a week. See *What We Do In Anguilla* for the current entertainment schedule.

THINGS TO BUY
There are a couple of galleries on the island. The Devonish Art Gallery, on the road between The Valley and Sandy

Ground, is the show room of Barbadian artist Courtney Devonish who creates pottery and modern wood sculptures. The gallery also carries antique maps and works by other Caribbean artists.

The New World Gallery, next to the tourist office in The Valley, features both regional and international art work.

The Anguilla Arts & Crafts Centre in The Valley sells locally made silk-screened clothing, T-shirts, pottery and baskets, and has a good collection of books about Anguilla.

Getting There & Away

AIR
There are no direct trans-Atlantic flights to Anguilla. However, it's possible to make same-day international connections to get to Anguilla via St Martin or San Juan, Puerto Rico.

American Airlines' New York-Anguilla (via San Juan) 30-day excursion ticket is about US$650, although discounted fares between the US mainland and San Juan can sometimes make it cheaper to buy separate New York-San Juan and San Juan-Anguilla tickets.

American Eagle (☎ 497-3131) has at least one flight a day to Anguilla from San Juan. A roundtrip excursion fare that allows a stay of up to 30 days is US$203 with a seven-day advance purchase. The one-way fare is US$138.

Winair (☎ 497-2748) has a few flights daily between St Martin and Anguilla. The fare is US$28 one way, US$29 for a same-day return ticket and US$53 for a regular roundtrip ticket.

LIAT (☎ 497-2238) has direct daily flights to Anguilla from St Martin, St Thomas, St Kitts and Antigua. The St Martin-Anguilla fare is US$30 one way, US$60 roundtrip; St Thomas-Anguilla is US$90 one way, US$146 roundtrip; St Kitts-Anguilla is US$69 one way, US$118 roundtrip; and Antigua-Anguilla is US$85 one way, US$161 roundtrip.

Tyden Air (☎ 497-2719, in the USA 800-842-0261) flies to Anguilla from St Martin where it connects with flights on American and Continental airlines. The cost is US$30 one way. Tyden has a day trip to St Barts on Monday, Wednesday and Friday, leaving Anguilla in the morning and returning in the late afternoon. The cost for a same-day roundtrip ticket (US$100) is the same price as the regular one-way fare.

Airport Information
Anguilla's Wallblake Airport is small and modern. There are counters for LIAT, Winair, American Eagle, Air Anguilla (a local charter airline) and Tyden Air. During the high season there's sometimes a staffed tourist information booth; you can find pay phones near the arrivals exit.

There are no car rental booths at the airport but two companies, Triple K and Island Car Rentals, are within a five-minute walk north of the airport.

SEA
Inter-Island Ferry
Ferries make the 25-minute run from Marigot Bay in St Martin to Blowing Point in Anguilla an average of once every 30 minutes from 8 am to 7 pm (from 7:30 am to 6:15 pm from Anguilla to St Martin). If you're planning on catching the last ferry, reconfirm that sailing once you arrive on the island as adjustments in schedules aren't uncommon.

The one-way fare is US$10 (US$12 on the last boat of the day). Sign the passenger registration list and pay the US$2 departure tax as soon as you arrive at the dock. The fare for the passage is paid on board the boat.

Yacht
The main port of entry is at Sandy Ground in Road Bay. The immigration and customs office is open daily from 8:30 am to noon and 1 to 4 pm (closed Saturday mornings).

LEAVING ANGUILLA
There's an airport departure tax of US$10 and a ferry departure tax of US$2.

ANGUILLA

Getting Around

There's no bus service on the island and travelers will find it difficult to get around Anguilla without renting either a car or a bicycle.

TAXI

Taxis are readily available at the airport and the ferry terminal. The minimum charge is US$5. Rates from the airport are US$10 to Sandy Ground or Shoal Bay East and US$14 to Meads Bay. From Blowing Point, it costs US$10 to Sandy Ground or The Valley, US$15 to Shoal Bay East. These rates are for one or two people; each additional person is charged US$3.

CAR & MOTORCYCLE
Road Rules

In Anguilla, you drive on the left-hand side of the road. The steering wheels on virtually all rental cars, however, are also on the left-hand side. This situation can be quite disorienting!

Visitors must buy a temporary Anguillian driver's license for US$6, which is issued on the spot by the car rental companies.

The roads are generally well maintained and relatively wide by Caribbean standards. Be cautious of stray goats that occasionally bolt onto the road.

There are gas stations in The Valley, in Island Harbour, on the west end of the island near the Sonesta Beach Resort and in Blowing Point.

Rerouting

Most roads on Anguilla are not marked with names or numbers, although hotel and restaurant signs point the way to many beaches. Beware of the occasional renegade restaurant sign that appears to point to someplace nearby but is actually an attempt to reroute you halfway across the island. ∎

Rental

Compact air-conditioned cars rent for about US$40 a day with free unlimited mileage. Jeeps cost just a few dollars more.

Triple K Car Rental (☎ 497-2934, fax 497-2503), Anguilla's Hertz agent, is on Airport Rd in The Valley. Other major rental agencies are Island Car Rentals (☎ 497-2723, fax 497-3723) on Airport Rd in The Valley and Connor's Car Rental (☎ 497-6433) at the intersection at the north end of Blowing Point Rd.

Boo's Cycle Rental (☎ 497-2323), on the road between The Valley and Sandy Ground, rents scooters for around US$20.

BICYCLE

Innovation Center (☎ 497-5810), on the main road half a mile west of the airport rotary, rents mountain bikes for US$10 a day.

ORGANIZED TOURS

Taxi drivers provide tours of the island for US$40 for one or two people, US$5 for each additional person.

Among the offshore islands, one of the most popular destinations is Prickly Pear Cays, which has excellent snorkeling conditions. Tour boats leave Sandy Ground for Prickly Pear at around 10 am, returning around 4 pm; the cost averages US$80, including lunch, drinks and snorkeling gear. If you want to pack your own lunch, you can also arrange to simply be picked up and dropped off; Garfield's Sea Tours (☎ 497-2956) charges US$35 per person with a minimum of three passengers.

Also popular are sails to secluded Little Bay, on Anguilla's east coast, which is a lovely cliff-backed cove north of The Valley with a little white-sand beach and fine snorkeling. The best deal is with Calvin (☎ 497-3939), who hangs out at Roy's Place in Crocus Bay and offers a boat shuttle from there to Little Bay for just US$10 per person roundtrip.

Chocolat (☎ 497-3394), a 35-foot catamaran, offers sails to Prickly Pear, sunset cruises and private charters.

For information on boats to Sandy Island see the Sandy Ground section.

The Valley

The Valley, the island's only real town, is the geographic, commercial and political center of Anguilla. Although it's not a very large town, it's rather spread out and rambling. In part because the British moved the administration of the island to St Kitts back in 1825, there are no quaint colonial government buildings or even a central square. Most buildings are the functional type, taking on the appearance of small shopping centers.

The **Anguilla National Trust**, in the center of town between Wallblake and Airport Rds, displays changing exhibits of Anguilla's history and natural environ-

ment; it's usually open from 10 am to 5 pm Tuesday to Saturday, with free admission.

The Valley's most interesting building is the **Wallblake House**, which was built in 1787 and is one of the oldest structures on the island. The house can only be viewed from the exterior as it's the rectory for the Roman Catholic church. You can, however, view the interior of the adjacent **church**, which has a unique design incorporating a decorative stone front, open-air side walls and a ceiling shaped like the hull of a ship.

Places to Stay

Casa Nadine Guest House (☎ 497-2358) is a local boarding house with 11 very basic rooms, each with a private shower and toilet. Singles/doubles cost US$20/30.

Lloyd's Guest House (☎ 497-2351, fax 497-3028) is an old-fashioned guest house with a dozen basic rooms. All are very

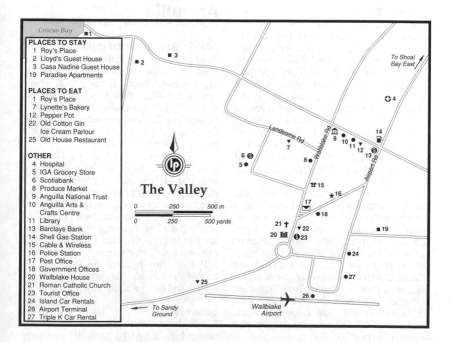

The Valley

0   250   500 m
0   250   500 yards

PLACES TO STAY
1 Roy's Place
2 Lloyd's Guest House
3 Casa Nadine Guest House
19 Paradise Apartments

PLACES TO EAT
1 Roy's Place
7 Lynette's Bakery
12 Pepper Pot
22 Old Cotton Gin
     Ice Cream Parlour
25 Old House Restaurant

OTHER
4 Hospital
5 IGA Grocery Store
6 Scotiabank
8 Produce Market
9 Anguilla National Trust
10 Anguilla Arts &
     Crafts Centre
11 Library
13 Barclays Bank
14 Shell Gas Station
15 Cable & Wireless
16 Police Station
17 Post Office
18 Government Offices
20 Wallblake House
21 Roman Catholic Church
23 Tourist Office
24 Island Car Rentals
26 Airport Terminal
27 Triple K Car Rental

Crocus Bay

To Shoal Bay East

Landsome Rd

Wallblake Rd

Airport Rd

To Sandy Ground

Wallblake Airport

straightforward, but they do have private baths and the year-round rate of US$50/70 for singles/doubles includes breakfast.

Paradise Apartments (☎ 497-2168) is opposite the Central Baptist Church in the Rey Hill area, not far from the airport. The two-story building has four modern apartments, each with a large bedroom, bathroom, separate kitchen, ceiling fans and a view of The Valley. Rates are US$60/85 in summer/winter.

Roy's Place (☎ 497-2470), on Crocus Bay, manages four inviting apartments adjacent to their restaurant. Each is clean and well equipped with full kitchen, aircon, phone, TV and balcony. The one-bedroom apartments cost US$65/110 in summer/winter for up to two people; the two-bedroom apartment US$85/165 for up to four people. The beach, which offers good swimming and snorkeling, is just a stone's throw away.

Places to Eat
Pepper Pot, west of Barclays Bank, has chicken or vegetarian rotis for EC$10, inexpensive sandwiches, and local dishes such as stewed goat or salt fish for around EC$20. It's open daily from 7 am to 10 pm.

The *Old House Restaurant*, a local favorite on the Sandy Ground road at the south side of town, has a varied menu at moderate prices. Breakfasts and lunchtime sandwiches start around US$6, while dinners begin at US$16, including the house specialty of Anguillian-style potfish served with peas and rice. It's open daily from 7 am to 10 pm.

Roy's Place, a pub-style restaurant and bar on Crocus Bay, has good food and a great beachfront location. The lunch menu includes sandwiches from US$5 and flying fish & chips for US$9, while at dinner, seafood dishes range from English-style fish & chips for US$17 to crayfish for US$30. It's busiest on Fridays from 6 to 7 pm, when there's a happy hour featuring half-price beer and a choice of two meals for US$10 or less. The kitchen is open from noon to 2 pm except Saturday and from 6 to 9 pm daily.

For The Valley's best breakfast deal, try *Lynette's Bakery* on Landsome Rd, where you can get a big slab of warm tasty bread pudding for EC$1.75 as well as cheap sandwiches to go. It's open from 6:30 am to 5 pm Monday to Saturday.

Above Lynette's in the same building is *Simply Natural*, a little health food store selling dried fruit, juices and a few packaged items. For a treat, the *Old Cotton Gin Ice Cream Parlour* serves up tropical-flavored ice cream from 10:30 am to at least 8 pm daily except Tuesday.

IGA, a new American-style grocery store, is the island's biggest. It's open from 8 am to 9 pm Monday to Saturday, 8 am to noon on Sunday. Near the corner of Wallblake and Landsome there's a produce market, but be prepared for high prices.

Central & West Anguilla

SANDY GROUND/ROAD BAY
Sandy Ground, a small village fronting Road Bay, is the closest thing Anguilla has to a travelers' haunt. It has a nice white-sand beach lined with beach-side restaurants, a dive shop and a few low-key places to stay. The fishhook-shaped bay is one of the most protected on the island and the main port of entry for yachts.

Sandy Ground is backed by a large salt pond that was commercially harvested until just a few years ago, when the cost of shipping the salt began to exceed its value. The former salt works, idle at the north end of the village, has recently been converted into a bar (The Pumphouse) and visitors are free to go in and take a look at the old salt-processing machinery.

If you enjoy birding, the quieter north end of the salt pond attracts egrets, stilts, herons and other wading birds.

Sandy Island
Sandy Island, lying a mile off Sandy Ground, is a small islet with gleaming

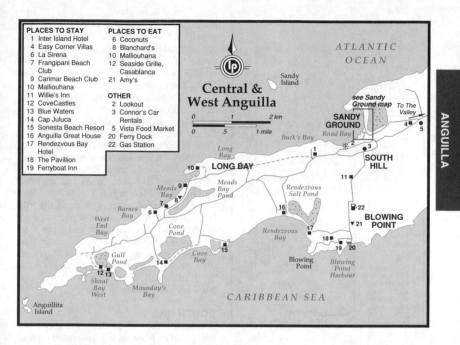

PLACES TO STAY
1 Inter Island Hotel
4 Easy Corner Villas
6 La Sirena
7 Frangipani Beach Club
9 Carimar Beach Club
10 Malliouhana
11 Willie's Inn
12 CoveCastles
13 Blue Waters
14 Cap Juluca
15 Sonesta Beach Resort
16 Anguilla Great House
17 Rendezvous Bay Hotel
18 The Pavillion
19 Ferryboat Inn

PLACES TO EAT
6 Coconuts
8 Blanchard's
10 Malliouhana
12 Seaside Grille, Casablanca
21 Amy's

OTHER
2 Lookout
3 Connor's Car Rentals
5 Vista Food Market
20 Ferry Dock
22 Gas Station

Central & West Anguilla

ATLANTIC OCEAN

white sands and a couple of coconut palms – you can walk around the whole thing in just 10 minutes. The island is surrounded by shallow reefs that offer reasonable snorkeling, with waving finger corals, sea fans and small tropical fish.

Boats leave from the pier in front of the immigration office, making the five-minute jaunt to the island on demand between 10 am and 3 pm. Buy tickets (US$8 roundtrip) at the booth next to Johnno's Beach Bar.

There's a beach bar on the island that sells US$2 beers and plate lunches from US$10 (chicken or fish) to US$20 (lobster).

Places to Stay

Located in the center of the village, the *Pond Dipper Guest House* (☎ 497-2315), on the 2nd floor of a family home, has a couple of simple rooms with a shared kitchen for US$50/60 in summer/winter.

Syd-An's Apartments (☎ 497-3180, fax 497-5381; in the USA ☎ 800-553-4939), on the beach road, has half a dozen very

pleasant apartments with separate bedrooms, full kitchens and TV. Rates are US$65/105 in summer/winter for rooms with fans, US$85/135 for rooms that have air-con.

If Syd-An's is full, the nearby *Sea View Guest House* (☎ 497-2427), has a couple of fan-cooled apartments at comparable rates.

Sandy Ground's only hotel, *Mariners Cliffside Beach Resort* (☎ 497-2671, fax 497-2901; in the USA ☎ 800-848-7938), is at the quieter south end of the beach. Many of the 67 rooms are in a cluster of attractive West Indian-style cottages with brightly painted shutters and gingerbread trim. Though it has an old-fashioned appeal, it's under new management and is in the process of being developed into an all-inclusive resort, with summer/winter rates beginning at US$140/220.

Places to Eat

Johnno's Beach Bar, a casual open-air restaurant right on the beach, has picnic

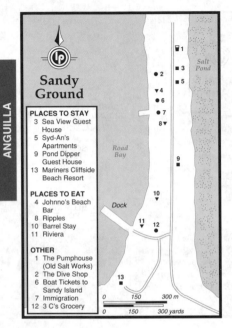

PLACES TO STAY
3 Sea View Guest House
5 Syd-An's Apartments
9 Pond Dipper Guest House
13 Mariners Cliffside Beach Resort

PLACES TO EAT
4 Johnno's Beach Bar
8 Ripples
10 Barrel Stay
11 Riviera

OTHER
1 The Pumphouse (Old Salt Works)
2 The Dive Shop
6 Boat Tickets to Sandy Island
7 Immigration
12 3 C's Grocery

tables and a simple menu. A burger with fries costs US$5.50, chicken or ribs US$10 and catch of the day US$12. It's open daily from noon to midnight, and is especially lively on Saturday nights and Sunday when there's a live band and a US$5 cover charge (no cover for diners).

Ripples, on the beach road, is a late-night place with pleasant decor and straightforward food. The varied menu has Mexican fare, fish & chips, pasta and local seafood, most priced from US$14 to US$20. It's open daily from noon to at least midnight.

The popular *Barrel Stay* has a romantic seaside setting and good fish dishes, with a number of creative preparations from around US$25 à la carte. Don't miss the fish soup, regarded as Anguilla's best. It's open daily for lunch and dinner in season.

Riviera has a pleasant beachfront veranda and serves reasonably good French fare. The kitchen does a nice job with grilled crayfish, which costs US$33. Prices on the other main dishes, such as lambi and

mahimahi, begin around US$22. There are usually a few good-value specials on offer that essentially throw in an appetizer and dessert for the same price as the main course alone. Riviera is open daily for lunch and dinner.

The Pumphouse, at the north end of Sandy Ground, is operated by a friendly couple, Laurie & Gabi Gumbs, whose family once operated a salt works in this same building. The Gumbs have turned this little historic site into an atmospheric bar, serving pub food such as kebabs and salads and offering live jazz, blues and acoustic guitar music a few nights a week.

3 C's, a small grocery store in the village, is open from 8 am to 4 pm and 5 to 8 pm Monday to Saturday and from 8 to 10 am on Sunday. For more extensive shopping, drive up to *Vista Food Market*, a well-stocked grocery store a mile away at the roundabout, open from 8 am to 6 pm Monday to Saturday.

SOUTH HILL

South Hill, the village that rises above the south end of Road Bay, is essentially a residential area although there are a couple of places to stay. There are no sights in South Hill, but you can take the one-way road that goes west to east above the cliffs for some fine views of Sandy Ground, Road Bay and Sandy Island.

Places to Stay

Easy Corner Villas (☎ 497-6433, fax 497-6410), PO Box 65, on a hillside just west of Vista Food Market, has a dozen self-catering apartments, with balconies overlooking Sandy Ground. Rates are US$160/195/240 for one/two/three-bedroom apartments in winter, US$125/155/195 in summer. Studio units cost US$90/110 in summer/winter. The office is at Connor's Car Rental, a mile to the west on the same road.

Inter Island Hotel (☎ 497-6259, fax 497-5381), PO Box 194, an older two-story hostelry at the side of the main road, has 14 plain units. Many rooms are on the small side, though some have balconies with distant ocean views. While the hotel is rather oddly located, several beaches are within a 10-minute drive. Rates are the big plus here: for standard rooms, singles/doubles cost US$40/70 in winter and US$35/60 in summer, while one-bedroom apartments cost US$85/95 in summer/winter.

BLOWING POINT

Blowing Point, where the ferry from St Martin docks, is mainly a residential area and not a major tourist center. There is a modest beach west of the immigration office as well as a few reasonably priced apartment-style places to stay, but most visitors arriving for a day visit will want to make their way to better beaches elsewhere around the island.

Places to Stay

The first two places listed are within a 10-minute walk from the ferry, on the first road to the left after leaving the terminal.

The *Ferryboat Inn* (☎ 497-6613, fax 497-6713) has eight apartments on the beach. The units are large and modern with rattan furnishings, sliding glass doors to a porch or balcony, ceiling fans and TV. Rates are from US$78/140 in summer/ winter.

The *Pavillion* (☎ 497-6395, fax 497-6234), directly opposite the Ferryboat Inn, is a modern three-story building with eight one-bedroom apartments for US$60 a night, US$300 a week. Units have full kitchens, balconies, ceiling fans and TV.

Willie's Inn (☎ 497-6225, fax 497-6819), a mile up from the ferry dock, is a two-story building with 16 units. They are simple but a good budget option, each with a fan and refrigerator; a few also have limited cooking facilities. Rates begin at US$40 a day, US$35 a day on weekly stays. Willie is negotiable on monthly rates.

Places to Eat

Up the road from the ferry terminal is *Amy's*, a small bakery with a handful of café-style tables. In addition to inexpensive slices of banana bread and moist carrot cake, you can get pancakes for breakfast

and sandwiches for lunch for around US$5 and afternoon chicken or fish meals for about twice that. It's open from 7:30 am to around 6 pm daily except Sunday.

On the right side of the road just north of the ferry terminal, there's sometimes a man with a smoke-grill who cooks some of the best grilled ribs and fish on the island.

Ferryboat Inn has a pleasant open-air beachside restaurant a few minutes west of the dock. A cheeseburger and fries cost US$9, grilled chicken US$12 and fresh fish a few dollars more. It's open for lunch and dinner.

RENDEZVOUS BAY

Rendezvous Bay is a gorgeous arc of white sand that stretches for more than a mile. There's a hotel at either end and one in the middle, but otherwise it's delightfully free of development. This sheltered bay has protected turquoise waters, a nice sandy bottom and a straight-on view of hilly St Martin to the south.

Rendezvous Bay is well known in local history as the site of a 1796 invasion by French forces who hastily plundered the island before British troops from St Kitts came to the rescue.

Beachgoers will find public beach access at the east side of the Anguilla Great House. After turning south off the main road towards the hotel, simply continue along the dirt road that skirts the salt pond until you reach the beach.

Places to Stay

The 47-room *Rendezvous Bay Hotel* (☎ 497-6549, fax 497-6026; in the USA ☎ 800-274-4893), PO Box 31, is at the east end of Rendezvous Bay and reached via Blowing Point. It has straightforward hotel rooms with twin beds and fan for US$90/120 in summer/winter, newer units with air-con, refrigerators and king beds from US$120/200 and more expensive units with kitchens. There's a restaurant and a common room with TV.

Anguilla Great House (☎ 497-6061, fax 497-6019, flemingw@zemu.candw.com.ai; in the USA ☎ 800-583-9247), PO Box 157,

ANGUILLA

sits by itself on a quiet stretch of beach at the center of Rendezvous Bay. It's a collection of cottages built in traditional West Indian design and furnished with colonial decor. The 27 rooms have ceiling fans and king or queen beds. There's a restaurant, bar and pool. Rates for up to two people begin at US$130/200 in summer/winter.

Sonesta Beach Resort (☎ 497-6999, fax 497-6899; in the USA and Canada ☎ 800-766-3782), PO Box 444, is a 100-room Moroccan-style resort at the west end of Rendezvous Bay. With its pink exterior and exotic arches, it certainly looks quite apropos for the desert if not necessarily an Anguillian one. The whole place exudes a fantasy element, from elaborate tile mosaics in the lobby to the Bogart-reminiscent Casablanca bar, and the spacious rooms have Moorish decor, Italian marble baths and modern amenities such as TV, air-con and minibar. There's a large pool, tennis courts and a fitness room. Rates begin at US$180/290 in summer/winter.

Places to Eat

The Sonesta has a couple of restaurants. The *Seaside Grille* has a US$35 buffet on Monday and Thursday, with salads, various side dishes and beef, chicken and fish main courses. More formal and expensive is the *Casablanca* restaurant, which serves Mediterranean and Caribbean-influenced cuisine.

MEADS BAY

Meads Bay boasts a lovely mile-long sweep of white sand with calm turquoise waters. It's a good beach for swimming and a great one for strolling.

Although a couple of the island's trendiest hotels and a few small condominium complexes are scattered along the beach, Meads Bay is certainly not crowded – some of the hotels are a good five-minute walk from their nearest neighbor. The bay is backed by a salt pond for most of its length. There are annual boat races from the beach on the first Thursday in August.

Places to Stay

La Sirena (☎ 497-6827, fax 497-6829; in the USA ☎ 800-331-9358, in London ☎ 0800-373-742), PO Box 200, is at the west end of Meads Bay. There are 36 attractive rooms in low-rise whitewashed buildings with red tile roofs, each room with ceiling fans, a phone and minibar. Even though it's the cheapest of the area's hotels, it's a pleasant place, with singles/doubles for US$110/145 in summer, US$190/245 in winter.

Carimar Beach Club (☎ 497-6881, fax 497-6071; in the USA ☎ 800-235-8667), PO Box 327, is a pleasant, contemporary, two-story beachfront condominium complex on the east side of Mead's Bay. The 23 units have ceiling fans, full kitchens, a living/dining room and a balcony or patio. One-bedroom apartments begin at US$225/300 in summer/winter, two bedrooms from US$280/400. From April 1 to December 15 there's a special rate for stays of seven nights or more that begins at US$130 per night.

The *Malliouhana* (☎ 497-6111, fax 497-6011; in the USA ☎ 800-835-0796), PO Box 173, on a low cliff at the east end of Meads Bay, is one of the island's most fashionable luxury hotels. The rooms are air-conditioned and have tile floors, marble baths, rattan furnishings, original art work and large patios. Rates begin at US$240 in summer, US$320 in autumn and spring and US$480 in winter. Credit cards are not accepted.

Frangipani Beach Club (☎ 497-6442, fax 497-6440; in the USA ☎ 800-892-4564), on the quiet west side of Meads Bay, is a small condominium complex of Spanish design. Its large suites have air-con, ceiling fans, full kitchens, individual washer/dryers, marbled bathrooms, king beds and beachfront terraces. Rates for one-bedroom suites are from US$250/450 in summer/winter. There are also some hotel-style rooms available from US$165/300.

Places to Eat

Blanchard's (☎ 497-6100) is an open-air restaurant that's on the beach between the

Frangipani and Carimar condo complexes. The food is good and the menu creative, with appetizers such as gazpacho with grilled shrimp, satay with apricot chutney and lobster tostadas. Main dishes, which range from US$26 to US$38, include the likes of balsamic-mango snapper, coconut shrimp and barbecued free-range chicken. It's open from 7 pm; closed on Sundays (and on Mondays in the low season).

There are also restaurants at the hotels. Most affordable is *Coconuts* at La Sirena, which has pasta, fish and chicken dishes from around US$20 and appetizers for half that. At the well-regarded *Malliouhana*, which has classic French cuisine and a lovely ocean view, dinner for two will top US$100.

SHOAL BAY WEST

Shoal Bay West is a curving half-moon bay fringed by a pretty white-sand beach. The waters are clear and sheltered. It's rather remote, with just two small resorts and a pink beach estate belonging to actor Chuck Norris. The salt pond that backs the beach was used to harvest salt until just a few decades ago.

There's another glistening white-sand beach, Maunday's Bay, to the east, but it's largely dominated by Cap Juluca, an exclusive resort of Moorish design.

Places to Stay

CoveCastles (☎ 497-6801, fax 497-6051; in the USA ☎ 800-223-1108), PO Box 248, is a complex of 13 stark white villas with a futuristic sculptural design that's won kudos in architectural circles. The island's most upscale retreat, the villas are handsomely decorated with all rooms facing the sea. They have cable TV, VCRs, phones, hammocks on the terraces, full kitchens right down to the crystal and rates that start at US$425/695 in summer/winter.

Blue Waters (☎ 497-6292, fax 497-6982), PO Box 69, is just down the beach from CoveCastles. A bit more conventional in design, it's a modern two-story building with nine apartments, each with a beach-front balcony or terrace, a kitchen, ceiling fans and TV. Summer/winter rates are US$115/195 for a one-bedroom unit, US$160/285 for a two-bedroom unit.

Places to Eat

The restaurant at *CoveCastles* (☎ 497-6801) has a new well-credentialed chef from New York and is the trendiest place to eat on Anguilla. It has a changing menu, but signature dishes include the crayfish ravioli appetizer (US$14), potato-crusted red snapper (US$30) and a souffle-like chocolate pudding cake (US$12). It's open to the public for dinner only, seating is limited and reservations are required.

East Anguilla

SHOAL BAY EAST

Shoal Bay, often referred to as Shoal Bay East to distinguish it from Shoal Bay West, is considered by beach connoisseurs to be Anguilla's premier strand. At the northeast side of the island, Shoal Bay East is broad and long with radiant white sands and clear turquoise waters that are ideal for swimming, snorkeling and just plain lazing. To add to its appeal there are a couple of small hotels and restaurants on the beach, but virtually no other development in sight.

A trailer behind Uncle Ernie's beach bar rents snorkel gear (US$8 a day), lounge chairs and umbrellas.

The Fountain

The island's top archaeological site is the Fountain, a huge underground cave located along a rocky pathway a few hundred yards southeast of the Fountain Beach Hotel.

The cave, which draws its name from its former importance as a freshwater spring, contains scores of Amerindian petroglyphs, including a rare stalagmite carving of Jocahu, the Arawak God of Creation. The Fountain is thought to have been a major regional worship site and a place of pilgrimage for Amerindians. A national

ANGUILLA

park, with the Fountain at its centerpiece, has been proposed. In the meantime the Fountain remains the domain of archaeologists only and the ladder leading down into the cave has been fenced off to protect the site from damage.

Places to Stay

Fountain Beach Hotel (☎ 497-3491, fax 497-3493), at the secluded west end of Shoal Bay, is a modern little hotel whose 10 units have a lightly posh Italian decor. There's a poolside hotel room without a kitchen that costs US$100/150 in summer/ winter, a junior suite for US$170/245 and larger one- and two-bedroom suites priced from 20% to 50% more. Suites have full kitchens, comfortable living rooms with sofabeds and beachfront porches.

Shoal Bay Villas (☎ 497-2051, fax 497-3631; in the USA ☎ 800-722-7045), PO Box 81, has a splendid beachfront location and 13 large, comfortable units with tropical decor. For two people in summer/winter, studios cost US$142/235, one-bedroom apartments US$167/255. Two-bedroom apartments cost US$257/385 for up to four people. All have ceiling fans, a kitchen and a patio or balcony. There's a pool.

There are two apartment-style places at the east side of Shoal Bay within walking distance of the beach. *Milly's Inn* (☎ 497-2465, fax 497-5591), about five minutes from the beach, is a modern two-story building with just four units, each with a full kitchen, ceiling fans, white tile floors and a large oceanview balcony. The rate is US$110 in summer, US$140 in winter.

Allamanda (☎ 497-5217, fax 497-5216, allamanda@offshore.com.ai), just a two-minute walk from the beach, has 16 studio and one-bedroom apartments in a three-story building. The one-bedroom apartments aren't fancy but they have a small separate kitchen, living room, balcony, TV and ceiling fans. They cost US$118 to US$165 depending largely on their size and whether there's a queen or king bed. There are also a couple of studios for US$85 but sleeping is on a pull-out sofa. There's a pool and restaurant.

Places to Eat

At *Uncle Ernie's*, a popular local beach bar west of Shoal Bay Villas, you can get barbecued chicken, ribs or a cheeseburger for US$6 and wash it down with a US$2 Heineken. There are also more expensive fish, crayfish and lobster offerings. It's open from 9 am to 8 pm daily.

A bit more upmarket, but still with a casual beachside setting, is *Le Beach Bar* at Shoal Bay Villas, which has lunchtime sandwiches, salads and burgers for around US$10 and dinnertime meat and seafood dishes from around US$20.

Zara's, the new poolside restaurant at Allamanda, is the domain of Shamash, a local chef who focuses on Caribbean-influenced dishes such as crusted snapper, Bahamian conch and 'Rasta Pasta.' Most dishes, with the exception of lobster, are priced between US$16 and US$20.

ISLAND HARBOUR

Island Harbour is a working fishing village, not a resort area, and its beach is lined with brightly colored fishing boats rather than chaise lounges. Still it does have a few places to stay and eat and some travelers make their base here.

The area's historic site, albeit sadly neglected, is **Big Spring**, a partially collapsed limestone cave 10 yards west of the Island Pub supermarket. The cave contains 28 Amerindian petroglyphs and an underwater spring that once served as the village water source. The good news is that Big Spring has recently come under the jurisdiction of the Anguilla National Trust and there are plans to clean it up and make it accessible to visitors.

Just off Island Harbour, in the center of the bay, is the tiny private island of **Scilly Cay**, which has an open-air restaurant and bar and is fringed with a beach of bone-white sands. It can make for a fun afternoon of food, music and swimming.

Scrub Island

Scrub Island is the 2½-mile-long island that lies just off Anguilla's northeastern tip. Befitting its name the island has scrubby vegetation and is inhabited only by goats. It has a beach on its west side, some good snorkeling spots, and a blocked-off airstrip that's rumored to have once been used by cocaine runners. If you don't have your own boat, Smitty's beachside bar (☎ 497-4300) can arrange one to take you to the island for around US$50. There are no facilities; bring your own picnic.

Places to Stay

Harbor Lights (☎ 497-4435, in the USA ☎ 800-759-9870), PO Box 181, a tidy little place right on the ocean at the east side of town, has the area's best-value accommodations. There are four pleasant waterfront studios, all with full kitchens and baths with solar-heated showers. Rates are US$90 to US$100 for the three units that have a queen bed, US$70 for the smaller unit with a double bed. You can snorkel just a few feet from the deck; diving and other water sports can be arranged. Bicycle rentals are available.

Arawak Beach Resort (☎ 497-4888, fax 497-4898), PO Box 98, a small hotel on the west side of Island Harbour, has a dozen units in rough two-story buildings that take design influences from the ancient Arawaks who once occupied this area. Units have ceiling fans, private baths and refrigerators. Unfortunately, the accommodations are a bit tired relative to the rates: doubles cost US$100/150 in summer/winter, US$140/210 for units with kitchenettes.

Places to Eat

Smitty's is a beachside bar and restaurant with simple barbecue fare: hamburgers cost US$5, ribs, chicken or fish US$10 and lobster about US$20. There's a live band on Thursday evenings and from noon on Sunday.

Hibernia (☎ 497-4290), half a mile east of Island Harbour in the Harbour View residential area, is one of the island's top restaurants and features Caribbean nouvelle cuisine with Asian hints. There's veranda dining and a hillside setting with a spectacular sea view. Starters cost US$7 to US$10. Main courses range from a US$20 chicken dish to creative seafood dishes such as Thai-style bouillabaisse or grilled crayfish in a lime-soya sauce for US$32. In winter it's open for lunch and dinner from Tuesday to Sunday; in summer it's open for dinner from Tuesday to Saturday.

Scilly Cay (☎ 497-5123) has a casual lunchtime restaurant with chicken plates for US$25, fresh lobster for US$40, and a bar that's open from 11 am to 5 pm. Guests can pick up a free boat shuttle by going to the Island Harbour pier and waving towards the island. A reggae band plays on Sunday, a guitarist on Wednesday, a steel pan band on Friday. It's closed on Monday.

ANGUILLA

Antigua & Barbuda

Antigua's chief drawing cards are its fine beaches and abundance of colonial-era historic sites. Old stone windmills from long-abandoned sugar plantations are so plentiful that they are the island's main landmarks. The renovated colonial-era naval base of Nelson's Dockyard now attracts yachters from around the world and the scattered ruins of an extensive hilltop fortress are found at neighboring Shirley Heights.

HIGHLIGHTS

- Renovated colonial-era sights, including a working sugar mill at Betty's Hope and the 18th-century Nelson's Dockyard
- Scenic Shirley Heights' lively barbecue, with steel pan and reggae bands
- Antigua and Barbuda's fringing white-sand beaches
- Touring the Caribbean's largest frigatebird rookery in Barbuda

---

Antigua's hotels are spread out along its sandy beaches; Dickenson Bay and neighboring Runaway Bay have the most places to stay but remote resorts are scattered around the island.

Barbuda, 25 miles to the north, is the other half of the dual-island nation of Antigua & Barbuda. This quiet, single-village island has less than 2% of the nation's population. Barbuda gets very few visitors, mainly bird watchers who come to see its frigatebird colony and a few yachters who enjoy its clear waters and remote beaches. Information on visiting Barbuda is at the end of this chapter.

In early September 1995, Hurricane Luis slammed Antigua and Barbuda with winds in excess of 125 mph. On Barbuda, all hotels were damaged and an estimated 50% of the homes were destroyed. On Antigua, nearly 75% of the homes received significant damage and many public buildings, including schools and the hospital, were rendered unsafe. In all, two people were killed, more than 100 people were injured and total damages were estimated at some US$375 million. The recovery has been a slow one, but at this point most homes have been rebuilt and the majority of hotels and guest houses have reopened.

Facts about Antigua & Barbuda

HISTORY

The first permanent residents are thought to have been migrating Arawaks who established agricultural communities on both Antigua and Barbuda about 2000 years ago. Around 1200 AD the Arawaks were forced out by invading Caribs, who used the islands as bases for their forays in the region but apparently didn't settle them.

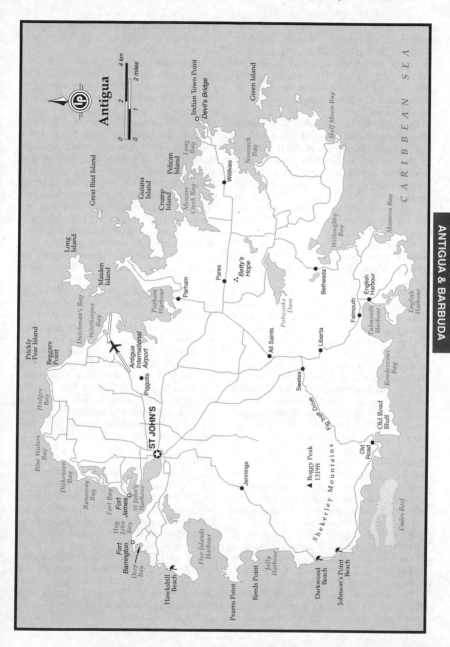

Columbus sighted Antigua in 1493 and named it after a church in Seville, Spain. In 1632 the British colonized Antigua, establishing a settlement at Parham on the east side of the island. The settlers started planting indigo and tobacco but a glut in the market for those crops soon undermined prices.

In 1674, Sir Christopher Codrington arrived on Antigua and established the first sugar plantation, Betty's Hope. By the end of the century, a plantation economy had developed, slaves were imported and the central valleys were deforested and planted in cane. To feed the slaves, Codrington leased the island of Barbuda from the British Crown and planted it with food crops.

As Antigua prospered, the British built numerous fortifications around the island, turning it into one of their most secure bases in the Caribbean. The military couldn't secure the economy, however, and in the early 1800s the sugar market began to bottom out. With the abolition of slavery in 1834 the plantations went into a steady decline. Unlike on some other Caribbean islands, as the plantations went under, the land was not turned over to former slaves but was consolidated under the ownership of a few landowners. Consequently, the lot of most people only worsened. Many former slaves moved off the plantations and into shanty towns, while others crowded onto properties held by the church.

A military-related construction boom during WWII and the development of a tourist industry during the post-war period helped spur economic growth, although the shanty towns that remain along the outskirts of St John's are ample evidence that not everyone has benefited.

After more than 300 years of colonial rule, in 1967 Antigua achieved a measure of self-government as an Associated State of the United Kingdom. On November 1, 1981, it achieved full independence.

Vere Cornwall Bird became the nation's first prime minister, and despite leading a government marred by political scandals he held that position through four consecutive terms. He stepped down in 1994 to be succeeded by his son Lester.

Another son, Vere Bird Jr, received international attention in 1991 as the subject of a judicial inquiry into his involvement in smuggling Israeli weapons to the Medellin drug cartel. His signature on documents, which were required by Israeli authorities to prove the weapons were bound for a legitimate buyer, allowed the cargo to be shipped to a nonexistent officer of the Antigua Defence Force.

After eight hours in port the weapons were transferred to a Columbian boat and shipped to the Medellin cartel without interference by customs. As a consequence of the inquiry, Vere Bird Jr was pressured into resigning his cabinet post but was allowed to keep his parliamentary position and remains a power figure in Antiguan politics.

Despite their stronghold on government, controversy continues to surround the Birds. In 1997, Prime Minister Lester Bird announced that a group of ecologically sensitive nearshore islands, including Guiana Island, which had been proposed for national park status, were being turned over to Malaysian developers. The deal, which calls for a 1000-room hotel, an 18-hole golf course and a world-class casino, sparked widespread criticism by environmentalists, minority members in parliament and the press.

GEOGRAPHY

The island of Antigua has a land area of 108 sq miles. It is vaguely rounded in shape, averaging about 11 miles across. Antigua's deeply indented coastline is cut by numerous coves and bays, many lined with white-sand beaches. The southwest corner is volcanic in origin and quite hilly, rising to 1319 feet at Boggy Peak, the island's highest point. The rest of the island, which is predominantly of limestone and coral formation, is given to a more gently undulating terrain of open plains and scrubland.

The island of Barbuda, 25 miles north of Antigua, has a land area of 62 sq miles. A low-lying coral island, Barbuda's highest point is a mere 145 feet. The west side of Barbuda encompasses the expansive Codrington Lagoon, which is bound by a long undeveloped barrier beach.

The country's boundaries also include Redonda, an uninhabited rocky islet, less than one sq mile in size, which lies 25 miles southwest of Antigua.

CLIMATE

In January and February, the coolest months, the daily high temperature averages 81°F (27°C), while the nightly low temperature averages 72°F (22°C). In July and August, the hottest months, the high averages 86°F (30°C), the low 77°F (25°C).

Antigua is relatively dry, averaging about 45 inches (1150 mm) of rain annually. The rainiest months are September to November, when measurable precipitation occurs on average eight days each month. February to April is the driest period, with an average of three rainy days each month.

FLORA & FAUNA

As a consequence of colonial-era deforestation most of Antigua's vegetation is dryland scrub. The island's marshes and salt ponds attract a fair number of stilts, egrets, ducks and pelicans, while hummingbirds are found in garden settings.

Guiana Island, off the northeast coast, has one of Antigua's largest remaining tracts of forest, is the sole habitat for the tropical mockingbird and supports the largest colony of nesting seabirds on Antigua. These include tropicbirds, roseate terns, brown noddies and endangered whistling ducks.

One of the world's rarest snakes, the Antiguan racer, is found on nearby Great Bird Island. The area also supports the fourth largest mangrove system in the Lesser Antilles. Unfortunately, the government is targeting Guiana Island and eight smaller adjacent islands for intensive resort development.

Barbuda's Codrington Lagoon has the largest frigatebird colony in the Lesser Antilles. For more information on frigatebirds see the Barbuda section.

GOVERNMENT & POLITICS

The nation of Antigua & Barbuda is a member of the Commonwealth and has a parliamentary system of government that's led by a prime minister and modeled after the British system. There's an elected 17-member House of Representatives and an appointed 17-member Senate. Elections are held at least once every five years.

The British monarchy is represented by a Governor-General who has a role in appointing members of the senate but is otherwise largely an advisory figure.

ECONOMY

Tourism is the island's main industry, accounting for about half of the workforce. Agriculture and fishing employ about 10% of the workforce. There's a bit of small-scale manufacturing, primarily in garment and electronics assembly.

POPULATION & PEOPLE

About 65,000 people live on Antigua. Approximately 90% are of African descent. There are also small minority populations of British, Portuguese and Lebanese ancestry. The population of Barbuda is approximately 1200. Most inhabitants are of African descent.

SOCIETY & CONDUCT

Away from the resorts, Antigua retains a traditional West Indian character. It's manifested in the gingerbread architecture found around the capital, the popularity of steel band, calypso and reggae music and in festivities such as Carnival. English traditions also play an important role, as is evident in the national sport of cricket.

Dos & Don'ts

Dress is casual and simple cotton clothing is suitable attire for most occasions. In a few of the most upscale resort restaurants, jackets and ties are required of men. To avoid offense, restrict swimwear to the beach.

RELIGION
Nearly half of all Antiguans are members of the Anglican Church. Other denominations include Roman Catholic, Moravian, Methodist, Seventh Day Adventist, Lutheran and Jehovah's Witness.

LANGUAGE
English is the official language, most often spoken with a distinctive Antiguan lilt.

Facts for the Visitor

ORIENTATION
Antigua's airport is at the northeast side of the island, about a 15-minute drive from either St John's or Dickenson Bay.

Finding your way around is difficult on Antigua. Virtually none of the roads are posted other than by private signs pointing the way to restaurants, hotels and a few other tourist spots. Beyond that the best landmarks are old stone windmills, which are shown on the Ordnance Survey map of Antigua – a very handy item to have if you intend to do extensive exploring.

Maps
The tourist office distributes a free color map of Antigua & Barbuda, which should suffice if you're touring by taxi or bus.

The best road map of Antigua is the 1:50,000 scale British Ordnance Survey map, *Tourist Map of Antigua*, reprinted in 1992. It can be bought at the Map Shop in St John's (EC$21) and a few other places around the island.

TOURIST OFFICES
Local Tourist Offices
The main tourist office is on Thames St in St John's. When requesting information by mail, write to: Antigua & Barbuda Department of Tourism (☎ 462-0480, fax 462-2483), PO Box 363, St John's, Antigua,

West Indies. There's a tourist information booth at the airport as well.

Tourist Offices Abroad
Tourist offices abroad include:

Canada
    Antigua & Barbuda Department of Tourism,
    60 St Clair Ave E, Suite 304,
    Toronto, Ontario M4T 1N5
    (☎ 416-961-3085, fax 416-961-7218)
Germany
    Antigua & Barbuda Department of Tourism,
    Thomasstr II, 61328 Bad Homburg
    (☎ 6172-21504, fax 6172-21513)
Italy
    Antigua & Barbuda Department of Tourism,
    Via Santa Maria alla Porta, No. 9,
    Milan 20123 (☎ & fax 2-877983)
UK
    Antigua & Barbuda Department of Tourism,
    High Commission, Antigua House,
    15 Thayer St, London W1M 5LD, England
    (☎ 0171-486-7073, fax 0171-486-9970)
USA
    Antigua & Barbuda Department of Tourism,
    610 Fifth Ave, Suite 311,
    New York, NY 10020
    (☎ 212-541-4117, 888-268-4227;
    fax 212-757-1607; antibar@ix.netcom.com)

VISAS & DOCUMENTS
Visitors from the USA, Canada and the UK may enter the country for stays of less than six months with either a valid passport or a birth certificate with a raised seal plus a photo ID.

Most other visitors, including citizens of Australia, New Zealand and West European countries, must have passports but do not need visas.

Officially all visitors need a roundtrip or onward ticket.

CUSTOMS
Arriving passengers may bring in a carton of cigarettes, one quart of liquor and six ounces of perfume duty free.

MONEY
The currency of Antigua & Barbuda is the Eastern Caribbean dollar (EC$) and the official exchange rate is US$1=EC$2.70.

US dollars are widely accepted. However, unless rates are posted in US dollars, as is the norm with accommodations, it usually works out better to pay for things in EC dollars.

MasterCard, Visa and American Express are widely accepted. Credit card charges are made in US dollars, so businesses that quote prices in EC dollars must convert the bill to a US dollar total. Whenever you intend to pay by credit card it's a good idea to ask about the exchange rate first, as some places use EC$2.60 or EC$2.65 to US$1, but others use EC$2.50, a hefty 8% overcharge.

A 10% service charge is added to most restaurant bills, in which case no further tipping is necessary.

POST & COMMUNICATIONS
Post
The main post office is in St John's and there are branch post offices at Nelson's Dockyard and the airport. The rate to send a postcard to North America or the UK is EC$0.45, to Australia or Europe EC$0.60; a half-ounce letter costs EC$0.90 and EC$1.20, respectively.

Mail sent to Antigua should have the post office box or street address followed by 'St John's, Antigua, West Indies.'

Telephone
Almost all pay phones have been converted to the Caribbean Phone Card system. Phonecards can be bought from vendors in areas near the phones and from the Cable & Wireless offices in St John's or English Harbour. They're priced from EC$10 to EC$60, depending on the number of time units they have.

Avoid the credit card phones found at the airport and in some hotel lobbies as they charge a steep US$2 per minute locally, US$4 to other Caribbean islands or the USA and as much as US$8 elsewhere.

When calling Antigua from overseas dial the 268 area code, followed by the seven-digit local phone number.

More information on phonecards and making long-distance calls is under Post &

Communications in Facts for the Visitor, in the front of the book.

The area code for Antigua & Barbuda is 268.

BOOKS
Antigua's best known writer is Jamaica Kincaid who has authored a number of novels and essays including *A Small Place* (1988), which gives a scathing account of the negative effects of tourism on Antigua. Other internationally recognized works by Kincaid include the novel *Annie John*, which recounts growing up in Antigua, and *At the Bottom of the River*, a collection of short stories.

Desmond Nicholson, president of the Historical and Archaeological Society of Antigua and Barbuda, has published several works on island history, including *Antigua, Barbuda & Redonda: A Historical Sketch*.

NEWSPAPERS & MAGAZINES
Antigua has two daily newspapers, the pro-government *Antigua Sun* and the opposition-leaning *Daily Observer*. Both concentrate on local issues.

Jamaica Kincaid

ANTIGUA & BARBUDA

The best source of tourist information is the glossy 80-page *Antigua & Barbuda Adventure*, a free magazine published annually, which has a couple of feature stories, lots of ads, and listings for most of Antigua's accommodations. It can be picked up at the airport tourist office counter and at some hotels.

RADIO & TV
Gem radio, at 93.9 FM, has hourly headline news and marine weather forecasts. Some hotels have Cable TV, which is predominantly US network programming.

ELECTRICITY
Most hotels operate on 110 volts AC, 60 cycles; however, some places use 220 volts. Check before plugging anything in.

WEIGHTS & MEASURES
Antigua uses the imperial system of measurement. Car odometers register in miles, speed limits are posted in miles per hour and gas is sold by the gallon.

HEALTH
Antigua's 225-bed Holberton Hospital (☎ 462-0251) is on the eastern outskirts of St John's, just off the Queen Elizabeth Highway.

DANGERS & ANNOYANCES
Visitors should be careful to not leave their valuables unattended and should be cautious about walking in secluded places after dark. Women traveling alone may find themselves the target of unwanted attention and sexual advances, particularly if they venture into less touristed areas.

EMERGENCIES
The police headquarters (☎ 462-0125) is on American Rd on the eastern outskirts of St John's. There are substations near Nelson's Dockyard at English Harbour and in central St John's on Newgate St.

BUSINESS HOURS
Typical business hours are 8 am to noon and 1 to 4 pm Monday to Friday; note that government offices generally close an hour early on Friday.

PUBLIC HOLIDAYS & SPECIAL EVENTS
Public holidays in Antigua & Barbuda are:

New Year's Day	January 1
Good Friday	late March/early April
Easter Monday	late March/early April
Labour Day	first Monday in May
Whit Monday	eighth Monday after Easter
Queen's Birthday	second Saturday in June
Carnival Monday	first Monday in August
Carnival Tuesday	first Tuesday in August
Antigua & Barbuda	
Independence Day	November 1
Christmas Day	December 25
Boxing Day	December 26

Carnival, Antigua's big annual festival, is held from the end of July and culminates in a parade on the first Tuesday in August. Calypso music, steel bands, masqueraders, floats and street jump-ups are all part of the celebrations.

Antigua Sailing Week is a major week-long yachting event that begins on the last Sunday in April. It generally attracts about 150 boats from a few dozen countries. In addition to a series of five boat races, there are rum parties and a formal ball, with most activities taking place at Nelson's Dockyard and Falmouth Harbour.

ACTIVITIES
Beaches & Swimming
Antigua's tourist office boasts that the island has 365 beaches, 'one for each day of the year.' While the count may be suspect, the island certainly doesn't lack in lovely strands. Most of Antigua's beaches have white or light golden sands, many are protected by coral reefs and all are officially public. You can find nice sandy stretches all around the island and, generally, wherever there's a resort there's a beach. Prime beaches on the east coast include: the adjacent Dickenson and Runaway beaches, Deep Bay and Hawksbill Beach to the west of St John's and Darkwood Beach to the south. On the east coast Half Moon Bay is a top contender. Those

based in the English Harbour area can make their way to Galleon Beach and the secluded Pigeon Beach.

The far ends of some public beaches, including the north side of Dickenson, are favored by topless bathers, and nude bathing is practiced along a section of Hawksbill Beach.

Diving

Antigua has some excellent diving with coral canyons, wall drops and sea caves hosting a range of marine creatures, including turtles, sharks, barracuda and colorful reef fish. Popular diving sites include the two-mile-long Cades Reef, whose clear calm waters have an abundance of fish and numerous soft and hard corals, and Ariadne Shoal, which offers reefs teaming with large fish, lobsters and nurse sharks. A fun spot for both divers and snorkelers is *Jettias*, a 310-foot steamer that sank in 1917 and now provides a habitat for reef fish and coral. The deepest end of the wreck is in about 30 feet of water while the shallowest part comes up almost to the surface.

Dive Shops The going rate is about US$45 for a one-tank dive, US$70 for a two-tank dive, US$55 for a night dive and US$450 for full certification courses. Non-divers who want to view the underwater world but not overly commit can opt for a half-day resort course that culminates with a reef dive for around US$85.

Dive shops in Antigua include:

Deep Bay Divers, PO Box 2150, at Heritage Quay in St John's (☎ / fax 463-8000)
Dive Antigua, PO Box 251, at Rex Halcyon Cove on Dickenson Beach (☎ 462-3483, fax 462-7787)
Dockyard Divers, PO Box 184, at Nelson's Dockyard (☎ 460-1178, fax 460-1179)
Jolly Dive, PO Box 744, at Jolly Harbour (☎ / fax 462-8305)
Octopus Divers, PO Box 2105, at Falmouth Harbour (☎ 460-6286, fax 463-8528)

Snorkeling

Paradise Reef, which has shallow waters and a variety of fish, is a popular destination for snorkel tours, and some of the dive

shops will take visitors there. However, it may be more convenient to go with one of the beach operators, such as Tony's Water Sports (☎ 462-6326) at Dickenson Bay, as they go out a few times a day. The going rate is US$20, snorkel gear included.

For snorkeling from the shore, the wreck of the *Andes* near the Royal Antiguan hotel at Deep Bay and the reef fronting nearby Hawksbill Beach are popular spots. You can rent snorkel sets for US$10 a day from Tony's Water Sports and from some dive shops.

For information on snorkeling with catamaran tours, see Organized Tours in the Getting Around section of this chapter.

Windsurfing

Antigua's sheltered west coast is best for beginners. The open east coast has conditions more suitable for advanced windsurfers, with onshore winds good for slalom and wave-slalom sailing.

At Dickenson Bay, the Rex Halcyon Cove hotel (☎ 462-0256) gives two-hour windsurfing lessons for US$40.

Windsurfing Antigua (☎ 462-9463), a windsurfing school at the Lord Nelson Beach Hotel on Dutchman's Bay, at the northeast side of Antigua, gives two-hour beginner lessons for US$50.

Rental gear for intermediate and advanced windsurfing costs US$20/50/225 an hour/day/week and lessons in waterstart, jibes and advanced windsurfing techniques cost US$25.

Fishing

Game fish caught in Antiguan waters include marlin, tuna and wahoo. Tony's Water Sports (☎ 462-6326) at Dickenson Bay offers a half-day deep-sea fishing trip for US$380, a full day for US$780, which covers up to four people. Most other deep-sea fishing boats, including *La Gioconda* (☎ 463-1665) charge around US$440 for a half day.

Hiking

The historical society, which operates the Museum of Antigua & Barbuda, sponsors a culturally or environmentally oriented hike once a month. Walks average about 90 minutes in duration and typically visit old estates or interesting landscapes. The walks are free, but donations are welcome. Call the museum (☎ 462-4930) for information on upcoming hikes.

If you want to move at a quicker pace, the local Hash House Harriers club does a morning jog on alternate Saturdays and welcomes visitors to come along. Call O'Grady's pub (☎ 462-5392) for the latest schedule.

Golf
The Cedar Valley Golf Club (☎ 462-0161), a 10-minute drive north of St John's, has an 18-hole course and green fees of US$35. The 18-hole Jolly Harbour Golf Course (☎ 480-6950) at Jolly Harbour has green fees of US$30, half that if you only want to play nine holes. Both have cart and club rentals.

Half Moon Bay Hotel (☎ 460-4300) has a nine-hole course that's been closed since the hurricane but is expected to eventually reopen.

ACCOMMODATIONS
Other than a couple of budget guest houses in St John's, Antigua has few truly inexpensive options. There are a few good-value, moderate-range places around the island, with prices beginning at about US$70 for a double in summer and closer to US$100 in winter. Still, most of what Antigua has to offer is easily priced at double that.

Top-end resorts average about US$300 in winter for 'standard' rooms – and many of these rooms really are quite standard, despite the price. If you want better amenities, more space or an ocean view, you often have to step up to a more expensive room category.

If you plan on traveling in late summer keep in mind that many of Antigua's hotels close for the month of September and some extend that a few weeks in either direction.

In addition to the rates given throughout this chapter, an 8.5% government tax and a

10% service charge are added to all bills for accommodations.

FOOD
There's a fairly good range of West Indian, French, Italian, English and North American food around the island. Most restaurants feature fresh seafood, with the catch of the day commonly being one of the better-value options.

For a good cheap local snack, order a roti, the West Indian version of a burrito that's filled with curried potatoes, chicken or beef.

Try one of the locally grown black pineapples, which are quite sweet, rather small and, despite the name, not at all black.

DRINKS
It's best to boil or otherwise treat tap water before drinking it. Bottled water is available in grocery stores.

Cavalier and English Harbour are two locally made rums and the island brews its own lager under the label Wadadli.

ENTERTAINMENT
The best music scene is at *Shirley Heights Lookout*, above English Harbour, which has back-to-back live steel band and reggae performances from mid-afternoon on Sunday and Thursday. *Millers By the Sea*, at Fort James, has nightly live music that ranges from jazz to calypso. *Spinnaker's* at Dickenson Bay has a band on Friday and Saturday nights and *Margaritas* at Redcliffe Quay in St John's has live reggae music on Sunday nights.

There are several casinos on Antigua, including one at Heritage Quay in St John's and another at the Royal Antiguan hotel on Deep Bay.

THINGS TO BUY
Caribelle Batiks in St John's sells quality Caribbean-made wall hangings and clothing. The Art Centre, near Limey's restaurant at Nelson's Dockyard, sells local artwork and inexpensive prints. T-shirts, jewelry and other souvenirs are available from vendors at the entrance to Nelson's

Dockyard and in St John's along Thames St between the two quays. Harmony Hall at Nonsuch Bay has a fine collection of quality arts and crafts, with changing exhibitions of work by local and regional artists.

You can buy 'duty-free' liquor at Heritage Quay or the airport departure lounge, with Johnny Walker Red selling for around US$15 and Antiguan rum for US$6. Rum can also be bought in local shops around the island for about the same price.

Getting There & Away

AIR
USA
American Airlines (☎ 462-0952) has three daily flights between Antigua and San Juan that connect with direct flights to Boston, New York and Miami. Continental (☎ 462-5353) flies from New York to Antigua daily in winter and a few times a week in summer. BWIA (☎ 462-0262) has daily nonstop flights to Antigua from New York and Miami. Fares depend on the season and current promotions, but from the US east coast they generally begin around US$500 for a ticket allowing stays of up to 30 days.

Canada
BWIA (462-0262) flies direct between Toronto and Antigua once a week and via Trinidad twice weekly. Air Canada (☎ 462-1147) flies direct between Toronto and Antigua on Saturday. With either airline the cheapest fare is around C$700 and allows a maximum stay of 21 days.

UK
British Airways (☎ 462-0876) has direct flights from London on Tuesday, Thursday and Saturday. Fares vary a bit with the season but are typically around £770 for a 21-day advance purchase ticket allowing stays of up to six months.

Europe
Air France (☎ 462-0983) has a weekly flight on Sunday between Paris and Antigua. The cheapest fare requires payment at the time of reservation but allows up to a one-year stay and costs 3460F.

Within the Caribbean
As LIAT is home-based in Antigua, you can get either a direct or a connecting flight from Antigua to any destination in LIAT's network.

LIAT flights from Antigua to Montserrat cost US$39 one way, US$73 roundtrip; to St Kitts they cost US$56 one way, US$106 roundtrip; to St Martin they cost US$86 one way, US$111 for same-day return and US$155 for a 30-day roundtrip; to Martinique it's US$133 one way, US$190 for a seven-day roundtrip and US$220 for a 30-day roundtrip ticket that allows a stopover in Dominica or Guadeloupe.

The LIAT ticketing and reservation office (☎ 462-0700) is at the airport, tucked behind the American Airlines check-in counter. It's open from 6:15 am to 6 pm daily.

Airport Information
Travelers island hopping through the Eastern Caribbean can expect to do some transiting through Antigua's VC Bird International Airport. The departure lounge has a couple of souvenir and duty-free liquor shops and coin and card phones. The bar sells drinks and sandwiches, and for long layovers you can order pizza and pasta from the upstairs restaurant via the bar.

Those not in transit will find a tourist information booth between immigration and customs. The staff distributes maps and brochures and can help with booking rooms.

Outside the arrivals exit, there are agents for a dozen car rental companies. Nearby is a post office, an exchange bank that's open from 9 am to 3 pm weekdays and an affiliated Bureau de Change window that's open weekdays from 3 to 9:30 pm and weekends from noon to 7 pm. There's also a 24-hour ATM that accepts Visa, MasterCard and Cirrus and Plus bank cards.

The middle phone of the three that are marked 'card' at the right of the airline ticket counters is a coin phone. A vending machine near the bank sells phonecards.

SEA

Yacht

A favorite place to clear customs is at Nelson's Dockyard in English Harbour (VHF channel 16; for more information see English Harbour later in this chapter). Other ports of entry are Falmouth Harbour, Jolly Harbour, St John's Harbour, and Crabbs Marina in Parham Harbour. If you're going on to Barbuda ask for a cruising permit, which will allow you to visit that island without further formalities.

Antigua has many protected harbors and bays and fine anchorages are to be found all around the island. Full-service marinas are located at English Harbour, Falmouth Harbour, Jolly Harbour and Parham Sound.

Boaters can make reservations at many restaurants around Falmouth Harbour and English Harbour via VHF channel 68.

Yacht charters can be arranged through Sun Yacht Charters (☎ 460-2615) at Nelson's Dockyard.

Cruise Ship

Antigua is a port of call for numerous cruise ships. The island's cruise ship terminal, at Heritage Quay in St John's Harbour, has a duty-free shopping center and a casino. Heritage Quay is within easy walking distance of St John's main sites: the museum, cathedral and historic Redcliffe Quay.

LEAVING ANTIGUA & BARBUDA

There's an EC$35 departure tax. Stays of less than 24 hours are exempt from the tax.

Getting Around

BUS

Antigua's buses are privately owned and they are predominantly minivans, although there are a few mid-sized buses. Buses from St John's to Falmouth and English Harbour are plentiful, cost EC$2 and take about 30 minutes. They start early and generally run until about 7 pm. Rush hour is particularly bustling, with lots of buses between 4 and 5 pm. There are very few buses on Sunday.

The main bus station in St John's is opposite the public market. Buses line up two or three across, all competing by revving up their engines and pretending to be on the verge of leaving so passengers will pile in – however, most buses don't actually leave until they're full.

Buses to Old Road also leave from St John's public market.

Buses to the east side of the island leave from the East Bus Station, near the corner of Independence Ave and High St, and go to Piggots and Willikies.

There's no bus service to the airport, Dickenson Bay or other resort areas on the northern part of the island.

TAXI

Taxi fares are regulated by the government, but confirm the fare with the driver before riding away. Fares from the airport are: US$7 to St John's, US$11 to Runaway or Dickenson Bays, US$16 to Jolly Harbour and US$21 to English Harbour.

From Nelson's Dockyard at English Harbour, taxi fares are US$20 to St John's, US$25 to Runaway Bay.

Could Be Dangerous

As is the case on other islands in the Eastern Caribbean, bus drivers on Antigua try to make their vehicles as distinctive as possible by giving them colorful names. Some of the buses, with names like 'Man Standing By' and 'Send Dem Come,' are making an obvious pitch to riders; others, such as 'Could Be Dangerous' or 'Don't Tes' Me,' sound anything but reassuring. Although there's an element of jest to it all, choosing a bus by the name may prove to have merit in avoiding some of the more reckless drivers. ■

In St John's there's a taxi stand opposite the public market and taxi drivers also hang around Heritage Quay. Most hotels have taxis assigned to them; if you don't find one, ask at reception.

CAR & MOTORCYCLE
Road Rules

To drive on Antigua you need to buy a temporary 90-day license, which is usually obtainable from car rental agents but can also be picked up at the Inland Revenue Department on Newgate St in St John's. Simply show your home license and dish out a hefty EC$50.

Driving is on the left. Many rental cars have steering wheels on the left, which can be disorienting.

Antigua has some of the most potholed roads in the Eastern Caribbean. Even the newer roads aren't maintained and can surprise you with unexpected craters.

Be aware of goats darting across the road and of narrow roads in built-up areas that can be crowded with children after school gets out.

The speed limit is generally 20 mph in villages and 40 mph in rural areas. There are numerous gas stations scattered around the island, including one just outside the airport terminal. Gas sells for EC$6.85 per gallon.

Rental

Car There are more than a dozen car rental agencies on Antigua, most of them with representatives at the airport. All of the agencies in the list that follows rent cars for around US$50 a day, and they offer slight discounts on longer rentals. Many of the companies also offer jeeps for the same rates.

In part because of the poor condition of the roads, all but the newest rental cars are generally quite beat. Your best bet (though by no means a sure bet) on getting a road-worthy car is to book with one of the international agencies. Most car rental firms will deliver cars to your hotel free of charge.

Rental companies include:

Avis	☎ 462-2840
Capital Rentals	☎ 462-0863
Dollar	☎ 462-0362
Hertz	☎ 462-4114
National Car Rental	☎ 462-0576
Oakland Rent-A-Car	☎ 462-3021
Stead's Rent-A-Car	☎ 463-9970
Thrifty Rent-A-Car	☎ 462-5364

Motorcycle Paradise Boat Sales (☎ 460-7125) at Jolly Harbour rents 80cc scooters for US$35 and 125cc motorcycles for US$45. Rates are 20% less on multiple-day rentals.

BICYCLE

Sun Cycles (☎ 461-0324), Nelson Drive, Hodges Bay, rents mountain bikes for US$15 the first day and US$13 for each additional day and will deliver and pick up bikes.

Paradise Boat Sales (☎ 460-7125) at Jolly Harbour rents mountain bikes for US$25 for single-day rentals and US$15 per day if you rent a minimum of two days.

ORGANIZED TOURS
Land Tours

Touring the island by taxi costs about US$80 per car for a half-day tour that takes in Nelson's Dockyard and Shirley Heights or US$150 for a full-day tour.

Boat Tours

Wadadli Cats (☎ 462-4792) offers a number of catamaran trips, including one that features snorkeling time at Cades Reef, and another at Great Bird Island, a small volcanic island a couple of miles off the northeast coast of Antigua. Both trips include lunch, cost US$60 and pick up their guests at Dickenson Bay and other points around the island. Wadadli also does a day-long circumnavigation tour of Antigua for US$75.

Kokomo Cat (☎ 462-7245), another large catamaran, has a full schedule of similar tours at prices comparable to Wadadli. They also offer a Sunday boat-land tour that includes snorkeling at a nearshore island, a tour of Nelson's Dockyard and a visit to the

Shirley Heights barbecue and steel-band party; it costs US$85.

The Jolly Roger 'pirate ship' (☎ 462-2064) is a party boat that offers a day trip of snorkeling, plank-walking, rope swinging and lunch for US$50.

St John's

St John's, Antigua's capital and commercial center, has a population of about 30,000, making it home to nearly half of the island's residents.

Most of the town's tourist activity is centered around two harborfront complexes, Heritage Quay and Redcliffe Quay, which are a few minutes walk apart along a street lined with sidewalk vendors.

Heritage Quay, where cruise ship passengers disembark, is a modern complex with a casino, a hotel and a few dozen duty-free shops selling designer clothing, perfumes, cameras and liquor.

Much more engaging is Redcliffe Quay, where a cluster of period stone buildings and wooden huts have been restored to house gift shops, art galleries and restaurants. Redcliffe Quay appeals to both islanders and tourists and is a popular spot for lunch.

Most of the rest of St John's is largely unaffected by tourism and remains solidly West Indian in flavor. The town center is a rather bustling scene, with shoppers making the rounds, taxis crowding narrow roads and businesspeople rushing to and from work. St John's also has depressed corners with deep poverty.

Information

Tourist Office The tourist office (☎ 462-0029), on Thames St, is open from 8 am to 4:30 pm Monday to Thursday, 8 am to 3 pm on Friday.

Money The Barclays Bank on Market St doesn't charge a commission on US dollar traveler's checks if the amount being exchanged is over US$150, but it charges EC$5 for amounts under that. It's open from 8 am to 2 pm Monday to Thursday, 8 am to 4 pm on Friday. The Swiss American Bank, at the east end of High St, charges no commission to cash traveler's checks and has the same opening hours as Barclays.

Post The post office, at the west end of Long St, is open from 8:15 am to 4 pm Monday to Thursday, to 5 pm on Friday.

Telephone Cable & Wireless on St Mary's St is open from 8 am to 6 pm Monday to Friday, 8 am to noon on Saturday. Card phones and a 24-hour phonecard dispenser can be found outside the building. If you need a coin phone, there's a row of them on Long St opposite the cathedral.

Bookstores The Map Shop on St Mary's St is the island's best bookstore and sells Caribbean charts, maps of Antigua & Barbuda and books on Caribbean history, culture, flora and fauna. The new store First Editions, at Woods Centre, is also worth a look.

Museum of Antigua & Barbuda

The Museum of Antigua & Barbuda, on the corner of Market and Long Sts, occupies the old courthouse, a stone building that dates from 1750. This community-run museum has a eclectic collection of displays on island history. There's a touchable section with stone pestles and conch shell tools, a reconstructed Arawak house and modest displays on natural history, the colonial era and the struggle for emancipation. It's open from 8:30 am to 4 pm Monday to Thursday, until 3 pm on Friday, and from 10 am to 2 pm on Saturday. Admission is free but an EC$7 donation is encouraged.

St John's Anglican Cathedral

The twin-spired St John's Anglican Cathedral between Newgate and Long Sts is the town's dominant landmark. The original church dated back to 1681 but the current baroque-style stone structure was erected in 1847, after a devastating earthquake.

ANTIGUA

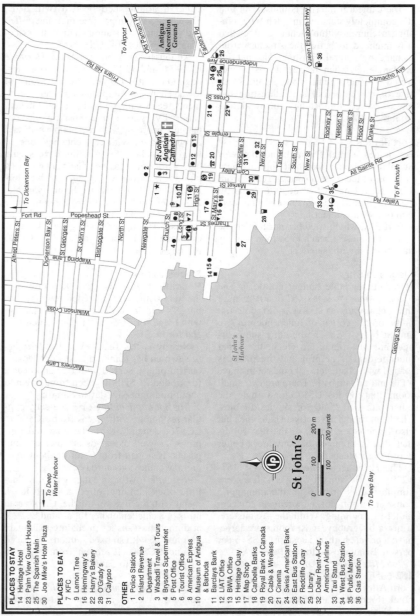

St John's

To Deep Bay

To Falmouth

St John's Harbour

To Deep Water Harbour

To Dickenson Bay

To Airport

Antigua Recreation Ground

0   100   200 m
0   100   200 yards

PLACES TO STAY
14 Heritage Hotel
23 Palm View Guest House
25 The Spanish Main
30 Joe Mike's Hotel Plaza

PLACES TO EAT
7   KFC
9   Lemon Tree
16 Hemingway's
22 Harry's Bakery
28 O'Grady's
31 Calypso

OTHER
1   Police Station
2   Inland Revenue
    Department
3   Wadadli Travel & Tours
4   Brysons Supermarket
5   Post Office
6   Tourist Office
8   American Express
10 Museum of Antigua
    & Barbuda
11 Barclays Bank
12 LIAT Office
13 BWIA Office
15 Heritage Quay
17 Map Shop
18 Caribelle Batiks
19 Royal Bank of Canada
20 Cable & Wireless
21 Cinema
24 Swiss American Bank
26 East Bus Station
27 Redcliffe Quay
29 Library
32 Dollar Rent-A-Car,
    American Airlines
33 Taxi Stand
34 West Bus Station
35 Public Market
36 Gas Station

The cathedral interior is unusual in that it's completely encased in pitch pine, creating a church-within-a-church effect that was intended to buffer the structure from damage by natural disasters. The interior can be viewed when the caretaker is around, which is usually until 5 pm. At the south side of the cathedral are interesting old moss-covered tombstones, many dating from the 1700s.

Fort James

Fort James, a small fort at the north side of St John's Harbour, was first built in 1675, but most of the present structure dates from 1739. It still has a few of its original 36 cannons, a powder magazine and a fair portion of its walls intact.

Fort Bay, which stretches north from the fort, is the closest beach to St John's and is thus popular with islanders.

Places to Stay

A recommendable budget option is *The Spanish Main* (☎ & fax 462-0660), a small inn occupying a 200-year-old colonial home on the corner of Independence Ave and St Mary's St. The building shows its age, but the rooms are clean, the expat management is helpful and the place is loaded with character. All nine rooms have a fan and private bath. There are two small rooms that cost just US$15 for a single, the others are US$25/40 for singles/doubles. The front rooms have private balconies but also catch street noise, so the rear rooms that share a common balcony are a better bet for light sleepers.

The *Palm View Guest House* (☎ 462-1299), 57 St Mary's St, has a few very simple rooms upstairs in the manager's house and a half-dozen more in an adjacent motel-like building. While they're austere, if not a bit grubby, most rooms are large, have a private bath and cost just US$15 per person. Bring mosquito repellent.

Joe Mike's Hotel Plaza (☎ 462-1142, fax 462-6056), PO Box 136, on the corner of Corn Alley & Nevis St, is an older central hotel. Rooms are rather basic, but adequate and clean, each with air-con, phone and either a double bed or two twin beds. There's a TV lounge, free morning coffee and an adjacent restaurant and mini-casino. Singles/doubles cost US$45/55.

Although it's a bit faded, the *Heritage Hotel* (☎ 462-1247, fax 462-1179) at Heritage Quay still has the fanciest rooms in town. There are 21 spacious, modern apartments, each equipped with a full kitchen, cable TV, phone, thermostatic air-con, bathtub, bedroom with two double beds and a living room with two couches, one of them a sofabed. Some units have scenic harborside verandas, but that's not always a plus as the harbor waters can get a bit odoriferous. While geared for businesspeople, this hotel could also be convenient for a family. Although the standard published rate is 50% higher, they generally offer everyone the business rate of US$80/100 for singles/doubles.

Places to Eat

Redcliffe Quay *The Quencher*, in one of the huts at the rear of Redcliffe Quay, has burgers and local dishes such as salt fish with bread for EC$6 and a daily lunch special for EC$13.

Nearby is the Tex-Mex-styled *Margaritas*, which has standard taco, enchilada or burrito plates, served with rice and beans, for around EC$20. It's open from 10 am to about midnight Monday to Saturday.

Big Banana Holding Co is a locally popular restaurant with pizzas from EC$22 to EC$76, depending on the size and toppings, as well as salads, sandwiches and pastas. It's open from 9 am to about midnight Monday to Saturday.

Redcliffe Tavern, in a nicely restored historic brick building, offers a varied lunch menu with the likes of quiche, Creole crab puffs or a chicken platter for around EC$25; at dinner most dishes, including mahimahi or fettucine with smoked salmon, are priced around EC$40. It's open from 8 am to 11 pm Monday to Saturday.

Around Town *The Spanish Main*, on Independence Ave, has a pleasant, old-fashioned dining room and bar. Breakfast pancakes or lunchtime rotis and sandwiches cost EC$12, while a range of other options such as vegie quiche or bangers and mash are around EC$20. Dinner features seafood and meat dishes averaging EC$40.

Hemingway's, at the west end of St Mary's St, has veranda dining on the 2nd floor of an attractive 19th-century West Indian building. At lunch, sandwiches or a Caesar salad cost EC$20 while catch of the day is about double that. Dinner offerings range from vegetarian pasta for EC$26 to lobster for EC$70. It's open 9 am to 10 pm Monday to Saturday.

Calpyso offers lunch in an attractive garden courtyard off Redcliffe St. Dishes, which range from EC$25 to EC$40, include pineapple stuffed with chicken salad, barbecued ribs and grilled swordfish, all served with rice or fries. Wash it down with a homemade ginger beer or passion fruit juice (EC$5). It's open from 10 am to 4 pm Monday to Friday.

The *Lemon Tree*, on Long St just west of the museum, is a popular upmarket restaurant with air-conditioned dining. At lunch, there are sandwiches with fries, omelets and specialty salads for around EC$20 and meat dishes for double that. Dinner options are snazzier, with escargot or conch fritter appetizers for EC$20, stuffed red snapper or tarragon shrimp main courses for EC$50. It's open from 11:30 am to 2 pm weekdays and 6:30 to 10 pm Monday to Saturday.

O'Grady's, on Lower Nevis St, is a popular expat hangout with pool, darts and moderately priced English pub grub such as fish and chips or steak and kidney pie. It's open from 10 am to 10 pm Monday to Saturday.

KFC, opposite the tourist office, has the standard two pieces of chicken with fries for EC$10.50 and is open from 10:30 am to 11 pm, to midnight on weekends.

Harry's Bakery on Cross St, is a good central bakery and a cheap breakfast option.

Brysons supermarket, near the post office, has a deli with inexpensive sandwiches and a moderate grocery selection; it's open from 8 am to 9 pm Monday to Saturday, to 4 pm on Sunday. *Discount Health Food Store*, behind the American Airlines office on Nevis St, has cereals, packaged natural foods, herbal teas and vitamins; it's open from 9 am to 6 pm Monday to Saturday.

The best place for fresh fruits and vegetables is the *public market* at the south end of Market St, open from 6 am to 6 pm Monday to Saturday.

Around Antigua

RUNAWAY BAY

Runaway Bay is a quiet area with an attractive white-sand beach, calm waters and a handful of small, reasonably priced hotels. Note, however, that the north end of the beach has lost virtually all of its sand since Hurricane Luis and the process of regeneration has been slow. But from Runaway Beach Club south there still is a gorgeous sandy strand and precious few beachgoers to share it with.

Although the area can seem quite sleepy, those staying here who want more action can simply wander over to the adjacent Dickenson Bay. A channel dug a few years back for a marina project (which was halted after hitting rock) cuts off shoreline access between Runaway and Dickenson bays but it's just a short walk along the road between the two areas.

Pelicans dive for food in the inlet created by the new channel and also along Corbinson Point, the rocky outcropping at the north end of the bay. The point is the site of an old fort, but there's little left to see there. A large salt pond stretches along the inland side of Runaway Bay, and in the evening egrets come to roost at the pond's southern end.

Places to Stay

The 14-room *Sand Haven Beach Hotel* (☎ and fax 463-4491), PO Box 2456, is a small English-run hotel right on the beach at the south end of Runaway Bay. Because it's a bit isolated, it's not a perfect choice if you don't have a car but there's a small restaurant on site and the hotel's rates are cheap enough to cover a few taxi fares. Each room has a private bath, oceanview terrace or balcony, ceiling fans and coffee-maker. Singles/doubles cost US$40/65 in summer, US$50/75 in winter.

Time A Way (☎ 462-1212, fax 462-2587), PO Box 189, is a small complex consisting of six good-value one-bedroom apartments. Each has air-con, a kitchenette, a balcony and a living room with a sofabed. Rates for up to three adults, or for two adults and two children, are US$60/85 in summer/winter. There's no front desk or on-site manager so reservations should be made in advance.

Once the largest hotel on Runaway Bay, the hurricane-battered *Runaway Beach Club* (☎ 462-1318, fax 462-4172; in the USA ☎ 800-742-4276), PO Box 874, has reopened a dozen rooms. Until it's fully renovated, rates are US$60/72 in summer/winter for a standard room with air-con and

private bath, US$90/110 for a studio unit with kitchenette. There's a pool.

Sunset Cove Resort (☎ 462-3762, fax 462-2684), PO Box 1262, has 33 modern units in two- and three-story buildings. Hotel rooms, which cost US$100/125 in summer/winter, have rattan furnishings, tiny kitchenettes, a balcony or porch, TV, air-con and ceiling fans. Ask for one of the top-floor units, which have high ceilings. Studio units, which cost US$125/145 for up to four people, have kitchens and a living room that doubles as the bedroom, with a pull-down double bed and a queen-sized sofabed. If things are slow they sometimes offer a 25% discount. There's a pool.

The *Barrymore Beach Club* (☎ 462-4101, fax 462-4101), PO Box 1774, is an overpriced 32-room complex. Cheapest are the hotel-style rooms, which are small and ordinary and cost US$72/115 in summer/winter. One-bedroom apartments with kitchens cost from US$115/180, and two-

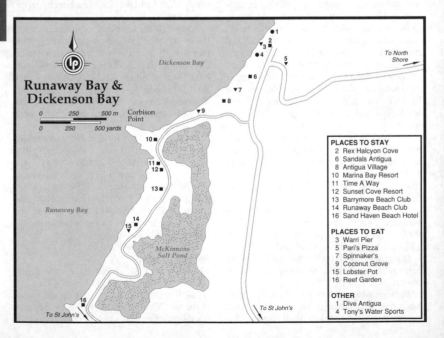

Runaway Bay & Dickenson Bay

PLACES TO STAY
2 Rex Halcyon Cove
6 Sandals Antigua
8 Antigua Village
10 Marina Bay Resort
11 Time A Way
12 Sunset Cove Resort
13 Barrymore Beach Club
14 Runaway Beach Club
16 Sand Haven Beach Hotel

PLACES TO EAT
3 Warri Pier
5 Pari's Pizza
7 Spinnaker's
9 Coconut Grove
15 Lobster Pot
16 Reef Garden

OTHER
1 Dive Antigua
4 Tony's Water Sports

bedroom apartments from US$180/295. Units have screened louvered windows and ceiling fans but no air-con. The 2nd-floor units, which have raised wooden ceilings, are the best.

Places to Eat

The *Lobster Pot* (☎ 462-2855) at Runaway Beach Club has an appealing beachside setting. At breakfast, from 7:30 to 11 am, you can get a fruit platter or a three-egg omelet with potatoes for under EC$20. At lunch, from noon to 3 pm, a chicken burger or flying fish sandwich with fries costs around EC$25, lobster Caesar salad about double that. Seafood is a specialty at dinner, from 6 to 10 pm, with catch of the day for EC$40, lobster for EC$80, but there are also moderately priced chicken and pasta dishes; call ahead to reserve one of the waterfront tables.

The *Reef Garden Restaurant* (☎ 462-4491) at Sand Haven Beach Hotel has waterside dining and a three-course dinner menu for EC$60 with a fish, chicken or rack of lamb main course, EC$85 with lobster thermidor.

DICKENSON BAY

Dickenson Bay, Antigua's main moderate-range resort area, is fronted by a long, lovely white-sand beach with turquoise waters and good swimming conditions.

All of Dickenson Bay's action is centered on the beach, where there are water sports booths, open-air restaurants and half a dozen hotels and condominiums. While it's more touristy than Runaway Bay, it's not over-touristed and can be a fun scene with reggae music, vendors selling T-shirts and jewelry, and women braiding hair.

Places to Stay

Marina Bay Resort (☎ 462-3254, fax 462-2151; in the USA ☎ 800-223-6510) is a condo complex on Corbison Point, which separates the two bays. The 27 units are sleek and contemporary with kitchens, air-con, cable TV, phone and balconies or patios. 'Super studios,' with a double bed in the bedroom and a queen sofabed in the

living room, cost US$80/100 in summer/winter for up to four people, while the standard efficiency studios cost the same but are smaller and hold only two people. One-bedroom units cost $100/130.

Antigua Village (☎ 462-2930, fax 462-0375; in the USA and Canada ☎ 800-742-4276), PO Box 649, is a well-maintained beachside condominium complex, with 100 units spread around landscaped grounds. They're individually owned so the decor varies, but most are quite pleasant and each has cooking facilities, air-con, ceiling fans and a patio or balcony. It's a good value in summer, when roomy studios cost US$95, one-bedroom apartments US$115 and two-bedroom apartments US$210. In winter it's a pricier US$170/210/380, respectively. Add another 20% for a beachfront unit. There's a pool.

The 210-room *Rex Halcyon Cove* (☎ 462-0256, fax 462-0271), PO Box 251, is a beachfront resort hotel at the north end of Dickenson Bay. The rooms have been renovated and are modern and pleasant but pricey. Fan-cooled standard rooms cost US$130/190 in summer/winter, and rooms with air-con begin at US$155/220. There's a pool and tennis courts.

Sandals Antigua (☎ 462-0267, in the USA ☎ 800-726-3257) is a busy couples-only beachside resort with 189 rooms, five pools, four bars, three restaurants, two tennis courts and a variety of water sports activities. All-inclusive rates per couple start at US$1620 for three nights.

Places to Eat

Pari's Pizza (☎ 462-1501), about 200 yards southeast of Rex Halcyon Cove on the inland road, is popular for takeout pizza. Cheese pizzas cost from EC$24 (small) to EC$43 (extra large), plus a few dollars more for each topping. You can also eat in or have your pizza delivered. Pari's is open from 11:30 am to 11:30 pm daily except Monday.

Spinnaker's, near Sandals, is a pleasant restaurant right on the beach. Breakfast, served until 10:30 am, features the usual fare at reasonable prices and a bottomless cup of coffee for EC$3. At lunch, served from 11 am to 5 pm, you can get salads, sandwiches and omelets for around EC$20 or a few hot seafood dishes for EC$35. At dinner (6:30 to 10:30 pm) there are vegetarian options for EC$40, while steak, red snapper or jumbo shrimp, all served with a side salad, are around EC$60.

Coconut Grove, on the beach at the south side of Antigua Village, is another casual waterfront restaurant with moderately priced breakfasts and lunchtime sandwiches. At dinner, dishes range from catch of the day for EC$55 to filet mignon or lobster for EC$75.

Warri Pier at Rex Halcyon Cove is set above the water on a private pier that juts out from the beach. Consequently, it makes a nice sunset spot for a drink or dinner. Pasta, fresh fish or spareribs cost around EC$40 at lunch or dinner. From noon to 6 pm you can also order sandwiches for EC$20. It's open daily until 10:30 pm.

There's a very small grocery store at Antigua Village that's open from 8:30 am to 7 pm daily.

NORTH SHORE

The northern part of the island between Dickenson Bay and the airport has the island's most well-to-do residential areas, a golf course, a few exclusive villa developments and small upscale resorts.

Places to Stay

The 117-room *Colonna Beach Resort* (☎ 462-6263, fax 462-6430, colonnabch@candw.ag), PO Box 591, is a newer complex at Hodges Bay with a Mediterranean style. Rooms there are modern and have air-con, TV, phones, minibars, hair dryers, etc. Singles/doubles cost from US$125/135 in summer, US$165/180 in winter. Three-bedroom villas that can house up to six people are available at US$300/400 in summer/winter.

The secluded, British-run *Blue Waters Beach Hotel* (☎ 462-0290, fax 462-0293), PO Box 256, is on a little sandy beach at Blue Waters Bay. This 50-room hotel is just completing hurricane-related repairs

and is expected to reopen shortly with rates of around US$150/250 in summer/winter.

Places to Eat

Le Bistro (☎ 462-3881) is a well-regarded restaurant serving traditional French food. Snapper, grilled lobster and meat dishes are priced around EC$65, while hors d'oeuvres are about half that. It's open for dinner only from 6:30 to 10:30 pm daily except Monday; reservations are recommended. Le Bistro is about a third of a mile south of Beggars Point and just a bit inland from the main road; a sign marks the turn-off.

Both the Blue Waters Beach Hotel and Colonna Beach Resort have moderately priced restaurants.

AROUND THE AIRPORT

There are no real sights around the airport and it's certainly not a prime tourist destination, but there are four relatively inexpensive places to stay, two just outside the airport and two others on small beaches a mile north of the runway.

Places to Stay

The *Airport Hotel* (☎ 462-1191, fax 462-0928), PO Box 700, is a concrete motel-style place next to the West Indies gas station, about a 10-minute walk from the airport terminal. The rooms are simple but clean, with TV and a fan, and the hotel provides free transport to and from the airport. Singles/doubles cost US$53/77 year round, or US$70/90 with air-con.

Also motel-style but spiffier is the *Antigua Sugar Mill Hotel* (☎ 462-3044, fax 462-1500), PO Box 319, half a mile from the airport terminal, north along the main road. There are 22 air-conditioned rooms with patios or balconies and the grounds have a pool and the remains of a sugar mill. The standard single/double rooms cost US$50/60 in summer, US$70/80 in winter.

The *Lord Nelson Beach Hotel* (☎ 462-3094, fax 462-0751), PO Box 155, is an unpretentious family-run operation with 16 simple ocean-fronting rooms right on the beach at Dutchman's Bay. There's a windsurfing school here and scuba diving can also be arranged. Singles/doubles cost US$60/70 in the summer, US$80/100 in the winter.

The 28-room *Antigua Beachcomber Hotel* (☎ 462-3100, fax 462-4012), PO Box 1512, on Winthorpes Bay, is 500 yards south of the Lord Nelson Beach Hotel, though a small headland topped with an oil depot separates the two. Rooms, which are on par with those of a mid-range motel, cost from US$65/85 for singles/doubles in summer, US$85/100 in winter. Although it's not the most pristine of locations there is a little sandy beach.

Places to Eat
Dining in this area is largely limited to the restaurants in the aforementioned hotels, with the most extensive menu at the *Antigua Beachcomber*. You can also get sandwiches, salads, pastas and reasonable pizza at moderate prices from *Big Banana Holding Co* on the 2nd floor of the airport terminal.

DEEP BAY
Deep Bay, west of St John's, is a pleasant little bay with a sandy beach and protected waters. The Royal Antiguan Hotel sits above the beach and there's a fair amount of resort activity, but it's a good-sized strand and a nice swimming spot.

The coral-encrusted wreck of the *Andes* lies in the middle of Deep Bay its mast poking up above the water. Nearly 100 years have passed since this barque caught fire and went down, complete with a load of pitch from Trinidad. The waters are shallow enough around the wreck to be snorkeled but divers tend to bypass it because ooze still kicks up pretty easily from the bottom.

The remains of **Fort Barrington**, which once protected the southern entrance of St John's Harbour, is atop the promontory that juts out at the northern end of the bay. Originally constructed in the mid-17th century, most of the present fortifications date to 1779. To hike up to the fort, simply begin walking north along the beach at Deep Bay; the trail takes about 10 minutes.

A salt pond separates Deep Bay from the smaller Hog John Bay, where there's another sandy beach and a couple of hotels.

Places to Stay
Yepton Beach Resort (☎ 462-2520, fax 462-3240; in the USA ☎ 800-361-4621, in the UK ☎ 514-284-0688), PO Box 1427, on Hog John Bay, has 38 modern air-con units with ocean-fronting balconies or patios. The studios are spacious with full kitchens and cost US$160/230 in summer/winter. Hotel-style rooms cost US$120/180 and one- and two-bedroom apartments are also available. This pleasant little resort has complimentary windsurfing, sailing, snorkeling and tennis.

With nine stories and 282 rooms, the *Royal Antiguan Hotel*, (☎ 462-3733, fax 462-3732; in the USA ☎ 800-345-0356, in the UK ☎ 561-994-5640), PO Box 1322, on Deep Bay, is the island's only high-rise resort. It has a casino, a pool, tennis courts, a fitness center and various water sports. Rooms are comfortable and well appointed, with TV, phone, minibar, bathtub and central air-con. Rates for standard rooms are US$150/190 in summer/winter; oceanview rooms with balconies cost US$200/250. There's a daily shuttle (US$7 roundtrip) to St John's. In summer the hotel commonly extends its corporate rate (US$85) to anyone calling from the airport.

Less than two miles south of the Royal Antiguan is the *Hawksbill Beach Resort* (☎ 462-0301, fax 462-1515; in the USA ☎ 800-223-6510), PO Box 108, an exclusive place that encompasses a couple of nice secluded beaches. There are 95 rooms, ranging from pleasant cottages to more traditional two-story buildings. Rates for singles/doubles begin at US$175/276 in summer, US$312/375 in winter, with breakfast included. The resort has an expensive restaurant, a pool, a tennis court and the usual water sports.

Places to Eat
Yepton Beach Resort's *Patio Caribe* has burgers, salads and fish & chips from US$7 to US$10 from noon to 2 pm.

ANTIGUA

The Royal Antiguan has a few dining options: the beach grill is primarily a lunch spot with US$10 burgers and similar fare; the *Lagoon Cafe* has a typical hotel menu with US$10 sandwiches and hot meals for about double that; and there's a fancier dinner restaurant.

JOLLY HARBOUR

Jolly Harbour is a marina and dockside condominium village on Antigua's west coast. Marina facilities include a pharmacy, a supermarket, a bakery, a liquor store, boat rentals and charters, restaurants and handicraft, beachwear and gift shops. The Swiss American Bank sells phonecards, changes traveler's checks free, and is open 9 am to 12:30 pm and 1:30 to 3 pm weekdays. There are free-use showers in the main complex.

Boaters will find 150 slips, fuel facilities, water, 110/220 volt power and a boat yard with a 70-ton lift and repair facilities.

There's a nice albeit busy white-sand beach south of the marina at Club Antigua and a quieter beach fronting Jolly Harbour.

Places to Stay

Jolly Harbour Beach Resort (☎ 462-6166, fax 462-6167), PO Box 1793, is a large complex with rows of condos built on artificial breakwaters. Each unit is townhouse-style, the downstairs with a full kitchen, living/dining room and a terrace that looks out onto a private boat mooring. Upstairs are two bedrooms (one with a double bed, the other with two twins), one or two bathrooms and a balcony. Partly because of the sheer number of units, the rates are relatively cheap at US$85/100 in summer/winter for up to two people, US$15 for each additional person. Add another US$15 a day if you want air-con. Monthly rates are around US$700. Facilities include a swimming pool, tennis courts and an 18-hole golf course.

Club Antigua (☎ 462-0061, fax 462-4900), PO Box 744, is a bustling all-inclusive beachfront resort with 470 rooms. Singles/doubles cost from US$100/200 in summer, US$115/229 in winter, including

all food, drinks, water sports, tennis and entertainment (but not the slot machines). For US$70 non-guests can use the resort facilities, including food and drinks, from 10 am until the disco closes, or pay US$40 for a half day.

Places to Eat

Most popular of the marina restaurants is *Al Porto*, which has harborfront dining with good pizza and pasta dishes in the EC$25 to EC$40 range and pricier meat dishes. Lunch is served daily from noon to 3 pm, dinner from 7 to 10:30 pm.

The marina's *Epicurean* market sells sandwiches, liquor and groceries.

JOHNSON'S POINT BEACH

Johnson's Point Beach, at the southwest corner of the island, is a fine stretch of white sand. Midway between St John's and English Harbour, it might suit some people who want to avoid the more touristed parts of the island without being totally secluded. It's not quite as out of the way as it seems, as buses (EC$1.50) go by about every half-hour (except on Sunday) on the way to St John's.

Places to Stay & Eat

The *Rex Blue Heron* (☎ 462-8564, fax 462-8005; in the USA ☎ 800-255-5859, in the UK ☎ 181-741-5333), PO Box 1715, is a quiet 40-room hotel right on the beach. Most of the units face the water; those on the upper floor have balconies, those on the ground level have patios. Rooms are modern but suitably straightforward with double beds, ceiling fans and showers. The 10 standard rooms cost US$87/102 in summer/winter, and the air-conditioned superior rooms cost US$107/120. Water sports activities, including diving and windsurfing, are available.

The hotel's restaurant serves a continental breakfast (EC$25) and a full breakfast (EC$30), while at lunch there are burgers, salads and sandwiches to choose from, for about EC$20. For dinner the menu features seafood main dishes beginning around EC$65.

FIG TREE DRIVE

After Johnson's Point Beach, the road passes pineapple patches, tall century plants and pastures with grazing cattle and donkeys. There are high hills on the inland side of the road, topped by the 1319-foot Boggy Peak, the island's highest point.

Old Road, a village with both a fair amount of poverty and the luxury Curtain Bluff Hotel, marks the start of Fig Tree Drive. From there the terrain gets lusher as the road winds up through the hills. The narrow road is lined with bananas (called 'fig' in Antigua), coconut palms and big old mango trees. It's not jungle or rainforest, but it is refreshingly green and makes a pleasant rural drive. There are a couple of snack bars that sell fresh fruit and juices along the way.

Fig Tree Drive ends in the village of Swetes. On the way to Falmouth Harbour you'll pass through the village of Liberta and by the St Barnabus Anglican Chapel, an attractive green stone and brick church built in 1842.

FALMOUTH HARBOUR

Falmouth Harbour is a large, protected, horseshoe-shaped bay. There are two main centers of activity: the north side of the harbor, where the small village of Falmouth is located, and the more visitor-oriented east side of the harbor, which has most of the restaurants. The east side of Falmouth Harbour is within easy walking distance of Nelson's Dockyard.

St Paul's Church

St Paul's Anglican Church, on the main road in Falmouth's center, was Antigua's first church. As one of the island's oldest buildings, dating to 1676, the church once doubled as Antigua's courthouse. You can get a sense of its history by poking around the overgrown churchyard, which has some interesting and quite readable colonial-era gravestones. Charles Pitt, the brother of the English prime minister, was buried here in 1780, and beside his site is the excessively loquacious memorial to Brigadier General Andrew Dunlop, who died of yellow fever.

Places to Stay

Falmouth Harbour Beach Apartments (☎ 460-1027, fax 460-1534), on the east side of Falmouth Harbour, has 22 straightforward studios in half a dozen two-story buildings. The studios have verandas or patios, full kitchens and ceiling fans, but no air-con. Though the beach fronting the hotel isn't anything special, there's a decent beach about 10 minutes walk to the east. Singles/doubles cost US$68/88 in summer, US$94/120 in winter. The complex has the same management as the Admiral's Inn in English Harbour.

The *Catamaran Hotel & Marina* (☎ 460-1036, fax 460-1339; in the USA ☎ 800-223-6510), PO Box 958, is on a little beach at the north side of Falmouth Harbour and has its own 30-berth marina. This pleasant 16-room hotel is one of the area's better value places. The deluxe rooms on the 2nd floor have bathtubs, four-poster queen-size beds and cost US$85/120 in summer/winter. The hotel also has four ground-level units with kitchenettes that cost US$70/80 in summer/winter and four simpler standard rooms with standing fans for US$55/65.

Places to Eat

The following restaurants are all within a few minutes of each other at the east side of Falmouth Harbour. Note that some of them close in the summer as business slacks off.

Malone's, a small grocery store just north of the entrance to Nelson's Dockyard, has a little deli counter that makes sandwiches for around EC$12 to EC$16.

Kwik Stop, on the main road, has sandwiches, rotis and omelets for EC$8 to EC$10 and more substantial meals for about double that.

Erma's Kitchen at Temo Sports complex serves omelets at breakfast and burgers with fries at lunchtime for EC$15, salads or fish of the day for EC$30. On the opposite side of the road is a harborside complex with a delicatessen, liquor store and *Southern Cross*, a moderately priced Italian restaurant.

ANTIGUA

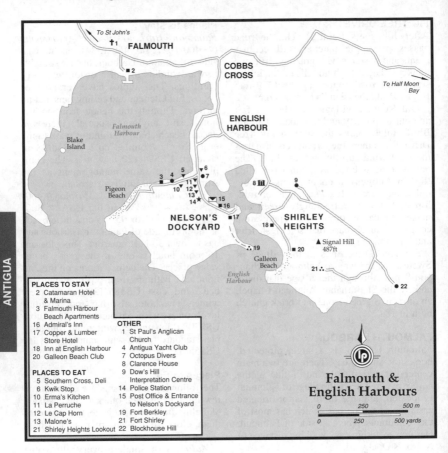

**Falmouth &
English Harbours**

PLACES TO STAY
2 Catamaran Hotel
& Marina
3 Falmouth Harbour
Beach Apartments
16 Admiral's Inn
17 Copper & Lumber
Store Hotel
18 Inn at English Harbour
20 Galleon Beach Club

PLACES TO EAT
5 Southern Cross, Deli
6 Kwik Stop
10 Erma's Kitchen
11 La Perruche
12 Le Cap Horn
13 Malone's
21 Shirley Heights Lookout

OTHER
1 St Paul's Anglican
Church
4 Antigua Yacht Club
7 Octopus Divers
8 Clarence House
9 Dow's Hill
Interpretation Centre
14 Police Station
15 Post Office & Entrance
to Nelson's Dockyard
19 Fort Berkley
21 Fort Shirley
22 Blockhouse Hill

Le Cap Horn (☎ 460-1194) has two sides: a pizzeria and a French restaurant. The pizzeria makes brick-oven pizza costing from EC$26 for tomato and cheese to EC$32 for a seafood version, as well as pasta dishes and a meal of the day in the same price range. The French restaurant, open from 6:30 to 11 pm daily, has daily specials such as red snapper in basil sauce for EC$39 and Creole lobster for EC$55.

La Perruche (☎ 460-3040) blends French and West Indian influences and specializes in dishes using fresh local produce and seafood. Starters and salads cost around EC$20, while main dishes range from seafood pasta for EC$40 to grilled lobster for EC$65. It's open from 7 pm Monday to Saturday.

ENGLISH HARBOUR

English Harbour has the richest collection of historic sites on the island; collectively, they are the centerpiece of the Antigua & Barbuda National Parks system.

Foremost is Nelson's Dockyard, an 18th-century British naval base named for the English captain Horatio Nelson, who spent the early years of his career here. Today, it's still attracting sailors as the island's most popular yacht haven.

ANTIGUA

There are also two hilltop forts flanking the entrance to the harbor and a couple of little museums. You could easily spend the better part of a day roaming around the sites. Bus routes from St John's end right at Nelson's Dockyard, but you'd need a car to explore the Shirley Heights area on the opposite side of the harbor.

English Harbour is separated from Falmouth Harbour by a slender neck of land that at its narrowest is just a few hundred yards wide.

Information

Money The Swiss American Bank, which is opposite the Admiral's Inn, exchanges US dollar traveler's checks to EC currency free of charge. It's open Monday to Thursday from 9 am to 1 pm and on Friday from 9 am to 2 pm.

Post & Communications The post office at the entrance of Nelson's Dockyard is open from 8:15 am to noon and 1 to 3:30 pm Monday to Friday. There are card and coin phones next to the post office; the bank sells phonecards.

For Boaters The following facilities are all inside Nelson's Dockyard. The customs office, on the ground level of the old Officer's Quarters building at the south side of the marina, opens from 8:30 am to 4 pm daily. Lord Jim's, south of the customs office, sells nautical charts and cruising guides. There are notices for crew wanted/available at Limey's. Showers (US$2) are open from 6 am to 6 pm daily, laundry facilities (US$8 a load) from 8 am to 6 pm daily.

Nelson's Dockyard

This historic dockyard is Antigua's most popular tourist sight as well as the island's main port of entry for yachts. The dockyard, which dates to 1743, was abandoned in 1899 following a decline in Antigua's economic and strategic importance to the British Crown.

Restoration work began in the 1950s and this former royal naval base now has a new life closely paralleling its old one – that of an active dockyard.

The handsome old brick and stone buildings have been converted into yachting and tourist-related facilities. Many duplicate the original use of the buildings. The bakery, for instance, was originally the officers' kitchen and still has the old stone hearth, while some of the hotel rooms that now house travelers were once used as quarters for sailors whose ships were being careened.

The dockyard is English Harbour's main center of activity, with a small market selling T-shirts and souvenirs, a handful of restaurants, two inns, a liquor shop, a dive shop, a travel agency, a pharmacy and numerous boating facilities – all of them occupying old naval buildings. Take time to stop at the interpretive plaques that explain the history of the various buildings.

Upon entering, pick up the free map that shows the dockyard sights and businesses. Admission is EC$6.50 for adults, free for children under 12.

Museum The dockyard's small museum occupies a former officers' house and features an assorted collection of nautical memorabilia, including clay pipes, rusty swords, muskets, cannonballs and one of Lord Nelson's telescopes. Models of a mid-19th-century schooner and naval brig round off the display. The museum's small gift shop sells books, maps and souvenirs. Admission is free.

Fort Berkley

A pleasant 10-minute stroll starting behind the Copper & Lumber Store Hotel leads to the site of this small fort, which overlooks the western entrance of English Harbour. The fort, dating to 1704, served as the harbor's first line of defense. You'll find intact walls, a powder magazine, a small guard house and a solitary cannon, the last of 25 cannons that once lined the fortress walls. There's also a fine harbor view at the top. The dirt path up is well maintained and passes lots of yucca and succulents, including tall dildo cactus and the stubby

Turk's-head cactus, easily identified by its round red head.

Clarence House

Clarence House, on the road to Shirley Heights, was built in 1786 for the Duke of Clarence, who later became King William IV. The aging Georgian-style residence has period furnishings and is now set aside as a rural residence of the governor. In years past, when the governor was not present, visitors could tour the house. However, the building was damaged by Hurricane Luis and remains closed until repairs can be made.

Shirley Heights

Shirley Heights is a fun place to explore with its scattered 18th-century fort ruins and wonderful hilltop views. A bit over a mile up Shirley Heights Rd you'll reach the **Dow's Hill Interpretation Centre**, which features a view point and an audio-visual presentation on island history and culture; it's open daily from 9 am to 5 pm and costs US$4.

For the best views and main concentration of ruins continue past the museum; the road will fork after about half a mile. The left fork leads shortly to **Blockhouse Hill**, where you'll find remains of the Officers' Quarters dating to 1787 and a clear-on view of sheltered Mamora Bay to the east. The right fork leads to **Fort Shirley**, which has more ruins, including one that has been turned into a casual restaurant and bar. There's a sweeping view of English Harbour from the rear of the restaurant while from the top of Signal Hill (487 feet), just a minute's walk from the parking lot, you can see Montserrat 28 miles to the southwest and Guadeloupe 40 miles to the south.

Places to Stay

The *Admiral's Inn* (☎ 460-1027, fax 460-1534; in the USA ☎ 800-223-5695, in the UK ☎ 181-940-3399), PO Box 713, built as a warehouse in 1788, has nine rooms above the restaurant in the original brick building and five rooms in a separate modern annex. Rooms vary in size and decor and some are

Turk's-head cactus

quite small. Room No 6 is larger and a good choice in the moderate category, while No 3, a quiet corner room with a fine harbor view, is recommended in the superior category; both have hand-hewn open beams. In summer, singles/doubles cost US$68/86 for moderate rooms, US$72/94 for superior rooms. In winter, moderate rooms cost US$92/120, superior rooms US$98/132. Complimentary transport is provided to nearby beaches.

The *Copper & Lumber Store Hotel* (☎ 460-1058, fax 460-1529; in the USA ☎ 800-633-7411, in the UK ☎ 01453-835-801) was built in the 1780s to store the copper and lumber needed for ship repairs. It now has 14 studios and suites, all with kitchens and ceiling fans. Rates range from US$195 to US$325 in winter, US$85 to US$175 in summer, with the higher rates for units with antique furnishings. The top-priced Georgian suite is so laden with historic character that you could almost imagine Lord Nelson stepping into the scene.

The *Galleon Beach Club* (☎ 460-1024, fax 460-1450; in the UK ☎ 081-767-7926), PO Box 1003, is a quiet resort on Galleon Beach at the southeast side of English Harbour. Accommodations are in cottages spread along the beach. All 28 units have a kitchen, a deck and a living room with a sofabed. In summer/winter one-bedroom cottages cost US$125/200, and for two-bedroom cottages the price is US$160/260. Each bedroom sleeps two people and two more can sleep on the sofabed at no extra cost. There's an Italian restaurant on site, a couple of tennis courts and some water sports activities.

The *Inn at English Harbour* (☎ 460-1014, fax 460-1603; in the USA ☎ 800-223-6510), PO Box 187, is another small beach resort on the southeast side of English Harbour. There are 28 rooms, most with beachfront balconies and rates of US$170/340 in summer/winter.

Places to Eat
The *Dockyard Bakery*, behind the museum at Nelson's Dockyard, has breads, meat patties, guava danish, carrot cake and other tempting pastries at reasonable prices. You can also get takeout coffee (EC$2) and sip it under the 300-year-old sandbox tree that fronts the bakery. It's open from 7:30 am to 4 pm weekdays, until 1:30 pm on Saturday.

Limey's is Nelson's Dockyard's cheapest spot for meals, serving inexpensive diner-quality food. There's an indoor dining room but it's better to grab one of the picnic tables out on the balcony and enjoy the harbor view. Sandwiches at Limey's cost EC$9, a cheeseburger or chicken and fries costs EC$18 and fresh fish goes for EC$25. It's open Monday to Saturday from 9 am to 5 pm in summer, longer hours in winter.

The *Admiral's Inn* is open for three meals daily. The changing chalkboard menu usually has such things as salads, burgers and curried conch for around EC$30 at lunch, while at dinner there are more elaborate dishes for about double that. There's both indoor dining and outdoor harborfront tables.

The *Copper & Lumber Store Hotel* has a pub serving continental breakfast for EC$18 and the likes of shepherd's pie, chicken salad and sandwiches for around EC$25. The hotel also has a more formal restaurant, *The Wardroom*, which is open in winter only.

Shirley Heights Lookout (☎ 460-1785), in a vintage 1791 guard house at Fort Shirley, has a fantastic view of English Harbour and serves lunch and dinner at moderate prices. It's best known for its Thursday and Sunday barbecues, which are accompanied with steel band music from 4 to 7 pm and reggae from 7 to 10 pm, with lots of dancing towards the end of the evening. There's no admission fee, drinks are reasonably priced and a simple hamburger or chicken plate with salad costs EC$22, a rib plate EC$42. All in all it's one of the island's nicest scenes.

HALF MOON BAY
Half Moon Bay, on the southeastern side of the island, is a C-shaped bay with a beautiful white-sand beach and turquoise waters. It's largely undeveloped, though there's a hotel at the south side of the bay and a little snack bar on the beach.

Places to Stay & Eat
The *Half Moon Bay Hotel* (☎ 460-4300, fax 460-4306, halfmoon@candw.ag; in the USA ☎ 800-745-0809), PO Box 144, is a 100-room resort on a rise overlooking the beach. Amenities include a pool, tennis courts and a nine-hole golf course. The hotel, which was damaged by Hurricane Luis, was still sorting through refinancing matters at press time, but expected to reopen with rates from US$275/375 in summer/winter, including meals, water sports and golf fees.

An interesting lunch option is *Harmony Hall* (☎ 460-4120, VHF 68) on Nonsuch Bay, a 10-minute drive north of Half Moon Bay. It has an atmospheric estate setting and offers moderately priced Caribbean-influenced food from noon to 4 pm. There's a dinghy dock for yachters.

LONG BAY

Long Bay, on the east side of Antigua, has clear blue waters and a quite appealing white-sand beach that's reef protected and good for snorkeling. There are two exclusive resorts at either end of the beach. Other than a few private homes there's little else in the neighborhood. Unless you're looking for total seclusion or don't mind paying some hefty taxi fares you'll need a car if you make a base in this area.

Devil's Bridge

Devil's Bridge is a modest little coastal sea arch at Indian Town Point, an area thought to have been the site of an early Arawak settlement. To get there, turn east onto the paved road a third of a mile before the Long Bay Hotel turnoff. The road ends after a mile at a turnaround; from there the arch is a minute's walk to the east. Be careful when you're walking near the arch, because the Atlantic breakers that have cut the arch out of these limestone cliffs occasionally sweep over the top.

Places to Stay & Eat

The *Long Bay Hotel* (☎ 463-2005, fax 463-2439), PO Box 442, on the east end of Long Bay, is an upscale family-run hotel. The 18 waterfront rooms there start at US$175/255 for singles/doubles in summer and US$285/365 in winter, including breakfast and dinner, while the six cottages start at US$200 in summer and US$300 in winter, with kitchen facilities but no meals. Tennis and water sports are available. The hotel restaurant has candlelight dining with an ocean view; there's a three-course dinner of the day for EC$105 or a range of main dishes from EC$45 to EC$75.

The *Pineapple Beach Club* (☎ 463-2006, fax 463-2452; in the USA ☎ 800-345-0356),

PO Box 54, is a 130-room all-inclusive resort on the west end of Long Bay. Single/double rates, which begin at US$260/330 in summer and US$330/390 in winter, include meals, drinks, water sports activities and airport transfers.

BETTY'S HOPE

Betty's Hope, just southeast of the village of Pares, was the island's first sugar plantation, built by Christopher Codrington in 1674 and named in honor of his daughter Betty. Ruins of two old stone windmills, a still house and a few other stone structures remain on the site, which is now under the jurisdiction of the Museum of Antigua & Barbuda. Through a combined local and international effort, one of the mills has been painstakingly restored and returned to working condition. The mill is only operated on special occasions but the windmill sails remain up all year, with the exception of the hurricane season.

The site's old stable has been converted into a visitor center focusing on Antigua's sugar era and the amiable caretaker, Lionel George, provides informative tours peppered with insights on the estate's history. The road into Betty's Hope is signposted. It's open from 9 am to 5 pm Monday to Saturday. A donation of US$2 is appreciated.

Barbuda

Barbuda, which is 25 miles north of Antigua, remains one of the Eastern Caribbean's least visited places. Other than its frigatebird colony and its beautiful beaches, most of which are best accessed by private boat, there's not much to attract tourists to this low scrubby island.

The only village, Codrington, is home to most residents and is the site of the island's airport. Barbuda has two small exclusive resorts at its southern tip, although these club-like places are so removed from the rest of the island that they have their own landing strip and haven't done much to upset Barbuda's isolation.

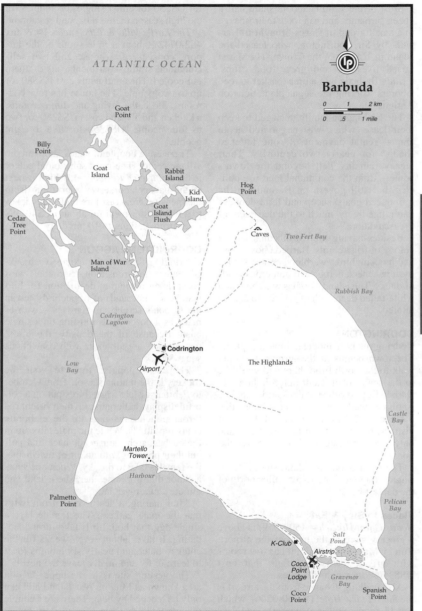

Most of the 1200 islanders share half a dozen surnames and can trace their lineage to a small group of slaves brought to Barbuda by Sir Codrington, who leased the island in 1685 from the Crown. The slaves raised livestock and grew food crops, turning Barbuda into a breadbasket to feed laborers working the sugar plantations on Antigua.

The Codrington family managed to keep their lease, which was negotiated at an annual rental payment of 'one fattened sheep,' for nearly two centuries. Their legacy remains well beyond the town's name – from the communal land-use policies that still govern on Barbuda to the introduced goats, sheep and feral donkeys that range freely, much to the detriment of the island flora.

Besides having the Caribbean's largest colony of frigatebirds, Barbuda hosts tropical mockingbirds, warblers, pelicans, ibis, oystercatchers, herons and numerous kinds of ducks. The island also has wild boar and white-tailed deer, both of which are legally hunted.

CODRINGTON

Codrington is a modest, low-key place. The town begins at the airport – simply walk to the north from there and you'll be in the center of it. Codrington is home to Barbuda's post office, it bank and its police station as well as a government house that dates to 1743. This is not a town set up for visitors, however: there are few signs and only one of the eateries there keeps regular hours.

The town is on the inland side of Codrington Lagoon, a hefty 3.5 miles north of the nearest beach.

Places to Stay & Eat

Nedds Guest House (☎ 460-0059) is above a grocery store at the head of the airport. Run by MacArthur Nedd, it has five rooms with private baths and fans that cost US$35/60 for singles/doubles.

Also walking distance from the airport is the *Sunset View Hotel* (☎ 460-0266), which has 11 rooms with private baths and fans

for US$50 for either singles or doubles. In the high season there's a bar and restaurant.

The Earl's Villa & Efficiencies (☎ & fax 462-0742), about a mile south of the airport, consists of a house and two self-contained studio apartments, all of them fan-cooled. The apartments cost US$80 for up to two people. The house has four bedrooms, 3½ baths, living and dining rooms, a kitchen and TV and costs US$250 for two to four people, US$350 for five to eight people.

There are a couple of snack shops in the village center. The most substantial eatery is the *Palm Tree Restaurant*, which is next to the bakery and serves everything from inexpensive breakfast fare and sandwiches to a full lobster meal for about EC$40. It's open from 7:30 am to 10 pm daily.

CODRINGTON LAGOON

Codrington Lagoon, the expansive brackish estuary that runs along Barbuda's west coast, is an intriguing destination for bird watchers. Thousands of frigatebirds nest in the lagoon's scrubby mangroves – with as many as a dozen birds roosting on a single bush. Because of the density, the birds' nesting sites are all abuzz with contentious squawking.

The most popular time to visit the rookery is the mating season, from October to February. Male frigatebirds put on a colorful display, ballooning up their bright red throat pouches as part of the elaborate courtship rituals. While the males line up in the bushes, arch their heads back and puff out their pouches with an air of machismo, the females take to the sky. When one spots a suitor that impresses her, she'll land and initiate a mating ritual.

After mating, a nest is built from twigs that the male gathers. The female lays a single egg that both birds take turns incubating. It takes about seven weeks for the chick to hatch and nearly six months for it to learn to fly and finally leave the nest.

The nesting site is in the upper lagoon area known as Man of War Island and can only be reached by boat. There are a couple of outboards that can take visitors out to the rookery, but arrangements generally need to be made a day in advance. If you're staying over on Barbuda you can arrange it through your guest house – the cost is about US$40 per boat for up to four people and the trip lasts about 75 minutes. If you're going over to Barbuda for the day, there are day tours that include the rookery (see the Organized Tours section near the end of this chapter).

WEST COAST

The west coast of Barbuda is lined with beautiful white-sand beaches and azure waters. From Palmetto Point northward there's a magnificent pinkish strand that extends 11 miles, most of it lining the narrow barrier of land separating Codrington Lagoon from the ocean. Because of its isolation, however, the beach remains largely the domain of a few lone boaters. More accessible beaches are found along the coast south of the harbor, with one of the finest sweeps along the stretch between the two resorts.

The **harbor** has a customs office and a sandloading operation – Barbuda's sands also glisten on some of Antigua's beaches! To the northwest of the harbor is the 56-foot-high **Martello Tower**, a former lookout station that from a distance looks like an old sugar mill. About half a mile north of Coco Point there's a nice white-sand strand with nearshore coral formations that provide good snorkeling.

The pristine waters of **Gravenor Bay**, between Coco Point and Spanish Point, is a favored yacht anchorage with reef formations and excellent snorkeling. Near the center of the bay is an old deteriorating

Frigatebirds

Frigatebirds skim the water's surface for fish but because their feathers lack the water-resistant oils common to other sea birds, they cannot dive into water. Also known as the man-of-war bird, the frigatebird has evolved into an aerial pirate that supplements its own fishing efforts by harassing other sea birds until they release their catch, which the frigatebird then swoops up in mid-flight.

While awkward on the ground the frigatebird, with its distinctive forked tail and six-foot wingspan, is mesmerizingly graceful in flight. It has the lightest weight-to-wingspan ratio of any bird and can soar at great heights for hours on end – making it possible for the bird to feed along the coast of distant islands and return home to roost at sunset without landing anywhere other than its nesting site. ■

pier, while the ruins of a small **tower** lie about half a mile away to the east.

Archaeologists believe the uninhabited peninsula leading to **Spanish Point** was once the site of a major Arawak settlement. A dirt track connects both ends of the bay and another leads northward from the east side of the salt pond.

Places to Stay & Eat

The *K-Club* (☎ 460-0300, fax 460-0305; in the USA ☎ 800-223-6800) is the handiwork of Italian fashion designer Mariuccia 'Krizia' Mandelli. This exclusive beachfront resort has 36 upscale, contemporary cottages and its own nine-hole golf course. While the K in the name stands for Krizia, the daily rate just happens to hover around a cool K, US$1000 inclusive. For US$100, non-guests can have dinner at the resort; lunch is also available, but it's not much cheaper.

Coco Point Lodge (☎ 462-3816, fax 462-5340), about a mile south of the K-Club, is a US-owned, members-only club situated on a lovely beach. The cheapest of the 36 rooms and suites begin at around US$500, plus membership fees. The lodge is open from November to April and does not welcome non-guests.

CAVES

If you feel like taking a look down under, there are some caves about five miles northeast of Codrington, though if it's been raining recently mud holes may well make it impossible to visit them. Dark Cave is an expansive underground cavern with pools of deep water while another cave near Two Feet Bay contains the faded drawings of Arawak Indians.

GETTING THERE & AWAY
Air

The only scheduled air service is into Codrington airport. LIAT (☎ 462-0700) has two daily flights making the 20-minute skip between Antigua and Barbuda. Flights leave Antigua at 8:35 am and 4 pm and depart Barbuda for Antigua 30 minutes later. The fare is US$34 one way, US$48

for a same-day roundtrip ticket or US$50 for a 21-day excursion ticket.

Carib Aviation (☎ 462-3147) has flights from Antigua to Barbuda at 7:15 am and 5 pm on Monday, Wednesday and Friday; flights return from Barbuda to Antigua 30 minutes later. There also is a 2 pm flight Thursday from Antigua to Barbuda open to passengers, but the return route is chartered by the bank. The fare is US$30 one way, or US$47 for a same-day roundtrip ticket.

Boat

Barbuda's reefs, which extend several miles from shore, are thought to have claimed a good 200 ships since colonial times – a rather impressive number considering Barbuda has never been a major port. Some reefs still remain poorly charted and the challenge of navigating through them is one reason Barbuda remains well off the beaten path. If you're sailing to the island bring everything you'll need in advance, because there are no yachting facilities on Barbuda.

There's no scheduled passenger boat service to Barbuda but if you want to try your luck hitching with a private yacht, check around at the marinas on Antigua.

Organized Tours

Barbuda has a reputation for tours that fail to materialize, a driver that doesn't show up at the airport or some other missing link. Confirm all reservations.

If you book a tour with LIAT be sure to get a contact number on Barbuda; consider calling that person in advance to reconfirm your tour directly with them.

LIAT charges US$125 for a day tour that includes airfare, a boat ride to the frigatebird rookery, a visit to the caves, some time on the beach and lunch. Some Antiguan travel agents, such as Wadadli Travel & Tours (☎ 462-2227) and Caribrep (☎ 462-3884), also offer the same package.

Claudia Richards of The Earl's Barbuda Day Tour (☎ & fax 462-0742) arranges a day trip to Barbuda that includes airfare, the rookery, a short land tour and a lobster lunch for US$130.

The Sunset View Hotel on Barbuda offers a tour to the rookery and beach that includes a lobster lunch but not the airfare to Barbuda and costs US$60 per person with a minimum of two people. Make reservations (☎ 460-0266) in advance.

GETTING AROUND

Barbuda has no public transportation. Distances are too great and the dusty dirt roads too hot to make walking a practical means of exploring. There isn't an established taxi service, but you might be able to arrange to hire someone to drive you around – ask the LIAT agent or inquire at your guest house.

Vehicle rental is another option, although the individuals who rent vehicles change from time to time and tracking them down can be tricky. A good place to start is with Claudia Richards (☎ 462-0742) or Eric Burton (☎ 460-0078); you should be able to arrange a jeep rental for about US$55 a day.

BARBUDA

Barbados

Barbados, the easternmost island in the Caribbean, is one of the most successful at luring visitors to its shores. It has fringing white-sand beaches, a good range of places to stay and eat and enough organized activities to make for a solid vacation destination.

The west and south coasts, which have the lion's share of visitor accommodations, are quite built up with an intermingling of tourist and residential areas. The interior is predominantly rural with undulating hills of sugar cane, grazing sheep and scattered villages.

Perhaps no other Caribbean island has been as strongly influenced by the British as Barbados. It's visible in the national passion for cricket, the old stone Anglican churches found in every parish, the well-tended gardens fronting islanders' homes and the Saturday horse races.

But the 'Little England' analogy only goes so far. Bajans, as islanders call themselves, also draw heavily from West Indian influences. Some of the finest calypso musicians in the Caribbean have hailed from Barbados. The countryside is dotted with rum shops, not pubs, and West Indian cuisine, not kidney pie, is the mainstay of Bajan diets.

For many visitors Barbados can make for a comfortable mix of the familiar peppered with just enough local flavor to feel exotic. The island handles tourism well, people are friendly and it makes a good choice for a tame destination.

HIGHLIGHTS

- Fine white-sand beaches that fringe the west and south coasts
- Grand 17th-century plantation homes and estate gardens
- Harrison's Cave, with its impressive stalactites and stalagmites
- The Barbados Museum and the adjacent history-laden Garrison area
- Joining the crowd at a cricket match or a Saturday horse race

Facts about Barbados

HISTORY

The original inhabitants of Barbados were Arawak Indians, who were driven off the island around 1200 AD by invading Carib Indians from Venezuela. The Caribs themselves abandoned Barbados around the time the first Europeans sailed into the region. Although the conditions of their departure are unclear, some historians believe the Spanish might have landed on Barbados in the early 1500s and taken some of the Caribs as slaves, prompting the rest of the tribe to flee to the safety of more protected, mountainous islands such as St Lucia.

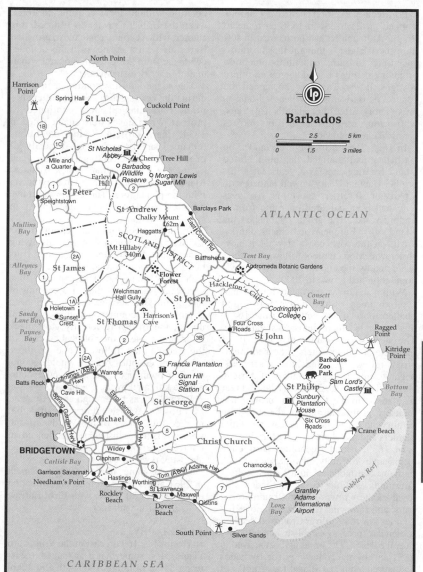

Portuguese explorer Pedro a Campos stopped on Barbados in 1536 en route to Brazil. Although he had no interest in settling the island it's thought that he introduced pigs to Barbados with the intention of having them as a food source on return voyages. It was Campos who named the island Los Barbados ('the bearded ones'), presumably after the island's fig trees, whose long hanging aerial roots have a beard-like resemblance.

In 1625 Captain John Powell landed on Barbados and claimed the uninhabited island for England. Two years later, his brother Captain Henry Powell landed with a party of 80 settlers as well as 10 slaves who had been captured en route from a trading vessel. The group established the island's first European settlement, Jamestown, on the west coast at what is now Holetown. More settlers followed in their wake and by the end of 1628 the colony's population had grown to 2000.

Within a few years the colonists had cleared much of the native forest and planted tobacco and cotton. In the 1640s they replanted their fields in sugar cane. The new sugar plantations were labor intensive and the planters, who had previously relied upon indentured servants, began to import large numbers of African slaves. Their estates, the first large sugar plantations in the Caribbean, proved immensely profitable and by the mid-17th century the islanders – or at least the white planters and merchants – were thriving.

In 1639, island freeholders formed a Legislative Assembly, only the second such parliament established in a British colony (Bermuda was the first). Barbados was loyal to the Crown during Britain's civil wars, and following the beheading of King Charles I in 1649, Oliver Cromwell decided to send a force to establish his authority over the island. The invading fleet arrived in 1651 and by the following year Barbados had surrendered and signed the Articles of Capitulation, which formed the basis for the Charter of Barbados. The charter guaranteed government by a governor and a freely elected assembly as well as freedom from

taxation without local consent. In 1660, when the British Crown was restored, this charter, with a certain ironic twist, provided Barbados with a greater measure of independence from the English monarchy than that of other British colonies.

The sugar industry continued to boom during the next century and even after abolition Barbadian planters continued to prosper. When slaves were emancipated in 1834, their difficult living conditions remained largely unchanged. Virtually all of the arable land continued to be owned by large estates and most black islanders found few options other than staying on with the plantations. Those who did move off often ended up living in shanty towns in abject poverty.

During the economic depression of the 1930s, unemployment shot upwards, living conditions deteriorated and street riots broke out. As a consequence the British Colonial Welfare and Development Office was established, providing sizable sums of money for Barbados and other Caribbean colonies. To counter growing political unrest, the British reluctantly gave black reformers a role in the political process. In the decade that followed one of those reformers, Grantley Adams, would become the first premier of Barbados and eventually be knighted by the queen.

Barbados was far enough afield to avoid the hostile British-French rivalry that marked the history of the Windward and Leeward Islands. Instead it experienced an unbroken period of British rule that lasted almost 350 years.

Barbados gained internal self-government in 1961 and became an independent nation on November 30, 1966, with Errol Barrow as its first prime minister.

GEOGRAPHY
Barbados lies 160km east of the Windward Islands. It is somewhat pear shaped, measuring 34km from north to south and 22km at its widest. The total land area of the island is 430 sq km.

The island is largely composed of coral accumulations built on sedimentary rocks.

Water permeates its soft coral cap, creating underground streams, springs and limestone caverns. The most notable of the caverns, Harrison's Cave, is one of the island's leading tourist attractions.

Most of the island's terrain is relatively flat, rising to low gentle hills in the interior. However, the northeastern part of the island, known as the Scotland District, rises to a relatively lofty 340 meters at the island's highest point, Mt Hillaby.

The west coast has white-sand beaches and calm turquoise waters, while the east side of the island has turbulent Atlantic waters and a coastline punctuated by coastal cliffs. Coral reefs surround most of the island.

CLIMATE

In January the average daily high temperature is 28°C (83°F) while the low averages 21°C (70°F). In July the average daily high is 30°C (86°F) while the low averages 23°C (74°F).

February to May are the driest months, with a mean relative humidity around 68%. The rest of the year the humidity averages between 74% and 79%. In July, the wettest month, there's measurable rainfall for an average of 18 days, while April, the driest month, averages seven days. Annual rainfall averages 1275 mm (51 inches). Visitors on the island can get the current weather forecast by calling ☎ 976-2376.

FLORA & FAUNA

As most of Barbados' native forest was leveled by early settlers who cleared the land for farming, the landscape is predominantly one of sugar cane fields, pasture and scrubland. The small sections of native woodlands that still remain are mainly in gullies and clifflands too steep for cultivation.

One of the island's more notable trees is the bearded fig tree (*ficus citrofolia*), for which the island was named. Other trees common to Barbados are palms, casuarina, locust, white cedar, mahogany and poinciana. There are also a fair number of flowering plants on the island and some

---

Green Monkeys

The green monkeys that inhabit Barbados were introduced as pets from West Africa some 350 years ago. The monkeys quickly found their way into the wild where they fared well, free of any predators other than humans.

Today the island's monkey population is estimated at between 5000 to 10,000. They are shy of people and live mainly in forested gullies, traveling in groups of about a dozen. Like most other primates, they are active from dawn to dusk and sleep at night.

Green monkeys are not rare or endangered either in Barbados or worldwide. Indeed, because monkeys have many of the same food preferences as humans, they are considered a pest by Barbadian farmers who can lose as much as a third of their banana, mango and papaya crops to the monkeys.

Consequently, the government has long encouraged the hunting of monkeys. The first bounties were introduced in the late 1600s, with five shillings offered for each monkey head delivered to the parish church. In 1975 the Ministry of Agriculture introduced a new bounty of B$5 for each monkey tail received. After the Barbados Primate Research Center was founded in 1982, it began to offer a more enticing B$50 reward for each monkey captured alive and delivered unharmed to the center. As a result many farmers now trap, rather than shoot, the monkeys. ■

---

attractive cultivated gardens that are open to visitors.

A few introduced mammals are found in the wild, including green monkeys, mongoose, European hares, mice and rats. Found only on Barbados is the non-poisonous and rarely seen grass snake *Liophis perfuscus*. The island also has a small harmless blind snake, whistling frogs, lizards, red-footed tortoises and eight species of bats.

Hawksbill turtles come ashore to lay their eggs on sandy beaches around Barbados on a regular basis, and the leatherback turtle is an occasional nester.

More than 180 species of birds have been sighted on Barbados. Most of them are migrating shorebirds and waders that breed in North America and stop over in Barbados en route to winter feeding grounds in South America. Only 28 species nest on Barbados; these include wood doves, blackbirds, bananaquits, guinea fowl, cattle egrets, herons, finches and three kinds of hummingbirds.

GOVERNMENT & POLITICS

Barbados is an independent state within the Commonwealth. It has a bicameral parliament consisting of a House of Assembly with 28 elected members, who serve for a maximum five-year term, and a Senate with 21 appointed members. Executive power is vested in the Prime Minister, who is generally the leader of the majority party in the Assembly. A Governor-General representing the Queen is the official head of state, but the role is mainly ceremonial in nature.

Universal suffrage dates from 1951. The two main political parties are the Barbados Labour Party (BLP), formed in 1938 by Grantley Adams, and the Democratic Labour Party (DLP), which splintered from the BLP in 1955. Both parties have moderate socialist platforms.

Early Tourists

In 1751 at age 19, some 38 years before he would become the first US president, George Washington visited Barbados as a companion to his half-brother Lawrence, who suffered from tuberculosis. It was hoped the tropical climate would prove therapeutic.

The two rented a house in the Garrison area south of Bridgetown (where the Bush Hill House now stands) and stayed on the island for six weeks. Unfortunately, George contracted smallpox while on Barbados, which left his face permanently scarred, and Lawrence died the following year. The Barbados trip was the only overseas journey George Washington ever made. ■

ECONOMY

Sugar, the mainstay of the Barbadian economy for 300 years, was nudged into second place by tourism in 1970. Since then tourism has continued to grow and now accounts for nearly 50% of the island's gross national product.

Sugar, and its byproducts of rum and molasses, are still leading exports, but the amount of land devoted to sugar cane is gradually declining and a policy of agricultural diversification is underway. Other crops include yams, sweet potatoes, peanuts, cut flowers and sea-island cotton.

In total, agriculture accounts for about 10% of the Barbadian labor force and the fishing industry accounts for another 5%. There's also a small light industry sector that includes the manufacturing of clothing, pharmaceuticals and computer components. Barbados meets nearly half of its energy needs from its domestic oil and natural gas supplies; there's a refinery in Bridgetown.

POPULATION & PEOPLE

The population of Barbados is approximately 265,000. More than 90% of Bajans are black, of African descent. The remainder are mostly English and Scottish, along with a small minority of East Indians. Although there are many small villages throughout Barbados, the vast majority of people live along the leeward side of the island, in an urban sweep running from Speightstown in the northwest to Oistins in the south.

SOCIETY & CONDUCT

The national sport, if not the national obsession, is cricket. Barbadians boast more world-class cricket players than any other nation, at least on a per capita basis. One of the world's top all-rounders, Bajan native Garfield Sobers, was knighted by Queen Elizabeth II during her 1975 visit to Barbados, while another cricket hero, Sir Frank Worrell, appears on the face of the Barbadian five-dollar bill.

Island architectural styles have their roots in the colonial era when virtually all

Frank Worrell, cricket hero

land belonged to large sugar estates. The island still has a number of grand plantation homes as well as numerous chattel houses, the latter being a simple rectangular wooden home built on stone blocks so that it could be moved.

Despite the British influence, West Indian culture is also strong in terms of family life, food and music. Barbadian contributions to West Indian music are renowned in the region, having produced such greats as the calypso artist the Mighty Gabby, whose songs on cultural identity and political protest speak for emerging black pride throughout the Caribbean.

One of the Eastern Caribbean's leading contemporary poets is Edward 'Kamau' Brathwaite, who hails from Barbados. Among his writings is *The Arrivants, A New World Trilogy*, which examines the lives of blacks in the Caribbean and the Americas.

The foremost contemporary Barbadian novelist is George Lamming, who has authored six novels and several collections of short fiction. Much of his writing critiques social and political conditions. His most acclaimed novel is *The Castle of My Skin*, which portrays what it was like

growing up black in a colonial Barbados struggling towards independence.

Dos & Don'ts

Shorts are not appropriate in nightclubs or in most restaurants at dinner time. Topless sunbathing is illegal.

RELIGION

The majority of the population is Anglican. Other religious denominations on Barbados include Methodist, Moravian, Roman Catholic, Pentecostal, Baptist, First Church of Christ Scientist, Jehovah's Witnesses, Seventh Day Adventist, Baha'i, Muslim and Jewish. For a current calendar of religious services see the 'Let Us Pray' page in the free tourist publication *Visitor*.

LANGUAGE

The island's language is English, spoken with a distinctive Bajan accent.

Facts for the Visitor

ORIENTATION

Barbados is divided into 11 parishes. The airport and the south coast resorts are in the parish of Christ Church, while most of the west coast resorts are in St James. Addresses commonly list both the village and parish name.

The island's major highways, numbered 1 to 7 from north to south, all begin in Bridgetown. The airport is on the southeast side of the island, 16km from Bridgetown. Hwy 7 leads from the airport through the south-coast resort area, but if you're heading to Bridgetown or the west coast, the bypass road, the ABC Highway, is much quicker than the coastal road. The ABC Highway is a combination of the Adams, Barrow and Cummings highways.

Most of the island's rural sights – plantation houses, gardens and parks – are scattered throughout the interior. With a car you could see the bulk of them in one frenetic day or all of them in a couple days of leisurely exploring.

BARBADOS

Maps

If you intend to explore the island on your own, a good map will certainly come in handy. The best overall map of the island is the Ordnance Survey 1:50,000 map of Barbados, which can be purchased at larger bookstores.

Although they don't show topographical detail, there are a couple of good free maps available as well, including a road map distributed by the tourist office.

TOURIST OFFICES
Local Tourist Offices

The Barbados Tourism Authority has its administrative office (☎ 427-2623, fax 426-4080) on Harbour Rd in Bridgetown, though most visitors will instead be using the convenient and very helpful booth (☎ 428-5570) at the airport. When requesting information by mail, write to: Barbados Tourism Authority, PO Box 242, Bridgetown, Barbados, West Indies.

Tourist Offices Abroad

Overseas offices of the Barbados Tourism Authority include:

Canada
    5160 Yonge St, 18th Floor, North York, Ontario M2N 6L9 (☎ 416-512-6569, 800-268-9122; fax 416-512-6581)
Germany
    Neue Mainer Strasse 22, D-60311 Frankfurt/Main (☎ 69 23 23 66, fax 69 23 00 77)
UK
    263 Tottenham Court Rd, London W1P OLA (☎ 0171-636-9448, fax 0171-637-1496)
USA
    800 Second Ave, New York, NY 10017 (☎ 212-986-6516, 800-221-9831; fax 212-573-9850)
    3440 Wilshire Blvd, Suite 1215, Los Angeles, CA 90010 (☎ 213-380-2198, fax 213-384-2763)

VISAS & DOCUMENTS

Citizens of the USA and Canada who are traveling directly from their home countries can enter Barbados without a passport for stays of less than three months, as long as they have an original birth certificate or naturalization certificate along with a photo ID such as a driver's license. Citizens of all other countries must have a valid passport.

Visas are required for citizens from the People's Republic of China, Taiwan, Pakistan, non-Commonwealth African countries and all South American countries except Argentina, Brazil and Venezuela.

Foreign Embassies in Barbados

Foreign embassies and high commissions in Barbados are:

Australia
    Australian High Commission, Bishop's Court Hill, Pine Road, St Michael (☎ 435-2834)
Brazil
    Embassy of Brazil, 3rd Floor, Sunjet House, Fairchild St, Bridgetown (☎ 427-1735)
Canada
    Canadian High Commission, Bishop's Court Hill, Pine Rd, St Michael (☎ 429-3550)
China
    Embassy of the People's Republic of China, 17 Golf View Terrace, Rockley, Christ Church (☎ 435-6890)
Colombia
    Embassy of Colombia, Rosemary, Dayrells Rd, Rockley, Christ Church (☎ 429-6821)
Cuba
    Embassy of the Republic of Cuba, Erin Court, Collymore Rock, St Michael (☎ 435-2769)
France
    French Consulate, Waverly House, Hastings, Christ Church (☎ 435-6847)
UK
    British High Commission, Lower Collymore Rock, St Michael (☎ 436-6694)
USA
    US Embassy, Broad St, Bridgetown (☎ 436-4950)
Venezuela
    Venezuelan Embassy, Hastings, Christ Church (☎ 435-7619)

CUSTOMS

Visitors may bring in one liter of spirits or wine, 200 cigarettes (or 50 cigars) and a reasonable amount of personal effects.

BARBADOS

MONEY

Banks exchange Barbados dollars at the rate of B$1.98 for US$1 in cash, B$1.99 for US$1 in traveler's checks. To exchange Barbados dollars back to US dollars the rate is B$2.04 to US$1. Cash and traveler's checks in British, Canadian and German currencies can also be readily exchanged at banks, with rates fluctuating daily according to international monetary markets.

Banks charge a stamp fee for each traveler's check cashed – 10 cents for up to the equivalent of B$50, 50 cents for larger checks – and generally a commission of B$1 to B$3, depending on the amount of money exchanged. American Express in Bridgetown cashes American Express traveler's checks without a commission charge.

You'll certainly want some Barbados dollars for incidentals but most larger payments can be made in US dollars or with a credit card. Hotels and guesthouses quote rates in US dollars, although you can use either US or Barbadian currency to settle the account; most give an exchange rate of B$2 to US$1 for traveler's checks or cash. When using a credit card, charges are made in Barbados dollars and calculated by the bank at the rate of B$1.97 to US$1.

Most restaurants, hotels and shops accept Visa, MasterCard and American Express cards. A few also accept the Discover Card.

Banks are easy to find in larger towns and major tourist areas. Credit card holders can obtain cash advances from automated teller machines (ATMs) at many branches of the Royal Bank of Canada and Barclays Bank. There's an ATM at the airport.

Currency

Notes come in B$2 (blue), B$5 (green), B$10 (brown), B$20 (purple), B$50 (orange) and B$100 (gray) denominations.

There are 1 cent copper coins, 5 cent bronze coins and 10 cent, 25 cent and B$1 silver-colored coins. All are round except the dollar coin which has seven sides.

POST & COMMUNICATIONS
Post

The general post office, in Cheapside, Bridgetown, is open from 7:30 am to 5 pm Monday to Friday. There are also district post offices in every parish, as well as one at the airport; most are open weekdays from 8 am to noon and 1 to 3:15 pm (3 pm on Monday).

Airmail postage rates for a postcard are B$0.65 to the Caribbean, the USA and Canada and B$0.70 to the UK and Europe. For a letter up to 10 grams it's B$0.70 to other Caribbean countries, B$0.90 cents to the USA and Canada and B$1.10 to Europe.

Mail service is quite efficient and mail is dispatched daily to both London and New York.

When addressing mail to Barbados from overseas, follow the town and/or parish name with 'Barbados, West Indies.'

Telephone

Local phone numbers have seven digits. When calling Barbados from overseas, add the area code 246.

Barbados has both coin and card phones. At coin phones, you'll get five minutes calling time to anywhere on the island for each 25 cents; 5, 10 and 25 cent coins are accepted.

There are card phones at the airport, Bridgetown Harbour, major shopping centers and in other heavily trafficked public places although, to date, card phones are not as widespread as coin phones.

Barbados phonecards are available in B$10, B$20, B$40 and B$60 denominations and are sold at the airport, phone company offices, convenience stores and supermarkets. If you're in possession of an Eastern Caribbean phonecard, it'll work in Barbados phones as well.

If you need to send a fax or telegram it can be done weekdays from 8 am to 4:30 pm at the telephone company office on McGregor St in Bridgetown.

More information on phonecards and making long distance calls is under Post & Communications in the Facts for the Visitor chapter at the front of the book.

The area code for Barbados is 246.

BOOKS
There are numerous books on Barbadian history and sights.

The Barbados Garrison and its Buildings by Warren Alleyne & Jill Sheppard is a well-written little book describing the many historic buildings that comprise the Garrison area.

Other books include *Barbados: Portrait of an Island*, a smart hardcover coffee-table book by Dick Scoones; *Treasures of Barbados*, a hardcover book on the island's architecture by Henry Fraser, president of the Barbados National Trust; and books on Barbadian political figures, including *Tom Adams: A Biography* and *Grantley Adams and the Social Revolution*, both by local historian FA Hoyos.

NEWSPAPERS & MAGAZINES
Barbados has two daily newspapers, *The Barbados Advocate* and *The Nation*. British and American newspapers are available at

convenience stores in the main tourist areas. Two free tourist publications worth picking up are the weekly *Visitor* and the bi-monthly *Sunseeker*, both of which have lots of ads and general information.

RADIO & TV
In addition to the government-owned TV station, CBC, which broadcasts on Channel 8, a number of international TV networks, including CNN, ESPN and TNT, are picked up by satellite. There are several local radio stations on Barbados.

ELECTRICITY
Electricity in Barbados is 110 volts AC, 50 cycles, with a flat two-pronged plug; many hotels have 240-volt converter outlets in the bathrooms.

WEIGHTS & MEASURES
Despite its British heritage, Barbados has gone metric. Road signs and car odometers are in kilometers, weights are in grams and kg. However, the transition to metric is fairly recent and many islanders still give directions in feet and miles.

HEALTH
There's a 600-bed government hospital in Bridgetown, the Queen Elizabeth Hospital (☎ 436-6450) on Martindales Rd, and several clinics around the island.

For divers who get the bends, the Barbados Defence Force (☎ 436-6185) maintains a decompression chamber in the Garrison area of Bridgetown.

Leptospirosis, which can be carried by mongooses, can be present in freshwater streams.

DANGERS & ANNOYANCES
Crime, including assaults on tourists, is certainly not unknown on Barbados. Still, the crime statistics are not alarming and the usual precautions should suffice.

Portuguese men-o-war (which are a type of poisonous jellyfish) are occasionally encountered in Barbadian waters, and poisonous manchineel trees grow along some beaches.

EMERGENCIES

Emergency telephone numbers in Barbados are:

Ambulance	☎ 115
Fire	☎ 113
Police	☎ 112

(☎ 436-6600 for routine police matters)

BUSINESS HOURS

Most banks are open from 8 am to 3 pm Monday to Thursday, until 5 pm on Friday. A few branches are also open from 9 am to noon on Saturday.

Most stores are open from 8 am to 4 pm Monday to Friday and to noon on Saturday. Supermarkets are generally open until 6 pm.

Many restaurants and visitor attractions are closed on public holidays.

PUBLIC HOLIDAYS & SPECIAL EVENTS

Public holidays are:

New Year's Day	January 1
Errol Barrow Day	January 21
Good Friday	late March/early April
Easter Monday	late March/early April
Labour Day	May 1
Whit Monday	eighth Monday after Easter
Kadooment Day	first Monday in August
United Nations Day	first Monday in October
Independence Day	November 30
Christmas Day	December 25
Boxing Day	December 26

The island's top event is the Crop-Over Festival, which originated in colonial times as a celebration to mark the end of the sugar cane harvest. Festivities stretch over a three-week period beginning in mid-July. There are spirited calypso competitions, fairs and other activities around the island. The festival culminates with a Carnival-like costume parade and fireworks on Kadooment Day, a national holiday.

In February, the Holetown Festival celebrates the February 17, 1627, arrival of the first English settlers on Barbados. Holetown's week-long festivities include street fairs, a music festival at the historic parish church and a road race.

One of the cultural highlights of the year is the Holders Season, a program of opera, music, theater and sporting events held during the month of March. Although performers vary with the year, among those taking the stage has been the renowned opera singer Luciano Pavarotti.

The Oistins Fish Festival, held over Easter weekend, commemorates the signing of the Charter of Barbados and celebrates the skills of local fisher folk. It's a seaside festivity with events focusing on boat races, fish-boning competitions, local foods, crafts and dancing.

The National Independence Festival of Creative Arts, held throughout November, features talent contests in dance, drama, singing and the like. Performances by the finalists are held on Independence Day, November 30.

There are also a handful of international sporting events, including the Barbados Windsurfing World Cup, held at Silver Sands in January; the Caribbean Surfing Championship, held in November at Bathsheba; Banks Field Hockey Festival, held in late August; and Run Barbados, a marathon held in early December.

ACTIVITIES

Barbados has a plethora of civic clubs and special interest groups, covering everything from flower arranging and Scottish dance to taekwondo and transcendental meditation. Many are open to short-term visitors; meeting times and contact numbers are listed in the *Sunseeker* and *Visitor* tourist publications.

Beaches & Swimming

Some of the island's prettiest beaches and calmest waters are along the west coast. Top spots include Paynes Bay, Sandy Bay and Mullins Bay – all lovely white-sand beaches that are easily accessible.

The southwest side of the island also has some fine beaches, including Sandy Beach in Worthing and Dover Beach. On the southeast side is Crane Beach, a scenic stretch of pink-tinged sand that's popular with bodysurfers but rough for swimming.

BARBADOS

The east coast has dangerous water conditions, including rocky nearshore shelves and strong currents, and only the most confident swimmers should take to the waters. The Bathsheba area, in particular, has been the scene of a number of visitor drownings.

Diving & Snorkeling

The west coast of Barbados has reef dives with soft corals, gorgonians and colorful sponges. There are also about a dozen shipwrecks. The largest and most popular, the 111-meter freighter *Stavronikita*, was scuttled by the government in 1978 to create an artificial reef. It now sits upright off the central west coast in 42 meters of water, with the rigging reaching to within six meters of the surface. The coral-encrusted tug *Berwyn*, which sank in 1919 at Carlisle Bay, lies in only seven meters of water and makes for good snorkeling as well as diving.

One-tank dives with gear average US$40, two-tank dives US$70. For beginners who want to try the waters, most dive companies offer a brief resort course and a shallow dive for US$45 to US$60. Many also offer full certification courses in either PADI or NAUI for US$350 to US$375.

Dive companies include:

Bubbles Galore,
    Sandy Beach Hotel, Worthing
    (☎ 435-8000, bubbles@caribsurf.com)
Dive Boat Safari at the Barbados Hilton,
    Aquatic Gap, St Michael
    (☎ 427-4350)
Dive Shop,
    Aquatic Gap, St Michael
    (☎ 426-9947)
Exploresub Barbados,
    St Lawrence Gap, Christ Church
    (☎ 435-6542, fax 428-4674)
Underwater Barbados,
    Carlisle Bay Centre, Bay St, Bridgetown
    (☎ 426-0655)

Snorkeling sets can be rented at beach water sports huts and dive shops around the island. Dive Boat Safari offers a one-hour snorkeling tour that often takes in the *Berwyn* for just US$15.

Windsurfing

Barbados has good windsurfing conditions, with the best winds and waves from December to June. Maxwell is a popular area for intermediate-level windsurfers, while the Silver Sands area, at the southern tip of the island, has excellent conditions for advanced windsurfing.

Club Mistral rents windsurfing gear daily all year round at its Windsurfing Club (☎ 428-7277) in Maxwell and from December to June at the Silver Sands Resort (☎ 428-6001). At Maxwell, a range of boards and wave and slalom sails rent for US$25/75/285 per hour/day/week. At Silver Sands, Club Mistral rents only short boards (sinkers) and wave sails, for US$30/65/350.

Club Mistral gives lessons to beginners in Maxwell. Group lessons cost US$140 for four hours, private lessons US$110 for two hours, including gear.

Windsurfing gear can also be rented from the Silver Rock Hotel (☎ 428-2866) in Silver Sands; Dread or Dead (☎ 437-3404) on the main road in Hastings; High Tide Watersports (☎ 432-1311) at the Sandy Lane Hotel in St James; Charles Watersports (☎ 428-9550) at Dover Beach; and the water sports hut at Sandy Beach in Worthing.

Surfing

Barbados has some excellent surfing action. The biggest swells hit the east coast, with the prime surfing taking place at the Soup Bowl, off Bathsheba.

South Point and Rockley Beach on the south coast are sometimes good for surfing and the west coast can have surfable waves as well.

Though winter sees the highest swells, surfers will generally find reasonably good conditions on Barbados year round. The water tends to be flattest in May and June.

Dread or Dead (☎ 437-3404) on the main road in Hastings rents boogie boards for B$20 a day, surfboards for B$30 a day, each requiring a B$100 deposit. Surfboards and boogie boards can also be rented from Charles Watersports at Dover

Beach and the water sports hut at Sandy Beach in Worthing.

Hiking
Each Sunday at 6 am and 3 pm, the Barbados National Trust (☎ 426-2421) leads guided hikes in the countryside. Hikers are divided into three categories ranked by pace: fast, medium and stop-and-stare. Hike leaders share insights into local history, geology, flora and fauna. Locations vary, but all hikes end where they start, last around three hours and cover about 8km. There is no fee. Schedule information can be found in the free tourist publications or is available by calling the trust.

Horseback Riding
The Wilcox Riding Stable (☎ 428-3610) near the airport and Tony's Riding Stables (☎ 422-1549) near Mullins Bay both offer one-hour rides, either along the beach or in the country, for B$65.

Tennis
There are tennis courts at several resort hotels, including the Casuarina Beach Club at Dover, Southern Palms Beach Club in St Lawrence, the Barbados Hilton in Bridgetown, Silver Sands Resort on the south coast and Sam Lord's Castle and the Crane Beach Hotel, both on the east coast. There are public tennis courts at Folkestone Park in Holetown and at the Garrison area south of Bridgetown center.

Golf
There's an 18-hole course at the Sandy Lane Hotel & Golf Club (☎ 432-1145) in St James. Green fees for non-guests are US$85/ 115 in summer/winter, plus US$25 for a cart. Rockley Resort Golf Club (☎ 435-7873) on the south coast has a nine-hole course, with green fees of US$50, including club and cart rentals.

The Belair Par 3 Golf Course (☎ 423-4653), on the east coast near Sam Lord's Castle, has rather affordable green fees of US$12.50 for nine holes; to rent clubs it costs US$2.50.

Other
For information on bicycle rentals, see the Getting Around section of this chapter. Information on various boat cruises, distillery tours, brewery tours and open houses is under Organized Tours in the same Getting Around section.

ACCOMMODATIONS
Barbados has a good variety of low and mid-range places to stay. Some could use a fresh coat of paint but most are comfortable and good value by Caribbean standards. There are also some fine top-end resorts.

Most of the upscale resorts are along the west coast in the parish of St James, a relatively quiet and subdued area. The south coast, which generally attracts a younger crowd, has most of the low and mid-range accommodations. There's a light scattering of places to stay elsewhere on the island, including a few secluded options on the east and southeast coast.

As most hotels don't include breakfast, many charge the same rate for single or double occupancy. Some places have three rate schedules: a low rate for summer, a marginally more expensive spring and autumn rate and a high rate for winter.

If you arrive without a reservation the tourist office at the airport can book you a room. There's no charge for the service and they can almost always come up with something in every price range. The tourist office also keeps a short list of families that rent out bedrooms in their homes, from about US$25 to US$50 a night. Most hotels add a 7.5% government tax and a 10% service charge.

Camping is generally not allowed on Barbados, except for organized outings by designated youth groups.

Reservation Service
The Barbados Reservation Service (☎ 402-398-3217 or 800-462-2526 from the USA, ☎ 800-822-2077 from Canada; fax 402-398-5484) books about half of the island's hotels. They don't cover the very cheapest budget hotels or guesthouses, but otherwise

book a full spectrum, from small hotels and apartments to luxury resorts.

There are no fees to make a reservation (although a credit card guarantee is usually required) and bookings are made at established rates. The only thing to keep in mind is that island hotels sometimes offer discounted promotional rates that are available only by booking directly with the hotel.

Villas

There are numerous individually owned villas available for rent on Barbados. They are generally quite exclusive; all have maid service, most have a cook and some also have a butler. About half of the villas have private pools.

WIMCO books 100 such properties, with weekly prices ranging from about US$1200 for a simple one-bedroom place to US$25,000 for an eight-bedroom great house. Summer prices are 30% to 60% cheaper. For reservations contact WIMCO (☎ 401-849-8012, fax 401-847-6290, wimco@well.com), PO Box 1461, Newport, RI 02840. Toll free numbers are ☎ 800-932-3222 in the USA, ☎ 01 30 81 57 30 from Germany and ☎ 0-800 89-8318 from the UK.

FOOD

Barbados has a range of Western fare from fast-food pizza and fried chicken to fine continental cuisine. In addition there's spicier Bajan and Caribbean food to choose from. Some of the more popular local foods, many of which borrow heavily from African and Indian influences, include conkies, cou-cou, cutter, flying fish, jug-jug and souse. For descriptions, see the food glossary in the Facts for the Visitor chapter.

Other common local foods include pigeon peas and rice, pumpkin fritters, fried plantains and coconut pie.

DRINKS

Tap water is safe to drink; it comes from underground reservoirs that are naturally filtered by the island's thick limestone cap.

Barbadian rum is considered some of the finest in the Caribbean, with Mount Gay being the largest and best-known label. A liter of rum costs about B$12. The island beer, Banks, is a reasonably good brew.

ENTERTAINMENT

The south coast of Barbados has a lively night scene. Most clubs open around 9:30 pm and continue into the wee hours of the morning, often until 3 am. The music is usually a mix of reggae, calypso and rock.

Harbour Lights, an open-air nightclub on Bay St at the south end of Bridgetown, has dancing and live bands most nights, with Friday generally the liveliest. While it's not gay-oriented, it is one of the more gay-friendly places.

Waterfront Cafe, at the Careenage in Bridgetown, has steel pan music on Tuesday and Wednesday and jazz Thursday to Saturday. There's no cover and the musicians usually play from 8 to 11 pm.

Ship Inn is the most happening place in the St Lawrence area. Tuesday and Saturday are the hottest, but there's a live band nightly. The cover charge is B$10, with B$5 redeemable in drinks or food. The nearby *After Dark* is a popular mingling place for locals and tourists and is generally at its best on Friday and Saturday.

'1627 and All That,' a colorful dramatization of the island's history through music and folk dance, is held from 6:30 to 10 pm each Thursday at the Barbados Museum. It's all good fun and the price of B$115 for adults, B$63 for children, includes the show, a Bajan dinner buffet, drinks, a museum tour and transportation. For reservations call ☎ 435-1627.

The *Plantation Restaurant* (☎ 428-5048) on Hwy 7 in St Lawrence puts on a flamboyant costumed cabaret show with music, dancing and fire eating at 8 pm Wednesday and Friday. The show and drinks cost B$55; with a buffet dinner (at 6:30 pm) and transportation it's B$115.

On weekends, the seaside fish market in Oistins is the sight of the island's most spirited night scene. Women grill Cajun-style fish; live soca and calypso bands perform to a gyrating audience; and a line of normally inconspicuous rum shops pack in a crowd. It's roughly 80% locals, 20% tourists, and makes a fun scene, whether you're out for partying or just getting a solid local meal at an honest price. The height of the action is between 10 pm and 2 am on Friday and Saturday.

Entertainment schedules are in the *Sunseeker* and *Visitor* tourist publications.

THINGS TO BUY

There are a couple of good places to shop in Bridgetown. The Women's Self Help Association on Broad St, adjacent to the Royal Bank of Canada, has island crafts, handmade dolls, pottery and T-shirts while the Verandah Art Gallery directly above sells quality paintings, prints and cards, mainly by Barbadian artists.

You can shop duty free (upon presentation of your passport) at a number of shops, including Cave Shepherd, the island's largest department store chain. It has a branch on Broad St, Bridgetown's main shopping street.

Best of Barbados, a small chain with shops around the island, including one at 34 Broad St in Bridgetown, has a good selection of crafts, books and other gifts.

Pottery made up on Chalky Mount is a good, if not lightweight, souvenir. Two lightweight items that make tasty gifts are locally made Cajun hot pepper sauce and concentrated ginger beer syrup. For an even more unusual souvenir you might want to pick up a packed box of frozen flying fish at the airport departure lounge.

Getting There & Away

AIR
Airlines

Most airlines have offices in Bridgetown: American Airlines is upstairs in the Cave Shepherd department store on Broad St; British Airways is on Fairchild St; BWIA is on the corner of Fairchild and Probyn Sts; and LIAT is on St Michael's Row opposite St Michael's Cathedral. All are open from 8 am to 4 pm weekdays.

You can also purchase tickets at the airport counters but it's best to avoid heavy flight times; in LIAT's case that's usually early morning and late afternoon.

Airline reservation numbers on Barbados are:

Aeropostal	☎ 427-7781
Air Canada	☎ 428-5077
Air Jamaica	☎ 420-7361
American Airlines	☎ 428-4170
BWIA	☎ 426-2111
	☎ 428-1650 (airport)
British Airways	☎ 436-6413
	☎ 428-1661 (airport)
LIAT	☎ 434-5428
	☎ 428-0986 (airport)
Mustique Airways	☎ 428-1638

USA

Both American Airlines and BWIA fly to Barbados daily from Miami and New York. Fares fluctuate with the period of travel and current promotions but during the low season both airlines commonly offer 30-day excursion fares from Miami for as low as US$350 and from New York for around US$450; in the high season fares are generally about 50% higher.

The newest entry into the market is Air Jamaica, which flies daily from New York (JFK) to Barbados with year-round midweek fares beginning around US$550.

Canada

Air Canada flies from Toronto to Barbados on Friday and Saturday and from Montreal to Barbados on Sunday. The cheapest excursion fare from either city, with a maximum stay of 14 days, costs C$590.

BWIA flies from Toronto to Barbados on Saturday with a fare of C$726 for an excursion ticket allowing a 21-day stay.

UK

British Airways flies to Barbados from London's Gatwick Airport on Monday, Wednesday, Thursday, Friday and Saturday. The least expensive regular roundtrip fare is UK£794, with a seven-day minimum stay and a 180-day maximum stay.

BWIA flies from Heathrow to Barbados on Monday, Thursday and Saturday and charges UK£885 for an excursion ticket allowing a stay up to 180 days.

Note that for both airlines these are the standard rates. Travel agents specializing in cheap airfares can often book a ticket for half these prices.

South America
Aeropostal flies to Barbados from Porlamar on Venezuela's Margarita Island on Tuesday and Saturday for US$85 one way and US$150 roundtrip. Aeropostal also has an excursion ticket between Caracas and Barbados, with a stopover on Margarita Island, for US$222 roundtrip.

In addition LIAT has direct flights between Barbados and Guyana's capital of Georgetown, and BWIA flies between Barbados and Georgetown via Trinidad. The one-way fare costs US$172, while a 30-day excursion ticket is US$193.

Within the Caribbean
LIAT has direct daily flights to Barbados from Antigua, St Lucia, Grenada and St Vincent. You can get connecting flights on LIAT to other islands throughout the Eastern Caribbean.

LIAT's fare between Barbados and St Lucia is US$78 one way, US$124 for a 30-day excursion. Other one-way/excursion fares to Barbados are US$110/164 from Grenada, US$95/144 from St Vincent and US$211/278 from Antigua.

Mustique Airways has daily flights to St Vincent and the Grenadines. One-way fares from Barbados are US$95 to St Vincent, $98 to Mustique or Bequia and US$110 to Union Island.

BWIA has direct flights daily between Barbados and Trinidad with a one-way fare of US$121 and a roundtrip fare of US$133. Everyday except Wednesday and Saturday BWIA flies between Barbados and Antigua for US$186 one way, US$194 roundtrip. These BWIA roundtrip fares allow stays of two to 12 days and require a one-day advance purchase.

Tickets purchased in Barbados for flights originating in Barbados have a 15% tax added on. However, if you buy a ticket in Barbados for flights originating on another island the tax is not added.

Airport Information
In season, a steel band greets the arriving passengers.

The friendly tourist office booth can help you book a room and is a good place to pick up tourist brochures; the booth is open from 8 am to 10 pm or until the last flight arrives. Opposite it is Barbados National Bank's exchange booth, open daily from 8 am to 9:30 pm. Near the airline counters there's an ATM that accepts Visa, MasterCard and Cirrus and Plus ATM cards.

The airport also has card and coin phones, a post office, a sit-down restaurant and a few stalls selling drinks, simple eats and souvenirs.

The departure lounge has shops selling duty-free liquor, watches and jewelry as well as a money-exchange window.

SEA
Because of Barbados' easterly position and challenging sailing conditions, it is well off the main track for most sailors and there is no yacht charter industry on the island.

There is a passenger/cargo boat, the M/V *Windward*, which links Barbados with St Lucia, St Vincent, Trinidad and Venezuela. Details are under Boat in the Getting Around chapter in the front of the book.

Cruise Ship
About 500,000 cruise ship passengers arrive in Barbados each year. Ships dock at Bridgetown Harbour, about a kilometer west of the city center. The port has the usual duty-free shops.

LEAVING BARBADOS
Barbados has a departure tax of B$25.

Getting Around

THE AIRPORT
If you're traveling light, it's possible to walk out to the road and wait for a passing

bus. Look for buses marked 'Sam Lord's Castle' if you're going east, 'Bridgetown' if you're going west; make sure the bus driver knows your destination.

Otherwise, if you're not renting a car, you'll find a line of taxis outside the arrival lounge. Taxi rates from the airport are about B$20 to St Lawrence, B$30 to central Bridgetown, B$38 to Holetown, B$48 to Bathsheba and B$55 to Speightstown.

BUS

It's possible to get to virtually any place on the island by public bus.

There are three kinds of buses on Barbados: government-operated public buses, which are blue with a yellow stripe and have the most extensive routes; a privately operated minibus system, which uses intermediate-sized buses painted yellow with a blue stripe; and route taxis, which are white with a burgundy stripe. The latter are individually owned minivans that have 'ZR' on their license plates and ply shorter, heavily traveled routes.

Some islanders prefer the minibuses, which are generally better maintained than the government buses and don't pack passengers as sardine-like as the route taxis. Others swear by the government buses, because the staff are on salary and not driving hell-bent to collect extra fares.

All three types of buses charge the same fare: B$1.50 to any place on the island. You should have exact change when you board the bus.

Most buses transit through Bridgetown although a few north-south buses bypass the city. Buses to the southeast part of the island generally transit through Oistins.

To get to the east coast, you can catch one of the hourly direct buses between Bridgetown and Bathsheba. There's also a bus service between Speightstown and Bathsheba; those buses leave Speightstown on odd-numbered hours (9 am, 11 am etc) and return from Bathsheba on the even hour.

Bus stops around the island are marked with red and white signs printed with the direction the bus is heading ('To City' or

'Out of City'). Buses usually have their destinations posted on or above the front windshield.

Buses along the main routes, such as Bridgetown to Oistins or Speightstown, are frequent, running from dawn to around midnight. You can get schedule information on any route by calling the Transport Board (☎ 436-6820).

Bridgetown Terminals

In Bridgetown, public buses going south and east leave from the Fairchild St Bus Terminal on the corner of Fairchild and Bridge Sts. Public buses going north up the west coast leave from the Jubilee (Lower Green) Terminal at the west end of Lower Broad St.

Minibuses use the River Bus Terminal, on the east side of the Fairchild St Public Market, for central and eastern routes. Minibuses going south leave from the corner of Probyn St and Jordan's Lane, while those going north up the west coast leave from near the general post office in Cheapside.

The route taxi terminal is on River Rd, east of the Fairchild St Public Market.

TAXI

Taxis have a 'Z' on the license plate and usually a 'taxi' sign on the roof. They're easy to find and often wait at the side of the road in popular tourist areas.

Although fares are fixed by the government, taxis are not metered, so you should establish the fare before you start off. The rate per kilomter is about B$1.50 and the flat hourly rate B$32.

Have a Good Day

In Bridgetown center you can expect to have taxi drivers approach and ask if you need a tour or a ride, whether you look like you do or not. This is not a hassle scene, however, and if you politely decline they generally smile and respond with the likes of 'just stretching legs?' or 'you have a good day then.' ■

BARBADOS

CAR & MOTORCYCLE
Road Rules
In Barbados, you drive on the left. Temporary driving permits are required; they cost B$10 and can be obtained through your car rental agency.

Highways are not very well marked, although key roundabouts and major intersections are usually signposted. The most consistent highway markings are often the low yellow cement posts at the side of the road; they show the highway number and below that the number of kilometers from Bridgetown.

Finding major tourist sights, many of which are on country roads, is not too difficult as most have signs en route pointing the way. If you get lost don't hesitate to stop and ask for directions; this is common practice and Bajans are generally very helpful.

All primary and main secondary roads are paved, although some are a bit narrow. There are lots of gas stations around the island, including one outside the airport. Some stations in the Bridgetown area are open 24 hours a day.

Rental
Barbados doesn't have any car rental agents affiliated with major international rental chains. There are, instead, scores of independent car rental companies, some so small that the number rings through to a private home. You simply call to book a car and someone will swing by your hotel to pick you up.

Despite the number of companies, prices don't seem to vary much. The going rate for a small car is about B$150 a day including unlimited mileage and insurance. Rental cars are marked with an 'H' on the license plate.

While most car rental companies don't have booths at the airport there are a number of nearby agencies that will pick you up there. You can make a reservation on the spot using the courtesy car/hotel phone located between immigration and customs.

Courtesy Rent-A-Car (☎ 431-4160, fax 429-6387) is one of the island's larger companies and has an airport location.

Other car rental companies include:

Corbins Car Rentals, Collymore Rock, St Michael (☎ 427-9531, fax 427-7975)
Direct Rentals, Enterprise, Christ Church (☎ 428-3133, fax 420-8190)
Hill's Car Rentals, Mason Hall St, St Michael (☎ 426-5280)
P & S Car Rentals, Cave Hill, St Michael (☎ 424-2052, fax 424-7591)
Rayside Car Rental, Charnocks, Christ Church (☎ 428-0264)
Sunny Isle Motors, Worthing, Christ Church (☎ 435-7979, fax 435-9277)
Sunset Crest Rent-A-Car, Sunset Crest, St James (☎ 432-2222, fax 432-1619)

BICYCLE
Rob's Bike Hire (☎ 437-3404), on the main road in Hastings, rents mountain bikes for B$20/100 a day/week, plus a deposit of B$100. They do not accept credit cards.

HITCHHIKING
Hitchhiking is tolerated but the practice is not widespread, in part because buses are cheap and frequent. All the usual safety precautions apply.

ORGANIZED TOURS
Sightseeing Tours
Bajan Tours (☎ /fax 437-9389, bajan@ caribnet.net) is one of the largest companies providing sightseeing tours and has relatively good prices. It has a couple of full-day island tours, including one that concentrates on the perimeter of the island, stopping at Edgewater Inn for lunch and visiting sights such as Sam Lord's Castle, Barbados Wildlife Reserve and Speightstown. A similar, second tour spends more time in gardens. Each costs B$100. Bajan also offers cheaper, half-day tours, such as one to Harrison's Cave and the Flower Forest for B$70. Tour prices include entrance fees.

Other companies offering island tours include LE Williams Tour Co (☎ 427-1043) and Topaz Tours (☎ 435-8451).

The going rate for custom tours by taxi drivers is B$32 an hour, but you can usually negotiate with individual drivers to work out your own deal.

Open Houses

From mid-January to mid-April, the Barbados National Trust (☎ 436-2421) has an Open House Programme offering visits to some of the island's grander private homes. A different house can be visited each Wednesday from 2:30 to 5:30 pm for an admission of B$15, which includes a drink. Should you be a member of the National Trust in another Commonwealth country, the fee is only B$6. The tourist office or most Barbados National Trust sites can provide a brochure describing the open houses and directions to them. If you don't have your own transportation, for B$35 you can book a tour that includes hotel pickup and admission; call ☎ 425-1103 for details.

Barbados National Trust Properties

The Barbados National Trust is a non-profit organization dedicated to the preservation of the island's historic sites and areas of environmental significance. Founded in 1961, the trust is the caretaker of many of the island's leading visitor attractions. In some cases it owns the property outright, but in other cases, as with the great houses, it primarily assists with managing visitor access to the property, which otherwise remains in private hands.

Properties under the Barbados National Trust umbrella include the Barbados Museum, Barbados Synagogue, Gun Hill Signal Station, Welchman Hall Gully, Francia Plantation House, Sunbury Plantation House, St Nicholas Abbey, Morgan Lewis Sugar Mill, Andromeda Botanic Gardens, Barbados Zoo Park and a handful of other sites.

The trust sells a Heritage Passport that provides free or discounted admission to all 15 affiliated sites for B$70 and three mini-passport options that each package five to seven sites together for B$36. The passports can be purchased at most of the above sites. Each property can also be visited by paying a single admission fee and if you don't intend to take in a lot of sites, that's generally the most economical way to go. ■

Distillery & Brewery

The Mount Gay Rum Visitors' Centre (☎ 425-9066) provides 45-minute tours of its bottling facility on weekdays, beginning every half hour from 9 am to 4 pm. The tours, which explain the distilling operation and cap off with rum tasting, cost B$11.50. There's also a special noon tour (reservations ☎ 425-8757) that includes a buffet lunch and hotel transfer for B$45. The center is on the coastal road about a kilometer north of Bridgetown Harbour.

Tours of the Banks beer brewery (☎ 429-2113) in Wildey, which is about 3km east of Bridgetown center, are conducted on Tuesday and Thursday. Call ahead for reservations.

Boat & Submarine Cruises

The *Jolly Roger* (☎ 436-6424), a party boat built to replicate a pirate ship, offers a four-hour excursion that includes lunch, an open bar and snorkeling for B$123. It leaves from Bridgetown at 10 am on Tuesday, Thursday and Saturday, anchoring off Holetown at lunchtime.

The *Bajan Queen* (☎ 436-6424), a replica of a Mississippi riverboat, has a four-hour sunset dinner cruise with an open bar and a live band on Wednesday and Saturday. The cost is B$103.

If you're looking for a mellower scene, there are also a number of small sailboat cruises available. One of the more affordable options is the 36-foot catamaran *Mona Lisa* (☎ 435-6565), which has a two-hour cruise with a stop for snorkeling for B$40. Other sailboat operations include *Limbo Lady* (☎ 420-5418), *Secret Love* (☎ 432-1972) and Heat Wave Sailing Cruises (☎ 423-7871).

The *Atlantis* (☎ 436-8929), a 28-seater submarine lined with portholes, takes visitors on underwater tours of the coral reef off the island's west coast. Tours operate weekdays on the hour from 9 am to 4 pm and cost B$142 for adults, half price for children under 12 (who must be at least 42 inches in height). The outing lasts 1¾ hours, with the underwater segment about 50 minutes.

You can also do a little coral viewing at half the price with the Atlantis' *Seatrec*, a semi-submersible glassbottom boat with a below-waterline seating deck. The cost is B$70 (half price for children) for a 1½-hour tour; there are several tours a day.

The Atlantis operations and most other sailing cruises leave from Bridgetown.

Tours to Other Islands

The most popular inter-island day tour from Barbados is to the Grenadines. The tour generally starts with an early morning flight to Mustique for breakfast at Basil's, followed by a continuing flight to Union Island and a sail in a catamaran around the spectacular Tobago Cays and Mayreau. The tour includes lunch, complimentary drinks and a bit of beach and snorkeling time, returning to Barbados around 6:30 pm. The cost is US$315.

There are various other day tours to Grenada, St Lucia, Martinique, Dominica and Tobago for about the same price.

Three of the largest inter-island tour companies are Caribbean Safari Tours (☎ 427-5100), Ship Inn Complex, St Lawrence Gap; Grenadine Tours (☎ 435-8451), 27 Hastings Plaza, Hastings, Christ Church; and Chantours (☎ 432-5591), Sunset Crest Plaza No 2, St James.

You can sometimes make an interesting weekend budget trip from Barbados to St Lucia aboard the passenger-cargo ferry M/V *Windward*, by taking the boat northbound Friday night and returning from St Lucia on Sunday. For details, see Boat in the Getting Around chapter in the front of the book.

Bridgetown

Bridgetown, the island capital, is a busy commercial city set on Carlisle Bay, the island's only natural harbor.

Architecturally, the city is a bit of a hodgepodge. Most of the main streets are quite modern and businesslike in appearance, but there's also a handful of nicely restored colonial buildings, as well as side streets that lead off into residential neighborhoods sprinkled with rum shops and chattel houses.

The Careenage, a finger-like inlet lined with recreational boats, cuts into the heart of the city. At the south side of the Chamberlain Bridge, which crosses the Careenage to Trafalgar Square, is Independence Arch, which commemorates Bajan independence and has plaques honoring the island's first prime minister, Errol Barrow.

Bridgetown center doesn't boast a lot of must-see sights but there's enough bustle for an interesting half-day of sauntering around. There are some good shopping opportunities, especially at the Broad St department stores and on Swan St, which is thick with vendors selling jewelry, sandals and fruit. Swan St can make a fun stroll whether you're in the mood for shopping or just soaking up a little local flavor.

Information

Tourist Office The tourist office (☎ 427-2623) is on Prescod Boulevard, at the west side of town. It's open from 8:15 am to 4:30 pm Monday to Friday.

Money There are numerous banks in the city, including Barbados National Bank and Scotiabank near the bus terminals on Fairchild St and Royal Bank of Canada and Barclays Bank on Broad St near Trafalgar Square.

The local American Express office, at Barbados International Travel Services (☎ 431-2400) on McGregor St, cashes American Express traveler's checks free of commission.

Post & Communications The general post office is in Cheapside and is open from 7:30 am to 5 pm Monday to Friday. You can make overseas calls and send faxes and telegrams weekdays from 8 am to 4:30 pm at the telephone company office on McGregor St.

Pharmacy Collins Pharmacy (☎ 426-4515) is on Broad St.

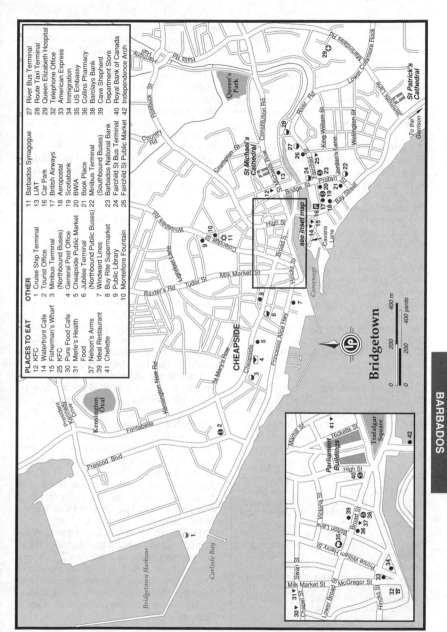

PLACES TO EAT
12 KFC
14 Waterfront Cafe
15 Fisherman's Wharf
25 KFC
30 Pure Food Cafe
31 Merle's Health Food
37 Nelson's Arms
39 Ideal Restaurant
41 Chefette

OTHER
1 Cruise Ship Terminal
2 Tourist Office
3 Minibus Terminal (Northbound Buses)
4 General Post Office
5 Cheapside Public Market
6 Jubilee Terminal (Windward Public Buses)
7 Windward Lines
8 Buy Rite Supermarket
9 Public Library
10 Montefiore Fountain
11 Barbados Synagogue
13 LIAT
16 Car Park
17 British Airways
18 Aeropostal
19 Scotiabank
20 BWIA
21 Book Place
22 Minibus Terminal (Southbound Buses)
23 Barbados National Bank
24 Fairchild St Bus Terminal
26 Fairchild St Public Market
27 River Bus Terminal
28 Route Taxi Terminal
29 Queen Elizabeth Hospital
32 Telephone Office
33 American Express
34 Immigration
35 US Embassy
36 Collins Pharmacy
38 Barclays Bank
39 Cave Shepherd Department Store
40 Royal Bank of Canada
42 Independence Arch

BARBADOS

Bookstores There are a few bookstores around town, including one in Cave Shepherd department store on Broad St, Brydens Bookshop behind Cave Shepherd on Victoria St and the Book Place on Probyn St. The last sells both new and used books, specializing in black and Caribbean literature and social issues. Cloister, on Hincks Street, is an institution in the Caribbean.

Library The public library, on Coleridge St, is open 9 am to 5 pm Monday to Saturday. Visitors may check out library books on payment of a B$20 refundable deposit.

Trafalgar Square

The triangular-shaped Trafalgar Square marks the bustling center of the city. The square, which fronts the parliament buildings, has an obelisk monument honoring WWI dead and a water fountain commemorating the bringing of piped water to Bridgetown in 1861. At the west side of the square is a bronze statue of Lord Horatio Nelson, who sailed into Barbados in 1805, just months before dying at the Battle of Trafalgar. The statue was erected in 1813, three decades before its larger London counterpart.

Parliament Buildings

On the north side of Trafalgar Square are two stone-block, Gothic-style government buildings constructed in 1871. The west-side building with the clock tower contains public offices. The building on the east side houses the Senate and House of Assembly and is adorned with stained-glass windows depicting British monarchs. The parliament building is not generally open for public viewing, but it's possible to visit when parliament is in session (generally on Tuesdays after 11 am); call ☎ 427-2019 during business hours for more information.

St Michael's Cathedral

St Michael's, the island's Anglican cathedral, is a five-minute walk east of Trafalgar Square. The original church, built in 1665 to accommodate 3000 worshippers, proved to be too much of a windscreen and came tumbling down in a hurricane a century later. The scaled-down, but still substantial, structure that stands today dates to 1789 and seats 1600. At the time of construction it was said to have the widest arched ceiling of its type in the world.

Also interesting is the adjacent churchyard, where many island notables are buried. Sir Grantley Adams, Barbados' first premier and the head of the West Indies Federation from 1958 to 1962, is buried at the north side of the church. His son Tom, prime minister of Barbados from 1976 to 1985, is buried in a separate plot.

Visitors are charged B$5 if they come simply to tour the cathedral; it's free to those who come to 'pray and reflect.'

Barbados Synagogue

This small synagogue, built in 1833 and abandoned in 1929, was restored a few years ago and is now under the jurisdiction of the Barbados National Trust. The distinctive white building has a simple but handsome interior with brass chandeliers, a checkerboard marble floor and a columned ladies' balcony.

The island's first synagogue was built on this site in the 1600s, when Barbados had a Jewish population of more than 300. Many were refugees who had fled Portuguese and Dutch oppression in South America and became plantation owners in Barbados. Today the island's Jewish population numbers about 50.

Lord Nelson

Over the years the Lord Nelson statue, which stands in Trafalgar Square fronting Parliament, has been the center of controversy among islanders, many of whom feel it too closely embraces the island's colonial past. In the 1970s, the Mighty Gabby, who is Barbados' leading calypso singer, had an immensely popular song called 'Take Down Nelson' that called for replacing Nelson's statue with one of a Bajan man. ■

The synagogue, on Coleridge St, a 10-minute walk from Trafalgar Square, is usually open for viewing from 9 am to 4 pm Monday to Friday. There's an old Jewish cemetery at the side.

Nearby, opposite the public library, is the **Montefiore Fountain**, a decorative little monument that was given to the city in 1864 by John Montefiore, a wealthy Jewish resident.

Queen's Park

A green space of grassy lawns, Queen's Park is a popular place for island families to picnic and relax on Sunday afternoons.

On a knoll at the top of the park is a rather grand two-story house that was once the residence of the commander of the British forces in the West Indies. Erected in 1786, it was thoroughly restored in 1973 and now houses a theater and a gallery of local art. Nearby are a few cages with green monkeys and exotic birds and a lunchtime restaurant serving inexpensive Bajan fare.

One of the park's more unique features is the huge baobab tree, 18 meters in circumference, at the edge of the playground. A plaque at the site estimates the tree to be 1000 years old, the claim somewhat complicated by the fact that the tree is native to Africa, a continent with which Barbados had no known contact until the early 17th century.

There's no admission fee to the park or gallery.

Harry Bayley Observatory

The Harry Bayley Observatory (☎ 426-1317), east of central Bridgetown in the Clapham area, off Rendezvous Rd, is the headquarters of the Barbados Astronomical Society. The observatory is open to the public on Friday evenings; arrive between 8:30 and 8:45 pm. The cost is B$8 for adults, B$5 for children.

The Garrison Area

About 2km south of central Bridgetown is the Barbados Garrison. Spreading inland from the south side of Carlisle Bay, the garrison was the home base of the British Windward and Leeward Islands Command in the 1800s.

A central focal point is the oval-shaped **Savannah**, which was once a large parade grounds and is now used for cricket games, jogging and Saturday horse races. Standing along the west side of the Savannah are some of the Garrison's more ornate colonial buildings, most notably the salmon-colored **Main Guard** with its four-sided clock tower. Fronting the Main Guard you'll find an impressive array of cannons. Barbados, incidentally, claims the world's largest collection of 17th-century iron cannons, including one of only two existing cannons bearing Oliver Cromwell's Republican Arms.

If you're interested in British military history, the entire Garrison area can be fascinating to explore. The first fortifications in the area went up as early as 1650, although many of the current buildings date to the mid-19th century, a consequence of the violent 1831 hurricane that destroyed virtually everything not made of stone or iron. In the grounds of the Hilton at Needham's Point you'll find the remains of the 17th-century **Charles Fort** and a nice coastal view.

Barbados Museum The Barbados Museum (☎ 427-0201), on the northeast side of the Savannah, is housed in an early 19th-century military prison. It has engaging displays on all aspects of the island's history beginning with its early Amerindian inhabitants. Not surprisingly, the most extensive collections cover the colonial era, with exhibits on slavery, emancipation, military history and plantation house furniture, all accompanied by insightful narratives.

Among the museum's other offerings are an African culture gallery, a children's gallery, natural history displays, changing exhibits of local contemporary art, a gift shop and a small café.

For a quick immersion into island history, you couldn't do better than to spend an hour or two here. The museum is open from 9 am to 5 pm Monday to Saturday, 2 to 6 pm on Sunday. Admission is B$10 for adults, B$5 for children. The museum also sponsors a dinner show; see the Entertainment section earlier in this chapter.

Places to Stay
Angle House (☎ 427-9010), Upper Bay St, at the southern outskirts of Bridgetown near the yacht harbor, is a good inexpensive guesthouse with a solidly local flavor that attracts mainly Caribbean visitors but appeals to other budget travelers as well. This large old house has nine simple but clean rooms for just US$12.50 per person. Guest have use of four kitchens and a common sitting area with TV. There's a beach, restaurants and a grocery store nearby.

The *Barbados Hilton* (☎ 426-0200, fax 436-8946; in the USA ☎ 800-445-8667), PO Box 510, Bridgetown, is at the tip of Needham's Point on the grounds of the former Charles Fort. It's a typical Hilton, with a pool, health club, tennis courts, restaurants and 184 rooms, each with a phone, TV, minibar, air-con and balcony. The area is pleasant enough, and has a nice beach considering its proximity to the capital. Behind the hotel are some fort remains and an embankment lined with replicas of the original cannons. Summer/winter rates are US$158/242 for doubles, though they occasionally run a special that includes breakfast for US$128. Singles are about US$20 less.

On the road into the Hilton, next to the Brown Sugar restaurant, is the *Island Inn Hotel* (☎ 436-6393, fax 437-8035), Aquatic Gap, St Michael. The hotel incorporates a restored 1804 garrison building that was originally a military rum store. There are 23 rooms with a king or queen bed, air-con and a phone. There's a bar, restaurant and pool. Singles/doubles cost US$135/175 in summer, US$185/225 in winter.

Places to Eat
The best places to buy fruit and vegetables are at the Fairchild St and Cheapside public markets, which are open from 7 am to late afternoon Monday to Saturday. Produce vendors can also be found along the streets near Trafalgar Square. There are a couple of large supermarkets in town, including the *Buy Rite Supermarket* on Lower Broad St.

Merle's Health Food, on the corner of Chapel and Milk Market Sts, has a B$10 takeout vegetarian lunch from 11 am until mid-afternoon Monday to Saturday. The meal is typically brown rice, vegetables and a salad. Merle's also makes lentil burgers and sells herbal drinks and a few packaged health food items.

For a healthy sit-down meal there's *Pure Food Cafe*, on the same block of Chapel St, which has simple inexpensive vegetarian fare and is open weekdays from 8 am to 5 pm, Saturdays until 2 pm.

Chefette, on Marhill St, 100 meters north of Trafalgar St, is a busy fast-food spot with cheap rotis, burgers and fried chicken. For more familiar fried chicken, there are a couple of *KFC's*, one around the corner from Chefette and another on Fairchild St.

A favorite lunch stop with office workers is *Ideal Restaurant*, a cafeteria with good, inexpensive island-style food upstairs in the Cave Shepherd department store. A solid meal of pigeon peas & rice, salad and fish costs B$13 and there are cheaper specials. It's open from 9 am to 3 pm on weekdays, to 1:30 pm on Saturdays.

Nelson's Arms in the Galleria Mall at 27 Broad St is a popular lunch spot with balcony dining and a pleasant pub atmosphere. Weekdays from 11 am to 4 pm, and Saturdays from 10 am to 3 pm, you can get hoagies or baguette sandwiches for B$12 and specials such as lasagna or cajun chicken for around B$20.

Bridgetown's busiest and arguably most pleasant lunch spot is *Fisherman's Wharf* (☎ 436-7778), which has a 2nd-floor waterfront setting overlooking the Careenage near Independence Arch. At lunch, you can get flying fish for B$22 or coconut shrimp for B$30. A particularly good lunch day is Friday, when there's a special Bajan buffet for B$26. At dinner, most main courses are B$35 to B$50. Lunch is from 11:30 am to 3 pm (except Sundays), dinner from 6:30 to 10 pm (except Mondays).

Also inviting is the *Waterfront Cafe* (☎ 427-0093), on the ground floor of the same building, which has both outdoor waterside tables and indoor seating. The food is good and includes sandwiches for around B$20 and specialty salads or fish of the day for around B$30. They also have gazpacho soup, vegetable samosas and Bajan fish cakes. On Tuesdays there's a Caribbean buffet (B$43) with steel pan music. Food is served Monday to Saturday from 10 am to 10 pm.

Brown Sugar (☎ 426-7684) at Aquatic Gap in the Garrison area, not far from the Hilton, is a veritable greenhouse of hanging plants complete with a waterfall and whistling frogs. It has a popular West Indian buffet weekdays from noon to 2:30 pm for B$35 and is also open from 6 to 9:30 pm daily for dinner served à la carte, with the likes of shrimp Creole for B$42 and lobster for B$72. Reservations are advised.

South Coast

The south coast, from Hastings to Maxwell, has most of the island's low to midrange accommodations. Virtually the entire strip is fringed with white-sand beaches and turquoise waters.

Hwy 7, a two-lane road, links the southcoast villages; buses and route taxis (No 11) run frequently along this route as they ply between Bridgetown and Oistins.

While the south coast is fairly well built up, some areas, such as the coastal roads in St Lawrence and Maxwell, are off the main strip and thus more lightly trafficked. As a rule the farther you go from Bridgetown the less developed it is.

All the communities described in this section are in the parish of Christ Church, which ends at the airport. For the region east of the airport see the Southeast section.

HASTINGS & ROCKLEY

The Hastings-Rockley area is the first major tourist area east of Bridgetown. The center of activity is Rockley Beach, a roadside white-sand beach with shade trees, snack wagons and clothing vendors. It's a halflocal, half-tourist scene and as Rockley Beach is a mere 10-minute bus ride from central Bridgetown, it attracts a crowd, especially on weekends.

Places to Stay

Abbeville Hotel (☎ 435-7924, fax 435-8502), Rockley, Christ Church, is on the inland side of Hwy 7, a couple of minutes walk from the beach. This older hotel has 19 straightforward rooms with private baths. Singles/doubles cost US$45/55 for a room with air-con, US$35/45 without air-con. Rates are US$5 cheaper in summer and major credit cards are accepted. The hotel's Bert's Bar is a popular local eating and drinking spot.

Also just a short walk to the beach is *Pink Coral Inn* (☎ /fax 435-3151), Hastings Main Road, Christ Church, a newly renovated colonial home with six cheery guest rooms. Each has a ceiling fan and sink; there are four shared baths in the hall and a couple of common rooms and porches. Rates, which include breakfast, are a reasonable US$35/50 for singles/doubles in summer, US$45/60 in winter.

The five-story beachfront *Coconut Court Hotel* (☎ 427-1655, fax 429-8198), Hastings, Christ Church, is a good-value package resort hotel especially popular with Canadians. There are 30 oceanview rooms with small refrigerators, coffeemakers and toaster-ovens that cost US$65/95 in summer/winter. There are also 60 spacious apartments with full kitchens that cost US$65/95 for a studio, US$75/105 for a one-bedroom apartment. Units have ceiling fans and balconies; some have a double sofabed in the living room. It has a beachside pool, a restaurant, a bar and water-sports rentals.

Places to Eat

At the east end of Rockley Beach on Hwy 7 is a *Shakey's Pizza* with the chain's usual pizza and fast-food offerings. On the same road 300 meters west of Shakey's is a *KFC*. The *Barbecue Barn*, opposite Rockley

Beach, is a modern steakhouse restaurant with grilled chicken or steak served with a baked potato and garlic bread for around B$20; add B$6 a simple salad bar. In the same complex is a branch of the fast-food chain *Chefette* with inexpensive burgers, rotis and fried chicken. All are open from around 11 am to 11 pm daily.

Sugar Reef Bar & Restaurant (☎ 435-8074), on the west side of Rockley Beach, has an inviting waterfront setting and good-value food. From noon to 3 pm daily there's a buffet that includes fish, chicken, lamb, salad and ice cream for B$25. At dinner (6:30 to 9 pm) if you stick with the simpler offerings, you can get a good meal for about B$40.

WORTHING

Worthing can make a nice base, particularly if you're on a tight budget but still want to be in the middle of things. It has inexpensive places to eat and a handful of cheap guesthouses that are either on the beach or a stone's throw from it.

Sandy Beach, which fronts Worthing, is a lovely broad beach of powdery white sand. The beach has just enough activity to

be interesting but not so much that it feels crowded.

From Worthing it's only a five-minute stroll to St Lawrence, a walk that can be made along the beach at low tide.

Information

There's a Scotiabank on Hwy 7 in front of Sandy Beach Hotel and a Barclays Bank with a 24-hour ATM on Rendezvous Rd. North of Barclays is the Worthing post office, which is open weekdays from 8 am to at least 3 pm.

The Southshore Laundermat (435-7438) on Hwy 7 has a token-operated laundry that charges B$8 to wash and dry a load of clothes. There's an adjacent used-book store; both are open from 8 am to 4 pm weekdays, to 2 pm on Saturdays.

Places to Stay

Guesthouses *Summer Place on Sea* (☎ 435-7424), Worthing, Christ Church, set right on the sand, is a funky place that has seven simple rooms, each with a fan and private bath. Two of the rooms have kitchenettes. A TV and phone are available in the common room. Owner George de Mattos is

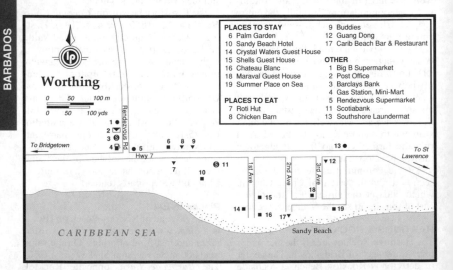

PLACES TO STAY	9 Buddies
6 Palm Garden	12 Guang Dong
10 Sandy Beach Hotel	17 Carib Beach Bar & Restaurant
14 Crystal Waters Guest House	
15 Shells Guest House	**OTHER**
16 Chateau Blanc	1 Big B Supermarket
18 Maraval Guest House	2 Post Office
19 Summer Place on Sea	3 Barclays Bank
	4 Gas Station, Mini-Mart
PLACES TO EAT	5 Rendezvous Supermarket
7 Roti Hut	11 Scotiabank
8 Chicken Barn	13 Southshore Laundermat

Worthing

CARIBBEAN SEA

Sandy Beach

a congenial host who hails from Trinidad but has been operating inns on Barbados for 25 years. Rates are US$40 for kitchenette units, US$20/30 a single/double for the others. As many repeat visitors stay here, it often books out during the peak months of January to March and July and August.

Nearby is the *Maraval Guest House* (☎ 435-7437), 3rd Ave, Worthing, Christ Church, which has small simple rooms with shared bath for US$20/30 singles/doubles. There's access to a well-equipped kitchen and a living room with TV and stereo.

Shells Guest House (☎ 435-7253), 1st Ave, Worthing, Christ Church, has a Scandinavian manager and is popular with budget travelers and gay visitors. There are seven sufficient rooms, each with a ceiling fan, sink, small dresser and lamp. Four rooms have private baths, while three rooms share two baths. Singles/doubles cost a reasonable US$20/35, or US$23/38 with private bath. Rates include a continental breakfast and there's a TV room and a bar.

Crystal Waters Guest House (☎ 435-7514), Worthing, Christ Church, is a small, older beachfront inn with a faded period character. The rooms are clean and have hardwood floors, twin beds with comfortable mattresses, dressers and private baths. There's a TV room on the 2nd floor and a casual beachfront bar. Singles/doubles cost US$25/35.

Hotels & Apartments *Chateau Blanc* (☎ 435-7518, fax 435-7414), Worthing, Christ Church, is a recommendable little apartment building smack on the beach. It has nine air-conditioned units, most of them with waterview terraces. They include a studio with a refrigerator and toaster oven for US$35/65 in summer/winter, a one-bedroom apartment with a separate living room and beachfront patio for US$75/105 and a two-bedroom apartment with four twin beds for US$100/140.

The 18-unit *Palm Garden* (☎ 435-6406, fax 435-7031), Worthing, Christ Church, on the inland side of Hwy 7, is an older but pleasant family-run place popular with Canadian visitors. Rooms with refrigerators cost US$60/75 in summer/winter and suites with two bedrooms and full kitchens are US$85/95. While there aren't any frills, all units have air-con. If you call from the airport and they're not full you can usually get a slightly discounted (US$10 off) walk-in rate. There's a pool.

Sandy Beach Hotel (☎ 435-8000, fax 435-8053), Worthing, Christ Church, is a modern if rather nondescript four-story beachfront hotel, formerly a Best Western. There are 40 comfortable rooms with one king or two twin beds for US$85/120 in summer/winter and 78 one-bedroom suites with kitchenettes for US$125/205. All units have phones, air-con and cable TV. The hotel has a pool and restaurant.

Places to Eat

The *Roti Hut*, on Hwy 7, has cheap rotis ranging in price from B$4 for a potato version to B$9 for a shrimp roti. It's open from 11 am to 10 pm Monday to Thursday, and until 11 pm on Friday and Saturday.

The *Chicken Barn*, diagonally opposite the Roti Hut, is a fried-chicken restaurant with both eat-in and takeout service. You can get burgers for B$4 or fried chicken & chips for B$12. There's also a simple salad bar. It's open from 10 am to 11 pm Monday to Saturday.

The little café at *Shells Guest House* offers a simple breakfast of juice, coffee, cheese and toast for B$7 from 8 to 10 am daily.

Buddies, on Hwy 7, is a friendly café serving good, reasonably priced food. Homemade soups, various salads, creative sandwiches and tasty pasta dishes with pesto or baby clams average B$10 to B$15. It's open from 11 am to 11 pm nightly.

Carib Beach Bar & Restaurant, an open-air eatery right on Sandy Beach, has a fish cutter sandwich with fries for B$12 and other fish meals for B$16 at lunch, B$24 at dinner. Food is available from 11 am to around 10 pm daily, but the bar stays open later. There's a two-for-one happy hour from 5 to 6 pm.

Guang Dong, on the corner of Hwy 7 and 3rd Ave, has sweet and sour pork with chop suey and fried rice or a couple of other combos for B$16 at lunch. Otherwise, there's a full menu of standard Cantonese main dishes, most from B$16 to B$25. It's open daily from 11 am to 2 pm and 6 to 10 pm.

The *Big B Supermarket*, just 100 meters up Rendezvous Rd, has a wide range of imported foods, a deli with inexpensive local food (stew, chicken legs etc) and a large liquor section. It's open from 8 am to at least 8 pm Monday to Saturday. The nearby *Rendezvous Supermarket*, on the corner of Hwy 7 and Rendezvous Rd, has a smaller selection but stays open until 10 pm daily, except on Sunday when it's open from 9 am to 1 pm. Some of the 24-hour gas stations along Hwy 7 have mini-marts.

ST LAWRENCE & DOVER

St Lawrence has the area's most active night scene as well as numerous mid-range restaurants and places to stay, many of which front the ocean.

The western end of St Lawrence is at the junction of Little Bay and Hwy 7, but most of St Lawrence lies along the St Lawrence Coast Rd, in the area known as the Gap. Although there's a lot happening in the Gap, the coastal road extends nearly 2km, so it's not a hectic scene.

Dover Beach, near the middle of the coastal road, is a nice broad white-sand beach that attracts swimmers, bodysurfers, windsurfers and board surfers, depending on the water conditions.

Information

On St Lawrence Coast Rd there's a Royal Bank of Canada beside Ship Inn and a Barclays Bank next to Shakey's Pizza.

If you need groceries, sundries or liquor, there are a couple of reasonably stocked convenience stores on St Lawrence Coast Rd that stay open daily until 10 pm.

Places to Stay – budget

Rio Guest House (☎ 428-2546, melden@ caribsurf.com), St Lawrence Gap, Christ Church, is a traveler's haunt with good unpretentious accommodations. There are seven fan-cooled rooms. Singles have a sink but share a bath and cost US$20/25 in summer/winter. Doubles, which have two beds and their own bath, cost US$26/35. There's a fully equipped guest kitchen and friendly Swiss-Bajan managers who speak French and German. It's a great location, off the main drag but just minutes from the beach.

Four Aces (☎ 428-9441), St Lawrence Gap, Christ Church, has 14 relatively inexpensive units with phones, private baths and a casual cottage-like setting. Large two-bedroom apartments with air-con, full kitchens and living rooms cost US$80 for up to four people. Studio and one-bedroom units cost from US$35 to US$60, with the cheapest ones without air-con.

Another reasonably priced place is the nearby *Salt Ash Apartment Hotel* (☎ 428-8753, fax 428-5140), St Lawrence Gap, Christ Church, a small family-run operation that caters to both overseas and Caribbean travelers. The eight units are roomy and have air-con, private bathrooms with tubs, kitchenettes and balconies, some with fine ocean views. While certainly not fancy, it's quite adequate, right on the beach and costs just US$35/58 in summer/winter.

St Lawrence Apartments (☎ 435-6950, fax 428-1970), St Lawrence Gap, Christ Church, comprises two apartment hotels with a total of 75 units. St Lawrence West has big studios with ceiling fans, air-con, phones, bathtubs, kitchens and large ocean-facing balconies that cost US$65/105 in summer/winter. St Lawrence East has essentially the same facilities, but its units are smaller and less spiffy; studios with simple kitchenettes cost US$60/85 and one-bedroom apartments with full kitchens cost US$65/95. Both complexes have swimming pools.

Little Bay Hotel (☎ 435-7246, fax 435-8574, lbay@ndl.net), St Lawrence Gap, Christ Church, is a pleasant little place on Little Bay. The 10 units are comfortable, with ceiling fans, refrigerators, TVs, phones and private baths; most have balconies

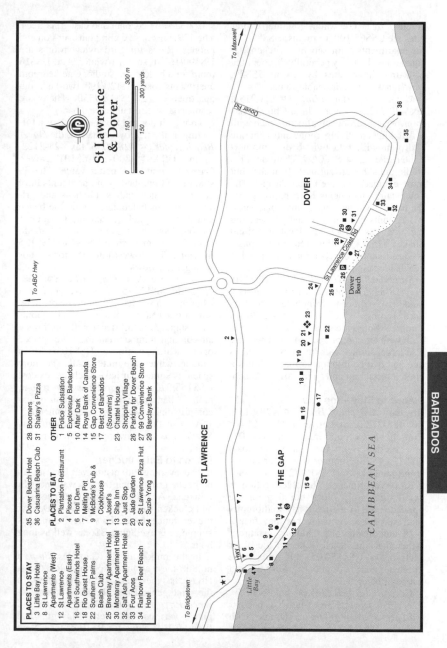

PLACES TO STAY
3 Little Bay Hotel
8 St Lawrence
   Apartments (West)
12 St Lawrence
   Apartments (East)
16 Divi Southwinds Hotel
18 Rio Guest House
22 Southern Palms
   Beach Club
25 Bresmay Apartment Hotel
30 Monteray Apartment Hotel
32 Salt Ash Apartment Hotel
33 Four Aces
34 Rainbow Reef Beach
   Hotel

35 Dover Beach Hotel
36 Casuarina Beach Club

PLACES TO EAT
2 Plantation Restaurant
4 Pisces
6 Roti Den
7 Melting Pot
9 McBride's Pub &
   Cookhouse
11 Josef's
13 Ship Inn
19 Just Stop
20 Jade Garden
21 St Lawrence Pizza Hut
24 Suzie Yong

28 Boomers
31 Shakey's Pizza

OTHER
1 Police Substation
5 Exploresub Barbados
10 After Dark
14 Royal Bank of Canada
15 Gap Convenience Store
17 Best of Barbados
   (Souvenirs)
23 Chattel House
   Shopping Village
26 Parking for Dover Beach
27 99 Convenience Store
29 Barclays Bank

St Lawrence & Dover

To Maxwell

Dover Rd

DOVER

St Lawrence Coast Rd

Dover Beach

To ABC Hwy

ST LAWRENCE

THE GAP

Hwy 7

Little
Bay

To Bridgetown

CARIBBEAN SEA

0   150   300 m
0   150   300 yards

BARBADOS

perched over the water. Summer/winter rates are US$65/100 for rooms, US$85/140 for apartments with separate kitchens. If business is slow they generally discount the walk-in winter rates by about US$20, which makes it a reasonable value.

Monteray Apartment Hotel (☎ 428-9152, fax 428-7722), Dover, Christ Church, has roomy one-bedroom apartments, each with a full kitchen, living room and separate bedroom with two twin beds; summer/winter rates are US$60/95. There are also studio units that are similarly furnished but more compact, and are US$5 cheaper. The downstairs apartments have patios while the upper-level ones have small balconies. All 22 units have air-con and phones, and the hotel has a pool. The location behind Shakey's Pizza isn't inspired, but the place is significantly cheaper than comparable beachside neighbors.

Rainbow Reef Beach Hotel (☎ 428-5110, fax 428-5395), Dover, Christ Church, is a modern 43-unit beachfront hotel. The standard rooms, which cost US$55/70 in summer/winter, are small but comfortable, each with air-con, phone and TV. There are also larger studios with kitchens, as well as one and two-bedroom apartments. It has a pool, a restaurant and a nice strip of beach.

Places to Stay – top end

Bresmay Apartment Hotel (☎ 428-6131, fax 428-7722), St Lawrence Gap, Christ Church, has 69 rooms in two sections. The new section is on the beach and costs US$125/150 in summer/winter for oceanfront studios, or US$190/250 for one-bedroom apartments. The older section, a small three-story block building on the opposite side of the road, has studio units that are pleasant enough, but they face a pool and the hotel's Chinese restaurant rather than the beach. Rates in the older section are US$65/105. All units have kitchen facilities, phones, air-con and patios or balconies.

Casuarina Beach Club (☎ 428-3600, fax 428-1970), Dover, Christ Church, is popular with package-tour groups and families with children. The hotel is on a nice beach and is surrounded by coconut and casuarina trees. The 129 units have ceiling fans, air-con and phones. Rates for gardenview rooms are US$90/165 in summer/winter. Add US$10 more for a beachfront studio. One-bedroom apartments cost US$120/190, two-bedroom apartments are US$180/330. There are tennis courts, a restaurant and bar.

Though it doesn't have as much of a following as the nearby Casuarina, the *Dover Beach Hotel* (☎ 428-8076, fax 428-2122; in the USA ☎ 800-223-6510), Dover, Christ Church, is a better value. The 39 studios and one-bedroom apartments have air-con, phones, radios, kitchens and private patios or balconies. It's on the beach and there's a pool, restaurant, TV lounge and bar. Double rates range from US$65 to US$82 in summer, from US$96 to US$125 in winter. The lowest rates are for studios with garden views.

Southern Palms Beach Club (☎ 428-7171, fax 428-7175), St Lawrence, Christ Church, is a modern 92-room resort hotel with a fine beachfront location. The rooms have standard resort decor with tile floors, air-con and minibars but the lower priced ones, which begin at US$105/180 in summer/winter, are quite small. The more spacious suites have kitchenettes cost US$155/270. The resort has two restaurants, a bar, two pools, tennis courts and complimentary water sports equipment.

Also in the area is the 150-room *Divi Southwinds*, a sprawling time-share resort.

Places to Eat – budget

In the evening, streetside vendors set up barbecue grills along the sidewalk near St Lawrence Apartments and sell burgers, fish and chicken for B$5 to B$7. *Roti Den*, at the entrance to St Lawrence Gap, has simple rotis averaging B$6 as well as long hours.

In the middle of the Gap, *Just Stop*, a hole-in-the-wall lunch spot near Rio Guest House, has inexpensive rotis and cutters. In the same general neighborhood is *St Lawrence Pizza Hut*, which has French bread pizza, various sandwiches, lasagna and flying fish & chips for B$10 or less. Next door is a little ice cream shop serving up both traditional and tropical flavors.

Boomers, a lively bar and restaurant in the Dover Beach area, has typical French toast and egg breakfasts for around B$12. At lunch there are burgers and sandwiches for around B$10, while dinner features the addition of a vegetarian plate for B$18, flying fish or Creole chicken for B$22 and seafood dishes for a few dollars more. It's open from 8 am to 10 pm.

Shakey's Pizza, near Boomers, has the usual pizza, sandwich and burger menu. In addition, local lunch specials, available from 11:30 am to 3 pm, feature a flying fish sandwich or barbecued chicken with a Coke and sweet potato pie for B$10.

Jade Garden, opposite the Southern Palms Beach Club, is an air-conditioned restaurant with a varied Cantonese and Sichuan menu. Most meat and fish dishes, as well as a handful of vegetarian offerings, cost B$16; add another B$4 for rice. At lunchtime there's a special that includes soup, a main dish and chow mein for B$17 or a simple takeout box lunch for B$8. Lunch is from 11 am to 2:30 pm, dinner from 6 to 10:30 pm daily.

Suzie Yong, a Chinese restaurant at Bresmay Apartment Hotel, has an open-air setting with prices similar to those at Jade Garden. Lunch specials of a main dish with fried rice or chow mein cost B$17, as do most à la carte menu items. It's open from 11:30 am to 3 pm and 6 to 10:30 pm daily.

You'll find a more homey setting up on Hwy 7 at the *Melting Pot*, a place run by a Canadian-Bajan couple. They serve good local dinners, such as a flying fish plate that costs B$22 or a full meal from soup to tea for B$30.

Ship Inn, at the west end of St Lawrence Coast Rd, has a couple of dining spots under one roof. The *Captain's Carvery*, the main restaurant, is pleasant enough but the food, served buffet-style, is undistinguished. Dinner (6:30 to 10:30 pm) features lamb, roast beef and ham or turkey accompanied by a simple salad bar for B$42, while a lighter buffet lunch (noon to 3 pm except on Saturday) costs B$24. The

adjacent *Ship Inn Bar* has a pub menu, with steak & kidney pie or chicken & chips for around B$20.

A couple of doors to the west is *McBride's Pub & Cookhouse*. The decor bears some resemblance to a chain steak house and may not appeal to everyone, but the food is good and it's a popular dinner place, serving chicken, pasta or fish dishes for B$30, plus B$12 for one trip to a small but decent salad bar. Dinner is served from 6 to 11 pm.

Places to Eat – top end

Pisces (☎ 435-6564), at the west end of St Lawrence Coast Rd, is a popular open-air restaurant with candlelight dining to the tune of lapping waves. While the atmosphere is special the food is not particularly notable for the money. Standard fish dishes or seafood fettucini average B$50, while the menu tops off with lobster for B$76. It's open daily for dinner only, from 5:30 pm.

A top choice for a special night out is *Josef's* (☎ 435-6541), a casually elegant restaurant with open-air dining and well-prepared seafood dishes. Starters such as smoked salmon or duck salad average B$22 while main courses range from B$45 for Cajun-style blackened fish or garlic shrimp to B$85 for rack of lamb. Lunch, from noon to 2:30 pm on weekdays, features lower priced specials, including Creole flying fish, seafood pasta or yakitori chicken for B$28. Dinner is daily from 6:30 to about 9:30 pm and dinner reservations are suggested.

MAXWELL

Maxwell has two distinct but adjacent areas. Maxwell Rd (Hwy 7) is predominantly residential with a few small businesses and a couple of the area's older hotels. Maxwell Coast Rd, which curves south from the highway, is the more touristed area.

Maxwell is generally a quieter, cheaper neighborhood than St Lawrence, and some of its beaches are equally appealing. The dining options in Maxwell can quickly wear thin, however, and there's little

BARBADOS

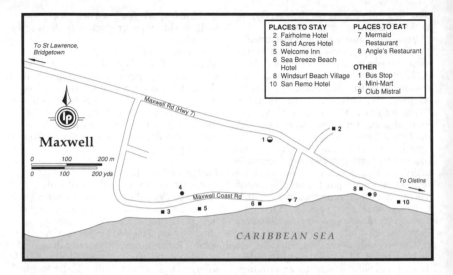

PLACES TO STAY
2 Fairholme Hotel
3 Sand Acres Hotel
5 Welcome Inn
6 Sea Breeze Beach Hotel
8 Windsurf Beach Village
10 San Remo Hotel

PLACES TO EAT
7 Mermaid Restaurant
8 Angie's Restaurant

OTHER
1 Bus Stop
4 Mini-Mart
9 Club Mistral

To St Lawrence, Bridgetown

Maxwell Rd (Hwy 7)

Maxwell

0   100   200 m
0   100   200 yds

To Oistins

Maxwell Coast Rd

CARIBBEAN SEA

nightlife. Depending on where you stay, St Lawrence is a 15- to 30-minute walk away, while the bus to Bridgetown takes roughly 20 minutes.

Places to Stay

Fairholme Hotel (☎ 428-9425), Maxwell, Christ Church, set back 150 meters from Maxwell Rd, has simple, inexpensive accommodations. There are studios with cooking facilities, two single beds, private baths and a faded decor; the 2nd-floor ones have balconies but their corrugated tin roofs can be noisy in the rain. The studios cost US$40/65 in summer/winter; optional air-con costs US$3 per eight hours. A better value, especially in winter, are the 11 fan-cooled rooms in the main house. These are quite basic but clean and cost US$25/28 for singles/doubles in summer, US$26/30 in winter. The hotel is quiet and the rear courtyard has a small pool. It's about five minutes on foot to the nearest beach or by bus to St Lawrence.

The *San Remo Hotel* (☎ 428-2816, fax 428-8826), Maxwell, Christ Church, is a two-story motel-style place that's long past its prime but it fronts the beach and the

rates, particularly in summer, are cheap. The 25 rooms vary but all have ceiling fans, private baths and cooking facilities – some with ovens, others just hot plates. Singles/doubles are US$33/38 in summer and US$65/70 in winter, though you can usually negotiate, especially on longer stays.

Windsurf Beach Village (☎ 428-9095), Maxwell, Christ Church, is a casual seaside hotel catering to windsurfers. There are 18 straightforward rooms with private baths and ceiling fans; some rooms have kitchenettes. It attracts an international crowd and there's a simple restaurant and an adjacent Club Mistral operation. Rooms for two cost US$35/55 in summer/winter, studios US$45/75. Note that it often books solid with windsurfing tours, so availability can be hit or miss. If you have a problem reaching the reception, Sea Breeze Beach Hotel will take messages.

Sea Breeze Beach Hotel (☎ 428-2825, fax 428-2872), Maxwell Coast Rd, Christ Church, is a pleasantly low-keyed beachfront resort. All 79 rooms have air-con, refrigerators and coffeemakers and many also have kitchenettes. Request an upper-level unit, as most have little balconies fronting the sea. Rates are US$80/140 in summer/winter; add US$10 for a kitchenette unit. There's a TV lounge and a pool.

Sand Acres Hotel (☎ 428-7141, fax 428-2524), Maxwell Coast Rd, Christ Church, has 134 spacious contemporary studios with kitchenettes, oceanview balconies, air-con, TV and phones. It has a restaurant, bar, tennis courts, a pool and a lovely stretch of beachfront. Studios cost US$82 in May, June, September and October; US$155 from mid-December through March and US$113 the rest of the year. There are larger one-bedroom apartments for about 20% more.

The seven-story *Welcome Inn* (☎ 428-9900, fax 428-8905), Maxwell Coast Rd, Christ Church, is a standard package-tour hotel with rooms that are average in both size and decor; all have air-con, phones and balconies, some have kitchenettes. Standard studios cost US$70/110 in summer/winter with a garden view, but it's worth the additional US$10 for an ocean view. Nicer still are the corner deluxe rooms that have queen beds and broad ocean views and cost US$95/130 in summer/winter. There's a TV lounge and a large swimming pool.

If you're staying in the area for a while, there are a handful of apartment-for-rent signs along the north end of Maxwell Coast Rd that might be worth checking.

Places to Eat

The dining room at the *Fairholme Hotel* offers a continental breakfast of toast, orange juice and coffee for B$6.50 or the same items with the addition of a cheese omelet for B$12. Breakfast is from 8 to 9:30 am.

The open-air *Angie's Restaurant*, on the waterfront at Windsurf Beach Village, has full breakfasts such as a cheese omelet or a flying fish-scrambled egg combo, both with toast, juice and coffee, for B$14. At lunch and dinner there are sandwiches, burgers, chicken and fish dishes for B$8 to B$25. It's open daily from 7:30 am to 11 pm.

The *Mermaid Restaurant* (☎ 428-4116), on the east end of Maxwell Coast Rd, has the atmosphere of an upmarket beach house

and a splendid waterfront view. From 7 to 10 am there's a simple buffet breakfast of eggs, bacon, pancakes, juice and fruit for B$20. Tuesday night features a Bajan barbecue buffet (B$40), which starts at 6:30 pm, is accompanied by a steel band and includes steak, fish, chicken, salads, dessert and coffee. On other nights there's an à la carte menu with main dishes from B$30.

The restaurant at *Sea Breeze Beach Hotel* has an pleasantly old-fashioned seaside setting and offers a buffet breakfast (B$20) from 7 to 10 am that includes fruit, bacon and eggs; lunch features sandwiches and other light fare.

The mini-mart opposite Welcome Inn is open from 8 am to 8 pm and sells beer, rum and a few grocery and snack items.

OISTINS

The Barbados Charter, the document that provided the island with its first constitutional protections, was signed in Oistins in 1652.

Today this decidedly local town, 2km east of Maxwell, is best known as the center of the island's fishing industry. The heart of town is the large, bustling seaside fish market that's open daily from morning to night.

On Friday and Saturday nights Oistins' fish market hosts the island's best party with soca music, vendors selling barbecued fish and plenty of rum drinking. Although it's quieter at other times there are a few stalls selling inexpensive fish sandwiches on weekdays.

SILVER SANDS

At the southernmost tip of the island, between Oistins and the airport, is the breezy Silver Sands area, a mecca for windsurfers. However, if you're not on Barbados for windsurfing, the location is a bit out of the way and the beaches to the west are better suited for tamer water activities.

Places to Stay & Eat

In addition to the following listings, there are a number of private places in the Silver Sands area that can be rented by the week.

BARBADOS

Many windsurfers stay a night or two in a hotel and then through word-of-mouth find a shared house or apartment nearby.

Round Rock Apartments (☎ 428-7500, fax 428-7970), Silver Sands, Christ Church, a two-minute walk from the beach, has seven self-catering units that cost US$45/65 in summer/winter for a studio, US$55/90 for a two-bedroom apartment.

Although it's not on the main windsurfing beach, the area's most appealing hotel is the suitably named *Peach and Quiet Hotel* (☎ 428-5682, fax 428-2467), Inch Marlow, Christ Church, which has 22 airy rooms with private baths and seaview patios for US$69 year round. There's an oceanside pool, a buffet breakfast of juice, cereal, eggs and toast for an additional B$15, and reasonably priced lunch and dinner offerings.

Silver Sands Resort (☎ 428-6001, fax 428-3758), Silver Sands, Christ Church, is a 106-room resort on a sandy beach surrounded by casuarina trees. All rooms have air-con, phones, radios and balconies; some have kitchenettes. There are two pools, two tennis courts, two restaurants and a Club Mistral windsurf shop. Rates begins at US$65 in summer, US$120 in winter.

The beachside *Silver Rock Hotel* (☎ 428-2866, fax 420-6982), Silver Sands, Christ Church, has 33 pleasant units, all with hot plates and refrigerators, that cost US$60/100 in summer/winter for a studio or US$80/135 for a one-bedroom unit. There's a pool, a windsurf shop and a reasonably priced restaurant serving three meals a day.

Southeast

St Philip, the diamond-shaped parish east of the airport, is relatively sparsely populated, with a scattering of small villages but no large towns. Along the coast are a couple of resort hotels, while inland, just north of Six Cross Roads, is one of the oldest and most interesting plantation houses on the island.

CRANE BEACH

Crane Beach, 7km northeast of the airport, is a broad white-sand beach backed by cliffs and fronted by aqua blue waters. Despite some storm erosion to the cliffs, this is still one of the loveliest beaches on the Atlantic coast. Public access to the beach can be found along the side roads north of the Crane Beach Hotel.

In terms of the view, the most spectacular angle is from the Crane Beach Hotel, which sits high on a cliff at the south end of the beach. So scenic is the setting that the hotel has managed to turn itself into a bit of a tourist attraction, charging B$10 to tour the grounds. In most cases no one is there to collect before 9:30 am and in any case the fee can be redeemed with a purchase at the restaurant and bar.

Places to Stay & Eat

Crane Beach Hotel (☎ 423-6220, fax 423-5343), St Philip, occupies an 18th-century mansion and has 18 spacious rooms and suites with mahogany furnishings, hardwood floors and bathrooms with tubs. The suites have kitchens, queen beds and either an ocean or pool view. Though each unit varies in size and decor, the rooms are some of the most atmospheric on the island. Rooms cost US$100/180 in summer/winter, suites begin at US$150/270.

The hotel's dining room has a fine view overlooking the beach. It offers a continental breakfast for B$14 and other breakfasts, such as a Bajan-style flying fish version, for B$20. Lunch features a buffet with chicken, fish, rice and dessert for B$25.

SAM LORD'S CASTLE

Sam Lord's Castle, the centerpiece of a resort hotel of the same name, is a limestone coral mansion with an interesting, albeit much embellished, history. The mansion was constructed on Long Bay in 1820 by Samuel Lord, who according to legend hung 'wrecker' lanterns off the point here to lure ships onto nearby Cobbler's Reef. After the ships, which thought they were entering a safe harbor, crashed on the reef, Lord purportedly scurried out to pilfer the

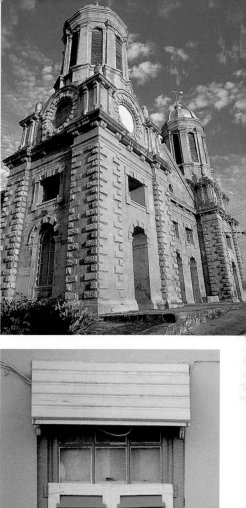

Top Left: Catholic church, The Valley, Anguilla
(Ned Friary)
Middle Left: Shoal Bay East, Anguilla (Ned Friary)
Bottom Left: Island Harbour, Anguilla (Tony Wheeler)

Top Right: St John's Cathedral, Antigua (Ned Friary)
Bottom Right: Colorful Barbados window shutters
(Tony Wheeler)

Top: Francia Plantation, Barbados (Ned Friary)
Bottom Left: Schoolgirls in Speightstown, Barbados
(Glenda Bendure)

Bottom Right: Chattel house, Barbados
(Glenda Bendure)

cargo. Although there's little doubt that Lord was a scoundrel, most historians discount the lantern story as folklore.

Lord's former home, which looks more like a stately residence than a castle, contains the hotel reception and a museum-like collection of antique furnishings and paintings. It's interesting enough, but not a major sight worth going out of your way to see. The hotel charges non-guests a B$12 fee to enter the grounds.

Places to Stay

Sam Lord's Castle (☎ 423-7350, fax 423-5918), Long Bay, St Philip, is a former Marriott affiliate with 248 rooms. A handful of these are on the 2nd floor of the 'castle' and have a colonial decor, but the rest of the accommodations are more typical chain hotel fare, most in smaller buildings spread around the grounds. The hotel beach has a broad stretch of white sand backed by coconut palms, but the waters can be dangerous. There are tennis courts and swimming pools. Summer rates begin at US$130, winter rates at US$195.

SUNBURY PLANTATION HOUSE

Sunbury Plantation House (☎ 423-6270) was built between 1660 and 1670 by an early Irish planter, Mathew Chapman. This handsome house changed hands once a century; the 1775 owners who hailed from Sunbury-on-Thames gave it its present name. In 1888 a Scottish planter purchased the property and after his two unmarried daughters died in 1981, the house was separated from the plantation and sold in auction. A fire swept through the house in 1995, closing down the property for more than a year and resulting in a major – and painstakingly faithful – restoration.

The house has 2½-foot-thick walls built of local coral blocks and ballast stones, the latter from the ships that set sail from England to pick up shipments of Barbadian sugar. The interior retains its plantation-era ambiance and is furnished in antiques, many made from Barbadian mahogany. The cellar has a horse-drawn carriage along with various riding paraphernalia.

To the benefit of visitors, the present owners do not live here, making this the only Barbados plantation house that can be toured in its entirety. The tours, given by guides who are well versed in local history, are conducted daily from 10 am to 4:30 pm. Admission costs B$12 for adults, B$6 for children under 12. Buses from Oistins can drop you at the gate.

Places to Eat

The *Sunbury Plantation House* has a pleasant little outdoor café at the rear of the main building. Offerings include English scones and a pot of tea for B$8 and quiche with salad for B$15. An elaborate period-style dinner is held twice weekly in the plantation house and includes a five-course meal, drinks and a house tour for US$60.

BARBADOS ZOO PARK

The Barbados Zoo Park (☎ 423-6203), a couple of kilometers northeast of Sunbury, is perhaps more interesting for its history than for its modest collection of caged creatures. The zoo has Brazilian tapirs, zebras, the ubiquitous Barbadian black belly sheep, South American macaws, parrots and cockatoos and a few boa constrictors.

The zoo is on the grounds of Oughterson House, a small plantation house that was rebuilt in 1820 after being the first of some 40 plantation estates torched during a short-lived but tumultuous slave uprising in 1816. The zoo and house can be visited from 9:30 am to 4:30 pm daily. Admission is B$12 for adults, B$6 for children under 12.

West Coast

Barbados' west coast has lovely white-sand beaches and the majority of the island's luxury hotels. Most are in the parish of St James, which in colonial times was a popular holiday area for the upper crust of British society. Over the years their seaside estates have gradually been replaced by resort hotels, many of which still cater to the well-to-do.

BARBADOS

Hwy 1, the two-lane road that runs north from Bridgetown to Speightstown, is bordered much of the way by a close mix of tourist facilities and residential areas.

PAYNES BAY

Paynes Bay is a gently curving bay with a fine stretch of white sand and good swimming and snorkeling. There are numerous beach access walkways clearly marked by roadside signs.

Places to Stay & Eat

Angler Apartments (☎ /fax 432-0817, gosain@sunbeach.net), Clarke's Rd No 1, Derricks, St James, is inland on a side road about 200 meters southeast of the Coconut Creek Hotel. This locally owned, unpretentious operation has 13 older but clean apartments. The eight one-bedroom units each have a kitchen, a living room with a small bed and ceiling fan, a bedroom with either a queen or two twin beds, a bathroom and a radio. The five studios are similar but lack the living room. Cribs can be provided. Studios cost US$55/80 in summer/winter, one-bedroom units cost US$63/85. There's a small patio bar and restaurant.

Coconut Creek Hotel (☎ 432-0803, fax 432-0272), PO Box 429, a kilometer south of Paynes Bay, is a low-key, upscale resort on a private beach. It has 50 air-con rooms in whitewashed Mediterranean-style buildings, as well as a pool and complimentary water sports. Singles/doubles begin at US$216/268 in the summer, US$297/346 in the winter, including breakfast and dinner.

Treasure Beach Hotel (☎ 432-1346, fax 432-1094), a 30-room hotel right on the beach at Paynes Bay, is a personable place that books heavily with repeat guests. Rooms have typical high-end amenities and cost from US$155/350 in summer/winter for either single or double occupancy. There's a pool and a pricey restaurant.

Fathom's (☎ 432-2568), on Hwy 1 near the south end of Paynes Bay, is a delightful open-air beachfront restaurant that's top value both for its setting and food. At lunch, starters such as vegie spring rolls or octopus salad average B$15, while pastas, grilled fish or Greek moussaka cost B$20. Dinner features fish and meat dishes with creative sauces for around B$40.

SANDY LANE BAY

Sandy Lane Bay has a wonderful white-sand beach backed by shade trees and fronted by lovely turquoise waters. It's popular for swimming and sunbathing. Much of the activity is centered near the Sandy Lane Hotel, where you'll often find a few jewelry vendors, hair braiders and someone offering horseback rides along the shore. When the surf is up there are usually a few surfers along the quieter south end of the beach.

There's public access to the beach on both sides of the Sandy Lane Hotel.

Places to Stay

Founded by former British parliamentarian Ronald Tree in 1961, the 121-room *Sandy Lane Hotel* (☎ 432-1311, fax 432-2954), St James, is the island's most exclusive resort, complete with marbled lobbies and grand facades. Rooms are posh with rates to match, beginning at US$700 (US$525 in summer) including breakfast. Guests have complimentary use of the fitness center, tennis courts and the 18-hole golf course. The hotel is planning major renovations, to the tune of US$75-million.

HOLETOWN

The first English settlers to Barbados landed at Holetown in 1627 aboard the *Olive Blossom*. An obelisk **monument** along the main road in the town center commemorates the event – albeit the date on the monument, which reads July 1605, is off by two decades.

Despite being the oldest town on the island, Holetown is a rather bustling place that's more modern than traditional in appearance.

St James Church on Hwy 1, just north of the town center, is the site of the region's oldest church. The initial church, built in 1660, was replaced by a more substantial structure in the mid-19th century. A few vestiges of the original church remain, including a bell that was cast in the late 1600s and inscribed with the name of King William.

At the north side of Holetown is **Folkestone Park**, a public park with a narrow beach. It has reasonable surfing when the waves are up and snorkeling when it's calm. The underwater trail that once existed at this park is long gone but snorkelers can still find some small tropicals, including angelfish and blue hunters. The park has a few picnic tables, a lifeguard, snorkel rentals and usually a couple of clothing vendors. The park also has a modest marine museum, open from 9 am to 5 pm weekdays, with displays on coral, shells, fishing and boat building. However, if you're just looking for a nice beach for sunbathing and swimming there are better ones in the area, including the strip that fronts Inn on the Beach.

Information

The Super-Centre supermarket complex, in the town center, has a CBIC bank, a travel agent and a Texaco gas station. The Sunset Crest Shopping Centre at the south side of town has a '99' convenience store and a fruit stand; there's a Barclays Bank south of that.

Places to Stay

Homar Rentals (☎ 432-6750, fax 432-7229), Sunset Crest, St James, handles two properties on the inland side of the road about 500 meters from the beach. The cozy *Travellers Palm* has 16 pleasant apartments, each with a full kitchen and a separate bedroom with two twin beds. In the same neighborhood is *Halcyon Apartments*, a rather sprawling complex with 73 apartments equipped with kitchenettes, living rooms and large bedrooms with twin beds. Both places have pools. Rates at either cost US$50/75 in summer/winter.

Inn on the Beach (☎ 432-0385, fax 432-2440), Holetown, St James, just south of Mr Comeback, is a quiet place despite being in the center of Holetown. There are

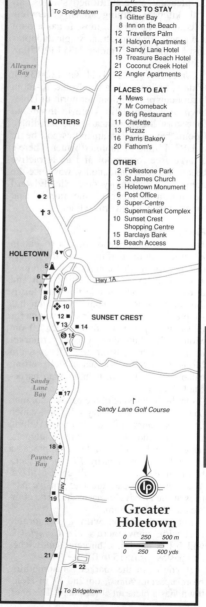

PLACES TO STAY
1 Glitter Bay
8 Inn on the Beach
12 Travellers Palm
14 Halcyon Apartments
17 Sandy Lane Hotel
19 Treasure Beach Hotel
21 Coconut Creek Hotel
22 Angler Apartments

PLACES TO EAT
4 Mews
7 Mr Comeback
9 Brig Restaurant
11 Chefette
13 Pizzaz
16 Parris Bakery
20 Fathom's

OTHER
2 Folkestone Park
3 St James Church
5 Holetown Monument
6 Post Office
9 Super-Centre Supermarket Complex
10 Sunset Crest Shopping Centre
15 Barclays Bank
18 Beach Access

Greater Holetown

BARBADOS

20 pleasant air-conditioned studios, all with kitchens, dining areas, oceanview balconies, phones and tubs. It has a pool and a beachfront location. Singles/doubles cost US$65/80 in summer, US$130/150 in winter.

Glitter Bay (☎ 422-4111, fax 422-1367), Porters, St James, is a handsome 70-room luxury complex a kilometer north of Holetown. Accommodations are in three and four-story Mediterranean-style buildings. Rooms have modern amenities and begin at US$215/300 in summer/winter. There's a large free-form pool and an attractive beach. The site, incidentally, was once the home of British tycoon Sir Edward Cunard, a member of the family that founded the Cunard cruise line.

Places to Eat

There's no shortage of places to eat in Holetown. In the parking lot of the *Super-Centre* supermarket complex you can usually find a few vendors selling fruit and drinking coconuts. Inside the complex is the open-air *Brig* restaurant, which has simple fare like fish & chips or lasagna for B$19; it's open from 8:30 am to 10 pm Monday to Saturday. The supermarket itself, open from 8 am to at least 8 pm Monday to Saturday, has a deli selling bakery items, B$5 rotis and cheap barbecued chicken.

On the beach side of the road is a branch of the Bajan chain eatery *Chefette*, which has long hours and serves up everything from rotis and salads to chicken nuggets, burgers and thick shakes. For pizza, a better bet is the nearby *Pizzaz* – prices begin at B$16 for a small cheese pizza. You can pick bread and inexpensive pastries at the *Parris Bakery* in the same complex as Barclays Bank.

For routine food with a memorable beachside view there's *Mr Comeback*, which has lunchtime burgers, sandwiches and pastas for B$15 to B$20.

If you're in the market for something more upscale, *Mews*, on 2nd St in Holetown, has a pleasant atmosphere. The chef,

an Austrian, cooks up good top-end food for reasonable prices.

Inn on the Beach has an enjoyable Tuesday night barbecue (B$32) that includes an appetizer-and-salad bar, vegetables and a choice of fish or steak – all accompanied by steel pan music.

MULLINS BEACH

Mullins is a popular roadside beach along Hwy 1 between Holetown and Speightstown. The waters are usually calm and good for swimming and snorkeling.

The landmark here is *Mullins Beach Bar & Restaurant*, a bustling watering hole with an open-air veranda right on the sand; in addition to drinks, you can get moderately priced burgers, rotis and fish.

SPEIGHTSTOWN

Now a shadow of its former self, Speightstown was a thriving port in the days when sugar was king. A main shipping line ran from Speightstown to Bristol, England, and trade was so extensive between the two areas that Speightstown was once dubbed 'Little Bristol.'

Today Speightstown is a decidedly Bajan town, its side streets thick with older wooden buildings with overhanging galleries. Unfortunately many of these historic buildings are in a state of disrepair, some abandoned and literally falling apart. If you have time to spare, the waterfront is worth a stroll, not for any particular sights but to soak up the town's overall character.

Places to Stay

If you're interested in staying in Speightstown, apartment and house rentals can be arranged at reasonable rates (from around US$30) through the amiable Clement 'Junior' Armstrong, who manages the Fisherman's Pub (☎ 422-2703).

There are also two top-end resorts: *Almond Beach Village* (☎ 422-4900), at the northern outskirts of town, and the exclusive *Cobblers Cove* hotel (☎ 422-2291) to the south.

Places to Eat

In the center of town, opposite the post office, is the Speightstown Mall which has a fruit stand, a *KFC* and an ice-cream shop (as well as a Barclays Bank). Vegetable and fruit vendors can be found along the main street.

Fisherman's Pub, on Queen St down by the waterfront, is a spirited, colorful place with a thoroughly Bajan atmosphere and inexpensive local food. Essentially an oversized beach shack, this is the town's most popular eating and drinking spot. You can get a good fish meal for around B$15.

A fancier dinner option is the town center is *Mango Cafe* (☎ 422-0704). Main dishes include mango chicken, seafood crêpes and fresh fish for around B$35. Shrimp cocktail or smoked salmon starters cost about half that.

Central & Eastern Barbados

From Bridgetown a series of highways fan out into the interior. Any one of these can make a nice drive and there are scores of secondary roads that add still more possibilities for exploration.

The most popular touring route, which takes in some of the finest scenery on Barbados as well as many of its leading attractions, starts along Hwy 2, running northeast from Bridgetown. The suburbs soon give way to small villages, sugar cane fields and scrubby pastureland with grazing black belly sheep. About 10km out of the city the road leads to Welchman Hall Gully, Harrison's Cave and the Flower Forest. Hwy 2 continues through the hilly Scotland District and then turns westward, leading to a scenic loop drive that takes in the Morgan Lewis Sugar Mill, the vista at Cherry Tree Hill, St Nicholas Abbey, Farley Hill and the Barbados Wildlife Reserve.

From there it's possible to head down the east coast to Bathsheba and return via Gun Hill Signal Station, with a detour to the Francia Plantation.

WELCHMAN HALL GULLY

Welchman Hall Gully, along Hwy 2 near the turn-off to Harrison's Cave, is a thickly wooded ravine with a walking track and nearly 200 species of tropical plants. Gullies like this were virtually the only places planters were unable to cultivate crops and thus represent an unspoiled slice of forest similar to the one that covered Barbados before the arrival of English settlers.

Geologically, this was once a part of the network of caverns that encompasses the nearby Harrison's Cave, but the caverns here collapsed eons ago, leaving an open gully. Admission is B$11.50 for adults, B$5.75 for children. It's open daily from 9 am to 5 pm. Parking for Welchman's Gully is a few hundred meters north of the entrance.

HARRISON'S CAVE

Harrison's Cave, just off Hwy 2, is a fascinating network of limestone caverns with dripping stalactites, stalagmites and subterranean streams and waterfalls. A tram goes down into the cave, stopping en route to let passengers get out and closely examine some of the more impressive sites, including the Great Hall, a huge domed-shaped cavern, and Cascade Pool, an impressive body of crystal clear water 50 meters beneath the surface. The air temperature inside the cave is 26°C (78°F).

The underground tram tour lasts about 35 minutes, but it's usually preceded by a short video, so the whole thing takes about an hour. At certain times of the day it can get very busy with tour groups; to avoid a wait, call ☎ 438-6640 for reservations. The cost is B$17.25 for adults, half price for children. There's a snack bar with drinks and sandwiches.

FLOWER FOREST

Flower Forest, 3km north of Harrison's Cave, at the western edge of the Scotland District, is a 50-acre botanical garden at the site of a former sugar estate. Paths meander through the grounds, which are now planted with virtually every plant found on Barbados, including lots of flowering species that bloom at a height ideal for photography. The gardens retain the estate's mature citrus and breadfruit trees, the latter having been introduced to Barbados from the South Pacific as an inexpensive food source for slaves.

Plaques display both the English and Latin names of flowers and trees, making this a particularly nice place to come if you want to identify flora you've seen around the island. The grounds also offer sweeping views of Chalky Mountain and the Atlantic Ocean to the east and of Mt Hillaby, the island's highest point, to the west. Some of the paths are wheelchair accessible.

The flower forest is open from 9 am to 5 pm daily. Admission is B$14 for adults, B$7 for children. There's a snack bar with moderately priced sandwiches and other simple fare.

MORGAN LEWIS SUGAR MILL

Morgan Lewis Sugar Mill, at the side of the road 2km southeast of Cherry Tree Hill, claims to be the largest intact sugar windmill surviving in the Caribbean. The mill interior has a simple display of historic photos, a few artifacts of the plantation era and the original gears, shaft and grinding wheel. A stairway leads up around the works to the top where you can get a bit of a view of the surrounding area. The mill is undergoing restoration, so hours may be a bit sketchy but it's usually open weekdays from 9 am to 5 pm. Admission is B$5 (B$2.50 for children).

CHERRY TREE HILL

Cherry Tree Hill, on the road that turns inland a kilometer north of Morgan Lewis Sugar Mill, offers a fine vista of much of the east coast. The best views are just beneath the summit at the roadside lookout next to the sugar cane fields. There's usually an elderly security guard there who is more than willing to spice up the view with a little local history.

A steep dirt track opposite the lookout leads to the top of the hill, but the view from there is largely blocked by trees. They are not cherry trees, incidentally; according to local lore, the cherry trees were chopped down long ago because passers-by kept taking the fruit.

ST NICHOLAS ABBEY

St Nicholas Abbey, 750 meters west of Cherry Tree Hill, is one of the oldest plantation houses in the Caribbean. This unique Jacobean-style mansion with curly Dutch gables dates from the 1650s.

One of its early owners, Sir John Yeamans, led a 1663 expedition that colonized Carolina and he went on to become governor of that North American colony. For the last five generations it's been in the family of Colonel Stephen Cave, who resides in the house and manages the surrounding plantation.

Visitors can tour the ground floor of the mansion which has a fine collection of 19th-century Barbadian and English furnishings. One peculiar feature of the house is the inclusion of fireplaces, apparently the result of a strict adherence to a design drawn up in England that didn't give consideration to Barbados' tropical climate.

Until the 20th century, each plantation on Barbados had its own windmill for crushing cane. The remains of this plantation's mill (and the tower from the former syrup factory) can be seen below the house. These days the sugar cane is hauled to the Portvale Sugar Factory near Holetown.

St Nicholas Abbey is open from 10 am to 3:30 pm Monday to Friday. If you time your visit accordingly you can also see a 15-minute film made in 1935 that shows some of the old sugar mills in action; it plays at 11:30 am and 2:30 pm. Admission is a bargain at B$10, with or without the movie.

FARLEY HILL

Farley Hill, off Hwy 2, is a pleasant hilltop park that would make a fine place to break out a picnic. The centerpiece of the park is the former mansion of Sir Graham Briggs, a wealthy 19th-century sugar baron whose guest list included the Duke of Edinburgh and King George V. In 1957, the stately Georgian-style mansion appeared in the movie *Island in the Sun*, starring Harry Belafonte. In 1965 a fire swept through the mansion, completely gutting the interior and burning away the roof. Today only the hollow coral block walls still stand – a rather haunting site that nonetheless retains a measure of grandeur.

Behind the mansion a hilltop gazebo offers a fine view clear out to East Point Lighthouse at the eastern tip of the island.

Farley Hill is open daily from 8:30 am to 6 pm. Admission is B$3 per car.

BARBADOS WILDLIFE RESERVE

The Barbados Wildlife Reserve, opposite Farley Hill, is a walk-through zoo with short paths that meander through a mahogany woods of scurrying green monkeys, sluggish red-footed turtles and a caiman pond. Other creatures that might be spotted in the reserve include brocket deer, iguanas and agoutis. There's also a small aviary with macaws and cockatoos, as well as some caged parrots and uncaged peacocks and pelicans.

The free-roaming monkeys are the highlight. They are generally easy to spot but if you want to stack the odds in your favor come around 4 pm when feedings take place.

Green monkeys are for the most part brownish-gray, with highlights of white fur, but flecks of yellow and olive-green give them a greenish cast in some light, hence the name. On average, adult females weigh about three kg, males about five kg.

There are also caged monkeys on the grounds. The reserve is a project of the non-profit Barbados Primate Research Center, which was established in 1985 with assistance from the Canadian International Development Agency. The center supports itself by supplying monkeys to laboratories in the USA and other countries for the production and testing of vaccines.

Adjacent to the reserve is the **Grenade Hall Forest & Signal Station**. Here you'll find a restored signal tower and a short loop trail through a shady forest of native trees, some identified by interpretive plaques.

The properties are jointly managed and open from 10 am to 5 pm daily. Admission to both costs B$23 for adults, B$11.50 for children under 12.

GUN HILL SIGNAL STATION

The 215-meter Gun Hill, off Hwy X in the center of the island, boasts a small hilltop signal tower and a clear view of the surrounding valleys and the southwest coast.

The island was once connected by six such signal towers that used flags and lanterns to relay messages. The official function of the towers was to keep watch for approaching enemy ships but they also served colonial authorities as a mechanism for signaling an alarm in the event of a slave revolt.

The Gun Hill tower, built in 1818, houses a couple of small displays of military artifacts and a pair of old cannons. The grounds are open from 9 am to 5 pm Monday to Saturday. Admission is B$8 for adults, B$4 for children.

Down the slope from the signal station is a British Regiment lion, carved from rock and painted white.

FRANCIA PLANTATION

Francia Plantation, on the side road just south of Gun Hill, is an elegant plantation house with an interior of rich woods, period furnishings and an interesting collection of antique maps and prints. There are pleasant formal gardens out the back and some surrounding fields of vegetable crops.

The plantation was built at the turn of the century and is still occupied by descendants of the original French owner. The narrow kilometer-long road into the plantation is lined with mahogany trees. Francia Plantation can be visited from 10 am to 4 pm Monday to Friday. Admission is B$9 for adults, half price for children under 12.

EAST COAST

The east coast has a predominantly rugged shoreline, turbulent seas and an unspoiled

BARBADOS

rural character. The East Coast Rd, which connects Hwy 2 with Bathsheba, is the only coastal road of any length on this side of the island.

Near the upper end of the East Coast Rd is **Barclays Park**, a public beach and picnic area donated to the government as an independence gift from Barclays Bank. Because of dangerous currents, the beach is best suited for picnicking and strolling.

Bathsheba, at the south end of the road, is the island's top surfing locale and has a picturesque coastline of high sea cliffs, untamed beaches and roaring Atlantic waters.

Chalky Mount, the white clay hills that rise inland of the East Coast Rd, are home to a couple of pottery shops. Visitors can view the operations and purchase items direct from the potters at reasonable prices. Access to Chalky Mount is from Hwy 2 near Haggatts.

Places to Stay & Eat

There's a beachside snack bar at Barclays Park that serves lunch fare such as burgers and flying fish sandwiches.

Atlantis Hotel (☎ 433-9445), at the south side of Bathsheba, St Joseph, has eight simple but adequate rooms, an interesting local flavor and agreeable prices. All rooms have private bath and half have oceanview balconies. Rates include breakfast and dinner; they are US$30/50 for singles/doubles in summer and US$35/55 in winter. Add another US$10 for a room with a view. The restaurant has an open-air oceanside setting and a B$25 lunch of chicken or fish with fried plantain, pumpkin fritters, candied

sweet potatoes and dessert, served from 11:30 am to 3 pm.

Edgewater Inn (☎ 433-9900, fax 433-9902, info@edgewaterinn.com), Bathsheba, St Joseph, has a fine cliffside setting overlooking the beach at the north side of Bathsheba. The inn has 20 modern and comfortable ocean-facing rooms, each with a sitting area, mahogany furnishings, a tub, ceiling fan and phone. Standard rooms cost US$75/95 in summer/winter, while air-conditioned suites cost US$90/110. Continental breakfast is included in the rates and there's a pool perched above the ocean and satellite TV in the lobby.

The Edgewater Inn's restaurant, which has alfresco dining, is a popular lunch stop for people on day tours. From noon to 2 pm there's a good Bajan buffet that includes flying fish, chicken, salad, fritters, macaroni pie, rice and peas, yogurt and coffee. It costs B$30, except on Sunday when it cost B$40, has more offerings and is served until 3 pm. Sandwiches and other simple eats are also available throughout the day.

ANDROMEDA BOTANIC GARDENS

Andromeda Botanic Gardens, off Hwy 3 a couple of kilometers south of Bathsheba, was the private garden of the late Iris Bannochie, one of Barbados' foremost horticulturists. The gardens cover six acres and have a wide collection of introduced tropical plants, including orchids, ferns, water lilies, bougainvillea, cacti and palms. The property is managed by the Barbados National Trust and is open from 9 am to 5 pm daily. Admission is B$12 for adults, B$6 for children.

Dominica

Whether you approach Dominica by air or sea, the island looms above the horizon like no other in the Eastern Caribbean. Its interior is solidly mountainous. Sharp steep ridges rise up from the coast and deep jungly river valleys run back down.

The island is strikingly rural and unspoiled. Most of the larger towns are set on the coast, but there are also tiny hamlets that snake along the mountain ridges. Even the capital of Roseau, whose sidewalks are lined with period wood and stone buildings, has the appearance of a forgotten frontier town.

Not only does Dominica have a rich West Indian tradition, the island is also home to the Eastern Caribbean's largest Carib Indian community.

Dominica, which fittingly dubs itself the 'Nature Island,' promotes itself as a 'non-tourist destination' for divers, hikers and naturalists. Indeed, it offers some of the Caribbean's most spectacular scenery, both above and below the water. Many of the diving spots are still virgin and there's scarcely a soul on most of the trails. Hikes range from short walks to all-day treks and take in rainforests, waterfalls, rivers, lakes, bird sanctuaries, hot springs and other volcanic sites.

Dominica has beaches, but they are not exceptional and they're mostly of black sand. Because of this and because overseas visitors have to touch down on a neighboring Caribbean island first (Dominica has no international jet traffic), the most popular way to see Dominica is as part of an island-hopping itinerary that also combines more traditional beach destinations.

HIGHLIGHTS

- Unsurpassed mountain and rainforest scenery
- Superb hiking, ranging from a stroll to Trafalgar Falls to an unforgettable trek to Boiling Lake
- Top-notch diving at unfrequented sites
- Roseau's expansive botanical gardens and parrot aviary
- Cabrits National Park, with its colonial fortress and fine views

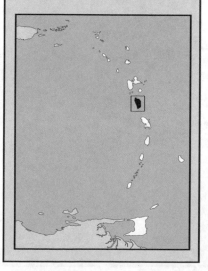

Facts about Dominica

HISTORY

The Caribs, who settled here in the 14th century, called the island Waitikubuli, which means 'tall is her body.' Christopher Columbus, with less poetic flair, named the island after the day of the week that he spotted it – a Sunday ('Doménica' in Italian) – on November 3, 1493.

Daunted by fierce resistance from the Caribs and discouraged by the absence of gold, the Spanish took little interest in Dominica. France laid claim to the island in 1635 and a few years later sent a contingent

Guadeloupe Channel

Cape
Melville
Carib
Point

Vieille Case

Toucari
Bay

Douglas
Bay

Woodford
Hill Bay

Cabrits
National
Park
Portsmouth
Anse Du Mé
Calibishie

Prince
Rupert
Bay
Indian River

Melville Hall
Airport
Londonderry
Bay

Northern Forest
Reserve
Melville Hall River
Marigot

Pagua
Bay

Dublanc

▲ Morne Diablotin
4747ft

Pagua River

Bataka
Salybia

Carib
Territory

Sineku

L'Escalier
Tête Chien

Salisbury

Layou River

Castle
Bruce

Mero

Castle Bruce River

St Joseph

Emerald
Pool

Layou

Rodney's
Rock

Pont Casse

Rosalie River

Rosalie
Point

Massacre

Canefield
Airport

▲ Morne Trois Pitons
4550ft

Boeri Lake

CARIBBEAN SEA

Pringles
Bay

Morne
Macaque ▲
4005ft

Freshwater
Lake

Boiling
Lake

La Plaine

Trafalgar
Laudat
Trafalgar
Falls

Watt
Mountain ▲
4015ft

Morne
Trois Pitons
National Park

★ ROSEAU
Castle Comfort

Delices

Woodbridge
Bay

Petite
Savanne

Point
Guignard
Soufriere

Grand
Bay

Dominica

Scotts
Head
Soufriere
Bay

Scotts
Head

Martinique
Channel

0   3   6 km
0   2   4 miles

of missionaries, who were driven off by the unwelcoming Caribs. In 1660 the French and English signed a neutrality treaty in which they agreed to allow the island to remain a possession of the Caribs. Nevertheless, by the end of the century, French settlers from the neighboring French West Indies began to establish coffee plantations on Dominica. In the 1720s France sent a governor and took formal possession of the island.

For the remainder of the 18th century, Dominica was caught up in the French and British skirmishes that marked the era, with the island changing hands between the two powers several times. In 1763, under the Treaty of Paris, the French reluctantly ceded the island to the British. The French made attempts to recapture Dominica in 1795 and again in 1805 when they burned much of Roseau to the ground.

After 1805 the island remained firmly in the possession of the British who established sugar plantations on Dominica's more accessible slopes. The British administered the island as part of the Leeward Islands Federation until 1939 when it was transferred to the Windward Islands Federation. In 1967 Dominica gained autonomy in internal affairs as a West Indies Associated State and on November 3, 1978, the 485th anniversary of Columbus' 'discovery,' Dominica became an independent republic within the Commonwealth.

The initial year of independence was a turbulent one. In June 1979 the island's first prime minister, Patrick John, was forced to resign after a series of corrupt schemes surfaced, including one clandestine land deal that attempted to transfer 15% of the island to US developers. In August 1979 Hurricane David, packing winds of 150 miles an hour, struck the island with devastating force, denuding vast tracts of forest, destroying the banana crops and wreaking havoc on much of Roseau. Overall, 42 people were killed and 75% of the islanders' homes were destroyed or severely damaged.

In July 1980 Mary Eugenia Charles was elected prime minister, the first woman in

the Caribbean to hold the office. Within a year of her inauguration she survived two unsuccessful coups, including a bizarre attempt orchestrated by Patrick John that involved mercenaries recruited from the Ku Klux Klan.

In October 1983, as chairperson of the Organization of East Caribbean States, Prime Minister Charles endorsed the US invasion of Grenada and sent a symbolic force of Dominican troops to participate. An appreciative USA responded by increasing foreign aid to Dominica, one consequence of which is the island's fine paved roads.

GEOGRAPHY
Dominica is 29 miles long, 16 miles wide and has a total land mass of 290 sq miles. It has the highest mountains in the Eastern Caribbean; the loftiest peak, Morne Diablotin, is 4747 feet high. The mountains, which act as a magnet for rain, serve as a water source for the more than 200 rivers that run down the mountain valleys. En route to the coast many of the rivers cascade over steep cliff faces, giving the island an abundance of waterfalls.

CLIMATE
In January the average high temperature is 85°F (29°C) while the low averages 68°F (20°C). In July the average high is 90°F (32°C) while the low averages 72°F (22°C).

The driest months are February to June, with a mean relative humidity of around 65%. During the rest of the year the humidity is in the low 70s. In August, the wettest month, there's measurable rainfall

---

Peaks & Valleys
It's said that when Christopher Columbus returned to Spain after his second voyage to the New World, King Ferdinand and Queen Isabella asked him to describe the island of Dominica. Columbus responded by crumpling up a piece of paper and tossing it, with all its sharp edges and folds, onto the table.

That, he said, was Dominica. ∎

DOMINICA

for an average of 22 days, while April, the driest month, averages 10 days. All these statistics are for Roseau – the mountains are cooler and wetter.

FLORA & FAUNA

More than 160 bird species have been sighted on Dominica, giving it some of the most diverse bird life in the Eastern Caribbean. Of these, 59 species nest on the island, including two endemic and endangered parrot species.

Dominica's national bird, the Sisserou *(Amazona imperialis)*, also called the imperial parrot, is about 20 inches long when full grown, the largest of all Amazon parrots. It has a dark purple breast and belly and a green back.

The Jaco *(Amazona arausiaca)* parrot is somewhat smaller and more green overall with bright splashes of varied colors. It is also called the red-necked parrot for the fluff of red feathers commonly found at the throat.

The island has large crapaud frogs, small tree frogs, many lizards, 13 bat species, 55 butterfly species, boa constrictors that grow nearly 10 feet in length and four other types of snakes (none poisonous).

Dominica is well known for its vast rainforests, but the island also has montane thickets, dry scrub woodlands, evergreen forests, fumarole vegetation, cloud forests and elfin woodlands. The most abundant tree on the island is the gommier, a huge gum tree that's traditionally been used to make dugout canoes.

The most colorful of Dominica's endemic plants is its national flower, the bwa kwaib, or Carib tree. A deciduous shrub, it's found on the island's drier west coast. In spring, the bare branches of this shrub suddenly become thick with hundreds of scarlet flowers, adding a bright splash to the countryside.

GOVERNMENT & POLITICS

Dominica, an independent republic within the British Commonwealth, has a unicameral Assembly comprising 21 elected members and nine appointed senators. Members of the Assembly normally sit for five-year terms. The executive branch is headed by a prime minister who represents the majority party in the Assembly.

In addition there's a well-developed system of local government that includes town councils in Roseau and Portsmouth and 25 village councils around the island.

ECONOMY

Dominica's principal economic earnings are from agriculture. Bananas enjoyed a protected market in England until 1993, when the dismantling of trade restrictions between Western European nations opened the English market to substantially cheaper Central American bananas. The result has been a steep drop in the export value of the Dominican crop. The government is encouraging farmers to diversify in hopes of reducing Dominica's economic dependency on bananas, which account for 75% of its agricultural production.

Coconuts are the other major agricultural commodity. The largest island employer, Dominica Coconut Products, uses most of the coconut crop to produce body soaps and oils. Spices, coffee and citrus fruits are also grown for export.

New cruise ship facilities in Roseau and Prince Rupert Bay have resulted in a five-

Tree frog

fold increase in cruise ship arrivals, with some 300 cruise ships now pulling into port annually. Tourism on Dominica is otherwise still small scale. Only about 90,000 overnight visitors come to the island each year. However, in a move that has some environmentalists worried, the government is making a concerted effort to boost those figures. Within the next five years it plans to expand the Melville Hall airport runway to accommodate jet aircraft and triple the current hotel room inventory. Some of the rooms will come from adding new wings to existing hotels, but negotiations for the first large resorts, including a proposed 150-room Four Seasons Resort with an 18-hole golf course, are being undertaken by the government.

POPULATION & PEOPLE
Dominica's population is approximately 71,000; about a third live in Roseau.

While the majority of islanders are of African descent, about 3000 native Caribs also reside on Dominica, most of them on a 3700-acre reservation on the eastern side of the island.

SOCIETY & CONDUCT
Dominica draws on a mix of cultures: there are as many French place names as English; African language, foods and customs mingle with European traditions as part of the island's Creole culture; and the Caribs still carve dugout canoes, build houses on stilts and weave distinctive basketwork. Rastafarian and black pride influences, including dreadlocks and clothing in the African colors of red, green and yellow, are common on the island as well. Cricket and soccer are the most popular sports.

Dominica's most celebrated author, Jean Rhys, was born in Roseau in 1890. Although she moved to England at age 16 and only made one brief return visit to Dominica, much of her work draws upon her childhood experiences in the West Indies. Rhys touches lightly upon her life in Dominica in her books *Voyage in the Dark* (1934) and her autobiography *Smile Please* (1979). Her most famous work,

Wide Sargasso Sea, a novel set in Jamaica, was made into a film in 1993.

RELIGION
In terms of religion, the French have had a more lasting influence on Dominica than the British and over 50% of the population is Roman Catholic. Other denominations include Anglican, Methodist, Pentecostal, Baptist, Seventh Day Adventist and Baha'i.

LANGUAGE
English is the national language, but a French-based patois is also widely spoken.

Facts for the Visitor

ORIENTATION
Most of Dominica's attractions and places to stay are along the west coast or in the mountains just inland from the capital, Roseau.

Dominica has two airports: Canefield, a 10-minute drive from Roseau, and Melville Hall, on the secluded northeast side of the island. If you're planning to base yourself in Roseau, try to avoid Melville Hall as it's a good 75-minute haul to the capital.

This is a large island, but the primary roads are well paved and getting around is easy. With a reasonably early start, it's possible to drive up the west coast from Roseau to Portsmouth, explore Cabrits National Park, travel down the east coast through the Carib Territory and stop at the Emerald Pool on your way back across the island, all in a full-day outing.

Maps
The best map of the island is the detailed 1:50,000 British Ordnance Survey map, last published in 1991. It can be bought at the tourist office in Roseau for EC$22.

TOURIST OFFICES
Local Tourist Offices
There are tourist information booths at each airport and at the Old Market in Roseau. When you're requesting information from

DOMINICA

overseas, address your mail to: Division of Tourism (☎ 448-2045, fax 448-5840), National Development Corp, PO Box 293, Roseau, Commonwealth of Dominica, West Indies.

Tourist Offices Abroad

Information on Dominica can be obtained from:

Belgium
   OECS Embassy,
   Rue des Aduatiques 100, 1040 Brussels
   (☎ 322-733-4328, fax 322-735-7237)
Canada
   OECS Mission in Canada, Suite 1050,
   112 Kent St, Ottawa, Ontario KIP 5P2
   (☎ 613-236-8952, fax 613-236-3042)
UK
   Caribbean Tourism Organisation,
   Suite 3.15, Vigilant House, 120 Wilton Rd,
   Victoria, London SW1V 1JZ
   (☎ 0171-233-8382, fax 0171-873-8551)
USA
   Dominica Tourist Office, 10 E 21st St,
   Suite 600, New York, NY 10010
   (☎ 212-475-7542, fax 212-475-9728,
   dominicany@msn.com)

VISAS & DOCUMENTS

Most visitors to Dominica must have a valid passport, but US and Canadian citizens can enter with just proof of citizenship, such as a photo ID and an official birth certificate. French nationals may visit for up to two weeks with a Carte d'Indentité. Only citizens of former Eastern Bloc countries require visas. A roundtrip or onward ticket is officially required of all visitors.

CUSTOMS

Visitors may bring in a liter of wine or spirits and 200 cigarettes.

MONEY

Dominica uses the Eastern Caribbean dollar (EC$). The bank exchange rate for US$1 is EC$2.68 for traveler's checks, EC$2.67 for cash. US dollars are widely accepted by shops, restaurants and taxi drivers, although you'll often get an exchange rate of about EC$2.60.

Most hotels, car rental agencies, dive shops, tour operators and top-end restaurants accept MasterCard, Visa and American Express cards.

POST & COMMUNICATIONS
Post

The main post office is in Roseau; there are sub-post offices in larger villages. All post office boxes listed in this chapter are in Roseau, therefore box numbers should be followed by 'Roseau, Commonwealth of Dominica, West Indies.' When there's no post office box, the address should include the recipient's town. The use of 'Commonwealth' is to help prevent mail from being sent to the Dominican Republic by mistake.

Letters sent from Dominica cost EC$0.65 to the Caribbean; EC$0.90 to Europe, the UK or North America; and EC$1.20 to Australia, Africa and the Middle East. It costs EC$0.55 to mail a postcard anywhere in the world.

Telephone

Local numbers have seven digits. When calling from overseas add the area code 767. For local directory information dial 118. For questions with international calls dial 0.

Dominica has both coin and card phones, commonly side by side. You can buy phonecards at telecommunications offices, the Roseau library and the Canefield Airport gift shop.

The area code for Dominica is 767.

NEWSPAPERS & MAGAZINES

Dominica has two weekly newspapers: The *Chronicle*, published on Friday, and the *Tropical Star*, published on Wednesday.

RADIO & TV

There are four local radio stations, including the government-owned DBS (88.1 FM, 595 AM).

Cable TV has a mix of US network fare and local programming, including regional cricket matches. Channel 7 provides general information, exchange rates, a calendar of events and videos on island sightseeing and culture.

ELECTRICITY
Electricity is 220/240 volts AC, 50 cycles. Incidentally, 70% of the island's electricity is hydro generated.

WEIGHTS & MEASURES
Dominica follows the imperial system of measurements. Car odometers and speed limits are given in miles.

HEALTH
The Princess Margaret Hospital (☎ 448-2231) is in the Goodwill area at the north side of Roseau, off Federation Drive.

See the introductory Facts for the Visitor chapter for information on travel health.

DANGERS & ANNOYANCES
While Dominica is generally a safe place, thefts are not unknown and you shouldn't leave valuables unattended. Around Roseau you can expect at least a few pestering hustlers to chat you up for change. You'll also have to be firm at places like Trafalgar Falls, where would-be guides try their utmost to attach themselves to you.

Roads on Dominica are narrow and you'll need to be quite cautious when walking in trafficked areas. That holds doubly true for Roseau, where cars zip around at a fairly fast pace with drivers expecting pedestrians to grant them the right of way.

EMERGENCIES
For police, fire or ambulance, call ☎ 999.

BUSINESS HOURS
Though they vary a bit, typical business hours are from 8 am to 1 pm and 2 to 4 pm Monday to Friday. Most government offices stay open an extra hour on Monday, closing at 5 pm.

PUBLIC HOLIDAYS & SPECIAL EVENTS
Public holidays on Dominica are:

New Year's Day	January 1
Carnival Monday & Tuesday	two days preceding Ash Wednesday
Good Friday	late March/early April
Easter Monday	late March/early April
May Day	May 1
Whit Monday	eighth Monday after Easter
August Monday	first Monday in August
Independence Day	November 3
Community Service Day	November 4
Christmas Day	December 25
Boxing Day	December 26

Dominica's Carnival celebrations are held during the traditional Mardi Gras period. In the two weeks prior to Lent, there are calypso competitions, a Carnival Queen contest, jump-ups and a costume parade.

Creole Day, usually held on the Friday before Independence Day, is a celebration of the island's Creole language and culture and includes traditional dancing, folklore, food and music.

ACTIVITIES
Beaches & Swimming
While Dominica doesn't have the sort of gorgeous strands that make it onto brochure covers, it's not without beaches. On the calmer and more popular west coast they're predominantly black-sand beaches, with the best of the lot in the Portsmouth area.

The east coast is largely open seas with high surf and turbulent water conditions. There are a few pockets of golden sands just south of Calibishie that are sometimes calm enough for swimming and snorkeling and a couple of roadside brown-sand beaches a bit farther south.

Diving
Dominica has superb diving. The island's rugged scenery continues under the water, where it forms sheer drop-offs, volcanic arches, pinnacles and caves.

Many of Dominica's top dive sites are in the Soufriere Bay area. Scotts Head Drop

DOMINICA

is a shallow coral ledge that drops off abruptly to over 150 feet revealing a wall of huge tube sponges and soft corals. Just west of Scotts Head is The Pinnacle, which starts a few feet below the surface and drops down to a series of walls, arches and caves that are rife with stingrays, snappers, barracudas and parrotfish.

Calmer waters more suitable for snorkelers and amateur divers can be found at another undersea mound, the Soufriere Pinnacle, which rises 160 feet from the floor of the bay to within five feet of the surface and offers a wide range of corals and fish. Also popular for snorkelers and beginners is Champagne, a sub-aquatic hot spring off Pointe Guignard, where crystal bubbles rise from underwater vents.

The north side of the island still has lots of unexplored territory. Popular sites north of Roseau include Castaways Reef, Grande Savane, Rodney's Rock, Toucari Bay and the wrecks of a barge and tug off Canefield.

Dive Shops Dive shops on Dominica include:

Anchorage Dive Center, PO Box 34; based at Anchorage Hotel in Castle Comfort (☎ 448-2638, fax 448-5680, anchorage@mailtod.dm)

Dive Castaways, PO Box 5; based at Castaways Beach Hotel in Mero, on the west coast (☎ 449-6244, fax 449-6246)

Dive Dominica, PO Box 63; the island's oldest dive shop, based at Castle Comfort Lodge, just south of Roseau (☎ 448-2188, fax 448-6088, dive@tod.dm; in the USA ☎ 888-262-6611)

East Carib Dive, PO Box 375; on a black-sand beach 1.5 miles north of Castaways Beach Hotel, run by a divemaster from Germany (☎ /fax 449-6575, in the USA ☎ 800-867-4764)

Nature Island Dive; based in Soufriere, just minutes from many of the island's best dive spots (☎ 449-8181, fax 449-8182)

The going rate is about US$45 for a one-tank dive, US$50 for a night dive and US$70 for a two-tank dive. Anchorage offers beginners a resort course with an ocean dive for US$80. A number of the shops offer full PADI certification courses for around US$400.

In addition, Dive Dominica, Nature Island Dive and Anchorage have one-week packages that include accommodations and multiple dives.

Snorkeling

There's good snorkeling in the Soufriere Bay area and at Cabrits National Park. All the dive shops listed in the previous section offer snorkeling tours or will take snorkelers out with divers. If you're chumming along with divers, make sure they're doing a shallow dive – staring down at a wreck 50 feet underwater isn't terribly interesting from the surface.

Anchorage Dive Center has a snorkeling trip to Champagne (see the previous Diving section) and Nature Island Dive offers a snorkeling tour of two sites in Soufriere Bay; both charge US$25, snorkeling gear included.

If you want to strike out on your own, Anchorage rents snorkeling gear for US$10 a day, Nature Island Dive for US$15.

Kayaking

Nature Island Dive (☎ 449-8181) in Soufriere rents sea kayaks for US$11 an hour, US$26 a half-day or US$42 a day. You can paddle around Soufriere Bay or take an excursion up the coastline where there are snorkeling sites that can't be reached by land.

Whale Watching

Whales and dolphins roam the deep waters off Dominica's sheltered west coast. Sperm whales, which grow to a length of 70 feet and have a blunt square snout, are the whales most commonly sighted; the main season is from October to March. Other resident toothed whales are the orca, pygmy sperm whale, pygmy killer whale, false killer whale and pilot whale. In winter, migrating humpback whales are occasionally spotted as well.

Anchorage Dive Centers (☎ 448-2638) and Dive Dominica (☎ 448-2188) run whale-watching boat tours a few times a week from around 2 pm to sunset. Anchorage charges US$40, Dive Dominica US$50.

Sperm whale

Fishing

Deep-sea fishing for marlin, tuna and wahoo aboard a 32-foot sport cruiser is offered by Rainbow Sportfishing (☎ /fax 448-8650, rollei@tod.dm), The cost per boat, with a maximum of six people, is US$400 for five hours, gear included.

Hiking

Dominica has some excellent hiking. Short walks lead to Emerald Pool and Trafalgar Falls, two of the island's most visited sights. Cabrits National Park has a couple of short hikes. In the Northern Forest Reserve, there's an easy hike through a parrot reserve and a rugged trail to the top of the island's highest mountain. The Morne Trois Pitons National Park offers serious treks into the wilderness, ranging from jaunts through verdant jungles to an all-day trek across a steaming volcanic valley that ends at a boiling lake.

The short hikes to the more popular destinations can generally be done on your own but most wilderness treks require a guide who's familiar with the route.

The Forestry Division publishes brochures on many of the trails; each can be purchased for a dollar or so at the forestry headquarters in Roseau's botanical garden.

Individual hikes are described in their relevant sections throughout this chapter.

Mountain Biking

Nature Island Dive (☎ 449-8181) in Soufriere rents mountain bikes for US$11 an hour, US$21 a half-day, US$32 a full day, helmets and water bottles included. You can explore old estate trails and the nearby sulphur springs; the staff can recommend longer outings for serious bikers. Nature Island also leads guided biking trips, with per-person rates of US$55 (with six people) to US$84 (with two people).

ACCOMMODATIONS

Dominica has only about 750 rooms available for visitors, mainly in small, locally run hotels and guesthouses along the west side of the island. There are also three mountain lodges (Papillote, Roxy's and Springfield) just west of Morne Trois Pitons National Park that can make delightful places to stay for those who want to be on the edge of the rainforest.

Bottom-end accommodations are comprised largely of guesthouses in the US$25 to US$50 range. The middle range, about US$60 to US$85, also includes some good values but even the top-end hotels are

---

New User Fees

Hoping to cash in a bit more on the rising number of cruise ship visitors touring the island, the government of Dominica has just instituted user fees for all foreign visitors entering 'ecotourist sites.' These include national parks and other protected areas.

The new fees are set at US$2 per site, US$5 for a day pass or US$10 for a weekly pass. Passes are sold by car rental agencies, tour operators, cruise ship personnel and the forestry department, as well as at some of the sites, such as Cabrits National Park and Emerald Pool. ■

DOMINICA

reasonably priced by Caribbean standards, averaging US$100 to US$125.

Dominica has a 5% room tax and hotels also add a 10% service charge to bills.

FOOD

Dominica's national dish is the mountain chicken, which is not a chicken at all but the legs of a giant frog called the crapaud *(Leptodactylus fallax)*, which is endemic to Dominica and Montserrat. Found at higher elevations, it's a protected species and can only be caught between autumn and February. Crapaud meat is white and tastes similar to chicken.

Creole food is quite prevalent on restaurant menus. Be sure to try callaloo soup. Although no two recipes are identical, on Dominica it's invariably a flavorful, creamy concoction.

The island produces numerous fresh fruits, including bananas, coconuts, papayas, guavas, pineapples and mangoes, the latter so plentiful they commonly drop along the roadside.

DRINKS

Rivers flowing down from the mountains provide Dominica with an abundant supply of pure, fresh drinking water. Water is generally safe to drink from the tap. Fresh fruit juices are inexpensive and readily available at most restaurants. You can also find good punch drinks made from fresh fruit and local rum. Dominica now brews its own beer under the Kubuli label.

ENTERTAINMENT

Friday is the big night for entertainment on Dominica: *Fort Young Hotel* has a happy hour from 6 to 8 pm and live steel-pan music from 7 to 9:30 pm, while the *Q Club Disco* on Bath Rd is the hot spot after 10 pm.

The Warehouse, a dance club in the Canefield area, attracts a crowd on Saturday night. The *Carib Theatre* on Old St has a mixed billing of Hollywood and kung-fu flicks. Other entertainment is largely limited to a sunset drink at one of the hotel bars.

THINGS TO BUY

Dominica produces high-quality baskets using native fibers and traditional Carib designs. Prices are surprisingly moderate and the baskets can be purchased at roadside stands in the Carib Territory or at handicraft shops in Roseau. The handicraft shops also sell woven placemats, hats, pocketbooks and Creole dolls.

At Tropicrafts, at the east end of Queen Mary St in Roseau, you can watch women weaving huge floor mats of verti-vert, a native straw-like grass. Tropicrafts sells a wide range of souvenir items, but you can often find cheaper prices at two smaller gift shops in the center of Roseau, Dominica Handicrafts on Hanover St and Caribana Handcrafts on Cork St.

Dominican Pottery, next to Club de Cave on Mary E Charles Blvd, has attractive, reasonably priced pottery, including some items made at the local prison.

Supermarkets in Rouseau carry locally made food items, such as hot pepper sauce, marmalade and Dominican coffee, as well as island-made coconut oil soap, shampoo and skin creams, all of which make can good inexpensive souvenirs.

Getting There & Away

AIR

There are no international flights into Dominica, so overseas visitors must first get to a gateway island. There are direct flights to Dominica from Antigua, Barbados, Guadeloupe, Martinique, Puerto Rico, St Lucia and St Martin.

If you're island hopping, LIAT has numerous through fares that allow free stopovers on Dominica, including one from Antigua to Martinique for US$133/190 one way/roundtrip. Otherwise, a regular ticket to Dominica from Antigua costs US$99/170 one way/roundtrip, from Martinique US$82/120, from Guadeloupe US$88/147 and from St Lucia US$90/161. Roundtrip fares allow stays of up to 30 days. There are flights to both Canefield and Melville

Hall airports. LIAT's ticketing office (☎ 448-2421) is on King George V St in Roseau.

Air Guadeloupe flies to Canefield airport on Dominica from Guadeloupe twice daily (once on Sunday). Fares are competitive with LIAT. In Dominica, bookings are handled by Whitchurch Travel (☎ 448-2181), Old St, Roseau.

Cardinal Airlines (☎ 448-7432) has at least two flights daily (one on Sunday) between Dominica's Canefield airport and Antigua, Barbados and St Martin. One-way fares are US$83 to Antigua, US$146 to St Martin and US$159 to Barbados; excursion tickets, valid for a seven-day stay, cost US$123 to Antigua, US$187 to Barbados and US$199 to St Martin.

American Eagle (☎ 448-0628) has a daily flight between San Juan and Dominica's Melville Hall airport with a US$210 one-way fare and a US$295 regular round-trip fare, both with no advance purchase required. Discounted promotional deals can drop the roundtrip fare to as little as US$190.

Airport Information

Dominica has two airports: Canefield, just outside Roseau, and Melville Hall, on the secluded northeast side of the island. On LIAT's printed schedule the letters C and M after the departure time indicate which airport is being used.

Canefield Airport There's a tourist information booth open daily from 7 am to 6 pm (closed from 11 am to 2 pm on Saturday and Sunday), a small gift shop that sells phonecards, a snack bar, restrooms and coin, card and USA Direct phones. Avis has a booth here and Budget and Valley car rentals have courtesy phones. If you plan on renting a car, it's usually quicker to get your local license at airport immigration even though you may have to wait until incoming passengers are cleared.

Melville Hall Airport Sitting in the midst of the countryside, this airport looks all but abandoned except at flight time. There's a gift shop, a snack bar, a tourist information booth, restrooms and coin and card phones.

SEA
Inter-Island Ferry

L'Express des Iles connects Dominica with both Guadeloupe and Martinique via modern catamarans that seat about 300 passengers. This is a convenient way to arrive in Dominica, as it leaves you right in the center of Roseau, within walking distance of hotels and guesthouses.

On its southbound run, a boat leaves Pointe-à-Pitre, Guadeloupe, at 8 am on Monday, Wednesday and Saturday, at noon on Friday and at 2 pm on Sunday, arriving in Roseau 1¾ hours later. It then departs from Roseau at 10:15 am on Monday, Wednesday and Saturday, at 2:15 pm on Friday and at 4:15 pm on Sunday, arriving in Fort-de-France, Martinique, 1½ hours later.

Northbound, a boat leaves Martinique for Dominica at 2 pm on Monday and Wednesday, 3 pm on Friday and Sunday and 9 am on Saturday. This boat then continues from Dominica to Guadeloupe at 4 pm on Monday and Wednesday, 5 pm on Friday and Sunday and 11 am on Saturday.

The cost in French francs is 305F one way to Dominica from either Martinique or Guadeloupe, but it's only 10F more to make the one-way trip between Martinique and Guadeloupe with a free stopover on Dominica. From either Martinique or Guadeloupe the roundtrip fare to Dominica is 450F.

From Dominica, the fares are paid in Eastern Caribbean dollars; the one-way fare is EC$104 to Guadeloupe, EC$122 to Martinique.

On Friday at 2:15 pm the boat can be taken from Dominica to Castries, St Lucia, and on Saturday at 7 am and Sunday at 1 pm it can be taken from Castries to Dominica. The St Lucia-Dominica trip takes 3½ hours and costs EC$157 one way; roundtrip fares are double.

There are discounts of 50% for children ages two to 11 and 10% for passengers under 26 or older than 60. Reservations are made on Dominica through Whitchurch

Travel (☎ 448-2181), Old St, Roseau. For information in Martinique call ☎ 63 12 11, in Guadeloupe ☎ 83 12 45 and in St Lucia ☎ 452-2211.

Yacht

Yachts can clear immigration and customs at Roseau, Portsmouth or Anse Du Mé and get a coastal permit that allows visits at other ports and anchorages along the coast. Mooring in Soufriere Bay, now a marine reserve, is no longer permitted.

Cruise Ship

A growing number of cruise ships call on Dominica, most docking at the new terminal in the center of Roseau.

In hopes of encouraging cruise ship visitors to spend more time in the northern part of the island, a smaller cruise ship berth was opened at Cabrits National Park, a scenic setting and the site of historic Fort Shirley.

LEAVING DOMINICA

Visitors ages 12 and older who have stayed more than 24 hours must pay an EC$30 (or a US$12) departure tax when leaving Dominica.

Getting Around

Dominica is a visitor-friendly island. Road signs mark most towns and villages, and major intersections are clearly signposted.

Primary roads are usually narrow but in good shape – most are well paved and pothole free. Secondary roads vary and while some are quite rutted it's possible to explore the island thoroughly by car. Be careful of deep rain gutters that run along the side of many roads – a slip into one could easily bring any car to a grinding halt.

THE AIRPORT

Avis is the only car rental agency at Canefield airport, but other agencies will provide customers with free airport pickup. Taxis are readily available but if you're traveling light you could also walk out to the road and catch a bus into town.

From Melville Hall airport, there are no car rentals, so visitors must take a shared taxi, even if they intend to rent a car during their stay.

BUS

Buses, which are mostly minivans, run regularly along the coastal routes between Roseau and both Scotts Head and Portsmouth, although the farther north you go past Canefield the less frequent they become. Evening buses are few and there's no Sunday bus service along most routes.

In Roseau you can catch buses heading south for Scotts Head (EC$3) from the Old Market. The same bus will drop you in the Castle Comfort area for EC$1. Buses heading to Canefield (EC$1.50), the Carib Territory (EC$7) and Portsmouth (EC$7.50) leave from the east side of the Roseau River near the public market. Buses to Trafalgar (EC$2.25) and Laudat (EC$3) leave from the north side of the police station.

TAXI

From Canefield Airport, the fares for one taxi (up to four people) are EC$20 to Roseau, EC$25 to the Castle Comfort area, EC$65 to Scotts Head, EC$75 to the Layou area and EC$110 to Portsmouth.

From Melville Airport, the taxis are shared and rates are charged on a per-person basis: EC$42 to Roseau; EC$44 to Castle Comfort and EC$30 to Portsmouth.

CAR
Road Rules

Dominicans drive on the left-hand side of the road. Visiting drivers must be between ages 25 and 65 and have a valid driver's license and at least two years' driving experience to drive in Dominica. In addition, a local driver's license (EC$30) is required, which can be picked up from immigration at either airport any day of the week. Licenses can also be obtained Monday to Friday at the Traffic Department, High St, Roseau. Hours are from 8:30 am to 1 pm and 2 to 3 pm (to 4 pm on

Monday). However, when there's a queue (and they move slowly!) the office door is commonly shut 10 to 15 minutes before closing time. As a courtesy, car rental agencies will usually pick you up and take you to get your license.

There are gas stations in larger towns around the island, including Canefield, Portsmouth and Marigot.

Rental

Avis (☎ 448-2481) is the only car rental company right at Canefield airport and also has an office at 4 High St in Roseau. Daily rates begin at US$48.

Budget (☎ 449-2080), in the village of Canefield, has a courtesy phone at the airport, provides free pickup and has relatively attractive rates, beginning at US$35.

There are many other car rental agencies on the island, including Courtesy Car Rental (☎ 448-7763), Wide Range Car Rentals (☎ 448-2198) and STL Rent-A-Car (☎ 448-2340), all in Roseau; and Valley Rent-A-Car, which has offices in both Roseau (☎ 448-3233) and Portsmouth (☎ 445-5252).

Note that although most car rentals include unlimited mileage, a few local companies cap the number of free miles before a surcharge is added, so be sure to inquire in advance.

In addition to rental fees, most companies charge US$6 to US$8 a day for an optional collision damage waiver (CDW), though even with the CDW you may still be responsible for the first US$600 or so in damages.

HITCHHIKING

Hitchhiking is quite popular among islanders. While some islanders walk out into the street and attempt to wave drivers down, the most acceptable stance is to stand at the side of the road and hold out an open hand. The usual safety precautions apply.

ORGANIZED TOURS

There are a number of small companies that provide standard sightseeing tours, wilderness hiking tours or both.

Raffoul Luxury Tours (☎ 448-2895) offers several bus tours, including a half-day outing that takes in Trafalgar Falls, Emerald Pool and Roseau's botanical gardens for US$20 and a six-hour round-the-island tour for US$48.

For other vehicle tours you might try Mally's Tour and Taxi Service (☎ 448-3114) or Whitchurch Travel (☎ 448-2181), and for hiking tours Ken's Hinterland Adventure Tours (☎ 448-4850) or Antours Dominica (☎ 448-6460).

Hiking guides can also be arranged through many hotels and guesthouses (Hagan, at Ma Bass Central Guest House, does a fine job) and in Laudat village, where the hikes begin.

Most taxis can be hired for sightseeing tours at a rate of EC$45 per hour for up to four people.

Roseau

Roseau is a colorful West Indian capital, its streets lined with old stone-and-wood buildings. Some are strikingly picturesque with jalousied windows, gingerbread trim and overhanging balconies, while others are little more than weathered shells leaning precariously out over sidewalks. Many of the buildings are two-story structures with shops below and living quarters above. There are a growing number of modern cement structures too, but for the most part walking Roseau's quieter back streets feels like stepping back a hundred years.

While Roseau is one of the region's poorer capitals, it's not one of the grimmer ones. Shopkeepers wash down the sidewalks every morning, police walk their beats with a rhythmic stride and most people are quite friendly.

Roseau's waterfront, which was severely damaged by Hurricane David, has undergone an ambitious reclamation and now boasts a new cruise ship dock and a promenade with a good view of Scotts Head to the south. A particularly scenic vantage is from the balcony of the new museum.

DOMINICA

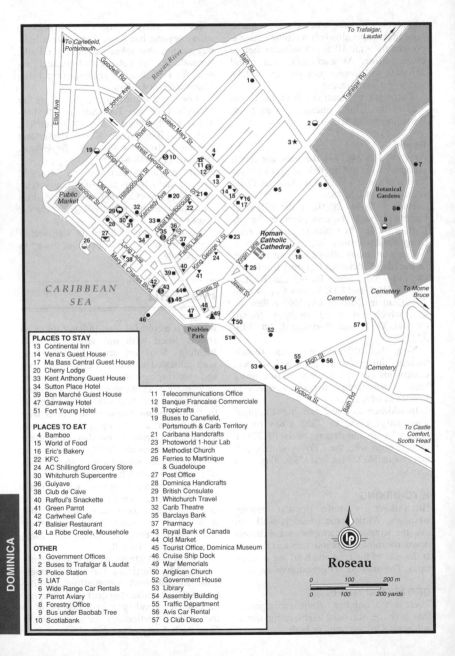

PLACES TO STAY
13 Continental Inn
14 Vena's Guest House
17 Ma Bass Central Guest House
20 Cherry Lodge
33 Kent Anthony Guest House
34 Sutton Place Hotel
39 Bon Marché Guest House
47 Garraway Hotel
51 Fort Young Hotel

PLACES TO EAT
4 Bamboo
15 World of Food
16 Eric's Bakery
22 KFC
24 AC Shillingford Grocery Store
30 Whitchurch Supercentre
36 Guiyave
38 Club de Cave
40 Raffoul's Snackette
41 Green Parrot
42 Cartwheel Cafe
47 Balisier Restaurant
48 La Robe Creole, Mousehole

OTHER
1 Government Offices
2 Buses to Trafalgar & Laudat
3 Police Station
5 LIAT
6 Wide Range Car Rentals
7 Parrot Aviary
8 Forestry Office
9 Bus under Baobab Tree
10 Scotiabank

11 Telecommunications Office
12 Banque Francaise Commerciale
18 Tropicrafts
19 Buses to Canefield,
   Portsmouth & Carib Territory
21 Caribana Handcrafts
23 Photoworld 1-hour Lab
25 Methodist Church
26 Ferries to Martinique
   & Guadeloupe
27 Post Office
28 Dominica Handicrafts
29 British Consulate
31 Whitchurch Travel
32 Carib Theatre
35 Barclays Bank
37 Pharmacy
43 Royal Bank of Canada
44 Old Market
45 Tourist Office, Dominica Museum
46 Cruise Ship Dock
49 War Memorials
50 Anglican Church
52 Government House
53 Library
54 Assembly Building
55 Traffic Department
56 Avis Car Rental
57 Q Club Disco

Roseau

0   100   200 m
0   100   200 yards

Roseau, incidentally, is pronounced 'rose-oh' and is named after a local reed.

Information
Tourist Office The tourist office, at the west side of the Old Market, is open weekdays from 8 am to 1 pm and 2 to 4 pm (to 5 pm on Monday) and from 8 am to noon on Saturday.

Money There are several banks in Roseau. Barclays Bank on Old St is open from 8 am to 3 pm Monday to Thursday, 8 am to 5 pm on Friday. Royal Bank of Canada near the Old Market has the same business hours, but also has a 24-hour ATM that accepts credit cards and Cirrus and Plus bank cards.

Post & Communications The post office, on Mary E Charles Blvd, is open from 8 am to 4 pm Tuesday to Friday, until 5 pm on Monday.

You can buy phonecards, make calls, send faxes and check email at the telecommunications office on the corner of Queen Mary St and Kennedy Ave; it's open from 8 am to 7 pm Monday to Friday. There's a row of coin and card phones at the corner of Hanover and Hillsborough streets.

Old Market
The cobblestone plaza and small covered arcade of the Old Market is the site of a former slave market. A wrought iron Victorian memorial marks the old block where the auctions took place. Today the area is used by vendors selling T-shirts, straw hats, baskets and other handicrafts.

Dominica Museum
This worthwhile little museum, on the 2nd floor of the same bayfront building that houses the tourist office, offers an insightful glimpse into the culture and history of the Dominican people.

You'll find Amerindian artifacts including stone axes and other tools, clay adornos and a dug-out gommier canoe. Informative displays delve into Carib lifestyles, Creole culture and the slave trade. There's also a collection of French and English colonial coins used on Dominica in the 18th and 19th centuries. It's open weekdays from 9 am to 4 pm, Saturday until noon. Admission is EC$2.

Public Market
The public market, along the riverfront at the west end of Mary E Charles Blvd, is open from sunrise to about 4 pm daily, except Sunday. You can find fresh fruit, vegetables and herbs – if you hear the blowing of a conch shell then there's also fresh fish for sale.

Churches
Roseau's Roman Catholic cathedral, on Virgin Lane above the Methodist Church, is an old stone edifice with an expansive interior. The windows are of typical Gothic shape but only the upper part is stained glass; the lower sections are wooden shutters that open to catch cross breezes. While the church is not a must-see sight, it's nicely maintained and worth a peek if you're in the area.

The Anglican Church, opposite the Fort Young Hotel, is a gray stone-block church that was left with only its shell standing in 1979 after Hurricane David ripped off the original roof, which has been replaced with tin.

Library Area
The public library on Victoria St was built in 1905 with funding from US philanthropist Andrew Carnegie. It has an old veranda with a sea view and a grand streetside cannonball tree that blooms in late spring. Government House, the white mansion with the expansive lawn, and a new Assembly building are opposite the library.

Botanical Gardens
The 40-acre botanical gardens, which date from 1890, are on the northeast side of town below Morne Bruce hill. It's a pleasant place to take a stroll. There are big banyan trees, flowering tropical shrubs and an aviary housing Jaco and Sisserou parrots, the two parrot species found in Dominica's rainforests.

Brochures describing the island's parks and trails are sold at the park headquarters. Nearby you'll find a monument of sorts to Hurricane David – a school bus crushed under the weight of a huge baobab tree that fell during the 1979 hurricane.

You can drive into the gardens from entrances off Bath Rd or Trafalgar Rd until 10 pm or walk in any time. Admission is free.

Places to Stay

Town Center The *Kent Anthony Guest House* (☎ 488-2730), 3 Great Marlborough St, is rather cheerless with sloping floors, peeling linoleum and furniture to match, but the rates are hard to beat at US$13/22 for singles/doubles. Add US$8 more for a room with a private bath.

Vena's Guest House (☎ 448-3286), is on a noisy corner at 48 Cork St. It occupies the site of author Jean Rhys' birthplace, but it's on the shabby side and the rooms are uninviting. Singles/doubles begin at US$20/25 for a room with shared bath.

Bon Marché Guest House (☎ 488-2083), 11 Old St, is a small guesthouse not far from the waterfront. The four rooms have foam mattresses, portable fans and private baths. There's a shared kitchen and living room with cable TV. Overall, it's a good value for the price range, with singles/doubles costing US$20/30 in a room with one double bed and US$30/40 in a room with two beds. The office is in the store below the guesthouse. On Sunday and after 5 pm you can reach the owners at ☎ 448-4194.

Ma Bass Central Guest House (☎ 448-2999), 44 Fields Lane, is Roseau's best guesthouse. The friendly owner, Theresa Emanuel (better known as Ma Bass), keeps the place spotlessly clean and goes out of her way to make guests feel at home. There are eight fan-cooled rooms that cost US$25/35 for singles/doubles with shared bath, US$45/50 with private bath. This three-story building rises above its neighbors and has a balcony with a good view of the town. For an additional US$5, there's a full kitchen guests can use, and with advance notice Ma Bass will cook up reasonably priced breakfasts and dinners.

Cherry Lodge (☎ 448-2366), 20 Kennedy Ave, a small family-run place, occupies an interesting old wooden building. The rooms are quite simple; the upper section of wall between them is open to allow air (and consequently noise) to circulate. Some rooms have balconies and a private shower and toilet, though the latter is separated from the rest of the room only by a vinyl curtain. Singles/doubles cost US$25/38.

Continental Inn (☎ 448-2214, fax 448-7022), 37 Queen Mary St, has a dozen rooms, most quite small and straightforward, but it's clean and ranks as one of the more comfortable of Roseau's budget accommodations. All rooms are freshly painted, some have just beds and a fan, others TV and air-con as well. The four rooms with shared bath cost from US$30/45 for singles/doubles, while those with private bath cost from US$40/55. Some of the walls are thin, so you might want earplugs. Credit cards are accepted and there's a small inexpensive restaurant.

Sutton Place Hotel (☎ 449-8700, fax 448-3045, sutton2@tod.dm), PO Box 2333, at 25 Old St, is a classy new boutique-style hotel in the town center. The five standard rooms have ceiling fans, air-con, cable TV, phones and hair dryers and cost US$75/95 for singles/doubles. The three suites also have antique furnishings, hardwood floors and kitchenettes and cost US$105/135. Continental breakfast is included in the rates.

Garraway Hotel (☎ 449-8800, fax 449-8807, garraway@tod.dm; in the USA ☎ 800-223-6510), PO Box 789, a new five-story hotel at the east end of the bay front, has Roseau's cushiest rooms. All 31 rooms are spacious with ocean views and full amenities, including fans, air-con, cable TV, phone, one king or two double beds, and bathrooms with tubs. Choicest are the top-floor units, which have a natural wood decor. Singles/doubles cost US$95/110. Commodious suites, which have the addition of a pull-out couch, cost from US$120 to US$155.

Fort Young Hotel (☎ 448-5000, fax 448-5006; in the USA ☎ 800-223-6510), PO Box 519, is on Victoria St, a few minutes south of the town center. This tourist-class hotel incorporates the walls of the 18th-century Fort Young, which once guarded the eastern flank of the capital. While they're not the spiffiest in town, the 33 rooms have hardwood floors, tiled baths, screened louvered windows, ceiling fans, air-con, cable TV and phone. Deluxe rooms, which are on the 2nd floor, also have private oceanview balconies and cathedral ceilings. Singles/doubles begin at US$95/115 in summer, US$105/125 in winter; add an extra US$10 for superior rooms.

Around Castle Comfort The following four hotels are all in a row on a rocky shoreline in the Castle Comfort area, a mile south of Roseau.

The *Sisserou Hotel* (☎ 448-3111, fax 448-3130), PO Box 134, has 24 small, ordinary rooms with air-con, TV and phone. Although the rooms have a fresh coat of paint, the place otherwise feels a bit neglected. The regular rates are US$75/95 for singles/doubles, but there's sometimes a more reasonable 'special rate' of US$42/57.

The *Anchorage Hotel* (☎ 448-2638, fax 448-5680, anchorage@mailtod.dm; in the USA ☎ 800-328-5336), PO Box 34, has 32 pleasant rooms with air-con, cable TV, phone and private balconies. Standard rooms have one double and one single bed and cost US$65/85 for singles/doubles. Superior rooms, which are larger, have two double beds and ocean views, cost US$80/110. Add US$15 more for a third person. There's a small pool, a squash court, a restaurant and a dive shop.

The *Evergreen Hotel* (☎ 448-3288, fax 448-6800), PO Box 309, is an appealing 16-room hotel with a tropical atmosphere. The buildings incorporate native woods and stonework, and the rooms are comfortable, each with air-con, cable TV, phone and

screened windows. The 2nd-floor rooms in the new wing have wonderful oceanfront balconies. Single/double rates, which include breakfast, are US$78/103 for standard rooms and US$88/118 for oceanview rooms. A third person is US$25 more. There's a restaurant, bar and small pool.

Castle Comfort Lodge (☎ 448-2188, fax 448-6088, dive@tod.dm; in the USA ☎ 888-262-6611), PO Box 2253, caters mostly to divers on dive packages. The 15 simple rooms vary in size and amenities, but all have air-con and ceiling fans and some have TVs. Rates are US$80/105 for singles/doubles, breakfast included.

Places to Eat – budget

The *Mousehole*, downstairs from La Robe Creole restaurant, has inexpensive rotis, meat pies, sandwiches and pastries. You can get a nice slab of banana bread for EC$1.25 and a large glass of fresh, creamy papaya or guava juice for EC$3.50. While most people order takeout, there's also a small counter where you can chow down. It's open from 8 am to 9 pm Monday to Saturday.

The *Cartwheel Cafe* on Mary E Charles Blvd is a pleasant little eatery in an historic waterfront building with thick stone walls. The menu, which includes standard breakfast items and lunchtime sandwiches, is priced mostly from EC$5 to EC$10. It's open weekdays from 7:30 am to 3:30 pm.

Guiyave, 15 Cork St, has dining on a pleasant 2nd-floor balcony. Breakfast, from 8 to 11:30 am, includes French toast and egg dishes, served with juice or coffee, for EC$12 to EC$21. From noon to 3 pm, sandwiches and burgers cost EC$5 to EC$12, goat and chicken meals around EC$20. On Saturday, local dishes such as rotis, goat water and souse are available. If you want value over atmosphere, there's a downstairs bakery/cafeteria with reasonably priced though rather average quiches and pastries as well as EC$14 plate lunches. It's closed on Sunday.

The *Green Parrot*, a little 2nd-floor eatery on King George V St, has sandwiches starting at EC$4, chicken & chips for EC$10 and full vegetarian, chicken and fish meals for EC$20. It's open weekdays from 8 am to 8 pm and Saturday from 8 am to 2 pm.

Club de Cave on Mary E Charles Blvd is a basement café serving good key lime pie for EC$5, full bacon and egg breakfasts or lunchtime fish & chips for under EC$15 and dinners for about double that. It's open daily from 8:30 am to whenever things get slow in the evening.

Bamboo, 72 Queen Mary St, is a small, tidy Chinese restaurant that's open daily to 11 pm. From 11 am to 3 pm there are lunch specials for EC$12. Otherwise, vegetarian dishes cost EC$15 and a range of chicken, pork or seafood dishes are EC$20 to EC$25. You can also call ahead for takeout (☎ 448-1921).

World of Food, an open-air courtyard restaurant at Vena's Guest House, 48 Cork St, is a popular spot for an after-work drink. Sandwiches cost around EC$5 and rabbit or goat meals are EC$20 at both lunch and dinner.

KFC, on Great George St, has the usual two pieces of fried chicken, fries and a Coke for EC$11 and is open from 10 am (noon on Sunday) to 11 pm daily.

For a cheap breakfast snack, pick up a tasty currant slice (EC$1.15) at *Eric's Bakery* on Queen Mary St; it's open weekdays from 8 am to noon and 3 to 6 pm.

Raffoul's Snackette, 13 King George V St, is essentially a bread outlet but also sells inexpensive sandwiches from 8:30 am to 4 pm weekdays.

There are a number of grocery stores around town, the largest being *Whitchurch Supercentre* on Old St, which has a deli with cooked chicken, sliced meats and bakery products. It's open from 8 am to 7 pm Monday to Thursday, to 8 pm Friday and Saturday. The *public market* is the place to get fruit and vegetables.

Places to Eat – top end

Sutton Grille at the Sutton Place Hotel, 25 Old St, has a nice historic atmosphere. Between 7 and 10 am, you can get a breakfast

of juice, coffee and a croissant for EC$13. At lunchtime, 11:30 am to 3 pm, a grilled chicken or tuna filet sandwich costs EC$10; the 'business lunch buffet' of chicken, fish, red meat, salad, rice and local vegetables is EC$25. At dinner the specialty is steak, with prices jumping to EC$75.

La Robe Creole, 3 Victoria St, has good Creole food and an engaging setting with stone walls, high-back chairs and waitresses in traditional Creole dress. The callaloo soup has a creamy coconut base and costs EC$8, while the Creole fish (EC$40) is a tasty main dish, accompanied by plantain, dasheen and sweet potato. The restaurant makes a powerful rum punch and good fresh fruit juices and desserts. There's also a varied snack menu and an inexpensive kids' menu. It's open from noon to about 10 pm Monday to Saturday.

The *Fort Young Hotel*'s restaurant incorporates the stone wall of the fort, though it's a bit too hall-like to make for an intimate dining experience. It has typical breakfast fare for around EC$20, a daily three-course lunch for EC$35 and main courses at dinner for around EC$40. The best time to visit is on Friday evenings, when there's a festive Caribbean buffet accompanied by live steel-pan music for EC$45.

The *Balisier Restaurant*, on the 2nd floor of the Garraway Hotel, has a great view of Scotts Head. A breakfast of coconut bread, muffin, coffee and juice costs EC$9, full breakfasts about double that. At lunch and dinner, curried goat, ginger pork and seafood main dishes average EC$50. On Friday from 12:30 to 2:30 pm there's a special EC$45 buffet lunch.

In the Castle Comfort area, the *Evergreen Hotel* has a very pleasant seaside terrace dining room. Breakfast and lunch has the usual fare at moderate prices. A full soup-to-dessert dinner costs EC$50 to EC$60, depending on the main course, which includes fish, chicken and a changing third choice. The restaurant at the nearby *Anchorage Hotel* has a vegetarian dinner plate for EC$30 and goat casserole or fresh fish for EC$50.

Around Dominica

MORNE BRUCE

Morne Bruce is a rather exclusive hillside suburb that's southeast of Roseau. It has a couple of places to stay but most people who venture up this way do so for the panoramic hilltop view of Roseau and its surroundings.

One way to get to the viewpoint is to drive up and park below the president's office. You can also hike up from the botanical gardens; the trail begins just east of the parrot aviary and takes about 15 minutes to walk.

Places to Stay & Eat

Itassi Cottages (☎ 448-7247, fax 448-3045), PO Box 1333, is in an exclusive hillside neighborhood with a view of Roseau and Scotts Head. These cottages, which have cooking facilities, phone and TV, cost US$60 for one or two people, US$90 for three or four and US$110 for five or six. There's also a studio unit that costs US$40 for one or two people. The manager prefers to rent the units on a weekly basis, which costs six times the daily rate, but accepts daily rentals when they're not full.

Reigate Hall Hotel (☎ 448-4031, fax 448-4034) is in the Reigate area on a hill above Morne Bruce. It has the character of a small mountain inn and a superb view of Roseau a mile below. The 17 rooms are rather simply appointed but they are modern and have air-con and private balconies. Single rooms, which are quite small, cost US$65, while doubles cost US$75 and larger, more comfortable suites cost US$145. There's a small pool, a sauna and a tennis court. The Reigate Hall Hotel is at the very end of a rather tortuous one-lane road.

Breakfast and lunch at Reigate Hall are moderately priced, while dinner features dishes such as fish Creole for around EC$50.

CANEFIELD AREA

Canefield, a 10-minute drive north of Roseau, is half suburbia, half industrial, and the site of the main inter-island airport. While Canefield isn't much of a tourist area there are a few places to stay, and because it's on a main bus route, getting into Roseau is fairly easy without a car.

Pringles Bay, just south of the airport, is a popular swimming spot for local residents despite being in an industrial setting with a commercial loading dock nearby. There are a couple of wrecks that can be dived in the area: a tugboat in about 65 feet of water near the river mouth and a barge about 10 feet below the surface at the side of a reef.

Half a mile south of the airport, you'll see the **Old Mill Cultural Centre**, an attractive stone building with gears from the old mill rusting on its grounds. Although the center doesn't have regular visitor hours, it occasionally opens for special functions.

In **Massacre**, a small village north of the airport, a mural along the main road commemorates the 1674 Carib massacre after which the town is named.

Massacre

Philip Warner, son of a 17th-century St Kitts governor, was responsible for a ruthless massacre of Carib Indians on Dominica in 1674, as well as for the murder of 'Indian' Warner, his half-brother.

Indian Warner, who had the same father as Philip but whose mother was a Dominican Carib, left his English upbringing on St Kitts to return to Dominica where he became a Carib chief. Philip Warner, leading a contingent of British troops intent on seeking vengeance for Carib raids on St Kitts, tricked his half-brother into meeting him on the west coast of Dominica in the village now known as Massacre, where Philip then ambushed Indian Warner along with his entire tribe. ■

Places to Stay & Eat

Nello Inn (☎ 449-1840), on the main road about a five-minute walk south of the airport, has four straightforward rooms with air-con, fans and shared bath for US$26/50 for singles/doubles. There's a little shop selling simple snacks and drinks downstairs.

The *Ambassador Hotel* (☎ 449-1501, fax 449-2304), PO Box 2413, is a rather lackluster place a minutes walk from Nello Inn. It has 10 rooms with foam mattresses, private baths, fans, phones and shared balconies. Singles/doubles cost US$50/68. There's a dining room in the hotel and the village grocer is across the street.

The *Hummingbird Inn* (☎ /fax 449-1042), PO Box 1901, on the main road midway between Canefield and Roseau, is 250 yards up a steep driveway just south of the West Indies gas station. All in all, it's not a terribly convenient location. There are 10 rooms with private baths from US$55/65 for singles/doubles. There's a dining room with good, albeit sometimes slow, food at moderate prices.

Springfield Plantation Guest House (☎ 449-1401, fax 449-2160, springfield@ tod.dm), PO Box 456, is a winding 10-minute drive inland from Canefield. This scenic mountain retreat, perched on a 1215-foot cliff, is part of the Archbold Tropical Research Station, a holding of the Clemson University of South Carolina. The former plantation is now used to house visiting scientists studying tropical ecosystems and as a center for nature tourism. The old plantation house is a bit weathered but quite atmospheric, and has large rooms with hardwood floors, eclectic furnishings, a smattering of antiques and grand veranda views. Rates begin at US$50/70 for singles/doubles. Breakfast and dinner can be included for an additional US$25 per person.

Springfield Plantation also has a few one- and two-bedroom apartments in an adjacent annex. These vary in size and have a mountain cabin decor, but they are quite adequate, have cooking facilities, phone, shower and private veranda, and cost US$60 for a one-bedroom unit, US$65 for two bedrooms.

LAYOU RIVER AREA

The Layou River, Dominica's longest, empties into the sea just south of St Joseph, at the center of the west coast. The river basin is a peaceful rural area, with bamboo leaning over the river banks and banana and coconut trees at the side of the road. When it's not running strong, the river is a popular place for freshwater swimming.

St Joseph, a simple fishing village of 2600 people, rises up the slope from a small black-sand beach, but the area's best beach is farther north at the Castaways Beach Hotel in Mero. There's good swimming in front of Castaways and fair snorkeling along the rock formations at the southern end of its beach – with a little luck you might even spot sting rays or octopus.

Just north of Mero, on the inland side of the coastal road, is the **Macoucherie Rum Distillery**. The distillery crushes sugar cane grown in the surrounding fields using an old-fashioned water wheel. There are no formal tours but you can view the operation from 7 am to 3 pm Monday to Friday. This rum is very popular on Dominica, with some islanders claiming it has aphrodisiac qualities.

The coastal road continues north along the leeward side of Dominica's highest mountain range, an effective rain screen that makes this region one of the driest on the island.

Places to Stay

The *Layou River Hotel* (☎ 449-6281, fax 449-6713), PO Box 8, has a pleasant waterside setting on the north side of the Layou River, 1.25 miles inland from the coastal road. The 34 air-conditioned rooms each have a bath, phone and either a double bed or two twin beds. Singles/doubles cost US$78/98 in the winter and US$70/82 in the summer. Guests can avail themselves of the pool; the hotel's owners are also in the process of building a new resort on the land across the road.

The *Castaways Beach Hotel* (☎ 449-6244, fax 449-6246, castaways@mail-tod-dom), PO Box 5, is an inviting place on a long, attractive gray-sand beach fronted by calm waters. There are 26 rooms in two wings. Those in the south wing have one double bed, while those in the north wing have two single beds and are a bit bigger. All are pleasant enough and have ceiling fans, shower, phone and ocean-fronting balconies. Singles/doubles cost US$82/ 110. There's a dive operation on site, a small dock and a tennis court.

Places to Eat

The *Castaways Beach Hotel* restaurant has a casual open-air setting overlooking the water and makes a nice place to stop for breakfast on your way north. Haitian, Creole and continental breakfasts cost from EC$18 to EC$24.

The restaurant at the *Layou River Hotel* has a less interesting setting and more standard fare, including continental (EC$23) and American (EC$26) breakfasts. Both restaurants also serve lunch and dinner at moderate prices.

NORTHERN FOREST RESERVE

The Northern Forest Reserve is an extensive area that encompasses 22,000 acres of land in the interior of the island, including the 4747-foot Morne Diablotin, the island's highest peak. The main habitat of Dominica's two endangered parrot species is in the eastern section of the reserve.

To get to the reserve, turn east on the signposted road that begins just north of the village of Dublanc and continue to the Syndicate Estate, about 4.5 miles inland. There you'll find an easy mile-long loop trail (Syndicate Trail) to a parrot observatory platform as well as the start of the trail leading up Morne Diablotin, a rugged hike that's best done with a guide (see Organized Tours in the Getting Around section earlier in this chapter). The best times for sighting parrots are in the early morning and late afternoon, when the birds are most active.

PORTSMOUTH

Portsmouth, Dominica's second-largest town, sits on the banks of Prince Rupert Bay. Columbus entered the bay during his

fourth voyage to the New World in 1504, and three decades later the Spanish established a supply station here for their galleons. It was visited by 16th-century buccaneers Sir Francis Drake and his rival John Hawkins, as well as by Prince Rupert of the Rhine.

In 1607, Captain John Smith and his followers stopped for a couple of days before heading north to establish Jamestown, North America's first permanent English settlement. Indeed, the harbor was so important to the British that they intended to make Portsmouth the island's capital until outbreaks of malaria and yellow fever thwarted the plan.

Cabrits National Park on the north side of town and Indian River to the south are the area's noteworthy attractions. Although Portsmouth center doesn't have any sights per se, there are a couple of oddities you might want to take a look at: the small but colorful monument at the bus stop dedicated to Lord Cathcart 'who died of the bloody flux off Dominica in 1741' and the nearby line of shipwrecks piled up in the shallow waters at the back of the police station.

Prince Rupert Bay is a lovely harbor whose grand scale is most easily appreciated when seen from the hills at Cabrits National Park. There are stretches of black

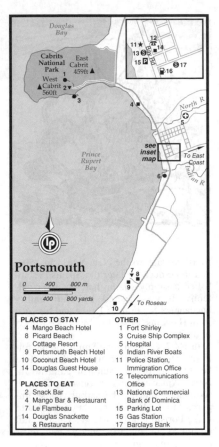

Portsmouth

PLACES TO STAY	OTHER
4 Mango Beach Hotel	1 Fort Shirley
8 Picard Beach	3 Cruise Ship Complex
Cottage Resort	5 Hospital
9 Portsmouth Beach Hotel	6 Indian River Boats
10 Coconut Beach Hotel	11 Police Station,
14 Douglas Guest House	Immigration Office
	12 Telecommunications
PLACES TO EAT	Office
2 Snack Bar	13 National Commercial
4 Mango Bar & Restaurant	Bank of Dominica
7 Le Flambeau	15 Parking Lot
14 Douglas Snackette	16 Gas Station
& Restaurant	17 Barclays Bank

sand along much of the bay, with the nicest beach fronting Portsmouth Beach Hotel. Snorkeling is reasonable along the north side of the hotel pier.

Douglas Bay, a couple of miles north of Portsmouth, also has a black-sand beach and decent snorkeling. A good paved road leads to Douglas Bay, but the area remains a bit of a backwater well off the tourist track.

Information

The police and immigration office is on Bay Rd, which is the main road that runs through the center of town. The National Commercial Bank of Dominica is south of the police station and south of that is a small parking lot where you can pick up the bus to Roseau. You'll find a Barclays Bank on the road to the east coast.

Indian River

Just south of town you can expect to be met by a handful of rowers ready and willing to take you on a boat ride up the Indian River. The boats wind up the shady river through tall swamp bloodwood trees whose buttressed trunks rise out of the shallows, their roots stretching out laterally along the river banks. It can be a fascinating outing, taking you into an otherwise inaccessible habitat and offering a close-up view of the creatures that live at the water's edge.

The rowers, who set up shop along the coastal road at the river mouth, charge EC$25 per person for a tour that takes about an hour.

Cabrits National Park

Cabrits National Park, on a scenic peninsula 1.25 miles north of Portsmouth, is best known as the site of Fort Shirley. In addition to the peninsula the park encompasses the surrounding coastal area as well as the island's largest swamp. The Cabrits Peninsula, formed by two extinct volcanoes, separates Prince Rupert Bay from Douglas Bay. The coral reefs and waters of the latter are also part of the park.

While the British built a small battery on Cabrits in 1765, it wasn't until 1774 that they began constructing the main elements of Fort Shirley. In 1778, the French captured the island and continued work on the fort. Between the two vying powers, a formidable garrison was built. France's effort proved to be counterproductive, as Dominica was returned to the British under the 1783 Treaty of Paris and the fort was subsequently used to repel French attacks.

Fort Shirley had more than 50 major structures, including seven gun batteries, quarters for as many as 600 officers and soldiers, numerous storehouses and a hospital. Following the cessation of hostilities between the British and French, the fort gradually slipped into disrepair and in 1854 was abandoned.

Today Cabrits is a fun place to explore. Some of the stone ruins have been cleared and partially reconstructed, while others remain half-hidden in the jungle. The powder magazine to the right of the fort entrance has been turned into a small museum with exhibits on the restoration and a display of artifacts unearthed during that work. From the nearby ruins of the Officer's Quarters there's a fine view of Prince Rupert Bay.

The fort is home to scores of ground lizards *(Ameiva fuscata)* that scurry about the ruins and along the hiking trails that lead up to the two volcanic peaks. The trail up the 560-foot West Cabrit begins at the back side of Fort Shirley and the hike takes about 30 minutes. Most of the walk passes through a wooded area but there's a panoramic view at the top.

There's a parking lot at the end of the road next to the cruise ship complex, where there's a handicraft center, restrooms and a dock. The path up to the fort begins at the nearby snack shop; it takes about five minutes to reach the main cluster of buildings and the museum.

Places to Stay

Douglas Guest House (☎ 445-5253), in town opposite the bus stop, has nine basic but clean rooms with shared bath for US$12/24 singles/doubles.

Mango Beach Hotel (☎ 445-3099) is a tidy two-story guesthouse on the beach at the northern end of town. There are eight straightforward rooms with two beds, a refrigerator, fan and private bath. Singles/doubles cost US$30/40.

Portsmouth Beach Hotel (☎ 445-5142), PO Box 34, is on a nice black-sand beach half a mile south of town. While there are 96 rooms, most are rented out to foreign students who attend the nearby Ross University medical school. However, the choicest wing, the one nearest the beach, sometimes has rooms available on a daily basis for US$60. Rooms are clean and straightforward with showers, phones, ceiling fans and screened

louvered windows. There's a pool and restaurant.

Picard Beach Cottage Resort (☎ 445-5131, fax 445-5599; in the USA ☎ 800-223-6510), which is next to Portsmouth Beach Hotel and shares the same management, has eight pleasantly rustic cottages with big oceanfront porches. Each has a separate bedroom, a small kitchenette and a dining/living room with two single beds. Cottages right on the beach cost US$120/140 for singles/doubles, while those a little farther back are US$100/120. In summer they'll sometimes discount these rates by a full 50%.

Coconut Beach Hotel (☎ 445-5393, fax 445-5693), PO Box 37, is on the beach a mile south of town. Good-sized rooms with kitchenettes on the terrace cost US$55/65 for singles/doubles and there are larger bungalows for US$90 a double.

Places to Eat

Douglas Snackette & Restaurant, on the ground floor of Douglas Guest House, has rotis (EC$6.50), chicken & chips (EC$8.50) and other simple inexpensive dishes.

Le Flambeau at the Portsmouth Beach Hotel is a pleasant al fresco restaurant on the beach. Simple breakfast items cost EC$10 and sandwiches and burgers are about the same price. There are also vegetarian plates and moderately priced fish and meat dinners.

Mango Bar & Restaurant, at the Mango Beach Hotel on the north side of Portsmouth, has a restaurant serving good Creole chicken (EC$20) and fish (EC$30) meals at lunch and dinner.

PORTSMOUTH TO THE EAST COAST

The route that cuts across the northern neck of the island from Portsmouth to the east coast is a delightful drive through mountainous jungle. The road is winding and narrow, the terrain is all hills and valleys, and the landscape is lush with tropical greenery. Once you reach the coast there are some fine ocean vistas, a couple of one-lane bridges, and plantations with seemingly endless rows of coconut palms. The road is

DOMINICA

paved, but be cautious of the deep gutters on the mountain side and steep drops on the cliff side.

CALIBISHIE TO PAGUA BAY

Calibishie, the first sizable village you'll reach on the east coast, is a good place to grab a bite to eat. In the center of the village is the *Almond Beach Restaurant & Bar*, a pleasant local seaside spot that serves lunch all afternoon and makes a refreshing homemade ginger beer.

There are a few small villages as you continue south but the area is made up predominantly of coconut and banana plantations. Occasionally the road winds from the jungle out to the coast. There are brown-sand beaches at **Woodford Hill Bay** and near Melville Hall Airport at **Londonderry Bay**. Both bays have rivers emptying into them where women gather to wash clothes; at Londonderry the airport fence doubles as the clothesline.

Surrounded by lush green hills, **Marigot**, the largest town on the east coast, is a pretty village of brightly painted houses, some of them built up on stilts. If you come by during the late afternoon there's a good chance you'll see villagers bringing in their fishing boats and sorting the day's catch.

CARIB TERRITORY

The 3700-acre Carib Territory, which begins around the village of Bataka and continues south for 7.5 miles, is home to most of Dominica's 3000 Carib Indians. It's a predominantly rural area with cultivated bananas, breadfruit trees and wild heliconia growing along the roadside. Many of the houses are traditional wooden structures on log stilts, but there are also simple cement homes and, in the poorer areas, shanties made of corrugated tin and tarpaper.

The main east coast road runs right through the Carib Territory. Along the road there are several stands where you can stop and buy intricately woven Carib baskets, mostly ranging in price from US$5 to US$30.

Salybia, the main settlement, has a couple of noteworthy buildings. One is the carbet, an oval-shaped community center designed in the traditional Carib style with a high-pitched ribbed roof; in pre-western times, these buildings served as collective living quarters. The Catholic church in Salybia, which also has a sharply pitched roof, is decorated with colorful paintings of Carib life and a unique altar made from a dugout canoe.

At Sineku a sign points oceanward to **L'Escalier Tête Chien**, a stairway-like lava outcrop that seems to climb out of the turbulent ocean. This unique natural formation was thought by the Caribs to be the embodiment of a boa constrictor and is significant in Carib legends.

After leaving the Carib Territory the road offers glimpses of the rugged coastline.

There's an intersection half a mile south of Castle Bruce; take the road marked Pont Casse to continue to the Emerald Pool and Canefield. This road takes you through a scenic mountain valley with a luxuriant fern forest and lots of rushing rivers.

Places to Stay & Eat

The *Carib Territory Guest House* (☎ 445-7256) at Crayfish River, just north of Salybia, consists of eight simple rooms at the home of Charles Williams. Singles/doubles cost US$30/40 with shared bath and US$40/50 with private bath. The guesthouse serves moderately priced lunch and dinner, using its own organically grown produce.

Floral Gardens (☎ 445-7636, fax 445-7333), PO Box 192, is in the Concord area, on the road leading inland from Pagua Bay. It has rooms with fans and private baths that cost US$45/60, apartments for US$80 and a restaurant with a varied menu at moderate prices.

EMERALD POOL

Emerald Pool, which takes its name from its lush green setting, is at the base of a gentle 40-foot waterfall. The pool, deep enough for a little dip, is reached via a five-minute walk through a rainforest of

Top Left: Nutmeg, Grenada (Ned Friary)
Middle Left: Houses in Roseau, Dominica (Ned Friary)
Top Right: House in Roseau, Dominica (Ned Friary)
Bottom: Island musicians, Dominica (Glenda Bendure)

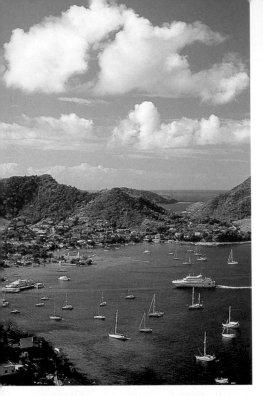

Top Left: Harbor, Bourg des Saintes, Terre-de-Haut, Guadeloupe (Kevin Schafer)
Bottom Left: Swing bridge, Parc National de la Guadeloupe (Glenda Bendure)

Top Right: Girl selling coconut cakes, Terre-de-Haut, Guadeloupe (Ned Friary)
Bottom Right: Bananaquit (Ned Friary)

ferns and tall trees. The path is well defined and easy to follow, although it can get a bit slippery in places. Emerald Pool is generally a serenely quiet area except on cruise ship days (Wednesday is the big one), when one packed minivan after another can pull up to the site.

Emerald Pool is on the road that runs between Canefield and Castle Bruce, a nice winding drive with thick jungle vegetation, mountain views and lots of beep-as-you-go hairpin turns. It's about a 30-minute drive from Canefield; the trailhead is marked with a roadside forestry sign.

TRAFALGAR FALLS

Trafalgar Falls, on the eastern edge of the Morne Trois Pitons National Park, is both spectacular and easily accessible. The 10-minute walk to the falls begins at Papillote Wilderness Retreat, about a mile east of the village of Trafalgar.

Start the walk at the bottom of the inn's driveway, where you'll find a cement track leading east. Follow the track until you reach a little snack bar, take the footpath that leads downhill from there and in a couple of minutes you'll reach a viewing platform with a clear view of the falls in a verdant jungle setting.

There are two separate waterfalls. Water from the upper falls crosses the Titou Gorge before plunging down the sheer 200-foot rock face that fronts the viewing platform. At the base of the waterfall are hot sulphur springs with a couple of basins that bathers can sit in – look for the yellow streaks on the rocks.

The lower falls flow from the Trois Pitons River, which originates in the Boiling Lake area. This waterfall, which is gentler and broader than the upper falls, has a pool at its base that's deep and wide enough for an invigorating swim.

Young men hang out at the start of the trail and tout their services as guides. Getting to the viewing platform is straightforward and doesn't require a guide, so if you plan to go only that far, save yourself the 'tip' (roughly EC$20), as the guides call their negotiable fee.

Going beyond the platform is trickier, as getting to the base of the falls requires crossing a river. Depending on how sure-footed you are, a guide could be helpful in climbing down the boulders to the lower pool and even more so in clambering over to the hot springs.

Guide or not, be very careful with your footing as the rocks get moss covered and can be as slippery as ice. This is a serious river, and during rainy spells it may be too high to cross. Flash floods are also a potential danger, as heavy rains in the upper slopes can bring a sudden torrent – if you're in the river and the waters start to rise, get out immediately.

Places to Stay & Eat

Papillote Wilderness Retreat (☎ 448-2287, fax 448-2285, papillote@tod.dm), PO Box 2287, is a delightful little inn nestled in the mountains above Trafalgar village. American owner and naturalist Anne Baptiste has planted the grounds with nearly 100 types of tropical flowers and trees. The rustic inn has eight simple units with private baths, wooden plank floors and patchwork bed quilts made at the local women's co-op. Singles/doubles cost US$50/70, plus an optional US$30 per person for breakfast and dinner. There's also a two-bedroom, two-bath cottage near a waterfall that costs US$150 as a unit but can be divided into two sections for US$85 with the kitchenette, US$70 without.

Papillote has good food with lunchtime salads for EC$20, a flying fish plate for EC$25 and a chicken plate for EC$30. Lunch is served from noon to 3 pm. Bring a bathing suit and top it off by relaxing in the inn's hot springs pool (EC$5). Dinner, a full meal for EC$50, is by reservation.

D'Auchamps Cottages (☎ 448-3346, honychurchs@tod.dm), PO Box 1889, on the road to Trafalgar Falls, is set on a nine-acre estate amidst a botanical garden. There are two cottages, each with a kitchen, veranda and bath. The smaller one, which has one bedroom, costs US$50; the larger has two bedrooms and costs US$60. The seventh night is free on weekly stays.

Getting There & Away

To get to Trafalgar from Roseau, take King George V St north from the town center. After crossing the Roseau River, continue up the Roseau Valley road for 2.3 miles, at which point the road forks; take the right branch. From here it's a 10-minute drive along a narrow potholed road to Papillote, 2 miles away.

Buses go from Roseau to the village of Trafalgar (EC$2.25), from where it's a 15-minute walk to Papillote. Taxis from Canefield Airport to Papillote cost EC$45.

MORNE TROIS PITONS NATIONAL PARK

This national park, in the southern half of the island, encompasses 17,000 acres of Dominica's mountainous volcanic interior.

Most of the park is primordial rainforest, varying from jungles thick with tall, pillarlike gommier trees to the stunted cloud forest cover on the upper slopes of Morne Trois Pitons (4550 feet), Dominica's second-highest mountain. The park has many of the island's top wilderness sites including Boiling Lake, Boeri Lake, Freshwater Lake and Middleham Falls. Hikes to all four start at Laudat (elevation 1970 feet), a small hamlet with fine mountain views.

The Emerald Pool, at the northernmost tip of the park, is described earlier in this chapter.

Middleham Falls

The trail to Middleham Falls, one of Dominica's highest waterfalls, is an interesting rainforest walk. More than 60 species of trees, including the tall buttressed chataignier, form a leafy canopy that inhibits undergrowth and keeps the forest floor relatively clear. The treetops provide a habitat for light-seeking flora, including climbing vines, bromeliads and various air plants. The forest is also home to numerous bird species and a tiny tree frog.

There are usually guides available at the trailhead; they charge about EC$50 and the hike takes about 1¼ hours each way. If you don't use a guide, carry a compass and be careful not to stray off the main trail, as it would be easy to lose your bearings in the surrounding wilderness.

Boiling Lake

Dominica's preeminent trek is the rugged day-long hike to Boiling Lake, the world's second-largest actively boiling lake (the largest is in New Zealand). Geologists believe the 207-foot-wide lake is a flooded fumarole, a crack in the earth that is allowing hot gases to vent from the molten lava below. The eerie-looking lake sits inside a deep basin, its grayish waters veiled in steam, its center emitting bubbly burps.

En route to the lake the hike passes through the Valley of Desolation, a former rainforest destroyed by a volcanic eruption in 1880. Today it's an active fumarole area with a barren-looking landscape of crusted lava, steaming sulphur vents and scattered hot springs. The hike follows narrow ridges, snakes up and down mountains and runs along hot water streams. Wear sturdy walking shoes and expect to get wet and muddy.

This strenuous six-mile hike, which begins at Titou Gorge, requires a guide. It's about EC$80 (plus EC$20 for a second person) if you arrange your own guide in Laudat. Benjamin and Julian Armentrading, two brothers who live in the village, are good knowledgeable guides.

Other Trails

The walk to **Freshwater Lake**, Dominica's largest lake, is a straightforward hike that skirts the southern flank of Morne Macaque. As the 2.5-mile trail up to the lake is along a well-established 4WD track, this hike doesn't require a guide. It's a relatively gradual walk and takes about 2½ hours roundtrip.

Hikers can continue another 1.25 miles from Freshwater Lake to **Boeri Lake**, a scenic 45-minute walk that passes mountain streams and both hot and cold springs. The 130-foot-deep Boeri Lake occupies a volcanic crater that's nestled between two of the park's highest mountains. En route are ferns, heliconia and various epiphytes, as well as the mossy trees of the elfin woodlands that surround the lake.

For a short walk and a dip there's the trail to **Titou Gorge**, where a deep pool is warmed by a hot spring. Just above the pool the gorge narrows and when the water's calm it's possible to swim upriver to a small cascading waterfall. Whenever there's any brown water being kicked up there's also a dangerous current and you should stay out of the pool. To get to the trail turn at the pay phone in Laudat and follow the short road to the utility station. The trail follows a narrow canal that feeds water to the hydroelectric plant. The walk takes about 15 minutes.

Serious hikers could also hire a guide to tackle **Morne Trois Pitons**, the park's tallest peak, but it's a rough trail that cuts through patches of sharp saw grass and requires scrambling over steep rocks. The trail begins at Pont Casse at the north side of the park and takes about five hours roundtrip.

Places to Stay & Eat

Roxy's Mountain Lodge (☎ /fax 448-4845), PO Box 265, in the village of Laudat, makes a great base if you're planning to do a lot of hiking. This friendly family-run place has 17 rooms and an engaging communal atmosphere. There's a TV room, a small bar and a restaurant with inexpensive lunchtime sandwiches and dinner meals for EC$35 to EC$60. Valerie Rock, who runs the guesthouse with her brother, can arrange reliable trail guides and is a fine source of information about the island. Room rates begin at US$30/46 for singles/doubles in winter, US$28/40 in summer. Rooms with private bath are a few dollars more and there are also studios for US$65 to US$75.

Getting There & Away

To get to Laudat, take King George V St north from Roseau. After crossing the Roseau River, continue up the Roseau Valley for 2.3 miles, at which point the road forks; take the left fork, marked Laudat. The road is narrow and a bit potholed, but

passable. The trail to Middleham Falls begins on the left 2.5 miles up; the trail to Freshwater and Boeri lakes begins opposite the shrine, half a mile farther.

There's regular but limited bus service. Buses (EC$3) to Laudat leave from the Roseau police station every other hour from 6:30 am; buses return to Roseau from Laudat about 45 minutes later. Taxis from Roseau to Laudat cost EC$70.

SOUTH OF ROSEAU

The coastal road south of Roseau is a delightful 30-minute drive that takes you through a couple of attractive little seaside villages and ends at Scotts Head. Most of the road skirts the water's edge, although there's a roller coaster section just before Soufriere that winds up the mountain and gives a bird's-eye coastal view before dropping back down to Soufriere.

Soufriere, population 950, has a picturesque old stone church on the north side of the village. There are steaming sulphur springs in the hills above Soufriere, including one about a mile inland on the road that leads east from the village center.

Scotts Head, population 800, on the southernmost tip of Dominica's west coast, is a picturesque fishing village and a fun place to kick around. It has a gem of a setting along the gently curving shoreline of Soufriere Bay, the rim of a sunken volcanic crater. Mountains form a scenic inland backdrop. At the southern tip of the bay is a promontory, also called Scotts Head, which is connected to the village by a narrow, rocky neck of land. It's a short, easy walk to the top of the promontory, where there's a fine coastal view.

The center of village activity is the waterfront, where brightly painted fishing shacks line the shore and colorful fishing boats are hauled up onto the sand. The bay offers good swimming and snorkeling conditions, as well as some of the island's best diving.

Places to Stay & Eat

Petit Coulibri Guest Cottages (☎ /fax 446-3150, barnardm@tod.dm), PO Box 331, occupies an old sugar estate on the hill slopes a couple of miles inland from Soufriere. Run by an American couple, this pleasant upmarket property consists of three two-bedroom, 1½-bath cottages with kitchens and verandas for US$200 and two smaller studio rooms with private baths for US$90. It's got a pool, splendid views and an engaging seclusion, though the road in can be rough in an ordinary car. Breakfasts (US$10) and dinners (US$25) are available.

Gachette's Seaside Lodge (☎ 448-7749, fax 448-2308), PO Box 2047, in the center of Scotts Head village, is a guesthouse with rooms and cottages from US$35 to US$70. A couple of people in Scotts Head rent out apartments for US$25 to US$50 a day or US$150 to US$200 a week. Two such places are *Lydiaville* (☎ 448-4313, fax 448-3045) and *Castille Apartment* (☎ 448-2926).

The *Seabird Cafe*, south of Nature Island Dive in Soufriere, is a good little café that's open for lunch and dinner. There's a bakery in Soufriere and small food shops in both villages.

Grenada

Grenada is colorful, robust and rough around the edges. Dubbed the 'Spice Island,' it is the Caribbean's leading producer of nutmeg and mace and also grows cinnamon, ginger and cloves.

The island has a mountainous interior of rainforests and waterfalls and an indented coastline with protected bays and beaches. The capital, St George's, has one of the prettiest harbor settings in the Caribbean and takes its character from the 19th-century stone and brick buildings that slope down to the waterfront.

Although a handful of larger hotels have recently been constructed on Grenada, most places to stay and eat are still small locally owned businesses that offer a reasonable balance between comfort and price. Almost all of the accommodations and tourist facilities are concentrated at the southwest tip of the island, leaving the rest of Grenada with an unaltered West Indian nature.

The nation is comprised not only of the island of Grenada, which has 90% of the land and population, but also of several Grenadine islands, a couple of which are inhabited. The largest of these, Carriacou, has the relaxed pace of an overlooked backwater. It makes a nice off-the-beaten-path destination that can easily be visited while island hopping between Grenada and the St Vincent Grenadines. The third significant island, Petit Martinique, is a real sleeper that's only beginning to awaken to tourism. Regularly scheduled boat services link all three islands.

HIGHLIGHTS

- St George's, Grenada's capital, with its picturesque harbor
- A scenic drive through Grand Etang National Park
- Laid-back Carriacou, with its unspoiled West Indian character
- A snorkeling trip to uninhabited nearshore isles
- Strolling the quiet island of Petit Martinique

Facts about Grenada

HISTORY

In 1498, during his third voyage to the New World, Christopher Columbus became the first European to sight Grenada. Columbus however, didn't land on the island and other colonists continued to bypass it during the century that followed. The first European attempt to settle Grenada was made in 1609 by a party of 208 English settlers who planned to establish tobacco plantations on the island. Within a year most of the colonists had fallen victim to raiding Caribs and the settlement was abandoned.

In 1650, Governor Du Parquet of Martinique 'purchased' the island of Grenada

GRENADA

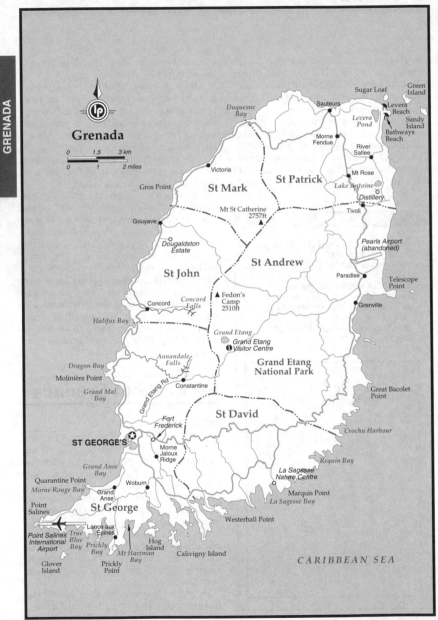

from the Caribs for a few hatchets, some glass beads and two bottles of brandy. Parquet immediately moved in 200 French settlers, complete with a prefabricated fort, and established a trading station, Port Louis, on a narrow strip of land that separated the Lagoon from St George's Harbour. (The land eventually sank and the site of Port Louis is today on a submerged sand spit near the mouth of the Lagoon.)

In 1651, the French, weary of ongoing skirmishes with the Caribs, sent a contingent of soldiers to drive the natives off the island. French troops routed the last of the Caribs to Sauteurs Bay at the north end of Grenada where, rather than submitting to the colonists, the remaining Caribs – men, women and children – jumped to their deaths from the precipitous coastal cliffs.

The French established plantations of indigo, tobacco, coffee, cocoa and sugar, which were worked by African slaves. Grenada remained under French control until 1762, when Admiral George Rodney captured the island for Britain. Over the next two decades Grenada see-sawed between the two powers, but in 1783, under the Treaty of Paris, the French ceded Grenada to the British, under whose colonial rule it remained until independence.

British colonists and Grenada's minority French settlers continued to have lingering animosities towards each other, however. In 1795 a group of French Catholics, encouraged by the French Revolution and supported by comrades in Martinique, armed themselves for a rebellion. Led by Julien Fedon, who owned a plantation in Grenada's central mountains, they launched their assault on the British in early March with a brutal attack on Grenville. They managed to capture the British governor, eventually executing him along with a number of other hostages. Fedon's guerrillas, who controlled much of the island for more than a year, were finally overcome by a fleet from the British navy. Fedon, incidentally, was never captured – he likely escaped to Martinique or drowned while attempting to get there, though some islanders believe he lived out the rest of his

Gre-NAY-duh

The Carib Indians called the island Camerhogne, and Columbus, in passing, named it Concepción. However, Spanish explorers soon began calling the island Granada, after the city of the same name in Spain. When the French moved in it became Grenade, which the British later changed to Grenada.

Pronounce it Gre-NAY-duh, with a long 'a' to rhyme with 'say.' ■

days as a recluse hiding in Grenada's mountainous jungles.

In 1877 Grenada was accorded the status of a Crown Colony and in 1967 became an associated state within the British Commonwealth. Grenada, Carriacou and Petit Martinique adopted a constitution in 1973 and became an independent nation on February 7, 1974.

The road to independence was a rocky one for Grenadians. Eric Garity, who rose to prominence after organizing a successful labor strike in 1950, became a leading voice in both the independence and labor movements. When independence came, the Grenada United Labour Party (GULP), which Garity headed, was swept into power with Garity as Grenada's first prime minister. His regime gained notoriety for patronage and corruption. It attempted to silence its critics with secret police tactics, largely carried out by a group of thugs known as the Mongoose Gang, who brutally attacked antigovernment critics and occasionally went on their own little looting campaigns. Garity's popular support evaporated as his rule became increasingly dictatorial.

Just before dawn on March 13, 1979, while Garity was overseas, a small group of armed rebels supported by the opposition party, the New Jewel Movement (NJM), led a bloodless coup. Maurice Bishop, head of the NJM, became prime minister of the new government, the People's Revolutionary Government (PRG).

The 34-year-old Bishop, a London-educated lawyer, immediately reinstated a measure of human rights and promised a

GRENADA

resolution of the country's economic problems. Bishop had widespread public support and proved a charismatic leader but his policy of nonalignment and socialist leanings didn't settle well with the USA and some of Grenada's more conservative Caribbean neighbors, such as Barbados.

Bishop built schools and medical clinics and created credit unions and farmers' cooperatives. Ostracized by the West, Bishop turned for aid to the Cubans, who undertook the construction of a new airport on Grenada. In the meantime divisions developed in the PRG between Bishop and those military leaders who wanted to take a more authoritarian approach.

In October 1983, a struggle between Bishop and the military hardliners resulted in Bishop's overthrow. On October 19, 1983, after learning of Bishop's house arrest, 30,000 supporters – the largest spontaneous crowd to ever gather in Grenada – forced his release. Together they marched to Fort George. At the fort the military opened fire on the crowd, killing an estimated 40 protesters. Bishop and several of his followers were taken prisoner and summarily executed in the courtyard.

In the turmoil that followed, the US government convinced a handful of Caribbean nations to pledge support to a US invasion of the island. On October 25, American troops, accompanied by symbolic forces from half a dozen Caribbean states, invaded Grenada. During the fighting that followed, 70 Cubans, 42 Americans and 170 Grenadians were killed, including 18 who died when the US forces mistakenly bombed the island's mental hospital. Most US forces withdrew in December 1983, although a joint Caribbean force and 300 US support troops remained on the island for two more years.

When elections were held again, in December 1985, Herbert Blaize and his newly formed New National Party won 59% of the vote and 14 of the 15 House seats. In July 1991 the death sentences for the 14 people who had been condemned to hang for the murder of Maurice Bishop and his supporters were commuted to life in prison.

GEOGRAPHY

The three-island nation of Grenada, Carriacou and Petit Martinique has a total land area of 133 sq miles. Grenada, with 121 sq miles, measures 12 miles in width and 21 miles in length. The island is of volcanic origin, although part of the northern end is comprised of limestone. Grenada's rainy interior is rugged, thickly forested and cut by valleys and streams. The highest point is the 2757-foot Mt St Catherine, an extinct volcano in the northern interior.

The south side of the island of Grenada has a markedly indented coastline of jutting peninsulas, deep bays and small nearshore islands, making it a favorite haunt for yachters.

Carriacou, a little under 5 sq miles, is the largest of the Grenadine islands that lie between Grenada and St Vincent.

CLIMATE

In St George's in January the average daily high temperature is 84°F (29°C) while the low averages 75°F (24°C). In July the average daily high is 86°F (30°C) while the low averages 77°F (25°C).

During the rainy season, June to November, rain falls an average of 22 days a month in St George's and the mean relative humidity is 78%. In the driest months, January to April, there's measurable rainfall 12 days a month and the humidity averages 71%.

Annual rainfall is about 60 inches (1520 mm) in St George's and about 160 inches (4060 mm) in the Grand Etang rainforest. Carriacou is substantially drier, averaging 40 to 60 inches of rain a year.

FLORA & FAUNA

Grenada has a varied ecosystem of rainforests, montane thickets, elfin woodlands and lowland dry forests. Breadfruit, immortelle, flamboyant and palms are some of the more prominent trees.

About a dozen troops of Mona monkeys, introduced from West Africa centuries ago, live in Grenada's wooded areas. Other mammals are nine-banded armadillos (tatou), opossum (manicou) and mongoose. Bird life includes hummingbirds, pelicans, brown boobies, osprey hawks, endangered hook-billed kites and hooded tanagers.

There are no poisonous snakes, but Grenada does have tree boas. These nocturnal serpents spend their daytime hours wound around branches high above the ground, however, so human contact with the creatures is quite limited.

Sea turtles nest along some of Grenada's sandy beaches. All sea turtles are endangered, but that doesn't stop them from making it onto the menu at a few restaurants around the island. Travelers should give pause before eating at any restaurant that serves turtle meat.

GOVERNMENT & POLITICS
Grenada, a member of the British Commonwealth, has a parliamentary government headed by a prime minister. The Governor-General, who represents the British Queen, has a largely advisory role but is responsible, on the advice of majority and opposition party leaders, for appointing the 13-member Senate. The 15-member House of Representatives is elected by universal suffrage.

The current prime minister, Keith Mitchell, is a member of the New National Party, which has been criticized for bringing Grenada into closer ties with the USA. Mitchell is currently considering a proposal to allow the US Coast Guard to open a base on Petit Martinique for the purpose of monitoring drug traffic in the region.

ECONOMY
Grenada is the world's second-largest producer of nutmeg. It also exports mace, cloves, cinnamon, cocoa and bananas. Although agriculture remains the most important sector of the economy, since the 1980s the government has been attempting to boost tourism, which is now the second leading source of the country's gross domestic product (GDP). In the past decade the number of overnight visitors to Grenada has more than doubled, while the arrival of cruise ship passengers has increased many

Nutmeg
The nutmeg tree (Myristica frangrans), originally from East India, was commercially introduced by the Dutch in the mid-19th century. It thrived so well that Grenada now produces a third of the world's nutmeg.

A fragrant evergreen that has glossy leaves and small yellow flowers, the nutmeg tree produces two spices: nutmeg and mace. The tree's yellow fruit, called the pericarp, splits open when ripe to reveal a brown nut, the nutmeg, which is covered with a lacy, orange-red webbing of mace.

Nutmeg is used to flavor baked goods, drinks, sauces and preserves. Mace is used as a seasoning and in cosmetics. The pericarp is used in nutmeg syrup. ■

times over. Of the 400,000 visitors who arrive annually, 285,000 are cruise ship passengers.

The government has encouraged foreign investors to fund new resorts on Grenada and is now eyeing both Carriacou and Petit Martinique, which have heretofore been spared any major hotel development.

The unemployment rate, while still substantial at 16%, is half of what it was four years ago.

POPULATION & PEOPLE
The population of Grenada is 97,600, nearly a third of whom live in St George's. Another 6000 people live on Carriacou and about 900 live on Petit Martinique. Approximately 82% of Grenadians are black, of African descent, while 13% have mixed origins. The other 5% is comprised of people of East Indian and European descent.

SOCIETY & CONDUCT
Grenadian culture is a mix of British, French, African and West Indian influences. A resurgence of Black Pride is visible in the widespread use of African names given to Grenadian children.

Steel band and calypso music are popular. Cricket and soccer are the most common sports; matches are held in St George's at Queen's Park and the Tanteen.

Dos & Don'ts
Dress is casual on Grenada and simple cotton clothing is suitable attire for any occasion. To avoid offense and unwanted attention, swim wear should be restricted to the beach.

RELIGION
Almost 60% of all Grenadians are Roman Catholic. There are also churches for Anglicans, Seventh Day Adventists, Methodists, Christian Scientists, Presbyterians, Scots Kirk, Baptists, Jehovah's Witnesses and the Baha'i faith.

LANGUAGE
The official language is English; a French-African patois is also spoken by some people.

Facts for the Visitor

ORIENTATION
The airport is at the southwestern tip of the island, 5.5 miles from the capital of St George's. Midway between the two lies Grand Anse Beach, Grenada's main tourist area.

It's possible to tour most of the island in a full-day outing. The most common sightseeing route is up the scenic Grand Etang Rd and north to Sauteurs via Grenville, Pearls and Bathways Beach, returning to St George's via the west-coast road.

Grenada is divided into six parishes. From north to south they are St Patrick, St Mark, St Andrew, St John, St George and St David.

Maps
The best road map of Grenada is the Ordnance Survey's 1:50,000 map, which can be bought for EC$15 at bookstores in St George's.

TOURIST OFFICES
Local Tourist Offices
When requesting information by mail, write to: Grenada Board of Tourism (☎ 440-2279, fax 440-6637), The Carenage, St George's, Grenada, West Indies.

There's a tourist office booth at the Point Salines Airport, just before immigration, where you can pick up tourist brochures; the staff can also help you book a room.

There are also tourist offices at the cruise ship dock in St George's and in Hillsborough on Carriacou.

Tourist Offices Abroad
Tourist offices abroad include:

Canada
    Grenada Board of Tourism,
    439 University Ave, Suite 820,
    Toronto, Ontario M5G 1Y8
    (☎ 416-595-1339, fax 416-595-8278)
Germany
    Marketing Services International,
    Johanna-Melber-Weg 12,
    D-60599 Frankfurt
    (☎ 069-611-178, fax 069-629-264)
UK
    Grenada Board of Tourism, 1 Collingham
    Gardens, Earls Court, London SW5 0HW
    (☎ 0171-370-5164, fax 0171-244-0177)
USA
    Grenada Board of Tourism, 800 Second
    Ave, Suite 400K, New York, NY 10017
    (☎ 212-687-9554, 800-927-9554;
    fax 212-573-9731)

VISAS & DOCUMENTS
Passports are not required of citizens of the USA, Canada or the UK, as long as they have proof of citizenship, such as an official birth certificate or naturalization papers, as well as a photo ID, such as a driver's license. Citizens of other countries must have a valid passport.

As immigration officials generally stamp in the exact number of days you tell them you intend to stay, be sure to include any time you plan to spend in Carriacou in your calculations. They also ask where you're staying, so it's best to have some place in mind to smooth the process – in the end you can stay anywhere.

Foreign Embassies & Consulates
The following countries have embassies or consulates in Grenada:

Guyana
  Consulate of the Cooperative Republic
  of Guyana, Gore St, St George's
  (☎ 440-2189)
Netherlands
  Consulate of the Netherlands,
  Huggins Building, Grand Etang Rd,
  St George's (☎ 440-2031)
UK
  British High Commission,
  14 Church St, St George's
  (☎ 440-3536)
USA
  US Embassy, Point Salines
  (☎ 444-1173)
Venezuela
  Venezuelan Embassy, Archibald Ave,
  St George's (☎ 440-1721)

CUSTOMS

Visitors can bring in 200 cigarettes and a quart of spirits duty free.

MONEY

The official currency is the Eastern Caribbean dollar (EC$2.70 equals US$1). Most hotels, shops and restaurants will accept US dollars, but you'll generally get a better exchange rate by changing to EC dollars at a bank and using local currency. Major credit cards are accepted by most hotels and upper-end restaurants as well as some car rental agencies. Make sure it's clear whether prices are being quoted in EC or US dollars, particularly with taxi drivers.

Barclays Bank exchanges traveler's checks free of commission if the exchange totals more than EC$500, and EC$5 for lesser amounts. Scotiabank charges an across-the-board 1% commission to exchange traveler's checks, while the National Commercial Bank charges EC$5 per transaction. Grenada currently has no ATMs and there are no banks at the airport.

An 8% tax and a 10% service charge is added to most hotel and restaurant bills. If no service charge is added, a 10% tip is generally expected.

POST & COMMUNICATIONS
Post

Grenada's general post office is in St George's and there are sub-post offices in many villages. The cost to mail an airgram is EC$.50. To mail an airmail letter under 20 grams costs EC$0.75 to the USA, Canada or the UK, EC$0.90 to Europe, EC$1.10 to Australia or the Far East.

When addressing a letter, include the street name or box number, the village and 'Grenada (or Carriacou), West Indies.'

Telephone

Local phone numbers have seven digits; when calling from outside the Caribbean add the area code 473.

Grenada has both coin and card phones. Coin phones take 25-cent coins (either EC or US) or EC$1 coins; each 25 cents allows three minutes on a call within the country. Card phones accept the same Caribbean Phone Card used on other Eastern Caribbean islands; cards are sold at the airport, harbors and numerous shops.

International phone calls can be made and faxes and telexes sent from the Grenada Telecommunications (Grentel) office at the Carenage in St George's from 7:30 am to 6 pm weekdays, until 1 pm on Saturday and from 10 am to noon on Sunday. Expect long queues.

More information on phonecards and making international phone calls is in the Post & Communications section in the introductory Facts for the Visitor chapter.

> **The area code for Grenada is 473.**

BOOKS

A good book to pick up if you want to learn more about geology, flora and fauna is *A Natural History of the Island of Grenada* by John R Groome, a past president of the Grenada National Trust. *The Mermaid Wakes: Paintings of a Caribbean Isle* is a hardcover book featuring paintings by

Carriacou artist Canute Caliste, with text about island life by Lora Berg.

Revolution in Reverse by James Ferguson, Monthly Review Press, presents a critical account of Grenada's development since the US invasion.

NEWSPAPERS & MAGAZINES
There are a handful of local newspapers, including the monthly *Barnacle*, which is distributed free. International newspapers, including *USA Today*, can be found in bookstores and large grocery stores.

The tourist office dispenses the handy *Discover Grenada*, a 65-page glossy magazine with general information on Grenada, Carriacou and Petit Martinique. Also useful is the 100-page magazine *The Greeting*, which is similar but has more accommodation details and is usually handed out by hotels and travel agents. Both publications are free.

RADIO & TV
Grenada has three local TV and four radio stations. Most hotels also have satellite or cable TV, which pick up major US network broadcasts.

ELECTRICITY
The electrical current is 220 volts AC, 50 cycles.

WEIGHTS & MEASURES
Grenada uses the imperial system.

HEALTH
St George's General Hospital (☎ 440-2051), the island's main medical facility, is in St George's near Fort George. There's a small hospital on Carriacou, the Princess Royal Hospital (☎ 443-7400). The quality of medical care on Grenada is not highly regarded and for serious health issues medical evacuation to Miami or Barbados is fairly common.

DANGERS & ANNOYANCES
Safety precautions are warranted in Grenada. There have been muggings of tourists in the Grand Anse area, mostly along the

beach at night, and the Lagoon area on the south side of St George's. Avoid walking in isolated areas after dark and don't carry an exposed camera bag or anything else that might make you stand out as a target. Yachters should have everything as secure as possible and belongings shouldn't be left unattended, especially in St George's.

Women traveling alone can expect to hear the occasional 'hey darlin' and other catcalls.

EMERGENCIES
For police and fire emergencies, dial ☎ 911.

BUSINESS HOURS
Shops are generally open from 8 am to noon and 1 to 4 pm Monday to Friday and 8 am to noon on Saturday, although some larger shops stay open through the lunch hour.

Banking hours are generally from 8 am to 3 pm (some close earlier) Monday to Thursday and 8 am to 5 pm on Friday.

PUBLIC HOLIDAYS & SPECIAL EVENTS
Public holidays are:

New Year's Day	January 1
Independence Day	February 7
Good Friday	late March/early April
Easter Monday	late March/early April
Labour Day	May 1
Whit Monday	eighth Monday after Easter
Corpus Christi	ninth Thursday after Easter
Emancipation Days	first Monday & Tuesday in August
Thanksgiving Day	October 25
Christmas Day	December 25
Boxing Day	December 26

Carnival, held on the second weekend in August, is Grenada's big annual festival. The celebration includes calypso and steel band competitions, all sorts of costumed revellers, a pageant and a big grand finale jump-up on Tuesday. Many of the events occur at Queen's Park at the north side of St George's.

Carriacou's Carnival usually takes place in February. The island also has a major sailing event, the Carriacou Regatta, held in late July or early August. The regatta features races to Grenada, Union Island and Bequia, various sporting events from volleyball competitions to donkey races, and plenty of music, including Big Drum performances.

Petit Martinique holds a home-grown regatta over Easter weekend that includes a swimming relay, rowboat races, kite flying, music and a beer-drinking competition.

ACTIVITIES
Beaches & Swimming
Grenada's most popular beach, Grand Anse, is a fine sweep of white sands. For somewhere less frequented, Morne Rouge Bay on the other side of Quarantine Point is both secluded and protected.

The southern tip of the island also has nice beaches on either side of the airport runway and along the Lance aux Épines peninsula.

Calivigny Island, east of Lance aux Épines, has a couple of pretty beaches, some walking tracks and the remains of an old hotel. If you don't have your own boat, The Moorings at Secret Harbour in Lance aux Épines shuttles people over for US$15 per person, or for even less you can sometimes arrange with fishers at Woburn Pier to drop you off on the island.

Diving
The waters around Grenada have extensive reefs, with a wide variety of corals, fish, turtles and other marine life. There are shallow reef dives, wall dives, drift dives and shipwrecks.

One popular dive is the wreck of the *Bianca C* ocean liner, off Grenada's southwest coast (see the sidebar The *Bianca C* later in this chapter). Because of strong currents, coupled with a depth of more than 100 feet, it's strictly for experienced divers; dive shops usually require at least one check-out dive in advance.

Other Grenada dive sites include Bose Reef, an extensive reef off Grand Anse that harbors manta rays and barracuda; Dragon Bay, a wall dive with rich marine life that

Sea anemone

includes moray eels and black coral; and Grand Mal Point, a reef and wall dive with varied soft and hard corals.

The islands between Grenada and Carriacou are also popular dive spots. These include Kick 'em Jenny, which has great visibility and marine life, and The Sisters, where there's a challenging wall dive with gorgonians and barracuda. Carriacou itself also has a number of decent dive sites.

Dive Shops Dive shops on Grenada and Carriacou include:

Dive Grenada, PO Box 441, St George's (☎ 444-1092, fax 444-6699, diveg'da@caribsurf.com); at Cot Bam on Grand Anse Beach. Dive Grenada offers dives to the *Bianca C* and night dives for US$50, a resort course that includes a reef dive for US$60 and open-water PADI certification for US$375 (US$325 if there are two or more people).

Grand Anse Aquatics, Grand Anse Beach (☎ 444-4129, fax 444-4808); at the Coyaba Beach Resort. This operation has dives to the *Bianca C* and night dives for US$55, other one-tank dives as low as US$35, resort courses for US$60 and open-water PADI certification for US$350 (US$300 if more than one person).

Scuba Express, PO Box 302, St George's (☎ 444-2133, fax 444-1247); at True Blue Bay. This small operation offers dives from US$32, discover scuba courses for US$75 and open-water PADI certification courses for US$325.

Tanki's Watersport Paradise, Carriacou (☎ 443-8406, fax 443-8391); at the Paradise Inn.

Operated by Tankred Mueller, a German divemaster with a long history on Carriacou, this operation offers single dives for US$45, 'discover scuba' courses for US$65 and open-water PADI certification for US$280 to US$350.

Carriacou Silver Diving, Carriacou (☎ /fax 443-7882); this German-run dive shop in Hillsborough offers one-tank dives for US$50, two-tank dives for US$90.

Snorkeling

Molinière Point, north of St George's, has some of the best snorkeling on Grenada, though land access is difficult. Grand Anse Aquatics offers daily two-hour snorkeling trips to Molinière Point at 2 pm for US$15; Dive Grenada offers an afternoon snorkel tour to the site for US$20.

Those who don't want to join a tour can find good coral and colorful reef fish at the south side of Morne Rouge Bay. If you're not too demanding and don't mind swimming out about five minutes, there are coral patches off Grand Anse Beach with some tropical fish, live conch and the occasional sand dollar.

If you haven't brought your own snorkeling gear, you can rent it at most dive shops.

Windsurfing

Grenada is not particularly known for its windsurfing, but you can rent boards at The Moorings, at Secret Harbour, for US$10 an hour; they offer lessons for US$15 an hour.

On the island of Carriacou, you can rent gear from Carriacou Silver Diving (☎ /fax 443-7882), on Main St in Hillsborough, for US$50 a day.

Sailing

The Moorings, at Secret Harbour, rents Sunfish for US$10 an hour, 14-foot Catalinas for US$15 an hour and 21-foot Impulses for US$20 an hour or US$100 a day. You must have sailing skills that are appropriate for the type of boat you want to rent.

For information on day sails see Organized Tours in the Getting Around section later in this chapter.

Fishing

Grenada offers good game fishing for blue marlin, white marlin, sailfish and yellowfin tuna. Winter is the best season. Tropix Sport Fishing (☎ 440-4961), Evans Chartering Services (☎ 444-4422) and Bezo Charters (☎ 443-5021) are three fishing charterers. Expect a boat to cost about US$500 a day.

The Spice Island Billfish Tournament, held yearly in January, attracts anglers from North America and around the Caribbean. Information is available from the Grenada Billfish Association, PO Box 14, St George's.

Hiking

The most popular hiking area in Grenada is the Grand Etang rainforest, where trails wind through a forest of mahogany and ferns and lead to a crater lake, waterfalls and mountain ridges. For details on specific trails, see the Grand Etang National Park, La Sagesse Nature Centre and Concord Falls sections.

The Hash House Harrier's Club sponsors a 'hash' on alternate Saturday afternoons, walking a different course each time. The trail is marked with scraps of paper and the object is to follow the route without getting lost. Visitors are welcome to join; schedules are posted at Rudolf's restaurant on Wharf Rd in St George's.

Tennis

Several hotels have tennis courts for guests' use. The Coyaba Beach Resort in Grand Anse allows non-guests access for EC$25 an hour, including use of rackets and balls.

Golf

The Grenada Golf Club (☎ 444-4128) near Grand Anse has a nine-hole course open to visitors daily from 8 am to 6 pm (to 1 pm on Sunday). Green fees are US$12 for nine holes, US$20 for 18 holes, and clubs can be rented.

People to People Tours

New Trends Tours (☎ 444-1236, fax 444-4836) arranges a 'People to People' program that offers visitors the opportunity to meet Grenadians of similar interests. There's no fee for the service.

Write to New Trends Tours, PO Box 797, St George's, and tell them a little about yourself, whether you'd like to meet a Grenadian family or someone with a specific profession, what you'd like to do (chat over lunch, go for a walk etc) and the dates you'll be on the island. The company maintains a list of islanders interested in meeting visitors and will attempt to make an introduction. Don't expect a reply to your letter. When you arrive in Grenada call New Trends to see if arrangements have been made. The office hours are from 8:30 am to 4:30 pm Monday to Friday at the Siesta Hotel in Grand Anse.

ACCOMMODATIONS

The main tourist areas are Grand Anse and Lance aux Épines; both have some good-value moderate and top-end places to stay. The island's handful of budget guesthouses are not on the beach, but are concentrated in St George's. In the Point Salines area there are a couple of moderately priced hotels and a few pricey beachside resorts. Beyond that, there are only a few scattered inns around the rest of Grenada.

Carriacou, which gets far fewer overnight visitors, has a number of good-value guesthouses.

In addition to booking direct, a few dozen hotels can be booked through the Grenada Hotel Association (☎ 444-2644, fax 444-4847; from the USA ☎ 800-322-1753), PO Box 440, St George's.

Camping

Camping is officially allowed in Grand Etang National Park but there are no established facilities and the park is in one of the rainiest parts of the island. Arrangements should be made through the park visitor center (☎ 440-6160); because so few people camp, the fee seems to be set at whim, but it should be modest. The park also has a lake house that can be rented, although it's often booked long term by visiting forestry officials or the medical school.

FOOD

You'll find Italian and French food as well as plenty of seafood and West Indian dishes. Popular local dishes include fish stew, curried lambi (conch) and the ubiquitous roti. Pigeon peas with rice, plantains, yams and callaloo soup are common side dishes.

Grenadians have a good appreciation of how a water view can add to a dining experience and many restaurants have good harbor and ocean views.

DRINKS

The official word is that water is safe to drink from the tap, but many expatriates boil their drinking water as a precaution and we recommend doing the same. Bottled water is available in grocery stores.

Carib beer is brewed on Grenada. Several rums are made using imported sugar, including Westerhall, a reasonably smooth rum that sells for about EC$12 a bottle.

Local nonalcoholic drinks worth a try are sorrel juice, mauby and ginger beer.

ENTERTAINMENT

Entertainment is limited on Grenada, though there's usually a steel band or other dinner entertainment at Grand Anse hotels a few nights a week. The main venues are the Renaissance Hotel, Spice Island Inn, Flamboyant Hotel and Coyaba Beach Resort.

Casablanca (☎ 444-1631), above Barclays Bank in Grand Anse, is a popular hangout with students from the medical college and has jazz and live music a few nights a week, a DJ on other nights. It's open nightly until at least 1 am. There's no cover charge.

Fantazia 2001 (☎ 444-3737), a disco on Morne Rouge Beach, has dancing from 9:30 pm to the wee hours on Wednesday, Friday and Saturday with a modest cover charge.

St George's is very quiet in the evening, although the *Regal Cinema* (☎ 440-2403) on Paddock St shows typical Hollywood fare each evening for EC$5.

THINGS TO BUY

Spices make nice, lightweight souvenirs. A good place to pick up quality spices at good prices is the Marketing & National Importing Board in St George's, which also sells local hot sauces, sorrel, nutmeg syrups and nutmeg and guava jams, some items gift-boxed.

Art Fabrik, next door on Young St, sells batik wall hangings and clothing that are made on site. For a general gift shop, Tikal on the opposite side of Young St, has a quality collection of local handicrafts, batiks and wood carvings.

White Cane Industries, at the south end of Wharf Rd in St George's, is a workshop for the blind where straw and cane baskets, place mats and serving trays are made and sold. The caliber of the work is good and the proceeds provide an income for the craftspeople working there.

Getting There & Away

AIR
Airlines

Airline reservation numbers are:

Airlines of Carriacou	☎ 444-3549
American Airlines	☎ 444-2222
British Airways	☎ 440-2796
BWIA	☎ 444-1221
LIAT, reservations	☎ 440-2796
at Point Salines Airport	☎ 444-4121
on Carriacou	☎ 443-7362

USA

American Airlines has a daily flight to Grenada from San Juan, Puerto Rico, which connects with the airline's flights from the USA. Excursion tickets to Grenada from the east coast of the US typically begin around US$450 in the low season, US$550 in the high season.

BWIA flies direct a couple of times a week from both New York and Miami, with fares that are competitive with American Airlines.

UK

British Airways has twice weekly direct flights from London to Grenada and BWIA offers London-Grenada flights a couple of times a week via Trinidad. Both charge around £850 for an excursion ticket with a seven-day minimum stay, a six-month maximum stay and a 21-day advance purchase.

Within the Caribbean

LIAT has daily nonstop flights between Grenada and Barbados, Carriacou, Trinidad, Tobago and St Vincent, with connecting flights to the rest of its Caribbean network.

The one-way/roundtrip fare to Grenada is US$110/164 from Barbados, US$111/172 from St Lucia and US$66/104 from St Vincent. A free stopover is allowed in Carriacou on flights between Grenada and St Vincent. The one-way/roundtrip fare from either Port of Spain or Tobago to Grenada is US$93/144.

LIAT has some good-value fares for flights that leave Grenada in the morning and return in the late afternoon. For instance, the airfare from Grenada for one-day outings to Barbados is US$82.

Air Carriacou flies from Grenada to Union Island in the St Vincent Grenadines for US$47 each way.

For information on flying between Grenada and Carriacou, see Getting There & Away in the Carriacou section.

Airport Information

Point Salines International Airport has car rental offices, pay phones and a reasonably priced 2nd-floor restaurant. You'll find a tourist office booth in the arrivals section *before* you reach immigration. Between immigration and customs you can find a courtesy phone that rings direct to a number of car rental agencies, hotels and guesthouses. There's no bank or exchange office – so if you're not already carrying EC currency it'll be very useful to have US currency in small denominations – taxis routinely accept either.

The departure lounge has a duty-free liquor store and gift shop.

SEA
For boats between Carriacou and Union Island, see Getting There & Away in the Union Island section of the St Vincent & the Grenadines chapter. For boats between Grenada and Carriacou, see Getting There & Away in the Carriacou section of this chapter.

Yacht
Customs and immigration can be cleared in Grenada at St George's or at Spice Island Marine Services on Prickly Bay; in Carriacou, clearance can be made at Hillsborough.

In St George's, customs is at Grenada Yacht Services (GYS) and most yachts anchor off GYS and the Grenada Yacht Club. Customs and immigration is generally open from 8 am to 3:45 pm weekdays.

The most frequented anchorages are along the southwest side of Grenada, including Prickly Bay, Mt Hartman Bay, Hog Island and True Blue Bay.

The Moorings (☎ 444-4439) bases its yacht charter operation at Secret Harbour and Sea Breeze Yacht Charters (☎ 444-4924) is at Spice Island Marine Services, both at Lance aux Épines.

Cruise Ship
Grenada is a port of call for a fair number of cruise ships. Ships dock at the southeast side of St George's center; at the dock there's a tourist office, waiting taxis and a line of souvenir shops. It's only a 10-minute walk to the opposite side of the harbor, where most of St George's sights and shops are situated.

Cruise ship passengers can expect to encounter young men touting their services as guides. It's not a good idea to follow an unknown person around and a guide is unnecessary anyway as St George's is easy to explore. You're better off strolling around the town with a few friends or arranging an island tour with one of the taxi drivers.

LEAVING GRENADA
There's an EC$35 departure tax for stays of longer than 24 hours (half price for children ages five to 10). Children under five are exempt from the tax.

There are no taxes or fees on flights between Grenada and Carriacou.

Getting Around

This section describes options for getting around Grenada. For information on getting around Carriacou, see the end of the Carriacou section.

BUS
Buses on Grenada are privately operated minivans. Using the bus is a good way to experience the rhythms of daily life on Grenada – most blast calypso and reggae music and provide a hair-raising ride. Most buses leave St George's from the Esplanade bus terminal at the west end of Granby St. Signs mark some of the routes and it's all fairly orderly. If you're not sure who's going where, any of the drivers can point you in the right direction. Generally, you're better off hopping into an almost-full bus as most buses leave only after they fill. You can catch buses bound for St David parish from the public market.

Fares in the greater St George's area are EC$1. From St George's fares are EC$1.25 to Grand Anse, EC$2.50 to La Sagesse, EC$3 to Gouyave or Grand Etang and EC$5 to Grenville or Sauteurs. Although it depends on how many passengers are picked up and dropped off, it takes about 45 minutes from St George's to Grenville, 1½ hours to Sauteurs.

Buses begin running around 7 am. Times for the last buses vary with location, but it's hard to catch any bus after 6 pm; head back early enough so as not to get stuck. There are very few buses on Sunday.

You can flag down a passing bus from the side of the road by sticking out your hand. To get off the bus, yell out 'drop one.'

TAXI

Taxi fares are regulated by the government. From the airport to Grand Anse or Lance aux Épines costs EC\$25, to St George's EC\$30. From central St George's it's EC\$8 to other parts of the city, EC\$20 to Grand Anse or Morne Rouge and EC\$32 to Lance aux Épines.

For trips elsewhere on Grenada, taxis charge EC\$4 per mile for the first 10 miles and EC\$3 per mile after that. The waiting charge is EC\$15 per hour. For sightseeing purposes, taxis can be hired at a flat rate of EC\$40 per hour. In addition an EC\$10 surcharge is added onto fares between 6 pm and 6 am.

CAR
Road Rules

Drive on the left-hand side. Many roads are narrow and curving and a few bus drivers seem a bit hell bound. For safety, slow down when approaching blind curves and toot your horn liberally. There are few road signs on the island, so a good road map and a measure of patience is essential for self-touring.

You'll need to buy a local driver's license for EC\$30 to drive in Grenada. You can get it from most car rental companies or from the Traffic Department booth (☎ 440-2267) at the fire station on the east side of the Carenage in St George's.

Grenada's larger towns, including Grenville, Sauteurs and Victoria, have gas stations; expect a gallon of unleaded to cost around EC\$6.

There are a lot of one-way streets in St George's but some of them are not marked, so be careful and watch the traffic flow; better yet, try to avoid driving around

the town center, especially on the north side of the Carenage.

Rental

There are a number of local car rental agencies but many of them have very small fleets and a three-day minimum rental period. For the most part, you're better off dealing with international companies.

Dollar (☎ 444-4786) has an office at the airport, while Budget has offices at both the airport (☎ 444-2877) and the Le Marquis Complex (☎ 444-2277) in Grand Anse. Avis (☎ 440-3936) is in St George's at the Shell station on the corner of Paddock and Lagoon roads but will pick up renters at the airport or their hotel at no charge.

Cars rent for around US\$50 a day, jeeps for US\$65. Optional CDW insurance, which limits your liability in the event of an accident, costs an additional US\$6 to US\$10 per day; note that even with the CDW you're still responsible for a deductible of at least US\$200 in damages.

ORGANIZED TOURS
Land Tours

Several small Grenadian-owned companies provide land tours of Grenada at competitive prices. Arnold's Tours (☎ 440-0531, fax 440-4118) offers a seven-hour circle-island tour for US\$40 that includes Concord Falls, the Dougaldston Estate, the Gouyave nutmeg station, Carib's Leap, lunch at the Morne Fendue Plantation House and return via Grenville and Grand Etang National Park.

Sunsation Tours (☎ 444-1594, fax 444-1103) offers a variety of tours including a seven-hour round-the-island jaunt that includes Grand Etang National Park, the River Antoine Rum Distillery, Lake Antoine, lunch at the Morne Fendue Plantation House and some time at Bathways Beach; the cost is US\$50. Both English and German-speaking guides are available.

If you want to take a packaged trek into the interior, Henry's Safari Tours (☎ 444-5313, fax 444-4460) specializes in hiking tours. There's a five-hour tour that includes a hike to the Seven Sisters Falls at US$80 for two people or US$30 per person for three or more. Another tour consists of a one-way five-hour trek to Fedon's Camp that begins in the national park and returns from the village of Mt Qua Qua via a minibus; the cost is US$110 for two people or US$55 each for three or more.

Some companies, including Arnold's, do a nicely packaged half-day triangle tour that takes in Concord Falls, the nutmeg station in Gouyave and Dougaldston Estate before turning inland to cut down through Grand Etang National Park on the return. The cost is US$25.

La Sagesse Nature Centre (☎ 444-6458) offers a tour that includes an hour-long guided nature walk through the nature center, some time on the beach, lunch and roundtrip transportation from your hotel for US$28.

Boat Tours

Several boats in Grenada offer trips to nearshore islands as well as sails through the Grenadines, often including snorkeling time. Tour frequency depends on demand and most require a minimum of four to six passengers. For the latest offerings, look for flyers, ask at your hotel or flip through the tourist magazines.

If you want to plan your own itinerary, The Moorings (☎ 444-4439) at Secret Harbour arranges yacht charters, with a skipper, for half-day (US$25) and full-day (US$40) sails. Rates are per person, with a minimum of four people.

The *Rhum Runner* (☎ 440-4386) is Grenada's version of a party boat, with rum punch, steel band music and limbo dancing. The cruise includes some snorkeling and beach time and costs US$20.

Day Tours to Other Islands

Fun Tours (☎ 444-3167) and Sunsation Tours (☎ 444-1594) both package day trips to the St Vincent Grenadines that include a flight to Union Island, and a sail from there to Mayreau, Tobago Cays and Palm Island; the cost is US$200.

St George's

St George's is a picturesque hillside town surrounding a deep horseshoe-shaped harbor called the Carenage. The main sights can easily be seen in a couple of hours. St George's has a small museum, two old forts offering fine views, a few churches, a colorful public market and a bustling waterfront.

You won't find wooden houses, which were banned in St George's following two catastrophic fires that swept through the town in the late 18th century. Instead, there's a predominance of 19th-century structures of brick and stone, many of them roofed with orange fish-scale tiles brought over as ballasts on ships from Europe.

The head of the Carenage makes a good place to begin a stroll of the town. Opposite the LIAT office is Christ of the Deep, a life-size bronze statue put up by Costa Cruise Line in honor of its ship, the *Bianca C*, which went up in flames inside the harbor

GRENADA

The *Bianca C*

At over 600 feet in length, the Italian liner *Bianca C* is the largest shipwreck in the Eastern Caribbean. In the early morning of October 22, 1961, the ship was anchored in St George's outer harbor preparing to sail when an explosion ripped through the engine room, setting off a fire that quickly engulfed the vessel.

A flotilla of yachts, fishing boats and inter-island schooners came to assist in the rescue efforts and all 400 passengers escaped without loss of life, although three of the 300 crew members died of fire injuries. A few days later a British warship towed the smoldering vessel out of the harbor and into deeper waters where it broke away and sank. Today the *Bianca C*, with its upper decks 100 feet below the surface, is the region's best-known dive wreck.

The cause of the explosion remains unknown. ∎

GRENADA

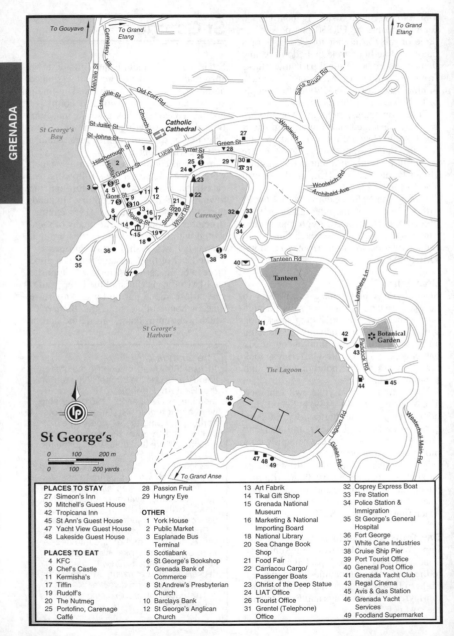

To Gouyave

To Grand Etang

To Grand Etang

Cemetery Hill

Melville St

Grenville St

Old Fort Rd

Sans Souci Rd

St George's Bay

St Juille St

St Johns St

Church St

Catholic Cathedral

Lucas St

Tyrrel St

Green St

Woolwich Rd

Hillsborough St

Halifax St

Granby St

Gore St

Young St

Scott St

Wharf Rd

Carenage

Woolwich Rd

Archibald Ave

Christ of the Deep Statue

Tanteen Rd

Tanteen

Lowthers Ln

St George's Harbour

The Lagoon

Botanical Garden

Paddock Rd

Lagoon Rd

Glean Rd

Westerhall Main Rd

St George's

0   100   200 m
0   100   200 yards

To Grand Anse

PLACES TO STAY
27 Simeon's Inn
30 Mitchell's Guest House
42 Tropicana Inn
45 St Ann's Guest House
47 Yacht View Guest House
48 Lakeside Guest House

PLACES TO EAT
4 KFC
9 Chef's Castle
11 Kermisha's
17 Tiffin
19 Rudolf's
20 The Nutmeg
25 Portofino, Carenage Caffé

28 Passion Fruit
29 Hungry Eye

OTHER
1 York House
2 Public Market
3 Esplanade Bus Terminal
5 Scotiabank
6 St George's Bookshop
7 Grenada Bank of Commerce
8 St Andrew's Presbyterian Church
10 Barclays Bank
12 St George's Anglican Church

13 Art Fabrik
14 Tikal Gift Shop
15 Grenada National Museum
16 Marketing & National Importing Board
18 Sea Change Book Shop
20 Sea Change Book Shop
21 Food Fair
22 Carriacou Cargo/ Passenger Boats
23 Christ of the Deep Statue
24 LIAT Office
26 Tourist Office
31 Grentel (Telephone) Office

32 Osprey Express Boat
33 Fire Station
34 Police Station & Immigration
35 St George's General Hospital
36 Fort George
37 White Cane Industries
38 Cruise Ship Pier
39 Port Tourist Office
40 General Post Office
41 Grenada Yacht Club
43 Regal Cinema
45 Avis & Gas Station
46 Grenada Yacht Services
49 Foodland Supermarket

in 1961. Boats that sail between Grenada and Carriacou are loaded nearby, on the west side of the Carenage. Farther along Wharf Rd are some 19th-century warehouses, including one restored building housing the National Library.

The winding maze of streets on the west side of the Carenage can be fun to wander through. At Scott and Lucas Sts a smartly uniformed police officer (locally dubbed 'cop in a box') directs traffic at a busy blind corner. On congested Young St, there are some interesting craft shops and art galleries – you can watch batik being made on site at Art Fabrik.

There's a modest botanical garden at the southeast side of town, a 10-minute walk from the post office, but it's not worth going out of your way to see.

At the cruise ship dock you'll find a line of stalls where island women sell fragrant spice baskets, cloth dolls and other souvenir items. On cruise ship days water taxis (US$2) shuttle from the cruise ship dock to the Renaissance Hotel at Grand Anse Beach.

Information
Tourist Office There are two tourist offices. Best-stocked is the one at the cruise ship dock, but you can also drop by the administrative office at the north side of the Carenage. Both are open Monday to Friday from 8 am to 4 pm.

Money Barclays Bank and Scotiabank are both on Halifax St and open from 8 am to 3 pm Monday to Thursday, 8 am to 5 pm on Friday.

Post & Communications The general post office, on the south side of the harbor, is open weekdays from 8 am to 3:30 pm.

You can make phone calls and send faxes from the Grentel office at the Carenage from 7:30 am to 6 pm weekdays, 7:30 am to 1 pm on Saturday and 10 am to noon on Sunday.

Bookstores St George's Bookshop on Halifax St has a fairly good collection of

Caribbean books, including ones about island flora and fauna. Sea Change Book Shop, below The Nutmeg restaurant, sells local and US newspapers. Both sell maps of Grenada.

Grenada National Museum
The Grenada National Museum, on the corner of Young and Monckton Sts, incorporates an old French barracks dating from 1704. The building served as a prison from 1766 to 1880 and as the island's first hotel in the 1900s.

The hodgepodge of exhibits includes Amerindian pottery fragments, an old rum still and a rather grubby marble bathtub that once belonged to the Empress Josephine. There's also a display on the events leading to the assassination of Maurice Bishop and the US invasion that followed.

The museum is open 9 am to 4:30 pm Monday to Friday, 10 am to 1:30 pm on Saturday. Admission is EC$5 for adults, EC$1 for children.

Fort George
Fort George, on the hilltop promontory at the west side of the Carenage, is Grenada's oldest fort, established by the French in 1705. While many of the fort buildings are used by the national police, the grounds are open to the public and offer some fine views of the surrounding area. The lookout opposite the police station provides one of the best vantages – a sweeping view of the west side of the city with its church spires and red-tile roofs and out across the Carenage to the hilltop Fort Frederick.

In the inner fort, just below the row of cannons, you'll find the courtyard where Maurice Bishop was executed. The bullet holes in the basketball pole were made by the firing squad and the spot is marked by fading graffiti that reads 'No Pain No Gain Brother.'

The entrance to the fort is at the end of Church St. There's no admission fee.

Churches
St George's boasts a number of 19th-century churches that add an appealing

element to the skyline, though the churches themselves are not extraordinary.

The most interesting is **St George's Anglican Church** on Church St. Built in 1825, it has a four-sided clock tower that doubles as the town's official timepiece; floor tiles in West Indian hues of red, black and yellow; and a marble tablet commemorating the English colonists killed in the French-inspired 1795 Fedon uprising.

The **Catholic cathedral**, the largest of the lot, has a brightly painted interior. It's opposite York House, a building of early Georgian architecture that holds the Supreme Court, House of Representatives and the Senate.

The yellow brick church immediately north of Fort George is **St Andrew's Presbyterian Church**, which dates from 1833 and sports a spired four-sided clock tower.

You may have to glimpse St Andrew's through the windows but the other two churches are usually open for viewing.

Fort Frederick

Fort Frederick, which is atop Richmond Hill, 1.2 miles east of St George's, was constructed by the French in 1779 after wresting control of the island from the British. After 1783, when the French were forced by treaty to return Grenada to the British, the fort served to guard against the threat of French attacks. The cessation of hostilities between the two powers led to the fort's abandonment in the 1850s. The fort now provides a fine panoramic view that includes Quarantine Point, Point Salines and Grover Island. Grover Island, incidentally, was used until 1927 as a Norwegian whaling station.

Fort Frederick remains well intact, in part due to a targeting blunder made during the US invasion of 1983. US forces intended to hit Fort Frederick, then in use by the Grenadian military, but instead mistakenly bombed Fort Matthew, just a few hundred yards to the north, which was being used as a mental hospital at the time of the attack. You can walk the grounds of the fort free.

Places to Stay

Yacht View Guest House (☎ 440-3607), on Lagoon Rd near the Foodland supermarket, is a clean, friendly family-run place with four simple rooms that share two baths. Guests have access to a common kitchen and a little balcony overlooking the yacht harbor. Singles/doubles cost only US$15/20 but it's often booked solid in winter.

A few doors away on Lagoon Rd is *Lakeside Guest House* (☎ 440-2365), where the amiable elderly proprietor, Mrs Haynes, rents clean, straightforward budget rooms with a bed and sink for US$15.

St Ann's Guest House (☎ 440-2717), 16 Paddock Rd, is on the southeast side of town, a 20-minute walk from the center but on a main bus route. It has a dozen clean, straightforward rooms, each with a sink. Singles/doubles cost US$18/26 for rooms with shared baths, US$20/31 with private baths.

Simeon's Inn (☎ 440-2537), on Green St opposite the Jehovah's Witnesses hall, has nine basic rooms with shared bath. Some have sinks, table fans are available on request and there's a harbor view from the shared balcony. Singles/doubles cost US$20/35.

Mitchell's Guest House (☎ 440-2803) is an older place on Tyrrel St in central St George's. There are 11 simple rooms with shared bath costing US$22/35 for singles/ doubles. It can be noisy.

The new *Tropicana Inn* (☎ 440-1586, fax 440-9797, tropicana@cpsnet.com) on Lagoon Rd is a recommendable place opposite the water at the quieter south side of town. The rooms have air-con, TV, phone, tile floors and either one double or two single beds. The rates are US$35/45 for singles/ doubles in summer, US$40/50 in winter; rooms with lagoon-view balconies are US$5 to US$10 more. There's a reasonably priced restaurant serving meals all day.

Mount Helicon Guest House (☎ 440-2444, fax 440-7168), on Upper Lucas St on the hillside above St George's, occupies a restored estate house. The guest rooms are pleasant but not fancy; all seven rooms have phones, fans and private baths and cost US$40/50 for singles/doubles. A couple of the rooms have air-con and one unit (US$10 more) has a kitchenette. The guesthouse is about 100 yards east of St George's northernmost traffic circle and can be reached via the St Paul's bus (EC$1).

Places to Eat – budget
Hungry Eye on the inner Carenage has good cheap eats with chicken rotis for EC$5 and plate lunches for EC$10. It's open from 7 am to around midnight, except on Sunday when it's open from 10 am to 10 pm.

At *KFC* on Granby St, two pieces of chicken and fries cost EC$11. It's open from 9:30 am (noon on Sunday) to at least 9 pm daily.

Chef's Castle on the corner of Halifax and Gore Sts is a modern fast-food restaurant with ice cream, hot dogs, burgers, fried chicken and rotis, all for EC$10 or under. It's open from 9 am to 10 pm Monday to Saturday.

For something healthier in the same price range try the nearby *Kermisha's*, tucked into the upper floor of the Singer building. This neat, friendly spot has rotis and sandwiches for around EC$7 and a generous meal of the day for EC$11. It's open weekdays from 9 am to 5 pm.

Passion Fruit on Tyrrel St is a popular spot with Peace Corps volunteers that serves inexpensive fish sandwiches, rotis and juices. It's open from 9 am to 4:30 pm Monday to Friday.

For an authentic English respite, there's *Tiffin* on Young St, which serves tea with scones for EC$10. They also have sandwiches, salads, croissants, cake, ice cream and wine by the glass. It's usually open from 7:30 am to 6 pm Monday to Friday, until 2 pm on Saturday.

The Italian-run *Carenage Caffé*, next to the LIAT office, has homemade ice cream for EC$1.50 a scoop and Italian cappuccino, juice, sandwiches, pizza and other light fare. It's open from 8 am to 11 pm Monday to Saturday.

Foodland on Lagoon Rd is the island's largest supermarket and the best place to find imported Western foods; it's open from 9 am to at least 7 pm Monday to Saturday. On the west side of the Carenage, *Food Fair* sells groceries.

Local fruits and vegetables are sold at the *public market*, though foreigners generally do better at the *Marketing & National Importing Board* on Young St, a farmers' cooperative with set prices and no haggling.

Places to Eat – middle
Get a harborview table at *The Nutmeg*, on the west side of the Carenage, and you'll see why it's one of the capital's most popular dining spots. At lunch and dinner, there are sandwiches and rotis for around EC$10, fish & chips for EC$18 and a good curried conch for EC$30. Specialties include a spicy callaloo soup and a potent nutmeg rum punch. It's open Monday to Saturday from 9 am to around 10:30 pm and on Sunday from 5 pm.

Rudolf's on Wharf Rd is a casual pub-style restaurant that packs in crowd, including many expats. There are fish sandwiches for EC$8, flying fish, mahimahi or chicken with chips for around EC$22 and lambi for a few dollars more. It's open from 10 am to midnight Monday to Saturday.

Portofino, on the Carenage, has pizzas from EC$16, pasta dishes from EC$25 and catch of the day for EC$35. At dinner they usually play recorded jazz, making for one of the area's mellower dining scenes. Ask for a window table and get a harbor view. It's open from 11 am to 11 pm Monday to Friday, from 5 to 11 pm on Sunday.

The restaurant at *Mount Helicon Guest House*, on Upper Lucas St, offers upmarket West Indian food in the atmospheric dining room of a colonial estate house. A traditional Grenadian breakfast of fish cakes and salt fish souse, or light lunch fare, costs around EC$15. At lunch and dinner you can also get main courses ranging from flying fish (EC$25) to lobster (EC$65). For details on getting there, see the above Places to Stay.

Around Grenada

GRAND ANSE

Grenada's main resort area is along Grand Anse Beach, a long attractive sweep of white sand fronted by turquoise blue waters. The beach has a few vendors selling T-shirts and spice baskets, others offering to braid hair, but overall the activity at Grand Anse is low key.

There are numerous places to eat and stay around Grand Anse. The most expensive hotels front the beach, while rates tend to drop proportionally as you get farther away. Grand Anse Beach is backed by hills and consequently many hotels are terraced along the hillside and have good views.

Information

The Grand Anse Shopping Centre, opposite the Renaissance hotel, has a Scotiabank, a gift shop called Imagine, and Food Fair, a large modern grocery store that's open from 9 am to 5:30 pm Monday to Thursday, to 7 pm on Friday and Saturday.

There's a drugstore, two banks and a fruit stand in a row a few hundred yards to the west. The Le Marquis Complex has a couple of travel agencies.

Tangie's Laundry, at the traffic circle, will wash and dry a load of clothing for EC$30. It's open from 8 am to 6:45 pm Monday to Saturday, to 3 pm on Sunday.

Places to Stay – budget

Palm Grove Guest House (☎ 444-4578, fax 444-0943), PO Box 568, St George's, is above the Grand Anse Shopping Centre, about a five-minute uphill walk from the beach. There are a dozen varied rooms, some quite cheerless but all with private bath. Guests have access to a shared kitchen. Singles/doubles cost US$25/35 and the rate drops US$5 for stays of more than two days.

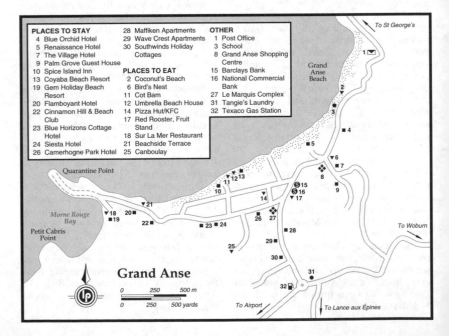

PLACES TO STAY
4 Blue Orchid Hotel
5 Renaissance Hotel
7 The Village Hotel
9 Palm Grove Guest House
10 Spice Island Inn
13 Coyaba Beach Resort
19 Gem Holiday Beach Resort
20 Flamboyant Hotel
22 Cinnamon Hill & Beach Club
23 Blue Horizons Cottage Hotel
24 Siesta Hotel
26 Camerhogne Park Hotel

28 Maffiken Apartments
29 Wave Crest Apartments
30 Southwinds Holiday Cottages

PLACES TO EAT
2 Coconut's Beach
6 Bird's Nest
11 Cot Bam
12 Umbrella Beach House
14 Pizza Hut/KFC
17 Red Rooster, Fruit Stand
18 Sur La Mer Restaurant
21 Beachside Terrace
25 Canboulay

OTHER
1 Post Office
3 School
8 Grand Anse Shopping Centre
15 Barclays Bank
16 National Commercial Bank
27 Le Marquis Complex
31 Tangie's Laundry
32 Texaco Gas Station

Grand Anse

In the same neighborhood but closer to the beach is *The Village Hotel* (☎ 444-4097, fax 444-4098), PO Box 602, St George's, which has a dozen simple self-catering rooms with private baths from US$50. It's a fair value for the money and they'll sometimes discount a bit on walk-ins.

Camerhogne Park Hotel (☎ 444-4587, fax 444-3111), a block from the beach, has 25 rooms in a few two-story apartment-like buildings. The rooms are straightforward and a bit wear-worn but have air-con, TV and phone. Singles/doubles cost US$45/55 year round. There are also self-contained apartments that can accommodate three to six people and cost from US$90 to US$130.

Southwinds Holiday Cottages (☎ 444-4310, fax 444-4404), PO Box 118, St George's, has 19 apartments in boxy two-story buildings about a 10-minute walk from the beach. The units are straightforward with kitchens, phones and TV. One-bedroom apartments cost US$50 with a ceiling fan, US$60 with air-con. Two-bedroom apartments, which have air-con, cost US$80 for up to four people. Rates are US$10 less during the summer.

Close by are the *Wave Crest Apartments* (☎ /fax 444-4116), at PO Box 278, St George's, a recommendable 18-unit complex. Attractive one-bedroom apartments with air-con, TV, phone, a separate kitchen and dining area and a small balcony cost US$50/55 for singles/doubles in summer, US$60/65 in winter. Two-bedroom apartments cost US$75/90 in summer/winter for up to four people.

Maffiken Apartments (☎ 444-4255, fax 444-2832), PO Box 534, St George's, offers good-value units with a full kitchen, air-con, phone, TV and veranda. One-bedroom apartments cost US$60/350 a day/week in summer, US$70/400 in winter, for one or two people. Two-bedroom apartments cost US$70/390 in summer, US$85/450 in winter for up to four people. The only problem is availability as it's often booked solid with medical students during the school year.

Blue Orchid Hotel (☎ 444-0999, fax 444-1846, dovetail@carib.com), PO Box 857, St George's, is a new 15-room hotel that's just a few minutes walk from the beach. The rooms, which have air-con, TV, refrigerators, private baths and balconies, cost from US$50/60 for singles/doubles in summer, US$60/70 in winter. Rooms with kitchenettes are US$10 more.

Places to Stay – middle

The 37-room *Siesta Hotel* (☎ 444-4645, fax 444-4647, siesta@caribnet.com), PO Box 27, St George's, is popular with European visitors. The rooms are pleasant with balconies, TV, air-con, bathtubs and tile floors. While it's not on the beach, it's only a few minutes walk away, the location is quiet and there's a pool. Singles/doubles cost US$60/80 in summer, US$90/110 in winter, a full breakfast included. You can also get a kitchenette unit without breakfast for the same rate or a roomy one-bedroom apartment for US$85/105 in summer, US$115/135 in winter.

Coyaba Beach Resort (☎ 444-4129, fax 444-4808, coyaba@caribsurf.com), PO Box 336, St George's, is a 70-room resort at the center of Grand Anse Beach. Rooms are comfortable with satellite TV, air-con, phones, hair dryers and terraces, and most have at least a partial ocean view. Singles/doubles cost US$80/100 in summer, US$125/175 in winter. There's a swimming pool and tennis court.

Places to Stay – top end

A good upscale choice is the *Flamboyant Hotel* (☎ 444-4247, fax 444-1234, email flambo@caribsurf.com), PO Box 214, St George's, an attractive hillside complex at the west end of Grand Anse Beach. The hotel has a variety of accommodations, mostly in buildings of two to four units. All have ocean-facing terraces, phones, TV, air-con and bathtubs; some have hardwood floors. There's a pool, fine views and steps leading down to the beach. Hotel rooms cost US$80/90 for singles/doubles in summer, US$110/125 in winter. Better value are the roomy one-bedroom suites, which have full kitchens and cost US$10 to US$20 more.

Cinnamon Hill & Beach Club (☎ 444-4301, fax 444-2874, cinhill@cpsnet.com), PO Box 292, St George's, has 26 units in two-story Spanish-style buildings. The units are large – all have full kitchens, big balconies and at least four beds and two bathrooms. The 2nd-floor apartments are best, as they have beam ceilings and many have water views. Rates for one or two people are US$85/130 in summer/winter for a one-bedroom apartment, US$125/160 in the two-bedroom apartments. It's US$15 each for a third and fourth person. There's a pool and an Italian restaurant on site.

Blue Horizons Cottage Hotel (☎ 444-4316, fax 444-2815, spiceisl@caribsurf .com), PO Box 41, St George's, is a pleasant place just a few minutes from Grand Anse Beach. The 32 suites, spread out in Mediterranean-style buildings, are spacious with kitchens, tile floors, ceiling fans, air-con, TV and phones. Rates begin at US$110/160 in summer/winter. There's a pool, restaurant and bar.

Renaissance Hotel (☎ 444-4371, fax 444-4800, higda@caribsurf.com), PO Box 441, St George's, is Grand Anse's largest hotel, with 186 rooms in a sprawling, low-rise complex of beachside buildings. The rooms are standard resort fare, comfortable with air-con, TV and phones, but without much Caribbean influence. The hotel has a beachfront pool and tennis courts. Singles/doubles begin at US$129/140 in summer, US$188/204 in winter.

Grenada's most expensive property is the *Spice Island Inn* (☎ 444-4258, fax 444-4807), PO Box 6, St George's, an all-inclusive beachfront resort. The 56 cottage-style rooms have a casual, tropical elegance and rates ranging from US$405 to US$835.

Places to Eat – budget
The Swedish-run *Rick's Cafe* in the Grand Anse Shopping Centre has ice cream in traditional and tropical flavors for EC$3 a cone. The shop also sells inexpensive sandwiches, burgers and pizza. It's open from 11 am to 9:30 pm, except on Sunday when it's open from 4 to 9:30 pm.

La Boulangerie in Le Marquis Complex is a popular café with mouthwatering raisin rolls and apple turnovers, fresh breads and Italian ice cream – each for around EC$4. There are also sub sandwiches, generous slices of pizza (EC$5) and whole two-person pizzas to order for EC$20. It's open from 8 am (when pastries are hot from the oven) to 8 pm Monday to Saturday, from 9 am to 2 pm on Sunday. There's a simple donut shop, *Donut World*, in the same center.

The new *Pizza Hut/KFC* offers standard pizza at high prices (from EC$30 for a medium), the usual KFC fried chicken and Colombo frozen yogurt at EC$3.50 a scoop. It's open from 11 am to 10 pm (11 pm on weekends).

Cot Bam, a large open-air bar and restaurant on Grand Anse Beach, has inexpensive rotis and sandwiches, chicken or fish & chips for EC$13 and a few more substantial fish dishes for around EC$30. It's open from 9:30 am to around 11 pm.

Umbrella Beach House, an eatery just east of Cot Bam, is run by the amiable Mrs Bowen. A fish or chicken sandwich is EC$4, a tasty roti is EC$6; wash it down with one of her homemade rum punches. It's open from 9 am to about 6 pm weekdays, from 11 am on Saturday.

Places to Eat – middle
Bird's Nest, a Chinese restaurant opposite the Renaissance hotel, has lunch specials for EC$12 to EC$25. Otherwise, à la carte Chinese dishes average EC$20 for chicken or fish and EC$40 for shrimp or beef. It's open from 9:30 am to 11 pm Monday to Saturday.

Red Rooster, on the main road in the center, has moderately priced local food with rotis for around EC$10 and full meals from EC$20. It's open daily from 11 am to 10 pm.

The casual veranda restaurant at the *Siesta Hotel* offers a continental breakfast for EC$15, full breakfast for EC$25 and a mix of local and Mediterranean dishes at dinner for around EC$35. It's open from 7:30 to 11 am and 6 to 9:30 pm.

The Flamboyant Hotel's *Beachside Terrace* is an open-air restaurant with a fine sea view. It has a EC$28 buffet breakfast or à la carte items for about half that. Daytime snacks such as fish & chips, rotis or fresh tuna salad cost around EC$20. At dinner, main dishes range from EC$35 for fish to EC$65 for lobster. It's open from 7:30 am to 10:30 pm daily.

The Renaissance's open-air *Terrace Cafe* has a good breakfast buffet of juices, fresh fruit, yogurt, pastries and omelets to order. It's served from 7 to 10 am and costs EC$20 continental style or EC$35 for the full selection.

The place to go for Italian food is *La Dolce Vita*, which has pleasant veranda dining at the Cinnamon Hill hotel. They make their own pasta and have a variety of dishes from EC$30 to EC$50. It's open for dinner daily except Monday from 7 to 11 pm.

Places to Eat – top end
Coconut's Beach (☎ 444-4644), known locally as the French Restaurant, is a casual place on the water at the east side of Grand Anse Beach. The food is predominantly French Creole. At lunch you can get a sandwich, a cheese and tomato crêpe or quiche lorraine for under EC$20. At dinner, à la carte main courses, such as curried lambi or fresh fish, average EC$45. Dine indoors or right on the sand under thatched umbrellas. It's open from 12:30 to 10 pm daily except Tuesday.

For a splurge dinner out, there's the acclaimed *Canboulay* (☎ 444-4401), a hillside restaurant with a panoramic view and creative cuisine that combines West Indian, African and European influences. An appetizer, salad or sorbet, main course, dessert and coffee cost from EC$75 to EC$95, depending upon the main dish selected. It's open for dinner from 6:30 pm nightly except Sunday; reservations are recommended.

La Belle Creole (☎ 444-4316) at the Blue Horizons Cottage Hotel is a well-regarded restaurant serving a blend of Grenadian and continental food. There's a fixed-price dinner (EC$110) that changes

nightly; it includes an appetizer, salad or soup, a choice of three main dishes accompanied by island-grown vegetables, dessert and coffee. Dinner is served from 7 to 9 pm nightly.

MORNE ROUGE
If Grand Anse seems a bit busy, you could follow the road to its end at Morne Rouge, a lovely little U-shaped bay that's fringed by white sand and backed by green hills. Still undeveloped, Morne Rouge Bay is but a 15-minute walk over the hill from Grand Anse. Around the point at the south side of the bay there's good snorkeling with sea fans and coral.

The long thin peninsula that separates Morne Rogue Bay from Grand Anse Beach was once a leper colony. For those who care to explore, a dirt road leads a few hundred yards out to the site, called Quarantine Point. While there's little to see in terms of the old colony, there's a good view of the coast in both directions. To the south you can see Point Salines, to the north as far as Molinière Point.

Places to Stay & Eat
Gem Holiday Beach Resort (☎ 444-4224, fax 444-1189), PO Box 58, St George's, has an enviable beachfront location on the north side of Morne Rouge Bay. This pleasant family-run place has 18 units, all with terraces, TV, phones and kitchenettes; the upper-story units have high ceilings as well. The only problem is getting in, as it books up quite heavily in winter. One-bedroom units cost from US$55 to US$90 for singles, US$60 to US$110 for doubles, depending on the view and season. Two-bedroom units are also available. If you call from the airport ask about discounted walk-in rates.

The *Sur La Mer Restaurant* on the beach has a nice water view and moderately priced lunch and dinner offerings, with an emphasis on seafood and West Indian dishes. Adjacent is the Fantazia 2001 nightclub, which has dancing until 2 am from Wednesday to Saturday.

GRENADA

POINT SALINES

The Point Salines area is dry and scrubby. Although there are beaches on either side of the airport runway, there's not much to do in the area. There are, however, two reasonably priced places to stay on the airport road and a couple of fancy beach resorts north of the airport. Keep in mind you'll probably want to spend most of the day elsewhere and thus will be dependent on some sort of transportation. Passing taxis are plentiful but bus traffic becomes lighter as you get closer to the airport.

Incidentally, St George's Medical School, a private school serving foreign students, is at the eastern tip of the airport runway. Former US president Ronald Reagan used the safety of the students at this small American-run facility as a rationale for invading Grenada following the 1983 military coup.

Places to Stay & Eat

No Problem Apartments (☎ 444-4634, fax 444-2803), PO Box 280, St George's, is on the main road midway between the airport and Grand Anse. The 20 apartments are spacious, each with a kitchen, living room, separate bedroom with two twin beds, aircon, TV and phone. There's a pool, free airport transfer, shuttles to Grand Anse Beach and a small moderately priced restaurant. Singles/doubles cost US$55/65 in summer, US$75/85 in winter.

Fox Inn (☎ 444-4123, fax 444-4177), PO Box 205, St George's, a mile east of the terminal, is closer to the airport but quite removed from everything else. It has 16 standard motel-style rooms for US$55/65 for singles/doubles in summer, US$65/70 in winter. There are also six studios for US$70/80 in summer, US$80/95 in winter. Rooms have TV and phones and there's a pool and restaurant.

Upmarket hotels include the all-inclusive *La Source* (☎ 444-2556) on Pingouin Beach, which has 102 rooms priced from US$240, and the 212-room *Rex Grenadian Hotel* (☎ 444-3333) on Magazin Beach, which has beachfront rooms from US$200.

LANCE AUX ÉPINES

Lance aux Épines, the peninsula that forms the southernmost point of Grenada, is a rather affluent and quiet area with fine coastal views and some good moderately priced places to stay, most with their own little beaches.

The west side of Lance aux Épines, where most of the activity is centered, fronts Prickly Bay, one of the island's most popular yachting anchorages. Lance aux Épines (pronounced 'lance-a-peen') is sometimes spelled L'Anse aux Épines, from the original French.

Information

Spice Island Marine Services (☎ 444-4257, VHF 16), a full-service marina on Prickly Bay, has a customs and immigration office, stern-to berths for 30 boats, fuel, water, electricity and public showers.

Places to Stay

Coral Cove (☎ 444-4422, fax 444-4718; in the USA ☎ 800-322-1753), PO Box 487, St George's, is a pleasant little place set on a quiet knoll at the east side of Lance aux Épines. It has an expansive view across Mt Hartman Bay to a run of peninsulas and islets. There are both apartments and cottages, all modern with full kitchens, high ceilings, screened louvered windows, tile floors and phones. The two-bedroom apartments (ask for the 2nd floor) have huge dining areas, balconies and two twin beds in each bedroom. Rates are a reasonable US$70/90 in summer/winter for a one-bedroom unit, US$90/120 for a two-bedroom unit. There's a swimming pool, a tennis court and a small beach.

Lance Aux Épines Cottages (☎ 444-4565, fax 444-2802, cottages@caribsurf.com), PO Box 187, St George's, sits on a peaceful tree-shaded cove with a nice sandy beach. There are 14 modern, large apartments, most in duplex cottages, all with full kitchens, screened windows, ceiling fans and TV. It's a good value and quite popular with return visitors. Summer/winter rates are US$75/100 for two people

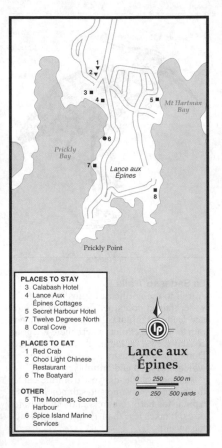

PLACES TO STAY
3 Calabash Hotel
4 Lance Aux
   Épines Cottages
5 Secret Harbour Hotel
7 Twelve Degrees North
8 Coral Cove

PLACES TO EAT
1 Red Crab
2 Choo Light Chinese
   Restaurant
6 The Boatyard

OTHER
5 The Moorings, Secret
   Harbour
6 Spice Island Marine
   Services

Lance aux Épines

0   250   500 m
0   250   500 yards

GRENADA

two people. Two-bedroom apartments cost US$225/300 for up to four people. Children under 12 are not allowed.

Secret Harbour Hotel (☎ 444-4548, fax 444-4819; in the USA ☎ 800-437-7880), PO Box 11, St George's, is a Club Mariner resort owned by The Moorings. Perched above Mt Hartman Bay, it has a pool, a restaurant and a swank Mediterranean decor. There are 20 suites with balconies, two four-poster double beds, refrigerators and air-con. Summer/winter rates are US$130/230 for one or two people. The resort is the site of a small marina that's home base for The Moorings yacht charter operation on Grenada.

The British-managed *Calabash Hotel* (☎ 444-4334, fax 444-5050, calabash @caribsurf.com), PO Box 382, St George's, is a pleasant, upmarket beachside resort. The 28 suites have ceiling fans, air-con, sitting areas, terraces and a tropical decor. Eight suites have their own private pools. Singles/doubles, which include breakfast, begin at US$205/235 in summer, US$310/355 in winter.

Places to Eat

The Boatyard at Spice Island Marine Services is open from 8 am to 11 pm every day but Sunday. The menu includes burgers with fries for EC$20, fish or chicken dishes for EC$30 and steaks for about double that. A steel band plays on most Fridays from 8 to 10 pm.

The marina mini-mart sells a good banana bread and is open from 9 am to 6 pm Monday to Saturday.

Choo Light Chinese Restaurant, near the Calabash Hotel, has a standard menu of Cantonese fare, ranging from sweet and sour chicken for EC$14 to garlic shrimp for EC$36. It's open daily from 11 am to 2:30 pm and 6 to 11 pm, except for Sunday when it's closed at lunch.

Next door, the *Red Crab* (☎ 444-4424) has consistently good food and a following with foreign residents, many of whom come here for the steaks. The most popular dish at lunch is the seafood platter at EC$26. There

in a one-bedroom unit, US$90/120 for up to four people in a two-bedroom unit.

Twelve Degrees North (☎ /fax 444-4580, 12degrsn@caribsurf.com), PO Box 241, St George's, is an exclusive beachside resort on the west side of Lance aux Épines. There are just eight apartments, each with its own housekeeper to do the cooking and cleaning. The apartments all have oceanview balconies and are comfortable but not luxurious. There's a pool, tennis court and small beach. One-bedroom apartments cost US$130/195 in summer/winter for up to

are also salads, hamburgers, omelets and seafood crêpes, all under EC$30. Dinner is à la carte, with a 'light bites' menu starting at EC$30 and other main dishes ranging from EC$46 for fish to EC$76 for lobster. It's open Monday to Saturday from 11 am to 2 pm and 6 to 11 pm.

In addition, the restaurant at the *Calabash Hotel* has a good reputation for fine dining.

LA SAGESSE NATURE CENTRE

La Sagesse Nature Centre fronts a deep coconut-lined bay with protected swimming and a network of hiking trails. The center occupies the former estate of the late Lord Brownlow, a cousin of Queen Elizabeth II. His beachside estate house, built in 1968, has been turned into a small inn, while the agricultural property is now operated by the government as a banana plantation. The beach has a nice sandy bottom and waters that are calm year round. Just outside the gate there's a water faucet where bathers can rinse off.

La Sagesse is about a 25-minute drive from St George's on the Eastern Main Rd. The entrance is opposite an old abandoned rum distillery and sugar mill, from where it's half a mile through banana fields to La Sagesse Bay. St David bound buses (EC$2) can drop you at the old distillery.

Brownlow's Gate

Lord Brownlow gained notoriety in the early 1970s when he built a gate at the entrance to La Sagesse, blocking public access to the area's best beach. The New Jewel Movement, the opposition party, gained momentum by targeting 'Brownlow's Gate' as a symbol of lingering colonialism and provoking islanders to tear the gate down. When the People's Revolutionary Government gained control of the island in 1979, the estate was taken over and turned into a public agricultural campus. After the military coup of 1983 the property was abandoned until 1986, when it was set aside and restored as the La Sagesse Nature Centre. ∎

La Sagesse Trails

A trail to the northeast begins opposite the water faucet, outside Brownlow's Gate, and leads 20 minutes through scrubby terrain to Marquis Point, where there are good coastal views, including that of a sea arch. Don't get too close to the edge of the point, which is eroded and crumbly.

Another trail leads west from the center to a mangrove swamp and salt pond that's a habitat for herons, egrets and other shorebirds. It takes less than 10 minutes to reach the swamp.

Places to Stay & Eat

La Sagesse Nature Centre (☎ /fax 444-6458, isnature@caribsurf.com; in the USA ☎ 800-322-1753), PO Box 44, St George's, has a handful of airy rooms with private baths, ceiling fans and double beds. A room with a kitchenette costs from US$65/85 in summer/winter, while a small budget room with a refrigerator but no kitchen costs US$50 year round.

The beachside restaurant, open daily, has fish sandwiches and burgers for EC$15 and fish or chicken dishes for about double that. Lunch is from 11 am to 3 pm, dinner from 7 to 9 pm.

GRAND ETANG RD

The Grand Etang Rd cuts across the mountainous center of the island through the Grand Etang National Park, taking in an easily accessible waterfall and a number of forest trails. To get started, you can take River Rd or Sans Souci Rd out of St George's, and when you reach the Mt Gay roundabout, take the road north.

While the road can be tortuously narrow and twisting (beware of deep roadside ditches), it's an otherwise delightful drive through the rainforest. The area is thick with ferns, bamboo groves, heliconia and buttressed kapok trees, as well as roadside plantations of nutmeg, cocoa and bananas.

Annandale Falls

Annandale Falls is an idyllic little waterfall with a 30-foot drop, surrounded by a grotto of lush vegetation. There's a pool beneath the falls that's deep enough for a refreshing swim. Avoid it on cruise ship days (Tuesday, Wednesday and Friday), however, as it's jam-packed with tourists and pesky young men hustling for tips.

In the village of Constantine, which is about 4 miles northeast of St George's, turn left on the road that leads downhill immediately past the yellow Methodist church. After three-quarters of a mile you'll reach the Annandale Falls visitor center. The falls are just a two-minute walk along a begonia-lined path that begins at the side of the center.

The visitor center is open from 8 am to 4 pm weekdays but the falls can be visited at any time. There's no entrance fee.

Grand Etang National Park

Two and a half miles north of Constantine, after winding steeply up to an elevation of 1900 feet, a roadside sign welcomes visitors to Grand Etang National Park.

Half a mile after entering the park you'll reach the visitor center, which overlooks Grand Etang Lake, a crater lake that forms the centerpiece of the park. The visitor center, open from 8:30 am to 4 pm weekdays (and on weekends if cruise ships are in), has displays on flora and fauna and sells trail maps. Near the parking lot there are a couple of stalls selling soft drinks and souvenirs.

Heading north from the park, the road hairpins down, offering views into valleys thickly forested with immortelle trees, which bloom bright red-orange in winter.

Park Trails The visitor center is the starting point for several trails that lead into the forest. Easiest is the **Morne LaBaye Trail,** an interpretive walk that starts behind the visitor center, takes in a few viewpoints and passes native vegetation, including the Grand Etang fern, whose sole habitat is in this area. The walk takes about 30 minutes roundtrip.

The **Grand Etang Shoreline Trail** is a 1½-hour loop walk around Grand Etang Lake. While this is a gentle hike, the going can get muddy as much of it is at shoreline elevation and it doesn't offer the same sort of views as the higher trails.

The **Mt Qua Qua Trail** is a moderately difficult three-hour roundtrip hike that leads to the top of a ridge offering some fine views of the interior forest.

Serious hikers could branch off shortly before the end of the Mt Qua Qua Trail to pick up the **Concord Falls Trail** for a long trek to Concord Falls, which takes about five hours one way from the visitor center. From Concord Falls, it's possible to walk about another 1.5 miles to the village of Concord on the west coast, where you can pick up a bus back to St George's.

A long, arduous hike leads deep into the forested interior to **Fedon's Camp**, the site where Julien Fedon, a rebel French plantation owner, hid out after a 1795 uprising in which he and his followers massacred the British governor and 47 other people.

One of the area's nicest hikes is to the **Seven Sisters Falls**, a series of seven waterfalls in the forested interior east of the Grand Etang Rd. The main hiking track is from the corrugated tin shed used by the banana association 1.25 miles north of the visitor center, on the right side of the Grand Etang Rd. The hike from the shed takes

GRENADA

about two hours roundtrip; there's a charge of EC$5 per person.

If you prefer a guide on the longer hikes the rangers at the visitor center (☎ 440-6160) can arrange one – the price depends on the trail and distance, but for a hike to Seven Sisters from the center expect to pay about EC$40.

GRENVILLE

Grenada's second-largest city, Grenville is the main port on the east coast and a regional center for collecting cocoa, nutmeg and other crops. The town, known as La Baye by the French, was established in 1763.

The center of town consists of a couple of blocks along the waterfront. Within a few minutes walk from the bus terminal there's a Barclays Bank, police station, post office, supermarket and public market. Near the public market is the island's largest nutmeg processing station.

While the town doesn't have a lot of interest for most visitors, there are a few older buildings of some note, including the Grenville Court House (circa 1886) near the market, the old police station and a couple of churches. The *Ebony Restaurant*, between Barclays and the police station, has reasonably priced West Indian fare.

Grenville is fairly easy to get to by bus and the ride (EC$5) from St George's, along Grand Etang Rd, is the island's most scenic.

Pearls Airport

The Grenville area's best-known site is Pearls Airport, 2 miles north of town, which served as the island's airport until the Cubans built the Point Salines Airport in 1983. The runway at Pearls still has an abandoned Russian biplane and a rusting Cubana aircraft, hastily left here after the US invasion in October 1983. The Grenada Defense Force maintains a barracks at the airstrip, but there's no problem driving into the site.

Because of Grenada's proximity to South America, it was one of the first islands that was settled by migrating Amerindians, and the airport area was a major settlement and burial ground. Thousands of pottery shards, adornos and grinding stones have been collected over the years, both by archaeologists and souvenir hunters. Although the construction of the airport in the 1940s damaged much of the site, the area north of the runway still has significant Amerindian remains; these are now protected by restrictions prohibiting souvenir hunting.

To get to the airport, head north out of Grenville and bear right in Paradise where the road forks. En route you'll pass a former horse race track, a river where local women wash clothes and the ruins of an old sugar mill.

NORTH OF GRENVILLE

As the road continues north from Grenville, it passes through a run of small towns with the occasional stone church and abandoned mill and lots of old wooden homes, some on stilts. When you reach the large church in the village of Tivoli, turn right to continue north to the distillery and Lake Antoine. However, if you prefer to bypass these sights follow the main road to Mt Rose and when you reach the post office take the right to get to Bathways Beach, the left to continue to Morne Fendue and Sauteurs.

The **River Antoine Rum Distillery** (☎ 442-7109) has been producing rum since 1785 and claims to have the oldest working water mill in the Caribbean. Perhaps what's most amazing about is that it works at all – considering how dilapidated the complex is. Not many tourists come this way but for EC$5 one of the workers will usually provide an ad hoc tour; it's open 8 am to 4 pm weekdays. The distillery is south of the lake and most easily accessed from the Tivoli direction.

Lake Antoine, a crater lake in an extinct volcano, is about a mile south of River Sallee; it's pleasant enough to add to a tour but not a must-see site.

BATHWAYS BEACH

From River Sallee, a good road leads to undeveloped Bathways Beach, where's there's a beach of speckled coral sands. At the north side of the beach a rock shelf parallels the shoreline, creating a very long, 30-foot wide 'pool' that's deep enough for swimming. The pool is protected, with a gentle current, while outside the shelf there are strong currents and rough Atlantic seas.

At the new visitor facility opposite the beach you'll find some simple displays on shells, coral and ecology, as well as restrooms. A vendor usually sets up along the beach selling soft drinks and barbecued chicken.

There are three islands off Bathways Beach. From west to east they are Sugar Loaf, a privately owned island with a cottage on its south shore; Green Island, which has a few abandoned buildings but no beach; and Sandy Island, an uninhabited island with a freshwater cistern. Sandy Island also has an abandoned hotel, crystal clear waters and a beautiful beach on its leeward side with fine swimming and snorkeling. It's possible to arrange for a boat in Sauteurs to take you to Sandy Island; make inquiries with the fishers on Sauteurs Beach – expect to pay about EC$150 per boat for the roundtrip.

LEVERA BEACH

Levera Beach is a wild beautiful sweep of sand backed by eroded sea cliffs. Just offshore is the high, pointed Sugar Loaf island (also called Levera Island), while the Grenadine Islands dot the horizon to the north. The beach, the mangrove swamp and the nearby pond have been incorporated into Grenada's national park system and are an important waterfowl habitat and sea turtle nesting site.

The road north from Bathways Beach to Levera Beach is usually passable in a vehicle, but it can be rough so most visitors end up hiking in. The walk from Bathways Beach takes about 30 minutes; stick to the road, as sea cliffs and rough surf make it impossible to walk along the coast between the two beaches.

SAUTEURS

Sauteurs, the largest town on the north side of Grenada, takes its name from the French word for 'jump' and its place in history as

the site where, in 1651, Carib families jumped to their deaths upon their final retreat from approaching French soldiers. Today these 130-foot-high coastal cliffs are called Caribs' Leap. They are the town's main tourist site.

The cliffs are on the north side of the cemetery behind St Patrick's Roman Catholic church. Simply walk straight through the cemetery to reach the site of Caribs' Leap.

From the ledge you can look down on the fishing boats along the village beach and get a view of the offshore islands. The largest is Isle de Ronde, home to a few fisher families. The small islets to the left are called The Sisters; to the right, and closer to shore, is London Bridge, an arch-shaped rock.

Places to Stay & Eat

There are a few local eateries in Sauteurs where you can get rotis and simple West Indian food.

Most people touring the island however, dine at *Morne Fendue Plantation House* (☎ 442-9330), 1.5 miles south of Sauteurs. Octogenarian Betty Mascoll, whose father built this plantation house in 1908 with river stones and a mortar of lime and molasses, serves a West Indian buffet on the veranda. Dishes include pepperpot, chicken fricassee, callaloo soup, pigeon peas and rice, christophene and plantain – many of the items grown right on the grounds. Lunch, available from 12:30 to 3 pm Monday to Saturday, costs EC$40. Reservations are advised.

If you want to soak up more atmosphere there are a couple of guest rooms upstairs that have creaky floors and are in a bit of disrepair, but abound in character. Rates range from US$40 to US$75 with breakfast and dinner included.

The house, marked by a small sign, is in the village of Morne Fendue.

VICTORIA

Although recently improved, the west coast road can still be a bit of a hair-raiser, as sections of it are along eroded cliffs that occasionally release falling rocks. One of the larger of the fishing villages that dot the west coast is Victoria, which has churches, schools, a post office, market, police station and health clinic. Grass Roots, at the Victoria Bridge at the south end of town, sells quality crafts.

While Victoria certainly isn't a tourist destination, it does have a decent place to stay if you want to immerse yourself in village life and be totally away from the tourist scene. Buses to St George's cost EC$3.50 and take about 30 minutes.

Places to Stay & Eat
Victoria Hotel (☎ 444-9367), Queen St, Victoria, is a clean 10-room hotel perched right on the water in the village center. The rooms, above a restaurant and bar, have high ceilings, fans, satellite TV and either a double or two single beds. They cost US$30/45 for singles/doubles. The hotel restaurant has reasonably priced West Indian fare at lunch and dinner. There's a small grocery store opposite the hotel and a few other places in town where you could also grab a bite.

GOUYAVE
Gouyave is the main town in the parish of St John. Many of the people here make a living from fishing and you can see their boats pulled up along the beach at the town's north end, which is called The Lance. There's a market, a bank and a couple of snack shops in the town center.

On Gouyave's main road there's a large **nutmeg processing station**. One of the workers is usually available to take visitors on a tour and explain the process, which can be quite interesting with its fragrant vats of curing nuts and various sorting operations. Tickets are sold at the office for US$1 and a tip to the guide of about the same amount is the norm. The station is open from 8 am to 4 pm weekdays.

Just south of the bridge on the south side of Gouyave, a rough road leads inland half a mile along the river to the **Dougaldston Estate**, where cocoa and spices are processed. If you're curious, someone is

generally around Monday to Friday from 8 am to 3:30 pm, Saturday to 1 pm; they'll give you a brief tour for a tip of about US$2 and you can buy little bags of spices for the same price.

CONCORD FALLS
There are a couple of scenic waterfalls along the Concord River. The lowest falls, a picturesque cascade of about 100 feet, can be viewed by driving to the end of Concord Mountain Rd, a side road leading 1.5 miles inland from the village of Concord. These falls, which have a swimmable pool, are on private property and the owner charges US$1 to visit them.

The trail to the upper falls begins at the end of the road and takes about 30 minutes to hike each way. Because of a history of muggings, the tourist office now provides a uniformed security guard, who will on request accompany visitors on the walk to the upper falls.

Back on the main road, just south of the turn-off to Concord Mountain Rd, there's a small roadside monument dedicated to nine people killed when a dislodged boulder crushed the minibus they were traveling in.

There's a lovely view of Halifax Bay as the road continues south to St George's.

Carriacou

Carriacou, 17 miles northeast of Grenada, is a rural island with small villages, good beaches and a delightfully slow pace. It's a hilly island, about 7 miles long and a third as wide. The landscape, which is dry and scrubby, is dotted with cactus and acacia, although dryland flowering plants such as bougainvillea add a splash of color. Carriacou has 6000 people and about as many goats and sheep.

While the island's low-key character and natural harbor have long attracted yachters, few other Caribbean visitors have Carriacou on their itinerary. Consequently, the beaches are uncrowded; finding a room is

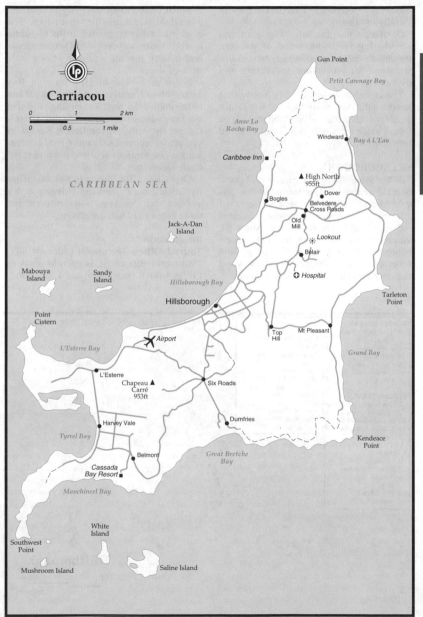

Carriacou

0   1   2 km
0   0.5   1 mile

CARIBBEAN SEA

Gun Point

Petit Carenage Bay

Anse La Roche Bay

Windward • *Bay á L'Eau*

Caribbee Inn ■

▲ High North 955ft

Bogles •   • Dover
         Belvedere
         Cross Roads
      Old Mill •

☀ *Lookout*

• Belair

Jack-A-Dan Island

✚ *Hospital*

Mabouya Island

Sandy Island

Hillsborough Bay

Hillsborough

Tarleton Point

Point Cistern

L'Esterre Bay

✈ *Airport*

Top Hill •   • Mt Pleasant

Grand Bay

L'Esterre •

Chapeau Carré ▲ 953ft

Six Roads

Harvey Vale •

Tyrrel Bay

• Dumfries

Belmont •

Cassada Bay Resort ■

Great Bretche Bay

Kendeace Point

Manchineel Bay

White Island

Southwest Point

Mushroom Island

Saline Island

seldom a problem and islanders are quite friendly to visitors.

Carriacou has fantastic views of the neighboring Grenadines and of its own nearshore islets, a few of which can readily be visited for picnicking, snorkeling and diving.

The island has a unique folk troupe that performs the African-influenced Big Drum Dance, which centers around the playing of drums made of small rum kegs covered with goatskin.

HILLSBOROUGH

Hillsborough, the administrative and commercial center of Carriacou, is an unspoiled and unhurried place – a mix of colorful wooden shops, cement buildings and ramshackle tin structures. Main St, which parallels the beach, has a few interesting 19th-century buildings with ground floors of stone and upper floors of wood that once served as seaside warehouses.

Much of the town's activity is centered around the pier where the ferries dock. The customs and immigration offices, public market, tourist office, post office, museum and bakery are all within a two-minute walk of the pier.

For a nice view of Hillsborough Bay and north to Union Island simply walk out to the end of the pier. Swimming is best at the far ends of town. To the north there's the beach at the Silver Beach Resort; if you prefer a completely untouristed scene, walk a few minutes south of town past the Catholic church.

Grenadians don't seem to have an affinity for botanical gardens; Hillsborough's version, on 1st Ave, is overgrown and more often than not, gated shut.

Information

Tourist Office The tourist office (☎ 443-7948), on Patterson St, is open Monday to Friday from 8 am to noon and 1 to 4 pm.

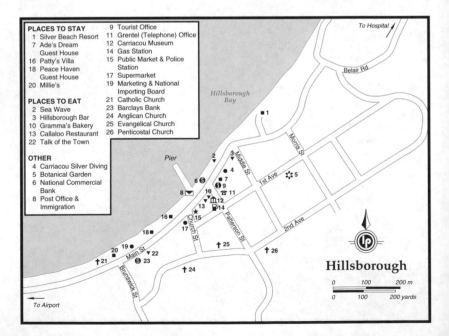

PLACES TO STAY
1 Silver Beach Resort
7 Ade's Dream Guest House
16 Patty's Villa
18 Peace Haven Guest House
20 Millie's

PLACES TO EAT
2 Sea Wave
3 Hillsborough Bar
10 Gramma's Bakery
13 Callaloo Restaurant
22 Talk of the Town

OTHER
4 Carriacou Silver Diving
5 Botanical Garden
6 National Commercial Bank
8 Post Office & Immigration
9 Tourist Office
11 Grentel (Telephone) Office
12 Carriacou Museum
14 Gas Station
15 Public Market & Police Station
17 Supermarket
19 Marketing & National Importing Board
21 Catholic Church
23 Barclays Bank
24 Anglican Church
25 Evangelical Church
26 Penticostal Church

Hillsborough Bay

To Hospital

Belair Rd

Morris St

Middle St

1st Ave

2nd Ave

Patterson St

Church St

Main St

Brunswick St

Pier

To Airport

Hillsborough

0   100   200 m
0   100   200 yards

Money Barclays Bank is on Main St at the south side of town, while the National Commercial Bank is opposite the pier; both are open from Monday to Friday with normal banking hours.

Post The post office, in front of the pier, is open from 8 to noon and 1 to 4 pm Monday to Friday.

Telephone At the Grentel office on Patterson St you can buy phonecards, send faxes or make international calls. It's open from 7:30 am to 6 pm weekdays, from 7:30 am to 1 pm on Saturday. The pay phones outside the office are accessible any time.

Carriacou Museum

Situated in a circa 1825 cotton ginnery, the little Carriacou Museum on Patterson St has a collection of island artifacts that includes Amerindian grinding stones and pottery fragments; a hodgepodge of items from the colonial era, such as clay pipes and China dishes; a small African display and a few works of local artists, including paintings by Canute Caliste.

It's open from 9:30 am to 3:45 pm Monday to Friday. Admission is EC$5 for adults, EC$2.50 for children, and your support will help keep this community-run museum in operation.

Places to Stay

Ade's Dream Guest House (☎ 443-7317, fax 443-8435), Main St, in the center of Hillsborough, has 16 rooms in a newer three-story building and seven rooms in an older wing. The older rooms, which cost US$21, are small and simple with shared baths but they have fans and there's a large group kitchen. The new rooms, which have kitchenettes, private baths, small balconies and fans, cost US$40 on the 2nd floor, US$45 on the 3rd floor. There's a grocery store on the ground floor of the hotel.

Millie's (☎ 443-8207), a new apartment building on Main St, has a variety of rooms that are spotlessly clean. The rooms are in three-bedroom apartments, so you rent one bedroom and share the kitchen and bath with other guests, if there are any. Rooms include fan-cooled ones for US$30, air-conditioned ones for US$35 and a master bedroom with private bath for US$41.

Peace Haven Guest House (☎ 443-7475), Main St, is a good central guesthouse. Rates range from around US$25 for a straightforward room with shared bath to US$50 for a comfortable apartment with full kitchen, two double beds and a balcony perched over the beach. Ask for No 1 or 2, which have ocean-fronting balconies and lovely views of Sandy Island.

Patty's Villa (☎ 443-8412), Main St, is a friendly place with two new apartments, each with a full kitchen and separate bedroom. The back yard is right on the beach. The cost is US$45.

Silver Beach Resort (☎ 443-7337, fax 443-7165), on a nice gray-sand beach at the north side of town, has 18 units, including a few wear-worn cottages. Some of the hotel rooms in the main building have balconies with pleasant ocean views but these too are otherwise ordinary for the money. Rates for either begin at US$70/85 for singles/doubles.

Places to Eat

Gramma's Bakery, in the town center, is a modern bakery with good coconut turnovers and loaves of raisin sweet bread (EC$2) that come warm from the oven in the morning. You can also get microwaved cheese sandwiches (EC$2.50), chicken rotis (EC$6) and drinks throughout the day. There are a few café-style streetfront tables. Gramma's is open Monday to Saturday from 7 am to 7 pm.

Callaloo Restaurant is a pleasant little 2nd-floor restaurant with lunch sandwiches for EC$10 and fish or chicken & chips for EC$15. At dinner, grilled fish or garlic shrimp, accompanied with fried plantains, rice and peas, cost EC$35. For another EC$10 you can add soup or salad and dessert. It's open weekdays from 10 am to 2 pm and 6 to 10 pm.

Sea Wave offers breezy seaside dining at reasonable prices, with a variety of full meals, including baked chicken or steamed fish, for EC$15 to EC$20. It's open daily from 7 am to 10 pm. It also doubles as the town's ice cream parlor.

Silver Beach Resort has an ocean-front al fresco restaurant serving three meals a day. At lunch, rotis, burgers and sand-wiches are priced from EC$12. Dinner main courses include chicken or fresh fish for around EC$30. The restaurant occa-sionally has a Big Drum performance or steel band at dinner.

Talk of the Town on Main St has rotis and other inexpensive local food at lunch. The *Hillsborough Bar*, at the opposite end of Main St, has pizza and other simple food and drinks.

You can find island fruits and vegetables at the small *public market* and get spices at the *Marketing and National Importing Board*, both on Main St.

NORTH OF HILLSBOROUGH

The northern section of Carriacou offers visitors some of the island's finest scenery, a couple of secluded beaches and a glimpse of rural areas that were formerly planted in sugar cane.

From the hilltop hospital, there's a splen-did view of Hillsborough Bay and the nearshore islands. Take Belair Rd, which begins about a third of a mile north of Silver Beach Resort, follow it uphill for half a mile and then bear right on the side road leading into the hospital. In addition to the view you'll find a couple of cannons on the hospital grounds, vestiges of a colonial-era British fort.

If you continue north after leaving the hospital, the road follows the crest of Belvedere Hill, providing some fine views of the east coast and the islands of Petit St Vincent and Petit Martinique. You'll then pass the remains of an old stone **sugar mill** just before reaching the Belvedere Cross Roads. From there, the route going north-east (called the High Rd) leads down to **Windward**, a small windy village backed by gentle hills that's home to the Scottish descendants of shipwrights brought to Car-riacou to build inter-island boats for the planters.

From Windward it's possible to continue another mile to **Petit Carenage Bay** at the northeastern tip of the island, where there's a good beach and views of the northern Grenadines.

If instead you were to go west from the Belvedere Cross Roads you'd soon come to the village of **Bogles**. There's a lovely secluded beach north of the village, at **Anse La Roche Bay**. Buses can drop you at Bogles (EC$2), from where it's about half an hour's walk to the beach.

Places to Stay & Eat

The Round House (☎ /fax 443-7841), right in the village of Bogles, consists of a couple of cottages on a seaside knoll. It's run by Sue and Kim Russell, two yachties who made a 'brief' stop on the island six years ago and never left. The cottages, which cost from US$65 a day for a unit that sleeps two to US$90 for one that sleeps four, have mosquito nets, fans, refrigerators and hot plates. Prices are negotiable in the low season. One of the cottages, an attractive round building made of stone, is being con-verted into a restaurant.

The *Caribbee Inn* (☎ 443-7380, fax 443-8142), Prospect, between Bogles and Anse La Roche Beach, is an upscale inn with a rural setting. Operated by British couple Wendy and Robert Cooper, it has eight bedrooms furnished with four-poster beds, ceiling fans, mosquito nets and private baths. Large louvered windows open to the trade winds and views. Doubles begin at US$130/170 in summer/winter; breakfast and dinner can be included for an extra US$40 per person.

There are no guesthouses or restaurants in Windward but there are small shops where you can buy cold drinks and snacks.

L'ESTERRE

L'Esterre is a small village southwest of the airport that retains a bit of French influ-ence, most noticeably in the French patois that many of the older villagers still speak.

The village's main sight is the home of Carriacou artist Canute Caliste, who paints uncomplicated visions of mermaids and sailing vessels. After many decades, his folk art has gained a bit of an international following and is the subject of the book *The Mermaid Wakes: Paintings of a Caribbean Isle*. To get to his shop, follow the road west at the main village T-junction rather than turning south towards Tyrrel Bay.

Places to Stay & Eat

Hope's Inn (☎ 443-7457) is a guesthouse on a pleasant sandy beach at the north side of L'Esterre on the road to the airport. There are six clean, straightforward rooms with fans and shared baths. Guests have use of two shared kitchens and a little sitting area. Singles/doubles cost US$25/29. There's also a roomy apartment with its own kitchen for US$40. A little store out front sells basic provisions.

Also near the beach is *Paradise Inn* (☎ 443-8406, fax 443-8391), which is run by Tankred Mueller, a German divemaster, and his native-born wife Ali. There are six large bedrooms with ceiling fans, rattan furnishings and private baths. Rates vary with the room but average US$45/55 for singles/doubles in winter, US$10 less in summer; discounts are available on weekly stays. Moderately priced meals are available at Ali's beachside bar.

TYRREL BAY

Tyrrel Bay is a deep protected bay with a sandy beach and the small low-key village of Harvey Vale. This is a popular anchorage for visiting yachters and the nearest that Carriacou has to a beach hangout. The deep, narrow lagoon at the north side of the bay is known by yachters as Hurricane Bay, because it's a safe harbor for them during severe storms. Local fishers know the bay as Oyster Bed, because of the oysters that grow on the roots of the lagoon's mangrove trees.

Opposite the beach are a couple of places to stay and eat, including a popular restaurant run by a young French couple. A relatively frequent bus route operates from Hillsborough to Belmont via Tyrrel Bay.

Places to Stay

Constant Spring (☎ 443-7396), a small guesthouse at the south side of Tyrrel Bay, has three simple rooms with shared baths and a shared kitchen. Singles/doubles cost US$17/32.

Scraper's Cottages (☎ /fax 443-7403), adjacent to the restaurant of the same name, consists of eight apartments in duplex cottages. Most are quite nice with a full kitchen, private bath and bedroom with two double beds. Singles/doubles cost US$45/50.

Alexis Apartment Hotel (☎ /fax 443-7179) has a dozen straightforward, clean rooms with private baths, opposite the beach at the center of Tyrrel Bay. Singles/doubles cost US$65/85 for rooms with kitchenettes, US$45/55 for those without; there's a 20% discount on weekly stays.

The new *Carriacou Yacht & Beach Club*, (☎ /fax 443-6292, VHF 16) on the south side of Tyrrel Bay, about a 15-minute walk from Harvey Vale, is geared primarily to visiting yachties. It has four simple but neat rooms with refrigerators, coffeemakers,

GRENADA

Boat Building

Carriacou islanders have long made their living from the sea as fishers, mariners and boat builders. Until recent times, it was possible to see wooden schooners being built along the beach in Windward, with boat builders using the same handcrafting techniques that the early Scottish settlers brought with them in colonial times. However, a penchant for steel hulls has undermined traditional boat building and, save for the occasional small fishing boat, little boat construction is done on Carriacou these days. The situation is similar to the more northerly Grenadine island of Bequia, which also has a sizable settlement of Scottish descendants. ∎

ceiling fans and private baths for US$50. The club has a dinghy dock, a small store with limited supplies and a moderately priced, open-air restaurant with a chalkboard menu.

Cassada Bay Resort (☎ 443-7494, fax 443-7672), between Tyrrel Bay and Belmont, about a 20-minute walk from either, has 16 hillside rooms and a splendid view. The weathered wooden duplex cottages have character, and were once part of a marine biology school, 'Camp Carriacou,' which catered to wealthy American children. The roomy cottages are pleasantly simple with oceanview decks, screened louvered windows, a table, couch and two single beds. Singles/doubles cost US$55/70 in winter, US$50/60 in summer.

Places to Eat
Poivre et Sel (☎ 443-8390, VHF 16), an open-air restaurant above Alexis Supermarket, is a high-energy place serving good French food. At lunch you can get pasta, omelets and salads for EC$10 to EC$20. At dinner, starters range from onion soup (EC$12) to shrimp Provençale (EC$20) and main courses include fresh fish preparations or lobster crêpes for EC$35. It's open from 10 am to 2 pm and from 5:30 pm to around midnight. Occasionally, there's live entertainment.

Scraper's Restaurant, sitting opposite the beach, has a varied menu that includes fish sandwiches or hamburgers for EC$8 and main dishes ranging from spaghetti for EC$15 to lobster for EC$45. It's open Monday to Saturday from 9 am to 11 pm and on Sunday from 11 am to 11 pm.

A couple of local eateries and bars opposite the beach, including *Al's*, provide inexpensive West Indian fare. You can pick up groceries and liquor at *Alexis Supermarket* near the center of the beach and *Barba's Supermarket*, closer to the dockyard.

Cassada Bay Resort has an open-air veranda restaurant and bar with a fine view and good food. At lunch, fish or meat burgers cost EC$10, while at dinnertime, chicken, catch of the day or curried lambi cost around EC$35.

NEARSHORE ISLANDS
The little islet of **Sandy Island**, off the west side of Hillsborough Bay, is a favorite daytime destination of snorkelers and yachters. It's the epitome of the reef island cliché – nothing but glistening sands dotted with a few coconut palms and surrounded by turquoise waters. Snorkelers take to the shallow waters fronting Sandy Island, while the deeper waters at the far side are a popular dive site. Unfortunately, the island's easy accessibility has resulted in it being 'loved to death,' with the surrounding coral gardens heavily damaged by dropped and dragging anchors.

A speedboat for up to two people costs EC$70 (EC$10 more for additional passengers) through the tourist office or call Cuthbert Snagg (☎ 443-8293), who runs a water taxi. Be clear as to when you want to be picked up – as the island takes only a couple of minutes to walk around, a whole afternoon here could tick by very slowly.

It's also possible to get there via the *Carriacou Islander*, a glass-bottom boat that provides day tours to Sandy Island for EC$95 (children half price), including a picnic lunch. The boat only goes out if there's a minimum of six passengers. You can make arrangements at Down Island Villa Rentals (☎ 443-8182), north of the tourist office.

Although it's often overlooked by travelers, **White Island** makes for a nice little outing. It has a good sandy beach for bathing and a pristine reef for snorkeling. This small hat-shaped island, about a mile off the southern tip of Carriacou, is also easy to get to.

Cassada Bay Resort will shuttle day trippers over to White Island, just a five-minute ride from the resort's pier, for EC$50 for up to five passengers. You can also make boat arrangements through the tourist office.

GETTING THERE & AWAY
Air
Airlines of Carriacou (☎ 444-3549) has three flights a day between Grenada and Carriacou, with the first northbound flight

leaving Grenada at 6:30 am on Monday, Wednesday and Friday and at 8 am other days, and the last flight returning from Carriacou at 4:50 pm. LIAT (☎ 443-7362) has two daily flights from Grenada to Carriacou, one at 9:30 am and the other at 5 pm. From Carriacou, LIAT flights leave for Grenada at 8:50 am and 4:15 pm. Region Air Caribbean (☎ 444-1117), the third carrier with flights between Grenada and Carriacou, has a schedule similar to LIAT's. The cost on any of these airlines is EC$93 one way, EC$127 for a same-day roundtrip ticket or EC$147 for a 21-day excursion ticket.

Air Carriacou and Region Air Caribbean each have a couple of daily flights between Carriacou and Union Island. The cheapest fare is with Region Air Caribbean, which charges EC$59 each way.

Airport Information Carriacou's airport, 1.2 miles west of Hillsborough, is such a modest facility that the island's main road cuts clear across the center of the runway, with traffic yielding to planes!

The terminal has a tiny souvenir shop, a bar, coin and card phones and a single check-in counter for LIAT, Air Carriacou and Region Air Caribbean.

Boat
There are two types of boats plying between Grenada and Carriacou. You can either hop an old-fashioned cargo boat that takes three to four hours, or ride on a modern express catamaran that takes half as long and costs twice as much.

Cargo/Passenger Boats The *Adelaide*, an older wooden boat that still uses its sail, departs from Grenada at 9:30 am Wednesday and Saturday and leaves Carriacou at 9:30 am Monday and Thursday. The *Alexia IV*, a steel-hulled ship that's a little more modern, has the same schedule as the *Adelaide*.

A sister ship, the *Alexia III*, departs from Grenada at 9:30 am Tuesday, 11 am Friday and 7 am Sunday, and leaves Carriacou at 9:30 am Wednesday and Saturday and 5 pm Sunday.

The fare on any of the three boats is EC$20 one way; buy your ticket on the boat. On Grenada the boats dock at the north side of the Carenage in St George's and on Carriacou at Hillsborough's town pier.

Catamaran The *Osprey* is a 144-seat motorized catamaran that connects Grenada's three populated islands. For reservations call ☎ 407-0470.

The following schedule covers the *Osprey's* sailings Monday to Saturday; Sunday's schedule is slightly different. The boat leaves Petit Martinique for Carriacou at 5:30 am and 3 pm (3:30 pm on Saturday), leaves Carriacou for Grenada at 6 am and 3:30 pm (4 pm on Saturday), leaves Grenada for Carriacou at 9 am and 5:30 pm (at 9 am only on Saturday) and leaves Carriacou for Petit Martinique at 11 am and 7 pm Monday to Friday.

The one-way fares are EC$10 between Petit Martinique and Carriacou and EC$40 between Grenada and Carriacou or Petit Martinique. Roundtrip fares from Grenada are EC$75.

GETTING AROUND
Bus & Taxi
Buses, which are privately owned minivans, charge EC$2 to go anywhere on the island (EC$1 if the distance is less than a mile). The two main routes run from Hillsborough, one south to Tyrrel Bay, the other north to Windward. Minibuses start around 7 am and stop around 4:30 pm – they're easiest to catch in the early morning when people are going to school and work and are less frequent during the late morning and early afternoon.

You can get a cheap island tour by hopping on a minibus departing from Hillsborough and either breaking en route or staying on the bus for the return ride. The Windward-bound buses usually take the High Rd one way and the Low Rd the other, making for a good loop tour.

Some minibuses double as taxis, and usually you can count on a couple of them swinging by the airport when a flight comes in. Taxis from the airport charge EC$10 to

Hillsborough and EC$20 to Tyrrel Bay, Cassada Bay or Bogles.

Car

The island's only gas station, which is on Patterson St in Hillsborough, is open daily from 8 am to 6 pm.

There are a couple of places to rent vehicles on Carriacou, with rates typically around US$40 to US$50 a day. Barba Gabriel (☎ 443-7454) at Barba's Supermarket in Tyrrel Bay rents both 4WD Suzukis and Geo Trackers, while Bullen Car Rental (☎ 443-7221) at the gas station rents jeeps.

Organized Tours

You can hire a taxi for a 2½-hour island tour that costs EC$150 for up to five people, or you could tour the northern half of the island, which takes half as long and costs EC$75.

Petit Martinique

Petit Martinique, 3 miles northeast of Carriacou, is a near-circular island, about a mile in width, with a volcanic cone rising 738 feet.

Most of Petit Martinique's 900 inhabitants make a living from the sea – largely from fishing, although a fair number of men work as mariners on regional ships.

It's a closely knit group of people; virtually all islanders are Catholic and most share a half-dozen surnames. They have a reputation for their independent character as well as a bit of notoriety for smuggling. There are a couple of schools and churches, a small restaurant and a few grocery stores. Homes are tidy and residents of Petit Martinique enjoy one of the region's highest per capita incomes.

There's one road along the west coast, but otherwise people get around on footpaths. While the beaches aren't special, it makes a pleasant place to walk around.

Places to Stay

At *Seaside View Holiday Cottages* (☎ 443-9210, fax 443-9113), Mrs Emma Logan rents out three self-contained cottages overlooking the harbor. The cost is US$25 for a one-bedroom cottage, US$35 for a two-bedroom.

Getting There & Away

The *Osprey* catamaran (☎ 407-0470) has introduced regular boat service connecting Petit Martinique with Grenada (EC$40 one way) and Carriacou (EC$10 one way). For the schedule, see the Getting There & Away section under Carriacou.

It's also possible to arrange through the tourist office for a speedboat to zip you over to Petit Martinique from Windward on Carriacou; it'll cost about EC$120 for the boat.

Guadeloupe

Guadeloupe, the center of the Caribbean's Creole culture, boasts a spirited blend of French and African influences. The island archipelago is largely provincial in nature and remains as well known for its sugar and rum as for its beaches and resorts.

Guadeloupe's shape inevitably invites comparison to a butterfly, as it has two abutting wing-shaped islands. The outline of the two islands is somewhat symmetrical, but the topography is anything but that. Grande-Terre, the eastern wing, has a terrain of gently rolling hills and level plains, much of which is cultivated in sugar cane. Basse-Terre, the western wing, is dominated by rugged hills and mountains that are wrapped in a dense rainforest of tall trees and lush ferns. Much of the interior of Basse-Terre has been set aside as a national park, which includes trails through the rainforest, the Eastern Caribbean's highest waterfalls and the island's highest peak, La Soufrière, a smoldering volcano.

The center of the island and its principal city is the bustling Pointe-à-Pitre, while the sleepy capital of Basse-Terre is on the remote southwestern side. Virtually all of the resort hotels, as well as the larger marinas, are along the southern shore of Grande-Terre.

Guadeloupe's surrounding offshore islands make interesting side excursions. The most visited, Terre-de-Haut, is a delightful place with a quaint central village and harbor, good beaches and restaurants and some reasonably priced places to stay. The other populated islands – Terre-de-Bas, Marie-Galante and La Désirade – have very little tourism development and offer visitors a glimpse of a rural French West Indies that has changed little in recent times.

HIGHLIGHTS

- Intriguing Creole culture, which permeates everything from local dress to restaurant menus
- Extensive national park with verdant rainforest, magnificent waterfalls and a steaming volcano
- Terre-de-Haut, a charming tourist haunt ideal for day trips
- Good beaches, breathtaking hikes and plenty of water sports
- Timeless rural character on the sleepy isles of La Désirade and Marie-Galante

Facts about the Guadeloupe Islands

HISTORY

When sighted by Columbus on November 14, 1493, Guadeloupe was inhabited by Carib Indians, who called it Karukera, 'Island of Beautiful Waters.' The Spanish made two attempts to settle Guadeloupe in the early 1500s but were repelled both times

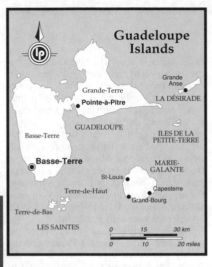

1674, a slavery-based plantation system was well established.

The English invaded Guadeloupe several times and occupied it from 1759 to 1763. During this time they developed Pointe-à-Pitre into a major harbor, opened profitable English and North American markets to Guadeloupean sugar and allowed the planters to import cheap American lumber and food. Many French colonists actually grew wealthier under the British occupation and the economy expanded rapidly. In 1763 British occupation ended with the signing of the Treaty of Paris, provisions of which relinquished French claims in Canada in exchange for the return of Guadeloupe.

Amidst the chaos of the French Revolution, the British invaded Guadeloupe again in 1794. In response to that invasion, the French sent a contingent of soldiers led by Victor Hugues, a black nationalist. Hugues freed and armed Guadeloupean slaves. On the day the British withdrew from Guadeloupe, Hugues went on a rampage and killed 300 Royalists, many of them plantation owners. It marked the start of a reign of reckless terror. In all, Hugues was responsible for the deaths of more than 1000 colonists and as a consequence of his attacks on US ships, the USA declared war on France.

In 1802 Napoleon Bonaparte, anxious to get the situation under control, sent General Antoine Richepance to Guadeloupe. Richepance put down the uprising, restored the prerevolutionary government and reinstituted slavery.

by fierce Carib resistance and finally in 1604 abandoned their claim to the island.

Three decades later, French colonists sponsored by the Compagnie des Iles d'Amérique, an association of French entrepreneurs, set sail to establish the first European settlement on Guadeloupe. On June 28, 1635, the party, led by Charles Liénard de l'Olive and Jean Duplessis d'Ossonville, landed on the southeastern shore of Basse-Terre and claimed Guadeloupe for France. They drove the Caribs off the island, planted crops and within a decade had built the first sugar mill. By the time France officially annexed the island in

---

Big Land, Flat Land

At first glance, the names given to the twin islands that make up Guadeloupe proper are perplexing. The eastern island, which is smaller and flatter, is named Grande-Terre, which means 'big land,' while the larger, more mountainous western side is named Basse-Terre, meaning 'flat land.'

The names were not meant to describe the terrain, however, but the winds that blow over them. The trade winds, which come from the northeast, blow *grande* over the flat plains of Grande-Terre but are stopped by the mountains to the west, ending up flat *(basse)* on Basse-Terre. ■

Guadeloupe

0   5   10 km

0   3   6 miles

GUADELOUPE

Guadeloupe was the most prosperous island in the French West Indies and the British continued to covet it, invading and occupying the island for most of the period between 1810 and 1816. The Treaty of Vienna restored the island to France, which has maintained sovereignty over it continuously since 1816.

Slavery was abolished in 1848, following a campaign led by French politician Victor Schoelcher. In the years that followed, planters brought laborers from Pondicherry, a French colony in India, to work in the cane fields. Since 1871, Guadeloupe has had representation in the French parliament and since 1946 has been an overseas department of France.

GEOGRAPHY

Guadeloupe proper is comprised of twin islands divided by a narrow mangrove channel called the Rivière Salée. The islands are volcanic in origin with a total land area of 1434 sq km. Grande-Terre, the eastern island, has a limestone cover, the result of having been submerged during earlier geologic periods. Basse-Terre, the larger western island, is rugged and mountainous. Guadeloupe's highest point is La Soufrière, a 1467 meter active volcano.

Of the nearby offshore islands, Les Saintes (14 sq km) are high and rugged, Marie-Galante (158 sq km) is relatively flat and La Désirade (22 sq km) has an intermediate topography with hills that rise up to 273 meters.

CLIMATE

Pointe-à-Pitre's average daily high temperature in January is 28°C (83°F) while the low averages 19°C (67°F). In July the average daily high is 31°C (88°F) while the low averages 23°C (74°F).

The annual rainfall in Pointe-à-Pitre is 1814 mm (71 inches). February to April are the driest months, when measurable rain falls an average of seven days a month and the average humidity is around 77%. The wettest months are July to November, when rain falls about 14 days a month and the average humidity reaches 85%.

Because of its height, the Basse-Terre side is both cooler and rainier than Grande-Terre. Its highest point, La Soufrière volcano, averages 9900 mm (390 inches) of rain a year.

The trade winds, called *alizés*, often temper the climate.

FLORA & FAUNA

Guadeloupe's diverse vegetation ranges from mangrove swamps to mountainous rainforest. Basse-Terre has an abundance of tropical hardwood trees, including lofty gommiers and large buttressed chataigniers, and thick fern forests punctuated with flowering heliconia and ginger plants.

Birds found on Guadeloupe include various members of the heron family, pelicans, hummingbirds and the endangered Guadeloupe wren. A common sighting is the bright yellow-bellied bananaquit, a small nectar-feeding bird that's a frequent visitor at open-air restaurants where it raids unattended sugar bowls.

The raccoon, whose main habitat is in the forests of Basse-Terre, is the official

symbol of the Parc National de la Guadeloupe. You can expect to see drawings of raccoons on park brochures and in Guadeloupean advertising as a means of projecting a 'natural' image.

Guadeloupe has mongooses aplenty, introduced long ago in a futile attempt to control rats in the sugar cane fields. Agoutis, a short-haired rabbit-like rodent with short ears that looks a bit like a guinea pig, are found on La Désirade. There are iguanas on Les Saintes and La Désirade.

GOVERNMENT & POLITICS

Guadeloupe is an overseas department of France and has a status on par with the 96 *départements* on the French mainland. The department of Guadeloupe, which also encompasses St Barts and St Martin, is represented in the French parliament by four elected deputies and two senators.

A prefect, who is appointed by the French Minister of the Interior and assisted by two general secretaries and two *sous-préfets* (sub-prefects), represents the central government and oversees island authorities. There are two locally elected legislative bodies, the Conseil Général and the Conseil Régional, each with about 40 members. Guadeloupe is further divided into three districts and 34 communes. Each commune has a municipal council elected by popular vote and a mayor elected from the council.

ECONOMY

Guadeloupe's economy is heavily dependent upon subsidies from the French government and upon its economic ties with metropolitan France, which absorbs the majority of Guadeloupe's exports and provides 75% of its imports. Guadeloupe has a sizable imbalance of trade; total exports are valued at an estimated US$130 million, while imports are valued at US$1.4 billion.

Agriculture remains a cornerstone of Guadeloupe's economy. The leading export crop is bananas, the bulk of which grow along the southern flanks of La Soufrière volcano. About two-thirds of all bananas eaten in France are from Guadeloupe.

Although the importance of sugar is diminishing, a third of Guadeloupe's cultivable land is still planted in cane. Much of the sugar is used in the production of rum, which is second only to bananas in export value.

In the industrial sector, Guadeloupe has about 150 small-scale enterprises including food processing, cement, plastics and furniture. Tourism is the fastest growing sector of the economy. Of the island's 165,000 annual overnight visitors, about 70% come from France, 13% from other parts of Europe and a little over 10% from the USA. In addition, about 75,000 cruise ship passengers call on Guadeloupe each year.

POPULATION & PEOPLE
The population of Guadeloupe (Basse-Terre and Grande-Terre) is about 350,000. In addition, about 3000 people live on Les Saintes, 1600 on La Désirade and 13,000 on Marie-Galante.

About three-quarters of the population is of mixed ethnicity, a combination of African, European and East Indian descent. There's also a sizable population of white islanders who trace their ancestry to the early French settlers, as well as a number of more recently arrived French from the mainland.

SOCIETY & CONDUCT
Guadeloupean culture draws on French, African, East Indian and West Indian influences. The mix is visible in the architecture, which ranges from French colonial to Hindu temples; in the food, which merges influences from all the cultures into a unique Creole cuisine; and in the local Creole language that predominates in the home.

Guadeloupe is one place where you're more apt to see women wearing traditional Creole dress, especially at festivals and cultural events. The typical costume consists of a full, brightly colored skirt, commonly a madras-type plaid of oranges and yellows, with a matching headdress, a white lace-trimmed blouse and petticoat and a scarf draped over the shoulder.

In the arts, the most renowned native son is Saint-John Perse, the pseudonym of Alexis Léger, who was born in Guadeloupe in 1887 and won the Nobel Prize for Literature in 1960 for the evocative imagery of his poetry. One of his many noted works is *Anabase* (1925), which was translated into English by TS Eliot.

Dos & Don'ts
Except for fine dining, dress is casual but generally stylish. Topless bathing is common on the island, particularly at resort beaches. Swim wear is not appropriate away from the beach.

RELIGION
The predominant religion is Roman Catholicism. There are also Methodist, Seventh Day Adventist, Jehovah's Witness and Evangelical denominations, as well as a sizable Hindu community.

LANGUAGE
French is the official language, but islanders commonly speak a local Creole dialect among themselves.

While English is not widely spoken, most desk clerks in larger hotels speak English and a fair number of other people in tourist-related areas are willing to communicate in a combination of slow French and broken English. If you don't speak French, bring a French-English dictionary and phrase book.

Keep in mind that even if you do speak French, the language – especially on the outer islands – is so peppered with Creole that it can be challenging to fully understand.

Facts for the Visitor

ORIENTATION
The airport is north of Pointe-à-Pitre, just a 10-minute drive from the city center and 20 minutes from Gosier, the largest tourist area. Roads are good and the island can readily be explored in a series of day trips, with a day given to circling Grande-Terre,

GUADELOUPE

another day to northern Basse-Terre and the Route de la Traversée and a third day to southern Basse-Terre.

Ferries link Guadeloupe to the islands of Terre-de-Haut, Marie-Galante and La Désirade, with schedules that allow day trippers to sail over to any of these islands in the morning and return to Guadeloupe in the late afternoon.

Maps

The best map of Guadeloupe is the No 510 (1:100,000) map published by the Institut Géographique National (IGN), which is sold at bookstores around the island for 55F. Although the paper quality is inferior, you can get the same detailed IGN map in a glossy version, free of charge, from island car rental agencies.

TOURIST OFFICES
Local Tourist Offices

The mailing address for the central tourist office on Guadeloupe is: Office Départemental du Tourisme de la Guadeloupe (☎ 82 09 30, fax 83 89 22), 5 Square de la Banque, BP 422, 97100 Pointe-à-Pitre, Guadeloupe, French West Indies.

There are also regional tourist offices in the towns of Basse-Terre (☎ 81 24 83) and Saint-François (☎ 88 48 74) and local information bureaus (syndicat d'initiative) in some smaller towns.

Tourist Offices Abroad

Overseas tourism representatives include:

France
 Office du Tourisme de Guadeloupe,
 43 Rue des Tilleuls,
 92100 Boulogne-Billancourt
 (☎ 01 46 04 00 08, fax 01 46 04 74 03)
Germany
 Bureau de la Guadeloupe en Allemagne,
 Bethmannstrabe 58, 6000 Frankfrut am
 Main 1 (☎ 69 28 33 15, fax 69 28 75 44)
Italy
 Ente Nationale Francese per il Turismo,
 5 Via Sant Andrea, 20121 Milan
 (☎ 258 31 64 71, fax 279 45 82)
UK
 French Government Tourist Office,
 178 Piccadilly, London W1V OAL
 (☎ 0171-491-7622, fax 0171-493-6594)

USA
 French Government Tourist Office,
 444 Madison Ave, New York, NY 10022
 (☎ 900-990-0040 – a toll call that costs 95
 cents per minute, fax 212-838-7855)

VISAS & DOCUMENTS

US and Canadian citizens can stay up to three months by showing proof of citizenship in the form of an expired (up to five years) passport or an official birth certificate accompanied by a driver's license or other government-authorized photo ID.

Citizens of the European Union (EU) need an official identity card, passport or valid French carte de séjour. Citizens of most other foreign countries, including Australia, need a valid passport and visa for France.

Visitors officially require a return or onward ticket.

CUSTOMS

Citizens of EU countries are allowed to bring in 300 cigarettes, 1.5 liters of spirits and four liters of wine duty free. Non-EU citizens are allowed to bring in 200 cigarettes, a bottle of spirits and two liters of wine duty free. All visitors are allowed to bring in 'large allowances of rum' as well.

MONEY

The French franc is the island currency. Hotels, larger restaurants and car rental agencies accept Visa (Carte Bleue), American Express and MasterCard (Eurocard). For most other situations, you'll need to use francs. Avoid changing money at hotel lobbies, where the rates are worse than at exchange offices or banks. More information is under Money in the Facts for the Visitor chapter at the front of the book.

POST & COMMUNICATIONS
Post

There are post offices in Pointe-à-Pitre, Basse-Terre, Gosier, Saint-François and other major towns. It costs 3F to send a postcard to France, 3.80F to the Caribbean or the USA, 4.40F to other parts of the Americas and 5.20F to the rest of the world. This rate also covers letters up to 20 grams.

Postage stamps can be purchased at tobacco shops *(tabacs)* and some hotels in addition to post offices.

Mail addressed to Guadeloupe should end with the postal code, town name and 'Guadeloupe, French West Indies.'

Telephone

Public phones in Guadeloupe accept French phonecards *(télécartes)*, not coins. The cards cost 37F or 89F, depending on the calling time, and are sold at post offices and at shops marked *télécarte en vente ici*. Public phones can be found at most post offices, the airport, city parks and other public places. For directory assistance, dial 12.

When making a local call, dial just the six-digit local number. When calling from outside Guadeloupe, add the 0590 area code to the six-digit local number.

More information on phonecards and making long-distance calls is under Post & Communications in the Facts for the Visitor chapter in the front of the book.

The area code for Guadeloupe is 0590.

BOOKS

There are many books about Guadeloupe and its flora and fauna in French, but books in English are harder to find. A good place to look is at the Boutique de la Presse in the Centre Saint-John Perse in Pointe-à-Pitre.

The leading contemporary novelist in the French West Indies is Guadeloupe native Maryse Condé. Two of her best-selling novels have been translated into English. The epic *Tree of Life* (Random House, 1992), centers around the life of a Guadeloupean family, their roots and the identity of Guadeloupean society itself. *Crossing the Mangrove* (Anchor Books, 1995), is a very enjoyable yarn that gently reveals nuances of rural Guadeloupean relationships as it unravels the life, and untimely death, of a controversial villager.

The bilingual French/English *A Cruising Guide to Guadeloupe*, part of the Guide Trois Rivières series (Edition Caripress, 30 Rue Montesquieu, 97200 Fort-de-France, Martinique), is a comprehensive sailing manual for cruising Guadeloupe and the offshore islands.

NEWSPAPERS & MAGAZINES

The island's local daily is the *France-Antilles*. Other French-language newspapers, such as *Le Monde*, are flown in daily from the mainland. Larger newsstands in Pointe-à-Pitre and major tourist areas sell the *International Herald-Tribune* and a few other English-language newspapers.

For tourist information these free and bilingual publications are useful: *Ti Gourmet*, a pocket-size restaurant guide offering a complimentary drink at many island restaurants; and *Le Guide Créole*, a more general publication with everything from historical background to entertainment listings.

RADIO & TV

Radio France Outre-Mer (RFO) provides public radio and TV broadcasting. Guadeloupe also has two private TV stations and a number of independent FM radio stations.

ELECTRICITY

Electricity is 220 volts AC, 50 cycles, as in France. Some hotels have adapted outlets in bathrooms that allow for the use of 110 volt electric razors.

WEIGHTS & MEASURES

Guadeloupe uses the metric system and the 24-hour clock.

HEALTH

The main hospital is the Centre Hospitalier (☎ 89 10 10) in Pointe-à-Pitre, at the east end of Faubourg Victor Hugo. There's also a hospital (☎ 80 54 54) in Basse-Terre and a number of smaller medical facilities around Guadeloupe.

Bilharzia (schistosomiasis) is found throughout Grande-Terre and in much of Basse-Terre, including Grand Étang lake. The main method of prevention is to avoid

GUADELOUPE

swimming or wading in fresh water. More information is in the Health section in the introductory Facts for the Visitor chapter.

DANGERS & ANNOYANCES
Guadeloupe's crime rate is relatively low compared to other large islands in the Eastern Caribbean. There are poisonous manchineel trees on some of the beaches, usually marked with a warning sign.

EMERGENCIES
In an emergency, dial ☎ 17 for police and ☎ 18 for the fire department. For more routine police assistance dial ☎ 89 77 17 in Pointe-à-Pitre, ☎ 81 11 55 in Basse-Terre.

BUSINESS HOURS
Although they vary, typical shop hours are from 9 am to 1 pm and 3 to 6 pm Monday to Friday. Many shops are also open on Saturday mornings.

Bank hours are commonly from 8 am to noon and 2 to 4 pm weekdays. During the summer, many banks change their hours to 8 am to 3 pm. Banks close at noon on the day before a public holiday.

PUBLIC HOLIDAYS & SPECIAL EVENTS
Public holidays in Guadeloupe are:

New Year's Day	January 1
Easter Sunday	late March/early April
Easter Monday	late March/early April
Labor Day	May 1
Victory Day	May 8
Ascension Thursday	40th day after Easter
Pentecost Monday	eighth Monday after Easter
Slavery Abolition Day	May 27
Bastille Day	July 14
Schoelcher Day	July 21
Assumption Day	August 15
All Saints Day	November 1
Armistice Day	November 11
Christmas Day	December 25

Carnival celebrations, held during the traditional week-long Mardi Gras period that ends on Ash Wednesday, features costume parades, dancing, music and other festivities.

The Fête des Cuisinières (Festival of Women Cooks) is a colorful event held in Pointe-à-Pitre in early August. Women in Creole dress, carrying baskets of traditional foods, parade through the streets to the cathedral where they are blessed by the bishop. It's followed by a banquet and dancing.

The Tour Cycliste de la Guadeloupe, a 10-day international cycling race, is also held in early August.

ACTIVITIES
Beaches & Swimming
There are white-sand beaches in the resort towns of Gosier, Sainte-Anne and Saint-François. At the north side of the peninsula leading to Pointe des Châteaux are a couple of picturesque remote beaches: Anse à la Gourde, a gorgeous sweep of white coral sands, and Anse Tarare, the adjacent nudist beach. While most of Grande-Terre's east coast has rough surf, there is a swimmable beach at Le Moule and a little protected cove at Porte d'Enfer. On the west side of Grande-Terre, Port-Louis is the most popular swimming spot, with a broad sandy beach that attracts weekend crowds.

On Basse-Terre, the nicest beaches are along the north side of the island. Choicest are Grande Anse beach, with its expansive golden sands, and Plage de Tillet, a secluded clothing-optional cove; both are just north of Deshaies. There are also a handful of black-sand beaches along Basse-Terre's southern shore.

Diving
Guadeloupe's top diving site is the Réserve Cousteau at Pigeon Island off the west coast of Basse-Terre. Spearfishing has long been banned in this underwater reserve and consequently the waters surrounding Pigeon Island, which is just a kilometer offshore, are teeming with colorful tropical fish, sponges, sea fans and corals.

Dive Shops There are numerous dive shops in Guadeloupe including the following three in the Réserve Cousteau area; each goes out daily at 10 am and 12:30 and

3 pm. Single dive rates average 200F, with discounts given on multiple dive packages.

Les Heures Saines, Rocher Malendure, 97132 Pigeon (☎ 98 86 63, fax 98 77 76); popular with English speakers, this well-regarded operation has modern equipment, a large catamaran, and both NAUI and CMAS programs.

Aux Aquanautes Antillais, Plage de Malendure, 97125 Bouillante (☎ 98 87 30, fax 90 11 85); a friendly local operation right on Malendure Beach.

Chez Guy et Christian, Plage de Malendure, 97132 Pigeon (☎ 98 82 43, fax 98 82 84); another beachside operator, it offers night dives in addition to day outings.

Snorkeling

Guadeloupe's most popular snorkeling spot is Pigeon Island. The company Nautilus (☎ 98 89 08) offers glass-bottom boat trips from Malendure Beach that include about 20 minutes of snorkeling time.

On Grande-Terre, there's reasonable snorkeling off Ilet du Gosier, which can be reached by boat from Gosier. Snorkeling equipment can be rented at many beachside tourist resorts.

Surfing

Le Moule, Port-Louis and Anse Bertrand commonly have good surfing conditions from around October to May. In summer, Sainte-Anne, Saint-François and Petit-Havre can have good wave action.

Windsurfing

Windsurfing is quite popular on Guadeloupe. Much of the activity is centered near the resorts on the south side of Grande-Terre and on the island of Terre-de-Haut. Windsurfing gear can be rented from beach huts for about 75F an hour. If you're new to the sport there are a number of reputable places offering courses, including Nathalie Simon Sport Away (☎ 88 72 04), at the south side of the marina in Saint-François, which has a 90-minute beginners course for 280F. The shop also rents surf and body boards for 70F a half-day.

UCPA, the Union des Centres de Plein Air (☎ 88 64 80), 97118 Saint-François,

has week-long windsurfing/hotel packages in both Saint-François and Terre-de-Haut.

Fishing

Deep-sea fishing can be arranged with Caraïbe Pêche (☎ 90 97 51), Evasion Exotic (☎ 90 94 17) and other boats at the Bas du Fort Marina.

Hiking

Guadeloupe has wonderful trails that take in waterfalls, primordial rainforest and botanical gardens. A number of them are simple 10- to 30-minute walks that can be enjoyed as part of a tour around the island.

Serious hikers will find many longer, more rigorous trails in the national park. The most popular are those leading to the volcanic summit of La Soufrière, the island's highest point, and to the base of Chutes du Carbet, the Eastern Caribbean's highest waterfalls. Both make for scenic half-day treks. Keep in mind that this is serious rainforest hiking, so be prepared for wet conditions and wear good hiking shoes. More information is found under individual sites in this chapter.

Horseback Riding

La Manade (☎ 81 52 21), a stable in Saint-Claude in the foothills of La Soufriére, offers half-day rainforest outings for 200F and full-day outings with lunch for 400F.

Golf

Guadeloupe's only golf course is the 18-hole, par 71 Golf de St François (☎ 88 41 87), designed by Robert Trent Jones, in Saint-François.

Tennis

Many resort hotels have tennis courts for their guests. In addition, municipal courts that are open to the general public can be found in many of the large towns.

ACCOMMODATIONS
Camping

The only established campground on Guadeloupe is Camping Traversée (☎ 98 21 23), which has a pleasant seaside setting

GUADELOUPE

south of Pointe-Noire on the northwest side of Basse-Terre.

Hotels

There are nearly 8000 hotel rooms in Guadeloupe, most in small to mid-sized hotels. The bulk of the accommodations are along the south coast of Grande-Terre, between Pointe-à-Pitre and Saint-François. Another 100 hotel rooms are on Les Saintes, there are 15 on La Désirade and there's a couple of dozen on Marie-Galante.

Some hotels have a three-night minimum stay in winter and as that's a busy season, advance reservations are a good idea.

By Caribbean standards rates are reasonable with good low-end choices available for around 320F a double, mid-range for around 600F and top-end around 1000F. As in France, taxes and service charges are included in the quoted rate; many hotels also include breakfast.

Gîtes de France

Some of the best-value places to stay are not hotels but small family-run facilities known as gîtes. Gîtes de France Guadeloupe (☎ 82 09 30), BP 759, 97171 Pointe-à-Pitre, is an association of homeowners who rent private rooms and apartments. Most of the gîtes are quite comfortable; all are rated on a scale of one to three by the association, the higher the number the higher the standard. The gîtes are spread around Guadeloupe, with the largest collection in the Gosier, Sainte-Anne and Saint-François areas. Generally they're booked by the week and arrangements can be made in advance through the association. Although rates vary, on average you can find a nice place for around 1600F a week for two people. Most hosts do not speak English, so a working knowledge of French is often essential. A full list of gîtes can be obtained from the association or at the tourist office.

FOOD

Guadeloupe has many restaurants with fine French and Creole food, the latter known for its savory flavors. Island cuisine draws upon a wide range of seafood including crayfish *(ouassous)*, octopus *(chatrou)*, conch *(lambi)* and more traditional fishes such as red snapper *(vivanneau)*. Some typical Guadeloupean dishes include *accras* (cod fritters), *crabes farci* (spicy stuffed land crabs), *colombo cabri* (curried goat), rice and beans, and breadfruit gratin. Another popular Creole dish is *blaff*, a seafood preparation poached in a spicy broth.

At the lower end, Guadeloupe has numerous pizzerias, pâtisseries with hearty inexpensive sandwiches and roadside snack wagons selling crêpes and grilled chicken. If you just want something quick while you are touring, gas stations along major roads often have convenience stores.

DRINKS

Tap water is safe to drink. There are lots of local rums and some distilleries have tasting rooms. Homemade flavored rums made by adding fruit are also popular; in bars and restaurants you'll commonly see these in large glass jars behind the counter. A common restaurant drink is ti-punch, where you're brought white rum, cane sugar and a fresh lime to mix to your own proportions. Corsaire beer is brewed in Guadeloupe.

ENTERTAINMENT

Most night-time entertainment, including dance clubs and dinner shows, is found in the resort areas, especially at Bas du Fort, Gosier, Sainte-Anne and Saint-François. Zouk, calypso, reggae and soca are popular. Trendy night spots include *Planet Caraïbes* (☎ 84 72 79) in Gosier and *Bet a Feu* (☎ 88 51 00) at the Méridien in Saint-François.

Guadeloupe has two casinos, one in Gosier and one in Saint-François. On a more local level, cockfighting is held on Saturday afternoons and Sunday from November to April in 'pitts' around the island and there are horse races at Hippodrome Saint-Jacques (☎ 22 11 08) near Anse Bertrand in northern Grande-Terre.

THINGS TO BUY

The most popular island souvenir is a bottle of Guadeloupean rum.

The harborfront market in Pointe-à-Pitre is a good place to buy island handicrafts, including straw dolls, straw hats and primitive African-style wood carvings. It's also a good spot to pick up locally grown coffee and a wide array of fragrant spices.

Getting There & Away

AIR
USA
American Airlines (☎ 21 13 66) has twice-daily flights to Guadeloupe from San Juan, Puerto Rico, which connect with mainland USA flights. Fares vary but in the low season a ticket allowing a stay of up to 30 days generally begins around US$500 from east coast cities such as Miami, New York and Boston. In the high season prices average about US$100 more.

Air France (☎ 82 61 61) has a flight from Miami to Guadeloupe on Tuesday and Saturday. The fare for a 21-day excursion ticket hovers around US$500.

Canada
Air Canada (☎ 83 62 49) has a Saturday flight from Montreal; fares depend on the season, beginning at C$750 roundtrip.

Europe
Air France (☎ 82 61 61) flies to Guadeloupe from Paris at least once daily, with connections throughout Europe.

Air Outre Mer or AOM (☎ 21 09 10), Air Liberté/Minerve (☎ 90 00 08) and Nouvelles Frontières (☎ 82 35 30) also have flights from Paris, with the frequency depending on the season.

It's a competitive market with the cheapest roundtrip fares from Paris to Pointe-à-Pitre generally beginning around 2600F.

South America
Air France has scheduled flights from Pointe-à-Pitre to Cayenne, in French Guiana, and Caracas, Venezuela. An excursion ticket that's good for a stay of two to 17 days costs around 2000F from either South American port.

Within the Caribbean
Air Martinique (☎ 21 13 42) has numerous daily flights between Pointe-à-Pitre and Fort-de-France, Martinique; fares are 539F one way and 836F roundtrip.

Air Guadeloupe (☎ 82 47 40) also has frequent flights from Pointe-à-Pitre and Fort-de-France at similar fares.

Air Guadeloupe and two smaller commuter airlines offer daily flights between Guadeloupe and St Martin with 614F one-way fares; Air Caraïbes (☎ 21 13 34) has the cheapest roundtrip deal with its 788F 'superpromo' fare, while Air St Martin (☎ 21 12 88) offers an 856F excursion fare.

LIAT (☎ 82 12 26) connects Guadeloupe with the English-speaking Caribbean. There are daily flights from Dominica to Guadeloupe for US$88/147 one way/roundtrip, from St Lucia for US$113/174 and from Antigua for US$73/115.

Airport Information
Guadeloupe Pole Caraïbes Airport is north of Pointe-à-Pitre, 6km from the city center on N5.

The terminal has a tourist information booth, car rental booths, a couple of restaurants, a pharmacy and gift shops. The two Tabac Presse newsstands sell phonecards and the IGN map of Guadeloupe.

During banking hours you can exchange money and traveler's checks at the Crédit Agricole bank in the arrival lounge and on a 24-hour basis you can exchange US and other major foreign currency notes using the currency-exchange ATM next to the bank. Another franc-dispensing ATM that accepts credit and bank cards can be found on the upper level next to the self-service restaurant.

SEA
Trans-Atlantic Boat
Compagnie Générale Maritime (☎ 83 04 43) operates weekly 'banana boats' that carry passengers between the French West Indies and mainland France. Information

GUADELOUPE

is in the Getting There & Away chapter in the front of the book.

Inter-Island Ferry

There are two companies providing regular boat service between Guadeloupe and Martinique; the larger of the two also has service to Dominica and St Lucia.

L'Express des Iles L'Express des Iles operates modern 300-seat catamarans between Guadeloupe and Martinique, some of which stop en route in Dominica. The boats have both air-conditioned and open-air decks and a snack bar.

Southbound, the boats leave Pointe-à-Pitre at 8 am Monday to Saturday and also at noon on Friday and 2 pm on Sunday. The Tuesday and Friday morning boats travel nonstop to Fort-de-France, Martinique, arriving there at 11 am. All other boats make an en route stop at Roseau, Dominica (a 1¾- hour ride), before arriving at Martinique 3¾ hours after leaving Guadeloupe.

In the opposite direction, boats depart from Martinique for Guadeloupe at 8 am and 2 pm Monday; 3:45 pm Tuesday; 2 pm Wednesday; 1 pm Thursday; 3 pm Friday; 9 am Saturday; and 3 pm Sunday. All boats except those that depart from Martinique on Monday morning and Tuesday and Thursday stop in Dominica. In addition, the Thursday boat (in either direction) stops en route in Les Saintes.

A couple of days a week there's also a boat between Guadeloupe and Castries, St Lucia. The boat leaves Guadeloupe at 8 am on Tuesday and noon on Friday (stopping en route in Martinique) and arriving in St Lucia about 5½ hours later. Northbound, boats leave St Lucia for both Martinique and Guadeloupe at 1:50 pm on Tuesday, 7 am on Saturday and 1 pm on Sunday.

The Guadeloupe-Martinique fare (in either direction) costs 325F one way, with a free stopover allowed in Dominica or Les Saintes. An excursion fare allowing a stay of up to seven days but no en-route stopover costs 470F. The Guadeloupe-St Lucia fare is 450F one way (Dominica or Martinique stopover allowed), or 700F for the excursion fare.

There are discounts of 50% for children ages two to 11 and 10% for passengers under 26 or age 60 and older. For reservations in Martinique call ☎ 63 12 11, in Guadeloupe ☎ 83 12 45, in Dominica ☎ 44 82 181, in Saint Lucia ☎ 452-2211, or check with any travel agent.

Brudey Frères Brudey Frères has a 350-passenger catamaran with service between Pointe-à-Pitre and Fort-de-France. The boat departs from Guadeloupe at 8:10 am Monday, Wednesday, Friday, Saturday and Sunday and from Martinique at 1 pm the same days. The fare is 304F one way, 513F roundtrip. Brudey offers discounts similar to the competition for youths and elders.

Reservation numbers are ☎ 91 60 87 in Guadeloupe, ☎ 70 08 50 in Martinique.

Yacht

Guadeloupe has three marinas. Marina de Bas du Fort (☎ 90 84 85), between Pointe-à-Pitre and Gosier, has 700 berths, 55 of which are available for visiting boats. It can handle craft up to 39 meters in length and has full facilities including fuel, water, electricity, sanitation, ice, chandlery and a maintenance area.

Marina de Saint-François (☎ 88 47 28), in the center of Saint-François, has about 250 moorings, fuel, water, ice and electricity.

Marina de Rivière-Sens (☎ 90 00 01), on the southern outskirts of the town of Basse-Terre, has 220 moorings, fuel, water and ice.

There are customs and immigration offices in Pointe-à-Pitre, Basse-Terre and Deshaies.

The yacht charter companies The Moorings (☎ 90 81 81), Stardust Marine (☎ 90 92 02) and Star Voyage (☎ 90 86 26) are based at the Bas du Fort Marina.

Cruise Ship

Cruise ships dock right in the city at Centre Saint-John Perse, Pointe-à-Pitre's new port complex, which has shops, restaurants and a hotel.

LEAVING GUADELOUPE
There's no departure tax.

Getting Around

THE AIRPORT
There are car rentals and a taxi stand at the airport, which is north of Pointe-à-Pitre. Currently, there's no airport bus service.

AIR
Air Guadeloupe has daily flights between Pointe-à-Pitre and Marie-Galante, La Désirade and Terre-de-Haut; see those island sections for details.

BUS
Guadeloupe has a good public bus system that operates from about 5:30 am to 6:30 pm, with fairly frequent service on main routes. On Sunday, service is much lighter and there's no operation on most secondary routes.

Many bus routes terminate in Pointe-à-Pitre. Schedules are a bit loose and buses generally don't depart Pointe-à-Pitre until they're near capacity. Jump seats fold down and block the aisle as the bus fills, so try to get a seat near the front if you're not going far.

The bus from Pointe-à-Pitre to Gosier costs 5.50F and takes about 15 minutes. If you're going to the Bas du Fort Marina, you can take this bus and get off just past the university. Other fares from Pointe-à-Pitre are 10F to Sainte-Anne, 15F to Saint-François, 20F to Pointe-Noire (via Route de la Traversée) and 30F to Basse-Terre.

Pay the driver as you get off the bus. Having the correct fare is not essential, although larger notes could be problematic.

Destinations are written on the buses. Bus stops have blue signs picturing a bus; in less developed areas you can wave buses down along their routes.

TAXI
Taxis are plentiful but expensive. There are taxi stands at the airport, in Pointe-à-Pitre and in Basse-Terre. The larger hotels commonly have taxis assigned to them with the drivers waiting in the lobby.

The fare from the airport is about 80F to Pointe-à-Pitre, 100F to Gosier, 200F to Sainte-Anne and 300F to Saint-François. Fares are 40% higher from 9 pm to 7 am and on Sunday and holidays. You can call for a taxi by dialing ☎ 82 00 00 or 83 99 99 in the Pointe-à-Pitre area, ☎ 81 79 70 in Basse-Terre.

CAR & MOTORCYCLE
Road Rules
In Guadeloupe drive on the right; your home driver's license is valid.

Roads are excellent by Caribbean standards and almost invariably hard surfaced, although secondary and mountain roads are often narrow. Around Pointe-à-Pitre there are multi-lane highways, with traffic zipping along at 110km per hour. Outside the Pointe-à-Pitre area most highways have a single lane in either direction and an 80km/h speed limit.

Traffic regulations and road signs are of European standards. Exits and intersections are clearly marked and speed limits are posted.

Rental
Car Several car rental companies have offices at the airport and in major resort areas. Some agents will let you rent a car near your hotel and drop it off free of charge at the airport, which can save a hefty taxi fare.

Companies generally drop their rates the longer you keep the car, with the weekly rate working out to be about 15% cheaper than the daily rate. Note that many companies have both an unlimited-kilometers rate and a cheaper rate with a per-kilometer charge; as the island is big, fees on the latter can rack up quite quickly.

Rates for small cars with unlimited kilometers are advertised from around 190F a day, although the rates offered on a walk-in basis can vary greatly with the season. It's a competitive market and when business is slow, it's possible to find something for as

GUADELOUPE

low as 150F. At the height of the season you might not find anything available for less than 300F, and sometimes all categories of cars are sold out completely. Certainly if you're traveling in winter, it's a good idea to book in advance.

Car rental companies include:

Avis	☎ 21 13 54 at the airport
	☎ 84 22 27 in Gosier
	☎ 85 00 11 in Saint-François
Budget	☎ 82 95 58 at the airport
	☎ 84 24 24 in Gosier
Citer	☎ 82 10 94 at the airport
Europcar	☎ 21 13 52 at the airport
	☎ 84 45 84 in Gosier
	☎ 88 69 77 in Saint-François
Hertz	☎ 93 89 45 at the airport
	☎ 84 23 23 in Gosier
Thrifty	☎ 91 42 17 at the airport
	☎ 90 86 32 in Bas du Fort
	☎ 84 51 26 in Gosier

Motorcycle CFM, which is on D119 in Gosier (☎ 84 41 81) and at Le Méridien hotel in Saint-François (☎ 88 51 00), rents scooters for 220F a day and has bigger bikes, up to 600cc, for 470F a day. Dom Location (☎ 88 84 81) on Rue Saint-Aude Ferly in Saint-François has attractive rates, with scooters for 170F a day, 125cc motorcycles for 290F and 600cc motorcycles for 390F.

BICYCLE
Dom Location (☎ 88 84 81), on Rue Saint-Aude Ferly in Saint-François, has mountain bikes for 80F a day or 25% less on a three-day rental. CFM, on D119 in Gosier (☎ 84 41 81) and at Le Méridien hotel in Saint-François (☎ 88 51 00), rents mountain bikes for 90F a day.

HITCHHIKING
Hitchhiking is fairly common on Guadeloupe. The proper stance is to hold out an open palm at a slightly downward angle. All the usual safety precautions apply.

BOAT
Ferries to Les Saintes leave from Pointe-à-Pitre, Saint-François and Trois-Rivières. Ferries to Marie-Galante leave from Pointe-

à-Pitre and Saint-François. Ferries to La Désirade leave from Saint-François.

Schedule and fare information is given later in this chapter under the individual islands.

ORGANIZED TOURS
Emeraude Guadeloupe (☎ 81 98 28) organizes 'green tourism' sightseeing outings with an emphasis on nature and hiking.

Pointe-à-Pitre

In 1654 a merchant named Peter, a Dutch Jew who settled in Guadeloupe after being exiled from Brazil, began a fish market on an undeveloped harborside jut of land. The area became known as Peter's Point and eventually grew into the settlement of Pointe-à-Pitre.

Guadeloupe's largest municipality, Pointe-à-Pitre is a conglomerate of old and new and is largely commercial in appearance. There are a couple of small museums, but other than that the most interesting sight is the bustling harborside market.

The hub of town is Place de la Victoire, an open space punctuated with tall royal palms that extends north a few blocks from the inner harbor. There are sidewalk cafés opposite its west side, a line of big old mango trees to the north and some older buildings along with the sous-préfecture office at the park's east side.

While it's not a major tourist destination, all visitors can expect to at least pass through Pointe-à-Pitre as it's the main port for ferries to Guadeloupe's outer islands and has the central bus terminal.

Central Pointe-à-Pitre is quite compact and nothing there is more than a five- or 10-minute walk from Place de la Victoire.

Information
Tourist Office The tourist office (☎ 82 09 30), opposite the northwest end of the harbor, at 5 Square de la Banque, is open from 8 am to 5 pm Monday to Friday, 8 am to noon on Saturday. A second office

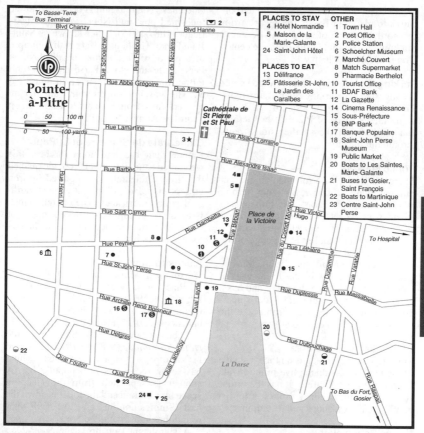

in the Centre Saint-John Perse, next to the police booth, is open when cruise ships are in port.

Money The BDAF bank next to the tourist office is open weekdays from 8 am to noon and 2 to 4 pm; there are a few more banks nearby on Rue Archille René Boisneuf.

Post & Communications The post office, a block north of the cathedral on Boulevard Hanne, is open from 8 am to 6 pm weekdays and to noon on Saturday; expect long, slow-moving lines. In addition to mail

services, you can also send faxes and telegrams from the post office.

Bookstores The Boutique de la Presse in the Centre Saint-John Perse sells English and French-language newspapers and Institut Géographique National maps of Guadeloupe and other French West Indies islands. La Gazette, the tobacco shop next to Délifrance, also sells maps of Guadeloupe and international newspapers.

Bus Terminals Buses to Gosier, Sainte-Anne and Saint-François leave from Rue

Dubouchage at the east side of the harbor. Buses to places in Basse-Terre leave from the northwest side of town near Bergevin Stadium, a 10-minute walk from the center along Boulevard Chanzy.

Parking On weekdays traffic in the center is congested and parking can be quite tight. There are parking meters (5F an hour) along the east side of Place de la Victoire and on many of the smaller side streets throughout the city.

Public Markets

There's a lively, colorful open-air market running along La Darse, the inner harbor. Women wearing madras cloth turbans sell island fruit, vegetables, flowers, pungent spices, handicrafts and clothing while a few fishing boats docked at the edge of the harbor sell fresh fish.

Another large public market, the Marché Couvert, is just a few blocks to the west at Rue Peynier and Rue Schoelcher and has a good collection of handicrafts and spices. To get there from the waterfront, take the pedestrian street Rue St-John Perse.

Centre Saint-John Perse

This large port complex is on the west side of the harbor, less than a five-minute walk from Place de la Victoire. It has the cruise ship dock, port authority offices, a tourist booth, boutiques, shops and restaurants.

Musée Schoelcher

This museum, which occupies an interesting period building at 24 Rue Peynier, is dedicated to abolitionist Victor Schoelcher. The main exhibits are personal objects belonging to Schoelcher and artifacts relating to slavery. The museum is open from 8:30 am to 12:30 pm Monday to Saturday, as well as from 2 to 5:30 pm on Monday and Tuesday and 2 to 6 pm on Thursday and Friday. Admission is 10F.

Musée Saint-John Perse

This municipal museum, at 9 Rue de Noziéres, occupies an attractive 19th-century colonial building with ornate wrought-iron balconies. The museum is dedicated to the renowned poet and Nobel laureate Alexis Léger (1887-1975), better known as Saint-John Perse. The house offers both a glimpse of a period Creole home and displays on Perse's life and work. Perse grew up a bit farther down the same street, in house No 54. The museum is open from 9 am to 5 pm on weekdays, from 8:30 am to 12:30 pm on Saturday. Admission is 10F.

Cathédrale de St Pierre et St Paul

Rather than the traditional arches, this weathered sand-colored church, nicknamed the 'Iron Cathedral,' is supported by iron girders intended to brace it against earthquakes and hurricanes. The church, which is a couple of minutes walk northwest of Place de la Victoire, doesn't win any honors for aesthetics but it is a curiosity.

Places to Stay

Maison de la Marie-Galante (☎ 90 10 41), 12 Place de la Victoire, 97110 Pointe-à-Pitre, is centrally located but run down. Basic rooms with twin beds and private baths cost 250/350F for singles/doubles.

A better bet, but also Spartan, is the *Hôtel Normandie* (☎ 82 37 15), 14 Place de la Victoire, 97110 Pointe-à-Pitre, which has seven rooms above a popular bar. A shower is separated from the sleeping space by a curtain and the toilet is down the hall. Singles/doubles are 250/300F year round, breakfast included.

A significant step up is the *Saint-John Hôtel* (☎ 82 51 57, fax 82 52 61), Centre Saint-John Perse, 97110 Pointe-à-Pitre, a member of the Anchorage chain, centrally located in the cruise ship complex. It has 44 compact but otherwise comfortable rooms with air-con, room safes, TV, phones and small shared balconies overlooking the harbor. Singles/doubles cost 362/462F in summer, 412/512F in winter, breakfast included.

Places to Eat

Délifrance, on the west side of Place de la Victoire, is a great place for a cheap breakfast. It has good croissants, pastries and mini-quiches for 6F to 13F, as well as inexpensive salads and sandwiches. This popular spot has sidewalk café tables and is open from 6:30 am every day but Sunday.

Pâtisserie St-John, at the side of the Saint-John Hôtel in Centre Saint-John Perse, also has good inexpensive sandwiches, quiches and pastries. For a sit-down restaurant, *Le Jardin des Caraïbes*, above the pâtisserie, is a good choice for Creole food at moderate prices.

There's a *Match* supermarket a minute's walk west of the tourist office.

Grande-Terre

The southern coast of Grande-Terre, with its reef-protected waters, is Guadeloupe's main resort area. The eastern side of the island is largely open Atlantic with crashing surf and a decidedly rural character. In the interior there's a mix of rolling hills and flat plains, the latter still largely given over to sugar cane.

BAS DU FORT

Bas du Fort, on the southern outskirts of Pointe-à-Pitre, has Guadeloupe's largest marina, a university and some new condo and hotel developments. The main hotel area is a couple of kilometers by road south of the marina. Bas du Fort takes its name from its location at the base *(bas)* of Fort Fleur-d'Épée.

Marina Bas du Fort

This expansive marina has full yachting facilities, a pharmacy, coin laundries, shops and eateries.

Crédit Agricole has a 24-hour change machine near Restaurant Shangai that will change US and Canadian dollars, British pounds and other major currencies to French francs.

Aquarium de la Guadeloupe

This harborside aquarium (☎ 90 92 38), rated as France's fourth best, has 60 species of tropical fish as well as turtles

and sharks. To get there turn off highway N4, east of the roundabout, between the Elf and Esso gas stations. The aquarium is open from 9 am to 7 pm daily and costs 38F for adults, 20F for children.

Fort Fleur-d'Épée

This small 18th-century hilltop garrison offers views of Gosier and the island of Marie-Galante. Much of the coral block walls and a few of the buildings stand intact and there are rusting cannons and flowering flamboyant trees on the grounds. To get there, turn off highway N4 at the 'Bas du Fort' sign and head south for about a kilometer; an inconspicuous sign on the left marks the side road that leads 800 meters up to the fort.

Places to Stay

A good-value place is *Village Viva* (☎ 90 98 98, fax 90 96 16), Bas du Fort, 97190 Gosier, on a point near the mouth of the marina. The 76 units, in contemporary four-story buildings, have air-con, TV, phone, balconies and kitchenettes. The shoreline is rocky, but there's a large pool. Rates for one or two people are 330F in summer, 560F in winter; optional breakfast is an additional 50F per person.

Fleur d'Épée Novotel (☎ 90 40 00, fax 90 99 07), Bas du Fort, 91790 Gosier, is an older but popular top-end resort. The 190 rooms are in three-story buildings and have all the standard amenities including room safes and balconies. There's a pool, tennis courts, a white-sand beach and a couple of restaurants and bars. Singles/doubles cost from 625/795F in summer and about 50% more in winter.

Places to Eat

You'll find a cluster of cafés and restaurants all within a few minutes walk of each other at the marina. The bakery, next to Thrifty car rental, has good pastries, crispy bread and filling baguette sandwiches for 12F to 18F.

For Chinese food, the nearby *Restaurant Shangai* has a soup-to-dessert plat du jour for 90F, vegetarian main dishes for 45F and

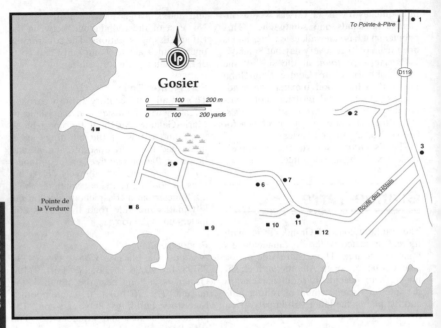

GUADELOUPE

pork and chicken dishes for 55F. There's also a cheaper takeout stand at the side of the restaurant.

Le Fregate is a simple harborside place with fresh fish dishes and daily chalkboard specials for around 70F. Nearby and also on the waterfront, *La Sirène* has pizza or half a chicken with fries for 50F, grilled fish for 60F and a tank of live lobsters at market prices. A popular place on the north side of the marina is *La Route du Rhum*, which has an open-air setting, salads from 50F and generous fish and meat main dishes for 70F to 120F.

North of the parking area is a supermarket and across the road a couple of vendors sell fruit and flowers.

GOSIER

Guadeloupe's largest tourist area is Gosier, 8km southeast of Pointe-à-Pitre. On the west side of Gosier there's a tourist strip with a run of resort hotels, a casino, car rental agents and restaurants. The beach forms a series of scalloped sandy coves, with a hotel backing each cove. The water is generally calm, the swimming good and there's a nice view across the channel to Basse-Terre.

Gosier's village center, which is about a 15-minute walk away, lacks the fine beaches found in the main hotel area, but it is more local in character. On the west side of the village center you'll find a park planted with flamboyant, white cedar and tropical almond trees. There's also a small but swimmable beach and a good view across the water to the Ilet du Gosier. The village's Catholic church is modernistic, with a cement steeple, and there's a cemetery with above-ground vaults and tombs opposite the post office.

In the evening, bird watchers can find scores of white egrets roosting on the bare trees in the roadside swamp that's west of the casino.

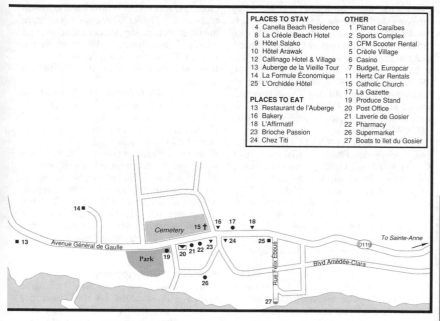

PLACES TO STAY		OTHER	
4	Canella Beach Residence	1	Planet Caraïbes
8	La Créole Beach Hotel	2	Sports Complex
9	Hôtel Salako	3	CFM Scooter Rental
10	Hôtel Arawak	5	Créole Village
12	Callinago Hotel & Village	6	Casino
13	Auberge de la Vieille Tour	7	Budget, Europcar
14	La Formule Économique	11	Hertz Car Rentals
25	L'Orchidée Hôtel	15	Catholic Church
		17	La Gazette
PLACES TO EAT		19	Produce Stand
13	Restaurant de l'Auberge	20	Post Office
16	Bakery	21	Laverie de Gosier
18	L'Affirmatif	22	Pharmacy
23	Brioche Passion	26	Supermarket
24	Chez Titi	27	Boats to Ilet du Gosier

GUADELOUPE

Information

Post The post office in the Gosier village center is open from 8 am to 5 pm on Monday, Tuesday, Thursday and Friday, and from 8 am to noon on Wednesday and Saturday.

Laundry Laverie du Gosier, a laundry near the post office, is open from 7:30 am to 7:30 pm Monday to Saturday. It costs 53F to wash and dry a load of clothes.

Bookstore La Gazette in the village center sells the IGN map of Guadeloupe, local newspapers, international newspapers including *USA Today* and *International Herald-Tribune* and a wide variety of French magazines.

Water Sports Equipment Beach huts in front of the resort hotels rent snorkeling gear for 40F a day, windsurfing equipment for 50F an hour, Sunfish sailboats for 80F an hour, larger Hobie Cat boats for 200F an hour as well as fun boards, pedal boats and other water activities gear.

Ilet du Gosier

Just 600 meters off Gosier village is lovely Ilet du Gosier, a little undeveloped island surrounded by calm turquoise waters. This relaxed place has an old lighthouse and attractive white-sand beaches, making it popular with swimmers, sunbathers and families out for a picnic. There's decent snorkeling on the northwest side of the island; if you go out about 20 meters from the dilapidated green shed, you'll come to a sunken boat hull harboring big-eye fish and a bit beyond you'll find a few coral heads.

Motorboats shuttle beach goers back and forth (15F roundtrip, three minutes each way) between Gosier and the island, departing from the little dock at the end of Rue Félix Éboué.

Places to Stay – budget

La Formule Économique (☎ 84 54 91, fax 84 29 42), 112/120 Lot Gisors, 97190 Gosier, is a small economy hotel with rates that are based on the amenities you select. A basic room with a double bed begins at 199F, studios at 250F. Add another 50F if you want air-con, 30F for TV. It's on the inland side of the D119 road, about 200 meters up a side road that passes the Jehovah's Witness temple.

Les Flamboyants (☎ 84 14 11, fax 84 53 56), Chemin des Phares et Blaises, 97190 Gosier, has a quiet hilltop location about a kilometer east of the village and a five-minute walk from the nearest bus stop. This cozy hostelry has a view of Ilet du Gosier, a small pool and personable management. The 14 compact rooms are spotlessly clean and suitably simple with comfortable beds, air-con and private baths. Singles/doubles cost 260/300F in summer, 320/360F in winter; add 60F to 80F more if you want a kitchenette. A simple breakfast is included in the rates. Popular with budget travelers, it commonly books up in advance during the high season; phone reservations generally require a command of French.

Places to Stay – middle

L'Orchidée Ho (☎ 84 54 20, fax 84 54 90), Avenue Général de Gaulle, 97190 Gosier, is a spiffy new place smack in the village center. All 20 units are modern and have kitchenettes and air-con; most of them also have balconies with partial sea views. Studios have a double bed, TV and sofabed and cost 300F in summer for one or two people, 450/650F for singles/doubles in winter. There are also larger apartments that can hold up to six people for 550/750F in summer/winter.

Callinago Hotel & Village (☎ 84 25 25, fax 84 24 90), BP No 1, 97190 Gosier, has two separate wings: the 'hotel' with 40 rooms and the 'village' with 93 studios. The village units have kitchenettes, while the hotel units have no cooking facilities but include breakfast in the rate. Both wings have air-con and phones. There's a beachside pool. While the Callinago is older and lackluster, it also has the lowest rates among Gosier's beachside resorts. In the hotel section, singles/doubles cost from 445/506F in summer, 510/634F in winter. In the village section, singles/doubles cost from 385/400F in summer, 445/506F in winter.

Canella Beach Residence (☎ 90 44 00, fax 90 44 44; in the USA ☎ 800-223-9815), Pointe de la Verdure, BP 73, 97190 Gosier, has 146 air-con units in two three-story buildings. The studios have rattan furniture, a queen or two twin beds, a little sitting area with a sofabed, TV, phone and a balcony with a kitchenette. Some studios on the ground level are handicapped-accessible. Singles/doubles cost 420/530F in summer, 627/816F in winter. There are also suites and duplex apartments. There's a pool and rates include the use of tennis courts, paddle boats and canoes.

Places to Stay – top end

The following are modern beachside resorts with standard 1st-class amenities including swimming pools, activity centers, restaurants and well-appointed rooms with balconies.

La Créole Beach Hôtel (☎ 90 46 46, fax 90 46 66), BP 19, 97190 Gosier, is a 156-room complex with contemporary units costing 575/660F for singles/doubles in summer, 750/1100F in winter.

The eight-story *Hôtel Arawak* (☎ 84 24 24, fax 84 38 45), BP 396, 97162 Pointe-à-Pitre, has 200 rooms that cost 600/700F for singles/doubles in summer, 750/1000F in winter.

The lobby of the 160-room *Auberge de la Vieille Tour* (☎ 84 23 23, fax 84 33 43), Montauban, 97190 Gosier, incorporates an 18th-century windmill, but most of the rooms are in more ordinary buildings. Standard rooms cost 680/845F for singles/doubles in summer, 890/1010F in winter.

Places to Eat

The center of Gosier has a number of inexpensive eating options. There are two bakeries right opposite each other at the main intersection. One of them, *Brioche Passion*, has a few sidewalk tables where you can have coffee and croissants, good inexpensive sandwiches and crêpes. For mouthwatering French pastries, cakes and fruit tarts, the bakery across the street is in a class by itself.

A stone's throw from the bakeries is *Chez Titi*, where a sidewalk barbecue stand cooks up inexpensive grilled chicken in the evenings. A plate of chicken with fries costs 32F; it's closed on Monday. Opposite is a supermarket, open from 8 am to 10 pm, and there's a daytime produce stand next to the post office.

L'Affirmatif is an inviting little place with delicious Creole food at reasonable prices. The 65F menu du jour includes salad with accras, christophene gratin, dessert and the seafood dish of the day. They also make good wood-fired pizza from 40F. It's open for dinner only, from 6 pm to midnight daily.

West of the village center, the *Restaurant de l'Auberge* at the Auberge de la Vieille Tour hotel has Gosier's most upmarket fine-dining restaurant, serving traditional French and Creole cuisine. Everything's à la carte; expect dinner to run around 300F per person, without wine. The hotel's beach-side restaurant, *Ajoupa*, has a nice open-air seaside setting and a 75F breakfast buffet, available from 7 to 10 am, that includes croissants, pastries, fresh fruit, cereal and juice. At lunch it serves grilled fare at moderate prices.

In the main beach hotel area, the Créole Village shopping center has half a dozen places to eat, including *Pizza Alisa*, which has salads for 25F and of pizzas, pastas and lasagna for 45F to 60F. There's also a small pâtisserie selling pastries and baguette sandwiches; an ice cream and crêpe shop; and a fine dining Creole restaurant, with a menu du jour for 90F.

SAINTE-ANNE
The village of Sainte-Anne has a pleasant French West Indian character. There's a seaside promenade along the west side of town and a fine white-sand beach stretching along the east side. The beach, which offers

good swimming and is shaded by sea grape trees, is particularly popular with islanders.

Also worth a visit is the town square, which has a statue of abolitionist Victor Schoelcher and is flanked by the Catholic church, post office and town hall. It makes a nice scene in the evening when people stroll to the square to buy homemade sorbet from street vendors.

A magnet for tourists is lovely, white-sand Caravelle Beach, stretching along the east side of the Caravelle Peninsula, about 2km west of the town center. Its main tenant is the Club Med hotel, but the entire beach is public, and it's a gathering spot for singles straight and gay. The beach has decent windsurfing and a couple of huts that rent gear. The unmarked road to Caravelle Beach is off N4, opposite Motel Sainte-Anne.

Places to Stay
In Sainte-Anne *Auberge le Grand Large* (☎ 85 48 28, fax 88 16 69), Route de la Plage, 97180 Sainte-Anne, is opposite Sainte-Anne Beach on the corner of the beach access road. It has 13 suitably casual bungalows with air-con and phones for 320F to 500F, with the rate based on whether you opt to use the kitchenette and on how long you stay.

Motel Sainte-Anne (☎ 88 22 40, fax 88 28 29), Durivage, 97180 Sainte-Anne, is on the N4 at the west side of town, about a 10-minute walk from Caravelle Beach. This two-story motel has 10 good-sized air-conditioned rooms, some with kitchenettes. Rates begin at a reasonable 250/500F in summer/winter; add another 35F per person if you want breakfast.

Le Rotabas (☎ 88 25 60, fax 88 26 87), BP 30, 97180 Sainte-Anne, is a friendly, laid-back place with a prime location at Caravelle Beach. It has 43 unpretentious bungalows and rooms, most with air-con, refrigerator and radio. Singles/doubles begin at 389/437F in summer and 631/679F in winter, breakfast included. There's a pool and the ocean is just a stone's throw away.

La Toubana (☎ 88 25 78, fax 88 38 90; in the USA ☎ 800-223-9815), BP 63, 97180 Sainte-Anne, 2km west of Sainte-Anne center, is on a quiet coastal cliff overlooking the Caravelle Peninsula. There are 32 comfortable bungalows terraced down the hillside and surrounded by flowering plants. Each has a kitchenette, air-con and a porch. There's a pool and tennis court. Singles/doubles begin at 547/697F in summer, 746/960F in winter, breakfast included.

Le Club Méditerrannée, or *Club Med* (☎ 88 21 00, fax 88 06 06; in the USA ☎ 800-258-2633), is a secluded 322-room all-inclusive hotel on the Caravelle Peninsula, 2km west of Sainte-Anne center. It has an attractive white-sand beach, its own dock and all the standard Club Med amenities. Weekly rates, which include meals and an array of water sports activities, are 6000/10,000F for singles/doubles in summer, 7800/13,000F in winter; prorated daily stays are accepted when they're not fully booked.

Around Sainte-Anne If you have a car an interesting option is the rural gîte *Les Hesperides* (☎ 88 96 50), c/o Annie Henry-Coûannier, 16 lot Eugénie, Montmain, 97180 Sainte-Anne, located in the hills between Gosier and Sainte-Anne, 9km from both. This attractive country home is in a tropical setting with lots of flowering bushes and the helpful proprietor speaks English and welcomes foreign visitors. Rooms, which have private baths and cooking facilities, begin at 1485F a week for doubles; two of the rooms can be combined to accommodate up to four people for 2440F. There's also a second property, 2km from the beach at Sainte-Anne, that has two new studios with kitchenettes on the veranda, each renting for 1800/2200F a week for doubles/triples.

Relais du Moulin (☎ 88 23 96, fax 88 03 92), Chateaubrun, 97180 Sainte-Anne, has a picturesque old sugar mill used as a reception area and nicely planted grounds. Accommodations are in 40 rather rustic, free-standing, one-bedroom bungalows with phones, porches and refrigerators. The hotel has a country setting on the south side of N4, 6km east of Sainte-Anne. There's a pool, tennis court, children's playground and an upscale Creole restaurant. Singles/doubles begin at 440/490F in summer, 650/700F in winter.

Places to Eat

Opposite Sainte-Anne Beach there's a row of simple open-air restaurants with tables in the sand and barbecue grills at the side. Recommended is *Le Coquillage*, which has meal specials that include fish blaff for 65F, lambi fricassee for 90F and crayfish for 115F; the food is delightfully spiced and the servings generous. Two other popular spots are *Chez Monique*, which has a Creole decor and big servings of straightforward food (chicken for 40F, grilled fish for 70F), and *Chez Jose*, which has sandwiches for around 15F as well as reasonably priced fish, chicken and beef dishes.

You'll find the best bread in Sainte-Anne at *Le Relais des Gourmands*, the green and white pâtisserie on N4, diagonally opposite the access road to Sainte-Anne Beach.

At Caravelle Beach, near La Rotabas hotel, there are snack shops selling crêpes, hot dogs, sandwiches and other simple eats as well as a couple of beachside spots offering plate meals from around 60F. *La Rotabas* has a restaurant serving more substantial Creole food at moderate prices.

On the opposite side of the Caravelle Peninsula, near La Toubana, the *Sicilienne Pizzeria* has pastas and a wide variety of good pizzas from 40F to 50F. The restaurant at *La Toubana* specializes in lobster with prices beginning at 165F.

SAINT-FRANÇOIS

Saint-François is a former fishing village that has boomed into Guadeloupe's second-largest tourist area. The west side of town is largely provincial in character while the east side has been given over to tourism development. The center of the action is the deep U-shaped harbor, which is lined with restaurants, hotels, car rental offices, boutiques and marina facilities. Just north of the marina there's a golf course.

A small beach fronts Le Méridien hotel and an undistinguished strand runs along the south side of the town center, but the

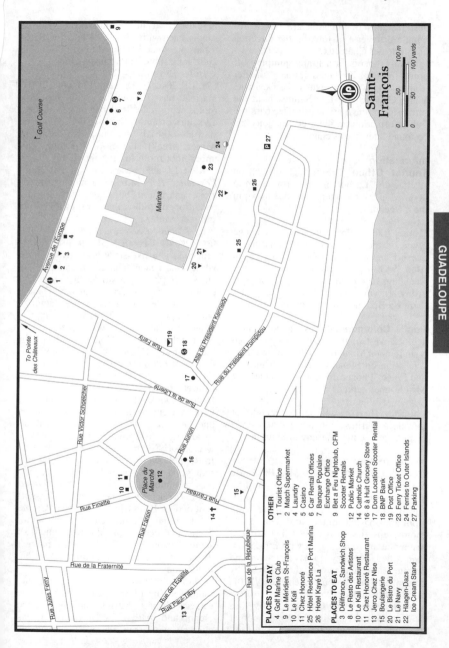

GUADELOUPE

PLACES TO STAY
4 Golf Marine Club
9 Le Méridien St-François
10 Le Kali
11 Chez Honoré
25 Hôtel Residence Port Marina
26 Hôtel Kayé La

PLACES TO EAT
3 Délifrance, Sandwich Shop
8 Le Resto des Artistes
10 Le Kali Restaurant
11 Chez Honoré Restaurant
13 Jerco Chez Nise
15 Boulangerie
20 Le Bistro du Port
21 Le Navy
22 Haagen-Dazs
Ice Cream Stand

OTHER
1 Tourist Office
2 Match Supermarket
4 Laundry
5 Casino
6 Car Rental Offices
7 Banque Populaire
Exchange Office
9 Bet a Feu Nightclub; CFM
Scooter Rentals
12 Public Market
14 Catholic Church
16 8 à Huit Grocery Store
17 Dom Location Scooter Rental
18 BNP Bank
19 Post Office
23 Ferry Ticket Office
24 Ferries to Outer Islands
27 Parking

best beaches in the area are just a 10-minute drive east of town in the direction of Pointe des Châteaux.

Saint-François is a major jumping-off point for trips to Guadeloupe's smaller islands. The dock for boats to La Désirade, Marie-Galante and Les Saintes is at the south side of the marina, as is free parking. Full information on these destinations can be found later in this chapter.

Information
Tourist Office The tourist office, on Avenue de l'Europe, is open from 8 am to noon Monday to Saturday and 2 to 5 pm most weekdays.

Money Banque Populaire has an exchange office on the north side of the marina. It doesn't charge commissions and is open from 7:45 am to noon and 2 to 4:45 pm weekdays, 7:45 am to 12:30 pm on Saturday. If you need a full-service bank, there's a BNP next to the post office.

Post & Communications The post office, a block west of the harbor, is open from 8 am to noon Monday to Saturday and from 2 to 4 pm on Monday, Tuesday, Thursday and Friday. Phonecards can be purchased at Match supermarket.

Laundry There's a self-service laundry at the Golf Marine Club hotel that's open from 6 am to 6 pm Tuesday to Saturday.

Places to Stay
Chez Honoré (☎ 88 40 61), Place du Marché, 97118 Saint-François, is an older local hostelry in the center of town opposite the market, about a 15-minute walk from the marina and beach. The seven rooms, upstairs above the Chez Honoré restaurant, are quite basic, with little more than a bed, but they do have air-con and private baths, and two of them have tiny balconies. Singles/doubles cost 240/320F, breakfast included.

Next door is *Le Kali* (☎ 88 40 10), Place du Marché, 97118 Saint-François, another old-time restaurant with upstairs accom-

modations. It has a handful of simple rooms, each with a bed, sink and fan. Bathrooms are shared. The cost is a reasonable 200F for doubles, breakfast included.

Hotel Kayé La (☎ 88 77 77, fax 88 74 67), BP 204, 97118 Saint-François, at the marina, has 75 pleasant contemporary rooms with waterfront balconies, phones, TVs, air-con and bathtubs. Singles/doubles start at 460/610F in summer, 650/800F in winter, breakfast included. Request an upper-floor room for a water view.

Kayé La also books the adjacent *Hotel Residence Port Marina*, a modern three-story apartment building with 33 air-conditioned studios that cost 410/650F in summer/winter.

Le Méridien St-François (☎ 88 51 00, fax 88 40 71), BP 37, 97118 Saint-François, is a five-story hotel with a little white-sand beach. The 265 rooms are 1st-class though not posh. Each has a TV, phone, air-con and a small balcony. There's a pool and tennis courts. Singles/doubles with breakfast cost 725/910F in summer, about double that in winter. It can be booked through Forte Hotels worldwide (in the USA and Canada ☎ 800-543-4300, in the UK ☎ 0800-404040).

Places to Eat
In the town center, opposite the market, two adjacent restaurants – *Chez Honoré* and *Le Kali* – offer multi-course seafood meals, with fish, conch or grilled lobster from 100F. South of the market, on Rue de la République, there's a local *boulangerie* with good croissants and breads.

A recommendable local favorite is *Jerco Chez Nise*, a pleasant neighborhood restaurant on Rue Paul-Tilby. It offers set Creole meals ranging from chicken colombo, accras and dessert for 55F to a nine-dish seafood meal for 95F. It's open for lunch Tuesday to Sunday and for dinner Tuesday to Saturday.

On the southwest corner of the marina, there's a line of inexpensive harborside eateries selling pastries, sandwiches, ice cream and grilled foods. *Le Navy* has chicken with fries, as well as various salads, for around 40F and seafood dishes for 60F. *Le Bistro du Port*, at the end of the row, has omelets for 30F, spaghetti for 45F and chicken colombo for 65F.

On the north side of the marina, near the car rental booths, *Le Resto des Artistes* has a waterfront setting and simple Italian fare. Pizza starts at 40F, while pasta is priced from 50F to 65F. It's open for lunch and dinner daily.

Clustered at the northwest side of the marina is a *Délifrance* and a second sandwich shop. There's also a large *Match* supermarket that's open daily from 8:30 am to 8 pm (to 1 pm on Sunday). In front of the supermarket is a sidewalk grill selling inexpensive chicken.

POINTE DES CHÂTEAUX
It's just a 10-minute drive from Saint-François to **Pointe des Châteaux**, the easternmost point of Grande-Terre. This intriguing coastal area has white-sand beaches, limestone cliffs and fine views.

From the end of the road you can make a couple of short hikes, including a 10-minute walk to the hilltop cross where there's a good view of the jagged nearshore bird islets and the island of La Désirade. The beach at the end of the point has rough surf and a steep shoreline, but there are more protected white-sand beaches to the northwest.

Anse Tarare is a nudist beach on a sheltered cove a couple of kilometers west of the road's end. The dirt road north of the main road is signposted 'Plage Tarare.'

A few minutes drive to the west, a side road (follow the signs for Chez Honoré) leads a kilometer north to **Anse à la Gourde**, a gorgeous sweep of white coral sands. The waters are good for swimming and snorkeling, but be careful of nearshore coral shelves.

Places to Stay & Eat
La Paillotte, a beach restaurant at the end of the road at Pointe des Châteaux, sells sandwiches and fresh tropical juices as well as a variety of Creole meals ranging from 60F for chicken to 150F for lobster.

Chez Honoré, an open-air restaurant facing the beach at Anse à la Gourde, specializes in seafood. A complete dinner that includes crab farci, grilled fish and dessert costs 100F; the same dinner with grilled lobster instead of fish costs 150F.

Chez Honoré also operates the adjacent *Village Bungalows* (☎ 85 03 93, fax 85 03 92), which consists of a row of pleasant one-room bungalows just a minute's walk from the beach. Each has air-con, a private bath and kitchenette; rates are 400F for one day, 750F for two days and 2500F for a week.

LE MOULE
Le Moule served as an early French capital of Guadeloupe and was an important Amerindian settlement in precolonial times. Consequently, major archaeological excavations have taken place in the area and Guadeloupe's archaeological museum is located on the outskirts of town.

Although the town itself is not a must-see sight, the center is worth a stroll if you've come this way. The town square has a few historic buildings, including the town hall and a neoclassical Catholic church. Along the river there are some discernible waterfront ruins from an old customs building and a fortress dating back to the original French settlement.

There's a tranquil beach with reef-protected waters at l'Autre Bord, about a kilometer east of town, while Baie du Moule on the west side of town is popular with surfers.

Edgar Clerc Archaeological Museum
This modern museum (☎ 23 57 57), on a coastal cliff in the Rosette area, has Amerindian petroglyphs, pottery shards, tools made of shells and stone and an exhibition on local excavations. It's closed on Wednesday afternoon but is otherwise open from 9 am to 12:30 pm and from 2 to 5:30 pm (on Saturday and Sunday until 6:30 pm). Admission is free for children under 12, 5F for children ages 12 and older and 10F for adults. The museum is about a kilometer north on La Rosette Rd (D123) on the western outskirts of Le Moule.

Places to Stay & Eat

The *Tropical Club Hotel* (☎ 93 97 97, fax 93 97 00), BP 121, 97160 Le Moule, is a 72-room hotel on a nice white-sand beach about a kilometer east of Le Moule. Rooms have balcony kitchenettes, TV, air-con and phones. There's a pool and a moderately priced French/Creole restaurant. Rooms begin at 550/650F in summer/winter.

There are reasonably priced restaurants in town including *Stardust* on the town square and *La Tortue* at the end of Rue St Jean.

NORTHERN GRANDE-TERRE

The northern half of Grande-Terre is a rural area of grazing cattle, cane fields and abandoned roadside sugar mills. The main sights are Porte d'Enfer and Pointe de la Grande Vigie, about a 40-minute drive north of Le Moule. The road can be a bit narrow, but it's in good condition and paved all the way.

From Le Moule, drive up past the museum in Rosette, then turn right on D120 and follow that road north. As you get closer to Porte d'Enfer the route will be signposted.

Porte d'Enfer

Despite its name, Porte d'Enfer ('Gate of Hell') is a lovely sheltered cove surrounded by cliffs and backed by a small beach. Inside the cove the water is shallow but deep enough for swimming, while the entire coastline outside of the cove is tumultuous, with pounding surf and strong currents. There are picnic tables and sea cotton trees near the beach – it would make a fine spot to break for a picnic lunch.

As you continue north there's a viewpoint about a kilometer beyond Porte d'Enfer that looks back at the beach and the area's craggy coastal cliffs. About a kilometer farther along if you look to the east you'll see a series of seven coastal points, the second of which has a blowhole.

Pointe de la Grande Vigie

Pointe de la Grande Vigie, the island's northernmost point, offers scenic views from its high sea cliffs. On a clear day you can see Antigua to the north and Montserrat to the northwest, both about 75km away. There's a good view of Grande-Terre's east side from the parking lot and you can take a short walk out to the farthest point for a view of the west side of the island.

Anse Bertrand

Anse Bertrand is a modest coastal town, a mix of concrete homes and simple wooden structures. The coastal section still shows signs of damage from Hurricane Hugo in 1989.

At Anse Laborde, about a kilometer north of town, there's an attractive little beach but it often has gusty winds and dangerous waves.

Port-Louis

Port-Louis is a sleepy fishing village full of character, from its aging wooden houses splashed in bright colors to the main street lined with turn-of-the-century iron lampposts.

At the north side of town is La Plage de Souffleur, a nice, long bathing beach that's especially popular on weekends. The beach is backed by white cedar trees *(poui)* that drop delicate pink flowers twice a year *(souffleur* means 'blowing flowers').

Places to Eat There are a couple of snack wagons selling crêpes, sandwiches, hamburgers and hot dogs on the beach. Down by the boat harbor at the south end of town there are some small unpretentious Creole restaurants, including the friendly *La Corrido du Sud*, which offers a complete fresh fish meal for 65F.

South to Morne-à-l'Eau

South of Port-Louis the road passes inland through a couple of agricultural towns. The coast, however, is largely mangrove swamp.

The main sight in Morne-à-l'Eau, the largest town in central Grande-Terre, is its cemetery, at the intersection of roads N5 and N6. Guadeloupe's most elaborate burial ground, it's terraced with raised vaults and tombs, many decorated in checkered black and white tiles.

Grands Fonds

The central part of Grande-Terre, known as the Grands Fonds, is an undulating landscape of mounded hills and deeply creviced valleys (*fond* means valley). It's a pretty rural area that's given over to small farms and lush green pastures and crossed by narrow winding roads.

The northern section of Grands Fonds is home to the Blancs Matignons, descendants of white colonists who settled these hills at the beginning of the 19th century and who have maintained a strict isolation ever since.

Grands Fonds is a fun place to drive – expect to get lost in the criss-cross of roads, but as long as you head in a southerly direction, you'll eventually come out to the coast.

To get into the heart of Grands Fonds simply take N5 east 1km from Morne-á-l'Eau and then turn south on D109.

Blancs Matignons

The northern section of Grands Fonds is settled by some 300 descendants of the Matignon family, French 'bluebloods' who fled to Guadeloupe to avoid persecution during the French Revolution. They've come to be dubbed the Blancs (white) Matignons.

Once on Guadeloupe they retreated to these remote hills, purchased slaves and took up small-scale farming. After the abolition of slavery in the mid-19th century, the Blancs Matignons continued to eke a modest living from the land as subsistence farmers. Over the years they've slipped deeper into poverty while still clinging to the concept that their heritage separates them from other Guadeloupeans. Not surprisingly, most other islanders – black, white or mulatto – tend to spurn them.

Two centuries after they arrived in exile, the Blancs Matignons still keep to themselves and maintain their blood line by not marrying outside the region. ∎

Basse-Terre

Shortly after entering Basse-Terre island from Pointe-à-Pitre, you have a choice of three main routes: north along the coast, south along the coast, or across the interior along the Route de la Traversée through the national park.

ROUTE DE LA TRAVERSÉE

The road that heads across the center of the island, Route de la Traversée (D23), slices through the Parc National de la Guadeloupe, the 17,300-hectare forest reserve that occupies the interior of Basse-Terre. It's a lovely mountain drive that passes fern-covered hillsides, thick bamboo stands and enormous mahogany and gum trees. Other rainforest vegetation en route includes orchids, heliconia and ginger.

Route de la Traversée begins off N1 about 15 minutes west of Pointe-à-Pitre and is well signposted. There are a few switchbacks but driving is not tricky if you don't rush and it's a good two-lane road all the way. Although the road could easily be driven in an hour, give yourself double that to stop and enjoy the scenery – more if you want to do any hiking or break for lunch.

Don't miss **Cascade aux Ecrevisses**, an idyllic little jungle waterfall that drops into a broad pool. From the parking area the waterfall is just a three-minute walk on a well-beaten but lushly green trail. The roadside pull-off is clearly marked on D23, 2km after you enter the park's eastern boundary.

At **Maison de la Forêt**, 2km farther west, there's a staffed roadside exhibit center with a few simple displays on the forest (in French only), open from 9:30 am to 4:30 pm daily. A map board and the trailhead for an enjoyable 20-minute **loop trail** is at the back of the center. The trail crosses a swing bridge over the Bas-David river and then proceeds through a verdant jungle of gommier trees, tall ferns and squawking tropical birds. If you want to extend the hike by an hour, you can take the **Sentier de promenade**, which splits off the main loop a few minutes after you cross the footbridge.

Picnic tables have been placed near the river side and at roadside spots throughout the park.

Continuing west, if the weather's clear you'll find a view of Pointe-à-Pitre from the rear of **Gîte de Mamelles**, a hilltop restaurant on the north side of the road. The restaurant takes its name from the smooth double-mounded hills to the south.

Before winding down to the coast there's a very modest **zoo** on the north side of the road with raccoons, birds and a few other creatures in small cages. On the same side of the road, a few minutes before the zoo, a signposted road leads up to **Morne á Louis**, which offers a nice hilltop view on a clear day.

Places to Stay

Auberge de la Distillerie (☎ 94 25 91, fax 94 11 91), Sommet Route de Versailles, 97170 Petit-Bourg, on the north side of D23 about 6km west of N1, is an unpretentious and inviting 15-room hostelry. Rooms have air-con, TV, phone, a small refrigerator and a patio strung with a hammock. There's a pool and lots of flowering plants on the grounds. Singles/doubles cost from 250/350F in summer, 450/650F in winter, breakfast included. It's a 15-minute drive from Pointe-à-Pitre and just a few minutes east of the national park.

Mr and Mrs Tiburce Accipe (☎ 94 23 92, fax 94 12 08), Barbotteau, 97170 Petit-Bourg, have two quite classy, three-star gîtes in Vernou on the eastern perimeter of the national park. One, *Le Mont Fleuri*, has five rooms, each with air-con and private bathroom, plus a shared kitchen and pool, which cost 1750F per week for two people. At the other, *Les Alpinias*, there are eight air-conditioned apartments with kitchenettes, balconies and TV that rent for 3500F a week for up to four people.

Places to Eat

If you want to grab something to eat on the way into the national park, the *Auberge de la Distillerie* has a small bakery with crispy baguettes and croissants. The hotel also has a restaurant with a full breakfast for 50F and a lunchtime plat du jour for 65F.

A popular lunch break for people touring the island is *Gîte de Mamelles*, which has a hilltop location on N11, a five-minute drive west of Maison de la Forêt. The menu includes grilled chicken for 50F and fish for 80F.

NORTHERN BASSE-TERRE

The northern half of Basse-Terre offers interesting contrasts. High hills and mountains rise above the west coast providing a lush green setting for the handful of small villages along the shoreline. Although much of the west coast is rocky there are a couple of attractive swimming beaches, the most popular of which is Grande Anse.

Once you reach the northern tip of the island the terrain becomes gentler and the vegetation dry and scrubby. Continuing down the east coast the countryside gradually gives over to sugar cane and the towns become larger and more suburban as you approach Pointe-à-Pitre.

Pointe-Noire

Pointe-Noire ('black point') is a good-sized town that gets its name from being in the shadow of the mountains that loom to

the east. Some residents make their living from fishing, others from working the coffee plantations in the hills above town.

The area is best known for its furniture and cabinet-making industries. Just off N2, at the south side of town, is **Maison du Bois**, a small museum of traditional woodworking tools and products (admission 5F). There's also a showroom selling furniture made of mahogany and other native woods harvested from the surrounding forests.

Places to Stay *Camping Traversée* (☎ 98 21 23) is a campground at Anse de la Grande Plaine, on the coast a few kilometers south of Pointe-Noire. It has a garden-like setting that attracts lots of hummingbirds and there are well-equipped facilities including hot showers and a laundry. Setting up a tent costs 50F per day for one person, 40F for each additional person, and there are also some rustic cabins with little verandas that rent for 200F a double. Breakfast is available for 30F.

Deshaies

Deshaies is an appealing little harborside village surrounded by green hills. It has a deep sheltered bay and is a popular stop with yachters; there's a customs office at the southernmost end of town.

Grande Anse, a mere 2km north of Deshaies, is an absolutely beautiful beach with no development in sight. There are scenic hills at either end of the beach and mounds of glistening sands along the shore. While it's arguably the finest beach in Basse-Terre, with the exception of weekends it's usually not crowded.

If you prefer to swim au naturel, **Plage de Tillet** is a lovely clothing-optional beach on a quiet cove; look for the roadside pull-off along N2, 1km northeast of the Fort Royal Touring Club. If you park along the edge of the pavement and continue on foot along the main path heading downhill to the north, you'll reach the beach in a couple of minutes.

Places to Stay There are a handful of gîtes on the road that leads inland from

Grande Anse beach towards Caféière. One of the larger and better priced ones is *Jacky Location* (☎ 28 43 53, fax 28 50 95), Plage de la Grande Anse, 97126 Deshaies, which has studios and apartments that rent from 1260F to 2900F per week, with the most expensive accommodating six people. It's about a five-minute walk from the beach and has a swimming pool.

Fort Royal Touring Club (☎ 25 50 00, fax 25 50 01), Pointe du Petit Bas-Vent, 97126 Deshaies, is on a sandy stretch a couple of kilometers north of Grande Anse. The hotel, which was formerly a Club Med, has 198 rooms and bungalows with TVs and phones. It has tennis courts, complimentary windsurfing equipment and two beaches, one of which is clothing optional. Singles/doubles cost 750/1200F in winter and from 485/680F in summer.

Places to Eat In the village of Deshaies there are a handful of restaurants that cater mostly to beach goers, sailors and weekend visitors. *Le Madras* is a quaint, moderately priced Creole restaurant opposite the waterfront on the north side of town. If you want to be right on the water there's *Le Mouillage*, a popular dockside restaurant specializing in seafood and Creole dishes with main courses averaging 75F.

In the parking area fronting Grande Anse beach you'll find a couple of food stalls selling inexpensive crêpes and sandwiches. *Le Fromager 2000*, opposite the parking lot, has excellent Creole fare at affordable prices. A tasty lambi fricassee or moist grilled fish, served with rice and beans, costs just 45F. If you have a big appetite *Edmonds*, at the south end of the parking lot, has a 65F 'menu complet' that includes accras, Creole crayfish, banana flambé and a ti-punch.

More upscale is *Le Karacoli* (☎ 28 41 17), a traditional Creole restaurant with a garden setting right on Grande Anse beach. A tasty starter is the crab farci while main courses include lobster, spicy colombo dishes and red snapper with cloves. Main courses are priced from 70F to 150F, while starters are half that. There's also a simpler menu du jour for 80F.

GUADELOUPE

Sainte-Rose

In days past Sainte-Rose was a major agricultural town and while sugar production has declined on Guadeloupe and a number of the mills have closed, sugar cane is still an important crop in this area. There are vast undulating fields of cane and a couple of rum-related tourist sights on the outskirts of town.

Musée du Rhum This museum, dedicated to the history of sugar and rum production, is at the site of the former Reimonenq Distillery, about 500 meters inland from N2 in the village of Bellevue, just southeast of Sainte-Rose. Exhibits include an old still, cane extraction gears and a vapor machine dating from 1707. It's open from 9 am to 5 pm Monday to Saturday. Admission is 40F for adults, 20F for children.

Domaine de Séverin A fun place to stop is Domaine de Séverin, a working mill and distillery that doesn't charge an entrance fee and has exhibits in English explaining the distillation process. Visitors are free to walk out back and get a close-up look at the distillery works, the antique water wheel and cane crushers and the foaming vats of rum. In the tasting room there are samples of the final products, including a nice light citron-flavored rum.

Domaine de Séverin is near the village of Cadet, which is off N2 midway between Sainte-Rose and Lamentin. The turn-off from N2, as well as the five-minute drive up to the site, is well signposted. It's open Monday to Saturday from 8 am to 12:30 pm and 2 to 5 pm.

SOUTH TO CAPESTERRE-BELLE-EAU

N1, the road that runs along the east coast of Basse-Terre, is for the most part pleasantly rural, a mix of sugar cane fields, cattle pastures, banana plantations and small towns.

Valombreuse Floral Parc, nestled in the hills west of Petit-Bourg, is a pleasant 14-hectare botanical garden. Trails wind through thick growths of flowering helico-

nias and gingers and there are lots of orchids, anthuriums and other tropical plants. The park is open from 9 am to 6 pm daily. Admission is 38F for adults, 20F for children. The road leading off N1 to the park, 5km inland, is well signposted.

In the center of the village of **Sainte-Marie** a bust of Columbus and two huge anchors comprise a modest roadside monument, honoring the explorer who landed on this shore in 1493. If you're up for a dip there's a brown-sand beach, **Plage de Roseau**, on the south side of town.

Two km farther south and visible from the roadside is a bone-white **Hindu temple** adorned with colorfully painted figures of Shiva and other Hindu gods, followed shortly by a galledrome where cockfights take place.

The road is lined with flamboyant trees on the north side of **Capesterre-Belle-Eau**, a good-sized town that has a supermarket, some local eateries and a gas station.

On the south side of Capesterre-Belle-Eau is the **Allée Dumanoir**, a stretch of N1 that's bordered on both sides by majestic century-old royal palms.

CHUTES DU CARBET

Unless it's overcast, the drive up to the Chutes du Carbet lookout will reward you with a view of two magnificent waterfalls plunging down a sheer mountain face.

Starting from Saint Sauveur on N1, the road runs 8.5km inland, making for a beautiful 15-minute drive up through a lush green rainforest. It's a good hard-surfaced road all the way, although it's a bit narrow and twisting. Three km before the end of the road there's a marked stop at the trailhead to **Grand Étang**, a placid lake circled by a loop trail. It's just a five-minute walk from the roadside parking area down to the edge of the lake and it takes about an hour more to stroll the lake's perimeter. (Due to the danger of bilharzia infection, this is not a place for a swim.)

The road ends at the **Chutes du Carbet lookout**. You can see the two highest waterfalls from the upper parking lot, where a signboard marks the trailhead to the base of the falls. The well-trodden walk to the second-highest waterfall (110 meters) takes 30 minutes; it's about a two-hour hike to the highest waterfall (115 meters). It's also possible to hike from the lookout to the summit of La Soufrière, a hardy three-hour walk with some wonderfully varied scenery.

There are picnic facilities at the lookout along with a few food stalls selling plate lunches of simple barbecue fare. This is a very popular spot for outings and can get quite crowded on weekends and holidays.

A nice stop on the way back is the flower nursery **Les Jardins de Saint-Eloi**, where there's a short path through a garden of ginger, heliconia and anthuriums. It's at the side of the road about 1.5km south of Grand Étang and there's no admission charge.

TROIS-RIVIÈRES

Most often visited as a jumping-off point to Les Saintes, Trois-Rivières has a sleepy town center of old leaning buildings with delicate gingerbread and rusting tin roofs. The town is surrounded by lush vegetation and has fine views of Les Saintes, just 10km offshore to the south.

Signs at the west side of the town center point the way from N1 to the dock, 1km away, where the ferry leaves for Terre-de-Haut. The restaurant La Roche Gravée, a few minutes walk from the dock, provides parking for ferry passengers at a cost of 12F a day.

There's a black-sand beach that's good for swimming at Grande Anse, a few kilometers west of Trois-Rivières.

Parc Archéologique des Roches Gravées

This intriguing park contains both a botanical garden and some impressive petroglyphs that date to around 300 AD. There are huge banyan trees, flowering tropical plants, scampering lizards and paths that wind up and around boulders, some of which are covered with Arawak carvings of human faces and simple designs thought to represent animals.

The park is on the road to the ferry dock, 200 meters north of the waterfront. It's open daily from 9 am to 4:30 pm and admission is a bargain at 10F.

Places to Stay

Le Joyeux (☎ 92 74 78), Faubourg, 97114 Trois-Rivières, is a pleasant little place in the village of le Faubourg, about a kilometer west of Trois-Rivières. It has rooms with air-con, cooking facilities and seaview terraces for 265F a double and smaller rooms without a view for 245F.

The *Grand Anse Hôtel* (☎ 92 92 91), Route Vieux Fort, 97114 Trois-Rivières, on the main beach road about 3km west of town, has 16 rooms with air-con, balconies, phones and kitchenettes from 300/400F for singles/doubles, breakfast included. It's just a short walk to the beach and there's also a pool.

Places to Eat

There are a few snack bars and restaurants on the waterfront near the ferry dock. *La Terrasse du Park*, in the center near the town hall, serves moderately priced Creole food.

West of town, the *Grand Anse Hôtel* has a Creole restaurant with a menu du jour for 70F. *La Paillote du Pêcheur*, a popular waterfront restaurant about 400 meters south of the Grand Anse Hôtel, has a menu that ranges from pizza to lobster.

LA SOUFRIÈRE

From Trois-Rivières there are a couple of ways to get to La Soufrière, the active volcano that looms above the southern half of the island.

If you have extra time you could take the D6 coastal road through Vieux-Fort, a town known for its eyelet embroidery, and then turn north to La Soufrière from Basse-Terre.

However, the most direct route to La Soufrière is to follow D7 northwest from Trois-Rivières, turn west on N1 for a few kilometers and then follow the signs north to Saint-Claude. This is a nice jungly drive

GUADELOUPE

into the mountains; you'll cross some small streams and pass banana plantations before reaching the village of Saint-Claude, just south of the national park boundaries. If you want to grab a bite to eat (there's no food available in the park), Saint-Claude has a couple of local restaurants and small grocers.

From Saint-Claude signs point to La Soufrière, 6km to the northeast on D11. The steep road up into the park has a few beep-as-you-go hairpin turns and narrows in places to almost one lane but it's a good solid road all the way. If it's fogged in, proceed slowly as visibility can drop to just a few meters.

Maison du Volcan, on the right about 2km after entering the park, has a small exhibit center (free admission) with displays on vulcanology and La Soufrière's last eruption in July 1976. The center is also the trailhead for a couple of hour-long walks, including one to Chute de Galleon, a scenic 40-meter waterfall on the Galleon river.

There are a couple of viewpoints and picnic areas as the road continues up the mountain for the 15-minute drive to **La Savane à Mulet**, a parking area at an elevation of 1142 meters. From here, there's a clear-on view straight up La Soufrière (when it's not covered in clouds or mist) and you can see and smell vapors rising from nearby fumaroles.

If you're up for a hardy 1½-hour hike to La Soufrière's sulphurous, moonscape-like

---

Precautions at La Soufrière

The higher you go into La Soufrière rainforest, the cooler it gets and the more likely you are to encounter rain. Even when it's sunny below it's a good idea to bring along rain gear if you plan to do any hiking. Hikers should also bring along a light jacket or sweater and a full canteen.

Young children and people with heart conditions or respiratory ailments should be cautious when hiking near the sulphur vents. ■

---

summit, a well-beaten trail starts at the end of the parking lot along a gravel bed and continues steeply up the mountain through a cover of low shrubs and thick ferns. In addition to a close-up view of the steaming volcano the hike offers some fine vistas of the island. It's also possible to make a four-hour trek from La Savane à Mulet to the Chutes du Carbet lookout.

The road continues east another 1.75km, taking in a lookout and views of sulphur vents before it dead-ends at a relay station.

BASSE-TERRE

Basse-Terre, the administrative capital of Guadeloupe, is home to a population of 14,000.

The south side of town, along the Boulevard Gouverneur Général Félix Eboué, has a couple of rather imposing government buildings including the Palais de Justice and the sprawling Conseil Général, the latter flanked by water fountains.

At the north side of town, opposite the commercial dock, is the old town square. It's bordered by the aging Hôtel de Ville (town hall), the tourist office, customs and some older two and three-story buildings that overall are more run-down than quaint. There's also a pharmacy on the square, a Crédit Agricole bank and a central parking area.

There's an unadorned cathedral near the river about five minutes walk south of the square and a modest little botanical garden on the west side of town about 250 meters beyond the police station.

The bus station is on the shoreline at the west end of Boulevard Gouverneur Général Félix Eboué. Opposite the north end of the station is the public market.

Fort Louis Delgres, which dates from 1643, is at the south side of town, as is the Rivière Sens Marina.

Places to Stay

A cheap budget option is *Hôtel Drouant* (☎ 81 28 90), 26 Rue Docteur Cabre, 97100 Basse-Terre, which has small rooms that are equipped with an old bed, a sink and a bidet. Singles/doubles cost 110/125F.

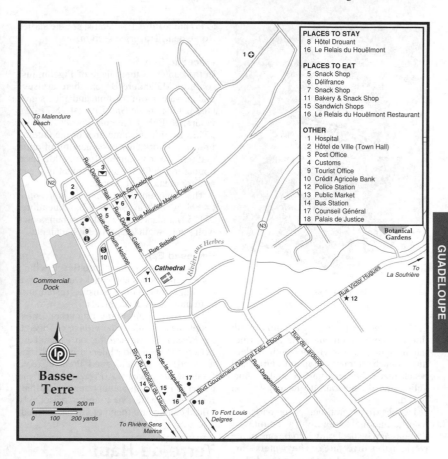

PLACES TO STAY
8   Hôtel Drouant
16 Le Relais du Houëlmont

PLACES TO EAT
5   Snack Shop
6   Délifrance
7   Snack Shop
11 Bakery & Snack Shop
15 Sandwich Shops
16 Le Relais du Houëlmont Restaurant

OTHER
1   Hospital
2   Hôtel de Ville (Town Hall)
3   Post Office
4   Customs
9   Tourist Office
10 Crédit Agricole Bank
12 Police Station
13 Public Market
14 Bus Station
17 Counseil Général
18 Palais de Justice

Botanical
Gardens

To
La Soufrière

Commercial
Dock

Basse-
Terre

0   100   200 m
0   100   200 yards

To Rivière Sens
Marina

To Fort Louis
Delgres

To Malendure
Beach

Cathedral

GUADELOUPE

Le Relais du Houëlmont (☎ 99 13 27), 34 Rue de la République, opposite the Conseil Général, has eight simple rooms, with either a double or two twin beds, a private bathroom and air-con. Singles cost 250F, doubles 280F to 350F.

Places to Eat

Opposite the bus terminal there are a handful of cheap, if somewhat scruffy, snack shops serving sandwiches from around 8F. There's a *Délifrance* a block west of the town square on Rue Docteur Cabre, selling good breads, pastries and

sandwiches. Other snack shops can be found nearby on Rue Schoelcher.

For something more substantial, *Le Relais du Houëlmont* at 34 Rue de la République is a well-regarded restaurant with salads for 50F and a menu of the day for around 100F.

MALENDURE BEACH & PIGEON ISLAND

The road up the west coast from Basse-Terre (N2) follows the shoreline much of the way, passing fishing villages, small towns and a few black-sand beaches. The

Jacques Cousteau

landscape gets drier as you continue north into the lee of the mountains. There's not much of interest for visitors until Malendure Beach, a rather popular dark-sand beach that's the departure point for snorkeling and diving tours to nearby Pigeon Island.

Jacques Cousteau brought Pigeon Island to international attention a couple of decades ago by declaring it to be one of the world's top dive sites. The waters surrounding the island are now protected as the Reserve Cousteau, an underwater park.

There are a few dive shops (see the Diving section earlier in this chapter) and a tourist information booth on Malendure Beach.

Nautilus (☎ 98 89 08) has a glass-bottom boat tour from Malendure Beach daily at 10:30 am, noon, 2:30 and 4 pm. It takes 1¼ hours and costs 80F; snorkeling gear is provided for those who want to jump in for a closer look.

It's a 4-km drive from Malendure Beach to the beginning of Route de la Traversée (D23) for the scenic 45-minute drive back

to Pointe-à-Pitre. For details, see the earlier Route de la Traversée section.

Places to Stay

In the center of the village of Pigeon, just south of Malendure Beach, there are several private room-for-rent and gîte signs. One is for *Gite de Guy Yoko* (☎ 98 71 42), la Grange Bel'O, Chemin Poirier, Pigeon, 97125 Bouillante, a member of the Gîte de France network.Guy has a handful of units that rent weekly, ranging from 2300F for a double to 5200F for an apartment that can accommodate eight people.

The restaurant *Le Rocher de Malendure* (☎ 98 70 84, fax 98 89 92), Malendure, 97125 Bouillante, has a couple of bungalows with sea views that rent for 350F a night.

Places to Eat

There are huts on Malendure Beach selling cheap sandwiches and snacks and a couple of simple open-air beachside restaurants with more substantial meals.

For something more upmarket, most people head south to the village of Pigeon. *Le Rocher de Malendure*, on a headland between Pigeon and Malendure Beach, has a seaside setting and good French/Creole food at fair prices. *Le Pigeonnier*, in the center of Pigeon, is an unpretentious restaurant with a water view and a reasonably priced chalkboard menu of Creole seafood.

Terre-de-Haut

Lying 10km off Guadeloupe is Terre-de-Haut, the largest of the eight small islands that make up Les Saintes. Terre-de-Haut's history stands apart from other places in Guadeloupe; since the island was too hilly and dry for sugar plantations, slavery never took hold. Consequently, the population is largely comprised of 'blue eyes' who still trace their roots to the early seafaring Norman and Breton colonists.

Terre-de-Haut is quaint and unhurried, quite French in nature and almost Mediterranean in appearance. Although it's a tiny

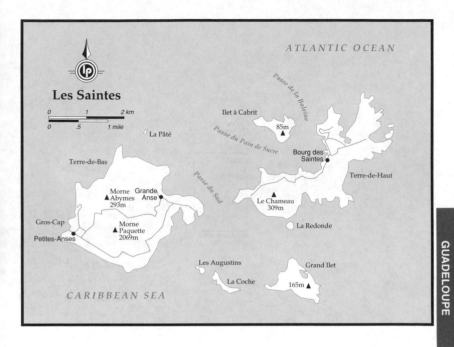

package it's got a lot to offer, including a strikingly beautiful landscape of volcanic hills and deep bays. The island has fine protected beaches with good swimming and windsurfing, a fort with a botanical garden, good restaurants and a range of places to stay at reasonable prices. In all, it's one of the most appealing little islands in the Eastern Caribbean, though it can get overrun with tourists on weekends and in the height of the season.

Although tourism is growing, many islanders still rely on fishing as a mainstay. You can often find the fishers mending their nets along the waterfront and see their colorful locally made boats, called *sain-toises*, lined along the shore.

Terre-de-Haut is only 5km long and about half as wide. If you don't mind uphill walks you can get around on foot, although many people opt to rent motorbikes. Ferries to Guadeloupe and Terre-de-Bas dock right in the center of Bourg des Saintes, the island's only village. The airstrip is to the east, a 10-minute walk from the village center.

BOURG DES SAINTES

Home to most of the island's residents, Bourg des Saintes is a picturesque village with a decidedly Norman accent. Its narrow streets are lined with whitewashed red-roofed houses with shuttered windows and yards of flowering hibiscus.

The ferry is met by young girls peddling *tourment d'amour* ('agony of love') cakes with a sweet coconut filling – an island treat that makes for a tasty light breakfast.

At the end of the pier there's a small courtyard with a gilded column commemorating the French Revolution; it's a bustling place at ferry times, quiet at others. Turn right and in a minute you'll be at the central town square, flanked by the *mairie* (town hall) and an old stone church.

It's a fun town to kick around. There are small restaurants, ice-cream shops, scooter

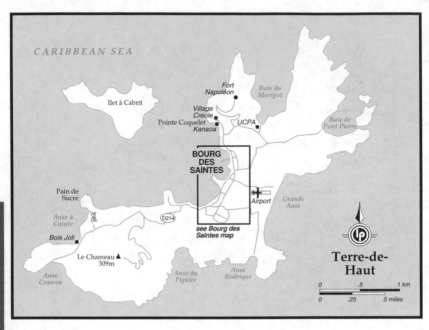

CARIBBEAN SEA

Ilet à Cabrit

Fort Napoléon

Baie du Marigot

Village Creole

Pointe Coquelet

Kanaoa

UCPA

Baie de Pont Pierre

BOURG DES SAINTES

Pain de Sucre

Anse à Cointe

trail

Bois Joli

D214

Airport

Grande Anse

see Bourg des Saintes map

Le Chameau ▲ 309m

Anse Crawen

Anse du Figuier

Anse Rodrique

Terre-de-Haut

0   .5   1 km
0   .25   .5 miles

rentals, art galleries and gift shops clustered along the main road, which is pedestrian-only during the day. Most shops close from noon to 2 pm.

Information
Money It's best to bring along sufficient francs to cover your stay as the island's sole bank, Crédit Agricole, is only open on Tuesday, Thursday and Friday from 9 am to 2:30 pm. Credit cards are accepted at hotels (but not bottom-end guesthouses) and by the motorbike rental companies.

Post & Communications There are card phones at the pier. The post office is on the main road a few minutes walk south of the town hall.

Places to Stay
In Town There are room-for-rent signs around the island but keep in mind that if you're traveling during the high season the competition for rooms can be over-whelming so it's wise to try to book ahead.

One good-value place is *Paul Maison-neuve* (☎ 99 53 38), 97137 Les Saintes, on the main road just south of the town hall. The three rooms are simple but bright, with comfortable foam beds, standing fans, lou-vered glass windows and a rate of 150F for doubles. The bathroom is shared and kitchen facilities are available. English is not spoken, but the owners are accommo-dating and it shouldn't be a problem if you don't speak French.

Jeanne d'Arc (☎ 99 50 41), 97137 Les Saintes, is a popular hotel on the water-front about 500 meters south of the town center. It has 10 straightforward rooms, each with a private bathroom, two beds and a fan, and there's a terrace with a good ocean view. Singles or doubles cost 300F with breakfast.

La Saintoise (☎ 99 52 50), 97137 Les Saintes, a 10-room hotel on the square

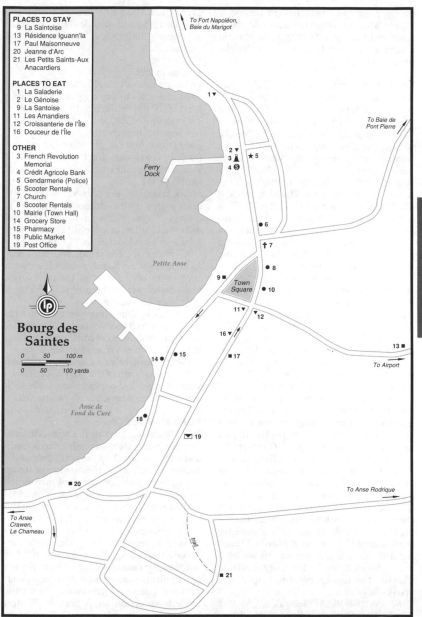

PLACES TO STAY
9 La Saintoise
13 Résidence Iguann'la
17 Paul Maisonneuve
20 Jeanne d'Arc
21 Les Petits Saints-Aux Anacardiers

PLACES TO EAT
1 La Saladerie
2 Le Génoise
9 La Santoise
11 Les Amandiers
12 Croissanterie de l'Île
16 Douceur de l'Île

OTHER
3 French Revolution Memorial
4 Crédit Agricole Bank
5 Gendarmerie (Police)
6 Scooter Rentals
7 Church
8 Scooter Rentals
10 Mairie (Town Hall)
14 Grocery Store
15 Pharmacy
18 Public Market
19 Post Office

To Fort Napoléon, Baie du Marigot

To Baie de Pont Pierre

Ferry Dock

Petite Anse

Bourg des Saintes

0   50   100 m
0   50   100 yards

Town Square

To Airport

Anse de Fond du Curé

To Anse Rodrique

To Anse Crawen, Le Chameau

trail

GUADELOUPE

opposite the town hall, has no particular charm but the rooms are clean and good-sized and have private bathrooms, air-con and phones. It costs 350F for a double, breakfast included.

Town Outskirts *Les Petits Saints-Aux Anacardiers* (☎ 99 50 99, fax 99 54 51), 97137 Les Saintes, is an eclectic hillside inn southeast of the town center, about a 15-minute walk from the pier. The 12 rooms, smallish but comfortable, have tropical decor, air-con and phones; some have balconies and TVs. Singles/doubles cost 350/400F in summer and 500/560F in winter for rooms with shared baths and 450/500F in summer and 650/700F in winter for nicer rooms with private bathrooms. Rates include breakfast. There's a pool with a great view of the harbor and a restaurant that specializes in lunchtime salads and Creole dinners.

Résidence Iguann'la (☎ /fax 99 57 69), Route de Grande Anse, 97137 Les Saintes, between town and the airport, has four cozy units within walking distance of Grande Anse Beach. All have air-con, TV, a kitchen and terrace. The three studios cost 400F for one or two people, the apartment 650F for up to four people. Each of the units can accommodate an additional two people, at a cost of 60F per person.

Village Creole (☎ 99 53 83, fax 99 55 55), Pointe Coquelet, 97137 Les Saintes, about a kilometer north of the pier, consists of 22 comfortable, contemporary, duplex apartments. Units are split level; there's a fully equipped kitchen and a living/dining room downstairs and two bedrooms with skylights upstairs. Each apartment has two bathrooms, two phones and a small safe. The coast is predominantly rocky, but there's a bit of a beach out front and the area is peaceful. Rates are a reasonable 460F a double in summer, plus 100F each for a third or fourth person. In winter it costs 640/840/960F for two/three/four people. The management is helpful and speaks English.

Kanaoa (☎ 99 51 36, fax 99 55 04), 97137 Les Saintes, adjacent to Village Creole, has 19 simple seaside rooms and bungalows. Singles/doubles cost 300/400F in summer, 500/650F in winter, breakfast included.

Places to Eat

There are lots of casual restaurants around town that cater to day trippers and offer a meal of the day in the 60F to 90F range.

Douceur de l'Île, south of the town hall, is a popular, unpretentious restaurant with good prices. You can get a simple breakfast for 25F, sandwiches for 15F and a plat du jour with the likes of colombo cabri or lambi for 45F.

Les Amandiers is a pleasant place on the town square with both indoor and outside dining. It specializes in Creole seafood dishes and offers a couple of good-value salad – dessert lunches for 60F to 75F.

A good place for salads and light seafood dishes is *La Saladerie*, a few minutes walk north of the pier on the main road. Most dishes are in the 50F to 75F range. It's closed on Tuesday.

Another healthy choice is the restaurant at *La Saintoise* hotel, which has generous salads, including good fruit, vegetable and seafood versions, for around 40F.

For pizza, there's *Le Génoise*, a grill and pizzeria just north of the ferry dock. *Croissanterie de l'Île*, opposite the town hall, sells fresh croissants, breads and pastries.

FORT NAPOLÉON

Fort Napoléon, built in the mid-19th century and never used in battle, stands intact and well preserved on the north side of the harbor. There's a fine hilltop view of Bourg des Saintes and you can look across the channel to Fort Josephine, a small fortification on Ilet à Cabrit. On a clear day you can also see Marie-Galante and La Désirade.

The grounds surrounding the fort are planted in cacti gardens. The fort's barracks contain a small museum with a few simple historical displays in both French and English. You can walk through on your own or join an informative 30-minute guided tour conducted in French. The fort is open daily, from 9 am to 12:30 pm only, and admission is 20F. Fort Napoléon is 1.5km north of the center of Bourg des Saintes; simply turn left as you come off the pier and follow the road uphill.

BAIE DU MARIGOT

Baie du Marigot is a pleasant little bay with a calm protected beach about a kilometer north of Bourg des Saintes. Even though it's just a 15-minute walk from town there's very little development in the area and the beach doesn't get crowded. It's fairly close to Fort Napoléon so you could combine a visit to the two; after visiting the fort turn left at the bottom of the winding fort road and bear left again a few minutes later as you near the bay.

Places to Stay

UCPA (☎ 99 54 94, fax 99 55 28), Baie du Marigot, 97137 Les Saintes, has 60 rooms in free-standing duplex and four-plex buildings. It sits alone above Baie du Marigot with its own jetty and a fine sea view. Geared for windsurfers, UCPA offers week-long packages that include accommodations, meals, lessons and unlimited use of sailboards and Hobie Cat catamarans.

BAIE DE PONT PIERRE

Baie de Pont Pierre is a lovely reef-protected beach with light brown sand and a splendid setting. This deep horseshoe-shaped bay is backed by sea grape trees and flanked on both sides by high cliffs, while an offshore islet at its mouth gives the illusion of closing the bay off as a complete circle. It's a very gentle place, with a nice mix of tourists and locals; there are even tame goats that mosey onto the beach and lie down next to sunbathers. The beach is an easy 1.5km walk northeast of Bourg des Saintes.

EAST COAST BEACHES

The long sandy beach **Grande Anse**, immediately east of the airport runway, has rough seas and water conditions that are more suitable for surfing than swimming. The north side of this windy beach is backed by clay cliffs.

South of Grande Anse beach and about 2km from town is **Anse Rodrique**, a nice beach on a protected cove that usually has good swimming conditions.

SOUTHWEST BEACHES

Two km southwest of Bourg des Saintes, **Anse à Cointe** is a good beach for combining swimming and snorkeling. The snorkeling is best at the north side of the beach. There's also good snorkeling and a sandy beach at **Pain de Sucre**, the basalt 'Sugarloaf' peninsula that's about 700 meters to the north.

Anse Crawen, 500 meters south of the Bois Joli hotel, is a secluded clothing-optional beach just a couple of minutes walk down a dirt path that starts where the coastal road ends. Anse Crawen has golden sands and a natural setting backed by trees.

Places to Stay & Eat

Bois Joli (☎ 99 50 38, fax 99 55 05), Anse à Cointe, 97137 Les Saintes, the island's only resort-like hotel, has 31 rooms fronting a golden-sand beach. Most accommodations are bungalow-style with small porches, air-con, showers, toilets and bidets; the cost is 1050F a double. There are also some small straightforward rooms with good views that cost 575/730F for singles/doubles. Rates include breakfast and dinner. The hotel's poolside restaurant has a fine sea view and features steak and seafood dishes priced around 100F, about twice that if you add a starter and dessert.

LE CHAMEAU

A winding cement road leads to the summit of Le Chameau, which at 309 meters is the island's highest point. There are picture-perfect views of Bourg des Saintes and Ilet à Cabrit on the way up and sweeping views of the other Les Saintes islands, Marie-Galante, Basse-Terre and Dominica from the top of the hill. The summit is capped by an old stone sentry tower that's deteriorated but still has metal steps leading to the top where there's an unobstructed view as far as the eye can see.

To get to Le Chameau, turn south from the Bourg des Saintes pier and continue 1km on the coastal road. At Restaurant Plongée turn inland on D214; 500 meters later, turn left on the cement road and follow it up 1.75km where it ends at the tower. From town it's a moderately difficult hour-long walk to the top or a fun five-minute motorbike ride.

GETTING THERE & AWAY
Air
Air Guadeloupe (☎ 99 51 23) flies to Terre-de-Haut from Pointe-à-Pitre at 8 am and 1:30 pm (the latter via Marie-Galante) Monday to Saturday and at 4:45 pm daily, returning 15 minutes later. The fare is 180F one way (135F for students) and 270F for a one-day excursion.

Sea
L'Express des Iles (☎ 83 12 45) leaves for Terre-de-Haut from the east side of Pointe-à-Pitre harbor at 8 am daily, returning from Terre-de-Haut at 4 pm. The crossing takes 50 minutes.

L'Express des Iles also has a seasonal boat service from the Saint-François marina (☎ 88 48 63). From mid-December to mid-May, and from mid-July to the end of August, the boat leaves Saint-François at 8 am on Tuesday and Thursday and returns from Terre-de-Haut at 4 pm. (Note that between mid-May and mid-July, there's usually a once-weekly service on Wednesdays.) The crossing takes 80 minutes, as the boat stops at Marie-Galante en route.

Brudey Frères (☎ 90 04 48) leaves Pointe-à-Pitre at 8 am daily for Terre-de-Haut, departing Terre-de-Haut at 3:45 pm. In the high season, there's also a Monday and Friday boat from Saint-François, with the same departure times.

The roundtrip fare with either company, from either Guadeloupean port, is 170F for adults, 90F for children.

The *Princesse Caroline* (☎ 86 95 83) departs from Trois-Rivières at 8:20 am daily for the 20-minute crossing to Terre-de-Haut, returning at 4 pm. The roundtrip fare is 80F.

GETTING AROUND
With advance reservations, most hotels will pick up guests free of charge at the airport or pier.

Motorcycle
Motorbikes are a great way to tour the island. Although roads are narrow there are only a few dozen cars (and no car rentals) on Terre-de-Haut, so you won't encounter much traffic. With a motorbike you can zip up to the top of Le Chameau and Fort Napoléon, get out to the beaches and explore the island pretty thoroughly in a day. The motorbikes are capable of carrying two people but, because the roads are so winding, unless you're an accomplished driver it's not advisable to carry a passenger.

There are lots of rental locations on the main road leading south from the pier, but the ones that set up dockside seem as good as any. If you arrive on a busy day it's wise to grab a bike as soon as possible as they sometimes sell out. Most charge 180F for day visitors (200F on a 24-hour basis) and require a 2000F deposit or an imprint of a major credit card. Motorbikes come with gas but not damage insurance, so if you get in an accident or spill the bike the repairs will be charged to your credit card.

Motorbike riding is prohibited in the center of Bourg des Saintes from 9 am to noon and 2 to 4 pm. Although you'll see people ignoring the law, if you run into a gendarme expect to get stopped.

Organized Tours
There are a few taxi minivans that provide two-hour tours of the island for about 50F per person, if there are enough people, or 350F for the whole van. Look for them parked along the street between the pier and the town hall right after the ferry arrives.

Terre-de-Bas

Terre-de-Bas, just a kilometer to the west of Terre-de-Haut, is the only other inhabited island in Les Saintes.

A bit less craggy than Terre-de-Haut, Terre-de-Bas once had small sugar and coffee plantations and is largely populated by the descendants of African slaves.

It's a quiet rural island and tourism has yet to take root, but there is a regular ferry service between the islands, making it possible for visitors to go over and poke around on a day excursion.

The main village, Petites-Anses, is on the west coast. It has hilly streets lined with trim houses, a small fishing harbor and a quaint church with a graveyard of tombs decorated with conch shells and plastic flowers.

Grande Anse, diagonally across the island on the east coast, is a small village with a little 17th-century church and a nice beach.

One-lane roads link the island's two villages: one of the roads cuts across the center of the island, passing between the two highest peaks – Morne Abymes and Morne Paquette – and the other goes along the south coast. If you enjoy long country walks it's possible to make a loop walk between the two villages (about 9km roundtrip) by going out on one road and returning on the other. Otherwise, there's sometimes an inexpensive jitney bus that runs between the villages.

Petite-Anses has a good bakery and pastry shop, and both villages have a couple of reasonably priced local restaurants.

GETTING THERE & AWAY
The boat *L'Inter* shuttles between Terre-de-Haut and Terre-de-Bas (30F) five times a day between 8 am and 4 pm.

Marie-Galante

Marie-Galante, 25km southeast of Guadeloupe proper, is the largest of Guadeloupe's outer islands. Compared to the archipelago's other islands, Marie-Galante is relatively flat, its dual limestone plateaus rising only 150 meters. It is roughly round in shape with a total land area of 158 sq km, much of which is planted in sugar cane.

The island is exceedingly rural in character and totally untouched by mass tourism. It offers visitors lovely, uncrowded beaches and some pleasant country scenery. Very few English -speaking tourists come this way and few islanders speak any English at all.

Marie-Galante has a population of about 13,000, half of whom live in Grand-Bourg, on the southwest coast. Most of the rest are evenly divided between its two smaller towns, Saint-Louis and Capesterre.

In the early 1800s the island of Marie-Galante boasted nearly 100 sugar mills and the countryside is still dotted with the scattered ruins of most of them. Today sugar production is concentrated at one mill, while cane is distilled into rum at three distilleries. Most of the cane is still cut by hand and hauled from the fields using ox carts.

The distilleries are among the island's main 'sights.' The Distillerie Poisson, midway between Saint-Louis and Grand-Bourg, bottles the island's best-known rum under the Père Labat label. Distillerie Bielle, between Grand-Bourg and Capesterre, offers tours of its age-old distillery operation. Both places have tasting rooms and sell rum.

GRAND-BOURG
Grand-Bourg is the commercial and administrative center of the island. The town was leveled by fire in 1901, and its architecture is a mix of early-20th-century buildings and more recent drab concrete structures.

The ferry dock is at the center of town. The post office, customs office and town hall are all within a couple of blocks of the waterfront. A BNP bank is two blocks inland on Place de l'Eglise, straight up from the dock.

Château Murat, about 2km from Grand-Bourg on the north side of the road to Capesterre, is an 18th-century sugar estate that's undergone extensive restorations. The grounds are open to the public all the time and there's a visitor center that's open sporadic hours.

GUADELOUPE

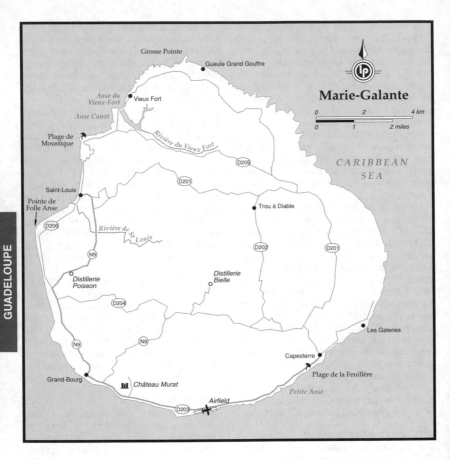

Places to Stay & Eat

Philippe Bavarday (☎ 97 83 94, fax 97 81 90), 97112 Grand-Bourg, a member of the Gîtes de France network, has an attractive home with four air-conditioned rooms that cost 240F per night or 1650F per week for two people. It's near the coast, a few kilometers east of town in the section of Les Basses, between the airport and Grand-Bourg center.

If you want to be in the center of town, there's *Auberge de l'Arbre à Pain* (☎ 97 73 69), Rue Docteur Etzol, 97112 Grand-Bourg, a few minutes walk from the dock.

Its seven small, straightforward rooms have private baths and cost 210/250F for singles/doubles. There's a Creole restaurant on site.

Opposite the dock you'll find a handful of local cafés and restaurants, most specializing in seafood. There's a bakery and a supermarket about two blocks inland.

SAINT-LOUIS

Saint-Louis, a fishing village of about 4000 residents, is the island's main anchorage for yachters and a secondary port for ferries from Guadeloupe. There's a little market at the end of the dock and a couple of restaurants and the post office are just east of that.

Although there are beaches along the outskirts of Saint-Louis, some of the island's most beautiful strands lie a few kilometers to the north. The golden sands of Plage de Moustique, Anse Canot and Anse du Vieux-Fort unfold one after the other once you round the point that marks the north end of Saint-Louis Bay.

Places to Stay & Eat

The island's largest hotel, the in-town *Le Salut* (☎ 97 02 67), 97134 Saint-Louis, has 15 simple rooms with sinks and showers for 170F without air-con and 250F with air-con. Toilets are in the hall.

A good gîte is *Le Refuge* (☎ /fax 97 02 95), Section Saint-Charles, 97134 Saint-Louis, about 2km southeast of Saint-Louis center. It offers air-conditioned double rooms for 300F and a good multi-course dinner of traditional island fare for 80F.

Chez Henri, just south of the dock, is quite popular for seafront dining and has good local food at moderate prices.

CAPESTERRE

Capesterre (population 4100), on the southeast coast, is a seaside town backed by hills. There are sea cliffs and hiking trails to the north of the village.

On the south side of town there's a beautiful beach, Plage de la Feuillère, and a second attractive beach, Petite Anse, is about a kilometer to the southwest.

Places to Stay & Eat

The *Hôtel Hajo* (☎ 97 32 76), 97140 Capesterre, which has a Mediterranean decor and six oceanview rooms, is about 2km southwest of Capesterre and a short walk from the beach. Rooms, which have fans and private bathrooms, cost 250/280F for singles/doubles and there's a reasonably priced French/Creole restaurant on site.

GETTING THERE & AWAY
Air

Air Guadeloupe (☎ 82 28 35) flies to Marie-Galante from Pointe-à-Pitre at 6:30 am, 1:30 and 6:15 pm Monday to Saturday and at 6:15 pm on Sunday. Flights return from Marie-Galante half an hour later. The fare is 180F one way (135F for students) and 290F for a one-day excursion. The airport is midway between Grand-Bourg and Capesterre, about 5km from either.

Sea

The inter-island crossing to Marie-Galante can be a bit rough, so if you're not used to bouncy seas it's best to travel on a light stomach and sit on deck.

There are two boat companies that make the run to Marie-Galante. On both, the roundtrip fare is 170F for adults, 90F for children.

L'Express des Iles L'Express des Iles (☎ 83 12 45) leaves from the east side of Pointe-à-Pitre harbor at 8 am, 12:30 and 5 pm Monday to Saturday and at 8 am, 5 and 7 pm on Sunday. The 12:30 pm boat goes via Saint-Louis, but all other sailings are to Grand-Bourg only. The boat leaves Grand-Bourg at 6 and 9 am and 3:45 pm Monday to Saturday and at 6 am, 3:45 and 6 pm on Sunday. The crossing takes 45 minutes.

In winter, L'Express des Iles has boat service to Saint-Louis from the Saint-François marina (☎ 88 48 63), leaving at 8 am on Tuesday and Thursday and returning from Marie-Galante at 4:45 pm. The trip takes 45 minutes. In summer, the schedule is more flexible, so you should call in advance.

Brudey Frères Brudey Frères (☎ 90 04 48) sails to Grand-Bourg, leaving Pointe-à-Pitre at 8 am and 3 pm on weekdays; at 8 am and 1 pm on Saturday; and 8 am and 4:45 pm on Sunday. The ferry departs Grand-Bourg at 1 and 4:30 pm on weekdays; 9:30 am and 4:30 pm on Saturday; and 3:30 and 6 pm on Sunday. Some boats go via Saint-Louis.

GETTING AROUND
Bus

During the day, except for Sunday, inexpensive minibuses make regular runs between the three villages.

GUADELOUPE

Car, Motorcycle & Bicycle

Cars, motorbikes and bicycles can be rented from Caneval (☎ 97 97 76) at the Shell station in Grand-Bourg. Other agents include Magauto (☎ 97 98 75), near the docks in both Grand-Bourg and Saint-Louis, and Location 2000 (☎ 97 12 83), south of the dockside town hall in Saint-Louis.

Bicycles can also be rented from the Bureau Touristique de Marie-Galante (☎ 97 77 48), 51 Rue du Presbytère, Grand-Bourg.

Cars generally cost from 250F to 300F a day, motorbikes 170F and bicycles about half that.

La Désirade

La Désirade, about 10km off the eastern tip of Grande-Terre, is the archipelago's least developed and least visited island. Looking somewhat like an overturned boat when viewed from Guadeloupe, La Désirade is 11km long and 2km wide, with a central plateau that rises 273 meters at its highest point, Grand Montagne.

The terrain is desert-like, with coconut and sea grape trees along the coast and scrub and cactus on the hillsides. It's too dry and arid for extensive agriculture and though some people raise sheep, most of La Désirade's 1600 inhabitants make their living from fishing and boat building.

The uninhabited north side of the island has a rocky coastline with rough open seas, while the south side has sandy beaches and reef-protected waters.

La Désirade's harbor and airport are on the southwest side of the island in **Grande Anse** (also called Le Bourg), the main village. The island's town hall, post office and library are also in Grande Anse. There are smaller settlements at **Le Souffleur** and **Baie Mahault**. La Désirade's main

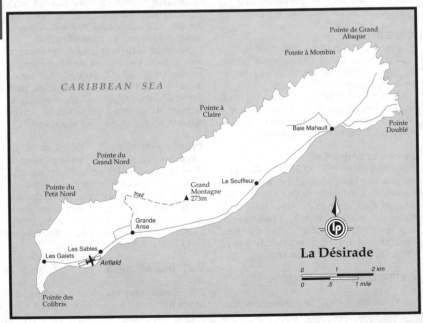

road runs along the south coast, joining the villages.

In 1725 Guadeloupe established a leper colony on La Désirade and for more than two centuries victims of the dreaded disease were forced to make a one-way trip to the island. The **leprosarium**, which was run by the Catholic Sisters of Charity, closed in the mid-1950s. Its remains, a chapel and a cemetery are just east of Baie Mahault.

There are white-sand beaches near all three villages and for a good view of the island there's an hour-long hike up Grand Montagne.

Places to Stay & Eat

The *L'Oasis du Désert* (☎ 20 02 12) hotel and restaurant and *Hôtel Le Mirage* (☎ 20 01 08) are both small hostelries in the Desert Saline quarter of Grand Anse with simple rooms at 200/220F for singles/doubles. There are also a few rooms in private homes around Grande Anse for 150F to 200F; help with bookings is available from Location 2000 (☎ 20 03 74).

Grande Anse and Baie Mahault both have a handful of moderately priced seafood restaurants and cheaper snack bars.

GETTING THERE & AWAY
Air

Air Guadeloupe flies to La Désirade from Pointe-à-Pitre at 7 am daily except on Sunday and at 4 pm daily except on Saturday; return flights depart from La Désirade 25 minutes later. The fare is 180F one way (135F for students).

Sea

There are two ferries to La Désirade. *Sotramade* (☎ 20 02 30) leaves from the Saint-François marina daily at 8 am and 5 pm, with an extra departure on Saturday at 11 am. It returns at 6:15 am and 4 pm daily, as well as at 2 pm on Saturday. The roundtrip fare is 120F and the ride takes about 45 minutes.

Imperiale (☎ 88 58 06) departs from Saint-François daily at 8 am and 5 pm, with an extra sailing on Saturday at 2 pm. On the return, the boat leaves La Désirade at 6:15 am and 4 pm daily. The roundtrip fare is 150F for adults, 80F for children.

GETTING AROUND

Bicycle and scooter rentals are available at the ferry dock for 70F to 150F a day.

Martinique

Martinique is a slice of France set down in the tropics. Its shops are full of Paris fashions, every village has a corner pâtisserie selling freshly baked baguettes and croissants, and its resorts are crowded with vacationers from mainland France.

The capital, Fort-de-France, is a bustling city of 100,000, the largest in the French West Indies. Most of the island's other large towns are modern and suburban-like, linked to the capital by multi-lane highways and fast-moving traffic.

HIGHLIGHTS

- The Eastern Caribbean's most cosmopolitan society, with a blended French/Creole culture
- Saint-Pierre's intriguing ruins from the 1902 volcanic eruption
- Route de la Trace, a scenic rainforest drive across the mountainous interior
- Fort-de-France, with its French colonial architecture

Nevertheless, nearly a third of Martinique is forested and other parts of the island are given over to pineapples, bananas and sugar cane fields. You can still find sleepy fishing villages untouched by development, remote beaches and lots of hiking tracks into the mountains.

Martinique is volcanic in origin, topped by the 1397-meter Mont Pelée, an active volcano. Pelée last erupted in 1902, gaining an infamous place in history by wiping out the then-capital city of Saint-Pierre, along with its entire population. Today the ruins of Saint-Pierre are Martinique's foremost tourist sight.

Facts about Martinique

HISTORY

When Columbus sighted Martinique it was inhabited by Carib Indians who called the island Madinina, 'Island of Flowers.' Three decades passed before the first party of French settlers, who were led by Pierre Belain d'Esnambuc, landed on the northwest side of the island. There they built a small fort and established a settlement that would become the capital city, Saint-Pierre. The next year, on October 31, 1636, King Louis XIII signed a decree authorizing the use of slaves in the French West Indies.

The settlers quickly went about colonizing the land and by 1640 had extended their grip south to Fort-de-France, where they constructed a fort on the rise above the harbor. As forests were cleared to make room for sugar plantations, conflicts with the native Caribs escalated into warfare and in 1660 those Caribs who had survived the fighting were finally forced off the island.

The British took a keen interest in Martinique as well, invading and holding the

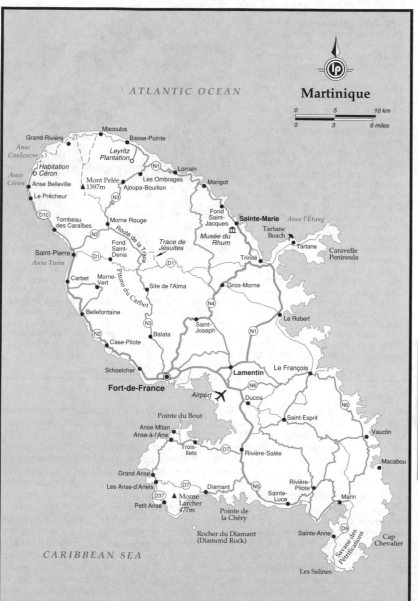

ATLANTIC OCEAN

Martinique

0   5   10 km
0   3   6 miles

Macouba
Grand-Rivière
Basse-Pointe
Anse Couleuvre
Leyritz Plantation
N1
Lorrain
Habitation Céron
Anse Céron
Mont Pelée 1397m
Les Ombrages
Marigot
Anse Belleville
Ajoupa-Bouillon
Le Prêcheur
N3
Fond Saint-Jacques
Sainte-Marie
Anse l'Étang
D10
Tombeau des Caraïbes
Morne Rouge
Musée du Rhum
Tartane Beach
Route de la Trace
Tartane
N2
Fond Saint-Denis
Trinité
Caravelle Peninsula
Saint-Pierre
D1
Trace de Jésuites
Anse Turin
D1
Carbet
Morne-Vert
Site de l'Alma
Gros-Morne
Pitons du Carbet
Bellefontaine
N4
N3
Le Robert
N2
Balata
Saint-Joseph
N1
Case-Pilote
Schoelcher
Le François
Fort-de-France
Lamentin
Airport
N6
Pointe du Bout
Ducos
Saint-Esprit
N6
Anse Mitan
Anse-à-l'Ane
Trois-Ilets
D7
Rivière-Salée
Vauclin
Grand Anse
D7
Macabou
Les Anse-d'Arlets
Diamant
N5
Rivière-Pilote
D37
Morne Larcher 477m
Sainte-Luce
Marin
Petit Anse
Pointe de la Chéry
D9
Rocher du Diamant (Diamond Rock)
Sainte-Anne
Savane des Pétrifications
Cap Chevalier
CARIBBEAN SEA
Les Salines

The Empress Josephine

Martinique's most famous colonial daughter was the Empress Josephine. Born in Trois-Ilets in June 1763 and baptized Marie Joseph Rose Tascher de la Pagerie, it is rumored that a soothsayer, upon seeing the child, declared that one day she would become queen. Her route to royalty wouldn't be a very direct one, however.

In 1779 she married a wealthy army officer, Alexandre de Beauharnais, and moved to France. A decade later de Beauharnais got caught up in the turmoil of the French Revolution and lost his neck to a guillotine. Shortly after, Josephine met a young, and still largely unknown, military officer named Napoleon Bonaparte.

A passionate love affair began and in 1796, at the age of 33, she married Napoleon. In the years that followed, Napoleon's victories in battle gained him world attention and in 1804, in a ceremony officiated by the pope and held at Notre Dame Cathedral, Napoleon was proclaimed Emperor of France and Josephine was crowned empress.

When Josephine married Napoleon she was six years older than he, a fact that she went to great lengths to conceal. Although she had two children by her first marriage, she was unable to bear Napoleon an heir. In 1809 Napoleon divorced Josephine and shortly after he married the Archduchess Marie Louise of Austria. Josephine retired to a chateau at Malmaison, outside Paris, and despite the divorce, Napoleon continued to call on her.

Curiously, Josephine's daughter from her first marriage, Hortense de Beauharnais, married Napoleon's brother and gave birth to a son, Louis, who would take the French throne as Napoleon III in 1852. ■

island for most of the period from 1794 to 1815. The island prospered under British occupation; the planters simply sold their sugar in British markets rather than French. Perhaps more importantly, the occupation allowed Martinique to avoid the turmoil and bloodshed of the French Revolution. By the time the British returned the island to France in 1815, the Napoleonic Wars had ended and the French empire was again entering a period of stability.

Not long after the French administration was reestablished on Martinique, the golden era for sugar cane began to wane, as glutted markets and the introduction of sugar beets on mainland France eroded prices. With their wealth diminished, the aristocratic plantation owners lost much of their political influence and the abolitionist movement, led by Victor Schoelcher, gained momentum.

It was Schoelcher, the French cabinet minister responsible for overseas possessions, who convinced the provisional government to sign the 1848 Emancipation Proclamation that brought an end to slavery in the French West Indies.

On March 8, 1902, in the most devastating natural disaster in Caribbean history, the Mont Pelée volcano erupted violently, destroying the city of Saint-Pierre and claiming the lives of its 30,000 inhabitants. Shortly thereafter, the capital was moved permanently to Fort-de-France. Saint-Pierre, which had been regarded as the most cultured city in the French West Indies, was eventually rebuilt, but it has never been more than a shadow of its former self.

In 1946 Martinique became an overseas department of France, with a status similar to those of metropolitan departments, and in 1974 it was further assimilated into the political fold as a region of France.

GEOGRAPHY

At 1080 sq km, Martinique is the second-largest island in the French West Indies. Roughly 65km long and 20km wide, it has a terrain punctuated by hills, plateaus and mountains.

The highest point is the 1397-meter Mont Pelée, an active volcano that is at the northern end of the island. The center of the island is dominated by the Pitons du Carbet, a scenic mountain range reaching 1207 meters.

Martinique's irregular coastline is cut by deep bays and coves while the mountainous rainforest in the interior feeds numerous rivers.

CLIMATE

Fort-de-France's average daily high temperature in January is 28°C (83°F) while the low averages 21°C (70°F). In July the average daily high is 30°C (86°F) while the low averages 23°C (74°F).

The annual rainfall in Fort-de-France is 1840 mm (72 inches). Measurable rain falls an average of 13 days a month in April, the driest month, and about twice as often in September, the rainiest month. Martinique's average humidity is high, ranging from 80% in March and April to 87% in October and November.

The mountainous northern interior is both cooler and rainier than the coast.

FLORA & FAUNA

Martinique has lots of colorful flowering plants, with the type of vegetation varying with altitude and rainfall. Rainforests cover the slopes of the mountains in the northern interior, which are luxuriant with tree ferns, bamboo groves, climbing vines and hardwood trees like mahogany, rosewood, locust and gommier.

The drier southern part of the island has brushy savanna vegetation such as cacti, frangipani trees, balsam, logwood and acacia shrubs. Common landscape plantings include splashy bougainvillea, red hibiscus and yellow-flowered allamanda trees.

Martinique has *Anolis* lizards, manicous (opossums), mongoose and venomous fer-de-lance snakes. The mongoose, which was introduced from India in the late 19th century, preys on eggs and has been responsible for the demise of many bird species. Some native birds, such as parrots, are no longer found on the island at all, while others have seen significant declines in their numbers. Endangered birds include the Martinique trembler, white-breasted trembler and white-breasted thrasher.

GOVERNMENT & POLITICS

Martinique, an overseas department of France, is represented in the French Parliament by four elected deputies and two senators.

A prefect, who is appointed by the French Minister of the Interior, represents the central government and oversees the execution of French law by island authorities. There are two island-wide legislative bodies, the Conseil Général and the Conseil Régional, each with about 40 members who are elected by universal suffrage.

Martinique is further divided into 34 *communes*; each has an elected municipal council, which in turn appoints a mayor. Quite a bit of political diversity and power rests at the municipal level.

ECONOMY

The economy of Martinique is heavily dependent upon outlays from the French government, whose expenditures account for more than 50% of the island's GNP. Although by Caribbean standards Martinique has a high per capita GNP at US$10,500, it's only about half of what prevails on the French mainland.

Agriculture accounts for many of the jobs in Martinique; sugar cane, bananas and pineapples are the leading crops. The cane is used by Martinique's 14 distilleries to produce rum, the island's best-known export item. Other export items include cut flowers and processed foods.

Tourism is the leading growth sector of the economy and has increased some 25% over the past decade as the government, in a drive to encourage more investment, subsidized the construction of new hotels. About 375,000 overnight tourists now visit the island annually; approximately 80% of them come from France and 10% from the USA and Canada. In addition, about 400,000 cruise ship visitors, 85% of them from the USA and Canada, make a stop on Martinique each year.

POPULATION & PEOPLE

The population of Martinique is about 400,000, of which more than a quarter live in the Fort-de-France area. The majority of residents are of mixed ethnic origin. The earliest settlers were from Normandy, Brittany, Paris and other parts of France; shortly after, African slaves were brought to Martinique; later, smaller numbers of immigrants came from India, Syria and Lebanon. These days Martinique is also home to thousands of aliens, some of them staying illegally, from poorer Caribbean islands such as Dominica, St Lucia and Haiti.

SOCIETY & CONDUCT

French and Creole influences are dominant in Martinique's cuisine, language, music and customs.

The Black Pride movement known as *négritude* emerged as a philosophical and literary movement in the 1930s largely through the writings of Martinican native Aimé Césaire, a poet and the long-time mayor of Fort-de-France. The movement advanced black social and cultural values and reestablished bonds with African traditions that had been suppressed by French colonialism.

The *biguine* (or beguine), an Afro-French dance music with a bolero rhythm, originated in Martinique in the 1930s. A more contemporary French West Indies creation, *zouk*, draws on the *biguine* and

other French Caribbean folk forms. With its Carnival-like rhythm and hot dance beat, zouk has become as popular in Europe as it is in the French Caribbean. The Martinique zouk band Kassav has made a number of top-selling recordings including the English-language album *Shades of Black*.

Dos & Don'ts

Except for fine dining, dress is casual but generally stylish. Topless bathing is common on the island, particularly at resort beaches.

RELIGION

An estimated 90% of all islanders are Roman Catholic. There are also Seventh Day Adventist, Baptist and Evangelical Christian denominations as well as Hindus, Baha'is and a small Jewish community.

LANGUAGE

French is the official language but islanders commonly speak Creole when chatting among themselves. English is spoken at larger hotels but is understood rather sporadically elsewhere so if you don't have a fair command of French, a dictionary and phrasebook will prove quite useful.

Facts for the Visitor

ORIENTATION

Martinique's only commercial airport is in Lamentin, 9km east of Fort-de-France. The main resort areas are on Martinique's southwest coast, from Pointe du Bout to Sainte-Anne. Roads on Martinique are good and despite the island's large size, no place is more than a two-hour drive from Fort-de-France.

Maps

The best road map of Martinique is the Institut Géographique National's No 511 map, which is sold around the island for 57F. However, this same map (on glossy paper, dotted with ads and labeled 'Carte

Routière') is distributed free by car rental agencies at the airport.

TOURIST OFFICES
Local Tourist Offices
Martinique's main tourist office is the Office Départemental du Tourisme (☎ 63 79 60, fax 73 66 93), 2 Rue Ernest Deproge, 97206 Fort-de-France, Martinique, French West Indies.

There is also a tourist information booth at the airport that usually stays open until the last flight comes in.

There are local information bureaus *(syndicats d'initiative)* in several towns including Sainte-Anne (☎ 76 73 45), Diamant (☎ 76 40 11), Saint-Pierre (☎ 78 15 41), Le Prêcheur (☎ 52 91 43) and Grand-Rivière (☎ 55 72 74). Most information distributed by the syndicats d'initiative is in French only.

Tourist Offices Abroad
Martinique has the following overseas tourist office representatives:

Canada
> Martinique Tourist Board,
> 1981 Ave McGill College, Suite 480,
> Montreal, Quebec PQH 3A 2W9
> (☎ 514-844-8566, fax 514-844-8901)

France
> Office du Tourisme de la Martinique,
> 2 Rue des Moulins, 75001 Paris
> (☎ 01 44 77 86 00, fax 01 49 26 03 63)

Germany
> Fremdenverkehrsamt Martinique,
> Westendstrasse 47, Postfach 100128,
> D60325 Frankfurt am Main
> (☎ 69 97 59 04 97, fax 69 97 59 04 99)

Italy
> Ente Nationale Francese per il Turismo,
> 5 Via Sant Andrea, 20121 Milan
> (☎ 258 31 64 71, fax 279 45 82)

UK
> French Government Tourist Office,
> 178 Piccadilly, London W1V OAL
> (☎ 0171-491-7622, fax 0171-493-6594)

USA
> Martinique Promotion Bureau, 444 Madison
> Ave, 16th Floor, New York, NY 10022
> (☎ 212-838-7800, 800-391-4909;
> fax 212-838-7855)

VISAS & DOCUMENTS
US and Canadian citizens can stay up to three months by showing proof of citizenship in the form of a current passport, an expired (up to five years) passport, or an official birth certificate accompanied by a driver's license or other government-authorized photo ID. Citizens of the European Union (EU) need an official identity card, valid passport or French *carte de séjour*. Citizens of most other foreign countries, including Australia, need a valid passport and a visa for France.

A roundtrip or onward ticket is officially required of visitors.

CUSTOMS
Citizens of EU countries are allowed to bring in 300 cigarettes, 1.5 liters of spirits and four liters of wine duty free. Non-EU citizens are allowed to bring in 200 cigarettes, a bottle of spirits and two liters of wine duty free. All visitors are allowed to bring in 'large allowances of rum' as well.

MONEY
The French franc is the island currency. Hotels, larger restaurants and car rental agencies accept Visa (Carte Bleue) and MasterCard (Eurocard). For most other situations, you'll need to use francs. Avoid changing money at hotel lobbies where the rates are worse than at exchange offices or banks. More information is under Money in the Facts for the Visitor chapter at the front of the book.

POST & COMMUNICATIONS
Post
There are post offices in all major towns. It costs 3F to send a postcard to France, 5.20F to other destinations in Europe, 3.80F to any place in the Caribbean or the USA and 4.40F to other parts of the Americas. This rate also covers letters up to 20 grams. You can buy postage stamps at some tobacco shops *(tabacs)*, hotels and souvenir shops in addition to post offices.

Mailing addresses given in this chapter should be followed by 'Martinique, French West Indies.'

Telephone

Public phones in Martinique accept French phonecards (télécartes), not coins. The cards cost 37F or 89F, depending on the calling time, and are sold at post offices and at shops marked télécarte en vente ici. Card phones can be found at post offices, the airport, city parks and other public places. For directory assistance, dial 12.

When making a local call, dial just the six-digit local number. When calling Martinique from outside the island, add the 0596 area code in front of the six digits.

More information on phonecards and making long-distance calls is under Post & Communications in the Facts for the Visitor chapter in the front of the book.

The area code for Martinique is 0596.

BOOKS

The bilingual French/English *A Cruising Guide to Martinique*, part of the Guide Trois Rivières series (Édition Trois Rivières, BP 566, 97242 Fort-de-France, Martinique), is a comprehensive sailing manual for cruising around Martinique.

Texaco, a novel by Patrick Chamoiseau that won the prestigious Prix Goncourt, recounts the social history of a shanty town in Martinique.

Le Quatrième Siècle (1962) and *Malemort* (1975) by Martinican native Édouard Glissant examine contemporary West Indian life against the backdrop of slavery and colonial rule.

NEWSPAPERS & MAGAZINES

The daily *France-Antilles* focuses on events occurring in the French West Indies. Other French-language newspapers, such as *Le Monde*, are flown in from the mainland. Larger newsstands in Fort-de-France and major tourist areas sell a few English-language newspapers including the *International Herald-Tribune*.

For tourist information the following free bilingual publications are useful: *Ti Gourmet*, a pocket-size restaurant guide offering a complimentary drink at many island restaurants; and the 100-page *Choubouloute*, with detailed listings of events, entertainment, ferry schedules and other current information.

RADIO & TV

Radio France Outre-Mer (RFO) has radio frequencies at 92 and 94.5 MHz. The TV networks RFO 1 and RFO 2 carry local programming, while other stations air standard programming from mainland France. CNN is available at some hotels, but that's usually the extent of English-language coverage.

ELECTRICITY

Electricity is 220 volts AC, 50 cycles, and plugs have two round prongs. Hotel bathrooms commonly have an adapted shaver outlet that accepts both 110 and 220 plugs.

WEIGHTS & MEASURES

Martinique uses the metric system, with elevations noted in meters, speed limit signs in kilometers and weights in grams. Time is given using the 24-hour clock.

HEALTH

Medical care is of high quality by Caribbean standards. There are a number of general hospitals on the island, including Hôpital de la Meynard (☎ 55 20 00) on D13 at the northeast side of Fort-de-France and Hôpital du Lamentin (☎ 57 11 11) on Blvd Fernand Guilon in Lamentin.

There is a risk of bilharzia (schistosomiasis) infection throughout the island; the main precaution is to avoid wading or swimming in fresh water. More information on this disease is under Health in the Facts for the Visitor chapter.

DANGERS & ANNOYANCES

The fer-de-lance, a large pit viper, can be found on Martinique, particularly in overgrown and brushy fields. The snake's bite is highly toxic and sometimes fatal; it's essential for victims to get an antivenin injection as soon as possible. Hikers should be alert for the snakes and stick to established trails.

Beware of manchineel trees on some beaches, as rainwater dripping off them can cause skin rashes and blistering.

EMERGENCIES

Emergency telephone numbers include:

Medical	☎ 75 15 15
Fire	☎ 18
Police	☎ 17
Sea rescue	☎ 71 92 92

BUSINESS HOURS

Although hours vary, many shops are open from 8:30 am to 6 pm Monday to Friday and until 1 pm on Saturday. Banks, and many other offices, are typically open from 7:30 am to 4:30 pm, with a two-hour lunch siesta beginning at noon. Note that banks close at noon on the day before a public holiday.

PUBLIC HOLIDAYS & SPECIAL EVENTS

Public holidays on Martinique are:

New Year's Day	January 1
Good Friday	late March/early April
Easter Sunday	late March/early April
Easter Monday	late March/early April
Ascension Thursday	40th day after Easter
Pentecost Monday	eighth Monday after Easter
Labor Day	May 1
Victory Day	May 8
Slavery Abolition Day	May 22
Bastille Day	July 14
Schoelcher Day	July 21
Assumption Day	August 15
All Saints Day	November 1
Armistice Day	November 11
Christmas Day	December 25

Martinique has a spirited Mardi Gras Carnival during the five-day period leading up to Ash Wednesday. The streets spill over with revelers, rum-fueled partying, costume parades, music and dancing. Much of the activity is centered around La Savane in Fort-de-France.

On a smaller scale, every village in Martinique has festivities to celebrate its patron saint's day. Saint-Pierre commemorates the May 8, 1902, eruption of Mont Pelée with live jazz and a candlelight procession from the cathedral.

The Tour de la Martinique, a week-long bicycle race, is held in mid-July. The Tour des Yoles Rondes, a week-long race of traditional sailboats, is held in early August. A 22-km semi-marathon around Fort-de-France is held in November. The biennial week-long Martinique Jazz Festival is held in December on odd-numbered years, while a guitar festival is held on even-numbered years.

ACTIVITIES

Beaches & Swimming

The beaches in the southern half of the island have white or tan sands while those in the northern half have gray or black sands. Many of Martinique's nicest beaches are scattered along the southwest coast from Grand Anse to Les Salines. In the Trois-Ilets area, Anse-à-l'Ane and Anse Mitan both have sandy beaches that attract a crowd. Popular east-coast beaches include Cap Chevalier and Macabou to the south and the Caravelle Peninsula beaches of Anse l'Étang and Tartane. Beaches along the northeast side of the island can have very dangerous water conditions and have been the site of a number of visitor drownings.

Diving

Saint-Pierre is one of the island's top dive sites with wrecks, coral reefs and plenty of marine life. More than a dozen ships that were anchored in the harbor when the 1902 volcanic eruption hit now lay on the sea bed, most in 10 to 50 meters of water; they include a 50-meter sailing ship, cargo ships and a tug.

Grand Anse, with its calm waters and good coral, is a popular diving spot for beginners. Cap Enragé, north of Case-Pilote, has underwater caves harboring lots of sea life. Rocher du Diamant (Diamond Rock) also has interesting cave formations but trickier water conditions. Ilet la Perle, a rock off the northwest coast, is a good place to see groupers, eels and lobsters when water conditions aren't too rough.

MARTINIQUE

The going rate is 200F to 250F for single dives, with the higher prices for night dives and more distant dive sites. There are discounts for packages of three or more dives.

Dive Shops Dive shops on Martinique include:

Corail Club Caraïbes, at the Frantour hotel in Anse à-l'Ane (☎ 68 42 99, fax 68 37 65)

Espace Plongée, at the Méridien hotel in Pointe du Bout (☎ /fax 66 01 79)

Planète Bleue, a dive boat that docks at the marina at Pointe du Bout (☎ 66 06 22)

Sub Diamond Rock, at the Novotel hotel in Diamant (☎ /fax 76 25 80)

Tropicasub, in Saint-Pierre, which specializes in wreck dives at 9:30 am and 3 pm (☎ 78 38 03, fax 52 46 82)

Snorkeling

Snorkeling is good around Grand Anse and Sainte-Anne and along the coast from Saint-Pierre to Anse Céron. Most larger hotels rent snorkeling gear and many provide it complimentary to their guests. Some of the dive shops offer snorkeling trips, others let snorkelers tag along with divers.

Windsurfing

Most beachfront hotels have beach huts and rent windsurfing gear. Rentals generally cost 70F to 80F an hour for non-guests, but are often complimentary to hotel guests.

Hiking

Martinique has numerous hiking tracks. From Route de la Trace a number of sign-posted trails lead into the rainforest and up and around the Pitons du Carbet. Also popular is the hike to the ruins of Château Dubuc on the Caravelle Peninsula.

There are strenuous trails leading up both the northern and southern flanks of Mont Pelée. The shortest and ·steepest begins in Morne Rouge and takes about four hours roundtrip. The hike up the northern flank is 8km long and takes about 4½ hours one way; two trails begin just east of Grand-Rivière and converge half-way up the mountain.

A bit less strenuous but still moderately difficult is the 20-km hike around the undeveloped northern tip of the island between Grand-Rivière and Anse Couleuvre. An easy way to do this trail is to join one of the guided hikes organized by the syndicat d'initiative (☎ 55 72 74) in Grand-Rivière, which conducts outings on Thursdays and Sundays. Hikers leave from Grand-Rivière's town hall, arriving in Anse Couleuvre about five hours later and then return to Grand-Rivière by boat. The outing costs 180F; make reservations in advance.

Other syndicats d'initiative organize hikes in other parts of the island and the Parc Naturel Regional (☎ 73 19 30), 9 Blvd du Général de Gaulle, Fort-de-France, leads guided hikes several times a week.

Horseback Riding

A number of stables offer horseback riding. The cost of guided outings varies with the destination and length, but is generally around 150F to 200F. Stables include Ranch Black Horse (☎ 66 00 04) in Trois-Ilets; Ranch Jack (☎ 68 37 69) near Anse d'Arlet; and La Cavale (☎ 76 22 94) in Diamant.

Mountain Biking

Mountain bike tours can be arranged with VT Tilt (☎ 66 01 01) in Anse Mitan. Half-day outings cost from 150F, full-day outings are 300F.

Golf

Martinique has one golf course, the 18-hole Golf de la Martinique (☎ 68 32 81) in Trois-Ilets. It costs 145/270F to play nine/18 holes. There's a pro shop; cart and club rentals are available.

Tennis

Most of the larger resort hotels have tennis courts that are free to their guests and some let non-guests use the courts at reasonable fees. There are also three lighted tennis courts at the golf course in Trois-Ilets that are open to the public at 70F per person.

MARTINIQUE

Top Left: Bibliotèque Schoelcher, Fort-de-France, Martinique (Ned Friary)

Top Right: Side street, Fort-de-France, Martinique (Ned Friary)
Bottom: Les Salines, Martinique (Glenda Bendure)

Top Left: Typical Saban house, Saba (Ned Friary)
Middle Left: Museum, Windwardside, Saba
(Glenda Bendure)
Bottom Left: Shutters, Gustavia, St Barts
(Glenda Bendure)

Top Right: St Jean, St Barts (Ned Friary)
Bottom Right: Rainforest, Mt Scenery trail, Saba
(Ned Friary)

ACCOMMODATIONS

Martinique has about 120 hotels. While the French shun the mega-resorts found elsewhere in the Caribbean, Martinique has about a dozen mid-size resorts with 100 rooms or more. Most of the island's other hotels range from 12 to 40 rooms. By Caribbean standards rates are moderate, with upper-end hotels averaging US$250, mid-range US$125 and the lower end about US$65.

As in France, taxes and service charges are included in the quoted rates.

Camping

There are established campgrounds with facilities at Vivre et Camper in Sainte-Anne and Le Nid Tropical in Anse à-l'Ane; for details see those destination sections.

Camping is also allowed along the beach at Les Salines and in a few other areas on weekends and during school holidays.

Fully equipped camper vans that sleep four can be rented by the week from West Indies Tours (☎ 54 50 71), Quartier Beauregard, Le François, for about the same cost as a moderately priced hotel.

Private Rooms & Apartments

Gîtes de France (☎ 73 67 92, fax 63 55 92; in Paris 01 49 70 75 75), BP 1122, 97209 Fort-de-France, offers rooms and apartments in private homes, with weekly rates beginning around 1100F for two people.

Centrale de Réservation (☎ 63 79 60, fax 63 11 64; in Paris ☎ 01 44 77 86 11), BP 823, 97208 Fort-de-France, opposite the tourist office, books studios, apartments and houses, with weekly rates from 1500F.

FOOD

Most restaurants serve either Creole or French food with an emphasis on local seafood. Red snapper, conch, crayfish and lobster are popular, although the latter is pricey at about 40F per 100 grams. The best value at many restaurants is the fixed-price menu, which is sometimes labeled *menu*

touristique – a three- or four-course meal that usually runs from 90F to 160F, depending on the main course.

For more moderately priced meals there are a number of Italian restaurants and pizzerias on the island. Bakeries make good low-budget places to grab a quick meal, because most of them make sandwiches to go and some have a few café tables out front.

The island of Martinique grows much of its own produce, including some very sweet pineapples.

DRINKS

Water is safe to drink from the tap. In restaurants, if you ask for water you'll usually get served bottled water; if you don't want to pay extra for that, ask for *l'eau du robinet* to get tap water.

The legal drinking age is 18. The local beer is Lorraine but island rums are far more popular than beer. Martinique's de rigueur apéritif is ti-punch, which is white rum, sugar cane juice and a squeeze of lemon. Also popular is planteur punch, which is essentially a mix of rum and fruit juice.

ENTERTAINMENT

The larger hotels in southern Martinique offer a good range of entertainment, including steel band music, dancing and various shows.

The most popular tourist show on the island is the performance by the 30-member folk troupe Ballet Martiniquais, which does a dinner show at a different hotel each night, including Thursday at Le Méridien Trois-Ilets and Friday at the Bakoua, both in Pointe du Bout.

There are a number of lively dance clubs in Fort-de-France including Manhattan at 18 Rue François-Arago and New Hippo at 24 Blvd Allègre.

The casino at Le Méridien Trois-Ilets hotel in Pointe du Bout offers slot machines, roulette and blackjack.

Cockfights are locally popular at various 'pitts' around the island.

THINGS TO BUY

The best place for shopping is Fort-de-France, where air-conditioned shops sell the latest Paris fashions, French perfumes, leather handbags, crystal, silk scarves etc. The main boutique area is along Rue Victor Hugo, particularly from Rue de la République to Rue de la Liberté. The department store Galeries LaFayette, near the cathedral, has a little of everything. Foreigners who pay with traveler's checks or a credit card get 20% off the posted price at Galeries LaFayette and at many of the fancier shops.

Local handicrafts such as wicker baskets, dolls in madras costumes, wooden carvings and T-shirts are sold by vendors at the northwest corner of La Savane and at craft shops around the island.

Island pottery at reasonable prices can be purchased directly from craftspeople at the potters village near Trois-Ilets.

Local rum makes a popular souvenir and sells from about 35F to 200F a liter, depending on the quality.

Getting There & Away

AIR

The following are airline reservation numbers on Martinique:

Air France	☎ 55 33 33
Air Guadeloupe	☎ 42 16 72
Air Liberté	☎ 42 18 34
Air Martinique	☎ 42 16 60
American Airlines	☎ 42 19 19
AOM	☎ 42 16 24
LIAT	☎ 42 16 03
Nouvelles Frontières	☎ 42 16 40

USA

American Airlines has daily service to Martinique via San Juan, Puerto Rico, which connects with American's mainland US flights. Fares vary but in the low season a ticket allowing a stay of up to 30 days generally begins at around US$500 from east coast cities such as Miami, New York and Boston. In the high season prices average about US$100 more.

Air France flies to Martinique from Miami on Tuesday and Saturday. The lowest fare of US$500 allows a stay of up to 21 days.

France

Air France, AOM, Air Liberté and Nouvelles Frontières have daily flights between Paris and Martinique. Fares are competitive, beginning at around 2700F roundtrip.

Within the Caribbean

Air Martinique flies daily between Martinique and Guadeloupe, St Martin and St Lucia. From Martinique to St Lucia there's a 586F same-day ticket for day visitors and a 650F roundtrip ticket allowing a stay of up to 21 days. From Martinique to Guadeloupe fares are 539F one way and 836F roundtrip, to St Martin they're 1100F one way and 1235F roundtrip. Air Guadeloupe and Air France also have frequent flights between Guadeloupe and Martinique.

LIAT flies between Martinique and the English-speaking Caribbean. A roundtrip ticket from Martinique allowing a 30-day stay costs 1250F to Antigua, 850F to Dominica and 836F to St Lucia; one-way fares are 780F to Antigua, 574F to Dominica and 556F to St Lucia.

Airport Information

The Lamentin International Airport has a friendly tourist information booth where you can get maps and brochures in English, car rental booths, a Délifrance snack bar, restaurants, souvenir shops, a newsstand and a pharmacy. The public phones take phonecards. You can buy phonecards and exchange money at the Change Caraïbes office, which occasionally changes its hours but is generally open daily from at least 8 am to 7 pm.

SEA

Trans-Atlantic Boat

Compagnie Générale Maritime (☎ 71 34 23), 8 Blvd du Général de Gaulle, Fort-de-France, has a weekly cargo/passenger boat between the French West Indies and mainland France. Information is in the Getting There & Away chapter in the front of the book.

Inter-Island Ferry

L'Express des Iles (☎ 63 12 11) operates modern catamaran ferries between Martinique, Guadeloupe, Dominica and St Lucia. The smaller Brudey Frères (☎ 70 08 50) has express catamarans between Martinique and Guadeloupe. Detailed information on both of these boats is in the Getting There & Away section of the Guadeloupe chapter.

Yacht

The main port of entry is in Fort-de-France but yachts may also clear at Saint-Pierre or Marin.

Yachting is very popular in Martinique and there are numerous yacht charter companies operating on the island. The Moorings (☎ 74 75 39), Stardust (☎ 74 98 17) and Sunsail (☎ 74 77 61) are based at the marina in Marin. Star Voyage (☎ 66 00 72) is based at the Pointe du Bout marina.

Cruise Ship

Cruise ships land at Pointe Simon in Fort-de-France, at the west side of the harbor and within easy walking distance of the city center and main sights. The arrival facilities have phones, restrooms, a taxi stand and a tourist information booth that opens on cruise ship days.

LEAVING MARTINIQUE

There's a 30F departure tax when leaving Martinique, although some air tickets already have the tax included in the fare.

Getting Around

THE AIRPORT

The airport is just a 10-minute ride from Fort-de-France, traffic permitting, and about 20 minutes from the Pointe du Bout resort area. Taxis are readily available at the airport but are expensive (about 100F to Fort-de-France), so if you plan to rent a car during your stay consider picking it up at the airport upon arrival. If you need to refuel a rental car, there are 24-hour gas stations on N5 near the airport.

Because of the taxi union, there's no direct bus service from the airport. However, on the return it's possible, if not terribly practical, to take a bus from Pointe Simon in Fort-de-France heading to Ducos (8.70F) and ask to be dropped off on the highway outside the airport.

BUS

Although there are some larger public buses, most buses are minivans, marked 'TC' (for *taxis collectifs*) on top. Destinations are marked on the vans, sometimes on the side doors and sometimes on a small sign stuck in the front window. Bus stops are marked *arrêt autobus* or with signs showing a picture of a bus.

Fort-de-France's busy main taxi collectifs terminal is at Pointe Simon, on the west side of the harbor. Buses to Saint-Pierre leave frequently on weekdays, less frequently on Sunday, take 45 minutes and cost 17F. Other bus fares from Fort-de-France are: 17F to Trois-Ilets, 19F to Diamant, 31F to Sainte-Anne and 40F to Grand-Rivière. You can pick up buses to the Balata Gardens and Morne Rouge alongside the cemetery south of the Parc Floral; they leave about every 30 minutes during the day, Sunday excepted.

TAXI

The taxi fare from the airport is 90F to 100F to Fort-de-France, 300F to Sainte-Anne and 180F to Pointe du Bout or Anse Mitan. There's a 40% surcharge on all fares between 8 pm and 6 am and on Sundays and holidays. To call a taxi, dial ☎ 63 63 62 or 63 10 10; both dispatch on a 24-hour basis.

CAR & MOTORCYCLE
Road Rules

In Martinique, drive on the right. Your home driver's license is valid. Traffic regulations and road signs are the same as in

Europe, speed limits are posted, and exits and intersections are clearly marked.

Roads are excellent by Caribbean standards and there are multi-lane freeways (and rush-hour traffic) in the Fort-de-France area. Be sure to give yourself extra time if you're driving to the airport during rush hour, as the N5 carries lots of commuters.

Rental

Car There are numerous car rental agencies at the airport. The daily rate for an economy car with unlimited kilometers ranges from 195F with the local company Euradom to 280F with Avis. During the sluggish summer season many agencies will discount an additional 20% (and sometimes even throw in free CDW), while at the height of winter you might not find anything available at the lower range without advance reservations.

Be aware that many companies also offer a rate that adds on an extra charge for every kilometer you drive; for example, an economy car from Euradom could be as cheap as 107F per day if you're willing to add an additional 1.1F per kilometer, or with Avis 160F a day plus 1.6F per kilometer. Be sure you know which deal you're getting; if you want to tour the island thoroughly, your best bet will likely be a car with unlimited kilometers.

Optional collision damage waiver (CDW) insurance that covers collision damage to the car, after a 2000F excess (a fixed payment in the event of an accident), costs 45F a day with Eurodom to 70F a day with most other companies. The minimum age to rent a car is 21 and some companies add an extra 100F surcharge for drivers under the age of 25.

Car rental companies include:

Avis	☎ 42 16 92 at the airport
	☎ 66 04 27 in Pointe du Bout
Budget	☎ 51 36 48 at the airport
	☎ 63 69 00 in Fort-de-France
	☎ 66 00 45 in Pointe du Bout
Citer	☎ 42 16 82 at the airport
	☎ 72 66 48 in Fort-de-France
	☎ 76 85 57 in Sainte-Anne
Euradom	☎ 42 17 05 at the airport
	☎ 60 43 62 in Fort-de-France
Europcar	☎ 42 16 88 at the airport
	☎ 73 33 13 in Fort-de-France
	☎ 66 04 29 in Pointe du Bout
Hertz	☎ 51 01 01 at the airport
Thrifty	☎ 42 16 99 at the airport
	☎ 66 09 59 in Pointe du Bout

Motorcycle Motorcycles can be rented from Funny (☎ 63 33 05), 80 Rue Ernest Deproge, Fort-de-France. The cost for a 50cc bike is 126F per day, helmet included. The cost for a 80cc bike that can hold both a passenger and driver is 155F per day. Optional insurance costs 44F a day; without it, you'll have to pay a 5000F deposit.

HITCHHIKING

Hitchhiking is fairly common on Martinique, although of course the usual precautions apply.

BOAT

There are a couple of regular ferries *(vedettes)* between main resort areas and Fort-de-France that provide a nice alternative to dealing with heavy bus and car traffic, allow you to avoid the hassles of city parking and are quicker to boot. In Fort-de-France the ferries dock at the quay fronting La Savane. Schedules are posted at the docks; the ferries leave promptly and occasionally even a few minutes early.

Fort-de-France to Pointe du Bout

Somatours Vedettes (☎ 73 05 53) runs a ferry between Fort-de-France and the Pointe du Bout marina. It's quite a pleasant way to cross and takes only 20 minutes. The boat runs daily from early morning to around midnight, with 22 crossings on the weekdays, 14 on the weekends. The fare is 19/32F one way/roundtrip for adults, 10/15F for children ages two to 10.

Fort-de-France to Anse Mitan & Anse-à-l'Ane

Madinina Vedettes (☎ 63 06 46) makes a triangle route between Fort-de-France, Anse

Mitan and Anse-à-l'Ane. The boats run daily, every 30 to 60 minutes, from about 6 am (8:30 am on Sunday) to about 6 pm.

The fare between Fort-de-France and Anse Mitan is 30F roundtrip (13F for children). The fare between Anse Mitan and Anse-à-l'Ane is 5F.

Fort-de-France to Trois-Ilets
Martinik Cruise Line (☎ 68 39 19 or 68 42 13) runs a ferry about every 75 minutes between Fort-de-France and the town dock in the village of Trois-Ilets. The first boat departs from Trois-Ilets at 6:10 am and the last boat returns from Fort-de-France at 5:45 pm. There are no boats on Sunday. The fare is 15F each way.

ORGANIZED TOURS
Taxi tours cost about 250F an hour, or about 600F for a half-day tour that typically includes a drive up the Route de la Trace, a visit to Saint-Pierre and a return to Fort-de-France down the west coast.

There are various catamaran tours and boat charters operating around the island. For the latest information check with the tourist office, ask at your hotel desk or leaf through the tourist magazines.

Fort-de-France

Fort-de-France, the island capital, is the largest and most cosmopolitan city in the French West Indies. It has a pretty harborfront setting with the Pitons du Carbet rising up beyond, a view best appreciated when approaching the city by ferry.

The narrow, bustling streets opposite La Savane (the harborfront central park) are lined with a mixture of ordinary offices and interesting turn-of-the-century buildings housing French cafés and designer boutiques. It has as much of the flavor of the side streets of Paris as it does of the Caribbean.

Give yourself a few hours to wander around and take in the handful of historic sites and museums the city has to offer, longer if you want to shop or enjoy a meal.

Information
Tourist Office The tourist office (☎ 63 79 60), 2 Rue Ernest Deproge, is open from 8 am to 1 pm and 2 to 5 pm on weekdays and from 8 am to noon on Saturday.

Money Change Caraïbes, 4 Rue Ernest Deproge, is open from 7:30 am to 6 pm on weekdays and 8 am to 12:30 pm on Saturday. Change Point, a block away, is open from 8 am to 5:30 pm on weekdays, until 12:30 pm on Saturday. Both exchange major currencies and don't charge commissions for most transactions.

Full-service banks can be found next door to Change Caraïbes on Rue Ernest Deproge and along Rue de la Liberté, opposite La Savane.

Post & Communications You can send faxes, buy phonecards, use a card phone or pick up mail sent poste restante at the central post office on the corner of Rue Antoine Siger and Rue de la Liberté. It's open from 7 am to 6 pm Monday to Friday, to noon on Saturday; expect long lines.

Other public card phones can be found in La Savane, opposite the post office, and around the city.

You can check your email or surf the Internet at Le Web Cyber Café, 4 Rue Blénac. The cost is 25F per 15 minutes. It's open from 11 am to 2 am Monday to Friday, from 6 pm to 2 am on Saturday.

Bookstores The newsstand at the west corner of La Savane sells the *International Herald-Tribune* and numerous French-language newspapers and magazines.

Centrale Catholique, 57 Rue Blénac, sells books in French about Martinique (history, flora and fauna and other topics) and the Institut Géographique National's map of Martinique.

Pharmacy There are several pharmacies around town, including Pharmacie Glaudon

MARTINIQUE

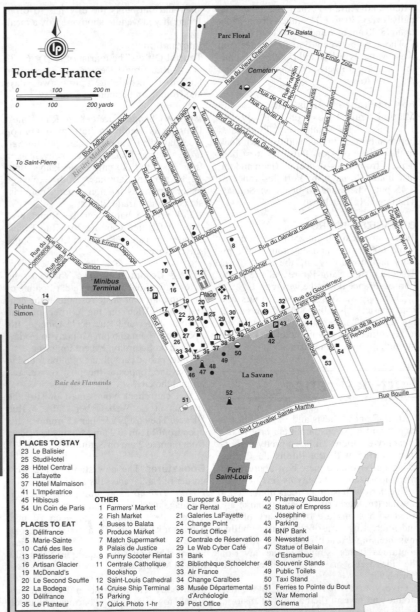

Fort-de-France

0   100   200 m
0   100   200 yards

Parc Floral

To Balata

Cemetery

To Saint-Pierre

Minibus Terminal

Pointe Simon

Place

Baie des Flamands

La Savane

Fort Saint-Louis

Rue Bouille

Blvd Chevalier Sainte-Marthe

MARTINIQUE

PLACES TO STAY
23 Le Balisier
25 StudiHotel
28 Hôtel Central
36 Lafayette
37 Hôtel Malmaison
41 L'Impératrice
45 Hibiscus
54 Un Coin de Paris

PLACES TO EAT
3   Délifrance
5   Marie-Sainte
10 Café des Iles
13 Pâtisserie
16 Artisan Glacier
19 McDonald's
20 Le Second Souffle
22 La Bodega
30 Délifrance
35 Le Planteur

OTHER
1   Farmers' Market
2   Fish Market
4   Buses to Balata
6   Produce Market
7   Match Supermarket
8   Palais de Justice
9   Funny Scooter Rental
11 Centrale Catholique
    Bookshop
12 Saint-Louis Cathedral
14 Cruise Ship Terminal
15 Parking
17 Quick Photo 1-hr

18 Europcar & Budget
    Car Rental
21 Galeries LaFayette
24 Change Point
26 Tourist Office
27 Centrale de Réservation
29 Le Web Cyber Café
31 Bank
32 Bibliothèque Schoelcher
33 Air France
34 Change Caraïbes
38 Musée Départemental
    d'Archéologie
39 Post Office

40 Pharmacy Glaudon
42 Statue of Empress
    Josephine
43 Parking
44 BNP Bank
46 Newsstand
47 Statue of Belain
    d'Esnambuc
48 Souvenir Stands
49 Public Toilets
50 Taxi Stand
51 Ferries to Pointe du Bout
52 War Memorial
53 Cinema

on the corner of Rue de la Liberté and Rue Antoine Siger.

Parking Parking is not a problem on weekends and holidays, but is quite a challenge on weekdays. There's a parking lot along the north side of La Savane that's entered at the intersection of Ave des Caraïbes and Rue de la Liberté; it costs 8F an hour or 70F for 12 hours from Monday to Saturday, 2F per hour on Sunday.

There's a parking lot off Blvd Alfassa between the tourist office and the minibus terminal which costs 9F an hour, 80F for 12 hours. There's also metered parking along many of the side streets running off Rue de la Liberté for 7F an hour, with a two-hour limit, and along La Savane on Ave des Caraïbes with a four-hour (18F) limit. Streetside parking is free in the evenings and on Sunday and holidays.

La Savane
This large central park sports grassy lawns, tall trees, clumps of bamboo and lots of benches. The harbor side of La Savane has souvenir stalls, a newsstand and statues dedicated to early settlers and fallen soldiers.

At the north side of the park, near the bustling Rue de la Liberté, there's a statue of the Empress Josephine holding a locket with a portrait of Napoleon – although in recent times her own head has been lopped off the statue. Despite all the Josephine hoopla on Martinique, the Empress is not highly regarded among islanders, many of whom believe she was responsible for convincing Napoleon to continue slavery so her family plantation in Trois-Ilets would not suffer.

Fort Saint-Louis
Opposite the south side of La Savane is Fort Saint-Louis. The original fort, built in the Vauban style, dates from 1640, although most of the extensive fort that stands today is the result of subsequent additions. The fort is still an active military base but visitors can join a 45-minute tour (25F), escorted by a guide and sailor; tours begin on the hour from 10 am to 3 pm.

Musée Départemental d'Archéologie
This archaeological museum, at 9 Rue de la Liberté, displays Amerindian artifacts, including stone tools, ritual objects and pottery. Most engaging are the 100 or so clay *adornos*, the decorative figurines that Amerindians used to adorn vases and bowls. There are also illustrations of the Caribs and a diorama of thatched huts. Overall, the presentation is simple if not a bit dry, and you can walk through it all in about 20 minutes. Most signs are in French only. It's open from 8 am to 5 pm Monday to Friday, from 9 am to noon on Saturday. Admission is 15F for adults, 5F for children under 12.

Bibliothèque Schoelcher
The Bibliothèque Schoelcher (Schoelcher Library), on Rue de la Liberté, is an elaborate, colorful building with a Byzantine dome. The work of architect Henri Pick, a contemporary of Gustave Eiffel, the library was built in Paris and displayed at the 1889 World Exposition. It was then dismantled, shipped in pieces to Fort-de-France and reassembled on this site. The ornate interior is also interesting; it's open on Monday from 1 to 5:30 pm, other weekdays from 8:30 am to 5:30 pm (5 pm on Friday) and on Saturday from 8:30 am to noon.

Saint-Louis Cathedral
With its neo-Byzantine style and 57-meter-high steeple, the Saint-Louis Cathedral on Rue Schoelcher, a block northwest of La Savane, is one of the city's most distinguished landmarks. Built in 1895 by Henri Pick, the church fronts a small square and is picturesquely framed by two royal palms. The spacious, ornate interior is well worth a look.

Palais de Justice
The Palais de Justice, a neoclassical courthouse built in 1906, is two blocks northeast of the cathedral. The design resembles a French railroad station, as the plaque out front unabashedly points out. The square fronting the courthouse has a statue of French abolitionist Victor Schoelcher.

Parc Floral & Public Markets

The Parc Floral, a public park at the north side of the city, is worth a stroll if you're already in the area.

A farmers' market runs along the west side of the Parc Floral and spills over into the street along the Rivière Madame. In addition to the island-grown fruits and vegetables, this open-air market sells drinking coconuts and cut flowers. The fish market is a block to the south, while a second and larger public produce market is on the north side of Rue Isambert.

Places to Stay

City Center The *Hibiscus* (☎ 60 29 59), 1 Rue de la Redoute Matouba, 97200 Fort-de-France, has Spartan rooms for 175/200F singles/doubles with shared bath; a double room with private bath costs 250F.

Un Coin de Paris (☎ 70 08 52, fax 63 69 51), 54 Rue Lazare Carnot, 97200 Fort-de-France Cédex, is a well-maintained place that's geared towards budget travelers rather than local boarders. There are 14 clean, straightforward rooms with private baths and air-con for 210/250F for singles/doubles.

The *Hôtel Malmaison* (☎ 63 90 85, fax 60 03 93), 7 Rue de la Liberté, 97200 Fort-de-France, has 20 rooms that vary in size and amenities. All have private baths and most have a TV. Although a few of the rooms have saggy mattresses and at least one has no windows, the rooms are clean and the desk clerk will usually let you look around and pick one to your liking. Singles/doubles cost 230/260F for fan-cooled rooms, 300/330F for rooms with air-con.

If you want to prepare your own meals the *StudiHotel* (☎ 63 70 32, fax 63 63 67), 21 Rue Blénac, 97200 Fort-de-France, has six rooms with kitchenettes, private baths, air-con and TV. They're compact but otherwise comfortable and cost from 270/285F for singles/doubles.

Le Balisier (☎ /fax 71 46 54), 21 Rue Victor Hugo, 97200 Fort-de-France, has 32 rooms in a couple of buildings. Best are the small but adequate rooms in the main hotel, which have TV, phones and private baths.

Ask for a room at the rear of the hotel, as they're quieter and some have partial ocean views. In an apartment building on the same street are a few studios that are OK for the price, each with a refrigerator, hot plate, TV, phone, air-con and a double and single bed. Hotel rooms cost 270/320F for singles/doubles, studio apartments cost 350F.

Hôtel Central (☎ 70 02 12, fax 63 80 00), 3 Rue Victor Hugo, 97200 Fort-de-France, is a small hotel with 18 rooms, most on the compact side but clean and adequate. Each has TV, air-con and private bath; the rates are 300/330F for singles/doubles and they are commonly discounted 10% in summer.

L'Impératrice (☎ 63 06 82, fax 72 66 30), 15 Rue de la Liberté, 97200 Fort-de-France, has standards and services that are a notch higher than other central hotels. All 24 rooms have air-con, private baths and phones; some have four-poster beds and balconies facing La Savane. In summer, singles/doubles begin at 300/350F, in winter at 340/400F. Breakfast is included in the rates.

Lafayette (☎ 73 80 50, fax 60 97 75), 5 Rue de la Liberté, 97200 Fort-de-France, is a three-story hotel with 24 rooms that have air-con, phones, TV, minibars and private baths. They're clean and adequate but a bit pricey at 340/400F for singles/doubles.

Around Fort-de-France The *Squash Hotel* (☎ 63 00 01, fax 63 00 74), 3 Blvd de la Marne, 97200 Fort-de-France, is 1km west of the town center. This modern, mid-priced hotel has 108 comfortable rooms with air-con, TV, phones and minibars. There's also a pool, restaurant, fitness center and three squash courts. Singles cost from 460F to 575F, doubles from 570F to 710F, breakfast included. It can be booked through Resinter (in the USA ☎ 800-221-4542).

La Batelière (☎ 61 49 49, fax 61 70 57), 97233 Schoelcher, a couple of kilometers west of central Fort-de-France, is a modern luxury hotel that caters in part to businesspeople. The hotel has a beach, a pool, a gym, a dive shop, tennis courts and restaurants. The 190 rooms and suites have heavy curtains, four-poster beds, marble baths and other top-end amenities. Doubles range from 845F for a standard room to 3515F for a suite in summer, from 960F to 3515F in winter.

Places to Eat
There are a number of cafés and restaurants opposite La Savane on Rue de la Liberté. If you want to eat cheaply you can easily find takeout food and freshly baked bread for a picnic in the park. Bakeries selling pastries and inexpensive sandwiches are scattered throughout the city. In the evenings food vans selling crêpes, barbecued chicken and other cheap local food park along the Blvd Chevalier Sainte Marthe at the south side of La Savane.

There are a couple of fast-food chains in the center, including a *McDonald's*, with 23F Big Macs, that's open to at least 11 pm daily. A good local alternative is the *Délifrance* on Rue Antoine Siger, which has good baguette sandwiches from 18F.

Café des Îles, 59 Rue Victor Hugo, is a small owner-run café with freshly squeezed orange juice (13F), salads (40F) and reasonably priced sandwiches. Nearby on the same street is *Artisan Glacier*, a stand with inexpensive crêpes and ice cream.

Le Second Souffle, diagonally opposite the cathedral at 27 Rue Blénac, is a good vegetarian restaurant. Salads are priced from 15F to 38F and there's a plat du jour for 50F. It's open weekdays from 10 am to 4 pm.

La Bodega, 28 Rue Ernest Deproge, is a pub-style restaurant with a variety of salads, pizzas and pasta dishes from 45F to 60F and a three-course menu du jour for 75F. It's open from 10 am to 11:30 pm daily.

If you're near the river, *Marie-Sainte*, 160 Rue Victor Hugo, is a popular little hole-in-the-wall serving moderately priced Creole food such as accras, lambi, fricassee and banana fritters. It's open for breakfast and lunch from 8 am to 3 pm Monday to Saturday.

More upscale is *Le Planteur*, overlooking La Savane at 1 Rue de la Liberté, which has good Creole and French food. Three-course set lunches range from 80F

for chicken to 150F for lobster. Otherwise, most à la carte main dishes cost 75F to 130F. It's open weekdays for lunch and nightly for dinner.

Match supermarket on Rue Antoine Siger is a good place to buy groceries; it's open from 8 am to 6:30 pm on weekdays, to 1:30 pm on Saturday. For vegetables and fruits, the produce market a block away is the best bet.

Northern Martinique

Several roads head north from Fort-de-France. The most interesting sightseeing routes are the coastal road (N2) to Saint-Pierre and the Route de la Trace (N3), which crosses the lush mountainous interior before ending in Morne Rouge. The two routes can be combined to make a nice loop drive; the highlights can be seen in a half day or the trip could be stretched into a leisurely full-day outing.

FORT-DE-FRANCE TO SAINT-PIERRE
N2, the coastal road north to Saint-Pierre, passes along dry, scrubby terrain and goes through a line of small towns, a merging of modern suburbia and old fishing villages. If you were to drive without stopping, it would take about 45 minutes to reach Saint-Pierre from Fort-de-France.

It's worth swinging off the highway at **Case-Pilote** to take a peek at the old village center. Turn west off N2 at the Total gas station and you'll immediately come to a quaint stone church, one of Martinique's oldest. Just 75 meters south is a pleasant town square with a water fountain, an historic town hall, a tourist office and a moderately priced café. In Case-Pilote, as well as in the next village, **Bellefontaine**, you can find brightly painted wooden fishing boats called *gommiers* (after the trees they're constructed from) lined up along the shore. At Bellefontaine, look inland at the hillside to spot one of Martinique's more unusual buildings, a blue and white house designed in the shape of a boat.

MARTINIQUE

The town of **Carbet**, where Christopher Columbus briefly came ashore in 1502, fronts a sandy beach and has a few tourist amenities, including a couple of restaurants and a rather forlorn little zoo.

Anse Turin, a long gray-sand beach that attracts a crowd on weekends, is along the highway 1.5km north of Carbet. Opposite the beach is the **Musée Paul Gauguin**, marked by an inconspicuous sign. One of the great post-impressionists of Europe, Gaugin (1848-1903) is best known for his paintings of Polynesian women, which were painted in the 1890s after he moved to Tahiti. This interesting museum contains Gauguin memorabilia, letters from the artist to his wife and reproductions of Gauguin's paintings including *Bord de Mer I* and *L'Anse Turin avec les raisiniers*, which were painted on the nearby beach during Gauguin's five-month stay on Martinique in 1887. The museum is open daily from 9 am to 5:30 pm. Admission is 15F.

Just north of the Gauguin museum is the driveway up to **La Vallée des Papillons** (☎ 78 18 07), where the scattered stone ruins of one of the island's earliest plantations have been enhanced with gardens and a butterfly farm. It's open from 9:30 am to 4:15 pm daily. Admission is 38F for adults, 28F for children, and there's a restaurant on site.

SAINT-PIERRE

Saint-Pierre is on the coast 7km south of Mont Pelée, the still-active volcano that laid the town to waste at the turn of the century. It's a fascinating town to wander around. There are ruins throughout Saint-Pierre, some of which are little more than foundations, others partially intact. Many of the surviving stone walls have been incorporated into the town's reconstruction, forming the base for the buildings that replaced them. Even these 'newer' buildings have a period character, with shuttered doors and wrought-iron balconies.

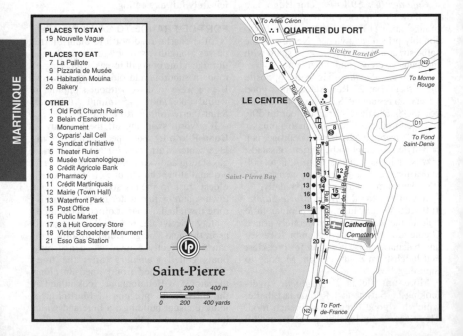

PLACES TO STAY
19 Nouvelle Vague

PLACES TO EAT
7 La Paillote
9 Pizzaria de Musée
14 Habitation Mouina
20 Bakery

OTHER
1 Old Fort Church Ruins
2 Belain d'Esnambuc Monument
3 Cyparis' Jail Cell
4 Syndicat d'Initiative
5 Theater Ruins
6 Musée Vulcanologique
8 Crédit Agricole Bank
10 Pharmacy
11 Crédit Martiniquais
12 Mairie (Town Hall)
13 Waterfront Park
15 Post Office
16 Public Market
17 8 à Huit Grocery Store
18 Victor Schoelcher Monument
21 Esso Gas Station

QUARTIER DU FORT

To Anse Céron

Rivière Roxelane

LE CENTRE

To Morne Rouge

To Fond Saint-Denis

Saint-Pierre Bay

Cathedral Cemetery

To Fort-de-France

Saint-Pierre

0   200   400 m
0   200   400 yards

MARTINIQUE

The center of town is long and narrow, with two parallel one-way streets running its length. All of the major sights have signs in both French and English and you can explore the area thoroughly in a few hours.

These days Saint-Pierre has 6000 residents, which is just one-fifth of the pre-eruption population. The central gathering spot is the waterfront town park, next to the market. A beach of soft black sand fronts the town and extends to the south.

Musée Vulcanologique

This small but very interesting museum, founded in 1932 by American vulcanologist Franck Perret, gives a glimpse of the devastating 1902 eruption of Mont Pelée. On display are items plucked from the rubble, including petrified rice, a box of nails melted into a sculpture-like mass, glass cups fused together by heat and the cast iron bell from the cathedral tower squashed like a saucer. There are also historic photos of the town before and immediately after the eruption. The displays are in both English and French.

There's free parking adjacent to the museum, which occupies the site of an old hillside gun battery. From the old stone walls along the parking lot you can get a good perspective of the harbor and city, and look down upon a line of ruins on the street below. The museum, on Rue Victor Hugo, is open from 9 am to 5 pm daily. Admission is 10F.

Ruins

Saint-Pierre's most impressive ruins are those of the old **theater**, just 100 meters north of the museum. While most of the theater was destroyed, enough remains to give a sense of the former grandeur of this building, which once seated 800 and hosted theater troupes from mainland France. A double set of stairs still leads up to the partial walls of the lower story.

The Eruption of Mont Pelée

At the turn of the 20th century Saint-Pierre, the capital of Martinique at that time, was a flourishing port city, so cosmopolitan it was dubbed the 'Little Paris of the West Indies.' Mont Pelée, the island's highest mountain, provided a scenic backdrop to the city.

In the spring of 1902, sulphurous steam vents on Mont Pelée began emitting gases, and a crater lake started to fill with boiling water. Authorities dismissed it all as the normal cycle of the volcano, which had experienced periods of activity in the past without dire consequences.

But in late spring the lake broke and spilled down the mountainside in Rivière Blanche, just north of the city, burying a plantation and its workers in hot mud. On April 25 the volcano spewed a shower of ash onto Saint-Pierre. Up until this point the volcanic activity had largely been seen as a curiosity, but now people became apprehensive and some sent their children to stay with relatives on other parts of the island. The governor of Martinique, hoping to convince residents that there was no need to evacuate the city, brought his family to Saint-Pierre.

At 8 am on Sunday, May 8, 1902, Mont Pelée exploded into a glowing burst of super-heated gas and burning ash, with a force 40 times stronger than the nuclear blast over Hiroshima. Between the suffocating gases and the fiery inferno, Saint-Pierre was laid to waste within minutes.

When rescuers from the French navy landed ashore that afternoon, they found only three survivors among the city's 30,000 inhabitants. Two of them had received fatal injuries, but the third, a prisoner named Cyparis, survived with only minor burns – ironically, he owed his life to having been locked in a tomb-like solitary confinement cell in the local jail. Following the commutation of his prison sentence by the new governor, Cyparis joined the PT Barnum circus where he toured as a sideshow act.

Pelée continued to smolder for months, but by 1904 people began to resettle the town, building among the crumbled ruins. ■

MARTINIQUE

On the northeast side of the theater you can look over the wall to the tiny, thick-walled **jail cell** that housed Cyparis, the town's sole survivor.

Another area rich in ruins is the **Quartier du Figuier**, along Rue Bouillé, directly below the vulcanology museum. Two sets of steps, one just north of the theater and the other just south of the museum, connect Rue Victor Hugo with the bayfront Rue Bouillé.

Places to Stay & Eat
The only in-town hotel is the aging *Nouvelle Vague* (☎ 78 14 34), 97250 Saint-Pierre, which has five very simple rooms for 250F and a waterfront restaurant that packs in a crowd at lunch.

There's an *8 à Huit* grocery store in the center of town; a *bakery* south of the cathedral; a wood-fired pizza place, *Pizzaria de Musée*, south of the museum, and another pizzeria, *La Paillote*, on the waterfront.

Habitation Mouina, a courtyard restaurant opposite the waterfront park, is a friendly family-run operation serving excellent Creole food, including a complete meal du jour for 60F; it's open from 11:30 am to 5 pm daily.

SAINT-PIERRE TO ANSE CÉRON
From Saint-Pierre, N2 turns inland but D10 continues north for 13km along the coast and makes a scenic side drive, ending in 20 minutes at a remote beach. The shoreline is rocky for much of the way and the landscape is lush, with roadside clumps of bamboo.

The limestone cliffs 4km north of Saint-Pierre, called **Tombeau des Caraïbes**, are said to be the place where the last Caribs jumped to their deaths rather than succumb to capture by the French.

The road goes through the town of **Le Prêcheur**, where green and orange fishing boats dot the shoreline, and **Anse Belle-ville**, a village so narrow that there's only room for a single row of houses between the cliffs and the sea.

Half a kilometer before the end of the road is **Habitation Céron** (☎ 52 94 53), a former sugar plantation that is open to visitors from 9:30 am to 5 pm daily. Admission is 35F for adults, 15F for children ages five to 12.

The road ends at **Anse Céron**, a beautiful black-sand beach in a wild, jungle-like setting. Anse Céron is backed by coconut palms and faces Ilet la Perle, a rounded offshore rock that's a popular dive site. Despite the remote location, the beach has a shower, toilets, picnic tables and a snack shop.

A very steep one-lane route continues for 1600 meters beyond the beach. This is the start of a six-hour, 20-km hike to Grand-Rivière.

ROUTE DE LA TRACE
The Route de la Trace (N3) winds up into the mountains north from Fort-de-France. It's a beautiful drive through a lush rainforest of tall tree ferns, anthurium-covered hillsides and thick clumps of roadside bamboo. The road passes along the eastern flanks of the pointed volcanic mountain peaks of the Pitons du Carbet. Several well-marked hiking trails lead from the Route de la Trace into the rainforest and up to the peaks.

The road follows a route cut by the Jesuits in the 17th century; islanders like to say that the Jesuits' fondness for rum accounts for the twisting nature of the road.

Less than a 10-minute drive north of Fort-de-France, you'll reach the **Balata Church**, a scaled-down replica of the Sacré-Coeur Basilica in Paris. This interesting domed church, in the Roman-Byzantine style, has a stunning hilltop setting – the Pitons du Carbet rise up as a backdrop and there's a view across Fort-de-France to Pointe du Bout below.

The **Jardin de Balata**, on the west side of the road a 10-minute drive north of the Balata Church, is a mature botanical garden in a rainforest setting. Walkways wind past tropical trees and flowers including lots of ginger, heliconia, anthuriums and bromeliads. Many of the plants are numbered; you can pick up a free corresponding handout listing 200 of the specimens with their Latin and common French names. This pleasant garden takes about 30 to 45 minutes to stroll through and is a great place to photograph flowers and hummingbirds. It's open from 9 am to 5 pm daily. Admission is 35F for adults, 15F for children.

After the garden, N3 winds up into the mountains and reaches an elevation of 600 meters before dropping back down to **Site de l'Alma**, where a river runs through a lush green gorge. There are riverside picnic tables, trinket sellers and a couple of short trails into the rainforest.

Four km later N3 is intersected by D1, a winding scenic drive that leads west 14km via Fond Saint-Denis to Saint-Pierre. Just beyond this intersection, N3 leads through a cobblestone tunnel and a kilometer beyond that, on the east side of the road, is the signposted trailhead for **Trace des Jésuites**. This popular hike is 5km long and takes about three hours one way. It winds up and down through a variety of terrain, ranging in elevation from 310 meters at the Lorrain River crossing to 670 meters at its termination on D1.

Continuing north on N3, the Route de la Trace passes banana plantations and flower nurseries before reaching a T-junction at Morne Rouge, on the southern slopes of Mont Pelée. From here, N2 winds west 8km down to Saint-Pierre, while N3 heads east to Ajoupa-Bouillon.

Morne Rouge was partially destroyed by Mont Pelée in August 1902, several months after the eruption that wiped out Saint-Pierre. At 450 meters it has the highest elevation of any town on Martinique, and it enjoys some nice mountain scenery.

About 2km north of the T-junction, a road (D39) signposted to Aileron leads 3km up the slopes of Mont Pelée, from where there's a rugged trail (four hours roundtrip) up to the volcano's summit.

LES OMBRAGES

Les Ombrages (☎ 53 31 90) is a naturalized botanical garden at the site of a former rum distillery. A trail passes by stands of bamboo, tall trees with buttressed roots,

torch gingers and the ruins of the old mill. It's a nice jungle walk.

The garden is open from 9 am to 5 pm daily. Tour guides lead 45-minute walks, in French only. Admission is 20F for adults and 10F for children. Les Ombrages is 250 meters east of N3, immediately north of the town of Ajoupa-Bouillon.

BASSE-POINTE

As N3 nears the Atlantic it meets N1, which runs along the coast both north and south. The northern segment of the road edges the eastern slopes of Mont Pelée and passes through banana and pineapple plantations before reaching the coastal town of Basse-Pointe.

Leyritz Plantation

Leyritz Plantation, dating from the early 18th century, is a former sugar plantation that now houses a hotel and restaurant.

It's an interesting place with a park-like setting. You can stroll around the grounds at your leisure and explore some of the old buildings. Most intriguing is the former plantation house, a weathered two-story building with period furnishings.

Inside the gift shop near the entrance is a 'museum' that's essentially a small collection of Victorian-style dolls made of dried plants and fibers.

If you're not eating at the plantation it costs 15F (children 5F) to explore the grounds and visit the museum. It's open every day from 9 am to 5 pm. The plantation is on D21, 2km southeast of Basse-Pointe.

Places to Stay & Eat

The *Leyritz Plantation* (☎ 78 53 92, fax 78 92 44), 97218 Basse-Pointe, has 67 guest rooms spread across its grounds, many in the old plantation quarters. Rooms vary, but most are comfortable and full of atmosphere. Some of the nicer ones are in the renovated stone cottages that once served as dwellings for married slaves. All rooms have air-con, TV and phones, some have minibars, and there's a pool and a tennis court. It's a popular place with returning retirees from mainland France, but its

MARTINIQUE

secluded country setting may prove too remote for first-time visitors intent on exploring the entire island. Singles/doubles cost 450/495F in summer, 790/825F in winter, breakfast included.

The Leyritz Plantation dining room, within the old stone walls of the refinery, has an engaging setting despite the rush of tour buses that arrive at lunchtime. A set lunch of various Creole foods costs 120F, otherwise salads and main dishes begin around 60F. It's open from noon to 2:30 pm and from 7 to 9 pm.

In the center of Basse-Pointe, along the main road, *Chez Mally Edjam* is a pleasant little family restaurant serving home-cooked food at honest prices. Chicken colombo is 65F, or you can get a daily set meal that includes dessert for the same price. If you're heading towards Grand-Rivière it's on the right, just before the cultural center, at Ruelle Saint-Jean.

GRAND-RIVIÈRE

From Basse-Pointe it's a pleasant 20-minute drive to Grand-Rivière along a winding, but good, paved road. En route you'll go through the coastal village of Macouba, where there's a rum distillery, pass two trails leading up the northern flank of Mont Pelée, cross a couple of one-lane bridges and finally wind down into Grand-Rivière.

Grand-Rivière is an unspoiled fishing village scenically tucked beneath coastal cliffs at the northern tip of Martinique. Mont Pelée forms a rugged backdrop to the south while there's a fine view of neighboring Dominica to the north.

The road dead-ends at the sea where there's a fish market and rows of bright fishing boats lined up on a little black-sand beach. The waters are sometimes good for surfing at the west side of town. The syndicat d'initiative, in the town center, has local tourist information and organizes guided hikes in the region.

While there's no road around the tip of the island there is a 20-km hiking trail leading to Anse Couleuvre, on the northwest coast. The trailhead begins on the

road opposite the quaint two-story *mairie* (town hall), just up from the beach. For more information see the Hiking section of this chapter.

Places to Stay & Eat

Chanteur Vacances (☎ 55 73 73), 97218 Grand-Rivière, is a restaurant and hotel with friendly management. There are seven straightforward rooms on the 3rd floor that cost 155/220F for singles/doubles, breakfast included. The 2nd-floor restaurant has fixed-price meals with soup or salad, Creole rice and ice cream or fruit. The cost depends on the main dish, ranging from 76F for fish blaff to 123F for lobster, the house specialty. Lunch is from noon to 4:30 pm.

Chez Tante Arlette (☎ 55 75 75), about 50 meters from the syndicat d'initiative, is another Creole restaurant with three-course meals (from 80F for chicken to 150F for lobster) and a handful of simple rooms (doubles 200F with breakfast) on the floor above. Meals are served from noon to 9 pm.

Yva Chez Vava, on the outskirts of town near the river, is slightly more upmarket and has fine Creole fare with an emphasis on seafood. A full meal will cost from 100F to 170F. It's open from noon to 5 pm.

BASSE-POINTE TO LAMENTIN

The highway (N1) from Basse-Pointe to Lamentin runs along relatively tame terrain and is not one of the island's most interesting drives, although there are a few worthwhile sights. The communities along the way are largely modern towns that become increasingly more suburban as you continue south.

Fond Saint-Jacques (☎ 69 10 12), 2km north of Sainte-Marie, is the site of an old Dominican monastery and sugar plantation dating from 1660. One of the early plantation managers, Father Jean-Baptiste Labat, created a type of boiler (the *père labat*) that modernized the distilling of rum. During the French Revolution, the plantation was confiscated by the state and it's now under the domain of the local government, which is developing it as a cultural center. The chapel and most of the living quarters are still intact and there are many ruins on the grounds including those of the mill, distillery basins, boiling house and sugar factory. This site, 150 meters inland from N1, is open from 8:30 am to 5 pm Monday to Friday and by appointment on weekends.

The **Museé du Rhum** (☎ 69 30 02), at the site of Saint-James Plantation's working distillery, is a fun place to stop. The plantation is on D24, 200 meters west of N1, on the northern outskirts of Sainte-Marie. There are both indoor and outside displays of old sugar-making equipment including steam engines, rum stills and cane-crushing gears. There's also a tasting room where you can sample different rums and if you don't get too heady you might want to go out back to check out the sugar mill and distillery. Admission is free for poking about on your own, or you can join a guided tour for 20F. It's open from 9 am to 5 pm on weekdays, to 1 pm on weekends.

The road continues south through cane fields and passes the **Caravelle Peninsula** (Presqu'île de Caravelle), which can make an interesting side trip if you have extra time. On the north side of the peninsula there are a couple of nice protected beaches, Tartane and Anse l'Étang. Tartane, the larger of the two, has lots of fishing shacks and colorful gommier boats; both places have plenty of beachside restaurants selling everything from crêpes and ice cream to pizza and Creole food. Out at the tip of the peninsula are the deteriorated ruins of Château Dubuc, an old 17th-century estate whose master gained notoriety by using a lantern to lure ships into wrecking off the coast and then gathering the loot. The site has trails and a small museum (10F).

Southern Martinique

The southern part of Martinique has many of the island's best beaches and most of its hotels. The largest concentration of places to stay is in the greater Trois-Ilets area, which encompasses Pointe du Bout, Anse

Mitan and Anse-à-l'Ane. Other important resort areas are Diamant and Sainte-Anne.

The interior of the southern half of the island is largely a mix of agricultural land and residential areas. Lamentin, the site of the international airport, is Martinique's second-largest city but like other interior towns has little that is targeted for tourists.

TROIS-ILETS

Trois-Ilets is a pretty little village with a central square that's bordered by a small market, a quaint town hall and the church where Empress Josephine was baptized in 1763. Despite its proximity to the island's busiest resort area, the village retains a delightful rural charm that's unaltered by tourism.

Pointe du Bout and Anse Mitan (both of which use Trois-Ilets as their postal address) are a few kilometers west of the village center, as are the island's golf course, the birthplace of Josephine and a small botanical park.

The area's other chief attractions, a sugar museum and a pottery village, are both east of Trois-Ilets center.

Musée de la Pagerie

This former sugar estate was the birthplace of Marie Joseph Rose Tascher de la Pagerie, the future Empress Josephine. A picturesque stone building, formerly the family kitchen, has been turned into a museum containing Josephine's childhood bed and other memorabilia. Multilingual interpreters relate anecdotal tidbits about Josephine's life, such as the doctoring of the marriage certificate to make Josephine, six years Napoleon's elder, appear to be the same age as her spouse.

A couple of other buildings on the museum grounds contain such things as the Bonaparte family chart, old sugar cane equipment, and love letters to Josephine from Napoleon.

The road leading up to the museum, 1km inland, begins opposite the golf course entrance. The museum is open from 9 am to 5:30 pm daily except Monday and admission is 20F.

MARTINIQUE

You can poke around in the ruins of the old mill directly opposite the museum for free.

Parc des Floralies

Parc des Floralies, halfway up the road to the Musée de la Pagerie, is a modest botanical park with a pond, picnic tables, a few birds in cages and identified plants and trees. It's open from 8:30 am to 5 pm on weekdays, 9:30 am to 1 pm on weekends. Admission is 10F for adults, 5F for children.

Maison de la Canne

This worthwhile sugar cane museum occupies the site of an old sugar refinery and distillery. Artifacts include an old locomotive once used to carry cane from the fields to the distillery, antique cane crushers and period photos. Displays are in both French and English. It's open from 9 am to 5 pm daily except Monday. Admission is 15F for adults, 5F for children ages five to 12. The museum is on D7, 1.5km east of Trois-Ilets' center.

Pottery Village

There's an interesting brick kiln and pottery village on the north side of D7 1km east of Maison de la Canne. A sign ('Village de la Poterie') marks the red clay road that leads 750 meters to the site.

The main workshop is International Atelier Caraïbe, but there are a few other potters in the village as well, all working out of old brick buildings. You can watch them at work making cups, vases, figurines and jewelry. The wares are quite nice and the prices are reasonable.

POINTE DU BOUT

Pointe du Bout has Martinique's most frequented yachting marina and three of its largest resort hotels. The point is a Y-shaped peninsula, with the hotels fringing the coast and the marina in the middle. All roads intersect south of the marina and traffic can get congested.

The three resorts (Bakoua, Le Méridien and Novotel Carayou) each have their own little sandy beaches. There's also a lengthy public beach, Plage de l'Anse Mitan, which runs along the western side of the neck of the peninsula between Pointe du Bout and Anse Mitan.

Information

Ferries to and from Fort-de-France leave from the west side of the marina, where a money changing office, a laundry, the port bureau and marine supply shops are all clustered together. Also at the marina is a newsstand, souvenir shops, boutiques and a Crédit Agricole bank, open from 7:30 am to 12:30 pm Tuesday to Saturday and from 2:15 to 4 pm Tuesday to Friday.

Thrifty, Budget and Avis car rental agencies have offices near the peninsula's main intersection. There's a pharmacy south of Bora Bora grocery store.

Places to Stay

The *Davidiana* (☎ 66 00 54, fax 66 00 70), 97229 Trois-Ilets, is a good-value 14-room hotel above a harborfront restaurant. The rooms are modern and comfortable with private bath, air-con and one or two beds; some have balconies. Nightly rates, which are the same for one or two people, are 250/350F in summer/winter; weekly rates are 1359/1750F.

Karakoli (☎ 66 02 67, fax 66 02 41), 97229 Trois-Ilets, is a pleasant little hotel in a quiet neighborhood, 100 meters uphill from the busy heart of Pointe du Bout. The 18 studios and apartments have air-con, phones, kitchenettes and fine ocean views. There's a TV room and a garden courtyard with a small pool. Studios for up to two people cost 275/430F in summer/winter. Apartments that hold up to four people cost 450F in summer, 705F in winter. Breakfast is available for an additional 40F.

Mercure Inn (☎ 66 05 30, fax 66 00 99), 97229 Trois-Ilets, is tucked between a busy intersection and the inner harbor. The hotel has 98 modern rooms, each with a balcony, air-con, TV, phone and a small refrigerator; some have kitchenettes. Overall, the atmosphere is similar to what you'd find in an apartment complex and services are minimal but there's a pool. Singles/doubles

MARTINIQUE

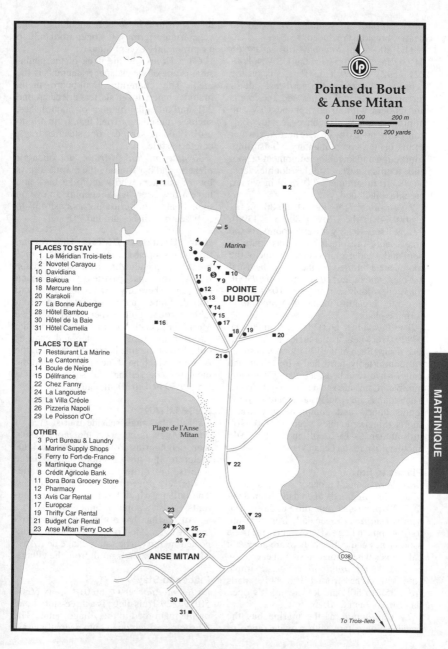

Pointe du Bout & Anse Mitan

Marina

POINTE DU BOUT

Plage de l'Anse Mitan

ANSE MITAN

To Trois-Ilets

PLACES TO STAY
1 Le Méridian Trois-Ilets
2 Novotel Carayou
10 Davidiana
16 Bakoua
18 Mercure Inn
20 Karakoli
27 La Bonne Auberge
28 Hôtel Bambou
30 Hôtel de la Baie
31 Hôtel Camelia

PLACES TO EAT
7 Restaurant La Marine
9 Le Cantonnais
14 Boule de Neige
15 Délifrance
22 Chez Fanny
24 La Langouste
25 La Villa Créole
26 Pizzeria Napoli
29 Le Poisson d'Or

OTHER
3 Port Bureau & Laundry
4 Marine Supply Shops
5 Ferry to Fort-de-France
6 Martinique Change
8 Crédit Agricole Bank
11 Bora Bora Grocery Store
12 Pharmacy
13 Avis Car Rental
17 Europcar
19 Thrifty Car Rental
21 Budget Car Rental
23 Anse Mitan Ferry Dock

MARTINIQUE

cost 510/640F in summer, 745/975F in winter, breakfast included.

The 200-room *Novotel Carayou* (☎ 66 04 04, fax 66 00 57; in the USA ☎ 800-221-4542), 97229 Trois-Ilets, sits on the peninsula that forms the northeast side of the marina. Recently renovated, the rooms are modern with air-con, phones, TV and minibars; many also have seaview balconies at no extra cost. There's a water sports center, complimentary windsurfing, snorkeling and kayaking equipment, a pool and tennis courts. Singles/doubles cost 645/830F in summer, 700/935F in winter, breakfast included.

Le Méridien Trois-Ilets (☎ 66 00 00, fax 66 00 74; in the USA ☎ 800-543-4300), 97229 Trois-Ilets, with 295 rooms, is the area's largest resort. It has tennis courts, a pool and a water sports center. Some of the rooms are a bit tired but they have the usual 1st-class amenities and cost from 670/800F for singles/doubles in summer, 1080/1480F in winter, breakfast included. A renovation is in the plans.

The *Bakoua* (☎ 66 02 02, fax 66 00 41), 97229 Trois-Ilets, is the area's most exclusive resort. Each of the 139 rooms and suites are comfortably furnished with either one king or two twin beds, air-con, TV, phone, minibar, room safe and a terrace or balcony. The grounds are spacious and there's a pool, tennis courts and complimentary water sports. Singles/doubles begin at 720/920F in summer, 1415/2060F in winter. Add another 15% for an ocean view.

Places to Eat

Bora Bora, a small grocery store just north of the Mercure Inn, is open daily from 8 am to 7:30 pm (to 1 pm on Sunday). The nearby *Délifrance*, open daily from 6:30 am to 7:30 pm, has good croissants, pastries, sandwiches and coffees; there are sidewalk café tables where you can sit and eat.

Next door is *Boule de Neige*, a simple café with crêpes from 15F to 40F, salads from 35F to 50F and ice cream. It's open daily from 7 am to 10 pm.

Le Cantonnais at the marina has the usual Chinese fare with a wide range of dishes from 55F to 60F, including some vegetarian offerings. It's open from 6:30 to 11 pm nightly except Sunday.

Chez Fanny, on the neck of the peninsula, is one of the cheaper restaurants in the area. The changing chalkboard menu includes half a dozen starters priced around 20F and an equal number of main dishes, such as couscous or fried fish, from 40F to 60F. Food is served from steamer trays, cafeteria style.

Restaurant La Marine, an open-air pizzeria and bar fronting the marina, draws lots of yachters who want to sit back and have a few beers while keeping an eye on their boats. Thin-crust pizzas cost 45F to 55F, seafood dishes around 75F.

Hotel Breakfast Buffets The *Novotel Carayou*'s open-air restaurant has a nice breakfast spread with fresh fruit, cereals, juices, croissants, pastries, yogurt, bacon and eggs. There are views across the bay to Fort-de-France and if you get a waterfront table it's quite a nice experience for 70F. *Le Méridien* puts on a similar spread with the addition of crêpes to order and charges 60F. Top of the line is the 75F buffet at the *Bakoua*, which has fancier pastries and the most upscale setting. All serve breakfast from 6:30 or 7 to 10 am daily.

ANSE MITAN

Overall, the small seaside tourist area of Anse Mitan is cheaper and more casual than neighboring Pointe du Bout, a kilometer to the north. There are no large resorts, but rather a number of smaller moderately priced hotels and guesthouses. The village, which has a cluster of restaurants, is also a popular dinner spot.

Anse Mitan has a pleasant view across the bay to Fort-de-France, to which it's connected by ferry. The sandy Plage de l'Anse Mitan beach extends north from the village.

Places to Stay

La Bonne Auberge (☎ 66 01 55, fax 66 04 50), 97229 Trois-Ilets, is a three-story hotel on the main road in the village center. The 32 rooms, which open onto a small garden courtyard, are simple with private baths, phones and either air-con or a ceiling fan. Singles/doubles cost 250/300F in summer, 350/500F in winter, breakfast included.

A good value is *Hôtel de la Baie* (☎ 66 06 66, fax 63 00 70), 97229 Trois-Ilets, on a hillside a few minutes walk from the main road, which has a dozen comfortable rooms with air-con, private bath, kitchenette and phone. Summer rates are 250F for a standard room, 320F for a room with a balcony, some of which have views of Fort-de-France. Winter rates range from 320F to 380F.

Hôtel Camelia (☎ 66 05 85, fax 66 11 12), 97229 Trois-Ilets, a member of the Best Western chain, is a modern, reasonably priced hotel about a five-minute uphill walk from the village center. Each of the 49 rooms is compact but pleasant, with air-con, TV, refrigerator, phone and private bath. About half of the units also have balcony kitchenettes for the same rate: 370F in summer, 580F in winter. Ask for a 2nd- or 3rd-floor room as they have views of Fort-de-France. There's a pool.

Hôtel Bambou (☎ 66 01 39, fax 66 05 05), 97229 Trois-Ilets, at the south end of the road between Anse Mitan and Pointe du Bout, is a sprawling complex with 118 cabin-like duplex bungalows that often fill with package tourists. The simple units have rustic pine interiors, air-con and private baths. The complex is set back from the beach and there's a pool and restaurant. Singles/doubles start at 476/550F in summer, 700/810F in winter, breakfast included.

Places to Eat

Pizzeria Napoli, in the village center, attracts a crowd with a menu that includes good pizzas and pasta from 39F to 70F and a handful of meat dishes, heavy on the veal, for around 85F. It's open for lunch and dinner.

Le Poisson d'Or, on the road between Pointe du Bout and Anse Mitan, has a friendly Creole atmosphere, good food, generous portions and reasonable prices. Best value is the menu du jour for 110F,

which includes accras or salad, Creole fish and dessert, but you can also order à la carte, with main dishes from 70F to 85F, or splurge on a three-course lobster meal for 200F. It's open for lunch and dinner daily except on Monday. There's a guitarist on Sunday evenings.

La Langouste, next to the Anse Mitan pier, is a popular bar and restaurant and the only place right on the water. There's a three-course meal for 100F that usually features grilled fish or chicken colombo. Otherwise, most beef or chicken main dishes average 65F, seafood dishes 80F, and lobster is available at market prices. It's open daily for lunch and dinner.

La Villa Créole, a top-end French/Creole restaurant, features two fixed menus at 160F and 250F. The cheapest includes a starter, grilled fish and dessert, while the more expensive pairs salmon pâté with half a lobster. There's also an à la carte menu with main dishes averaging 90F and a fixed children's menu for 55F. It's open for dinner daily except on Sunday.

ANSE-À-L'ANE

Anse-à-l'Ane is a modern seaside village with a nice beach of light gray sand. The north side of the village is largely residential, while the south side is developed for tourism; it's quite compact and nothing is more than a few minutes walk from anywhere else. The bay, which is generally calm, is a rather popular anchorage for yachts. At night you can see the lights of Fort-de-France twinkling across the water.

Anse-à-l'Ane is connected to Fort-de-France by ferry and on weekends the beach attracts a crowd. The ferry dock is in the center of the beach, near Le Nid Tropical.

Places to Stay

Le Nid Tropical (☎ 68 31 30), 97229 Trois-Ilets, has simple bungalows along the beach for 250F; add another 50F if you want air-con. If you have your own gear, it's also possible to camp on the beach. It costs 50F for one person, 90F for two people, to pitch a tent.

MARTINIQUE

Le Tulipier (☎ 68 41 21, fax 68 41 54), 7 Rue des oursins, 97229 Trois-Ilets, family run and a good value, consists of a dozen simple units with air-con and kitchenettes in a quiet residential area, a five-minute walk from the beach. Though weekly rentals are preferred, they'll rent out by the day if space is available: studios cost 300F for two people, one-bedroom apartments cost 400F for up to four people. Rates drop about 10% in summer. Not much English is spoken, but the managers are patient with non-French speakers.

The *Frantour* (☎ 68 31 67, fax 68 37 65), 97229 Trois-Ilets, is a pleasant contemporary resort hotel conveniently located in the center of the beach. The 77 rooms have air-con, ceiling fans, TV, minibars, room safes and small balconies or terraces. There's a pool and a water sports center. Singles/doubles begin at 470/600F in summer, 790/1200F in winter.

Places to Eat

There are a number of places to eat on or near the waterfront. The beachside snack shop in front of *Le Nid Tropical* has ice cream, beer, omelets and Creole snacks. *Chez Jojo*, a popular local bar and eatery near the Texaco gas station, has sandwiches and a 55F daily lunch special. On weekends, you can buy inexpensive barbecued chicken at the roadside grill in front of Chez Jojo.

GRAND ANSE

Grand Anse, on Grand Anse d'Arlet Bay, is lined with brightly painted fishing boats and beach-side restaurants. On weekends the area is packed with urbanites from Fort-de-France, yachters and other tourists.

Grand Anse has lots of boat traffic, but good snorkeling can be found along the south end of the bay just off Morne Champagne, the volcanic peninsula that separates Grand Anse from Anse d'Arlet. A trail at the south end of the beach leads up to the top of Morne Champagne.

Places to Eat

The beachfront road has a score of restaurants with reasonably priced meals, and it's easy to stroll along the beach and compare menus. A number of places offer a three-course menu du jour for 65F to 90F. *Chez Gaby*, a pleasant spot near the pier at the south end of the bay, also has inexpensive sandwiches.

GRAND ANSE TO DIAMANT

The coastal road south of Grand Anse passes through **Anse d'Arlet** and **Petit Anse**, two seaside villages off the tourist track, and then winds around the south side of **Morne Larcher** (477 meters). As you come around a curve, the offshore islet Rocher du Diamant (Diamond Rock) pops into view before the road drops down to the town of Diamant. Beware of tortuously high speed bumps near the beach on the western outskirts of Diamant.

DIAMANT

Diamant is a small seaside town facing Diamond Rock. The center of Diamant is far more local than touristy in character and even though a number of hotels list Diamant as their address, most are on the outskirts of town, with the biggest resorts a couple of kilometers to the east.

A long and narrow gray-sand beach extends nearly 2km along the west side of Diamant. Despite being less than 100 meters from D37, the beach has a delightfully natural setting with a wooded strip of sea grape, coconut and tropical almond trees providing a buffer between the waterfront and the road. The whole beach is quite popular; several pull-offs along the main road provide beach access.

Places to Stay

Diamant les Bains (☎ 76 40 14, fax 76 27 00), 97223 Diamant, is a small in-town hotel with a pleasant West Indian character. It has a pool, a landscape of flowering plants and a nice beachfront view, although the beach itself is narrow and not terribly appealing. The rooms are small and straightforward, but not uncomfortable, and have air-con, twin beds and phones, while the bungalows also have refrigerators. In summer, rooms cost 310/380F for

Diamond Rock

The 176-meter-high Rocher du Diamant, or Diamond Rock, is a gumdrop-shaped volcanic islet 3km off the southwestern tip of Martinique. It is a haven for sea birds and favored by scuba divers, but most intriguing of all is its history.

In 1804 the British landed 120 sailors on Diamond Rock who quickly established barracks and warehouses within the rock's caves and cliffs, reinforcing it all with cannons. In one of the more unusual moments of British military history, the Royal Navy then registered the rock as a fighting ship, the unsinkable HMS *Diamond Rock*, and for the next 17 months used it to harass French vessels trying to navigate the passage. French attacks proved unsuccessful until French Admiral Villaret de Joyeuse devised a plan to catch the enemy off balance. According to the French account, the admiral cut loose a skiff loaded with rum in the direction of Diamond Rock, the isolated British sailors chugged down the hooch and the French forces retook the island. ∎

singles/doubles, bungalows cost 380/450F. In winter, rooms cost 380/500F, bungalows 480/600F. Rates include breakfast.

The beachside *Village du Diamant* (☎ 76 28 93), La Dizac, 97223 Diamant, is a three-story hotel 2.5km west of Diamant's center. The 59 modern studio-style rooms have air-con, balconies, kitchenettes and phones. There's a pool and a TV lounge. Singles/doubles cost 600/690F in winter, 490/550F in summer.

The *Marine Hôtel* (☎ 76 46 00, fax 76 25 99), Pointe de la Chéry, 97223 Diamant, is a modern 150-room resort hotel on a predominantly rocky shoreline about 2km east of Diamant's center and on the same peninsula as the Novotel hotel. Rooms have air-con, both a king bed and a sofabed, room safes, kitchenettes on the balconies and nice ocean views. There's a restaurant, a large pool, tennis courts and water sports. Singles/doubles cost 475/565F in summer, 625/850F in winter.

The *Novotel Diamant* (☎ 76 42 42, fax 76 22 87), Pointe de la Chéry, 97223 Diamant, has a secluded location at the end of the peninsula that forms the eastern edge of Diamant Bay. This is the area's largest and most exclusive resort. The 180 rooms feature air-con, TV, phones and room safes. There are a couple of restaurants, a car rental agency, a pool, a white-sand beach and complimentary water sports. Singles/doubles cost 680/850F in summer, 1000/1175F in winter.

Places to Eat

For cheap eats in the town center, there's a snack shop with sandwiches, burgers and fried chicken on the waterfront opposite the church. For pizza there's *Pizza Pépé*, a couple of minutes walk southeast of the town hall, by the Esso station.

There are half a dozen cozy little restaurants on either side of the town hall. *Chez Lucie* has an enviable waterfront location and good local Creole food at reasonable prices. At lunch and dinner you can get a three-course meal with goat colombo or lambi fricassee for 95F, with lobster for 125F.

MARIN

Marin, at the head of a deep protected bay, is one of the island's two sub-prefectures and the region's commercial center. A large marina on the west side of town offers full yachting services and is home port to Martinique's yacht charter industry.

In the center of town, opposite the tourist office, there's a handsome stone church that dates from 1766. To get there turn south off the main road at Rue Schoelcher; the church is on the plaza just 200 meters down.

SAINTE-ANNE

Sainte-Anne, the southernmost village on Martinique, has an attractive seaside setting. Its most popular swimming beach is the long, lovely strand that stretches along

MARTINIQUE

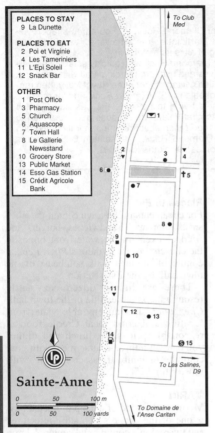

PLACES TO STAY
9 La Dunette

PLACES TO EAT
2 Poi et Virginie
4 Les Tameriniers
11 L'Epi Soleil
12 Snack Bar

OTHER
1 Post Office
3 Pharmacy
5 Church
6 Aquascope
7 Town Hall
8 Le Gallerie
   Newsstand
10 Grocery Store
13 Public Market
14 Esso Gas Station
15 Crédit Agricole
    Bank

To Club Med

Sainte-Anne

0   50   100 m
0   50   100 yards

To Les Salines, D9

To Domaine de
l'Anse Caritan

MARTINIQUE

Places to Stay

There's camping at *Vivre & Camper* (☎ 76 72 79, fax 76 97 82), BP 8, Pointe Marin, 97227 Sainte-Anne, opposite the beach near Club Med. At this well-organized campground, you can rent an equipped tent for 160F a day (minimum three nights) or set up your own tent and pay just 50F. The campground is very popular and often fills during the summer and on holiday weekends.

The in-town *La Dunette* hotel (☎ 76 73 90, fax 76 76 05), 97227 Sainte-Anne, has 18 modern rooms with air-con, TV, hair dryers and phones. Some of the rooms look out over the water and there's a beach fronting the hotel. Singles/doubles cost 300/400F in summer, 500/600F in winter, breakfast included.

Hameau de Beauregard (☎ 76 75 75, fax 76 97 13), 97227 Sainte-Anne, is a modern condo-like hotel on D9, about 500 meters southeast of the village center. A family-oriented hotel, it has 90 studio and one-bedroom units with kitchenettes, air-con, TV, phones and balconies. Rates start at 390F in summer, 690F in winter. There's a pool.

Domaine de l'Anse Caritan (☎ 76 74 12, fax 76 72 59), 97227 Sainte-Anne, has a secluded location 1km south of the village center. This modern hotel has 96 contemporary rooms with kitchenettes, air-con, phones and terraces or balconies. There's a restaurant, a pool and a white-sand beach. Singles/doubles cost 518/737F in summer, 897/1077F in winter.

Club Med's Buccaneer's Creek (☎ 76 72 72, fax 76 72 02), 97227 Sainte-Anne, is at the end of the Pointe Marin peninsula that juts out north of Sainte-Anne. It's fronted by a lovely white-sand beach and is virtually a little village unto itself. There are 300 rooms with air-con, queen or twin beds and the usual Club Med amenities. Weekly rates for singles/doubles, including meals, begin at 4200/8400F in summer and 6300/10500F in winter.

Places to Eat

There are numerous reasonably priced eateries on the beach near the campground north of Sainte-Anne center, serving up

the peninsula to Club Med, a kilometer north of the town center. Despite the number of visitors that flock to the town on weekends and during the winter season, Sainte-Anne remains a casual, low-key place.

The area waters have abundant nearshore reef formations that make for good snorkeling. If you want to see the underwater world without getting your feet wet, Aquascope, a semi-submerged vessel with viewing windows, operates daily at 9:30 and 11 am, 2 and 3:30 pm and charges 120F for adults, 60F for children.

everything from sandwiches, pizzas and crêpes to three-course meal du jours (60F to 90F).

In the town center, there's a snack bar on the coastal road in front of the public market and a grocery store a minute's walk to the north. In the same area, *L'Epi Soleil* sells pastries, bread and sandwiches and has a small dining area.

Also in the village is the upscale *Poi et Virginie*, which has a cozy waterfront setting. Starters and desserts are priced from 35F, while main courses range from goat colombo for 67F to grilled lobster for 190F.

Les Tameriniers, immediately north of the church, has salads and appetizers from 40F and main courses ranging from grilled Creole fish for 60F to lobster for 150F.

LES SALINES

Les Salines, at the undeveloped southern tip of the island, is a long, gently curving beach with golden sands. Shaded by coconut palms and tropical almond trees, it is widely regarded as Martinique's finest beach. Because the area is arid, Les Salines is often sunny when other parts of the island are not. The beach attracts scores of visitors on weekends and holidays, but it's big enough to accommodate everyone without feeling crowded.

Les Salines is 5km south of Sainte-Anne at the end of D9. There are showers and food vans near the center of the beach and about 500 meters farther south you'll find snack shops selling reasonably priced sandwiches, burgers and chicken. Camping is allowed at the west side of the beach on weekends and during school holidays.

Les Salines gets its name from Étang des Salines, the large salt pond that backs it. Beware of poisonous manchineel trees (most marked with red paint) on the beach, particularly at the southeast end.

Savane des Pétrifications

From the end of D9 at Les Salines, the road continues southeast along the beach for another 2km to the site of a petrified forest that unfortunately has been heavily scavenged by decades of souvenir hunters. There's a blazed trail through the former forest, which begins at the end of the road. It's also possible to continue walking up the coast; the track continues all the way to Macabou, about 25km away.

MARTINIQUE

Montserrat

Montserrat, a small island that has long prided itself on its unspoiled rural character, has had its serenity shattered by an awakening volcano.

Ever since July 18, 1995, when the Soufrière Hills Volcano ended 400 years of dormancy, the island has slipped deeper into volcanic throes. Plymouth, the island's capital and only significant town, had the misfortune of being just a couple of miles from the volcano and was abandoned soon after the initial eruptions, as drifting ash settled over it.

With the evacuation of Plymouth and nearby villages, more than half of the island's 11,000 residents suddenly became homeless. Some went overseas; others resettled elsewhere on the island, particularly in the Salem area, which became a makeshift boomtown. Islanders tried to go on with their lives as normally as possible

and overall managed to keep an upbeat spirit with the expectation that the situation would be temporary.

Shortly after the eruptions began, a cadre of vulcanologists and other scientists from the UK, Trinidad and the USA rushed to Montserrat to study the Soufrière Hills Volcano and advise the government on its status. Based on the data they provided, the island was divided into seven 'volcanic risk zones,' rated from A for high risk to G for low risk. Every place riskier than the midrange – essentially all parts of the island south and east of Plymouth – was declared off-limits.

Nonetheless, since much of the island's food was grown on small farms in an exclusion zone that ran from the hazardous northeast slopes of the volcano to just south of the airport, farmers continued to tend livestock and work many of the off-limit fields.

On June 25, 1997, the volcano erupted violently with avalanches of fiery debris and ash that raced down its northeastern slope, engulfing a half-dozen villages in the off-limits zone between Soufrière Hills and the airport. Helicopters searched the charred villages for survivors and airlifted five burn victims to hospitals on Guadeloupe and Martinique. In all, more than 50 people were rescued by the helicopters, which had to lower harnesses because the earth was too hot for landings. Nineteen people, most of them farmers, were killed.

In the wake of the eruption, the safety zone was redrawn, cutting the still-habitable area of the island by half. Salem, which had become the island's temporary capital after the evacuation of Plymouth, was now on the wrong side of the exclusion zone. For many people, it meant an unwelcome second evacuation and the need to start over once again. The island's largest and last remaining hotel, the Vue Pointe Hotel, was

North West Bluff

▲ Silver Hill
1323ft

Rendezvous Bay

Little Bay

CARIBBEAN
SEA

Carr's Bay

Davy
Hill

Gerald's

Northern Zone: Area with
significantly lower risk, suitable
for residential and commercial
occupation.

Central Zone: Residential area
only; residents on heightened
state of alert. All residents must
have hard hats, dust masks and
rapid means of exit.

Exclusion Zone: No admittance
except for scientific monitoring
and national security matters.

St John's

St Peters

Bunkum Bay

Northern Zone

ATLANTIC
OCEAN

Woodlands Bay

Woodlands

Laquers River

Pelican Ghaut

▲ Katy Hill
2429ft

*Blackburne
Airport
(closed)*

*Lime Kiln
Bay*

Salem

Central Zone
Centre Hills

Nantes River

Spanish Point

Vue Pointe Hotel

Old Road Bay

*Air
Studios*

Windy Hill

Harris

Bethel

Golf Course

Belham River

Fox's Bay

Cork Hill

St George's
Hill

Bransby
Point

Exclusion Zone

Richmond Hill

Gages

Soufrière Hills
Volcano
▲ 3180ft

▲ Chances Peak
3000ft

◉ **Plymouth**

Sugar Bay

Kinsale

Galways
Soufrière

South Soufrière Hills

*Roche's
Bluff*

Great Alps Falls

St Patrick's

White River

Montserrat

0   1.5   3 km
0   1   2 miles

Old Fort Point

Pyroclastic Flows & Lava Domes

Pyroclastic flows, which are common to Caribbean volcanoes, are comprised of hot rocks, ash, pumice and gases that can move at speeds of more than 100 miles per hour and reach temperatures in excess of 1000°F. They usually result from an explosive eruption or the collapse of a lava dome.

The lava domes themselves are made up of thick walls of extruded lava that build up in a cone shape atop an active volcano. These domes often have steep sides and become increasingly unstable as they grow. Under building pressure, entire sections of a lava dome can simply break away and tumble down the mountainside, filling the valleys below with volcanic debris. ■

forced to shut down. Even the Montserrat Volcano Observatory, which had its operations at Cork Hill, moved its seismographs and computers farther north.

In August 1997, a superheated pyroclastic flow entered the abandoned town of Plymouth, setting it on fire. One of the Caribbean's most appealing West Indian capitals, lined as it was with period wood-and-stone houses, was lost as the blaze destroyed an estimated 80% of the buildings.

For now, approximately 4000 to 5000 people remain on Montserrat. The population has been concentrated into the northern third of the island where new schools, housing and a hospital have been constructed.

While Montserrat can still be visited, accommodations are extremely limited and at this point it's certainly not a vacation destination. Most visitors to the island are working on reconstruction or involved in other aid projects.

Soufrière Hills Volcano

No one knows why the Soufrière Hills Volcano, which had been dormant since before the island was colonized in 1632, came to life when it did.

The first indications that an eruption could be in the making occurred in 1992, when seismographs began to record a growing number of minor earthquakes. The earthquakes led to the onset of the current eruption, beginning with a relatively small phreatic explosion that released steam and ash on July 18, 1995.

Since spring 1996, the volcano has been periodically producing superheated fast-moving pyroclastic flows that travel from the crater toward the ocean, destroying everything in their paths. These flows, along with noxious clouds of hot ash that can reach more than 15,000 feet high, have provided the main hazards to life on Montserrat.

The nature of the buildups and subsequent collapses of the lava dome within the volcano allows flows to move down the mountainside in different directions. Areas that have been hit by pyroclastic flows include the White River, south of the volcano; Plymouth, on the volcano's western slope; and the airport and nearby villages northeast of Soufrière Hills.

While scientists cannot predict exactly how the volcano will play out, many feel that volcanic activity on Montserrat will probably continue for at least a few more years.

Some volcanoes give off a powerful explosion à la Mt St Helens and then die down. Indeed, just a year after the Caribbean's most famous volcano, Mont Pelée on Martinique, blew violently in 1902, killing the 30,000 inhabitants of the capital Saint-Pierre, people began to resettle among the ruins.

The situation is different on Montserrat. So far, following each eruption, material has continued to build up within the volcanic dome. The volcano's proximity to the capital – a mere 2½ miles – casts doubts that Plymouth will ever be deemed safe for rebuilding. The general consensus is that the entire southern part of the island may not be considered habitable for at least 20 years after the eruptions stop.

The latest scientific assessment announced by the Montserrat government

---

Volcano Online

One might think that an island as remote and undeveloped as Montserrat would be totally cut off from the rest of the world when disaster strikes. In reality, what's happening there is being followed blow by blow as it occurs.

When scientists at the Montserrat Volcano Observatory (http://vulcan.wr.usgs.gov/volcanoes/montserrat/framework.htm) set up shop on Cork Hill, just a couple of miles from the fuming Soufrière Hills, they installed a live camera on their back porch with a permanent fix on the volcano. Off-island scientists, would-be vulcanologists and just plain web-browsers could then go online and watch the volcano as it erupted, belched or – on quiet days – simply let off a bit of steam.

On a more personal level, people living on Montserrat remain connected to the outside world via an email service (glaseran@musc.edu) dubbed the 'Electronic Evergreen' for a once-popular meeting place in the abandoned capital of Plymouth. Subscribers to the email service not only receive daily reports on the volcano, but the Electronic Evergreen also acts as a conduit for residents to report eruptions as they occur and to help friends and family living overseas keep in touch with folks back on the island.

In addition, the Montserrat government's website (http://www.geo.mtv.edu/volcanoes) publishes daily reports on volcanic activity, island news and issues important to the now far-flung Montserrat community. ∎

---

considers the possibility of a cataclysmic Krakatau-style eruption to be virtually negligible, but concludes that the possibility of a smaller, yet still significant, explosion that could affect the populated north and result in serious injury to be somewhere between the odds of 1 in 30 and 1 in 300.

Just in case a major volcanic eruption does occur, French and Montserrat authorities have drawn up an emergency evacuation plan dubbed 'Operation Exodus' that calls for rapid disaster assistance from Guadeloupe, which has the region's most developed infrastructure.

Facts about Montserrat

HISTORY

Amerindians called the island Alliouagana, meaning 'Land of the Prickly Bush.' When Columbus sighted the island in 1493, he named it Montserrat, as its craggy landscape reminded him of the serrated mountains above the Monastery of Montserrat near Barcelona, Spain.

The first European settlers were Catholics, mainly Irish, who moved to Montserrat in 1632 to escape persecution from Protestant rule on neighboring St Kitts. In the years that followed, Montserrat continued to attract Catholics from other New World colonies as well as new immigrants from Ireland. Many came as indentured servants who paid off their passage by toiling in the fields of the early plantations.

By the mid-17th century Montserrat was thick with sugar cane fields and the need for labor had outstripped the supply of Irish field hands. Over the next century thousands of African slaves were brought to Montserrat as the island developed the same slavery-based plantation economy found throughout the rest of the British West Indies.

For two centuries sugar production flourished and in its heyday in the 1760s more than 100 sugar plantations dotted the island. By the early 1800s the sugar market had deteriorated and with the abolition of slavery in 1834 many of the plantations slipped into decline. Some were divided up among small farmers and planted with lime trees, a crop that attained a certain measure of success, but other estates were simply abandoned.

Montserrat has been under British control almost continuously since 1632. There were, of course, the usual skirmishes with the French, who held the island briefly in 1665 and 1712, thanks in part to assistance from Irish-born islanders who distrusted the English. The French moved in again in 1782 but the Treaty of Paris, signed in 1783, returned Montserrat permanently to the British.

With the breakup of the Federation of the West Indies in 1962, Britain offered self-government to all its Caribbean dependencies. Montserrat, too small to stand alone, balked at being lumped into a coalition government with either Antigua or St Kitts and successfully petitioned the British to remain a Crown Colony.

GEOGRAPHY
Montserrat is shaped like a teardrop, about 11 miles in length and 6 miles at its widest point. The total land area is 39 sq miles.

Three distinct mountains run down the center of the island. In the north, Silver Hill reaches a height of 1323 feet. In the middle are the Centre Hills, topped by the 2429-foot Katy Hill. The south is home to the Soufrière Hills, whose highest point before the volcano was the 3000-foot Chances Peak. Since the volcano has begun erupting, an active lava dome to the east of Chances Peak has grown to heights of 3180 feet.

CLIMATE
The coolest months are December to February, when average temperatures range from a low of 70°F (21°C) in the evening to a high of 83°F (28°C) in the day. From May to October, the average low is 74°F (23°C) and the average high is 88°F (31°C). The annual rainfall is about 59 inches (1500 mm). Although there's no clearly defined rainy season, the driest time is generally between February and May.

FLORA & FAUNA
Montserrat has rainforests, tree fern forests, montane thickets and elfin woodland. The island is home to iguanas, agouti, large crapaud frogs, seven bat species and numerous bird species.

The long-term impact of the volcano on native flora and fauna remains unknown, but

it certainly will be profound. For example, the national bird, the endemic Montserrat oriole, survives solely in Montserrat's mountains. Prior to the volcanic eruptions, fewer than 500 pairs existed. A bamboo forest on the slopes of the Soufrière Hills contained the largest known oriole colony, but that forest was literally turned into an ash heap by the volcano.

Concerns about environmental damage reach beyond the land to Montserrat's surrounding coral reefs, some of which have been severely damaged by volcanic ash and flows.

GOVERNMENT & POLITICS
Montserrat remains, by its own volition, a British Crown Colony. A governor, who represents the Queen, presides over both the executive council and the legislative council. Seven members of the legislature are elected in general elections while four others are appointed.

Many Montserratians feel that the British were less than forthcoming in responding to the current crisis. There was confusion as to just what relocation aid would be provided to those who fled the island and to the level of commitment the British would make to rebuild Montserrat for those who stayed. Indeed, the British minister in London responsible for aid to Montserrat issued a dire warning of a possible cataclysmic eruption that could threaten the entire island, even while scientists on Montserrat were discounting the possibility of such an apocalyptic event.

In August 1997 a British offer to evacuate all remaining Montserratians was met with street protests by islanders who felt that the British, faced with the high costs of resettlement projects in the northern part of the island, were more concerned with keeping a lid on expenditures than they were in the well-being of Montserratians. The lack of clarity in government policy so frustrated islanders who were trying to decide whether to leave or stay that Montserrat's chief minister, perceived as being weak in his dealings with the British, was forced to resign.

ECONOMY

Before the volcano began erupting, Montserrat was self-sufficient in fruit and vegetable production, and even exported some small-scale crops such as herbal teas. Although only about 30,000 tourists visited Montserrat annually, tourism accounted for roughly 25% of the island's GNP. Tourism slowed to a trickle after the evacuation of Plymouth, and by the end of 1997 the island's last remaining hotel had closed. All in all, the local economy has been obliterated and Montserrat is now virtually reliant on outside aid.

Britain has been much criticized for failing to live up to its underlying obligations to Montserrat, and for keeping the hardships of the colony at arm's length. Partly to blame is the fact that Britain funds its few remaining dependent territories from the same overseas aid pool that it uses to fund development projects in unrelated Third World countries – meaning that Montserrat's claim has to be measured against those of some of the world's poorest nations. When perceived simply as aid to an overseas people, Britain's contributions to Montserrat could seem generous, but when viewed as disaster relief to colonial subjects by their own government, it's been tight-fisted.

Among the aid that Britain has provided to Montserrat residents has been a stipend of US$3850 per adult, US$1000 per child, for those willing to relocate off the island. As this package had no additional provision for airfare, the amounts fell well short of what most people needed to adequately relocate.

Still, about 1000 islanders have managed to move to Britain, where most qualify for public housing. About 1000 more evacuees have made their way to US territories and have been offered work permits and temporary asylum in the USA.

Most Montserratians remain close to home, however. An estimated 3000 have relocated in nearby Antigua, some moving in with relatives, others living as refugees. The Antiguan government, facing its own economic problems and high unemployment, has pressed the British government to provide financial assistance if the refugees are to remain.

Stung by criticism in the press, the British government has upped its funding to US$80 million in aid to redevelop the northern third of Montserrat.

In November 1997, Prince Andrew arrived on the island to reassure the remaining residents of Britain's renewed commitment. He toured some of the 32 schools, churches and purpose-built structures that were being used as shelters for Montserrat residents. The shelter situation has significantly improved with the completion of 100 new government-funded homes in early 1998.

POPULATION & PEOPLE

The pre-volcano population was about 11,000. Between 4000 and 5000 people remain on Montserrat. Most Montserratians are of African descent, although there is an admixture of Irish blood.

SOCIETY & CONDUCT

Although the island's African heritage remains strong, it blends uniquely with

---

Montserrat's Rock Music Connection

During the height of the rock era, George Martin, the man responsible for producing most of the Beatles' albums, established a state-of-the-art recording studio – Air Studios – on a hillside north of Plymouth. Over the years, many top-name rock stars came to Montserrat to record albums, relax and unwind. Although it's been a decade since Air Studios has been used for recording purposes, Montserrat's rock connection remains strong. In September 1997, a group of musicians with Air Studios ties – including Elton John, Sting, Paul McCartney, and Eric Clapton – performed a benefit concert in London, raising over US$1.5 million for new housing and relocation efforts on Montserrat. ■

MONTSERRAT

Irish influences. For instance, island folk dances incorporate Irish steps enlivened with an African beat.

Montserrat plays up its Irish connection. Green shamrocks show up in business logos and are stamped into visitors' passports. There are nearly 100 Montserratian families with the surname Ryan and dozens of O'Briens, Galloways and Sweeneys; village names include the likes of St Patrick's, Kinsale and Cork Hill.

These days, the Montserratian most recognized throughout the Caribbean is Alphonsus Cassell, otherwise known as Arrow, whose tune "Hot! Hot! Hot!" is a soca classic; he continues to live on the island despite the volcano.

RELIGION
Most people are Anglican, but Methodist, Pentecostal, Roman Catholic and Seventh Day Adventist denominations are also represented.

LANGUAGE
English is the main language on Montserrat, usually spoken with an island patois. Some islanders have a noticeable Irish brogue as well.

Facts for the Visitor

TOURIST OFFICES
You can request information from the Montserrat Department of Tourism (☎ 491-2230, fax 491-7430, mrattouristboard @candw.ag), PO Box 7, Montserrat, West Indies. In addition, up-to-date information is available on Montserrat websites; see the Appendix of Online Services in the back of the book.

VISAS & DOCUMENTS
All visitors must have a valid passport, with the exception of US, Canadian and British citizens who may instead present an official ID, such as a birth certificate, as proof of citizenship.

MONEY
The Eastern Caribbean dollar (EC$) is the official currency, but US dollars are also widely accepted.

POST & COMMUNICATIONS
Post and telephone services continue despite the volcano. When writing, follow the business name with 'Montserrat, West Indies.'

When calling from overseas add the area code 664 to the seven-digit local number.

The area code for Montserrat is 664.

ELECTRICITY
The electric current is 220 volts AC, 60 cycles.

WEIGHTS & MEASURES
Montserrat uses the imperial system.

DANGERS & ANNOYANCES
Because prevailing winds seldom blow in a northerly direction, the northern part of Montserrat does not receive much volcanic ash fallout. Nevertheless, on high-ash days, residents do commonly don dust masks as a health precaution.

PUBLIC HOLIDAYS & SPECIAL EVENTS
Public holidays on Montserrat are:

New Year's Day	January 1
St Patrick's Day	March 17
Good Friday	late March/early April
Easter Monday	late March/early April
Labour Day	first Monday in May
Whit Monday	eighth Monday after Easter
Queen's Birthday	second Saturday in June
August Monday	first Monday in August
Christmas Day	December 25
Boxing Day	December 26
Festival Day	December 31

Montserrat observes March 17 not only for its Irish connection but also to commemorate a rebellion by island slaves in 1768.

MONTSERRAT

Montserrat's main festival begins on Christmas Eve and culminates with a jump-up on New Year's Day.

ACTIVITIES

Recreational activities have been curtailed by the volcano.

There are a couple of pleasant beaches in the north at Rendezvous Bay and adjacent Little Bay. Although the island's new jetty is at Little Bay, there was minimal disruption to the beach during its construction; sections of the coral reef were transplanted and a new underwater snorkel trail was created 75 yards west of the jetty.

The best hiking trails were in the southern part of the island, but being close to the eruption site most of those are now buried deep in ash. A network of new trails is being planned for northern Montserrat.

Montserrat has an 11-hole golf course in Belham Valley but since it's within the exclusion zone it's currently off-limits.

Getting There & Away

A new ferry service, which uses a 300-seat French *Antilles Express* boat, operates between Montserrat and Antigua daily except Sunday. The ferry leaves Montserrat's new jetty at Little Bay at 8 am and departs from St John's in Antigua at 4 pm. The ride takes about an hour and costs EC$75 each way. For tickets and more information contact Carib World Travel (☎ 268-460-6101), Heritage Quay, Antigua.

The airport, which has a volcanic flow across its runway, has been closed since June 1997. The government is surveying possible sites for a new airport in the northern part of the island.

In the meantime, a helicopter service operates between Antigua and Montserrat, but it's mainly for officials, so other passengers are taken only on a space-available basis. The fare is EC$89 one way. Information can be obtained from Carib Aviation (☎ 268-462-3147) in Antigua.

Getting Around

Minivans provide bus service between the villages, with fares ranging from EC$1.50 to EC$3, depending on the distance. Taxis are also available and generally meet the ferry.

Around Montserrat

Currently the only inhabited part of Montserrat is the northern third of the island. Consequently, northern villages that were once tiny and rural, such as Davy Hill and St John's, are now the island's main population centers. Only lightly settled prior to the volcano, the north is an attractive area with green landscapes, low mountains and a couple of Montserrat's better beaches.

Carr's Bay, a fishing village on the west coast, is thought to have been the landing site of the first Irish settlers. It has a roadside black-sand beach with a view of uninhabited Redonda Island to the northwest and on a clear day you can also see Nevis beyond.

North of Carr's Bay is **Little Bay**, where there's a black-sand beach backed by hilly pastures. Little Bay now serves as the island's main port. About a half-mile beyond Little Bay is appealing **Rendezvous Bay**, which has broad golden sands.

From Carr's Bay the main road cuts east across the island between Silver Hill and the Centre Hills. Midway is the village of **St John's**, where most island services are now centered. **Gerald's**, north of St John's, has the island's new heliport. East of St John's are a run of largely uninhabited valleys. The road access ends just north of the old airport, where lava crosses the runway and the villages become ghost towns.

Places to Stay

Accommodation options are few in number and visitors should make sure they have a room squared away before heading off to the island.

There are a couple of cottages within walking distance of Woodlands Bay, where there's a small gray-sand beach. *Erindell* (☎ 491-3655), PO Box 36, Woodlands, is a studio apartment at the home of Shirley and Lou Spycalla. It has two comfortable twin beds and limited cooking facilities. Complimentary breakfast is provided on the first morning and you can join the Spycallas at other meals at reasonable prices. Singles/doubles cost US$35/45.

Egret House (☎ 491-5316), General Delivery, Woodlands, is a 400-sq-foot apartment at the home of Salo and Gloria Boekbinder Mulder, an Anglo-Dutch couple. The unit, which has a queen bed, sitting area and kitchen, costs US$55.

David Lea (☎ 491-5812) in St Peter's rents out a couple of rooms in his home at rates similar to the guesthouses.

Montserrat guesthouses can also be booked through the ferry vendor: Carib World Travel (☎ 268-460-6101), Heritage Quay, Antigua.

Although it's presently closed and in the exclusion zone, the *Vue Pointe Hotel* (☎ 491-5210, fax 491-4813), PO Box 65, on the beach at Old Road Bay, is the most northerly of Montserrat's hotels and will likely be the first to reopen when the volcano quiets down. It's a pleasant family-run place with 36 cottages and hotel rooms that prior to closing had costs from US$90 to US$160.

Montserrat previously had about 100 private villas that were rented by the week. However, many are in the hills above the golf course and are now in the exclusion zone. Others are being rented by British officials involved in reconstruction projects. For information on villa rentals, contact Neville Bradshaw Agencies (☎ 491-5270, fax 491-5069), PO Box 270, Montserrat.

Places to Eat

There are a couple of dozen small eateries on the island, with at least a few in each populated village and others working out of mobile wagons. Most have simple food such as rotis, pizza, sandwiches and barbecued chicken. If you're looking for vegetarian items, there's *Roots Man Beach Bar* at Carr's Bay.

St John's has a bakery as well as *Morgan's Place*, where the colorful Mrs Morgan still cooks up – as she has for decades – the island's best goat-water stew.

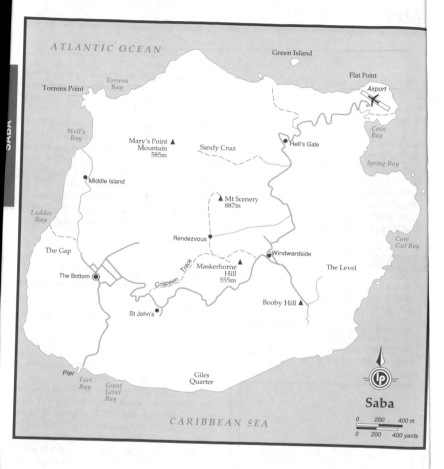

ATLANTIC OCEAN

Saba

GEOGRAPHY

Saba's land area is just 13 sq km but, because of its topography of folding mountains, Saba is far more substantial than any mere area measurement would indicate. The island is the emerged peak of an extinct volcano that rises to 887 meters at Mt Scenery, Saba's highest point.

There are no rivers or streams on the island. The leeward western side is dry with cacti and scrub, the windward eastern side has thicker vegetation and the mountainous interior is given over to lush jungle growth.

CLIMATE

Saba's rainfall averages 1070 mm (42 inches) a year. The mean monthly temperature is 27°C (80°F), with about a 2°C degree variance from summer to winter. Because of the difference in elevation, temperatures are a bit cooler in Windwardside than in The Bottom. In winter, evening temperatures often dip to around 17°C (63°F), and while summers are generally a little cooler than on neighboring islands, hot and sticky summer nights are not unknown.

Top Left: Wooden house, Nevis (Ned Friary)
Bottom Left: St Eustatius from the cane fields of St Kitts (Ned Friary)

Top Right: Petroglyphs, Old Road Town, St Kitts (Ned Friary)
Middle Right: Old sugar mill, Nevis (Glenda Bendure)
Bottom Right: Charlestown and Nevis Peak at sunset, Nevis (Ned Friary)

Top Left: Mural in the Cathedral of the Immaculate Conception, Castries, St Lucia (Ned Friary)
Bottom Left: Rum shop, Gros Islet, St Lucia (Ned Friary)

Top Right: Soufrière kids greeting yachters, St Lucia (Glenda Bendure)
Bottom Right: Gros Islet Beach with Pigeon Island in background, St Lucia (Ned Friary)

Saba

Dubbed the 'Unspoiled Queen,' Saba is both the smallest and loftiest of the islands that comprise the Netherlands Antilles. This ruggedly steep island has beautiful scenery, good hiking, pristine diving and strikingly little tourism.

At first glance Saba appears more like a misplaced Alpine community than part of the West Indies. As the tip of an immense underwater mountain, the island looms out of the sea, with no pause for lowlands or beaches. Saba's central volcanic peak, Mt Scenery, is cloaked in clouds. Its slopes are dotted with quaint white houses with green shutters, red roofs and gingerbread trim, while tiny vegetable plots sprout between rock-strewn hillsides.

The island has four villages, all spotlessly neat. Although The Bottom is the island's capital, Windwardside is the largest village and the most popular base for visitors. The villages of St John's and Hell's Gate are largely residential areas.

With only 1200 inhabitants, everyone on Saba knows everyone else and it's certainly one of the gentlest and friendliest places in the Caribbean.

HIGHLIGHTS

- Saba's crisp mountain air and bucolic serenity
- Diving the pristine waters of the Saba Marine Park
- Making a hardy sunrise walk to the top of Mt Scenery
- Strolling Windwardside, with its lace makers and art galleries

---

Facts about Saba

HISTORY

Because of the island's rugged terrain, Saba was probably not heavily settled in pre-Columbian times. However, artifacts uncovered in the Spring Bay area indicate the existence of a small Arawak settlement at that site about 1300 years ago.

During his second trip to the New World on November 13, 1493, Christopher Columbus became the first European to sight Saba. The Dutch laid claim to the island in 1632 and sent a party of colonists from St Eustatius in 1640 to form a permanent settlement. These early colonists originally lived at Middle Island and Mary's Point, where bits of a few cisterns and stone walls can still be found, but soon moved to The Bottom, which still remains the administrative center of the island.

Because the steep topography of the island precluded large-scale plantations, colonial-era slavery was quite limited on Saba. Those colonists who did own slaves generally had only a few and often worked side by side with them in the fields, resulting in a more integrated society than on larger Dutch islands.

The Road That Couldn't Be Built

Until a few decades ago, Saba's villages were connected solely by footpaths. For years engineers from low-lying Holland had declared that the island's steep terrain made road construction impossible.

One skeptical islander, Josephus Lambert Hassell, decided to take matters into his own hands. He enrolled in an engineering correspondence course and then organized a local construction team.

In the 1940s Hassell's 20-man crew constructed the first section of the concrete road from Fort Bay to The Bottom, and over the next 20 years they gradually extended the road to Hell's Gate. They built the entire road by hand, and though it may be narrow and twisting, it is free of the patchwork potholes that characterize so many roads elsewhere in the Caribbean. ■

FLORA & FAUNA

Saba has a wide variety of flowering plants, ranging from the prolific oleander and hibiscus that decorate yards to the wildflowers and orchids that thrive in the rainforest. Bird life is also abundant and varied with more than 60 species sighted on Saba. Bridled terns, sooty terns and brown noddys breed on the island, tropicbirds nest on the cliffs and frigatebirds soar near the coast. Red-tailed hawks can be spotted on the lower slopes, while thrashers and hummingbirds are found at higher elevations.

Saba has a harmless racer snake that's quite common to spot as it suns itself along trails and roadsides, although it generally darts off as people approach. Expect to see the friendly little *Anolis sabanus* lizard that's endemic to the island and to hear the tiny tree frogs whose symphony can be almost deafening at night.

GOVERNMENT & POLITICS

Saba is part of the Dutch kingdom, one of five islands in the Netherlands Antilles, whose central administration is in Curaçao. As with the other four islands, Saba is treated as a municipality and has its own lieutenant governor who, along with two elected commissioners, is responsible for running the island's daily affairs. Will Johnson, Saba's senator, represents the island in Curaçao.

ECONOMY

Although the scale of tourism is quite moderate, it is a major source of revenue for the island, second only to government employment. The largest growth of visitors has been among divers, who are attracted in ever increasing numbers by Saba's pro-environmental stance and its fine diving conditions.

Until a few years ago Saba was a popular destination for young Dutch who flew there to obtain their driver's licenses and escape strict and costly regulations in Holland. It was a thriving business for a handful of driving schools and for guesthouses that catered to them, but new regulations put an end to the practice. One of the old driving schools in The Bottom has been converted into a small medical school for overseas students.

Sabans grow much of their own food, from Irish potatoes and taro to hydroponically grown lettuce. Locally caught fish and lobster are exported to neighboring islands. There's also a small quarry that exports crushed stone and gravel.

POPULATION & PEOPLE

Saba's permanent population is about 1200. It's fairly evenly divided between descendants of African slaves and descendants of the early Scottish, Irish and Scandinavian settlers. Most people can trace their lineage to one of half a dozen families, and just two names, Hassell and Johnson, account for almost a third of the phone-book listings. Incidentally, despite its Dutch government, Saba is home to very few people of Dutch descent.

RELIGION

Catholicism is the predominant religion on Saba, but the island's eight churches also include Anglican, Wesleyan Holiness and Seventh Day Adventist denominations.

LANGUAGE

Although Dutch is the 'official' language, English is the primary language of the island and the language most commonly spoken in the home. To accommodate this reality the Dutch government recently allowed the Saban school system to switch from Dutch to English as the principal classroom language. Schoolchildren now study Dutch as a second language.

Facts for the Visitor

ORIENTATION

It's virtually impossible to get lost on Saba. There is only one main road, which runs from the airport at the northeast side of the island, through the villages of Hell's Gate, Windwardside, St John's and The Bottom, and continues down to Fort Bay, the island's main port. A second road connects The Bottom with Well's Bay, on the island's northwest side.

Maps

The tourist office has free island maps that show the roads and hiking trails.

TOURIST OFFICES
Local Tourist Office

The helpful Saba Tourist Bureau (☎ 62231, fax 62350) has its office in Windwardside.

When requesting information by mail, write to: Saba Tourist Bureau, PO Box 527, Windwardside, Saba, Netherlands Antilles.

Tourist Offices Abroad

Overseas tourism representatives include:

Netherlands
    Antillen Huis (Kabinet van de Gevol-machtigde Minister van de Nederlandse Antillen), Badhuisweg 173-175, 2597 JP 'S-Gravenhage (☎ 070-3512811, fax 070-3512722)

USA
    Saba Tourist Office, PO Box 6322, Boca Raton, FL 33427 (☎ 561-394-8580, 800-722-2394; fax 561-488-4294)

VISAS & DOCUMENTS

Valid passports are required of all visitors except for US and Canadian citizens, who need only proof of citizenship, such as an official birth certificate plus a driver's license. A roundtrip or onward ticket is officially required.

CUSTOMS

Saba is a free port and there are no customs regulations.

MONEY

The official currency is the Netherlands Antilles guilder or florin, but US dollars are accepted everywhere. Islander-geared businesses such as grocers and shops post prices in guilders while visitor-related businesses such as hotels, restaurants and dive shops post prices in US dollars. The exchange rate is 1.77 guilders to US$1. Generally, there's no advantage in changing your money to guilders unless you're planning a lengthy stay. For more information see Money in the Facts for the Visitor chapter.

The island's two banks, Barclays and the Commercial Bank, are both in Windwardside. Credit cards are accepted at most hotels and some restaurants.

POST & COMMUNICATIONS
Post

Saba's two post offices are in Windwardside and The Bottom. When writing to Saba from abroad, just address mail with the individual or business name, followed by the town and 'Saba, Netherlands Antilles.'

It costs Fls 1.10 to mail a postcard and Fls 2.25 to mail a letter to the USA, Canada, UK or Europe; and Fls 1.30 for a postcard and Fls 3.25 for a letter to Australia, Asia or Africa.

Telephone

Local phone numbers have five digits. The area code, which must be added when calling Saba from overseas, is 599-4.

There are two card telephones on the island: one at Scout's Place restaurant in

Windwardside and one at the Antelecom office in The Bottom. You can buy phonecards at either location. There are also two coin phones – at Fort Bay and the airport. For more information see Post & Communications in the Facts for the Visitor chapter at the front of the book.

The area code for Saba is 599-4.

Fax & Email
Faxes can be sent and received from the Antelecom office, and email can be checked at the main library. Both are in The Bottom.

BOOKS
Guide to the Saba Marine Park by marine biologist Tom van't Hof (Saba Conservation Foundation, 1991) is an authoritative guide to underwater Saba. Van't Hof, who spearheaded the development of the Saba Marine Park, gives detailed descriptions of each of Saba's 26 dive sites, accompanied by color photos illustrating coral and marine life.

Saban Cottages, a hardcover book by artist Heleen Cornet, contains lovely watercolor drawings of scores of the island's picturesque buildings.

Both books can be purchased in shops and art galleries on the island.

NEWSPAPERS & MAGAZINES
As Saba has no newspaper, local news and announcements are posted on bulletin boards in the villages. St Martin's *The Daily Herald*, which includes Saba news, can be purchased at Big Rock Market in Windwardside.

RADIO & TV
Radio PJF-1, 'The Voice of Saba,' is at 94.7 FM. The island has cable TV with US network programming.

ELECTRICITY
Electricity is 110 volts AC, 60 cycles, and a flat two-pronged plug is used.

WEIGHTS & MEASURES
Saba uses the metric system.

HEALTH
In The Bottom, the AM Edwards Medical Center (☎ 63289) is the island's medical facility.

There's a decompression chamber for divers at Fort Bay, which also serves divers who get the bends on neighboring islands.

BUSINESS HOURS
Shops and offices are commonly open from 8 or 9 am to noon and from 1 to 5 pm.

PUBLIC HOLIDAYS & SPECIAL EVENTS
Public holidays on Saba are:

New Year's Day	January 1
Good Friday	Friday before Easter
Easter Sunday	late March/early April
Easter Monday	late March/early April
Queen's Day	April 30
Labor Day	May 1
Ascension Thursday	40th day after Easter
Christmas Day	December 25
Boxing Day	December 26

The Saba Summer Festival, held in late July, is the island's Carnival. The week-long event includes jump-ups, a queen contest, a calypso king competition and a costumed parade around The Bottom and a grand finale fireworks display.

Saba Days, held in early December, features sporting events, steel bands, dancing, donkey races and barbecues.

ACTIVITIES
Beaches & Swimming
Saba is not the place to go if you want to lay out on sandy strands. The main swimming spot is Well's Bay at the northwestern side of the island, which has a small, rocky beach. All the island hotels have swimming pools.

Diving & Snorkeling
Saba's stunning scenery extends beneath the surface, with steep wall drops just offshore and some varied nearshore reef

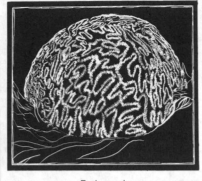

Brain coral

dives. Most of the island's 26 dive spots are along the calmer leeward side, between Tent Bay and Diamond Rock.

Some of the more exciting dives include Tent Reef Wall, which has colorful tube sponges and corals and lots of fish activity; Third Encounter and Twilight Zone, adjacent sponge and coral-encrusted pinnacles that rise about 30 meters from the ocean floor; and Diamond Rock, which has a great variety of marine life, including stingrays, black-tip sharks and bull sharks.

The waters surrounding Saba are protected under the auspices of the Saba Marine Park, which has undertaken a number of conservation efforts, including installing permanent mooring buoys at dive sites. To help cover the park's operating expenses, a US$3 marine park fee is added onto each dive.

For snorkelers, Well's Bay and the adjacent Torrens Point are popular spots and there's even a marked underwater trail.

Dive Shops Saba has three dive shops. Sea Saba (☎ 62246, fax 62362, seasaba@aol.com), based in Windwardside, generally does a 10 am and noon dive daily and night dives on request. Single-tank dives cost US$50, double-tank dives US$90 and night dives US$60. Masks and fins can be rented for US$8. Sea Saba also does a resort course for beginners for US$80 and

a five-day certification course for US$350. There's a three-person minimum for courses. Snorkelers can go out with the dive boat for US$25.

Saba's original dive shop, Saba Deep (☎ 63347, fax 63397, diving@sabadeep.com; in the USA ☎ (888) 348-3722) at Fort Bay, goes out at 9 and 11 am and 1 pm, taking no more than eight divers per boat. The first dive of the day is a deep dive, the second intermediate and the last a shallow dive. Rates, which include all gear, are US$50/90/110 for single/double/triple tank dives and US$65 for a night dive.

Saba Reef Divers (☎ 62541, fax 62653, sabareef@aol.com), the newest operation, has a shop in Windwardside. It goes out four times a day and charges US$50/90/125 for single/double/triple tank dives, US$60 for a night dive. Rates include gear. PADI open-water certification and advanced open-water courses are available. Dedicated snorkeling tours are offered for US$30, including gear and use of a wet suit.

Live-Aboard Boats The live-aboard dive boat M/V *Caribbean Explorer* generally starts and ends its week-long trips in St Martin, but spends much of its time around Saba. For more information see Organized Tours in the Getting There & Away chapter.

Kayaking
Saba Reef Divers (☎ 62541) offers guided two-hour sea-kayak tours from Fort Bay for US$50 for a single kayak, US$70 for a double kayak.

Hiking
Saba has some excellent and varied hiking opportunities. There are seven signposted and maintained hikes, ranging from a 15-minute walk to tide pools just beyond the airport to a steep climb up through a cloud forest to the top of Mt Scenery, Saba's highest point. Interpretive plaques describing natural history and trailside bird and plant life have been erected along the trails by the Saba Conservation Foundation.

As the trails cross private property, hikers should stick to established paths.

Saba Marine Park

Established in 1987, the Saba Marine Park encompasses all the waters surrounding the island from the high-water mark to a depth of 71 meters. The park has established zones for different marine uses. For example, it limits anchoring to the Fort Bay and Ladder Bay areas and sets aside the waters between the two bays exclusively for diving. Fishing is permitted in most other Saba waters, but some restrictions will apply, and there are quotas for at-risk creatures like conch.

The park was established with funding from the World Wildlife Fund and from the Saba and Dutch governments. It is administered by the Saba Conservation Foundation, a nonprofit group. ■

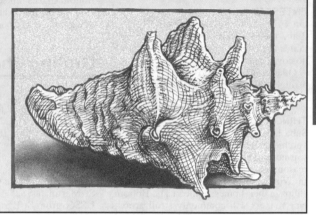

There are no poisonous creatures on Saba and it's one of the safest places in the Caribbean, so this is one island where you can feel free to concentrate all your attention on the environment.

Some of the trails, such as the Crispeen Track between The Bottom and Windwardside, follow the old footpaths that linked the villages before the first vehicle roads were built. A simple trail brochure and map is available free at the tourist office.

ACCOMMODATIONS

Most of Saba's accommodations fall in the moderate price range with rates averaging around US$100. If you're on a budget, there is one delightful low-end option, El Momo Cottages in Booby Hill, at just US$35. There are also a couple of pampering top-end hotels with rooms from US$150 to US$400.

In addition to the hotels listed in this chapter, there are a handful of cottages and apartments for rent on Saba, with prices ranging from US$50 to US$125 nightly,

US$300 to US$700 weekly. The Saba Tourist Bureau will send out an annually updated list with rates and contact numbers. While you can book these cottages on your own, it's also possible to do it through the tourist office and generally that's an easier route to take, as the tourist office staff know which cottages are available at any given time.

To rates given in this chapter add a 5% government room tax. Many hotels also add a 10% service charge (15% at Scout's).

FOOD

Food in Saba has continental and Creole influences, with an emphasis on fish and seafood, though popular local dishes also include goat meat, johnny cakes and barbecued ribs. A variety of fruit is grown on the island, including bananas, papayas, mangoes, avocados, and soursop.

DRINKS

Water is by catchment, but generally OK to drink from the tap – although you should inquire first.

Be sure to try Saba Spice, a rum-based liqueur spiced with a 'secret concoction' that varies depending on whose liquor you buy. It can be purchased in bars for US$1 a shot or US$10 a 750ml bottle.

ENTERTAINMENT

On Friday and Saturday from 9 pm to 2 am, Guido's Restaurant pushes the pool tables aside and turns into a disco; there's no cover charge.

Otherwise, the island is generally quiet at night, with only a bit of action at the hotel bars.

THINGS TO BUY

Saba lace handwork in the form of handkerchiefs, table runners, place mats, bun warmers and similar items are available at reasonable prices from local craftswomen. In Windwardside, the women have small shops in their homes, while in The Bottom, lace makers will commonly stroll around with boxes of their work. A good island-wide selection can be found at the community center in Hell's Gate.

The women at the Hell's Gate community center also sell homemade Saba Spice liqueur. Most varieties have a licorice-like flavor, as one of the common ingredients is the fennel that's planted at the side of some Saban homes.

Saba has attracted a number of good contemporary artists whose paintings and drawings take their inspiration from the island's natural scenery. Original oils and watercolors, glass jewelry, cards and prints can be found at several island shops, the best of which is the Breadfruit Gallery in Windwardside.

The Saba Artisans Foundation in The Bottom makes silkscreen cotton bags and clothing on site; it also sells T-shirts, Saba Spice liqueur and pareos.

Getting There & Away

AIR

The only scheduled flight service to Saba is with Winair (☎ 62212 or 62255), which has at least four flights a day from St Martin, a 15-minute hop. Winair also has a daily flight from St Eustatius and a flight on Tuesday and Thursday from St Barts.

The one-way fare to Saba is US$42 from St Martin, US$25 from St Eustatius and US$66 from St Barts. Roundtrip fares are double.

Airport Information

Saba's seaside airstrip is a mere 400 meters long, the region's shortest. It's similarly narrow, with the plane touching down just meters away from a sheer cliff, all of which makes for a thrilling landing.

The small airport has a Winair booth, restrooms, a coin telephone and a stall selling beer and soda.

SEA
Inter-Island Ferry

Two motorized catamarans run between Dutch St Maarten and Saba.

The Edge (☎ 42640) leaves Pelican Marina in Simpson Bay at 9 am on Wednesday, Friday and Sunday.

Voyager I (☎ 24096) departs from Bobby's Marina in Philipsburg at 8:30 am on Thursday and Saturday (only on Thursday in summer).

Both boats arrive at Saba's Fort Bay around 10 am, depart from Saba around 4 pm and charge US$60 for the roundtrip journey.

Saba Lace

The craft most associated with the island is Spanish work, or Saba lace, a drawn threadwork first introduced to Saba in the 1870s by a woman who learned the stitching technique in a convent in Venezuela. While this lace-like embroidery work is high quality, the market for it is so limited that the craft is not being practiced by the younger generation and is a dying art. ∎

Yacht

Saba has two designated anchorages: the harbor at Fort Bay and the area from Well's Bay to Ladder Bay. Under normal conditions, Well's Bay is the best anchorage and offers excellent holding in sand. Ladder Bay also has good holding but has some tricky downdrafts as well as boulders in the shallower waters. There are yellow buoys in the Ladder and Well's Bay anchorage area that can be used by visiting yachts; however, the white and orange buoys are reserved for dive boats.

People arriving by boat should first clear immigration at the harbor office at Fort Bay. The office monitors VHF channels 16 and 11. If there's no one at the harbor office, check in at the adjacent Saba Marine Park office.

To help support the Saba Marine Park, there is a yacht visitor fee of US$3 per person.

Cruise Ship

Saba does not have a deep-water port that is capable of handling large cruise ships. However, Windjammer Barefoot Cruises and a few other small ships stop over at Saba by anchoring in Fort Bay and bringing passengers ashore by dinghy.

ORGANIZED TOURS

The catamaran shuttle *The Edge* (☎ 42640) offers a day package that includes lunch, an island tour and roundtrip boat passage from Dutch St Maarten for US$90.

Dive packages that include accommodations and airport transfers can be arranged from all three dive shops, or in the USA through Dive Saba Travel (☎ 713-467-8835, 800-883-7222; fax 713-461-6044). Rates vary according to the accommodations you select, but average about US$500/575 in summer/winter for a five-night, six-dive package, based on double occupancy.

LEAVING SABA

The departure tax, for people aged two and older, is US$2 for those going to a Nether- lands Antilles island and US$10 for those going to a non-Dutch island.

Passengers connecting with an international flight from St Martin pay US$10; be sure to pick up a transit pass at your airline check-in counter in St Martin, which exempts you from paying an additional departure tax there.

Getting Around

There are no public buses and no scooters or bicycles for rent on Saba.

THE AIRPORT

Taxis meet the flights. There are no car rentals at the airport.

TAXI

Taxi fares are set by the government. The price from the airport is US$8 to Windwardside and US$12.50 to The Bottom for up to four people, plus 50 cents for each piece of luggage.

From Windwardside it costs US$6.50 to The Bottom, US$9.50 to Fort Bay. A sight-seeing tour, which lasts 1½ to two hours and covers most of the island, costs US$40 per taxi.

As there are only a dozen full-time taxis, they can get tied up at busy times; if you're unable to find one, the tourist office (☎ 62231) will try to hunt one down for you.

CAR

Saba has very narrow and steep roads that may intimidate some drivers. Even Sabans are challenged by tight corners in Windwardside – you'd be hard pressed to find a car that doesn't bear scrape marks from kissing at least one stone wall!

Road Rules

Drive on the right side of the road. Your home driver's license is valid for driving on Saba. The island's sole gas station is in Fort Bay; it's open from 8 am to 3 pm Monday to Saturday.

SABA

Rental
There aren't many rental cars on the island, so if you want one you may need to book in advance. The going rate for a small car is around US$45 a day. The main rental agents are Johnson's Rent a Car (☎ 62269), which is at Juliana's hotel, and Scout's Place (☎ 62205), both in Windwardside.

HITCHHIKING
Hitchhiking is a common means of transportation. In Windwardside, the main hitching spot is near the wall by the Big Rock Market and in The Bottom it's by the Department of Public Works.

Around Saba

HELL'S GATE
When you stand at the airport and look up the mountain, you see the village of Hell's Gate, whose houses seem to cling precariously to the side of the mountain slopes. The road from the airport to Windwardside passes directly through the village.

The main landmark in Hell's Gate is the Holy Rosary Church, a seemingly old stone church that was built just three decades ago. Behind the church is the Hell's Gate community center, which sells the best collection of Saba lace on the island, as well as bottles of homemade Saba Spice liqueur. The community center is usually open daily from 9 to 11 am.

The ride from Hell's Gate to Windwardside is steep and winding. It passes through a variety of terrains, offering some fine scenic views of Saba itself and glimpses of the neighboring islands of St Eustatius, St Kitts, Nevis and St Barts.

Places to Stay & Eat
The Gate House (☎ 62416, fax 62550, sabagate@aol.com; in the USA ☎ 708-354-9641) has six cheery rooms with private baths, tile floors and either one king or two single beds. Two rooms also have kitchenettes. All have a stylish decor with works by American artist Jim Siegel, who

runs the place along with his Dutch partner Manuella. There's a pool and wrap-around balconies with fine views. Singles/doubles cost US$75/85 in summer, US$85/95 in winter, breakfast included. In the evening a set dinner with salad, dessert and a main dish, such as jerk pork or coconut shrimp, is available for US$23.

WINDWARDSIDE
The island's largest hamlet, Windwardside has curving alleyways lined with picturesque cottages and flower-filled gardens. Being on the windward side of the island, just below Mt Scenery, this hillside village is pleasantly green and a tad cooler than other parts of the island. It's a delightfully unhurried and friendly place.

Windwardside makes the best base for visitors, as it has the most hotels, restaurants and shops, as well as the tourist office, the museum, a good art gallery and the trailhead for the island's most popular hike. While you are walking around you'll probably notice that many homes have Dutch doors. The top half of these doors are commonly kept open in the evening, allowing people to chat from their living rooms with neighbors strolling by.

Information
Tourist Office The Saba Tourist Bureau (☎ 62231) is at the northwest side of town and is open from 8 am to noon and 1 to 5 pm Monday to Friday.

Money Barclays Bank, near the crossroads, is open from 8:30 am to 2 pm Monday to Friday. Barclays cashes Visa traveler's checks for free and others for a 1% fee. The island's only other bank, the Commercial Bank, is opposite the post office and open weekdays from 8.30 am to 3 pm (to 4 pm on Thursday and Friday).

Post The Windwardside post office is open from 8 am to noon and 1 to 5 pm Monday to Thursday, to 4:30 pm on Friday.

Library The library, which is next to the post office, is open from 8 am to noon on

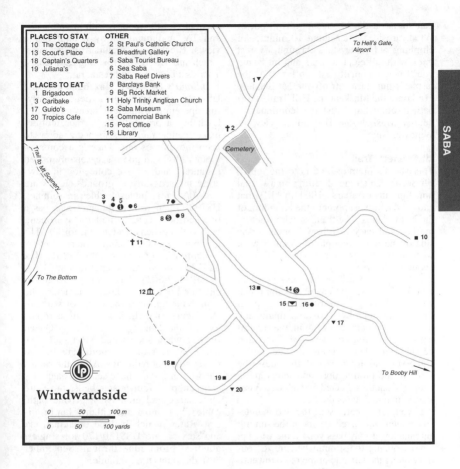

PLACES TO STAY
10 The Cottage Club
13 Scout's Place
18 Captain's Quarters
19 Juliana's

PLACES TO EAT
1 Brigadoon
3 Caribake
17 Guido's
20 Tropics Cafe

OTHER
2 St Paul's Catholic Church
4 Breadfruit Gallery
5 Saba Tourist Bureau
6 Sea Saba
7 Saba Reef Divers
8 Barclays Bank
9 Big Rock Market
11 Holy Trinity Anglican Church
12 Saba Museum
14 Commercial Bank
15 Post Office
16 Library

To Hell's Gate,
Airport

Trail to Mt Scenery

Cemetery

To The Bottom

To Booby Hill

Windwardside

0   50   100 m
0   50   100 yards

SABA

Monday, 2 to 5 pm on Tuesday and Thursday and 7 to 9 pm on Saturday.

Saba Museum

The Saba Museum is in a garden-like setting surrounded by wildflowers, including black-eyed susans, the official island flower. The museum is in a typical Saban home, whitewashed with green-shuttered windows, and re-creates the living quarters of a 19th-century Dutch sea captain. It has a four-poster bed with period decor, a collection of pottery fragments, Amerindian hand tools and lots of memorabilia including maritime documents, sextants and a compass. Curiously, there's also a bust of the South American revolutionary Simón Bolívar on the grounds, which was presented to Saba by the Venezuelan government. The museum is open from 10 am to noon and 1 to 4 pm Monday to Friday. Admission is US$2.

Maskehorne Hill Trail

For a quick sense of what Saban wilderness is like, take this 45-minute roundtrip hike that starts on the Mt Scenery Trail out of Windwardside. After about 10 minutes of climbing old stone steps through a forest thick with tall elephant ears and birdsong, you'll reach a small dasheen farm. At the farmer's hut, turn left off the Mt Scenery Trail onto the Maskehorne Hill Trail, a dirt path through the forest that continues to nearby Maskehorne Hill and a view of Windwardside.

Mt Scenery Trail

The island's premier hike is to the top of Mt Scenery, a strenuous climb up a virtual nonstop run of stairs (1064 in all!) that ends at the highest point in the Kingdom of the Netherlands. The trail, which is clearly marked and easy to follow, begins at the side of the road a couple of minutes walk west of the tourist office. Hiking time is about 2½ hours roundtrip.

As ample reward for a good workout you'll get a close-up view of an elfin forest with its lush growth of ferns, tropical flowers and epiphyte-covered mahogany trees, and if clouds don't roll in, the summit provides panoramic views of Saba and neighboring islands. There are interpretive signboards along the trail that describe some of the prolific flora and fauna and a couple of shelters erected by Cable & Wireless, which maintains the trail.

If you get an early start the two maintenance men who hike to work at the summit antenna tower may pass you on the way up. After reaching the summit be sure to continue along the left side of the radio tower to reach a scenic lookout 100 meters beyond.

The trail can be very slippery in places; wear shoes with good traction, watch your footing and be especially careful where there are fallen leaves. This hike is only partially shaded and can get very hot at midday. Bring water; most hotels will provide guests with canteens.

Places to Stay

Windwardside Center *Scout's Place* (☎ 62205, fax 62388) is a casual 15-room inn with a cliffside location in the village center. The rooms are simple but perfectly

adequate for the money, with private baths and TV, and many enjoy distant ocean views. Breakfast is included in the rates, which are US$65/85 for singles/doubles. There's a pool, bar and restaurant.

Juliana's (☎ 62269, fax 62389; in the USA ☎ 800-365-8484) is a friendly family-run operation with eight pleasant rooms. Each has a private bath, terrace, coffee-maker, ceiling fan, and screened windows to keep mosquitoes out. There's a common room with TV, a pool, a reasonably priced restaurant and a prize collection of flowering hibiscus on the grounds. Rates are US$70/90 for singles/doubles in summer, US$90/115 in winter. Juliana's also has a two-bedroom cottage and an apartment, both with kitchens, which rent for US$115 in summer and US$135 in winter.

Captain's Quarters (☎ 62201, fax 62377, sabacq@aol.com; in the USA ☎ 212-289-6031) has a dozen rooms, a cliffside pool and a classic character. The main building, once the home of sea captain Henry Hassell, has two guest rooms (which, incidentally, were used by Queen Beatrix when she visited Saba in 1993), while the rest of the rooms are in two newer adjacent buildings. All of the rooms are different, some have seaview balconies and canopied four-poster beds, most are quite large and all have a private bath, cable TV, minibar and either a fan or air-con. Rates, which include breakfast, tax and service, are US$130/170 for singles/doubles. From June through September 30% discounts are available.

If you're planning on preparing your own meals consider *The Cottage Club* (☎ 62386, fax 62476), which has five duplex cottages with fine hillside views. The 10 roomy studio-style units each have a full kitchen, a dining table, a queen bed and cable TV. There's a pool and it enjoys a rural setting at the eastern edge of the village, but it is still within easy walking distance of the center. Singles/doubles cost US$94/105 in summer, US$126/136 in winter.

Booby Hill Booby Hill, a rural area about a kilometer south of Windwardside center, has two interesting new hotels – one the island's cheapest, the other its priciest.

El Momo Cottages (☎ /fax 62265), PO Box 519, on the edge of the rainforest, is a delightful traveler's haunt with a Robinson Crusoe charm. Run by a friendly Dutch couple who treat their grounds like a nature sanctuary, the cottages are linked by flower-lined paths that are used by sunning lizards. Clean and simple, the cottages have gables with gingerbread trim, a porch and two twin beds. Showers are out in the open air (with a privacy screen), utilizing solar-heated water bottles. Guests share a pool, a barbecue and a lounge with a view. Full breakfast is available for US$5.75, sandwiches for half that. Rates are US$30/35 for singles/doubles. As there are only five cottages, advance reservations are usually essential – German and French are spoken.

Willard's of Saba (☎ 62498, fax 62482) is a small American-run luxury hotel with a scenic cliffside location and seven attractive rooms. There's a hot tub, a large heated lap pool, a tennis court and an upmarket restaurant. The least expensive room, which lacks a balcony, begins in summer at US$150/200 for singles/doubles, while the top-priced 'Room in the Sky,' a honeymoon suite with splendid 180° views, costs US$400. Winter rates are US$50 to US$100 higher.

Places to Eat

Caribake, a bakery tucked behind the tourist office, is open from 7 am to 3 pm Monday to Friday, to noon on Saturday. The specialty is the pastries, which include Danish, turnovers and huge cinnamon-raisin rolls, all under US$2. Coffee is available and there are tables on the porch where you can sit and eat. At lunchtime, there are also deli sandwiches, kosher hot dogs and pizza and quiche slices.

Another good-value spot is *Tropics Cafe* (☎ 62469), next to the pool at Juliana's. Tasty tropical-flavored muffins cost a mere US$1. Breakfasts such as French toast or an omelet with coffee, as well as lunchtime burgers with fries, average US$6. They'll also prepare sandwich-and-fruit box lunches for US$5. It's open 7 to 9:30 am

daily and from noon to 2:30 pm Monday to Saturday.

Guido's (☎ 62230) is the Windwardside party place, serving as the island's pool hall during the week and a disco on weekends. Guido's has burgers with fries for US$5.50 and pizzas from US$7.50. It's open for dinner only, from 6 to 10 pm Monday to Thursday, to 9 pm on Friday and Saturday when the dancing starts.

Scout's Place (☎ 62205) has nice views, good straightforward food and generous servings. At lunch, sandwiches cost US$5.50, while hot dishes, including fresh fish or goat stew, are US$13. Reservations are required for dinner, which starts at 7:30 pm and is a set three-course meal, usually priced at US$17. The bar is a popular drinking hole.

Brigadoon (☎ 62380) has pleasant alfresco dining and good food with tasty homemade sauces. Salads and starters begin around US$5, while main dishes such as snapper in spicy Creole sauce, curry-coconut grilled shrimp or Jamaican jerk chicken cost US$12 to US$16. Desserts include a delicious key lime pie. It's open for dinner daily from 6:30 pm.

Captain's Quarters (☎ 62201) has cliffside, oceanview dining and some good deals. On Fridays there's a three-course curry dinner for US$15 and on Saturdays a poolside barbecue featuring a choice of grilled chicken, ribs or local fish for US$12 to US$15. On Monday and Wednesday evenings there's a menu of fish, lobster and meat dishes. Dinner is served from 6:30 to 8:30 pm. Full breakfasts (US$9) are served daily from 7:30 to 9:30 am.

Big Rock Market, Saba's largest grocery store, has beer, wine and a wide selection of food items. It's open from 8 am to noon and 2 to 6 pm Monday to Saturday.

ST JOHN'S

The road from Windwardside to The Bottom passes by the village of St John's. The most notable site along the way is the roadside plaque to Josephus Lambert Hassell, the man responsible for constructing the island's road, a nearby section of which bears a striking resemblance to China's Great Wall.

St John's has Saba's only school, which provides all island children with primary and secondary education.

There is a lovely view of The Bottom as you drive down from St John's. The trailhead for the Crispeen Track begins at the side of the main road 500 meters before reaching The Bottom. This rural track leads to Windwardside, connecting with the Mt Scenery trail after about an hour.

THE BOTTOM

The Bottom, on a 250-meter plateau surrounded by hills, is the island's lowest town. It's also Saba's administrative center.

As you first enter The Bottom you'll come upon the Department of Public Works, a quaint former schoolhouse flanked by three-meter-high night-blooming cacti that give off a wonderful fragrance in the evening. On the next corner is the Anglican church, a picturesque stone structure more than 200 years old. The church is followed by the police and fire station, in front of which you'll find a bell that was rung every hour on the hour until just a few years ago.

The Bottom also has a couple of cobblestone streets lined with old stone walls, a public library and the island's government offices.

The attractive 'governor's house' (actually home to the lieutenant governor) is on the left as you leave The Bottom for Well's Bay. The gate is marked with orange balls, for the House of Orange, which rules the Netherlands.

Information

The post office and the phone company (Antelecom) are at the government center; both are open from 8 am to noon and 1 to 5 pm Monday to Friday.

Saba's small rural hospital is at the northwest end of the village.

Places to Stay

Cranston's Antique Inn (☎ 63203, fax 63469) is an old-fashioned and neglected inn in the center of town. It has six rooms,

hardwood floors, a smattering of antiques and a pool. A couple of the rooms have private baths – the others share a bath. There are no fans or screens and some windows have broken panes. Singles/doubles cost US$44/58.

Midtown Apartments (☎ /fax 63263), above the grocery store, has nine modern apartments with full kitchens, cable TV and air-con. They're a good value, with doubles costing US$60/75 in summer/winter, but like most rental apartments in The Bottom they are usually booked solid with students from the medical school.

Queen's Gardens Resort (☎ 63494, fax 63495; in the USA ☎ 800-599-9407), PO Box 4, is a new 12-unit luxury condo resort in a verdant setting 800 meters east of town. The units are pleasant with cable TV, phone, four-poster beds, a fully equipped kitchen and a separate living room. In addition, the one- and two-bedroom units have a veranda jacuzzi with a view. The facility has a fitness center, a tennis court and a well-regarded restaurant. In summer, studios cost US$128, one-bedroom apartments US$170 and two-bedroom units US$255. In winter they cost US$150/200/300, respectively. Rates include breakfast for two.

Places to Eat

The Bottom has a few eateries serving local food in simple surroundings. The largest is the *Sunset Bar & Restaurant*, which has reasonably priced sandwiches and goat and chicken dishes, and is open for lunch and dinner.

My Store, immediately south of the government center, is a well-stocked grocery store that sells fresh pastries from Windwardside's bakery. It's open from 8 am to noon and 2 to 6:30 pm Monday to Saturday.

Mango Royale at Queen's Gardens Resort is the trendiest restaurant in Saba. Lunch is reasonably priced, with Greek and Caesar salads or barbecue chicken for under US$10. At dinner, chef Michael Sylva of Boston makes an unbeatable goat and black bean burrito (US$9), while main dishes such as chicken breast in lobster sauce or kingfish with cilantro butter average US$19. It's open for lunch from noon to 2:30 pm and for dinner from 6:30 pm.

LADDER BAY

Before Fort Bay was enlarged as a port, Saba's supplies were commonly unloaded at Ladder Bay. They were then hauled up to The Bottom via the Ladder, a series of hundreds of steps hewn into the rock. Everything from building materials and school books to a Steinway piano entered the island via the Ladder.

These days there's not much at Ladder Bay, other than an abandoned customs house and the coastal views, but the curious can still walk the route, which takes about half an hour down and a bit longer back up. The road to the bay leads steeply downhill to the left after the last house in The Bottom, not far from Nicholson's store.

FORT BAY

The main road continues south from The Bottom to Fort Bay, the island's commercial port. This winding section of road, which is 1.2km long, leads down through dry terrain punctuated by Turk's-head cacti. Fort Bay has dive shops, the marine park office, the island's power station, a water desalination plant and Saba's only gas station.

The Saba Marine Park office has a few brochures to give away and sells marine park logo T-shirts and books on diving. The office is usually open weekdays from 8 am to noon and 1 to 5 pm and on Saturday morning. The region's only hyperbaric facility is also at Fort Bay.

While there's no beach at Fort Bay, it's possible to join the local kids swimming at the pier – there's even a shower.

Places to Eat

In Two Deep, a cozy little restaurant and bar above the Saba Deep dive shop, has reasonably priced breakfasts and lunchtime sandwiches and salads.

There's also a snack shop, *Pop's Place* (Pop's motto: 'cold beer and warm conver-sation'), which sells hot dogs, soda and ice-cold beer.

WELL'S BAY

Saba's newest stretch of road runs from The Bottom to Well's Bay, where it terminates at the island's only beach. Just before the road itself nose-dives for Well's Bay there's a fine view of the coast that invites you to pull over for a snapshot.

The beach at Well's Bay has a small patch of chocolate-colored sand, though the amount of sand varies with the season, with the best conditions in summer. The shoreline is generally quite rocky. Those thinking of sunbathing might pause to look up at the cliffs towering above the beach – an eroding conglomerate of sand and boulders with many rocks hanging precariously directly overhead.

The bay, which is part of the Saba Marine Park, offers good swimming and snorkeling. You can find some coral-encrusted rocks in shallow waters along the north side of the bay, but the best snorkeling is near **Torrens Point** at the northeast end of the bay, about a 15-minute swim from the beach. About 50 meters short of the point a partially emerged sea tunnel cuts through the rock leading to deeper waters where there's good coral, schools of larger fish and an occasional sea turtle and nurse shark.

Off Torrens Point is glistening **Diamond Rock**, the tip of an underwater pinnacle and a bird nesting site. All that glitters, in this case, is simply guano.

There are no facilities at Well's Bay and you should bring water.

COVE BAY

Although the waters off Saba's east coast are often turbulent, Cove Bay, near the airport, has a little boulder-protected pool that provides a safe spot for cooling off on a hot day. The bay is reached after a five-minute walk along the side road that begins just outside the terminal.

Along the road into Cove Bay there's a signposted trail that begins at an old leather factory (it's now a classroom for medical

SABA

students) and goes out along coastal bluffs to some nice tidal pools at **Flat Point**, behind the airport. The hike takes about 15 minutes one way.

Situated to the south of Cove Bay is **Spring Bay**, which was named after a freshwater spring and was the site of an Arawak settlement.

St Barthélemy (St Barts)

St Barthélemy, more commonly called St Barts, is the smallest of the French West Indies, a mere 10km long and at its widest just 4km across.

St Barts has lovely beaches and a relaxed pace. The island is hilly and dry, with a landscape that includes rock-strewn pastures, deeply indented bays and villages of trim white houses with red-tiled roofs. There's such a quintessential French flavor to the place that it's easy to forget you're in the Caribbean and to instead imagine little St Barts as some Mediterranean isle off the

coast of France. The architecture, lifestyle, culture and food are all solidly French.

St Barts' low-key character has long appealed to wealthy escapists. Decades ago the Rockefellers and Rothschilds built estates here and in more recent times the island has become a chic destination for the well-heeled, attracting royalty, rock stars and Hollywood celebrities.

Although the island has a reputation for being an expensive destination, it's possible to get by in reasonable comfort on a moderate budget. St Barts can also be visited inexpensively as a day trip aboard one of several catamaran shuttles from St Martin.

HIGHLIGHTS

- Classy French ambiance, fine restaurants and upscale hotels
- Day tripping in quaint Gustavia
- Lovely, secluded beach of Anse de Colombier and the scenic coastal hike leading to it
- Windsurfing at Grand Cul-de-Sac and St Jean

Facts about St Barts

HISTORY

In pre-contact times, Carib Indians made fishing expeditions to St Barts but the absence of a reliable freshwater source on the island hindered the establishment of permanent Amerindian settlements. During his second New World voyage in 1493, Christopher Columbus sighted the island and named it after his brother Bartholomew.

The first European attempt to settle the island was not until 1648, when a party of French colonists arrived from St Kitts. After Caribs raided the island in 1656 and massacred the entire colony, St Barts was abandoned. In 1673 Huguenots from Normandy and Brittany established the first permanent settlement. The island's prosperity didn't come from fishing and farming, however, but from the booty captured by French buccaneers who used St Barts as a base for their raids on Spanish galleons.

Conditions on arid St Barts didn't favor the development of sugar plantations, so unlike other Caribbean islands where large numbers of slaves were brought in, the population remained predominantly European.

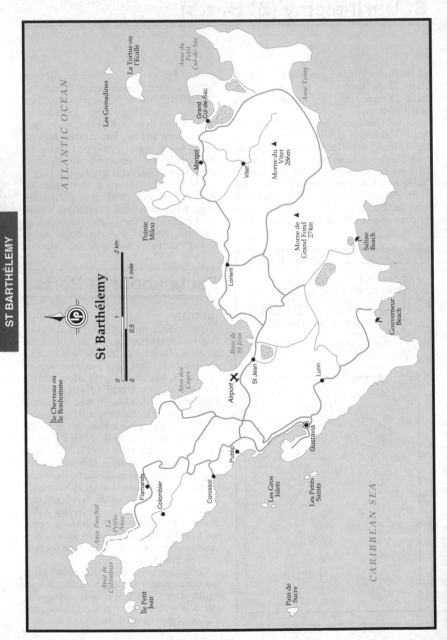

In 1784, King Louis XVI ceded the island to his friend King Gustaf III of Sweden in exchange for trading rights in the Swedish port of Gothenburg. The Swedes changed the name of St Barts' port from Carenage to Gustavia, built a town hall and constructed three small forts named Gustaf, Octave and Karl. Hoping to make money on their new outpost, the Swedes turned St Barts into a duty-free port and by 1800 the population had swelled to 6000.

In 1852 a catastrophic fire swept across much of Gustavia. By this time a change in European-American trade routes had led to a decline in both trade and population and most of the city was not rebuilt. In 1878 the Swedes, anxious to cut their losses on St Barts, sold the island back to France for the sum of 320,000F. Although today St Barts is decidedly French, traces of the Swedish era still remain in the form of a few period buildings and Swedish street names, and in the island's duty-free status.

GEOGRAPHY
St Barts' total land area is a mere 21 sq km, although its elongated shape and hilly terrain make it seem larger. The island lies 25km southeast of St Martin.

St Barts has numerous dry and rocky offshore islets. The largest, Île Fourchue, is a half-sunken volcanic crater whose large bay is a popular yacht anchorage and a destination for divers and snorkelers.

CLIMATE
The island is dry; the temperature averages 26°C (79°F) in the winter, 28°C (82°F) in the summer. The water temperature averages about one degree warmer than the air temperature.

FLORA & FAUNA
St Barts has an arid climate with dryland flora such as cacti and bougainvillea. Local reptiles include lizards, iguanas and harmless grass snakes. From April to August sea turtles lay eggs along the beaches on the northwest side of the island. The numerous islets off St Barts support seabird colonies, including those of frigatebirds.

GOVERNMENT & POLITICS
St Barts, together with St Martin, is a sub-prefecture of Guadeloupe, which in turn is an overseas department of France. While the sub-prefect resides in St Martin, St Barts has its own mayor who is responsible for administering local affairs.

ECONOMY
Some islanders still make a living from fishing, but tourism is the mainstay of the economy these days. St Barts gets about 160,000 visitors annually; more than half of them come by boat, mostly on day trips from St Martin. In winter the majority of visitors come from the USA, in the summer from France.

POPULATION & PEOPLE
St Barts has a population of nearly 5000. While most native islanders trace their roots to the 17th-century Norman and Breton settlers, the island is also home to the descendants of latter-day Swedish merchants and more recent arrivals from mainland France.

Iguana

SOCIETY & CONDUCT

The island's culture is very French, with a rural character that's manifested in the local dialect, the architecture and the slow-paced lifestyle of the islanders.

Dos & Don'ts

Although topless bathing is de rigueur, nudity is officially banned on St Barts. Still, on some of the more secluded beaches, such as Saline, the restriction is not strictly adhered to.

While the island has some very exclusive restaurants, jackets and ties are not required for dining.

RELIGION

Catholicism is the dominant religion. There are Roman Catholic churches in Gustavia and Lorient and an Anglican church in Gustavia.

LANGUAGE

French is the official language, although the type spoken by many islanders is heavily influenced by the old Norman dialect of their ancestors.

Many people speak some English, particularly those in hotels and restaurants. A French-English dictionary and phrasebook will come in handy, but a working knowledge of French is not essential.

Facts for the Visitor

ORIENTATION

The airport is at the western end of St Jean, just a kilometer from Gustavia. As there aren't many roads on the island and most destinations are signposted, it isn't difficult to find your way around.

Maps

There are free tourist maps of the island that are suitable for most purposes. If you want something more detailed, there's the Institut Géographique National's Serie Bleue map 4608-G (1:25,000), which includes St Martin and St Barts and shows both roads and topography.

TOURIST OFFICES

The St Barts Tourist Office (☎ 27 87 27, fax 27 74 47) is on the harborfront in Gustavia at Quai du Général de Gaulle. When requesting information by mail, write to: Office Municipal du Tourisme, Gustavia, 97133 St Barthélemy, French West Indies.

Tourist representatives abroad are listed under Tourist Offices in the Facts for the Visitor section of the Guadeloupe chapter.

VISAS & DOCUMENTS

US and Canadian citizens can stay up to three weeks by showing proof of citizenship in the form of a current passport, an expired (up to five years) passport, or an official birth certificate accompanied by a driver's license or other government-authorized photo ID. Citizens of the EU need an official identity card, valid passport or French *carte de séjour*. Citizens of most other foreign countries, including Australia, need both a valid passport and a visa for France.

A roundtrip or onward ticket is officially required of visitors.

CUSTOMS

St Barts is a duty-free port and there are no restrictions on items brought in for personal use.

MONEY

The French franc is the official currency and most transactions on St Barts are calculated in francs. US dollars are readily accepted everywhere, though each shop sets its own exchange rate, so if you're going to be on the island any length of time you'll probably be better off paying in francs. Major credit cards are widely accepted in shops and at most hotels and restaurants.

More information can be found under Money in the introductory Facts for the Visitor chapter.

POST & COMMUNICATIONS
Post
There are post offices in Gustavia, St Jean and Lorient. It costs 3F to send a postcard (or lightweight letter) to France, 3.80F to the USA and the Caribbean, 4.40F to other places in the Americas and 5.20F to the rest of the world.

To address mail to the island, follow the business name (and the post office box number – BP – when there is one) with the town or beach name and '97133 St Barthélemy, French West Indies.'

Telephone
Almost all pay phones are card phones. Phonecards, called *télécartes*, are sold at post offices and some shops.

If you're calling within St Barts or from Guadeloupe or French St Martin, dial the six-digit local number. If you're calling from outside these areas, add the area code 0590 in front of the six-digit local number.

More information can be found under Post & Communications in the introductory Facts for the Visitor chapter.

The area code for St Barts is 0590.

NEWSPAPERS & MAGAZINES
The free monthly *St-Barth Magazine* newspaper has local news in French and tourist information in both French and English. *Le Journal de St Barth* is a free weekly newspaper in French that's published on Wednesday.

Discover Saint Barthélemy and *Tropical St Barth* are substantial glossy magazines with history and destination articles, as well as ads for shops, restaurants and hotels. Both are published annually and distributed free by the tourist office.

RADIO & TV
There are two radio stations: Radio St-Barth at 98 FM and Radio Transat at 100.3 FM. As there's currently no cable network, TV on St Barts is limited to a couple of channels from Guadeloupe, except for places with satellite dishes.

ELECTRICITY
The electric current is 220 volts AC, 50/60 cycles. Many hotels have dual voltage (110/220) shaver adapters.

WEIGHTS & MEASURES
St Barts uses the metric system and the 24-hour clock.

HEALTH
There's a small medical facility, Bruyn Hospital (☎ 27 60 35), in Gustavia, and there are pharmacies in Gustavia and St Jean.

DANGERS & ANNOYANCES
St Barts has very little crime, and no unusual safety precautions are necessary.

EMERGENCIES
For police emergencies dial ☎ 27 60 12.

BUSINESS HOURS
While business hours vary, offices and shops are generally open weekdays from about 8 am to 5 pm, with most taking a lunchtime siesta. Note that many places shut down completely on Wednesday afternoon.

Banking hours are from 8 am to noon and 2 to 3:30 pm Monday to Friday.

PUBLIC HOLIDAYS & SPECIAL EVENTS
Public holidays on St Barts are:

New Year's Day	January 1
Easter Sunday	late March/early April
Easter Monday	late March/early April
Labor Day	May 1
Ascension Thursday	40th day after Easter
Pentecost Monday	seventh Sunday after Easter
Bastille Day	July 14
Assumption Day	August 15
All Saints Day	November 1
All Souls Day	November 2
Armistice Day	November 11
Christmas Day	December 25

ST BARTHÉLEMY

A number of festivals are celebrated on St Barts throughout the year. The St Barth Music Festival, in mid-January, features two weeks of jazz, chamber music and dance performances.

Carnival is held for five days before Lent and includes a pageant, costumes and street dancing, ending with the burning of a King Carnival figure at Shell Beach, Gustavia. Many businesses close during Carnival.

Festival of St Barthélemy, celebrated on August 24, the feast day of the island's patron saint, includes fireworks, a public ball, boat races and other competitions.

St Barts is the setting for several regattas including St Barth's Cup, a three-day yachting race sponsored by the St Barth's Yacht Club, held in late January; St Barth Regatta, a colorful four-day regatta in mid-February; and International Regatta of St Barthélemy, held for three days in mid-May. There's also a biennial transatlantic race, the Transat AG2R, that leaves Lorient, France, in mid-April in even-numbered years.

ACTIVITIES
Beaches & Swimming
St Barts, with its numerous bays and coves, boasts nearly two dozen beaches. For 'in-town' beaches, St Jean, Flamands, Lorient and Shell Beach all have beautiful sandy strands. For more secluded spots, Colombier, Saline and Gouverneur beaches are all fine choices.

Diving
The most popular diving spots are off the islets surrounding St Barts, which are rich in marine life and coral.

Two of the largest dive shops are West Indies Dive at Marine Service (☎ 27 70 34, fax 27 70 36) and La Bulle (☎ 27 62 25, fax 27 68 93) at the Océan Must Marina, both at La Pointe in Gustavia. Single dives average 250F; for beginners, there are three-day open-water certification courses for 2400F.

Snorkeling
Popular snorkeling spots include Anse de Colombier, La Petite Anse and Lorient.

For snorkel/sail day trips see Organized Tours in the Getting Around section of this chapter.

Snorkeling gear can be rented for 75F a day from Marine Service (☎ 27 70 34) in Gustavia.

Windsurfing
Grand Cul-de-Sac, the main windsurfing center, has a large protected bay that's ideal for beginners and some nice wave action beyond the reef good for advanced windsurfers. Wind Wave Power (☎ 27 82 57) at St Barts Beach Hotel in Grand Cul-de-Sac gives 1½-hour windsurfing lessons for 380F and rents equipment for 130F an hour.

There's also good windsurfing at St Jean, where the St Barth Bic Center (☎ 27 71 22) rents beginners' equipment from 100/300F per hour/day. Lessons cost 245F an hour for one person, 360F for two people.

Surfing
The main surfing spots are at Lorient, Anse des Cayes and Anse Toiny. Hookipa Surf Shop (☎ 27 71 31) in St Jean rents surfboards and bodyboards for 120F a day.

Fishing
Tuna, dorado, marlin and wahoo are caught in the waters off St Barts. Marine Service (☎ 27 70 34), a member of the Big Game Fishing Club of France, can arrange charter boats for deep-sea fishing. The cost is 4100F for a full day with drinks and lunch, 2600F for a half day.

Horseback Riding
Ranch de Flamands (☎ 27 80 72) offers two-hour excursions for beginning and experienced riders for 235F, departing most days at 3:30 pm.

ACCOMMODATIONS
Accommodations on St Barts are all small scale. The island has about 40 hotels, with a combined capacity of only 650 rooms. Virtually all are in the moderate to high range; there are none of the local-style guesthouses that shore up the bottom range on many other Caribbean islands.

Some hotels set prices in US dollars, others set them in French francs. As the exchange rate between the two currencies can fluctuate rather substantially, we've listed rates in the currency quoted by each hotel.

Most hotels include the tax and service charge in their quoted rates, although a few places add 5% to 10% onto the bill.

Villas
In addition to hotels, St Barts has numerous villas for rent. The biggest agent is Sibarth (☎ 27 62 38, fax 27 60 52, email 105062.1516@compuserve.com), BP 55, on Rue du Général de Gaulle in Gustavia, which handles around 200 villas and apartments. Weekly rates range from US$900/1200 in summer/winter for a one-bedroom apartment to US$10,000/20,000 for a five-bedroom five-bath villa with a pool.

Sibarth's representative in the USA is WIMCO (☎ 401-849-8012, 800-932-3222; fax 401-847-6290). In France, Sibarth can be reached toll free at ☎ 0800 90 16 20; in the UK at ☎ 0800-89-8318; in Germany at ☎ 01 30 81 57 30.

FOOD
St Barts has many fine French restaurants and if money is no object you can eat very well indeed. There are also moderately priced places to eat but as most of the island's food is imported the only inexpensive options are pretty much limited to grocery stores and bakeries.

DRINKS
St Barts lacks a freshwater source. The island has a desalination plant but water prices are so high that many places maintain their own rainwater catchment systems. If your tap water is from catchment, the best policy is to boil it before drinking. You can buy bottled water at grocery stores.

Wine is the drink of choice on St Barts and French wines and champagnes can be purchased from grocery stores around the island at duty-free prices, which make them one of the best buys to be found on St Barts. Restaurants generally have extensive wine lists, although their prices are much higher.

ENTERTAINMENT
In terms of entertainment on St Barts, an evening out is most commonly a dinner affair. However, there are a few places where you can find dancing; for the latest in entertainment information, pick up a copy of *St-Barth Magazine*.

THINGS TO BUY
There are plenty of shops in Gustavia selling duty-free perfumes, French and Italian designer clothing, Swiss watches and jewelry. L'Carré d'Or, a shopping complex on Rue de la République, has the largest collection of quality shops.

The most traditional island-made crafts are the straw products from the lantania palm made and sold in the village of Corossol.

Getting There & Away

AIR
The landing strip at St Barts can't handle anything larger than 20-seater STOL aircraft and is not equipped for night landings. While there are no long-distance direct flights to St Barts, there are frequent

ST BARTHÉLEMY

flights from the islands of St Martin and Guadeloupe.

Air Caraïbes (☎ 27 99 41) flies to St Barts twice daily from Guadeloupe with 'superpromo' fares of 404F one way, 798F roundtrip. It also flies a couple of times a day between French St Martin and St Barts for 250F one way, 450F roundtrip.

Air Guadeloupe (☎ 27 64 44) flies to St Barts a few times daily from both French and Dutch St Martin for 264F one way, 528F roundtrip, and from Guadeloupe to St Barts from 500F one way.

Air Saint-Barthélemy (☎ 27 71 90) flies to St Barts daily from Guadeloupe and from both French and Dutch St Martin. The fare from Guadeloupe is 574F one way, 888F roundtrip. From French or Dutch St Martin the fare is 269F one way, 528F roundtrip.

Winair (☎ 27 61 01) flies to St Barts a few times a day from Dutch St Martin, targeting day trippers. The flight costs US$58 one way or US$78 on a same-day excursion. Winair also flies on Tuesday and Thursday between Saba and St Barts for US$78 one way and US$109 for a same-day excursion.

Airport Information

St Barts' modest airport terminal has a liquor store, a small gift shop and a magazine stand that sells a few English-language newspapers.

SEA
Inter-Island Ferries

There's regular boat service between St Martin and St Barts. As the seas can be a bit choppy, all of the companies use stable catamaran-type boats.

The main company is *Voyager* (☎ 87 10 68 in Marigot, 24096 in Philipsburg, 27 77 24 in Gustavia), which has two modern high-speed boats. One leaves daily from Marigot at 9 am and 5:45 pm for the 1½-hour journey; it departs from Gustavia at 7:15 am and 4 pm. The second boat leaves from Bobby's Marina in Philipsburg at 8:30 am and returns from Gustavia in the late afternoon daily

except Thursday and Saturday. The cost is US$50 roundtrip.

A couple of other boats ply between Dutch St Maarten and Gustavia a few times a week. *The Edge* (☎ 42640), a high-speed catamaran that departs from Pelican Marina on Simpson Bay and takes just 45 minutes, charges US$50. *Quicksilver* (☎ 22869), a more leisurely motorized catamaran with sails, departs from Great Bay Marina in Philipsburg, takes about 1½ hours and commonly cuts its rate to US$40 or less.

Yacht

Those arriving by yacht can clear immigration at the port office (VHF: 16 or 10) on the east side of the Gustavia Harbor. In the high season, it's open from 7 am to 6 pm Monday to Saturday, 9 am to noon on Sunday. In the low season, it's open from 7:30 am to 12:30 pm and 2:30 to 5:30 pm Monday to Saturday only.

Gustavia Harbor has mooring and docking facilities for about 40 yachts. Popular anchorages can be found up the coast at Public, Corossol and Colombier.

LEAVING ST BARTS

St Barts has a US$7 passenger tax that's generally added onto the air or boat fare when you purchase your ticket.

Getting Around

St Barts has no public bus system so hiring a vehicle is essential to thoroughly explore the island.

THE AIRPORT

Many hotels will provide free transportation from the airport with advance notice. There are usually taxis parked in front of the airport, though occasionally it's necessary to wait a few minutes for one to show.

TAXI

In addition to the taxi terminal at the airport, there's one in Gustavia near the tourist office. To call for a taxi dial ☎ 27 66 31.

A taxi from the airport to either St Jean or Gustavia costs about US$8. For US$40 day trippers can get a one-hour tour of the island, be dropped off at a beach or in town and be picked up at a prearranged time and driven back to the airport.

CAR & MOTORCYCLE

The most popular rental vehicle on the island is the open-air Mini Moke, although small cars can be rented for about the same price. Scooters and motorcycles are also available; however, this option is best suited to experienced motorcycle drivers as the island's roads have a cement surface that can get slippery when wet and many roads are narrow, winding and steep. There are two gas stations on St Barts: one opposite the airport and the other in Lorient.

Road Rules

Drive on the right. Your home driver's license is valid in St Barts. The speed limit is 45 km/h unless otherwise posted.

Rental

A dozen car rental companies have booths at the airport, including Hertz, Avis, Budget and Europcar/National. Cars can also be rented from most hotels and in Gustavia. There's a lot of competition and prices fluctuate but in summer you can generally get a Mini Moke or a small car for about US$35 per day, in winter for about US$50.

Chez Beranger (☎ 27 89 00) on Rue du Général de Gaulle in Gustavia rents motor scooters for US$25, motorcycles (125cc and 175cc) for US$30 and cars for US$40.

HITCHHIKING

Hitchhiking is legal and common on St Barts. The usual safety precautions apply.

ORGANIZED TOURS
Sightseeing Tours

The tourist office organizes minibus tours that depart from its Gustavia office. There's a 45-minute tour (150F) of the western side of St Barts, an hour tour (200F) of the eastern side and a 90-minute tour (250F) of the whole island. The cost covers up to three people; add 50F for more than three.

Sailing/Snorkeling Tours

Marine Service (☎ 27 70 34) offers a full-day sail aboard the catamaran *Ne Me Quitte Pas* that takes in Île Fourchue and Anse de Colombier for 480F; snorkel gear is included, as is an open bar and lunch. Marine Service also has a half-day snorkel sail to Anse de Colombier for 290F and a 1½-hour sunset sail for 230F.

Océan Must Marina (☎ 27 62 25) in Gustavia also offers sailing and snorkeling cruises.

Gustavia

Gustavia, the island's capital and main port, is an appealing horseshoe-shaped town built up around a deep harbor. It has streetside cafés where day visitors linger the afternoon away, a couple of historic sites worth a stroll and a nice beach within walking distance. As Gustavia is a duty-free port, there are also numerous jewelry shops and exclusive boutiques, with the highest concentration along the Rue de la République.

The old *mairie* (town hall), built during the Swedish period, is at the end of Rue Couturier. There's a small fruit and vegetable market 100 meters east of the mairie and adjacent to that is a little war memorial. As you walk around, you'll notice that some of the street signs in this neighborhood still bear Swedish names, ending in the suffix '-gaten.'

At the inner harbor, in the area around Rue du Centenaire, you'll find a stone Anglican church dating from 1855 and the town's landmark Swedish tower, which houses an antique clock that is still hand-wound daily.

Information

Tourist Office The helpful tourist office (☎ 27 87 27) is on the east side of the harbor at Quai du Général de Gaulle. In summer

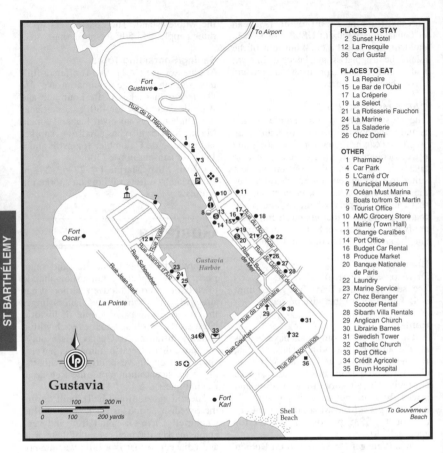

ST BARTHÉLEMY

PLACES TO STAY
2 Sunset Hotel
12 La Presquile
36 Carl Gustaf

PLACES TO EAT
3 La Repaire
15 Le Bar de l'Oubil
17 La Créperie
19 La Select
21 La Rotisserie Fauchon
24 La Marine
25 La Saladerie
26 Chez Domi

OTHER
1 Pharmacy
4 Car Park
5 L'Carré d'Or
6 Municipal Museum
7 Océan Must Marina
8 Boats to/from St Martin
9 Tourist Office
10 AMC Grocery Store
11 Mairie (Town Hall)
13 Change Caraïbes
14 Port Office
16 Budget Car Rental
18 Produce Market
20 Banque Nationale
    de Paris
22 Laundry
23 Marine Service
27 Chez Beranger
    Scooter Rental
28 Sibarth Villa Rentals
29 Anglican Church
30 Librairie Barnes
31 Swedish Tower
32 Catholic Church
33 Post Office
34 Crédit Agricole
35 Bruyn Hospital

Gustavia

Fort Gustave

Fort Oscar

Fort Karl

Gustavia Harbor

La Pointe

Shell Beach

To Airport

To Gouverneur Beach

Rue de la République

Rue du Roi Oscar II

Rue de Centenaire

Rue de Général de Gaulle

Rue de Bord de Mer

Rue Jeanne d'Arc

Rue Aralien

Rue Sadocleher

Rue Jean Bart

Rue Courbet

Rue des Normands

0   100   200 m
0   100   200 yards

the office is open from 8:30 am to 12:30 pm Monday to Friday, from 9 to 11 am on Saturday; in winter it opens half an hour earlier.

Money You can change money at Change Caraïbes on Rue de la République or Crédit Agricole on Rue Jeanne d'Arc. Crédit Agricole has a 24-hour automatic money exchange dispenser that can convert major currencies to French francs or US dollars, as well as a standard ATM. If you need a full-service bank, there's a branch of the Banque Nationale de Paris on Rue du Bord de Mer.

Post The Gustavia post office, on the corner of Rue Jeanne d'Arc and Rue du Centenaire, is open from 8 am to 3 pm on Monday, Tuesday, Thursday and Friday, and from 8 am to noon on Wednesday and Saturday.

Bookstore Librairie Barnes on Rue Courbet has French-language books and newspapers as well as the English-language *International Herald-Tribune*. It's open from 7:30 am to 5:30 pm Monday to Saturday.

Le Musée de St-Barth

The Municipal Museum of St-Barthélemy, at the northwest side of La Pointe, is a modest but developing museum, established in 1989. On the ground floor of an atmospheric stone warehouse, it has period photo exhibits, engravings and some simple displays that give a glimpse into the island's history. It's open from 8:30 am to 12:30 pm and 2:30 to 5:30 pm on weekdays, from 8:30 to 11 am on Saturday. Admission is 10F.

Shell Beach

Shell Beach, the common name for Anse de Grand Galet, is a nice sandy beach with a shoreline packed high with tiny shells. Only a 10-minute walk from the harbor, the beach makes a fine swimming spot.

To get there go south on Rue Gambetta, turn right, go past the Catholic church and continue on that road until you reach the beach.

Fort Gustave

The site of old Fort Gustave has a couple of cannons and a mild-bottle-shaped lighthouse, but most people come here for the fine view of Gustavia and the harbor. An interpretive plaque points out local sights and landmarks. Across the harbor to the south is Fort Oscar, which is still used as a military installation, and on a clear day you can see the islands of St Kitts and St Eustatius.

To get there, take the Gustavia road 700 meters from the airport crossroads and then as the road curves left down to Gustavia, pull off to the right where there's space for a couple of cars. The fort isn't marked, but you'll see a Meteo France sign here. It's just a minute's walk up the hill to the fort.

Places to Stay

La Presquile (☎ 27 64 60, fax 27 72 30), on Rue Avaler in La Pointe, has 12 good-value rooms. While they're not fancy, they're clean and all have refrigerators, air-con and private baths -some also sport nice harbor-view balconies. There's a pleasant young manager and singles/doubles cost a reasonable 220/330F.

Sunset Hotel (☎ 27 77 21, fax 27 81 59), BP 102, Rue de la République, is an unpretentious hotel with eight pleasant rooms, each with air-con, TV, phone, minibar and private bath. From its 3rd-floor balcony there are fine views of the harbor and Gustavia. Singles/doubles cost 330/420F in summer, 480/520F in winter; add another 100F for one of the two larger 'superior' rooms with harbor views.

Carl Gustaf (☎ 27 82 83, fax 27 82 37), Rue des Normands, on a hillside overlooking the harbor, is a modern luxury hotel with 14 suites, each with a VCR, fax, a couple of phones and a private plunge pool. Rates begin at US$350 in the low season, US$680 in the high season.

Places to Eat

La Rotisserie Fauchon on Rue du Roi Oscar II has excellent French pastries, deli items, mini-quiches and rotisserie chicken at moderate prices. It's open daily from 7 am to 7 pm.

The outdoor patio of *Le Select*, on the corner of Rue de France and Rue du Général de Gaulle, is a popular spot to hang out and down a few drinks. Famed as the place where Jimmy Buffett, who once was a part-owner of the bar, wrote *Cheeseburger in Paradise*, it specializes – not surprisingly – in cheeseburgers (US$5), which are available from 10:30 am to 2:30 pm and 6 to 10 pm Monday to Saturday.

The little *La Crêperie* on Rue du Roi Oscar II attracts a crowd with a variety of main-course crêpes and sandwiches from about 25F and dessert crêpes ranging from 14F to 45F. You can also get a continental breakfast with coffee for 35F. It's open from 7 am to 10 pm Monday to Saturday.

Chez Domi, an inviting café on Rue du Général de Gaulle, blends French and West Indian cuisines. Main dishes such as conch stew, octopus with dumplings or fish in Creole sauce average 75F, while salads and appetizers start at 45F. There's also a daily special for around 50F. It's open daily from noon to 3 pm and 6:30 to 10 pm.

Le Repaire, a streetside restaurant opposite the harbor, is open for lunch and dinner, serving grilled steak with fries for 75F, grilled fish for 95F and a range of salads and warm starters from 40F to 80F. It's closed on Sunday.

La Saladerie, a waterfront café on the west side of the harbor, specializes in salads, from simple green for 20F to seafood salad for 68F. There are also pizzas and a few grilled dishes at moderate prices. It's open from noon to 2:30 pm and 7 to 10:30 pm except on Monday.

The nearby *La Marine* (☎ 27 68 91), also on the harborfront, is open for lunch and dinner Monday to Saturday. Burgers and omelets cost 35F to 70F, fish and meat dishes start at around 100F. The restaurant is packed on Thursday nights (reserve early) when they serve mussels (79F) that are flown in from France and prepared in a garlic-wine broth.

Carl Gustaf has an exclusive French restaurant where dinner for two can easily top 1000F.

AMC, a large grocery store on Rue de la République, sells everything from pastries and wine to deli foods. It's open from 8 am to at least 5 pm Monday to Saturday, except for Wednesday when it closes at 1 pm.

Around St Barts

COROSSOL

About 2km northwest of Gustavia is Corossol, one of the island's most traditional fishing villages. The brown-sand beach is lined with blue and orange fishing boats and stacks of lobster traps. Women here still weave the leaves of the lantania palm into straw hats, baskets and place mats, which they line up on the walls in front of their homes to attract buyers.

On the southeast end of the beach, just 50 meters down a dirt road, is the Inter Oceans Museum, a collection of 9000 seashells in the home of Ingénu Magras,

who started the museum half a century ago. It's open from 9 am to noon and 2 to 5 pm Tuesday to Sunday; admission is 20F.

FLAMANDS

Flamands, a small village on the northwestern side of the island, retains a pleasantly rural character. The village stretches along a curving bay whose long, broad white-sand beach and clear waters are popular with beach goers. There's easy beach access with streetside parking at the westernmost end of Flamands Bay.

The peninsula on the west side of the beach separates Flamands from nearby La Petite Anse, where rocky waters afford good snorkeling. To get there, continue west past Flamands for about 200 meters and take the short spur that curves down to the right before the main road reaches a dead end.

Places to Stay & Eat

Auberge de La Petite Anse (☎ 27 64 60, fax 27 72 30), BP 117, has 16 condo-like units above a rocky coastline. It's within walking distance of Flamands Beach and right at the trailhead to Anse de Colombier. Each unit has a bedroom with two beds, a kitchenette, ocean-facing terrace and air-con. Singles/doubles are a reasonable 300/400F in summer, 500/700F in winter.

St-Barth Isle de France (☎ 27 61 81, fax 27 86 83), BP 612, a luxury hotel at the east end of the bay, has 30 spacious rooms and suites that cost from US$300/420 in summer/winter, breakfast included.

Restaurant options are limited. For something quick and cheap, there's *Epicerie Sainte Helen*, a small bakery on the village's main road about 50 meters before the beach.

ANSE DE COLOMBIER

Anse de Colombier is a beautiful, secluded white-sand beach fronted by turquoise waters and backed by undulating hills. It's reached by boat or via a scenic 20-minute walk that begins at the end of the road in La Petite Anse, just beyond Flamands.

The well-trodden trail leads through a fascinating desert-like terrain punctuated by organ pipe cacti and wildflowers. En route it provides some wonderful coastal views of La Petite Anse and the rugged shoreline of Anse Paschal before crossing a ridge and ending at the north side of Colombier Bay, where there are steps leading down to the beach.

The sandy bottom at the beach is ideal for swimming and there's fairly good snorkeling at the north side. Take water, as the trail is unshaded and there are no facilities.

ST JEAN

St Jean, the island's most touristed area, is spread along a large curving bay lined with a white-sand beach.

St Jean has no real center and from the road it can seem like a nondescript strip of small shopping complexes, hotels and restaurants. However, it's quite appealing once you're on the beach, where reef-protected turquoise waters provide good conditions for swimming, snorkeling and windsurfing. The beach is divided into two separate sections by a quartzite hill topped by the picturesque Eden Rock Hotel. The airport is at the west end of St Jean.

Places to Stay

Village St Jean (☎ 27 61 39, fax 27 77 96; in the USA ☎ 800-633-7411), BP 623, is a pleasant family-run hotel five minutes walk uphill from the beach. There are 20 modern cottages with kitchens, air-con, ceiling fans and private terraces. The hotel has a pool with a view of the bay, a jacuzzi and a small 'honor store' with soft drinks and snacks. Standard cottages begin at US$110/160 in summer/winter, deluxe cottages at US$170/265. There are also six hotel rooms, without kitchens but including breakfast, for US$89/140 in summer/winter.

The *Tropical Hotel* (☎ 27 64 87, fax 27 81 74), BP 147, on a hillside a couple of minutes walk from the beach, has 20 rooms with air-con, refrigerators, TV and balconies. Singles/doubles start at US$95/130 in summer, US$185/220 in winter, for gardenview rooms with breakfast. It's closed in June and July.

Emeraude Plage (☎ 27 64 78, fax 27 83 08) is a pleasant beachfront hotel

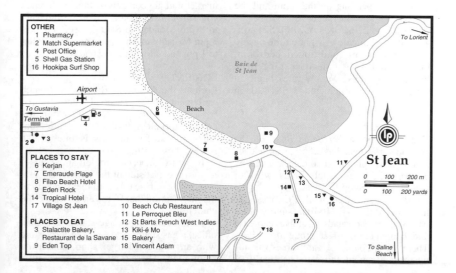

OTHER
1 Pharmacy
2 Match Supermarket
4 Post Office
5 Shell Gas Station
16 Hookipa Surf Shop

Airport
To Lorient
Baie de St Jean
To Gustavia
Terminal
Beach

PLACES TO STAY
6 Kerjan
7 Emeraude Plage
8 Filao Beach Hotel
9 Eden Rock
14 Tropical Hotel
17 Village St Jean

PLACES TO EAT
3 Stalactite Bakery, Restaurant de la Savane
9 Eden Top

10 Beach Club Restaurant
11 Le Perroquet Bleu
12 St Barts French West Indies
13 Kiki-é Mo
15 Bakery
18 Vincent Adam

St Jean

0   100   200 m
0   100   200 yards

To Saline Beach

ST BARTHÉLEMY

landscaped with oleander and hibiscus. It has 24 bungalow-style units, each with a kitchenette that opens onto a terrace, and contains a TV, phone, air-con and ceiling fan. Rates, which vary depending on the size of the bungalow and its proximity to the beach, begin at 650/920F in summer/winter for one-bedroom bungalows.

Filao Beach Hotel (☎ 27 64 84, fax 27 62 24), BP 667, has 30 rooms in one-story duplex buildings. This upmarket hotel has attractive grounds, amiable staff and a nice beachfront location. Rooms are comfortably furnished with a TV, ceiling fan, air-con and a queen or king-sized bed. Rates, which include breakfast, are 1000F to 2200F in the summer, 1800F to 3500F in the winter.

Eden Rock (☎ 27 72 94, fax 27 88 37, edenrock@saintbarts.com), St Barts' first hotel, sits on the rocky promontory that separates the two sandy strands of St Jean Beach. Although the new English owners have modernized the property, many of the 14 rooms still have antique furnishings and a pleasant old-fashioned decor. You can even sleep in the same four-poster bed that Greta Garbo slept in. The only drawback is the price, which ranges from US$220 to US$1040 depending on the room and the season, breakfast included.

Kerjan (☎ 27 62 38, fax 27 60 52) consists of five bungalows right on the beach. Each has an air-conditioned bedroom, kitchen and TV; some have nice little lounging porches. Weekly rates begin at US$950 in summer and US$1800 in winter.

Places to Eat

Town Center *Le Perroquet Bleu*, on the east side of St Jean, has crêpes, sandwiches and other simple fare, and there's a nearby bakery with a few deli items west of Hookipa Surf Shop.

Kikié Mo, in a colorful little roadside hut, has deli-style Italian sandwiches, pastas, antipasto salads, tiramisu, espresso and cappuccino, all at moderate prices. There are a couple of café tables outside where you can sit and eat. The nearby *St Barts French West Indies* has ice cream, sandwiches and cold drinks.

Eden Rock's *Beach Club Restaurant*, with its alfresco waterside dining, is the area's most popular lunch spot. Salads and light fare cost around 80F, while meat, duck and fish main dishes average 100F to 160F. The hotel's *Eden Top* is a fine-dining dinner restaurant with an pleasant balcony setting and expensive continental fare.

Vincent Adam (☎ 27 93 22) features a 190F three-course French dinner with your choice of starter, main dish and dessert selected from a varied menu. Some of the main dishes are filet mignon, hunter's hare and duck rolled in juniper berries. The food is good and there's a tranquil setting overlooking a salt pond. It's open from 7 pm nightly.

Around the Airport *Stalactite*, a bakery opposite the airport terminal, has good croissants, pastries and bread; it's open from 7 am to 1 pm and 3 to 7 pm Monday to Saturday. The adjacent *Restaurant de la Savane* has 20F sandwiches and a 50F salad buffet from noon to 2:15 pm every day but Monday.

In the same center is a large *Match* supermarket with a good deli section and French wines from 15F a bottle. It's open from 8 am to 8 pm Monday to Saturday (closed 1 to 3 pm Monday to Thursday) and from 9 am to 1 pm and 4 to 7 pm on Sunday.

LORIENT

Lorient, the site of St Barts' first French settlement (1648), is a small village fronted by a nice white-sand beach. When it's calm, snorkelers take to the water, but when the surf's up, this is one of the island's best surfing spots.

To get to the beach, turn left at the cemetery on the east side of the village. Be sure you don't confuse this with the cemetery at the intersection that fronts an attractive old church.

Lorient has a postage-stamp-size post office, a gas station and Jojo's grocery store with an attached burger shop, all on the main road. There's an inexpensive little

French-Vietnamese café, *Traiteur Asiatique*, at the south side of the church cemetery.

Places to Stay

The village has two recommendable accommodation options on the inland road within easy walking distance of the beach. The more conventional is *La Normandie Hôtel* (☎ 27 61 66, fax 27 98 83), which has eight pleasant rooms with refrigerators, ceiling fans and air-con from 200/300F for singles/doubles in summer and 250/350F in winter. There's a pool.

Le Manoir (☎ 27 79 27, fax 27 65 75) is a delightful place with accommodations in 17th-century-style cottages surrounding a manor house that was built in Normandy in 1610 and reconstructed here in 1984. The brainstorm of Jeanne Audy-Roland, creator of the 'M' natural cosmetic line, Le Manoir was designed for visiting artists and other like-minded travelers. The cottages are rustic with mosquito nets over the beds, small kitchens and private gardens. Singles/doubles cost 250/450F.

LORIENT TO GRAND CUL-DE-SAC

On the eastern outskirts of Lorient the road climbs up into the hills, offering some fine coastal views. The area encompasses the coastal headland of **Pointe Milou**; the hamlet of **Vitet**, at the foothills of 286-meter Morne du Vitet; and **Marigot**, a little seaside village on a small bay.

Places to Stay & Eat

Hubert Delamotte, a New Age astrologer and chef, operates *Hostellerie des 3 Forces* (☎ 27 61 25, fax 27 81 38) in Vitet. The site has a dozen simple rooms, each named for a sign of the zodiac; all of them have private bathrooms and balconies, mosquito nets and mini-refrigerators. Fan-cooled singles/doubles cost US$65/75 in summer, or US$120/140 in winter. Air-conditioned rooms are about 20% higher. The restaurant serves French and Creole food. Lunch offerings range from omelets (45F) to beef brochette (105F), while dinner features a 230F three-course meal with a choice of seafood, vegetarian or red meat main dishes.

Christopher Hotel (☎ 27 63 63, fax 27 92 92; in the USA ☎ 800-221-4542), BP 571, on Pointe Milou, is an upscale resort with 40 luxurious rooms. Each has an oceanview patio, separate bathtub and shower, silent air-con, ceiling fan, minibar, room safe, TV and phone. While the beach is rocky, the hotel has a large, free-form swimming pool and a fitness center. Rates are from US$240/340 in summer/winter, full breakfast included. For guests staying more than a couple of nights, there are often some good-value package deals that cut the rates by a third. The hotel's seaside restaurant, *L'Orchidée,* offers a three-course dinner of the day for 220F.

GRAND CUL-DE-SAC

Grand Cul-de-Sac has a sandy beach and a reef-protected bay with good water sports conditions. The area attracts an active crowd that includes lots of windsurfers. The beach is along a narrow strip of land that separates the bay from a large salt pond (sand fleas can be a nuisance). Fronting the bay are a couple of hotels and restaurants, along with a windsurfing and water sports center.

Places to Stay

St Barths Beach Hotel (☎ 27 60 70, fax 27 75 27), BP 581, is in fact right on the beach, with 36 rooms in two-story buildings, each with air-con, a balcony, phone, TV and minibar. Rates are pricey at US$121/170 for singles/doubles in summer, US$206/294 in winter.

At the north end of the beach is the *Sereno Beach Hotel* (☎ 27 64 80, fax 27 75 47), BP 19, which has 20 rooms surrounding a central courtyard garden. While each has a TV, small refrigerator, air-con and room safe, the rates are steep, beginning at US$175/300 in summer/winter. There's a pool.

Places to Eat

Le Rivage at St Barths Beach Hotel is a popular restaurant with a fine beachfront setting. Sandwiches start at 40F and main dishes such as Creole chicken or lambi

ST BARTHÉLEMY

begin around 85F. It's open daily from noon to 3 pm and 7 to 10 pm.

The *West Indies Café*, at Sereno Beach Hotel, offers French and Creole food, including seafood salad, curry chicken and grilled salmon for 75F to 100F. It's open daily from noon to 2:30 pm and 7 to 10 pm.

BEYOND GRAND CUL-DE-SAC

From Grand Cul-de-Sac the road makes a curving sweep around the base of the 286-meter Morne du Vitet and the 274-meter Morne de Grand Fond, the island's highest mountains. It's a nice country drive, passing grassy green slopes, handsome stone walls, grazing cows and the occasional farmer, creating a scene that's often compared to rural Normandy.

SALINE BEACH

Anse de Grande Saline is a long lovely beach, broad and secluded, named after the large salt pond that backs it. Stilts and other waterbirds flock to the pond, but so do biting gnats that sometimes can be an obstacle to enjoying the beach. Saline Beach is off the main tourist track but is considered a special place by islanders and return visitors.

The cement road into Saline Beach ends about half a kilometer before the beach, but you can often continue to drive along the south side of the salt pond on a rutted dirt road that will take you within a two-minute walk of the beach.

For an enjoyable lunch *Le Tamarin*, on the way to the beach, has a pleasant setting and offers a melange of good Creole and French food at moderate prices.

GOUVERNEUR BEACH

Anse du Gouverneur is a gorgeous sandy beach lining a U-shaped bay that's embraced by high cliffs at both ends. The beach is broad and secluded and makes a nice spot for sunbathing and picnics. There are no facilities.

To get there from Gustavia, head southeast past the Carl Gustaf hotel. The road becomes increasingly steep until you reach the mountain crest in Lurin, where you turn right and wind down a narrow cement road that will test your brakes (use low gear). There are some spectacular glimpses of the coast en route.

St Eustatius (Statia)

St Eustatius – spelled Sint Eustatius in Dutch and usually called Statia for short – is a tranquil little outpost with an intriguing colonial history. Part of the Netherlands Antilles, the island has interesting historical sites and some good hiking and diving opportunities.

Just a few kilometers wide, Statia is essentially a one-town island, with the airport and a few residential neighborhoods on the town's outskirts.

Although it's only a 20-minute flight from St Martin, Statia is one of the most overlooked destinations in the Leeward Islands, partly because it has none of the tourist-luring beaches that St Martin's closer neighbors boast. Of course the lack of crowds is part of the appeal for travelers who do come this way. In many ways landing in Statia is a bit like stepping back into a niche of the Caribbean from the 1950s – islanders enjoy striking up a conversation, stray chickens and goats mosey in the streets and the pace is delightfully slow. Statia offers a nice, quiet break for those looking to get away from the more touristed islands.

HIGHLIGHTS

- Hiking up to The Quill, Statia's extinct volcano
- Ambling around Oranjestad's colonial sites and historic fort
- Visiting the 18th-century Simon Doncker House, now a superb historical museum

Facts about Statia

HISTORY

The Caribs called the island Alo, which means cashew tree, while Columbus named the island after St Anastasia. Although the French began construction of a fort in 1629, the first permanent settlement was established by the Dutch in 1636 after they routed the small French contingent off the island. Statia subsequently changed hands 22 times between the Dutch, French and British.

In the 18th century, as the British and French buried their colonies in taxes and duties, the Dutch turned Statia into a duty-free port. As a result, West Indian and North American colonies were able to circumvent duties by shipping goods via Statia, which boomed into a thriving entrepôt and a major trade center between the Old and New worlds.

During its heyday in the 1770s, as many as 300 trading ships pulled into port each month and the island's population swelled to 20,000. The resulting prosperity earned Statia the nickname 'Golden Rock of the Caribbean.'

Many of the goods destined for the rebellious North American colonies passed

353

through Statia. Along with 'legal' cargoes of molasses and slaves, the merchant ships sailing from Statia also smuggled in arms and gunpowder to New England, much to the ire of British officials, whose protest to the mercantile Dutch drew little response.

One event that particularly irritated the British took place on November 16, 1776, when Statia, rather inadvertently, became the first foreign land to recognize the American colonies' Declaration of Independence by returning a cannon salute to the passing American war brig *Andrew*

Doria. Unfortunately for Statia, another American vessel went on to capture a British ship in nearby waters, adding an element of significance to the gesture.

In 1781, British admiral George Rodney settled the score by launching a naval attack on Statia, ransacking the warehouses, exiling the island's merchants and auctioning off their goods. The Dutch regained possession of the island a few years later but the British invasion marked the end of Statia's predominance as a trade center.

Ironically, US independence, and the signing of a peace treaty between the USA and Britain in 1783, allowed the former American colonies to establish more direct trade routes and bypass Statia altogether. To this day Statia remains well off the beaten path.

GEOGRAPHY

St Eustatius is 8km long and 3km wide, with 21 sq km of land. The island is 61km south of St Martin and 27km southeast of Saba.

The Quill (whose name is derived from the Dutch word *kwil*, meaning volcano) looms above the southern half of the island. This extinct volcano, which reaches 600 meters at Mazinga, the highest point on the rim, is responsible for the high conical appearance Statia has when viewed from neighboring islands.

Cliffs drop straight to the sea along much of the shoreline and the island has precious few beaches. At the north side of Statia there are a few low mountains, while the island's central plain contains the airport and town.

CLIMATE

In January the average daily high temperature is 29°C (85°F) while the low averages 22°C (72°F). In July the average daily high is 32°C (90°F) and the average low is 24°C (76°F).

The annual rainfall in St Eustatia averages 1145 mm (45 inches) and is fairly evenly dispersed throughout the year. Humidity is in the low 70s from March to December and in the mid-70s in January and February.

FLORA & FAUNA

Most of the island is dry, with scrubby vegetation, although oleander, bougainvillea, hibiscus and chain of love flowers add a splash of color here and there. The greatest variety of flora is in The Quill, which collects enough cloud cover for its central crater to harbor a rainforest with ferns, elephant ears, bromeliads, bananas and tall trees. The island also has 18 varieties of orchids, all but three of which are found within The Quill.

There are 25 resident species of birds on Statia, including white-tailed tropicbirds that nest on the cliffs along the beach north of Lower Town. There are also harmless racer snakes, iguanas, lizards and tree frogs. Other than that, most animal life is limited to goats, cows and donkeys.

GOVERNMENT & POLITICS

St Eustatius is part of the Dutch kingdom, one of five islands in the Netherlands Antilles, whose central administration is in Curaçao. As with the other four islands, Statia is treated as a municipality and has its own lieutenant governor, appointed by Queen Beatrix of the Netherlands. The lieutenant governor and two elected commissioners are responsible for running Statia's daily affairs.

ECONOMY

A large proportion of Statia's work force is employed in government administration. The rest of the island's economy is dependent upon a mix of fishing, small retail businesses and a bit of tourism. There are large, unsightly oil tanks on the northwest side of the island where oil is off-loaded and stored for transshipment to other islands.

ST EUSTATIUS

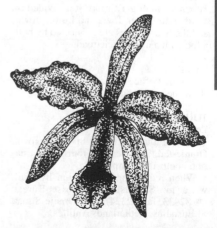

POPULATION & PEOPLE
The population of Statia is about 2100. The majority of the people are black, largely the descendants of African slaves brought to Statia to work in the warehouses in Lower Town and on a handful of long-vanished plantations.

SOCIETY & CONDUCT
The culture is a mix of African and Dutch heritage, similar to that found on other Dutch islands. The lifestyle is casual, but a bit more conservative than on neighboring islands – bathing suits should certainly be limited to beach areas and hotel pools.

RELIGION
There are Methodist, Roman Catholic, Seventh Day Adventist, Anglican, Baptist, Apostolic and Baha'i churches on Statia.

LANGUAGE
While Dutch is the official language, English is most commonly spoken.

Facts for the Visitor

ORIENTATION
Statia has few roads and is easy to get around. Oranjestad, the island's town, is 1.5km south of the airport. It is divided by a cliff into Upper Town and Lower Town, and the two sections are connected by both a footpath and a vehicle road.

Maps
The tourist office has free island maps that show the roads and hiking trails.

TOURIST OFFICES
Local Tourist Offices
The main tourist office is in Upper Town, Oranjestad, and there's a tourist information booth at the airport.

When requesting information by mail, write to: St Eustatius Tourist Bureau (☎ 82433, fax 82324), Fort Oranje Straat, St Eustatius, Netherlands Antilles.

Tourist Offices Abroad
Overseas tourism representatives include:

Netherlands
  Antillen Huis (Kabinet van de Gevol-machtigde Minister van de Nederlandse Antillen), Badhuisweg 173-175, 2597 JP 'S-Gravenhage (☎ 070-3512811, fax 070-3512722)
USA
  St Eustatius Tourist Office, PO Box 6322, Boca Raton, FL 33427 (☎ 561-394-8580, 800-722-2394; fax 561-488-4294)

VISAS & DOCUMENTS
Valid passports are required of all visitors except for US and Canadian citizens, who need only proof of citizenship, such as an official birth certificate accompanied by a driver's license. A roundtrip or onward ticket is officially required.

CUSTOMS
Statia is a free port and there are no customs regulations.

MONEY
The Netherlands Antilles guilder or florin is the official currency, but US dollars are accepted everywhere. Hotel, car rental and dive shop prices are given in dollars, while islander-geared businesses post prices in guilders. The exchange rate is officially 1.77 guilders to US$1. For more information see Money in the Facts for the Visitor chapter in the front of the book.

Credit cards are accepted by car rental agencies, larger hotels and a few shops.

POST & COMMUNICATIONS
Post
Statia's only post office is in Oranjestad on Cottageweg. When writing to Statia from abroad, if a post office box number is not listed, simply address mail with the individual or business name, followed by 'St Eustatius, Netherlands Antilles.'

It costs Fls 1.10 to mail a postcard and Fls 2.25 to mail a letter to the USA, Canada, UK or Europe; and Fls 1.30 for a postcard and Fls 3.25 for a letter to Australia, Asia or Africa.

Telephone
There are card phones at the airport, the port and in a number of places around town. Phonecards at sold at the Antelecom telephone office, airport and several stores.

To call Statia from overseas add the area code 599-3 in front of the five-digit local number.

For more information see Post & Communications in the Facts for the Visitor chapter at the front of the book.

The area code for Statia is 599-3.

NEWSPAPERS & MAGAZINES
There currently is no island newspaper or magazine published on Statia, but St Martin's *Daily Herald* has a bit of Statia news and is sold around the island.

RADIO & TELEVISION
Statia has its own radio station at 92.3 FM. Cable TV delivers two dozen channels, heavy on American programming.

ELECTRICITY
Electricity is 110 volts AC, 60 cycles, and a flat two-pronged plug is used, the same type as in the USA.

WEIGHTS & MEASURES
Statia uses the metric system.

HEALTH
Statia's hospital, the Queen Beatrix Medical Center (☎ 82211), is at Prinsesweg 25 on the east side of Oranjestad.

DANGERS & ANNOYANCES
There is little crime on Statia, and most locals don't even lock their doors. However, it's best not to leave things unattended on the beach – snorkeling gear is one item that sometimes seems to wander off.

BUSINESS HOURS
Shops and offices are commonly open from 8 or 9 am to noon and from 1 to 5 pm.

PUBLIC HOLIDAYS & SPECIAL EVENTS
Public holidays on St Eustatius are as follows:

New Year's Day	January 1
Good Friday	Friday before Easter
Easter Sunday	late March/early April
Easter Monday	late March/early April
Queen's Day	April 30
Labor Day	May 1
Ascension Thursday	40th day after Easter
Christmas Day	December 25
Boxing Day	December 26

The Statia Carnival, which is held during mid-July and culminates on a Monday, is the island's biggest festival. Music, jump-ups, competitions and local food are the highlights.

Fort Oranje is the site of ceremonies held on Statia-America Day, November 16, which commemorates the date in 1776 when Statia became the first foreign land to salute the US flag.

ACTIVITIES
Beaches & Swimming
No one visits Statia for its beaches, which are few in number and undistinguished. The island's best beach for swimming is the usually calm Oranje Beach in Lower Town. Zeelandia Bay on the east coast, which has rough surf and undertows, is not recommended for swimming but nonetheless rates as Statia's second beach.

Diving & Snorkeling
Statia has a couple of dozen dive sites, the majority of which are coral formations on old lava flows. There are also a few wrecks of colonial trading ships, although the remains are basically piles of ballast stones as the ships themselves have disintegrated. To protect the island's historical remains from souvenir hunters, all divers are required to be accompanied by a guide.

ST EUSTATIUS

The *Stingray* wreck (1768), a few minutes from Lower Town in 15 meters of water, is near a ledge with a rich concentration of marine life, including stingrays, spotted eels and octopuses.

Hangover Reef, at the southwest side of the island, is a popular reef dive with a wide variety of sponges, corals and sea fans. It also has many ledges and crevices harboring lobsters, sea turtles and numerous species of fish.

For a deep dive, Doobie Crack, a large cleft in a reef at the northwest side of the island, has black-tip sharks and schools of large fish.

Snorkeling tours of some of the shallower reefs are available from the dive shops for around US$25.

Dive Shops Despite Statia's light tourism, there are three dive shops offering competitive rates. One-tank dives average US$45, two-tank dives US$75. Night dives, certification courses and multi-dive packages are also available. Dive shops include:

Blue Nature Watersports & Diving
  (☎ 82725, fax 82756, akegel@ibm.net)
Dive Statia (☎ 82435, fax 82539)
Golden Rock Dive Center (☎ /fax 82964;
  in the USA ☎ 800-311-6658)

Hiking

The tourist office has a free hiking brochure with descriptions of 11 trails and can provide information on current trail conditions. Most of the trails are signposted and some of them are marked with orange ribbons.

The most popular hike is to The Quill, Statia's extinct volcano. The trail leading up the mountain begins at the end of Rosemary Laan in Oranjestad and takes about 50 minutes to reach the edge of the crater. From there you can continue in either direction along the rim. The trail to the right (southeast) takes about 45 minutes and ends atop the 600-meter Mazinga, Statia's highest point. The shorter Panorama Track to the left offers spectacular views and only takes about 15 minutes. A third option is the steep track leading down into

the crater, where there's a thick rainforest of tall trees, some with huge buttressed trunks. This track, which takes about 30 minutes each way, can be very slippery so sturdy shoes are essential.

ACCOMMODATIONS

Most accommodations are in Oranjestad or near the airport. All places are quite modest in scale and prices are moderate by Caribbean standards.

There's a 7% government tax on accommodations in Statia and hotels tack on a 10% to 15% service charge.

FOOD & DRINKS

Considering its size, Statia has a reasonable number and variety of restaurants; most are moderately priced. There are several small grocery stores in Oranjestad, with the Windward Islands Supermarket on Heilligerweg being one of the better stocked.

Most tap water comes from individual rainwater catchment systems and should be boiled before drinking. Bottled water is available at grocery stores.

ENTERTAINMENT

The main entertainment spot is *Lago Heights Club* in Upper Town, which has dancing on weekends to live music and DJs. *Stone Oven Bar* on Faeschweg also has dancing some weekends. *Blue Bead* in Lower Town is a nice place to sit and sip a tropical drink.

THINGS TO BUY

Mazinga Gift Shop on Fort Oranje Straat in Upper Town sells a little bit of everything, including T-shirts, jewelry and other souvenirs.

Getting There & Away

AIR

The only scheduled flights to Statia are with Winair (☎ 82381 or 82362), which has four flights a day from St Martin.

Statia can be easily visited as a day trip. The first flight from St Martin leaves at 7 am and the last flight returns at 6 pm weekdays and 9 pm on weekends. The fare is US$44 one way, and from US$68 roundtrip.

Winair also makes the 10-minute hop from Saba to Statia every afternoon, as well as a couple of mornings a week, for US$25 one way, US$50 roundtrip.

Airport Information
Statia's little airport has a staffed tourist information booth, a card phone, a refreshment stand and a Winair counter.

SEA
Statia has a new 210-meter L-shaped breakwater at the south end of Lower Town. The harbor includes an anchorage for fishing boats and space for visiting yachts. Yachters should check in with the harbormaster upon arrival.

Cruise Ship
Statia does not have a deep-water port capable of handling large cruise ships, but the island is visited by Windjammer Barefoot Cruises' schooners and a few other small cruise ships.

LEAVING ST EUSTATIUS
For stays of more than 24 hours, there's a departure tax of US$5 for flights within the Netherlands Antilles, US$10 to other destinations.

Getting Around

Statia has no buses, so renting a car is useful if you want to explore the island properly, which could be done in a day. If you're staying on in Oranjestad, you probably won't need a car for most of your stay but expect to do some serious walking as the town is spread out.

THE AIRPORT
There are usually one or two taxis on hand to meet flights. If you miss the taxis, look

for Rosie, the cheery ex-St Martiner who owns Rainbow Car Rental, as she'll drop you off in town for the same rate. Otherwise, the person at the tourist information booth can call a taxi for you.

TAXI
Taxis charge US$4 between the airport and Upper Town, US$3 from Upper Town to Lower Town, US$5 from the airport to the jetty and US$3 from town to the Quill trailhead; add US$1 after sunset.

CAR
Road Rules
Drive on the right-hand side of the road. Your home driver's license is valid for driving on Statia.

By Caribbean standards Statia's roads are good, albeit sometimes narrow, and you need to watch out for stray animals on the road. Surprisingly, Oranjestad has quite a few one-way streets.

Statia's only gas station is in Lower Town opposite the pier. It's usually open from 7:30 am to 7 pm Monday to Saturday.

Rental
Rainbow Car Rental (☎ 82811) rents cars for US$35, insurance included; although there's no booth, Rosie, who manages Rainbow, is often at the airport to meet flights.

Avis (☎ 82421), which is the only company with a booth at the airport, rents cars for US$40 a day plus US$9 for CDW insurance.

Other rental companies include ARC Car Rental (☎ 82595), Brown's Car Rental (☎ 82266) and Lady Ama's Services (☎ 82451).

HITCHHIKING
Hitchhiking is practiced on Statia, but traffic is light to the more distant parts of the island, and, of course, the usual precautions apply.

ORGANIZED TOURS
A two-hour taxi tour of the island costs US$40 for up to four people.

Oranjestad

Oranjestad, the island's capital and its only town, is a pleasant place with a fine sense of history. It consists of Lower Town, which is the area down along the waterfront, and Upper Town, which is on the bluff above.

Lower Town was the location of the original port town and still has some ruins from the colonial era, as well as the island's best beach and Statia's harbor.

Upper Town is Oranjestad's main commercial and residential area. It has numerous historical sites, all of which can easily be explored on foot in a few leisurely hours. Bay Rd, a steep cobbled lane that was once used to march Africans from the slave ships, provides a pedestrian route up the coastal cliff to link the two parts of town.

You can pick up a useful historical walking tour book and map of Oranjestad for US$2 at the museum.

Information

Tourist Office The helpful St Eustatius Tourist Bureau (☎ 82433) is behind Government Guesthouse in an old stone building that once served as a debtor's prison. It's open from 8 am to noon and 1 to 5 pm Monday to Thursday, to 4:30 pm on Friday.

Money There are two banks in the town center: Barclays Bank, between the library and museum, and Windward Islands Bank, on Fort Oranje Straat. Barclays Bank is open from 8:30 am to 3:30 pm Monday to Thursday, from 8:30 am to 12:30 pm and 2 to 4:30 pm on Friday. Windward Islands Bank has similar hours, but closes at noon for an hour.

Post & Communications The post office, on Cottageweg, is open from 7:30 am to noon and 1:30 to 5 pm Monday to Thursday, to 4:30 pm on Friday. Antelecom, the telephone office, is to the south.

Library The public library is open from 1 to 5 pm on Monday and from 8 am to noon and 1 to 5 pm Tuesday to Friday.

Fort Oranje

Right in the center of town, Fort Oranje is an intact fort complete with cannons, triple bastions and a cobblestone courtyard. It's perched on the cliffside directly above Lower Town and offers a broad view of the waterfront below. The first rampart here was erected by the French in 1629 but most of the fort was built after the Dutch took the island from the French in 1636. They added to the fort a number of times over the years, enlarging it into the largest fortress on Statia.

The courtyard has a couple of memorials, including a plaque presented by US president Franklin Roosevelt to commemorate the fort's fateful 1776 salute of the American war vessel *Andrew Doria*. The fort is always open and there's no admission fee.

Sint Eustatius Museum

This museum, operated by the Sint Eustatius Historical Foundation, gives visitors a glimpse of upper-class colonial life on Statia and is one of the Eastern Caribbean's finest historical museums.

It occupies the Simon Doncker House, a restored 18th-century Dutch merchant's home that's decorated with period furnishings and holds collections of nautical artifacts, china and hand-blown bottles. The basement, formerly a wine cellar, houses the museum's pre-Columbian collection.

The house's history includes a stint as the headquarters of Admiral George Rodney following the British invasion of the island in 1781. The museum is open from 9 am to 5 pm weekdays and from 9 am to noon on Saturday. Admission is US$2.

Government Guesthouse

The Government Guesthouse is the handsome 18th-century stone and wood building opposite Barclays Bank. It was thoroughly renovated in 1992 with funding from the EU and is now the government

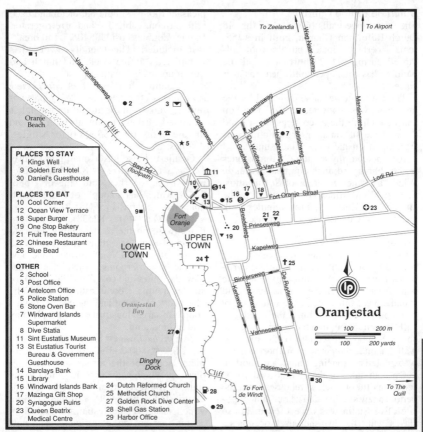

PLACES TO STAY
1 Kings Well
9 Golden Era Hotel
30 Daniel's Guesthouse

PLACES TO EAT
10 Cool Corner
12 Ocean View Terrace
18 Super Burger
19 One Stop Bakery
21 Fruit Tree Restaurant
22 Chinese Restaurant
26 Blue Bead

OTHER
2 School
3 Post Office
4 Antelcom Office
5 Police Station
6 Stone Oven Bar
7 Windward Islands
    Supermarket
8 Dive Statia
11 Sint Eustatius Museum
13 St Eustatius Tourist
    Bureau & Government
    Guesthouse
14 Barclays Bank
15 Library
16 Windward Islands Bank
17 Mazinga Gift Shop
20 Synagogue Ruins
23 Queen Beatrix
    Medical Centre
24 Dutch Reformed Church
25 Methodist Church
27 Golden Rock Dive Center
28 Shell Gas Station
29 Harbor Office

Oranjestad

ST EUSTATIUS

headquarters, with the offices of the lieu-tenant governor and commissioners on the ground floor and the courtroom on the upper floor.

The building, which once served as the Dutch naval commander's quarters, de-rived its name from its 1920s spell as a guesthouse.

Synagogue Ruins
The roofless and slowly decaying yellow-brick walls of the Honen Dalim, an aban-doned synagogue that dates from 1739, can be found 30 meters down the alleyway

opposite the south side of the library. The synagogue is the second oldest in the western hemisphere.

Statia's rising influence as a trade center was accompanied by a large influx of Jewish merchants beginning in the early 1700s. With their livelihoods closely linked to trade, most of the Jewish community left the island around the turn of the 19th cen-tury, when Statia's importance as a port declined.

About half a kilometer east of the syna-gogue ruins is a Jewish cemetery with gravestones dating from 1742 to 1843.

Dutch Reformed Church

The thick stone walls (600 cm) of the old Dutch Reformed Church, built in 1755, remain perfectly intact, but the roof collapsed during a 1792 hurricane and the building has been open to the heavens ever since.

The church tower, also damaged by the hurricane, was renovated in 1981 and you can now climb the steep steps for a good view of the surrounding area. Entrance is free, and it's usually open until sunset.

Also noteworthy are the old tombstones in the churchyard, including that of Jan de Windt, a former governor of St Eustatius, Saba and St Martin, who died in 1775. The church is on Kerkweg, a few minutes walk south of the Government Guesthouse.

Lower Town

Lower Town is a narrow coastal area backed by steep cliffs. High seas and hurricanes have taken their toll on the historic waterfront; however, the remains of the old foundations from some of the 18th-century warehouses that once lined the coast can still be seen jutting into the water along the shore. Submerged sections of the old seawall that once protected the harborfront can be explored by donning a mask and snorkel.

On both sides of the coastal road you'll see a handful of brick warehouses from the period, a few still in use. The building opposite Dive Statia was once used to house slaves, while the dive shop itself occupies a former lighthouse.

With a little imagination, the fading ruins can help conjure up an image of the past, when the area was bustling with traders and merchants and the bay was chock full of ships.

Oranje Beach, at the north end of Lower Town, has gray sands and generally calm waters. Modest as it may be, it's the island's best all-round beach and a popular swimming spot for Statian families. There's a new harbor at the south end of Lower Town.

Places to Stay

Country Inn (☎ /fax 82484) in Concordia, a 10-minute walk east of the airport, has six pleasant rooms, simple but clean and each with air-con, cable TV and a refrigerator. Singles/doubles cost US$40/55, full breakfast included. The friendly owner, Iris Pompier, is a fine cook, and lunch and dinner are available on request.

If Country Inn is full, *Airport View Apartments* (☎ 82299, fax 82517), a two-minute walk from the airport terminal, has five one-bedroom apartments with TV and private baths for US$50/60 for singles/doubles.

Oranjestad also has a small guesthouse, *Daniel's Guesthouse* (☎ 82358) on Rosemary Laan, on the south side of Upper Town, which has a couple of rooms available on a daily basis for US$40.

Kings Well (☎ /fax 82538), on Van Tonningenweg, on the road winding down to Lower Town, has nine straightforward rooms with cable TV and refrigerators. Best are the upstairs rooms, which have ocean-view balconies and cost from US$55/70 for singles/doubles, breakfast included. The place is very casual and the owners have a couple of large dogs that some people may find intimidating.

Talk of the Town (☎ 82236, fax 82640; in the USA ☎ 800-223-9815) is half a kilometer south of the airport on LE Saddlerweg, which is the first side street to the right as you drive from the airport towards Oranjestad. The hotel's original section, which is above the restaurant, has eight rooms that are quite sufficient. The new poolside wing has 11 modern, comfortable rooms with high ceilings and one king or two double beds. Rooms in both sections have air-con, phones and cable TV. Year-round rates are US$57/72 for singles/doubles in the older section, US$69/88 in the newer section, both including breakfast.

Golden Era Hotel (☎ 82345, fax 82445; in the USA ☎ 800-223-9815), in the center of Lower Town on a rocky shoreline, is a two-story hotel with 20 adequate but ordinary rooms, each with a TV, phone and air-con, and most with refrigerators. There's an oceanfront pool. Rates are US$60/75 for singles/doubles in summer, US$70/88 in winter.

Places to Eat
One Stop Bakery, near the Dutch Reformed Church in Upper Town, has inexpensive breads, fruit pies, salt fish and meat patties, cheese rolls and sandwiches. It's open from 5:30 am to 7:30 pm weekdays and to 1 pm on Saturday.

Super Burger, a friendly spot at the south end of De Graafweg, has ice cream, milk shakes and good inexpensive sandwiches. For a treat, try the johnny cake and swordfish. Nothing costs more than US$5. It's open from 8 am to 11:30 pm daily.

Fruit Tree Restaurant on Prinsesweg, is an inviting little place with tables under a fruit tree. It has a variety of fresh tropical fruit juices for US$1.50 and home-cooked Caribbean fish, goat and chicken meals for around US$7.50. It's open weekdays for lunch and dinner and Sundays for brunch.

Cool Corner, a bar and restaurant in the center of town, offers Chinese-Caribbean style food with curries, chop suey and similar dishes from about US$10. It's open daily from 10 am to midnight. For more conventional Chinese food, there's the *Chinese Restaurant* on Prinsesweg.

Ocean View Terrace, in the courtyard next to the tourist office, has a quiet open-air setting. A breakfast of eggs, ham and home fries or lunchtime burgers with fries cost US$6, while dinner dishes are double that. It's open from 9 am to 11:30 pm daily except Wednesday.

Blue Bead, a bar and restaurant at Oranjestad Bay, offers pleasant waterview dining and reasonable prices. At lunch everything is under US$10, including salads, burgers, chicken sate, calamari or fish & chips. At dinner a main dish with salad averages US$20 but you can also order from a 'lite dishes menu' for half that. It's open daily from 11:30 am to 2:30 pm and 6 to 9 pm.

Talk of the Town, between the airport and Upper Town, is run by a Dutch family and has straightforward food. Breakfast, from 7 to 11 am, is a simple Dutch-style buffet that includes cold cuts, eggs, corn flakes and juice for US$7.75. At lunch, burgers

and sandwiches are around US$5. Dinner, which requires reservations, features a three-course meal that changes daily and averages US$25, depending upon the main course. There's also a bar. For directions, see the earlier Places to Stay section.

The restaurant at the *Golden Era Hotel* in Lower Town has an attractive oceanfront setting. At lunch you can get sandwiches for US$5, while standard chicken, meat and seafood dishes are US$12 to US$20 at dinner.

Around Statia

FORT DE WINDT
The road south from Oranjestad ends abruptly at Fort de Windt, where a couple of rusty cannons sit atop a cliffside stone wall. While there's not much else to this small 18th-century fort, you'll be rewarded with a fine view of St Kitts to the southeast. The most interesting geological feature in the area is the white cliffs to the east of Fort de Windt, a landmark readily visible from neighboring islands.

To get there, take the road that runs past the old Dutch Reformed Church and follow it south, through a dry terrain of cacti and stray goats, to its end 3km away.

ZEELANDIA
Zeelandia, 3km northeast of Oranjestad, takes its name from Statia's first Dutch settlers, who were from Zeeland province in the Netherlands.

The dark-sand beach at Zeelandia Bay collects a fair share of flotsam and is not a good beach for swimming; the Atlantic side of the island is turbulent and there are dangerous currents and undertows. It is a reasonable strolling beach, however, and you can find private niches by walking south along the beach towards the cliffs.

If you're up for a longer walk, a track from the main road leads north to the semi-secluded Venus Bay. There's no beach, but it makes for a nice hike, taking about 45 minutes one way.

ST EUSTATIUS

Places to Stay & Eat

La Maison Sur la Plage (☎ 82256, fax 82831), the only development at Zeelandia Bay, has 10 rooms in five duplex cottages, each with a private bath and TV. There's also a pool. Singles/doubles cost US$60/75. As this is an isolated area, you'll need a car.

La Maison Sur la Plage has one of the best restaurants on the island, serving traditional French cuisine for lunch and dinner. It has an open-air setting above the beach with a view of The Quill. Prices are relatively expensive and reservations are required.

St Kitts & Nevis

The islands of St Kitts and Nevis are linked by ferry, making it easy to visit both halves of this two-island nation on a single trip. Most visitors to the islands fly into St Kitts, which on a clear day provides a wonderful introduction to that island. You'll get a glimpse of the mountainous interior, the patchwork of cane fields that carpets the lowlands and the curving southeast peninsula with its rugged hills, salt ponds and deeply indented bays.

While St Kitts has 80% of the population, both islands are small, rural and lightly populated. On both St Kitts and Nevis the colonial past is evident in the numerous old sugar mills and plantation estates found throughout the countryside. Many of the grander plantation houses have been converted into atmospheric inns.

The island known today as St Kitts was called Liamuiga, 'Fertile Island,' by its Amerindian inhabitants. When Columbus sighted the island on his second voyage to the New World in 1493, he named it St Christopher after his patron saint. St Kitts, the shortened name that came later, is today used by virtually everyone, including government offices.

Columbus used the Spanish word for snow, *nieves*, to name Nevis, presumably because the clouds shrouding its mountain reminded him of a snow-capped peak. Native Caribs knew the island as Oualie, 'Land of Beautiful Waters.'

These low-keyed islands can make for a nice quiet holiday, but keep in mind there's not a great deal of activity on either. Some people find the islands' relaxed nature ideal, while others get restless after a few days.

Facts about St Kitts & Nevis

HISTORY

St Kitts, settled by Sir Thomas Warner in 1623, was the site of the first British colony in the West Indies. The following year the French also settled part of St Kitts, a situation Warner tolerated in part to gain an upper hand against the native Caribs living on the island.

After they massacred the Caribs in a series of battles, the British and French turned on each other and St Kitts changed

ST KITTS & NEVIS

hands between the two colonial powers several times before the 1783 Treaty of Paris brought the island firmly under British control. During this era, sugar plantations thrived on St Kitts.

Nevis had a similar colonial history. In 1628 Sir Warner sent a party of about 100 colonists to establish a British settlement on the west coast of Nevis. Although their original settlement, near Cotton Ground, fell to an earthquake in 1680, Nevis went on to prosper, developing one of the most affluent plantation societies in the Eastern Caribbean. As on St Kitts, most of the

island's wealth was built upon the labor of African slaves who toiled in the island's sugar cane fields.

By the late 18th century Nevis, buoyed by the attraction of its thermal baths, had become a major retreat for Britain's rich and famous.

In 1816 the British linked St Kitts and Nevis with Anguilla and the Virgin Islands as a single colony. In 1958 these islands became part of the West Indies Federation, a grand but ultimately unsuccessful attempt to combine all of Britain's Caribbean colonies into a united political entity. When the federation dissolved in 1962, the British opted to lump St Kitts, Nevis and Anguilla together as a new state.

In February 1967 the three islands were given independence from the Crown as an Associated State, with its capital in Basseterre. Within months Anguilla, fearful of domination by a larger St Kitts, rebelled and eventually found its way back into the British fold as a colony.

Nevis was also wary of bonding with St Kitts and threatened to follow suit, but after a period of unrest it agreed to the union with the stipulation that it be given a heightened measure of internal autonomy and the right to secede in the future if it so desired. It was only after these conditions were guaranteed to Nevis under a new constitution that St Kitts and Nevis, in September 1983, were linked as a single federated state within the Commonwealth.

Kennedy Simmons, head of the predominant political party, the People's Action Movement (PAM), held the nation's prime minister post from the eve of independence in 1980 to 1995. Toward the end of his rule, however, Simmons found himself leading an increasingly unpopular party marred by corruption issues and alleged links to drug smuggling.

In national elections held in November 1993, PAM failed to win a majority, leaving it with only four of the 11 parliamentary seats. PAM captured just 41% of the popular vote, versus the 54% cast for the opposition Labour Party, which also carried four seats. Protests and street violence erupted after PAM made a deal with a minority splinter party that excluded the Labour Party from the ruling coalition.

In the fall of 1994, a son of the deputy prime minister was found murdered and two other sons were arrested on drug and firearms charges. In December of that year, when the two jailed brothers were abruptly released from prison, their fellow inmates rioted and all 150 of them broke out of the Basseterre prison. The situation got so out of hand that a regional security force from Barbados and Trinidad was brought in to assist local police.

The riots, corruption and civil unrest solidified the end of Simmons' 15-year rule. In parliamentary elections called in 1995, PAM won just a single seat and was overwhelmingly ousted by the Labour Party.

While St Kitts sorted out its dirty laundry, a secession movement simmered on Nevis. In 1997 the pro-independence Concerned Citizens Movement, lead by Nevis premier Vance Armory, won three of Nevis' five parliamentary seats – just one seat short of the four seats required to call a plebiscite on independence from St Kitts.

GEOGRAPHY

St Kitts is 23 miles long and 6.5 miles wide, with a land area of 68 sq miles. It has a central mountain range dominated by Mt Liamuiga, a dormant 3792-foot volcano. The higher mountain slopes are covered by rainforest, while the drier foothills and lowlands are largely planted with sugar cane.

Nevis, a couple of miles south of St Kitts, is a nearly round island of 36 sq miles that's dominated by a central volcanic peak, the 3232-foot Nevis Peak. Rainforests form Nevis' hilly interior while dry scrub lowlands predominate near the coast.

CLIMATE

In January the average daily high temperature is 81°F (27°C) while the low averages 72°F (22°C). In July the average daily high is 86°F (30°C), the average low 76°F (24°C).

Annual rainfall averages 55 inches (1400 mm) and is fairly consistent throughout the year. The driest months are February to June, when there's an average of 11 days of measurable rain a month and a mean relative humidity around 70%. The rest of the year the humidity averages 73%, with measurable rain falling an average of 16 days each month.

FLORA & FAUNA

Vegetation on both islands ranges from grassy coastal areas to a rainforested interior of ferns and tall trees. Flowering plumeria, hibiscus and chain of love are

ST KITTS & NEVIS

common along roadsides and in garden landscaping. St Kitts' uninhabited southeast peninsula has a sparse desert-like cover of dryland grasses dotted with cacti, yucca and century plants.

Salt ponds on the southeast peninsula provide feeding grounds for a variety of shorebirds, including plovers, stilts and oystercatchers. Pelicans and frigatebirds are common along the coast, and you can spot Antillean crested hummingbirds and nectar-feeding bananaquits wherever there are flowering plants. The country's only endemic bird, the St Kitts bullfinch, was recently spotted after having been considered extinct for decades.

The most commonly spotted wild mammal is the mongoose, introduced to the islands by plantation owners for the purpose of controlling rats in the cane fields; these slender ferret-like creatures hunt during the day when the nocturnal rats

sleep so the two seldom meet. Another exotic, the green vervet monkey, is found in the interior of both islands.

GOVERNMENT & POLITICS
St Kitts & Nevis is a federation officially headed by the British monarch, who is represented by a Governor-General. Legislative power is vested in a unicameral 11-member National Assembly – eight of whose members are elected from St Kitts and three from Nevis – and in the Prime Minister, who is leader of the majority party.

Nevis has internal home rule and a separate legislature, and an island administration that mirrors that of the federation.

Incidentally, the federation of St Kitts & Nevis forms the smallest nation in the Western Hemisphere.

ECONOMY
Although sugar production is declining, St Kitts remains heavily planted in sugar cane and agriculture still accounts for nearly 25% of the work force. Small-scale garment manufacturing, electronic assembly and a brewery and bottling plant account for 15% of St Kitts' labor force, while tourism, which is being actively promoted by the government, accounts for 12%.

On Nevis, where the economy is more sluggish, sugar has long been abandoned, but honey and some vegetables are produced and attempts are being made to revive one traditional crop, sea island cotton. Tourism is Nevis' largest employer; the Four Seasons Resort employs over 600 people – roughly a quarter of the island's labor force.

POPULATION & PEOPLE
The population is approximately 45,000, with 35,500 on St Kitts and 9500 on Nevis. Over 90% are of African descent. The rest of the population is predominantly of European, or mixed European and African, descent.

People on St Kitts are called Kittitians (Kit-TEE-shuns), while on Nevis they are called Nevisians (Nee-VEE-shuns).

SOCIETY & CONDUCT

Culturally, the islands draw upon a mix of European, African and West Indian traditions. Architecture is predominantly British in style and cricket is the national sport.

The cultural mix is evident in island dance and entertainment. Masquerades, St Kitts' popular folk troupe, performs dances ranging from a traditional French quadrille to a spirited African war dance. The troupe wears colorful costumes of a unique West Indian design.

Dos & Don'ts

Dress is very casual on both St Kitts and Nevis. Cotton clothing is suitable attire for any occasion; swim wear should be restricted to the beach.

RELIGION

Just over one-third of all islanders are Anglican. The rest are Methodists, Roman Catholics, Baptists, Adventists, Moravians and Jehovah's Witnesses.

LANGUAGE

The language of the islands is English.

Facts for the Visitor

ORIENTATION

St Kitts' shape resembles a cricket bat, with an oval road running around the perimeter of its main body and another extending down the spine of its southern arm. It takes about 1½ hours to make a nonstop loop around the northern road and about 30 minutes to drive from Basseterre, the capital, to the end of the southeast peninsula.

St Kitts' airport is on the northern outskirts of Basseterre, just a five-minute drive from the center.

On Nevis the airport is in Newcastle at the north side of the island, about a 20-minute drive from Charlestown, the main town. A loop road circles the island, making exploring quite straightforward.

Maps

The simple maps handed out by the tourist office will be suitable for most visitors.

The best map is the Ordnance Survey's map of St Kitts & Nevis (1:50,000), which includes inset maps of Basseterre, Brimstone Hill Fortress and Charlestown. It can be purchased for EC$25 at Wall's Deluxe Record & Bookshop in Basseterre and at the gift shop at Brimstone Hill Fortress National Park.

TOURIST OFFICES
Local Tourist Offices

St Kitts' main tourist office is in the Pelican Mall in Basseterre and there's also an information booth at the airport. The Nevis Tourist Office is on Main St in Charlestown.

When requesting information by mail, write to: St Kitts & Nevis Department of Tourism (☎ 465-2620, fax 465-8794), PO Box 132, Basseterre, St Kitts, West Indies.

Tourist Offices Abroad

Overseas St Kitts & Nevis tourist offices include the following:

Canada
    11 Yorkville Ave, Suite 508,
    Toronto, Ontario M4W IL3
    (☎ 416-921-7717, fax 416-921-7997)
UK
    10 Kensington Court, London W8 5DL
    (☎ 0171-376-0881, fax 0171-937-3611)
USA
    414 East 75th St, New York, NY 10021
    (☎ 800-582-6208, 212-535-1234;
    fax 212-734-6511)

VISAS & DOCUMENTS

Passports are required of all visitors except US and Canadian citizens, who may enter with proof of citizenship such as an official birth certificate and a photo ID.

Visas are not required of most visitors, including citizens of the UK, Western Europe and Commonwealth countries, for stays of up to six months. Visitors are required to be in possession of a roundtrip or onward ticket.

CUSTOMS
One bottle of wine or spirits and 200 cigarettes can be brought in duty free.

MONEY
The Eastern Caribbean Dollar (EC$) is the official currency (EC$2.70=US$1).

Larger tourist-related charges, such as car rental and hotel bills, are generally quoted in US dollars, although you can pay in either US or EC dollars. Most hotels, car rental agencies and restaurants accept major credit cards. Note that many businesses will use an exchange rate of EC$2.65=US$1 when converting a bill from EC to US dollars, a slight disadvantage if you're paying in US dollars.

Hotels and restaurants add a 7% tax and usually a 10% service charge as well. When a restaurant doesn't add a service charge, a 10% tip is appropriate.

POST & COMMUNICATIONS
Post
The main post offices are in Basseterre and Charlestown.

Airmail postage costs EC$0.50 for a postcard and EC$0.80 for a 10-gram letter sent to Canada, the UK, the USA and most Caribbean countries. Postcards to Europe cost EC$0.80, letters EC$1.

When mailing a letter to the islands, follow the addressee's name with the town and then 'St Kitts, West Indies' or 'Nevis, West Indies.'

Telephone
St Kitts phone numbers start with 465 or 466, Nevis numbers with 469. To make a local call, dial all seven digits. When calling the islands from overseas, add the area code 869 to the local number.

The islands have both coin and card phones. To use a coin phone, insert a minimum of EC$0.25, dial the number and as soon as the phone is answered push the pound (£) key. If you want to make another call push the 'follow-on call' button on the left under the hook, rather than hanging up the receiver.

Card phones, common in busier public places, take Caribbean Phonecards, which can be purchased at the airports, Skantel (telephone) offices and numerous shops.

For an international operator dial ☎ 0; for directory assistance phone ☎ 411. More details can be found under Post & Communications in the introductory Facts for the Visitor chapter.

> **The area code for St Kitts & Nevis is 869.**

NEWSPAPERS & MAGAZINES
There are three local newspapers: *The Democrat* and *The Observer*, both published on Saturday, and the twice-weekly *Labour Spokesman* published on Wednesday and Saturday.

The *St Kitts & Nevis Visitor* magazine, published annually, is a good source of general tourist information and can be picked up free at tourist offices and hotels.

RADIO & TELEVISION
The government radio station, ZIZ, can be heard on 555 AM and 96 FM. The Voice of Nevis is on 895 AM and there's a gospel station at 825 AM. There's a government-operated TV station as well as US-network TV via cable.

ELECTRICITY
Most electric current is 230 volts, 60 cycles AC; however, some hotels supply electricity at 110 volts.

WEIGHTS & MEASURES
St Kitts uses the imperial system of measurement. Speed limit signs are in miles and rental car odometers are usually in miles.

HEALTH
The main hospital on St Kitts, the JNF General (☎ 465-2551), is at the west end of Cayon St in Basseterre. On Nevis, the small Alexandra Hospital (☎ 469-5473) is on Government Rd in Charlestown.

DANGERS & ANNOYANCES

Manchineel trees, whose sap can cause a skin rash, grow along the coast, particularly on the leeward side of the islands.

EMERGENCIES

For police and ambulance dial ☎ 911.

BUSINESS HOURS

Business hours for offices and shops are generally from 8 am to noon and 1 to 4 or 4:30 pm Monday to Friday; however, on Thursday some shops close for the afternoon. Most banks are open from 8 am to 3 pm weekdays and until 5 pm on Friday.

PUBLIC HOLIDAYS & SPECIAL EVENTS

Public holidays on St Kitts & Nevis are:

New Year's Day	January 1
Good Friday	late March/early April
Easter Monday	late March/early April
Labour Day	first Monday in May
Whit Monday	eighth Monday after Easter
Queen's Birthday	second Saturday in June
August Monday	first Monday in August
Independence Day	September 19
Christmas Day	December 25
Boxing Day	December 26

On St Kitts, the biggest event is the week-long Carnival held from December 24 to January 2, with calypso competitions, costumed street dances and steel band music. Many businesses are closed during Carnival.

In the last week in June, the four-day St Kitts Music Festival brings together top-name soca, salsa and jazz performers from throughout the Caribbean.

Nevis has a week-long 'Culturama' from late July to early August featuring music, crafts, parade and cultural events.

ACTIVITIES

Beaches & Swimming

These islands aren't particularly known for their beaches, but there are reasonable strands on St Kitts and a couple of attractive options on Nevis.

St Kitts' best beaches are on the south end of the island at Frigate Bay and in the sheltered bays along the southeast peninsula. Beaches along the main body of the island are mostly thin strands of black and gray sands.

On Nevis, Pinney's Beach, which runs north from Charlestown, is a long, lovely beach backed by coconut palms. There's also a nice white-sand beach fronting the Nisbet Plantation Beach Club on the north shore in Newcastle and a pleasant little beach at Oualie Bay.

Diving & Snorkeling

St Kitts has healthy, expansive reefs and varied marine life that includes rays, barracuda, garden eels, nurse sharks, sea turtles, sea fans, giant barrel sponges and black coral.

One popular dive spot is Sandy Point Bay below Brimstone Hill, which has an array of corals, sponges and reef fish as well as some coral-encrusted anchors from the colonial era. Among a handful of wreck dives is the 148-foot freighter *River Taw*, which sank in 50 feet of water in 1985 and now harbors soft corals and reef fish. Nevis has good diving off its west side, including some colorful caves at a depth of about 40 feet.

On St Kitts, Pro-Divers (☎ 465-3223, fax 465-0265) at Turtle Beach offers single-tank dives for US$40, two-tank dives for

US$60, night dives for US$50, an introductory resort course for US$75, a three-day PADI certification course for US$300 and a half-day snorkeling trip for US$35.

There are two other dive operations on St Kitts offering similar services at comparable rates: St Kitts Scuba (☎ 465-1189, fax 465-3696) at Bird Rock Beach Hotel and Kenneth's Dive Centre (☎ 465-2670, fax 465-6472) on Bay Road at the east side of Basseterre.

On Nevis, Scuba Safaris (☎ 469-9518, fax 469-9619) at Oualie Beach offers single-tank dives for US$45, two-tank dives for US$80, night dives for US$60 and a half-day snorkeling trip for US$35.

A favorite place for snorkeling is White House Bay on St Kitts' southeast peninsula. All of the dive companies rent snorkel gear for around US$10 a day, as does Mr X Watersports at Frigate Bay Beach, which also offers a snorkeling tour for US$25.

Windsurfing

Oualie Bay, at the northwest side of Nevis, catches the trade winds and offers a sandy launch in shallow waters that's good for beginners. There are also opportunities for wave jumping and other advanced techniques.

Windsurfing Nevis (☎ /fax 469-9682) at Oualie Beach rents boards for US$35 for two hours, US$65 a day, and offers beginner lessons for US$50.

Other Water Sports

On St Kitts, Mr X Watersports (☎ 465-4995) on Frigate Bay Beach rents Sunfish and Hobie Cat sailboats for US$20 to US$30 an hour, offers water skiing for US$15 a circuit, and provides a shuttle to South Friar's Bay for US$5 roundtrip. Pro-Divers at Turtle Beach rents one-person ocean kayaks for US$10 an hour.

Hiking

Tracks into the interior of St Kitts and Nevis are not well defined, so it's advisable to do any major trekking with a guide.

Greg's Safaris (☎ 465-4121) has a half-day hike into the rainforest of St Kitts for US$35. The guide moves at a comfortable pace suitable for all ages, identifies flora and fauna and stops to sample fruits along the way. Greg's also offers a full-day volcano tour for US$60.

The amiable Kriss Berry of Kriss Tours (☎ 465-4042) also offers a full-day trek that goes through the St Kitts rainforest to the volcano. It costs a reasonable US$45, lunch included.

On Nevis, Top to Bottom (☎ 469-9080) offers a choice of more than a dozen hikes, ranging from walks to estate ruins to monkey-spotting hikes in the jungle. Each outing costs US$20, except for the strenuous and muddy trek up to Nevis Peak, which costs US$30.

Mountain Biking

Mountain bike rentals are available on Nevis for US$20 a day from Windsurfing Nevis (☎ 469-9682) at Oualie Beach Hotel.

Horseback Riding

Horseback riding is available on St Kitts from Royal Stables (☎ 465-2222) and Trinity Stables (☎ 465-9603). On Nevis it's offered by Nevis Equestrian Centre (☎ 469-2638) and The Hermitage (☎ 469-3477); the latter also has carriage rides.

Golf

The Four Seasons Resort on Nevis has a championship 18-hole golf course designed by Robert Trent Jones II. Green fees are US$125 for 18 holes, including cart rental.

On St Kitts, the 18-hole Royal St Kitts Golf Club (☎ 465-8339) at Frigate Bay has green fees of US$35. The green fees are waived for guests at some of Frigate Bay's hotels and condominiums, so golfers might want to inquire when booking a place to stay. Carts can be rented for another US$40.

Both courses offer club rentals and have lower rates for nine-hole play.

ACCOMMODATIONS

There are only two large resorts, the Jack Tar Village Beach Resort & Casino on St Kitts and the Four Seasons Resort on Nevis, each with about 200 rooms.

Other than that, accommodations are mostly in small-scale hotels and condominiums. There are also some fine upscale inns in converted plantation estate homes.

Places in St Kitts can book up pretty solidly in winter, so early reservations are a good idea, particularly if you want to stay in one of the better-value options. Hotels add a 7% tax and a 10% service charge on top of their rates.

FOOD
Reasonably priced local fresh fish and other seafood are plentiful on the islands and are generally the best bet. Beef and many other items are imported and tend to be expensive, particularly on Nevis. In Basseterre and Charlestown there are a few good inexpensive local restaurants, while the plantation inns on both islands offer some fine upscale opportunities for romantic dining.

DRINKS
Tap water is safe to drink on both islands. Cane Spirit Rothschild, more commonly known as CSR, is a clear sugar cane spirit distilled on St Kitts. CSR is often served on the rocks with Ting, a popular grapefruit soft drink. Ting, Ginseng Up and Carib beer are bottled on St Kitts.

ENTERTAINMENT
Nightlife is not a highlight on St Kitts or Nevis, but there are a few options. On St Kitts, there's a casino at Jack Tar Village Beach Resort in Frigate Bay; changing dinner entertainment at Ocean Terrace Inn in Basseterre; and occasional live entertainment at a few of the restaurants, including Fisherman's Wharf in Basseterre, which has music a few nights a week. Still, the busiest place is Basseterre's cinema, which shows first-run Hollywood movies.

There's also a bit of weekend entertainment on Nevis, but it's mostly in the winter season.

THINGS TO BUY
St Kitts' Caribelle Batik makes high-quality batik clothing, including shirts, pareos and skirts. A good selection of Caribelle batiks is available at Island Hopper shops in Charlestown and Basseterre.

Spencer Cameron Gallery, on the north side of Basseterre's Independence Square, has island artwork and prints at reasonable prices. Kate Design, on Bank St in Basseterre, features attractive watercolors, prints, cards and silks by island artist Kate Spencer. There are duty-free shops selling jewelry, watches and liquor at Basseterre's Pelican Mall.

On Nevis, there's a handicraft co-op next to the tourist office on Main St in Charlestown. The Sand-Box Tree, next to Super Foods in Charlestown, is a quality gift shop that sells, among other items, cotton clothing silkscreened on Nevis.

Getting There & Away

See the Getting Around section for information on traveling between St Kitts and Nevis by air and boat.

AIR
International Destinations
American Airlines (☎ 465-2273) flies from the USA to St Kitts daily via San Juan, Puerto Rico. The regular fare for a 30-day excursion ticket is about US$600 from Miami and US$650 from New York or Boston.

There's currently no scheduled service to St Kitts from the UK, Europe or Canada; travel from those areas is via other Caribbean islands, most commonly Antigua, St Martin or San Juan.

Within the Caribbean
LIAT LIAT (☎ 465-2286) has daily nonstop flights to St Kitts from Antigua and St Martin and connecting flights from those hubs to the rest of its Caribbean network.

The fare from St Martin to St Kitts is US$66 one way, US$85 for a one-day excursion and US$125 for a 30-day excursion.

LIAT flights from Antigua to St Kitts or Nevis cost US$56 one way and US$106 for a 30-day excursion ticket.

ST KITTS & NEVIS

Winair Winair (☎ 465-8010) has daily flights from St Martin to St Kitts and Nevis. Fares to either are US$58 one way, US$76 for a one-day excursion, US$95 for a four-day excursion and US$111 for a 21-day excursion.

Carib Aviation Carib Aviation (☎ 465-3055) is primarily a charter airline, but currently offers scheduled service between Antigua and Nevis from US$70 roundtrip.

Airport Information
St Kitts' Bradshaw Airport, on the outskirts of Basseterre, has limited facilities but a major renovation is underway. The tourist office booth, which is just before customs, distributes the standard tourist handouts.

SEA
Yacht
The two ports of entry are Basseterre and Charlestown. On both islands, customs is near the ferry dock and is open from 8 am to noon and 1 to 4 pm on weekdays. Yachters will need cruising permits to visit other anchorages and a special pass to go between the two islands.

White House Bay, Ballast Bay and Major's Bay on St Kitts' southeast peninsula make good anchorages. On Nevis, Pinney's Beach is the most popular anchorage.

Cruise Ship
Numerous cruise ships visit St Kitts, docking at Basseterre's deep-water harbor. Charlestown has recently undertaken an expansion of its pier, so sleepy Nevis may soon be added to the itinerary of a few smaller cruise lines.

LEAVING ST KITTS & NEVIS
The departure tax is EC$27.

Getting Around

AIR
LIAT (☎ 465-2286) has three flights a day between St Kitts and Nevis, with an early morning, midday and late afternoon flight in each direction. The fare is US$22 one way, US$42 roundtrip.

Nevis Express (☎ 469-9755, or email reservations@nevisexpress.com) operates a small prop plane shuttle between St Kitts and Nevis about 10 times a day. The fare is US$20 one way during the day and US$35 to US$50 at night.

BUS
The buses are privately owned minivans. In Basseterre, most leave from the bus stop on Bay Road. From Basseterre it's EC$2 to Sandy Point Town, EC$2.50 to St Paul's and EC$3 to Dieppe Bay Town.

Bus service is fairly sporadic and there's no schedule, although buses are generally most plentiful in the early morning and in the late afternoon. The last bus is usually around 6 or 7 pm. Frigate Bay is outside regular bus routes. For information on buses on Nevis see the end of the Nevis section.

TAXI
Taxis meet scheduled flights. On St Kitts, a taxi from the airport costs EC$16 to Basseterre, EC$25 to Frigate Bay, EC$42 to St Paul's.

From the Circus in Basseterre, the main taxi stand, it costs EC$10 to points within town, EC$20 to Frigate Bay and EC$35 to Brimstone Hill. Rates are 25% higher between 11 pm and 6 am. There's an EC$3 charge for each 15 minutes of waiting time. To call for a taxi, dial ☎ 465-4253. Information on taxis on Nevis is at the end of the Nevis section.

CAR & MOTORCYCLE
Road Rules
Drive on the left side of the road. Speed limits are posted in miles per hour, and are generally between 20 and 40 mph. Gas costs about EC$6 a gallon.

Basseterre has quite a few one-way streets, some of which are not clearly marked. Keep an eye out for road signs and when in doubt, simply follow the rest of the traffic.

Driver's Licenses

Foreign visitors must purchase a visitor's driver's license, which costs EC$50 (or US$20) and is valid for 90 days. The easiest place to get them is at the fire station on Pond Rd at the east side of Basseterre, which is open 24 hours and has a separate window designated for issuing visitor licenses. If you're flying into St Kitts and renting a car, the rental agency will usually pick you up at the airport and then stop at the fire station on the way to their office.

During weekday business hours, driver's licenses can also be obtained at the Inland Revenue Office, above the post office on Bay Rd.

In Nevis, visitor's driver's licenses can be obtained at police stations.

Rental

There are numerous car rental agencies on St Kitts. Rates begin at about US$35/200 a day/week with unlimited mileage for a small car such as a Nissan March or Suzuki Swift. In addition, optional collision damage waivers cost about US$10 a day. With some companies you're still responsible for the first few hundred dollars worth of damage, while with others the CDW waives all liability.

In Basseterre, three of the largest agents are Avis (☎ 465-6507) on South Independence Square, TDC Auto Rentals (☎ 465-2991) on West Independence Square and Sunshine Car Rental (☎ 465-2193; in the USA and Canada ☎ 800-621-1270) on Cayon St. All three provide free airport or hotel pick-up.

Other car rental agents include Delisle Walwyn Rentals (☎ 465-8449), Liverpool Row, Basseterre; Caines Rent-A-Car (☎ 465-2366), Princes St, Basseterre; and Ken's Car Rental (☎ 465-3706), Crab Hill, Sandy Point Town.

Information on renting cars on Nevis is at the end of the Nevis section.

BOAT

The government-run passenger ferry *Caribe Queen* runs between St Kitts and Nevis daily except Thursday and Sunday. The ferry docks are in central Basseterre and Charlestown, which for most people makes the ferry more practical than flying between the two islands.

From Basseterre the boat departs for Charlestown on Monday at 8 am and 4 pm; on Tuesday at 1 pm; on Wednesday at 7 am, 4 pm and 7 pm; and on Friday and Saturday at 8:30 am and 4 pm.

From Charlestown the boat departs for Basseterre on Monday at 7 am and 3 pm; on Tuesday at 7:30 am and 6 pm; on Wednesday at 8 am and 6 pm; and on Friday and Saturday at 7:30 am and 3 pm.

The ferry strictly enforces its 150-passenger limit and sells tickets on the day of travel only (if you're going over for a day trip you can, and should, buy a return ticket in the morning). Dockside booths begin selling tickets about an hour before the scheduled departure time. As sailings occasionally reach capacity, it's wise to arrive early. Also note that if a boat does reach capacity it sometimes sails a few minutes before its scheduled departure time – so don't stroll too far away after you've bought your ticket!

The fare is EC$10 each way. The ride, which takes about 45 minutes, is usually a smooth trip and offers good views of both islands, best from the small outdoor deck at the front of the boat.

ORGANIZED TOURS

On St Kitts, Tropical Tours (☎ 465-4167) and Annie's Caribbean Tours (☎ 465-7043) both have half-day circle-island tours for US$15. The same companies also offer catamaran cruises and deep-sea fishing.

Taxis charge about US$50 (for one to four people) for a half-day island tour.

Basseterre

Founded and named by the French in the 17th century, Basseterre is not one of the grander Caribbean capitals, in part because of a fire that swept through the town

ST KITTS

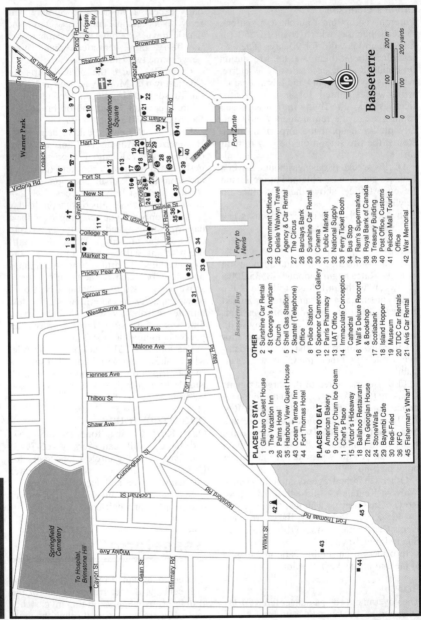

Basseterre

0   100   200 m
0   100   200 yards

PLACES TO STAY
1 Glimbaro Guest House
3 The Vacation Inn
26 Palms Hotel
35 Harbour View Guest House
43 Ocean Terrace Inn
44 Fort Thomas Hotel

PLACES TO EAT
6 American Bakery
9 Country Churn Ice Cream
11 Chef's Place
15 Victor's Hideaway
18 Ballahoo Restaurant
22 The Georgian House
24 StoneWalls
29 Bayembi Cafe
30 Redi-Fried
36 KFC
45 Fisherman's Wharf

OTHER
2 Sunshine Car Rental
4 St George's Anglican Church
5 Shell Gas Station
7 Skantel (Telephone) Office
8 Police Station
10 Spencer Cameron Gallery
12 Parris Pharmacy
13 LIAT Office
14 Immaculate Conception Cathedral
16 Wall's Deluxe Record & Bookshop
17 Scotiabank
19 Island Hopper
20 Museum
21 Avis Car Rental

23 Government Offices
25 Delisle Walwyn Travel Agency & Car Rental
27 The Circus
28 Barclays Bank
29 Sunshine Car Rental
30 Cinema
31 Public Market
32 National Supply
33 Ferry Ticket Booth
34 Bus Stop
37 Ram's Supermarket
38 Royal Bank of Canada
39 Treasury Building
40 Post Office, Customs Office
41 Pelican Mall, Tourist Office
42 War Memorial

in 1867, destroying most of its early colonial buildings.

Nonetheless, Basseterre has a fair number of appealing Victorian-era stone block structures topped by wooden second stories and decorated with fancy latticework and gingerbread trim. The town center is the **Circus**, a roundabout featuring a four-sided clock tower. It's supposedly modeled on London's Piccadilly Circus, but the most noticeable similarity lies in its traffic congestion. Most of the island's banks, airline offices and travel agents are in the streets radiating out from the Circus, while taxis, clothing and souvenir shops cluster at the roundabout.

The nearby **Independence Square**, once the site of slave auctions, is now a small public park with a central water fountain. The square is flanked by some of Basseterre's more substantial buildings, including a few Georgian-style houses and the twin-towered Immaculate Conception Cathedral that dates from 1927.

On the west side of town, Fort Thomas Hotel sits at the site of the old **Fort Thomas**. Though it's not a major sight, just below the hotel pool you can find a bit of the fort walls ringed with half a dozen cannons.

An extensive reclamation project is modernizing the waterfront. The ambitious undertaking, known as Port Zante, boasts a deep-water harbor capable of handling cruise ships and a new marina for yachts; there are plans to eventually add a hotel, a casino, office buildings and a cultural center.

Information

Tourist Office The tourist office (☎ 465-4040), in Pelican Mall, is open from 8 am to 4:30 pm Monday and Tuesday, to 4 pm on Wednesday, Thursday and Friday.

Money There are three banks near the Circus: Scotiabank, Barclays Bank and Royal Bank of Canada. The latter has a 24-hour ATM that accepts MasterCard and Visa as well as Cirrus and Plus bank cards. The banks are open from 8 am to 3 pm Monday to Thursday, to 5 pm on Friday.

Post The general post office on Bay Rd is open from 8 to 11 am on Thursday and 8 am to 3 pm on Monday, Tuesday, Wednesday, Friday and Saturday. Colorful commemorative stamps are sold at the philatelic bureau at Pelican Mall.

Telephone You can make international phone calls and send faxes and telegrams from the Skantel office on Cayon St; credit cards are accepted there. The office is open from 7:30 am to 6 pm Monday to Friday, 7:30 am to 1 pm Saturday and 6 to 8 pm on Sunday and holidays.

Bookstore Wall's Deluxe Record & Bookshop on Fort St sells maps and a fairly good selection of books on the Caribbean.

Museum

The St Christopher Heritage Society on Bank St, next to the US Peace Corps office, plans to eventually establish a substantial national museum in the waterfront Treasury Building. Meanwhile there's a small room with a few historic photos, Amerindian conch-shell tools and pottery shards. It's open from 8:30 am to 1 pm and 2 to 4 pm weekdays (mornings only on Wednesday) and 9 am to noon on Saturday. Admission is free, but donations are appreciated.

Brewery

St Kitts Breweries (465-2309), which brews Carib beer, usually offers visitors an informal tour during weekday business hours. The brewery is along the south side of the circle-island road just west of the hospital. There's no fee, but a tip to the worker who gives you the tour is the norm.

Places to Stay – budget

Town Center The best budget option is the conveniently located *Harbour View Guest House* (☎ 466-6759) on Bay Rd, opposite the harbor front. It has 10 rooms that are simple but clean and adequate, with air-con and private baths. Singles/doubles cost US$25/50.

The Vacation Inn (☎ 465-0363, fax 465-5403), on the corner of Cayon and College

Sts, has 10 cheerless rooms with air-con, TV and private baths for US$30 single or double. There's a shared kitchen.

The nearby *Glimbaro Guest House* (☎ 465-2935, fax 465-9832), on Cayon St, has 10 Spartan rooms with air-con, TV and phones. The six rooms with private baths cost US$45/55 for singles/doubles, while the four that share a bath cost US$25/35.

A good value is *Earle's Vacation Home* (☎ 465-7546, fax 466-7868), PO Box 604, in the Shadwell neighborhood at the north side of town and within walking distance of the center. There are two one-bedroom and four two-bedroom apartments, each with a full kitchen, dining area, washing machine and cable TV. Rates are US$50/60 in summer/winter for one-bedroom units and US$80/90 for two bedrooms. Two of the units have air-con (no extra charge), while the other two have ceiling fans.

Around Basseterre *Trinity Inn Apartments* (☎ 465-3226, fax 465-9460), Palmetto Point, is a small apartment building on the coastal road 4 miles west of Basseterre. There are 10 one-bedroom units with kitchens that rent for US$50/60 in summer/winter or US$700 monthly. There's a pool.

If you want to be closer to the water consider *Coral Reef Beach Cottages* (☎ 465-8154), c/ó Mrs Zenaida Katzen, PO Box 323, two cottages on Conaree Beach, about a mile northeast of the airport. Each has two bedrooms, two bathrooms, a living room, kitchen, phone and veranda. Rates, for up to four people, are US$35 a day with a three-day minimum stay, or US$225/750 a week/month, utilities included.

Places to Stay – top end
Town Center *Palms Hotel* (☎ 465-0800, fax 465-5889), PO Box 64, overlooking the Circus in Basseterre center, is a modern business hotel with 10 spiffy units. Roomy junior suites, which have two double beds, TV, air-con, phones, refrigerators and coffeemakers, cost US$75/85 in summer/winter. One-bedroom suites, which have a separate living room, are US$88/105, and

two-bedroom suites cost US$110/150. When occupancy is low they often run specials that cut rates by about US$20.

Fort Thomas Hotel (☎ 465-2695, fax 465-7518, dssdss@caribsurf.com; in the USA ☎ 800-851-7818), PO Box 407, is on the quiet western side of town. It has 64 comfortable rooms, each with two double beds, air-con, a phone, cable TV, a bath and a balcony from US$80/90 singles/doubles in summer, US$95/105 in winter. There's a moderately priced restaurant, an Olympic-sized pool and a free daily beach shuttle to Frigate Bay. Plans for expansion and the addition of a casino may alter the hotel's tranquil appeal.

Ocean Terrace Inn (☎ 465-2754, fax 465-1057; in the USA ☎ 800-524-0512), PO Box 65, is Basseterre's biggest hotel with some 76 rooms. Known locally as OTI, it's popular with both tour groups and business travelers. Accommodations are spread across three sites and vary greatly, ranging from cramped streetside cottages and standard hotel rooms to commodious split-level oceanview apartments perched above Fisherman's Wharf. All rooms have air-con, cable TV and phones. In winter, singles/doubles begin at US$93/116 for the cheapest rooms and US$121/165 for the split-level apartments. Summer rates average about 15% less. There's a pool, a fitness center and a complimentary shuttle to Turtle Beach.

Around Basseterre *Bird Rock Beach Hotel* (☎ 465-8914, fax 465-1675, birdrock@caribbeans.com; in the USA ☎ 800-621-1270), PO Box 227, in the suburbs 2 miles east of central Basseterre, has 38 pleasant rooms. All are well appointed with cable TV, air-con, fans, phones, tubs and cliffside, oceanview balconies. The studios and suites have simple kitchenettes as well. There's a moderately priced restaurant, tennis courts, a pool and a small black-sand beach. The units are spread across six contemporary two-story buildings; the farthest two are the newest and have the best views. Summer/winter rates are US$75/150 for a room, US$80/165 for a studio and US$125/295 for a two-bedroom suite.

Fairview Inn (☎ 465-2472, fax 465-1056; in the USA ☎ 800-223-9815), PO Box 212, is situated above a working cane field 4 miles west of town, on the north side of the circle-island road. A former plantation estate, Fairview is quite ordinary in comparison to other plantation inns on the island. The main house serves as a restaurant, while accommodations are provided in 30 cottages, some nondescript and others more atmospheric with old stone walls. All have private bathrooms and some have TV and a separate dining area. Superior rooms, which cost US$80/140 in summer/winter, have air-con, while moderate rooms (US$75/130) are fan cooled. Standard rooms (US$70/120) have neither air-con nor fans! There's a pool.

Morgan Heights Condominiums (☎ 465-8633, fax 465-9272), PO Box 536, is on the circle-island road in the Canada Estate area 2 miles northeast of the airport. While the location is a bit out of the way, the units are large and modern with full kitchens, air-con, cable TV, phones and patios. Summer/winter rates are US$75/125 for one-bedroom suites, US$125/175 for two-bedroom suites. You can also rent just a bedroom, hotel-style, for US$50/75. There is a restaurant and a pool.

Places to Eat

Redi-Fried, a hole-in-the-wall next to the cinema on Bay Rd, has two pieces of chicken with fries for EC$9. If you prefer to dine in air-conditioned comfort you can get similar fare at *KFC*, which is also on Bay Rd, for slightly higher prices. Redi-Fried is open until midnight daily, KFC to at least 11 pm.

The new *Bayembi Cafe*, on Bank St near the Circus, has an arty decor and Basseterre's best coffee. It serves bagels and croissants, vegie rotis (EC$9) and hot sub sandwiches (EC$16). Hours are from 9 am to 9 pm Monday to Saturday.

Chef's Place on Church St has good food and streetside patio dining. Various breakfasts cost EC$15, while at lunch and dinner there are four or five choices from the chalkboard, with such items as garlic chicken, grilled fish and butterfly shrimp – all around EC$20 and served with rice, a green salad and island vegetables. They also sell burgers and a good chicken roti (EC$10). It's open from about 8 am to 11 pm daily except Sunday.

Victor's Hideaway on Stainforth St serves up good local food. Generous plates of mutton, chicken, conch or pork, with vegetables, salad and rice, cost around EC$25. It's open from 11:30 am to 3 pm and 6 to 10 pm Monday to Saturday.

The popular *Ballahoo Restaurant* has a cheery 2nd-floor balcony overlooking the Circus. Full breakfasts, including Creole salt fish or pancakes with bacon, cost EC$17. At lunch, rotis, burgers and sandwiches start at EC$9, while the meal of the day is EC$20. Dinner offerings, which include vegetarian stuffed peppers, chicken kebabs, parrotfish fillet and lobster, range from EC$30 to EC$60. The banana-and-rum toasted sandwich topped with vanilla ice cream is a delicious finale. Another treat is the tangy fresh-squeezed ginger beer. It's open from 8 am to 10 pm daily except Sunday.

Fisherman's Wharf is a good-value, fun place to eat with dining at picnic tables on a waterfront dock below Ocean Terrace Inn. Dinners, cooked to order over an open grill, are accompanied by a self-service buffet of salad, Creole rice, sauteed potatoes, local vegetables and garlic bread. The price depends on the main dish you select: various fresh fishes cost EC$45, while meats range from barbecued chicken for EC$27 to sirloin steak for EC$69. Or just go vegetarian with the buffet alone for EC$18. It's open from 6:30 to 11 pm nightly.

StoneWalls (☎ 465-5248), a trendy pub on Princes St, is run by a Canadian-English couple, has a pleasant courtyard setting and offers Creole, Cajun and Caribbean cuisine. Dinner without drinks averages EC$50. It's open from 5 to 11 pm Monday to Saturday; reservations are suggested.

The Georgian House (☎ 465-4049) has romantic dining in a restored manor house on Independence Square. Main dishes, which average EC$65, include the likes of seared salmon, rack of lamb or ginger duck. Add another EC$13 for soup or salad. It's open from 6:30 pm daily except Sunday and reservations are advised.

American Bakery on Victoria Rd specializes in fresh bread and pastries and is open from 6 am to 6 pm weekdays, to 2 pm on Saturday. *Country Churn Ice Cream* on Cayon St serves homemade ice cream, including a rich chocolate flavor.

The green-walled, tin-roofed *public market* on Bay Rd is the best place to pick up fruits and vegetables. There are a couple of grocery stores between the public market and the post office – *National Supply* and *Ram's Supermarket* – but hands down the best food selection is at the new *Valu Mart*, an American-style supermarket on Wellington St, a third of a mile northeast of the Cayon St rotary on the way to the airport.

Around St Kitts

FRIGATE BAY

Frigate Bay, 3 miles southeast of Basseterre, is the main beach resort area for St Kitts. It has two beaches, North Frigate Bay (also called Atlantic Beach) and Frigate Bay Beach (also known as Caribbean Beach or Timothy Beach). It's a 15-minute walk between the two bays.

The calmer Frigate Bay Beach, on the south side of the peninsula, is the island's most popular bathing spot. The facilities at this gray-sand beach include water sports huts and an open-air drinking spot, the Monkey Bar, which attracts a crowd on weekends. The beach is backed by a salt pond while the nearshore waters are a feeding ground for pelicans and frigatebirds.

North Frigate Bay has waters that are a bit rough and a long stretch of golden sand. Most of the area's development is along North Frigate Bay, with condominiums and shops lined up along the beach, opposite the golf course and Jack Tar Village.

Despite the fact that Jack Tar has a casino, Frigate Bay is nonetheless a pretty low-key, uneventful area.

Buses generally don't run to Frigate Bay, so if you don't have your own rental car you'll have to plan on doing some hefty walking or rely on taxis.

Places to Stay

Gateway Inn (☎ 465-7155, fax 465-9322, gateway@caribsurf.com), PO Box 1253, is off by itself at the side of the main road between Basseterre and Frigate Bay. This unpretentious one-story apartment complex has 10 furnished units, each with a full kitchen, living room, separate bedroom, air-con, phone and cable TV. Rates are US$60/80 in summer/winter. On weekly rentals the seventh day is free.

Timothy Beach Resort (☎ 465-8597, fax 466-7085, tbeach@caribsurf.com; in the USA ☎ 800-777-1700), PO Box 1198, is a small condo-style hotel affiliated with the Colony resort chain. The rooms have seen better days but the resort does have a good beachside location on the east side of Frigate Bay Beach. Mountainview rooms are the cheapest; they have a tiny balcony, mini-refrigerator, air-con and phone and cost US$65/95 in summer/winter. Studios with a kitchen costs US$85/130, one-bedroom apartments US$95/165.

Frigate Bay Resort (☎ 465-8935, fax 465-7050; in the USA ☎ 800-266-2185), PO Box 137, is a contemporary 64-room hotel on a hillside above Frigate Bay. Rooms are pleasant with tiled floors, ceiling fans, air-con, bathtubs and phones. The cheapest rooms, which have hillside views, cost US$77/145 in summer/winter, while suites with kitchenettes start at US$175/267. There's a restaurant, a large pool and it's possible to walk down to Frigate Bay Beach via a path behind the hotel.

If you need a lot of space, *SeaLofts* (☎ 465-1075, fax 466-5034), PO Box 813, is one of Frigate Bay's better-value places to stay. The two-bedroom townhouse-style units each have a living room with sofabed, wicker and rattan furnishings, dining area,

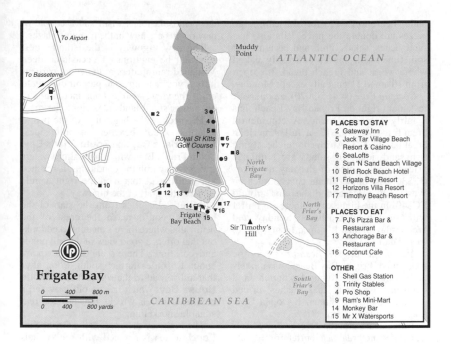

Frigate Bay

0   400   800 m

0   400   800 yards

CARIBBEAN SEA

PLACES TO STAY
2 Gateway Inn
5 Jack Tar Village Beach
   Resort & Casino
6 SeaLofts
8 Sun 'N Sand Beach Village
10 Bird Rock Beach Hotel
11 Frigate Bay Resort
12 Horizons Villa Resort
17 Timothy Beach Resort

PLACES TO EAT
7 PJ's Pizza Bar &
   Restaurant
13 Anchorage Bar &
   Restaurant
16 Coconut Cafe

OTHER
1 Shell Gas Station
3 Trinity Stables
4 Pro Shop
9 Ram's Mini-Mart
14 Monkey Bar
15 Mr X Watersports

full kitchen, large balcony, cable TV and a washing machine and dryer. It's on the beach and there are two tennis courts and a pool. Rates are US$140 to US$175 in winter, depending on the view, US$105 to US$130 in summer. There's no housekeeping service and thus no service charge. Credit cards are not accepted.

Sun 'N Sand Beach Village (☎ 465-8037, fax 465-6745; in the USA ☎ 800-223-6510), PO Box 341, has 18 fully equipped condo-style two-bedroom cottages and 32 motel-style studio apartments, with aircon, ceiling fan, cable TV and phones. The studios have toasters, refrigerators and microwave ovens while the cottages have full kitchens. There's a pool and tennis courts. The studios cost US$90/160 in summer/winter for up to two people, the cottages US$150/270 for up to four people.

Horizons Villa Resort (☎ 465-0584, fax 465-0785, horizons@caribsurf.com), PO Box 1143, is a large new development with

spacious contemporary units spread along an oceanside knoll. Suites, which have a seaview balcony, king bed, TV, VCR, thermostatic air-con, refrigerator, hot plate and coffeemaker, cost US$130/190 in summer/winter. Split-level one-bedroom units that have the addition of a separate living room and full kitchen cost US$160/240; there are also two-, three- and four-bedroom units. The resort has two pools, a tennis court and a restaurant.

Jack Tar Village Beach Resort & Casino (☎ 465-8651, fax 465-1031; in the USA ☎ 800-999-9182), PO Box 406, is a 244-room all-inclusive resort-cum-casino. Rates, which include meals, drinks and activities, cost from US$170/280 for singles/doubles.

Places to Eat

PJ's Pizza Bar & Restaurant (☎ 465-8373), run by two Canadian women, is a popular place with both eat-in and takeout service. Small pizzas cost from EC$15 for

ST KITTS

plain cheese to EC$25 for Mexican; large pizzas are double the price. PJ's also has sandwiches, salads, chili and lasagna and sometimes sells loaves of freshly baked whole wheat and French bread. It's open from 10 am to 11 pm daily except Monday.

Coconut Cafe (☎ 465-3020), an open-air restaurant right on Frigate Bay Beach, has a fairly extensive menu. A continental breakfast costs EC$13, a full American breakfast EC$21. At lunch, quiche, flying fish sandwiches or salads are similarly priced, while catch of the day averages EC$30. The dinner menu concentrates on West Indian seafood dishes for around EC$40. In the high season there's a buffet with steel band music on Sunday and Wednesday nights. It's open from 7 am to 11 pm daily.

Anchorage Bar & Restaurant, at the west end of Frigate Bay Beach, has moderately priced sandwiches for lunch, and chicken, fish and steak dishes priced around EC$40 for dinner. It's open from noon to around 10 pm.

The restaurant at the *Frigate Bay Resort* has a decent breakfast buffet for EC$25 and lunchtime sandwiches and salads from EC$14 to EC$22. On Wednesday there's a West Indian buffet and on Saturday a barbecue buffet; both cost EC$55 and are accompanied by a steel band. On other nights main courses average EC$55. It's open from 7:30 am to 9:30 pm daily.

Near Sun 'N Sand, there's a mini-mart, *Ram's*, open from 9 am to 6 pm daily except Sunday.

SOUTHEAST PENINSULA

St Kitts' southeast peninsula is wild and unspoiled. The scenery has a certain stark beauty, with barren salt ponds, grass-covered hills and scrubby vegetation. The main inhabitants are green vervet monkeys, which you may see bounding across the road, and a few wild deer.

Until the early 1990s, when the 6.5-mile Dr Kennedy Simmonds Hwy was constructed along its twisting spine, most visitors to this rugged peninsula arrived by boat. The highway signals grand plans to develop

the peninsula for tourism and a couple of new resorts are now in the planning stages.

The new highway is the island's best road but be cautious of occasional deep V-shaped rain gutters at the edge, particularly if you're tempted to pull off quickly to enjoy the view. Also, it's not uncommon to encounter small landslides along the road.

The neck at the beginning of the peninsula has sandy beaches on both sides: **North Friar's Bay** and **South Friar's Bay**. South Friar's Bay, which has calmer waters and better swimming conditions, is reached via a dirt road that's on the right a mile south of the start of the highway.

About 2.25 miles from the start of the highway, you'll reach the crest of the peninsula, where there's an unmarked lookout that offers a good view of the salt ponds and coastline. There's another viewpoint about 1.5 miles farther south. Soon after that a dirt road to the right leads to **White House Bay**, which has an old jetty and a couple of minor wrecks that provide reasonable snorkeling.

The highway then passes the **Great Salt Pond**, which is rimmed with salt crystals and attracts plovers, oystercatchers, stilts, whimbrels and other shorebirds. After that the road forks. The right fork leads to **Major's Bay**, which has a predominantly rocky shoreline, though if you walk west a few minutes from road's end you'll discover a quiet little sandy strand. The left fork leads to **Cockleshell Bay**, which has a pleasant gray-sand beach and a wonderful view of Nevis. On the road to Cockleshell Bay, just past an old sugar mill, a sign points to **Turtle Beach**, which also has a sandy beach and Nevis view. Turtle Beach is used by Ocean Terrace Inn and has a restaurant and dive shop.

Places to Eat

The only place to eat on the southeast peninsula is at the *Turtle Beach Bar & Grill* at Turtle Beach. The restaurant is open from 10 am to 6 pm daily (to 11 pm on Saturday) with simple offerings such as EC$15 sandwiches and chicken or fish dishes for about double that.

CIRCLE-ISLAND ROAD

The major sightseeing spot on St Kitts is Brimstone Hill Fortress, but the circle-island road passes a few other points of interest as well, including petroglyphs, a batik factory and the crumbling stacks of numerous abandoned sugar mills.

It's a pleasant rural drive with scenery dominated by fields of sugar cane, broken up here and there by scattered villages. The narrow gauge tracks of the sugar cane train run alongside the road and odds are good that you'll see these vintage trains hauling loads of freshly cut cane from the fields to the mill.

The villages themselves, with their weathered stone churches and old wooden houses with rusty tin roofs, offer a closer glimpse of island life. All have small stores or rum shacks that sell sodas, liquor and a few basic provisions.

The road is paved and in fairly good condition, though you'll have to slow down for potholes, rain gutters and the occasional stray goat. The circle-island tour can easily be done in half a day; however, giving yourself a few more hours would allow for a more leisurely exploration.

Bloody Point

A little over 4 miles west of Basseterre, at the north end of the village of Challengers, a sign marks Bloody Point, the site where more than 2000 Caribs were massacred by joint British and French forces in 1626.

Shortly after that sign there's a curve in the road and a small place to pull off – stop here for a scenic view of the coast and Brimstone Hill.

Old Road Town

After Bloody Point the road swings down to the seaside village of Old Road Town, the landing site of the first British settlers in 1623. Amerindians left an earlier mark in the form of petroglyphs, and a 17th-century sugar estate has been turned into a well-regarded batik factory.

In the center of the village a sign pointing to Caribelle Batik marks Wingfield Rd. Immediately after turning inland on Wingfield,

there's a yellow nursery school on the left. At the side of the road just past the school you'll find three large black stones with **petroglyphs**; the middle one has two distinct human-like figures carved by Caribs. There are no fees to visit the site.

The road continues another half-mile through corn and cane fields and up past the ruins of the mill, chimney and stone arches of the Wingfield Estate before reaching Romney Manor, the old estate grounds that now contain **Caribelle Batik**.

The estate is located at the edge of a rainforest and this drive makes a nice diversion from the more arid lowlands that edge the coast. Although the manor house itself burned down a few years ago, Romney Manor still has interesting landscaping, with lush vegetation and grand flowering trees.

Batiks are made and sold on site and you can watch wax being painted on cloth in a small demonstration area. It's open from 8:30 am to 4 pm weekdays.

Middle Island

The village of Middle Island is the site of the tomb of Sir Thomas Warner, the leader of the first British landing party on St Kitts, who died in March 1648. His marble-topped tomb with its verbose epitaph is under a white wooden shelter fronting the aging St Thomas church, which sits on a rise in the middle of town.

Brimstone Hill Fortress National Park

This rambling 18th-century compound, which in its day was nicknamed 'Gibraltar of the West Indies,' is one of the largest forts in the Caribbean. As a major British garrison, Brimstone Hill played a key role in battles with the French, who seized the fort in 1782 but returned it the next year under terms of the Treaty of Paris. The treaty ushered in a more peaceful era and by the 1850s the fort was abandoned.

After the 1867 fire swept through Basseterre, some of the fort structures were partially dismantled and the stones used to rebuild the capital. In the 1960s major restoration was undertaken and much of

ST KITTS

the fortress has been returned to its earlier grandeur. Queen Elizabeth II inaugurated the fort as a national park during her visit to St Kitts in October 1985.

The main hilltop compound, the Citadel, is lined with 24 cannons and provides excellent views of St Eustatius and Sandy Point Town. Inside the Citadel's old barrack rooms are museum displays on colonial history that feature cannonballs, swords and other period odds and ends. There's also a small collection of Amerindian adzes, a few pottery fragments and a rubbing of the Carib petroglyphs in Old Road Town. Another room contains a display on the American Revolution and the West Indian role in that revolt.

Also worthwhile is the short stroll above the cookhouse to the top of Monkey Hill, which provides excellent coastal views. A small theater next to the gift shop plays a brief video on the fort's history; a nearby canteen sells drinks and sandwiches.

Brimstone Hill, upon which the fortress stands, is an 800-foot volcanic cone named for the odoriferous sulphur vents that you will undoubtedly detect as you drive past the hill along the coastal road.

Buses from Basseterre to Sandy Point Town can drop you off at the signposted road leading up to the fortress, from where it's a 1.25-mile uphill walk on a narrow winding road. If you're driving up, be sure to beep your horn as you approach blind curves.

The fortress is open from daily 9:30 am to 5:30 pm. Admission for foreign visitors costs US$5 for adults, US$2.50 for children.

Northeast Coast

As you continue from Brimstone Hill Fortress, you'll pass through lowlands of cane while circling **Mt Liamuiga**, the 3792-foot volcano that dominates the interior of the island. The north side of St Kitts has two exclusive resorts, Rawlins Plantation, in the hills east of St Paul's, and the Golden Lemon, down on the coast at Dieppe Bay. **Dieppe Bay Town** is a seaside fishing village with the requisite stone mill but not much else of note.

At the south end of Sadlers, you'll spot an old stone church down in the cane fields and shortly beyond that a sign points to **Black Rocks**. A short drive down that side road ends at coastal cliffs and a view of some seaside lava rock formations. If the road proves too rough to drive on, the cliffs are only a five-minute walk from the circle-island road.

As the circle-island road continues south along the east coast, it passes more small towns, old sugar mills peeking above the cane fields and some stone churches, though there are no particular sights to stop for along the way. One of the villages on this side of the island, **Ottley's**, is the site of another exclusive plantation estate.

Places to Stay *Rawlins Plantation* (☎ 465-6221, fax 465-4954; in the USA ☎ 800-346-5358, in the UK ☎ 071-730-7144), PO Box 340, a mile inland from St Paul's, is the most gracious of St Kitts' plantation inns. A former sugar estate that's still bordered by cane fields, it nicely incorporates its historic buildings. A period stone mill has been turned into a romantic honeymoon suite, while other accommodations are in comfortable cottages with wooden floors, four-poster beds and separate sitting rooms or verandas. There's a pool. Single/double rates for the 10 rooms, which include breakfast, afternoon tea and dinner, are US$190/275 in the summer, US$280/395 in the winter.

The *Golden Lemon* (☎ 465-7260, fax 465-4019; in the USA ☎ 800-633-7411) is on a stony black-sand beach right in Dieppe Bay Town. A 17th-century plantation house is the centerpiece of the complex; however, most units are in a modern condo-like facility next door. Singles/doubles begin at US$160/245 in summer, US$218/333 in winter, breakfast included.

Ottley's Plantation Inn (☎ 465-7234, fax 465-4760, ottleys@caribsurf.com; in the USA ☎ 800-772-3039), PO Box 345, is a handsome 18th-century plantation house inland from Ottley's village. There are 15 air-con rooms in the main building and surrounding cottages. All are comfortably furnished, each with a ceiling fan and a queen- or king-size bed, and some with antiques. Summer/winter rates, breakfast included, range from US$215/290 for a room in the 'great house' to US$275/410 for the two-room English cottage where Princess Margaret once stayed. It's US$25 less for single occupancy. There's a pool and a daily shuttle to the beach and town.

Places to Eat *Rawlins Plantation*, with its splendid view across cane fields to St Eustatius, is the choice place to have lunch on a circle-island tour. The West Indian lunch buffet, served daily on the patio from 12:30 to 2 pm, includes numerous dishes, such as chicken and breadfruit curry, beef brochettes, flying fish fritters and fresh fruit sorbet. The cost is EC$65. Dinner, a set four-course meal costing EC$120, is available at 8 pm by reservation only. The plantation is a mile up a signposted cane road that begins half a mile east of St Paul's.

The *Golden Lemon* in Dieppe Bay Town serves lunch from noon to 2:30 pm, offering salads, sandwiches and fish & chips for EC$27 to EC$40. Dinner, by reservation only, changes daily but commonly includes a seafood main dish complete with an appetizer, soup and dessert for around EC$120.

Ottley's Plantation Inn has pleasant alfresco dining within the partial stone walls of a former sugar warehouse. At lunch, the menu features sandwiches and simple dishes such as flying fish or Jamaican jerk chicken for around EC$30, lobster quesadillas for EC$50. At dinner a four-course meal is offered for EC$135.

Nevis

Despite the opening of its first resort hotel, Nevis is still a sleepy little backwater. It's a friendly island with a delightfully rural character and some reasonably good beaches.

Sightseeing on Nevis is limited mainly to poking around the old stone churches and sugar plantation ruins scattered about

the countryside. A paved road circles the island and there are inexpensive car rentals, making it easy to explore Nevis on a day trip. The island has a forested interior rising to scenic Nevis Peak, which is often cloaked in clouds. The coastal lowlands, where the larger villages are located, are much drier and support bougainvillea, hibiscus and other flowering bushes that attract numerous hummingbirds.

While most visitors arrive on the St Kitts ferry for a one-day outing, Nevis has some interesting accommodations options for those seeking a quiet West Indian getaway.

CHARLESTOWN
The ferry from St Kitts docks in Charlestown, the island's largest town and commercial center. The town has a few buildings with gingerbread trim, some old stone structures and a center that's marked by two tiny squares. Flanking one square is the tourist office and taxi stand, while the second square, a block to the south, fronts the courthouse and library.

The greater Charlestown area can be readily explored on foot – the museums and the bath house are within walking distance. Just a 15-minute jaunt north of the center will put you on a lovely stretch of Pinney's Beach that's lined with coconut trees and invites long strolls.

Information
Tourist Office The Nevis Tourist Office (☎ 469-5521), a two-minute walk east of the pier, is open from 8 am to 4 pm weekdays and 9 am to 1 pm on Saturday. There's also a smaller tourist information booth at the ferry ticket office but it's generally busier as it's managed by the ticket agent.

Money The St Kitts and Nevis National Bank will cash traveler's checks in any amount free of commission, while Barclays Bank charges an EC$2 commission for amounts under US$100. Banking hours are 8 am to 3 pm Monday to Wednesday, 8 am to 2 pm on Thursday and 8 am to 5 pm on Friday.

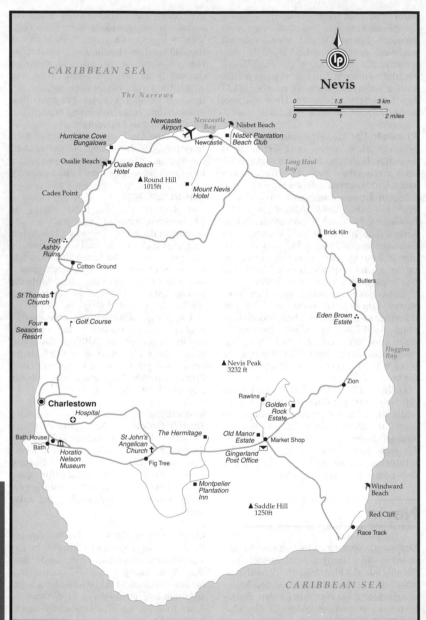

CARIBBEAN SEA

The Narrows

Nevis

0   1.5   3 km
0   1   2 miles

Hurricane Cove
Bungalows

Newcastle
Airport

Newcastle
Bay

Nisbet Beach

Newcastle

Nisbet Plantation
Beach Club

Oualie Beach

Oualie Beach
Hotel

Long Haul
Bay

▲ Round Hill
1015ft

Cades Point

Mount Nevis
Hotel

Brick Kiln

Fort
Ashby
Ruins

Cotton Ground

Butlers

St Thomas †
Church

Golf Course

Eden Brown
Estate

Four
Seasons
Resort

Huggins
Bay

▲ Nevis Peak
3232 ft

Zion

Rawlins

Charlestown

Hospital

Golden
Rock
Estate

Bath House

The Hermitage

Old Manor
Estate

Market Shop

Bath

Horatio
Nelson
Museum

St John's
Angelican
Church †

Gingerland
Post Office

Fig Tree

Windward
Beach

Montpelier
Plantation
Inn

Red Cliff

▲ Saddle Hill
1250ft

Race Track

CARIBBEAN SEA

NEVIS

Post The post office, on Main St in Charlestown, is open from 8 to 11 am on Thursday, 8 am to 3 pm other weekdays and 8 am to 11:30 am on Saturday. Commemorative stamps are sold at the Nevis Philatelic Bureau, which is near the public market and open from 8 am to 4 pm Monday to Friday.

Telephone You can make international phone calls and send faxes and telegrams from the Skantel office on Main St, which is open from 8 am to 5 pm on weekdays, to noon on Saturday.

Museum of Nevis History
The Museum of Nevis History occupies a Georgian-style building at the site where American statesman Alexander Hamilton was born in 1757 (the original home was toppled by an earthquake in the mid-1800s). In addition to portraits of Hamilton, this pleasant little museum has period photos with interpretive captions and other bits and pieces of Nevis culture and history. It's open from 8 am to 4 pm Monday to Friday and from 10 am to noon on Saturday. Admission is EC$5 or you can purchase a joint ticket that also covers the Horatio Nelson Museum (see below) for EC$8.

Incidentally, history still unfolds at this site, as Nevis' pro-independence House of Assembly holds its meetings upstairs.

Jewish Cemetery
A couple of minutes walk up Government Rd from the town center there's a small and largely forgotten Jewish cemetery, which consists of a grassy field of horizontal gravestones. The oldest stone dates from 1684 and quite a few others date from the early 1700s, when an estimated 25% of the non-slave population on Nevis was Jewish.

In addition it's now believed that the site of the original synagogue, which may be the oldest in the Caribbean, has been identified. An excavation is currently being undertaken about 75 yards south of the cemetery; to get there, take the dirt path that begins opposite the cemetery's south-

west corner and follow it to the ruins just beyond the government offices.

Horatio Nelson Museum
The Horatio Nelson Museum, on Building Hill Rd about 100 yards east of the old Bath House Hotel (see below), contains memorabilia relating to Lord Nelson, who stopped off on this island in the 1780s, where he met and married Fanny Nisbett, the niece of the island's governor. This former private collection consists largely of mugs and dishes painted with Nelson's image, ceramic statues of the admiral and a few everyday items once used by Nelson. The museum is open from 9 am to 4 pm Monday to Friday and 10 am to 1 pm on Saturday. Admission is EC$5.

Bath House
The Bath House, a 15-minute walk south of Charlestown center, is a defunct hotel dating from 1778 that sits above thermal springs. Its mineral-laden waters, thought to have regenerative qualities, were the island's main attraction in colonial days, when wealthy visitors flocked here to soak in the warm baths. While its days of glory are long gone, the stone bath house just below the old hotel still occasionally opens to the public, allowing visitors to soak in its shallow 108°F (42°C) waters for EC$5.

Some islanders skip the fees and simply bathe in the stream that runs below the bath house.

Places to Stay
Daniel's Deck (☎ 469-5265) has a handful of rooms for rent above a little grocery store on Main St in the town center. The rooms are simple but clean and all have fans and private baths. Singles/doubles cost US$19/30. The owner, Roosevelt Daniel, can also arrange short-term apartment rentals.

Sea Spawn Guest House (☎ 469-5239), Old Hospital Road, is a couple of minutes walk from Pinney's Beach and a 10-minute walk from the Charlestown pier. This 18-room guesthouse has small simple rooms, each with a private bathroom and portable

NEVIS

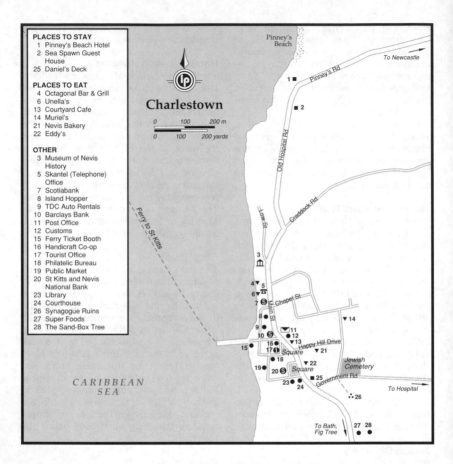

PLACES TO STAY
1 Pinney's Beach Hotel
2 Sea Spawn Guest House
25 Daniel's Deck

PLACES TO EAT
4 Octagonal Bar & Grill
6 Unella's
13 Courtyard Cafe
14 Muriel's
21 Nevis Bakery
22 Eddy's

OTHER
3 Museum of Nevis History
5 Skantel (Telephone) Office
7 Scotiabank
8 Island Hopper
9 TDC Auto Rentals
10 Barclays Bank
11 Post Office
12 Customs
15 Ferry Ticket Booth
16 Handicraft Co-op
17 Tourist Office
18 Philatelic Bureau
19 Public Market
20 St Kitts and Nevis National Bank
23 Library
24 Courthouse
26 Synagogue Ruins
27 Super Foods
28 The Sand-Box Tree

Charlestown

Pinney's Beach

To Newcastle

Pinney's Rd

Old Hospital Rd

Craddock Rd

Low St

Ferry to St Kitts

Chapel St

Main St

Happy Hill Drive

Square

Square

Jewish Cemetery

Government Rd

To Hospital

CARIBBEAN SEA

To Bath, Fig Tree

fan. While the downstairs rooms are a bit austere, the upstairs rooms are bigger and brighter. There's a large common space that includes a TV room, kitchen and dining room. Rates, tax and service included, are US$35/41 for singles/doubles downstairs and US$47 for the upstairs doubles.

The 55-room *Pinney's Beach Hotel* (☎ 469-5207), PO Box 61, is an older, neglected place on the water at the south end of Pinney's Beach. The rooms, which have orange carpets and a standard motel ambiance, are rather pricey for what you get. The cheapest, which cost US$55/80 for singles/doubles in summer and US$75/100 in winter, have air-con, phones and private baths. Add US$15 more if you want a room with a TV.

Places to Eat

The *Courtyard Cafe* serves ordinary fare in a quiet garden courtyard shaded by banana trees. Breakfast pancakes and lunchtime sandwiches or burgers cost around EC$12. It's open from 7:30 am to 3:30 pm Monday to Saturday. *Eddy's*, run by a Canadian-West Indian couple, has a pleasant 2nd-floor veranda dining area that overlooks

Main St. There's homemade soup and bread for EC$12, salads and burgers for EC$20 and chicken stir-fry for EC$25. It's open for lunch, from noon to 3 pm, daily except Thursday and Sunday.

There are a few restaurants just north of the dock. *Octagonal Bar & Grill* offers barbecued chicken (EC$15) and fish (EC$25) meals in a casual seaside setting, complete with reggae music and ice-cold beer. The nearby *Unella's*, a 2nd-floor open-air restaurant, has a water view and standard fare with fish burgers for EC$12 and various hot meals for about EC$25.

For local food without a view, there's *Muriel's*, an unpretentious little spot just beyond Happy Hill Drive, at the back of the Lime Tree store. The dinner menu includes chicken or fish for EC$35 and lobster for EC$45, served with rice and peas, christophene and fried plantain. Lighter and cheaper lunches are available from noon to 3 pm. It's open daily except on Sunday.

Nevis Bakery on Happy Hill Drive has breads, tasty pineapple-cinnamon rolls and inexpensive rotis.

The best place to go for produce is the *public market*, which is open from around 7 am to 4:30 pm daily except Sunday. There are a handful of small food markets in the town center. *Super Foods*, at the south side of Main St, is the island's biggest supermarket; it's open from 8 am to 8 pm Monday to Saturday.

SOUTH NEVIS

The circle-island road crosses the southern part of Nevis between cloud-shrouded Nevis Peak and Saddle Hill, passing through the districts of Fig Tree and Gingerland. This area was the center of Nevis' sugar industry in colonial days and there are many crumbling sugar mill stacks that evoke that era. A few of the former plantation estates have been converted into atmospheric inns.

St John's Anglican Church

St John's, on the main road in the village of Fig Tree, is a stone church that dates from 1680. A copy of the church register, dated March 11, 1787, which records the marriage of Lord Horatio Nelson and Francis Nisbett, can be found in a glass case at the rear of the church. If you peek beneath the red carpet in the center aisle you'll find a continuous row of tombstones of island notables who died in the 1700s.

Windward Beach

Windward Beach, also known as Indian Castle Beach, is the only easily accessible beach on the southern part of the island. Backed by beach morning glory and low scrubby trees, the beach has fine gray sand and fairly active surf. Unless it's a weekend, the odds are good that, with the exception of a few rummaging goats, you'll have the beach to yourself.

To get there, turn south at the Gingerland Post Office in Market Shop and continue straight ahead for 2 miles. (Be aware of humps and dips in the road; just south of the church there's an especially sharp dip that's not visible until you're on top of it.) Then turn left and follow the road for another three-quarters of a mile. After passing the racetrack (where horse races are held on holidays), the road turns to dirt and becomes somewhat rough but it should be passable unless it's been raining heavily. There are no facilities at the beach.

Places to Stay

The following four plantation inns are all on the grounds of former sugar estates. All are within 3 miles of each other and none is more than a few minutes drive from the circle-island road.

The Hermitage (☎ 469-3477, fax 469-2481, nevherm@caribsurf.com; in the USA ☎ 800-682-4025), St John's Parish, about a mile northeast of Fig Tree, is a quiet 14-room inn run by an American couple. The main plantation house, which is 250 years old and furnished with antiques, serves as a parlor and evening gathering spot. Accommodations are in one- and two-story cottages spread around the grounds. The cottages are pleasantly rustic with four-poster beds, hardwood floors, sitting rooms, ceiling fans, mini-refrigerators and lattice-shuttered windows. There's a pool and tennis court. Prices range from US$160 to US$250 in summer, US$295 to US$410 in winter, breakfast included.

Montpelier Plantation Inn (☎ 469-3462, fax 469-2932, montpinn@caribsurf.com), PO Box 474, 1.5 miles southeast of Fig Tree, is an exclusive 17-room cottage-style English inn. The estate was the site of Horatio Nelson's marriage in 1787 and in more recent times it hosted the late Princess Diana. Despite a regal guest list, the inn has a relaxed and personable appeal that has won it numerous accolades, including top place in Condé Nast reader polls. It has flower gardens, a beach shuttle and a swimming pool scenically set beside the ruins of an old sugar mill. All cottages have seaview balconies, a pleasant subdued decor and a king or two double beds. Singles/doubles cost US$175/195 in summer, US$265/295 in winter, breakfast included.

Old Manor Estate (☎ 469-3445, fax 469-3388; in the USA ☎ 800-892-7093), PO Box 70, at the north side of Market Shop, has an engaging setting. The grounds are scattered with the remains of an 18th-century sugar plantation, including a mill stack, a nearly intact boiler and the huge steel rollers that until 1936 were used to crush the plantation's cane. The inn's 13 atmospheric rooms, which occupy some of the estate's renovated buildings, are very large, cooled by ceiling fans and furnished with either king or queen beds; some also have separate sitting rooms. Rooms cost from US$125 in summer, US$195 in winter, breakfast for two included. There's a complimentary beach and town shuttle.

The 16-room *Golden Rock Estate* (☎ 469-3346, fax 469-2113), PO Box 493, is a casual family-run inn in the countryside between Market Shop and Zion. The main stone-block plantation house, circa 1815, has a bar, library and sitting room. Most accommodations are in cottages with four-poster beds and there's also a stone sugar mill that's been converted into a two-bedroom, two-bathroom suite. There's a

pool, tennis court, nature trails and a complimentary beach shuttle. Singles/doubles cost US$110/130 in summer, US$185/200 in winter.

Places to Eat

The Hermitage (☎ 469-3477) has pleasant open-air dining. Lunch selections include sandwiches, rotis and salads from EC$22 to EC$40. There's also a complete breakfast for EC$33 and a four-course set dinner available by reservation for EC$120. A good night for dinner is Wednesday during the winter season, when there's a string band and a hearty West Indian buffet for the fixed dinner price.

Montpelier Plantation Inn (☎ 469-3462) has a casual terrace where lunch is served from 12:30 to 2:30 pm; sandwiches, a chef's salad or simple pastas average EC$30. A traditional English tea with scones and sponge cake is served from 3:30 to 5:30 pm for EC$20. Dinner, a more pampering affair that's served on the main veranda overlooking spotlit gardens, is prepared by the inn's Welsh chef and features a changing four-course menu for EC$150; advance dinner reservations are required.

The *Cooperage Restaurant* (☎ 469-3445), at the Old Manor Estate, occupies an old cooperage and offers alfresco dining with a distant ocean view. A full breakfast or light lunch costs around EC$35. At dinner, there's a range of main dishes including Jamaican jerk pork, grilled fresh fish or filet mignon for EC$40 to EC$55; soup or salad costs another EC$10. Reservations are suggested.

Golden Rock Estate (☎ 469-3346) has outdoor dining on a cobblestone patio. At lunch, from noon to 2:30 pm, lobster salad for EC$50 is a specialty and there are sandwiches from EC$16 to EC$32. Dinner features a changing fixed-course meal and requires advance reservations.

EAST NEVIS

As you continue around the circle-island road up the east coast, the villages become smaller and houses fewer. The area's main sight is the **Eden Brown Estate** on the inland side of the main road just south of Mannings. The estate house, built around 1740, is most interesting for its macabre history.

Shortly after Julia Huggins inherited this estate from her father, she got engaged to be married. However, the plans were shattered when, on the eve of the wedding in 1822, her celebrating groom and his best man got into a drunken duel and killed each other. After the jolting event, Julia became a recluse in this house and was seldom seen by Nevisians. Following her death, the house was abandoned and to this day some islanders still believe it to be haunted by Julia's ghost.

There are extensive stone ruins of the old plantation, including the remains of a mill behind the house. The estate, now owned by the government, is marked by a sign and free to explore.

NEWCASTLE

Newcastle, at the north end of the island, has Nevis' airport, a handful of places to stay and eat and a roadside pottery shop where traditional coal pots are made and sold.

Newcastle's biggest attractions are its beaches. The fine strand of white sand fronting the Nisbet Plantation Beach Club is Nevis' best. To get there follow the road that runs along the side of the hotel down to the shore, where there's beachside parking. There's also a little beach along Newcastle Bay, where there's a restaurant and a seasonal water sports shop.

Places to Stay

Yamseed Inn (☎ 469-9361) is a contemporary Mediterranean-style home on the north side of the airport. Owner Sybil Siegfried rents four comfortable and airy rooms, each with a private bath, ceiling fan, screened louvered windows and either a queen bed or two extra-long twin beds that can be converted into a king bed. It's on a small private beach with good swimming and a scenic view across the channel to St Kitts. Rooms cost US$100, including a full breakfast of fresh fruit, homemade

granola, banana pancakes and other such goodies. There's a three-night minimum, and in winter it's best to book well in advance.

The *Mount Nevis Hotel* (☎ 469-9373, fax 469-9375, mountnevis@aol.com; in the USA and Canada ☎ 800-756-3847), PO Box 494, is an upmarket family-run hotel with a peaceful setting on the slopes of Mt Nevis. The 32 rooms, which are in four contemporary two-story buildings, have full amenities, including cable TV, VCRs, phones, ceiling fans, air-con, refrigerators and terraces. There's a fine view of St Kitts from the pool and from many of the rooms. The hotel has a complimentary beach shuttle. Double rooms cost US$130/190 in summer/winter, while suites with cooking facilities cost US$190/270. Rates include continental breakfast.

Nisbet Plantation Beach Club (☎ 469-9325, fax 469-9864, nisbetbc@caribsurf .com) is a contemporary beach resort on the site of a former plantation. It's a pleasant place with cottages spread across an expansive lawn that fronts a white-sand beach. There are tennis courts, a beachside pool, a restaurant and a beach bar. The cheapest rooms, which cost US$255 for doubles in summer, US$425 in winter, have wicker furnishings, tiled floors, a screened porch, ceiling fan and minibar. Larger rooms are US$70 to US$100 more. Rates include breakfast and dinner.

Places to Eat

The *Nisbet Plantation Beach Club* has a beachside café serving burgers, rotis and sandwiches for around EC$25, Caesar salad for a couple of dollars more. At dinner there's formal dining in the hotel's Great House (☎ 469-9325), which has a five-course menu du jour for EC$120.

The *Mount Nevis Beach Club Restaurant*, a seasonal place on the beach at Newcastle Bay, has good pizza, salads and sandwiches at moderate prices.

Mount Nevis Hotel (☎ 469-9373) has a chef who hails from New York, a great view and some of the best food on the island. The changing menu features creative

NEVIS

Caribbean and continental cuisine. At dinner, à la carte seafood and meat main dishes range from EC$50 to EC$70, while at breakfast and lunch there are simpler, moderately priced offerings.

OUALIE BEACH

Oualie Beach is a long, thin strip of light gray sand fronted by waters that are shallow and generally calm. It's a very low-keyed area but there are a couple of places to stay and the Oualie Beach Hotel has a dive and water sports shop.

Places to Stay

Oualie Beach Hotel (☎ 469-9735, fax 469-9176, oualie@caribsurf.com; in the USA ☎ 800-682-5431) is a pleasant place right on the beach. It has a dozen rooms, mostly in duplex waterfront cottages. The rooms are comfortable with a four-poster queen bed or two double beds, tiled floor, ceiling fan, refrigerator and screened oceanview patio. Singles/doubles cost US$100/140 in summer, US$155/195 in winter. A studio with air-con and a kitchen costs US$60 more.

Hurricane Cove Bungalows (☎ /fax 469-9462) has a clifftop location at the north end of Oualie Beach. Accommodations are in pleasantly rustic wooden cottages, each with a kitchen, porch and ceiling fan. The one-bedroom cottages cost from US$95/145 in summer/winter, two-bedroom cottages from US$155/225. In spring and late autumn there's a mid-range rate, and in winter a minimum three-day stay is required.

Places to Eat

Oualie Beach Hotel has an open-air beachside restaurant with standard breakfast offerings and lunchtime salads and sandwiches at moderate prices. At dinner there's a three-course meal that includes conch chowder or salad, a choice of six main dishes and dessert for EC$60.

PINNEY'S BEACH

Pinney's Beach is a long stretch of soft white sand that runs along the west coast down to the north side of Charlestown. The

beach, which is backed almost its entire length by tall coconut palms, has lovely views of St Kitts across the channel.

The site of **Fort Ashby**, which was built around 1702, is on the beach just north of Cotton Ground. It's the last of eight small fortifications that once extended along the coast north of Charlestown, but not much remains other than a few cannons and some partially reconstructed walls. This area was also the site of Jamestown, the island's original settlement, which was washed into the sea by an earthquake and tidal wave in 1680.

Places to Stay & Eat

Four Seasons Resort (☎ 469-1111, fax 469-1040; in the USA ☎ 800-332-3442, in Canada ☎ 800-268-6282), PO Box 565, is an upscale resort on a quiet stretch of Pinney's Beach. There's an 18-hole golf course, 10 tennis courts, a pool and health club. The posh 196 rooms each have tiled floors, marble baths, terraces, ceiling fans, air-con, phones, TV and VCRs. Rates are US$250 in summer and US$575 in winter for a golf-course view, and US$50 more for an oceanfront room.

There are a couple of expensive dinner restaurants at Four Seasons and a few small local restaurants scattered along the coast.

GETTING THERE & AWAY
Air

Nevis Express shuttles between St Kitts and Nevis throughout the day; LIAT has 6:40 am, noon and 6:20 pm flights daily from St Kitts to Nevis and a few daily flights from Antigua. For more information, see Getting There & Away and Getting Around at the beginning of this chapter.

Airport Information Nevis' airport, in Newcastle, is a small operation with Win-air, LIAT, Nevis Express, Carib Aviation and a couple of charter desks.

Boat

Information on the ferry between St Kitts and Nevis is in the Getting Around section at the beginning of this chapter.

NEVIS

GETTING AROUND
Bus

Buses are privately owned minivans. Those going up the west coast leave from the square in front of the tourist office on Charlestown's Main St. Some west-coast buses go only as far as Cotton Ground, others go to Newcastle and a few continue on to Butlers. Buses going east to Gingerland and Zion leave from Charlestown's courthouse square. Now there's rarely a bus between Butlers and Zion, and thus no circle-island bus route. Also service is sketchy and it's risky relying on buses if you're trying to see Nevis on a day tour.

Generally, buses don't leave Charlestown until they are full, which might be as often as every 15 minutes in the morning and late afternoon, or as infrequently as every hour in the middle part of the day. On Sunday there's virtually no service. The one-way fare to the farthest point is EC$3.

Taxi

Taxis congregate by the Charlestown pier and charge about EC$120 for a three-hour sightseeing tour. One-way taxi rates from Charlestown center are EC$10 to Bath or Pinney's Beach, EC$23 to Oualie Beach and EC$36 to Newcastle. Taxis also meet scheduled flights at Newcastle Airport.

Car

There are no gas stations on the east side between Fig Tree and Newcastle, so make certain you have enough gas before heading off to explore the island.

Rental Parry's Car Rental (☎ 469-5917) is a friendly, locally owned operation. If you're arriving by ferry, call Parry in advance and he'll meet you at the harbor (give him a few minutes) and when returning the car you simply park it near the dock with the keys in the ignition. Rates begin at US$33.

TDC Auto Rentals (☎ 469-5690 on Nevis, 465-2991 on St Kitts) has an office that's opposite the Charlestown ferry dock. Rates are US$35 for a small car. If you rent a car for a minimum of three days their exchange program allows you to use vehicles on both St Kitts and Nevis at no extra cost, but this option is based on availability, so be sure to confirm both islands when you make a reservation.

Other companies are, in Newcastle, Nisbett Rentals (☎ 469-9211) and Skeete's Car Rental (☎ 469-9458), and, in Fig Tree, Avis (☎ 469-1240). All three rent cars for about US$35.

Most places charge US$10 a day more for a collision damage waiver.

St Lucia

St Lucia is a high green island with a mountainous interior and a coastline pocketed with secluded coves and beaches. Its most dramatic scenery is in the south, where the twin peaks of the Pitons rise sharply from the Soufrière shoreline to form one of the Eastern Caribbean's most distinctive landmarks.

In recent years, St Lucia has seen a spurt of new resort development, much of it intended to make the island a trendy packaged tourism destination. Fortunately, there has also been a rise in the number of small family-run hotels and guesthouses geared towards individual travelers. Most hotels and visitor facilities are on the northwest coast, along the road that runs north from the capital city of Castries.

Once you go south beyond Castries, St Lucia is markedly rural in nature, a mix of small fishing villages, sprawling banana plantations and untamed jungle. The interior rainforest is home to tall hardwood trees, climbing vines, tree ferns and one of the last remaining species of parrots in the Eastern Caribbean.

HIGHLIGHTS

- Pigeon Island, which offers fort ruins, hiking and a white-sand beach
- Castries' Cathedral of the Immaculate Conception, with its unique African-Caribbean influences
- The Soufrière area for its fine scenery, steaming sulphur vents and good diving
- The colorful Friday night jump-up at Gros Islet

Facts about St Lucia

HISTORY

Archaeological finds on the island indicate that St Lucia was settled by Arawaks between 1000 and 500 BC. Around 800 AD migrating Caribs conquered the Arawaks and established permanent settlements on the island.

St Lucia was outside the routes taken by Columbus during his four visits to the New World and was probably first sighted by Spanish explorers during the early 1500s. The first attempt at European colonization wasn't made until 1605, when a party of English settlers was quickly routed off the island by unreceptive Caribs. A second attempt by about 400 British colonists from St Kitts was made in 1638, but the settlement was abandoned within two years after most of the settlers were killed in Carib attacks.

After the British left, the French laid claim to the island and attempted to reach an agreement with the Caribs. The French established the island's first town, Soufrière, in 1746 and went about developing plantations. St Lucia's colonial history was marred by warfare, however, as the

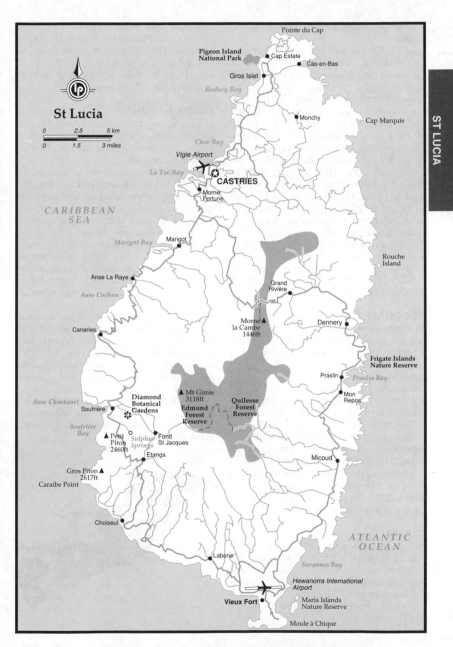

St Lucia

0   2.5   5 km
0   1.5   3 miles

Pointe du Cap

Pigeon Island National Park

Cap Estate

Cas-en-Bas

Gros Islet

Rodney Bay

Monchy

Cap Marquis

Choc Bay

Vigie Airport

La Toc Bay

CASTRIES

Morne Fortune

CARIBBEAN SEA

Marigot Bay   Marigot

Rouche Island

Anse La Raye

Grand Rivière

Anse Cochon

Canaries

Morne ▲ la Cambe 1446ft

Dennery

Frigate Islands Nature Reserve

Praslin

Praslin Bay

Anse Chastanet

Diamond Botanical Gardens

▲ Mt Gimie 3118ft

Quilesse Forest Reserve

Mon Repos

Soufrière

Edmund Forest Reserve

Soufrière Bay

▲ Petit Piton 2460ft

Sulphur Springs

Fond St Jacques

Etangs

Micoud

Gros Piton ▲ 2617ft

Caraibe Point

Choiseul

ATLANTIC OCEAN

Laborie

Savannes Bay

Hewanorra International Airport

Vieux Fort

Maria Islands Nature Reserve

Moule à Chique

British still maintained their claim to the island.

In 1778 the British successfully invaded St Lucia and established naval bases at Gros Islet and Pigeon Island, which they used as staging grounds for attacks on the French islands to the north. For the next few decades St Lucia seesawed between the British and the French. In 1814 the Treaty of Paris finally ceded the island to the British, ending 150 years of conflict during which St Lucia changed flags 14 times.

Culturally, the British were slow in replacing French customs and it wasn't until 1842 that English nudged out French as St Lucia's official language. Other customs linger, and to this day the majority of people speak a French-based patois among themselves, attend Catholic church services and live in villages with French names.

St Lucia gained internal autonomy in 1967 and full independence, as a member of the Commonwealth, on February 22, 1979.

GEOGRAPHY

St Lucia is teardrop shaped, roughly 27 miles in length and 14 miles in width, with a land area of 238 sq miles. The interior is largely mountainous, reaching its highest point at the 3118-foot Mt Gimie in the southwest. Deep valleys, many of which are planted with bananas and coconuts, reach down from the mountains.

The Soufrière area has the island's best-known geological features: the twin volcanic cones of the Pitons, which rise up some 2500 feet from the shoreline, and the hot bubbling Sulphur Springs just inland from the town. Despite this little show of geological activity, there hasn't been a volcanic eruption on St Lucia since 1766.

CLIMATE

In January the average daily high temperature in Castries is 81°F (27°C) while the low averages 68°F (20°C). In July the average daily high is 85°F (29°C) while the low averages 72°F (22°C).

Annual rainfall ranges from 59 inches (1500 mm) on the coast to 136 inches (3450 mm) in the mountains. In Castries, measur-able rain falls an average of 11 days a month from January to March, the driest months. The rainiest months, June to December, have an average of 18 days of rain. Humidity ranges from 76% in February to 83% in November.

FLORA & FAUNA

St Lucia's vegetation ranges from dry and scrubby areas of cacti and hibiscus to lush jungly valleys with wild orchids, bromeliads, heliconia and lianas.

Under the British colonial administration much of St Lucia's rainforest was targeted for timber harvesting. In many ways the independent St Lucian government has proved a far more effective environmental force and while only about 10% of the island remains covered in rainforest, most of it has now been set aside as nature reserve. The largest indigenous trees in the rainforest are the gommier, a towering gum tree, and the chatagnier, a huge buttress-trunked tree.

Island fauna includes the St Lucia parrot, St Lucian oriole, purple-throated Carib hummingbird, bats, lizards, iguana, tree frogs, introduced mongoose, the rabbit-like agouti and several snake species, including the venomous fer-de-lance and the boa constrictor.

It's illegal to damage, collect, buy or sell any type of coral on St Lucia and nothing should be removed from any of the island's many marine reserves.

St Lucia Parrot

The rainforest is home to the St Lucia parrot *(Amazona versicolor)*, locally called the jacquot, the island's colorful endemic parrot. Despite the jacquot's status as the national bird and its appearance on everything from T-shirts to St Lucian passports, it has teetered on the brink of extinction.

However, a successful effort to educate islanders on the plight of the parrot and new environmental laws seem to be working to save the parrots, which occasionally made it onto island dinner tables in times past. Fines for shooting or capturing parrots have been increased a hundredfold while much of the parrots' habitat has been set aside for protection. The efforts have resulted in an increase in the population from about 100 birds in the late 1970s to around 400 today. Most of the parrots nest in the adjacent Edmond and Quilesse Forest Reserves, east of Soufrière. ■

GOVERNMENT & POLITICS

St Lucia is an independent state within the Commonwealth, with the British monarchy represented by an appointed Governor-General. The bicameral parliament has an 11-member Senate that's appointed by the Governor-General and a more powerful 17-member House elected by universal suffrage for five-year terms. The prime minister, a member of the majority party of the House, is the effective head of state.

ECONOMY

Agriculture still accounts for nearly one-third of St Lucia's employment and gross national product. The leading export crop is bananas, followed by coconuts and cocoa. Tourism, which has been booming in recent years with the construction of new hotels and resorts, represents the fastest growing segment of the economy and either directly or indirectly accounts for about 15% of the labor force.

POPULATION & PEOPLE

The population is about 150,000, one-third of whom live in Castries. Approximately 85% of all islanders are of pure African ancestry. Another 10% are an admixture of African, British, French and East Indian ancestry, while about 4% are of pure East Indian or European descent.

SOCIETY & CONDUCT

St Lucia has a mix of English, French, African and Caribbean cultural influences, which are manifested in many ways. For instance, if you walk into the Catholic cathedral in Castries, you'll find a building of French design, an interior richly painted in bright African-inspired colors, portraits of a black Madonna and child, and church services delivered in English.

Derek Walcott, the renowned Caribbean poet and playwright and winner of the 1992 Nobel Prize for Literature, is a native of St Lucia. Walcott, who teaches at Boston University, still maintains his connections with the island and is spearheading a movement to renovate the buildings on Rat Island, a former quarantine station off Choc Beach, and turn it into a retreat for writers and artists.

Another nobel laureate with island connections is the former Princeton University professor Sir Arthur Lewis (1915-91), who was born in Castries but as a teenager moved to England where he was educated in the field of political economy. Lewis, who eventually returned to the Caribbean to teach at the University of the West Indies (1959-63), was a founder of the Caribbean Development Bank (1970) and the creator of the 'Lewis Model,' which explores the transition developing countries experience as they move from an agrarian to an industrial economy. Lewis received the Nobel Prize for Economics in 1979.

St Lucia's scenic landscape has been the backdrop for several foreign films, including the British movies *Water* (1985) starring Michael Caine and *Firepower* (1979) with

Sophia Loren as well as Hollywood's *Doctor Dolittle* (1967) and *Superman II* (1980).

Dos & Don'ts
Dress is casual and simple cotton clothing is suitable attire for any occasion. To avoid offense, swim wear should be restricted solely to the beach.

RELIGION
About 85% of St Lucians are Roman Catholics. Anglican, Baptist, Christian Science, Methodist, Pentecostal and Seventh Day Adventist denominations are also represented on the island.

LANGUAGE
The official language is English. When chatting among themselves islanders commonly speak a French-based patois that's spiced with African and English words.

Facts for the Visitor

ORIENTATION
St Lucia has two airports: international flights land at Hewanorra, at the southern end of the island, while most inter-island flights land at the more conveniently located Vigie Airport near Castries, the capital.

Maps
The best island map is the 1:50,000 Ordnance Survey map of St Lucia, which can be bought in island bookstores for EC$30. A reduced black and white print of the map can be found on the centerfold of *Tropical Traveller*, the free tourist newspaper.

TOURIST OFFICES
Local Tourist Offices
The St Lucia Tourist Board has an office opposite the port police office on Jeremie St in Castries and booths at the two airports and the cruise ship dock in Pointe Seraphine.

When requesting information by mail, write to: St Lucia Tourist Board (☎ 452-4094, fax 453-1121), PO Box 221, Castries, St Lucia, West Indies.

Tourist Offices Abroad
The St Lucia Tourist Board has the following overseas offices:

Canada
    130 Spadina Ave, Suite 203,
    Toronto, Ontario
    (☎ 416-703-0141, fax 416-703-0181)
France
    53 Rue François 1er, 7th floor, Paris 75008
    (☎ 01 47 20 39 66, fax 01 47 23 09 65)
Germany
    PO Box 1525, 61366 Friedrichsdorf
    (☎ 6172 778013, fax 6172 778033)
UK
    421a Finchley Rd, London NW3 6HJ
    (☎ /fax 0171-437-7920)
USA
    820 2nd Ave, 9th floor,
    New York, NY 10017
    (☎ 212-867-2950, 800-456-3984)

VISAS & DOCUMENTS
Citizens of the USA and Canada can enter St Lucia with proof of citizenship, such as an official birth certificate, and a photo ID, such as a driver's license. French citizens can enter with a national identity card. Citizens of the UK, Australia and most other countries must be in possession of a valid passport. For all foreign visitors, stays of over 28 days generally require a visa.

An onward or roundtrip ticket or proof of sufficient funds is officially required.

CUSTOMS
Visitors are allowed to bring in 200 cigarettes and one bottle of spirits.

MONEY
The Eastern Caribbean dollar (EC$) is the island currency. One US dollar equals EC$2.70. US dollar traveler's checks are the most convenient, but Canadian dollar and UK sterling checks can also be changed without difficulty. Other currencies are more problematic – many banks, including Barclays, commonly tag on an EC$80 fee per transaction to exchange French francs and EC$54 to exchange Dutch guilders or German marks.

Barclays, which has branches in Castries, Soufrière, Rodney Bay Marina and

Vieux Fort, will cash traveler's checks in US, Canadian and UK currencies free of charge for transactions of EC$500 or more, and with an EC$2 charge for lesser amounts. (The fee is waived for Barclays/ Visa traveler's checks.) In addition, all banks charge a EC$0.30 government stamp fee per check.

You can get 24-hour cash advances using Visa or MasterCard, or make withdrawals from your bank account using a Cirrus or Plus bank card, from ATMs at the Royal Bank of Canada branches in Castries and Rodney Bay.

Visa, MasterCard and American Express are the most widely accepted credit cards and can be used for car rentals and at most mid-range and top-end restaurants and hotels.

An 8% tax and a 10% service charge are added onto the bill at all but the cheapest hotels and restaurants; there's no need for additional tipping.

POST & COMMUNICATIONS
Post
There are post offices in major towns and villages around St Lucia. When addressing mail to the island, the town name should be followed by 'St Lucia, West Indies.'

Telephone
There are both card and coin phones around the island. Phonecards are sold at tourist office booths, Cable & Wireless offices and the Rodney Bay Marina office.

You can send international faxes, telexes and telegrams and make phone calls from the Cable & Wireless office on Bridge St in Castries.

For local calls, dial all seven numbers. When calling St Lucia from overseas, add the area code 758. More information on phonecards and on making long-distance calls is in Post & Communications in the introductory Facts for the Visitor chapter.

The area code for St Lucia is 758.

Email
You can check email messages and surf the Net for EC$20 per 30 minutes at Snooty Agouti, a café in the Reduit Beach area of Rodney Bay.

NEWSPAPERS & MAGAZINES
St Lucia's main newspaper is the *Voice*, which is published three times a week, and there are a handful of weeklies that hit the newsstand on Saturday. You can buy local, US and UK newspapers at Sunshine Bookstore at the Gablewoods Mall and at Pieces of Eight at Rodney Bay Marina.

In addition there's *Tropical Traveller*, a useful monthly tourist newspaper loaded with promotional articles, ads and visitor information, and *Visions of St Lucia*, a glossy magazine with detailed hotel listings; both of these free publications can be picked up at tourist offices or hotel lobbies.

RADIO & TV
Several radio stations can be received on St Lucia. Most hotels have cable TV, which has about 40 channels and provides a combination of programming from the US, Caribbean and Europe.

ELECTRICITY
Electricity is 220 volts AC, 50 cycles. Many hotels have adapter outlets in the bathrooms that allow 110-volt shavers to be used.

WEIGHTS & MEASURES
St Lucia follows the imperial system: distances and car odometers are measured in miles and maps note elevations in feet.

HEALTH
The island's two largest hospitals, Victoria Hospital (☎ 452-2421) in Castries and St Jude's Hospital (☎ 454-6684) in Vieux Fort, both have 24-hour emergency service. For more serious medical conditions people often obtain medical evacuation to Barbados, Martinique or Miami.

Bilharzia (schistosomiasis) is endemic to St Lucia; the general precaution is to avoid wading or swimming in fresh water. St Lucia also has the fer-de-lance snake, a poisonous pit viper. More information on both the fer-de-lance and bilharzia is under Health in the introductory Facts for the Visitor section.

DANGERS & ANNOYANCES

If you get into the local partying scene, such as the Friday night jump-up at Gros Islet, dress casually and be cautious not to flash a wad of money or wear expensive jewelry. Theft can be a problem and these precautions will help you avoid becoming a target. Note also that the streetside loudspeakers at Gros Islet can blare out music at ear-splitting volumes, so it's best to avoid walking directly in front of them.

Hikers should keep in mind that the poisonous fer-de-lance snake favors brushy undergrowth, so stick to well-trodden trails.

EMERGENCIES

For medical, fire and police emergencies dial ☎ 999.

BUSINESS HOURS

Government and business hours are generally from 8:30 am to 12:30 pm and 1:30 to 4:30 pm Monday to Friday. Many stores are also open on Saturday mornings from 8 am to noon. Bank hours are usually from 8:30 to 3 pm on Monday to Thursday, and to 5 pm on Friday. A few bank branches, particularly in resort areas, are open on Saturday mornings as well.

PUBLIC HOLIDAYS & SPECIAL EVENTS

St Lucia has the following public holidays:

New Year's Day	January 1
New Year's Holiday	January 2
Independence Day	February 22
Good Friday	late March/early April
Easter Monday	late March/early April
Labour Day	May 1
Whit Monday	eighth Monday after Easter
Corpus Christi	ninth Thursday after Easter
Emancipation Day	August 3
Thanksgiving Day	October 5
National Day	December 13
Christmas Day	December 25
Boxing Day	December 26

Note that when some holidays fall on a Sunday, they're celebrated on the following Monday.

St Lucia's Carnival takes place on the two days before Ash Wednesday, with calypso tents, costume parades, music contests and the like.

The biggest music event of the year is the four-day St Lucian Jazz Festival, which takes place in mid-May and has featured musicians such as Herbie Hancock, Chaka Khan and Chuck Mangione.

The Atlantic Rally for Cruisers (ARC), one of the largest transatlantic yacht races, is held in December, starting in the Canary Islands and ending at Rodney Bay Marina, St Lucia's largest yacht port. About 150 boats cross the finish line.

ACTIVITIES
Beaches & Swimming

All of St Lucia's beaches are public. On the touristed northwest side of the island there's a fine white-sand beach along the causeway linking Gros Islet and Pigeon Point and nice golden strands at Choc Beach, which stretches north from Sandals Halcyon, and Reduit Beach, the resort strip south of Rodney Bay.

Along the southwest coast there are numerous coves and bays, many accessible by boat only, that offer good swimming and snorkeling.

The east side of the island is less protected, with rougher water conditions.

Diving & Snorkeling

St Lucia's rugged mountain terrain continues beneath the sea as underwater mounts, caves and drop-offs. Most of the diving takes place on the western side of the island, with some of the top sites in the south-central area.

Anse Chastanet, near Soufrière, has been designated as a marine park and boasts spectacular nearshore reefs with a wide variety of corals, sponges and reef fish; it's excellent for both diving and snorkeling.

A popular dive just a bit farther south is Key Hole Pinnacles, consisting of coral-encrusted underwater mounts that rise to within a few feet of the surface.

There are a couple of wreck dives, including *Lesleen*, a 165-foot freighter that was deliberately sunk in 1986 to create an artificial reef. It now sits upright in 65 feet of water near Anse Cochon, another popular dive area. Anse Cochon is also a favored snorkeling stop on day sails to Soufrière.

In addition, there's good snorkeling and diving beneath both Petit Piton and Gros Piton, the coastal mountains that loom to the south of Soufrière. In the main resort area north of Castries, Pigeon Island offers fair snorkeling.

Dive Shops There are a number of dive shops on St Lucia.

Scuba St Lucia (☎ 459-7000, fax 459-7700) at Anse Chastanet Hotel, PO Box 7000, Soufrière, is a well-regarded PADI facility. It offers one-tank dives for US$30, an introductory scuba course for US$75, open-water certification courses for US$425 and referral courses for US$220. Boat transport from Castries to Anse Chastanet is available.

Buddies Scuba (☎ /fax 452-5288), PO Box 565, Castries, another PADI facility, is based at the Vigie Marina in Castries and has dives to Anse Chastanet and Anse Cochon, charging US$60 for a two-tank dive. They also offer an introductory scuba course for US$60.

The island's other PADI facility is Rosemond's Trench Divers (☎ 451-4761, fax 453-7605), PO Box 1809, Castries, which operates out of Marigot Bay, offering two-tank dives for US$70, night dives for US$65 and an introductory scuba course for US$75.

Other dive shops include Dolphin Divers (☎ 452-9485), PO Box 1538, Castries, at Rodney Bay Marina, and Frog's Diving (☎ 452-0913, fax 452-1494), PO Box 3049, Castries, at the Windjammer Landing hotel.

Windsurfing
Some of the large beachfront hotels, including the Royal St Lucian at Reduit Beach and the Windjammer Landing between Castries and Gros Islet, rent windsurfing equipment. The going rate is US$10 an hour for rentals, US$30 for a three-hour lesson.

The Vieux Fort area, at the southern tip of the island, and Cas-en-Bas on St Lucia's northeast side are popular spots with experienced windsurfers.

Hiking
There are three main trails into the mountainous interior on public lands administered by the Department of Forest & Lands. To help maintain the trails the department has initiated an EC$25 per person park fee for hikers.

The Barre de L'isle Trail is a good choice if you're on a budget as you can get to the trailhead from Castries for EC$2.50 by hopping a Vieux Fort bus (about 30 minutes). This lush rainforest hike, which is in the center of the island along the ridge that divides the eastern and western halves of St Lucia, leads to the top of the 1446-foot Morne la Cambe. It provides some fine views along the way and takes about three hours roundtrip. The trailhead, which begins at the south side of the highway, is clearly marked; on weekdays Department of Forest & Lands personnel wait at the trailhead to collect the park fee and are available as guides.

Because trailhead access for the other two forest reserve hikes are inland from major roads and bus routes, these hikes are usually undertaken as part of an organized tour. The Des Cartiers Rainforest Trail at the Quilesse Forest Reserve begins 6 miles inland from Micoud and passes through the habitat of the rare St Lucia parrot. The Edmund Forest Reserve Trail begins about 7 miles east of Soufrière, crosses a rainforest of tall trees interlaced with orchids and bromelaids and offers a fine view of St Lucia's highest peak, the 3118-foot Mt Gimie.

Although the latter two forest reserve hikes take only a few hours to walk, the travel time to either trailhead is about 90 minutes each way from Castries, so the hikes are full-day outings. The Department

ST LUCIA

of Forest & Lands (☎ 450-2231) and the island's main tour agencies arrange outings several days a week.

Horseback Riding

Trim's National Riding (☎ 450-8273) offers a US$30 hour-long ride along the beach in Cas-en-Bas and a US$45 two-hour ride that also includes crossing the interior to Gros Islet.

Fox Grove Inn (☎ 455-3271) offers horseback trail rides along the central Atlantic coast at Mon Repos, charging US$20 for a ride that last about 75 minutes.

Tennis & Squash

Most of the larger hotels have tennis courts. The St Lucia Yacht Club (☎ 452-8350) at Reduit Beach has squash courts open to visitors for a fee.

Golf

St Lucia Golf & Country Club (☎ 450-8523), on the northern tip of the island, has a nine-hole course. When played as 18 holes, green fees are US$27, golf clubs can be rented for US$10 and carts cost US$25.

ACCOMMODATIONS

St Lucia has a number of good-value, moderately priced guesthouses, with the lion's share in the Gros Islet area.

The island's main resort area, at nearby Reduit Beach, has reasonably priced mid-range hotels, as do other places scattered around the island.

St Lucia also has some good, albeit pricey, upper-end offerings and a growing number of all-inclusive resorts, including two Sandals resorts and half a dozen others.

FOOD

Standard Western fare predominates at most hotels. In contrast, local restaurants generally feature West Indian and Creole dishes – even those booked into an all-inclusive hotel will find it's worth slipping away for at least one good local meal. St Lucia has numerous restaurants in all price ranges, with the better ones invariably featuring fresh seafood.

DRINKS

Water is generally safe to drink from the tap. The island's local beer, Piton, is a decent lager that's brewed in Vieux Fort. The locally distilled Lucian Rhum, like the beer, has a logo incorporating the island's twin Piton peaks.

ENTERTAINMENT

In the Reduit Beach area, *The Late Lime*, a nightclub above The Lime restaurant, has music and dancing on Wednesday, Friday and Saturday nights. The cover of EC$15 is waived if you have dinner at the restaurant. Nearby, right on Reduit Beach, *Spinnakers* has calypso and other music several nights a week. *Indies*, a nightclub adjacent to Bay Gardens Hotel, has reggae and other lively Caribbean music on weekends; there's an EC$20 cover.

Still, the hottest scene isn't in a club. On Friday nights the streets in the town of Gros Islet are blocked off, women grill food on the corners, the rum shops spill out onto the sidewalks and live music and partying roll into the wee hours of the morning. This long-established 'jump-up,' as the partying is called, is popular with both tourists and locals but there are safety concerns, so it's best to arrive and leave by taxi, stick to the main strip and be careful with valuables.

THINGS TO BUY

On Jeremie St in Castries, on the west side of the public market, you'll find vendors selling T-shirts, dolls, wood carvings and other handicrafts and souvenirs. The Book Salon, nearby on the corner of Laborie and Jeremie streets, sells books about the Caribbean.

Pointe Seraphine, the main cruise ship dock, has a duty-free shopping complex with about 25 shops selling jewelry, watches, liquor, crystal, china and other imported goods. There are also a couple of clothing shops, including Bagshaws, which sells island-made silk-screened clothing. Although its business hours fluctuate a bit with the season, the complex is generally open from 9 am to 5 pm weekdays, 9 am to

2 pm on Saturday, and on Sunday if cruise ships are in port.

Getting There & Away

AIR

St Lucia has two airports: Hewanorra International Airport in Vieux Fort at the remote southern tip of the island and Vigie Airport in Castries, near the main tourist area.

International jet flights land at Hewanorra, which has a longer runway, while flights from within the Caribbean generally land at Vigie. Most visitors will find it significantly more convenient to book a flight that lands at Vigie.

Airlines

Offices for the main airlines serving St Lucia are in central Castries. The LIAT office, on Derek Walcott Square, also takes care of bookings for BWIA and is open weekdays from 8 am to 4 pm, Saturdays to noon.

British Airways is above Scotiabank on William Peter Blvd and American Airlines is on the corner of Micoud and Mongiraud Sts.

The following are the airline reservation numbers on St Lucia:

Air Canada	☎ 452-6406
Air Jamaica	☎ 454-6263
Air Martinique	☎ 452-2463
American Airlines	☎ 454-6777
British Airways	☎ 452-7444
BWIA	☎ 452-3778
LIAT	☎ 452-3051
	☎ 452-2348 after hours

USA

American Airlines has flights to each of St Lucia's airports at least once daily from San Juan, Puerto Rico, with connections to its USA flights. Fares vary with the season and current promotions but generally start at around US$500 for midweek travel from the US east coast.

BWIA flies to St Lucia twice weekly from both Miami and New York, while Air Jamaica flies four times weekly from New York. Their rates are comparable to those charged by American Airlines.

Canada

Air Canada flies to St Lucia from Toronto on Saturday. A roundtrip ticket with a minimum stay of seven days and a maximum stay of 14 days costs C$634.

UK

British Airways has flights from London's Gatwick Airport to St Lucia on Wednesday, Friday and Sunday, and BWIA flies from Heathrow Airport on Tuesday, Saturday and Sunday. The roundtrip fare with either airline is UK£762 with a minimum stay of seven days and a maximum stay of six months.

South America

LIAT has flights between St Lucia and Caracas on Tuesday and Friday. The one-way fare costs US$198 and a 21-day excursion ticket is US$297.

Within the Caribbean

LIAT has daily nonstop flights to Vigie Airport from Antigua, Barbados, Dominica, Martinique, St Vincent and Trinidad, and connecting flights from the rest of LIAT's network.

LIAT's one-way fares to St Lucia are US$142 from Trinidad, US$78 from Barbados, US$64 from Martinique, US$90 from Dominica, US$142 from Antigua and US$51 from St Vincent.

LIAT also has roundtrip excursion fares, good for 30 days, between St Lucia and Trinidad (US$177), Martinique (US$101), Dominica (US$161), Antigua (US$265) and Barbados (US$124).

Air Martinique has flights from Martinique to St Lucia for US$108 roundtrip with a 21-day maximum stay.

Airport Information

Both Vigie and Hewanorra airports have tourist information booths, taxi stands, card and coin phones and booths for Avis, Hertz, National and a few small local car rental agencies. The tourist information booths book rooms, sell phonecards and will exchange US cash into EC dollars at slightly disadvantaged rates.

SEA
Inter-Island Ferry
L'Express des Iles operates an express catamaran between Castries and Fort-de-France, Martinique. The boat, which takes 80 minutes, leaves Castries at 1 pm on Sunday, 1:50 pm on Tuesday and 7 am on Saturday. Departures from Fort-de-France are at noon on Tuesday, 4:30 pm on Friday and 5 pm on Saturday. The one-way/roundtrip fare is EC$104/175 from Castries, 305/450F from Fort-de-France. On St Lucia, tickets can be purchased from Cox & Co (☎ 452-2211), a block southwest of the tourist office in Castries. More information on this boat – which also connects with Dominica and Guadeloupe – is in Guadeloupe's Getting There & Away section.

Yacht
Customs and immigration can be cleared at Rodney Bay, Castries, Marigot Bay or Vieux Fort. Most yachties pull in at Rodney Bay, where there's a full-service marina and a couple of marked customs slips opposite the customs office.

It's also easy to clear in at Marigot Bay, where you can anchor in the inner harbor and dinghy over to the customs office. Castries is a more congested scene and yachts entering the harbor are required to go directly to the customs dock; if there's no room, anchor east of the customs buoy. At Vieux Fort, you can anchor off the big ship dock, where customs is located.

Popular anchorages around the island include Reduit Beach, the area southeast of Pigeon Island, Rodney Bay Lagoon, Marigot Bay, Anse Chastanet, Anse Cochon and Soufrière Bay.

Yacht charters are available from Sunsail (☎ 452-8648) and DSL Yachting (☎ 452-8531), both at Rodney Bay Marina, and from The Moorings (☎ 451-4357) at Marigot Bay. For addresses and booking information see the Yacht Charters section in the introductory Getting Around chapter.

Cruise Ship
Cruise ships dock in Castries. There are a number of berths, some on the east side of the harbor near the town center and others at Pointe Seraphine on the north side of the harbor, where there's a duty-free shopping complex.

Wednesday and Friday are the big days for cruise ships, when three or four liners are usually docked in the harbor.

LEAVING ST LUCIA
Air passengers leaving St Lucia must pay an EC$27 departure tax.

Getting Around

THE AIRPORTS
Hewanorra Airport
A taxi from Vieux Fort costs about EC$120 to Castries, EC$135 to Reduit Beach; travel time is about 1½ hours. If you're traveling light and in no hurry, there are inexpensive local buses from Vieux Fort to Castries (EC$6), but they're not terribly frequent and are loathe to carry large bags.

Vigie Airport
Taxi fares from Vigie Airport are EC$12 to Modern Inn or Halcyon Beach Club, EC$30 to Reduit Beach, EC$35 to Rodney Bay Marina, EC$12 to Castries center and EC$60 to Marigot.

In part because of the pressure from the taxi union, minibuses avoid Vigie Airport; the nearest bus stop is about a mile away, at the northern end of the runway.

BUS
Bus service is via privately owned minivans. They're a cheap way to get around and the means by which most islanders get to town, school and work. Buses are frequent on main routes (such as Castries to Gros Islet) during the work day but drop off

quickly after the evening rush hour, so that getting a bus after about 7 pm can be challenging. Very few buses run on Sunday.

If there's no bus stop nearby, you can wave buses down en route as long as there's space for the bus to pull over. Pay the fare directly to the driver.

If you're trying to circle the island by bus, note that afternoon service between Soufrière and Castries is unreliable so it's best to travel in a counterclockwise direction, catching a morning bus from Castries to Soufrière and returning via Vieux Fort (up the east coast) in the afternoon.

Sample fares from Castries are: EC$2 to Gros Islet (Route 1A) or Marigot (Route 3C), EC$6 to Vieux Fort (Route 2H), EC$7 to Soufrière (Route 3D). Route numbers are displayed on the buses.

In Castries, buses going south to Soufrière can be picked up at the east side of the public market, while buses to Gros Islet and Vieux Fort can be found nearby on Darling Rd.

TAXI
Taxis are plentiful at the airports, in Castries and in the main resort areas. Always establish the fare with the driver before you get in, doubly so if you want to do anything 'unusual,' like stopping to see a view.

From your guesthouse or hotel you can ask the receptionist to call a taxi; the rates are the same as waving one down and the odds of having to squabble over the fare are lower. To call a taxi yourself: ☎ 452-1599 in Castries, ☎ 454-6136 in Vieux Fort.

CAR & MOTORCYCLE
Road Rules
On St Lucia, drive on the left. Unless you have an International Driving Permit, you'll need to purchase a local license, which can be picked up from immigration at either airport and costs EC$30. If you don't get it upon arrival, most car rental companies will either issue you a license or take you to a nearby police station to get one.

Roads vary greatly around the island, with some sections being newly surfaced

and others deeply potholed. Make sure you have a workable jack and spare tire. Be cautious when driving around Castries, where many of the roads are very narrow and lined with deep rain gutters. Many of the interior and southern roads are also very winding and narrow. Speed limits are generally 15 mph in towns and 30 mph on major roads. Gas stations are distributed around the island.

Rental
Car Avis, Hertz and National operate out of both airports. All three companies allow 100 free miles per day on their standard rentals and charge US$0.40 for each additional mile.

The cheapest cars, usually little Daihatsu Cuores or Suzuki Altos, rent for US$49 a day from National (☎ 450-8500); from Avis (☎ 452-2046) they're US$63, and from Hertz (☎ 452-0680) they're US$55. Renters can sometimes get better deals with the international companies by booking in advance from their home country.

Car rental companies offer optional collision damage waiver (CDW) for about US$16 a day, which covers theft and collision damages to the car, but the renter is still responsible for the first US$300 to US$500 in damages. If the CDW is not taken, the renter is usually responsible for the first US$1200 to US$2000 in damages.

One local company offering good prices with unlimited mileage is CTL Rent A Car (☎ 452-0732, fax 452-0401), which operates out of Rodney Bay Marina. Rates begin at US$45 a day for a Coure and CTL provides free hotel pick-up.

Motorcycle Wayne's Motorcycle Center (☎ 452-2059), on the main road between Castries and Rodney Bay, rents 500cc Honda motorcycles for EC$75 a day, helmet included.

BICYCLE
An unnamed shop (☎ 452-9385) in a house opposite Candyo Inn in the Reduit Beach area rents mountain bikes for US$12 a day.

ORGANIZED TOURS

Sightseeing tours by taxi cost about US$15 to US$20 an hour. A taxi tour of the Soufrière area and back to Castries generally costs around US$120, with up to four passengers.

Local tour companies offer a range of land tours of the island, boat tours around St Lucia and air tours of neighboring islands. Most land tours average US$50, including a hiking outing to the Des Cartiers rainforest in the Quilesse Forest Reserve or a round-the-island van tour that stops at Marigot, Soufrière and the sulphur springs. Other tours take in estate homes and plantations that are otherwise inaccessible to individual travelers.

Two of the main tour companies are Sunlink Tours (☎ 452-8232) at Reduit Beach and Pitons Travel Agency (☎ 450-1486) in Castries. Most hotels can book tours as well.

The St Lucia National Trust (☎ 452-5005, natrust@isis.org.lc) can arrange tours to the island's coastal nature reserves: the Maria Island Nature Reserve off the southeast coast and the Frigate Islands Nature Reserve off the east coast.

Boat Tours

Day-long sails down the coast from Rodney Bay to Soufrière are very popular. They stop at Marigot Bay, include a minivan tour of Sulphur Springs and Diamond Botanical Gardens, and take you snorkeling at Anse Cochon or Anse Chastanet on the return trip.

The sailing time between Rodney Bay and Soufrière is about two hours each way, and the tours tend to last from about 9 am to 5 pm.

Several companies offer these sails, which can be booked directly or through tour agencies or hotels. The cost is about US$75 including hotel pick-up and lunch.

From Rodney Bay you can make the trip on the 56-foot *Endless Summer* (☎ 450-8651) catamaran or, if you want to go in style, on the *Brig Unicorn* (☎ 452-8232), a 140-foot-long tall ship that replicates a 19th-century brigantine.

Castries

Castries, the island's commercial center and capital, is a bustling port city set on a large natural harbor. The liveliest part of the city is just southeast of the port, at Jeremie and Peynier Sts, where the colorful Castries Market houses scores of produce, handicraft and souvenir stands.

The city, which was founded by the French in the 18th century, was ravaged by fire three times between 1785 and 1812 and again in 1948. Consequently, most of the city's historic buildings have been lost.

One area that survived the last fire was Derek Walcott Square, a quiet central square surrounded by a handful of 19th-century wooden buildings with gingerbread trim balconies, an attractive Victorian-style library and the imposing Cathedral of the Immaculate Conception. Opposite the cathedral at the east side of the square is a lofty saman tree that's estimated to be 400 years old.

Information

Tourist Office The tourist office (☎ 452-2479), opposite the port police office on Jeremie St, is open from 8 am to 12:30 am and 1:30 to 4 pm Monday to Friday, 9 am to 12:30 pm on Saturday.

Money The Royal Bank of Canada, on William Peter Blvd, is open from 8 am to 3 pm Monday to Thursday, to 5 pm on Friday. There's a Scotiabank a block to the west and a Barclays Bank farther west on Bridge St.

Post The GPO (general post office), on Bridge St a block south of the port, is open Monday to Friday from 8:15 am to 4 pm. Stamp collectors can buy commemorative stamps at the philatelic bureau inside the GPO.

Communications Phone calls can be made and faxes can be sent from the Cable & Wireless office on Bridge St, open from

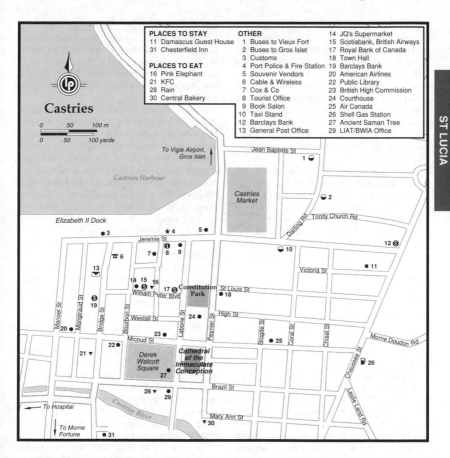

ST LUCIA

PLACES TO STAY
11 Damascus Guest House
31 Chesterfield Inn

PLACES TO EAT
16 Pink Elephant
21 KFC
28 Rain
30 Central Bakery

OTHER
1   Buses to Vieux Fort
2   Buses to Gros Islet
3   Customs
4   Port Police & Fire Station
5   Souvenir Vendors
6   Cable & Wireless
7   Cox & Co
8   Tourist Office
9   Book Salon
10 Taxi Stand
12 Barclays Bank
13 General Post Office
14 JQ's Supermarket
15 Scotiabank, British Airways
17 Royal Bank of Canada
18 Town Hall
19 Barclays Bank
20 American Airlines
22 Public Library
23 British High Commission
24 Courthouse
25 Air Canada
26 Shell Gas Station
27 Ancient Saman Tree
29 LIAT/BWIA Office

Castries

0   50   100 m
0   50   100 yards

7:30 am to 6:30 pm Monday to Friday, 8 am to 12:30 pm on Saturday.

Library The public library is open from 9 am to 6 pm Monday to Friday, to 12:30 pm on Saturday. Visitors can check out books for a refundable deposit of EC$50.

Cathedral of the Immaculate Conception

The city's Catholic cathedral, built in 1897, is a grand stone structure with a splendidly painted interior of trompe l'oeil columns and colorfully detailed biblical scenes. The island's patron saint, St Lucia, is portrayed directly above the altar. The church richly incorporates both Caribbean and African influences, including images of a black Jesus and Mary and the liberal use of bright tones of red, green and yellow.

Morne Fortune

Sitting atop the 2795-ft Morne Fortune, about 3 miles south of Castries center, is Fort Charlotte, whose construction began under the French and was continued by the British. Because of its strategic hilltop vantage overlooking Castries, the fort was a source of fierce fighting between the French and British in colonial times. In recent years the fort buildings have been renovated and given a new life as the Sir Arthur Lewis Community College.

At the rear of the college a small obelisk monument commemorates the 27th Inniskilling Regiment's retaking of the hill from French forces in 1796. Near the monument you'll also find a couple of cannons and a fairly good view of the coast north to Pigeon Point.

If you just want a good view of the city, there's no need to venture as far as the college. The scenic lookout opposite Government House, about a half-mile south of Castries, has a fine view of the port and capital and also gives a glimpse of the attractive crown-topped Victorian mansion that serves as the residence of the Governor-General.

Places to Stay

Damascus Guest House (☎ 452-1544), 20 Victoria St, Castries, is a local boarding house above a bar in the center of town. Rooms are basic with just a bed and fan, while showers and toilets are in the hall. For what you get, rates are pricey at US$19/30 for singles/doubles.

Chesterfield Inn (☎ 452-1295), PO Box 415, Castries, is on Bridge St, about a five-minute uphill walk from central Castries. The inn has a dozen adequate rooms with air-con, TV and private baths for US$35/45 singles/doubles; there's a commodious common area with antiques but otherwise the place is quite straightforward.

Seaview Apartel (☎ 452-4359), PO Box 527, Castries, has 10 big units, each with TV, air-con, phones, refrigerators, bathtubs and balconies. Although the 'sea view' is but a distant glimpse, it's still a good value at US$53 (US$59 for a unit with an oven). The main drawback is the odd location, on the east side of the airport runway, but it is on the Castries-Gros Islet bus route. Reception is at the Shell gas station next door.

Bon Appetit (☎ 452-2757), PO Box 884, Castries, at the south side of town near the top of Morne Fortune, has a lovely ocean view with Martinique on the horizon. It's

run by an Italian couple, Renato and Cheryl Venturi, who operate a small restaurant at the same site. There are four spotlessly clean rooms, each with a double bed, fan, private bath and cable TV. Singles/doubles cost US$37/42, including tax and breakfast.

Green Parrot (☎ 452-3399, fax 453-2272), PO Box 648, Castries, has 50 nice large rooms with air-con, cable TV, private baths, comfortable furnishings and balconies with fine views. There's a pool and a good restaurant. The main disadvantage is that, like Bon Appetit, Green Parrot is a bit out of the way, on the hillside of Morne Fortune, about 3 miles from central Castries. Singles/doubles cost US$80/90 in summer, US$90/110 in winter.

Places to Eat

Town Center For good cheap rotis and local dishes try the food stalls at the south side of Castries Market; the stalls are open Monday to Saturday from 11 am to around 2:30 pm. You can get drinking coconuts for EC$1 at the market and at the Darling Rd bus stand.

If you just want cheap eats on the run, you could pick up some fruit at the market and then walk over to the *Central Bakery* at the south end of Peynier St for fresh-baked bread and inexpensive coconut pies. For conventional fast food, there's a *KFC* on Bridge St that's open from 9:30 am to at least midnight daily.

The *Pink Elephant*, off William Peter Blvd, is the town's most popular lunch spot. Breakfast omelets and lunchtime sandwiches cost EC$8, chicken & chips EC$12 and a hefty lunch of the day is EC$16. The only problem is finding a free table as it packs solid at lunch. It's open weekdays from 7 to 10 am and from noon to 2 pm.

Rain, in a classic West Indian building that dates from 1885, offers balcony dining overlooking Derek Walcott Square. Castries' oldest restaurant, it has a full menu that ranges from sandwiches, rotis and salads for around EC$15 to fish dishes for double that. It's open from 8:30 am to 10 pm Monday to Saturday.

JQ's Supermarket on William Peter Blvd is a large, well-stocked grocery store that's open from 8 am to at least 5 pm on weekdays, to 4 pm on Saturday.

Morne Fortune For a French-inspired treat, head up to the *Green Parrot Restaurant* (☎ 452-3399), which serves a weekday business lunch from noon to 3 pm for EC$25 or sandwiches and salads for EC$10 to EC$20. Dinner is a more expensive proposal, with a four-course meal, selected from a full menu, priced at EC$90. Be sure to get one of the window tables to enjoy the restaurant's fine hilltop view of Castries and the northwest coast. The restaurant is in Morne Fortune, 3 miles from Castries center (EC$10 by taxi).

Bon Appetit (☎ 452-2757), also in Morne Fortune, is an intimate little restaurant with home-cooked food and a wonderful view. It's open from noon to 2 pm on weekdays and from 7 to 11 pm nightly. Main dishes range from EC$40 for fish to EC$90 for freshwater crayfish, the house specialty. As there are only five tables, reservations are recommended.

Northern St Lucia

NORTH OF CASTRIES

Gros Islet Rd runs up the coast connecting northern Castries to Rodney Bay. This area has a number of beachside resort hotels, as well as some moderately priced guesthouses. Most of the guesthouses are on the inland side of the road but within walking distance of the beach.

Gablewoods Mall, just south of the Halcyon, has a supermarket, eateries, a bank, a pharmacy, clothing shops and a bookstore.

Places to Stay – budget

The following are on Gros Islet Rd, a couple of miles north of the airport and a 10-minute walk from Gablewoods Mall.

Modern Inn (☎ 452-4001, fax 453-7313), PO Box 457, Vide Bouteille, Castries, is a good-value family-run hostelry with five guest rooms and a small common sitting area with cable TV and a refrigerator. The rooms are straightforward but clean and have comfortable mattresses and air-con. Rates are US$20 for singles, which share a bathroom, and US$30 for doubles, which have private baths. There are also three adjacent apartments with kitchens, cable TV, air-con and phones for US$40.

The 10-room *Paradise Inn* (☎ 452-1987) has a quiet hilltop location a five minute walk uphill from the Friendship Inn. There's a fine view of the coast and the inn is pleasant enough, though the rooms are simple, essentially just a bed, fan, night table and lamp. Singles/doubles cost US$25/40 with shared bath, US$30/50 with a private bath. There are also a few units with kitchenettes for not much more.

The roadside *Friendship Inn* (☎ 452-4201, fax 453-2635) is a small concrete two-story building with a line of simple motel-style rooms. Each has cable TV, phone, small kitchenette, air-con and private bathroom. Singles/doubles cost US$55/65. There's a small pool.

Places to Stay – top end

Windjammer Landing (☎ 452-0913, fax 452-0907; in the USA ☎ 800-743-9609, in the UK ☎ 800-373-742), PO Box 1504, Castries, on a quiet beach at Labrelotte Bay, is a sprawling villa-style complex with an upscale Mediterranean appearance. Units are contemporary with beam ceilings, rattan furnishings, kitchenettes, living rooms, terraces and air-conditioned bedrooms. There are two tennis courts, three restaurants and four pools. Rates vary throughout the year, with one-bedroom villas costing US$225 to US$385, two-bedroom villas from US$375 to US$590.

Sandals Halcyon (☎ 452-3081, fax 452-1012; in the UK 0171-581-9895), PO Box 399, Castries, is a 178-room all-inclusive resort on a nice sandy beach a couple of miles north of the airport. Per-person rates for a seven-night stay there start around US$1800, including meals, water sports and other activities.

ST LUCIA

ST LUCIA

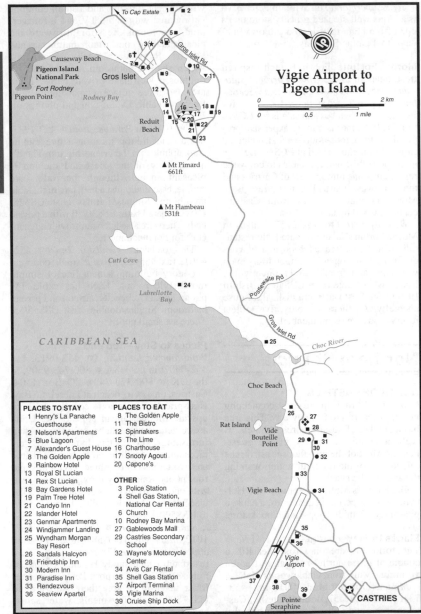

Vigie Airport to Pigeon Island

To Cap Estate

Causeway Beach

Pigeon Island National Park

Fort Rodney

Gros Islet

Pigeon Point

Rodney Bay

Gros Islet Rd

Reduit Beach

▲ Mt Pimard 661ft

▲ Mt Flambeau 531ft

Cuti Cove

Labrellotte Bay

CARIBBEAN SEA

Postewaite Rd

Gros Islet Rd

Choc River

Choc Beach

Rat Island

Vide Bouteille Point

Vigie Beach

Vigie Airport

Pointe Seraphine

CASTRIES

| 0 | 1 | 2 km |
| 0 | 0.5 | 1 mile |

PLACES TO STAY
1 Henry's La Panache Guesthouse
2 Nelson's Apartments
5 Blue Lagoon
7 Alexander's Guest House
8 The Golden Apple
9 Rainbow Hotel
13 Royal St Lucian
14 Rex St Lucian
18 Bay Gardens Hotel
19 Palm Tree Hotel
21 Candyo Inn
22 Islander Hotel
23 Genmar Apartments
24 Windjammer Landing
25 Wyndham Morgan Bay Resort
26 Sandals Halcyon
28 Friendship Inn
30 Modern Inn
31 Paradise Inn
33 Rendezvous
36 Seaview Apartel

PLACES TO EAT
8 The Golden Apple
11 The Bistro
12 Spinnakers
15 The Lime
16 Charthouse
17 Snooty Agouti
20 Capone's

OTHER
3 Police Station
4 Shell Gas Station, National Car Rental
6 Church
10 Rodney Bay Marina
27 Gablewoods Mall
29 Castries Secondary School
32 Wayne's Motorcycle Center
34 Avis Car Rental
35 Shell Gas Station
37 Airport Terminal
38 Vigie Marina
39 Cruise Ship Dock

Wyndham Morgan Bay Resort (☎ 450-2511, fax 450-1050; in the USA ☎ 800-327-8321) is a modern all-inclusive hotel with 238 rooms at the north side of Choc Bay. The rooms have full amenities and there's a fitness center, tennis courts, a pool and a water sports center. Singles/doubles begin at US$265/360 in summer, US$300/430 in winter.

Places to Eat

Gablewoods Mall has a few fast-food stalls around a central dining court. The eateries include *Peppino's Pizza*, with prices from EC$5 for a quarter of a small cheese pizza to EC$47 for a large pizza with the works; *Miss Saigon*, with Thai, Malaysian and Vietnamese dishes from around EC$15; and *El Burrito*, with Mexican burritos for EC$10. The stalls are open daily from late morning to about 9 pm.

There's also an air-conditioned sit-down restaurant, *Tacrose*, which has sandwiches or burgers for EC$6 and plate lunches with curried chicken or fried fish for EC$13. In addition, the mall has a good deli that sells bagels, luncheon meats and cheeses.

RODNEY BAY

Rodney Bay is a large protected bay that encompasses the resort area of Reduit Beach and the village of Gros Islet. An artificial channel cuts between Reduit Beach and Gros Islet, opening to a large lagoon that's the site of Rodney Bay Marina, the island's largest yachting port.

Rodney Bay Marina is a modern facility with a car rental agency, dive shops, a launderette, a bookshop, a travel agency, marine supply shops, a grocery store and some good eating spots – many of which are run by expatriates. There are also two banks, the Royal Bank of Canada and Barclays Bank, open from 8:30 am to 3 pm Monday to Thursday, to 5 pm on Friday and to noon on Saturday. The marina is a bustling yachters' scene and a good place to make contact with sailors if you're looking to hitch a ride or find a crew job.

In contrast, Reduit Beach, just southwest of the marina, is a more typical tourist resort with a fine sandy beach and a range of places to stay and eat. It's a 30-minute roundabout walk by road between the marina and the beach but there's a small ferry that crosses the lagoon between the two areas several times a day for US$4 roundtrip.

Places to Stay

Genmar Apartments (☎ 452-0834, fax 452-0165), PO Box 213, Reduit, is a recommendable little apartment cluster off Gros Islet Rd, near the bus route and about a 10-minute walk from Reduit Beach. The dozen units are straightforward but have private bathrooms, refrigerators, stoves and fans. Single/double rates for a studio are US$35/45 in summer, US$45/60 in winter. For a one-bedroom unit, the rates are US$40/50 in summer, US$50/65 in winter. To get there, turn left on the first dirt road after the Texaco gas station and then take the first right and look for the 'Gene' sign.

Candyo Inn (☎ 452-0712, fax 452-0774), PO Box 386, Rodney Bay, a five-minute walk from Reduit Beach, is a pleasantly upscale inn with four rooms at US$75 and eight roomy suites with full kitchens, living rooms and separate bedrooms for US$90. All are neat and comfortable with air-con, phones and cable TV. Rates are US$15 cheaper in summer. There's a pool, flower-laden landscaping and a friendly staff.

The *Rainbow Hotel* (☎ 452-0148, fax 452-0158), PO Box 3050, Castries, is just a minute's walk from the water but half the price of its beachfront neighbors. This spiffy new three-decker hotel has a large courtyard pool, tennis court and fitness center. Rooms are well appointed with thermostatic air-con, ceiling fans, phones, cable TV, queen beds and balconies. The rate is US$75.

If you don't mind being on the main road about 10 minutes from the beach there are two other new hotels with moderate prices. The 53-room *Bay Gardens Hotel* (☎ 452-8060, fax 452-8059, destangd@candw.lc), PO Box 1892, Castries, has a pleasant Caribbean decor and inviting rooms with air-con, cable TV, phones, refrigerators and coffeemakers for US$77/94 in summer/winter and kitchenette units for US$106/112. Next door the *Palm Tree Hotel* (☎ 452-8718), PO Box 2233, Rodney Bay, is a smaller hotel with similar rooms and rates.

The *Islander Hotel* (☎ 452-8757, fax 452-0958; in the USA ☎ 800-223-9815), PO Box 907, Castries, is an older complex with straightforward rooms for US$60 in summer, US$85 in winter. All rooms have air-con, refrigerators and cable TV. Add another US$10 for a unit with a kitchenette on the deck.

Rex St Lucian (☎ 452-8351, fax 452-8331; in the USA ☎ 800-255-5859), PO Box 512, Castries, fronts a fine section of Reduit Beach. The hotel is a rambling place, with 260 rooms spread across a series of two- and three-story buildings. All rooms have phones, a room safe, a king or two twin beds and a patio or balcony. Fan-cooled standard rooms cost US$115/135 in summer/winter, air-conditioned superior rooms cost US$140/175.

Royal St Lucian (☎ 452-9999, fax 452-9639), PO Box 977, Castries, is a modern three-story complex on Reduit Beach. It has 98 upmarket suites, each with a separate sitting area, private patio, TV, room safe, and minibar; rates begin at US$310/385 in summer/winter.

Places to Eat

Marina *Key Largo Pizza* (☎ 452-0282) has excellent pizza cooked in an outdoor brick oven. Calzones cost EC$15 and pizzas are EC$20 to EC$45, depending on the toppings. It opens around 11:30 am and stays open until at least 10 pm.

The *Yacht Club*, an informal dockside restaurant, has light meals and drinks. Sandwiches and rotis cost EC$8, fish & chips EC$18. Fuller meals are available at dinner – which is sometimes prepared as a barbecue. It's open from 7:30 am to 10 pm daily.

The *Bread Basket* bakery sells good breads, including whole wheat and a crispy French loaf, as well as sandwiches, muffins and pastries. It's a popular place for a light breakfast and they make a good egg and bacon sandwich for EC$8. You can take your food outside and dine on the waterfront. It's open from 7 am to 5 pm Monday to Saturday, to 1 pm on Sunday.

Le Marché de France is a small market with a fair selection, including meal-sized chunks of cheese, imported foods and moderately priced wines. It's open from 8:30 am to 7 pm Monday to Saturday, 9 am to 1 pm on Sunday and holidays.

The Bistro (☎ 452-9494), on the waterfront at Rodney Bay, is often crowded with yachters who can literally jump off their boats and into the restaurant. This popular watering hole has an extensive chalkboard menu that includes various chicken, beef and fish dishes from EC$35 to EC$60. It's open from 5 pm daily. There's a 20% discount on food orders made before 6:30 pm.

Reduit Beach For West Indian food, *The Lime* is the place to go. It has a good-value lunch buffet from 11 am to 3 pm for EC$19, excellent rotis for just EC$8. At dinner, from 6:30 to 10 pm, The Lime features fresh seafood dishes in the EC$30 to EC$45 range. In addition, there's a barbecue on Wednesday, Friday and Saturday evenings, with inexpensive chicken, ribs and fish by the piece. The Lime is closed on Tuesday.

Capone's has a casual patio section with inexpensive pizza and grilled chicken and a recommendable EC$18 fish, chips and salad plate. There's also a fine dining indoor section with Italian-style pasta, fish and meat offerings in the EC$35 to EC$50 range. The patio is open from 11 am to midnight, the fine dining section serves dinner only.

Charthouse (☎ 452-8115) has an appealing waterfront setting and is popular for its grilled steaks and baby back ribs; it also has chicken and fish dishes. Prices average EC$40 to EC$55; add another EC$8 for a green salad. It's open daily except Sunday from 6 pm.

If you want to dine on the beach there's *Spinnakers*, a thatch-roofed eatery right on Reduit Beach. The chalkboard menu includes lunchtime burgers for EC$12 and fish dishes for EC$30; dinner adds on pricier seafoods such as lobster. It's open from 9 am to 11 pm daily.

Snooty Agouti, behind Capone's, is the place to go for espresso and homemade desserts, including a tasty carrot cake. It also has Internet access and a used book exchange. Hours are from 9 am (3 pm on Sunday) to midnight daily.

The coffee shop at the *Rex St Lucian* has a tempting variety of tropical ice creams (EC$2.50 a cone) and is open from 7 am to 10 pm daily.

There are a couple of small stores selling groceries and spirits, including *SK Mini Mart*, near the Islander Hotel and a full-size grocery store is slated for the new shopping center south of Palm Tree Hotel.

GROS ISLET

Gros Islet is a small fishing village of simple wooden houses with rusting tin roofs, lots of rum shops and a shore dotted with gaily painted wooden boats. If you hear a conch shell being blown, it's the signal that fishing boats have arrived with a catch to sell.

Though the town doesn't have any sights per se, St Joseph's Church is a formidable structure at the north side of town and there's a small market near the shore where you can often find fishermen and women mending nets. Gros Islet is also famous for its spirited Friday night jump-up (see Entertainment in the Facts for the Visitor section).

From Gros Islet, walk a couple of minutes north along the shore and you'll come to an expansive stretch of white-sand beach that curves around to Pigeon Island. You're likely to find cows lazing along the beach under shade trees, a couple of pigs milling around and only a handful of people. The beach is quite beautiful and the calm turquoise waters are inviting but it's unfortunately littered with broken bottles and trash, especially at the village end. There are no facilities.

Most buses making the coastal drive north from Castries terminate in the center of Gros Islet.

Places to Stay

Alexander's Guest House (☎ 450-8610, fax 450-8014), Marie Therese St, Gros Ilet, is a newer guesthouse right in the village and just a minute's walk from the water. There are 10 rooms with fans and hot showers for US$20/30 singles/doubles; a couple of units also have kitchenettes and cost US$25/45. Alexander's commonly books solid in the winter.

The Golden Apple (☎ 450-8056), Dauphin St, Gros Islet, in the village center, just a block from the water, has four tidy new rooms above the restaurant of the same name. The rooms have ceiling fans, private baths and balconies; rates are US$35, except for the corner suite, which has a sea view and costs US$45.

The *Blue Lagoon* (☎ 450-8453, fax 450-0617), PO Box 637, Castries, is a family-run place with options that range from adequate budget rooms that have access to a common kitchen for US$18/30 singles/doubles to free-standing cottages with kitchenettes for US$45. It's a short walk to the nearest bus stand, 10 minutes to Rodney Bay Marina or the beach at Gros Islet.

Henry's La Panache Guesthouse (☎ 450-0765, fax 450-0453), Cas-en-Bas Rd, Gros Islet, is a relaxed and friendly place about a five-minute walk west of the highway in Gros Islet. The rooms are straightforward but have refrigerators, fans and private bathrooms, and the setting is pleasantly natural. Singles/doubles cost US$27/38. There's an outdoor dining area where meals can be arranged at reasonable prices. Henry also books self-catering apartments in his neighbor's contemporary house for US$50.

Nelson's Apartments (☎ 450-8275), PO Box 1174, Castries, is 75 yards west of Henry's. It has six good-value apartments with full kitchens, cable TV, portable fans and mosquito netting above the beds. Singles/doubles cost US$25/38.

Places to Eat

Blue Heaven on Dauphin St, the main road into the village, is a local eatery with good breakfasts, snacks and dinners at reasonable prices, though service can be very slow.

ST LUCIA

A bit more upmarket is *The Golden Apple*, which is closer to the water on Dauphin St. On Saturday it features island dishes such as cow-heel soup or pigtail bouillon – otherwise, the menu includes the likes of Creole fish or tuna kebabs for around EC$20. Golden Apple is mainly a dinner restaurant but during the high season is usually opens for lunch as well.

You can find simple breads and fresh coconut buns at *Everybody Bakery*, a little hole-in-the-wall on the inland side of the highway opposite the Shell gas station.

PIGEON ISLAND NATIONAL PARK

Pigeon Island has a spicy history dating back to the 1550s when St Lucia's first French settler, Jambe de Bois ('Wooden Leg'), used the island as a base for raiding passing Spanish ships. Two centuries later British admiral George Rodney fortified Pigeon Island, using it to monitor the French fleet on Martinique. Rodney's fleet set sail from Pigeon Island in 1782 for his most decisive military engagement, the Battle of the Saintes.

With the end of hostilities between the two European rivals, the fort slipped into disuse in the 19th century, although the USA established a small signal station here during WWII.

In the 1970s a sandy causeway was constructed between Gros Islet and Pigeon Island, turning the island into a peninsula, and in 1979 Pigeon 'Island' was established as a national park.

It's a fun place to explore, with walking paths winding around the scattered remains of Fort Rodney, whose partially intact stone buildings create a certain ghost town effect. The grounds are well endowed with lofty trees, including a few big banyans, and fine coastal views.

As soon as you go through the entrance gate, you'll see the remains of an 1824 kitchen and officers' mess. While some people make a beeline from here to the main fortress at Fort Rodney Hill on the outer point, a walk which takes about 15 minutes, it's enjoyable to just mosey

through the ruins and gradually work your way in that direction. A good route is to continue northwest from the officers' mess past the soldiers' barracks (1782) and then loop down towards the bay where you can pick up the main path.

At the top of Fort Rodney Hill, you'll find a small but well-preserved fortress, a few rusting cannons and a spectacular view. You can see south across Rodney Bay to the gumdrop-shaped hills dotting the coast and north past Pointe du Cap to Martinique. For more views, continue north past the stone foundations of the ridge battery to the top of 359-ft Signal Peak, about a 20-minute walk.

Pigeon Island, administered by the St Lucia National Trust, is open from 9 am to 5 pm daily. Admission, which includes entry to an interpretation center with multimedia historic displays, costs EC$10 for foreign visitors. There's a pub and restaurant selling sandwiches at moderate prices.

Most of the coastline around Pigeon Island is rocky, though there's a nice little sandy beach just east of the jetty.

The walk along the causeway from Gros Islet to Pigeon Point takes about 20 minutes.

Southern St Lucia

The main road in the southern part of the island makes a loop that can be done as a full day trip.

The road to Soufrière is a scenic drive, winding in and out of lush jungle valleys and up into the mountains. It goes through banana plantations, passes the fishing villages of Anse La Raye and Canaries and offers fine coastal and mountain vistas, including some lovely views of the Pitons as you approach Soufrière.

Choiseul, a little village south of Soufrière, has an active handicraft industry and its roadside arts and crafts center is a good place to pick up locally made dolls, baskets, pottery and wood carvings.

MARIGOT BAY

Marigot Bay is a lovely sheltered bay that's backed by green hillsides and sports a little palm-fringed beach. The inner harbor is so long and deep that an entire British fleet is said to have once escaped French warships by ducking inside and covering their masts with coconut fronds. The bay was the setting for the 1967 musical *Doctor Dolittle*, starring Rex Harrison.

Marigot Bay is a popular anchorage for yachters and the site of a marina with a customs office, a small market, water, ice and fuel. The Moorings (☎ 451-4357) bases its bareboat charters here and runs the marina facilities.

A little pontoon boat shuttles back and forth on request (EC$2 roundtrip), connecting the two sides of the inner harbor.

Places to Stay & Eat

The Moorings' *Marigot Bay Hotel* (☎ 451-4357, fax 451-4353; in the USA and Canada ☎ 800-437-7880), PO Box 101, Castries, is on the south side of the bay. It has 16 pleasant stone cottages, each with tasteful tropical decor, rattan furniture, a refrigerator, coffeemaker, ceiling fan and lots of open-air screened windows; singles/doubles cost US$70/85 in the summer, US$120/135 in the winter.

Marigot Beach Club (☎ 451-4974, fax 451-4973; in the USA and Canada ☎ 800-278-5842), PO Box 101, Castries, is a similar property on the north side of the bay. There are fan-cooled studios with kitchenettes for US$103/129 in summer/winter, and one- and two-bedroom hillside villas priced from US$129 to US$205 in summer, US$155 to US$232 in winter. It's an older place but it has character and many units have patios with idyllic water views.

Dolittle's Restaurant & Beach Bar, a pleasant waterside spot at the Marigot Beach Club, has lunchtime sandwiches and salads for around EC$20 and chicken and fish dishes for EC$30.

The *Rusty Anchor*, a poolside restaurant and bar at the Marigot Bay Hotel, has sandwiches, burgers, rotis and omelets for about EC$20 at lunch and fresh seafood dinners from around EC$50.

There are late afternoon happy hours at both Dolittle's and the Rusty Anchor.

A popular local eatery is *JJ's Restaurant & Bar* (☎ 451-4076) in the village, a 10-minute walk up the hill from the harbor. The fish Creole and chicken curry are both tasty dinner dishes that cost EC$37 and include rice, salad, vegetables and dessert. From noon to 3 pm JJ's has a lighter lunch menu that includes inexpensive rotis and chicken with chips. On Wednesday and Friday nights there's live music.

SOUFRIÈRE

Founded by the French in 1746 and named after the nearby sulphur springs, the town of Soufrière has a lovely bay setting. The coastal Pitons provide a scenic backdrop to the south and the island's highest peaks rise above the rainforest just a few miles inland.

Like other fishing communities along the coast, Soufrière has lots of old weathered buildings, some still adorned with delicate gingerbread trim, others more ramshackle. There is an interesting stone Catholic church in the town center. At the north side of the dock is the Soufrière Market, where you can buy baskets, straw hats, T-shirts and spices.

The main sights, the Sulphur Springs, Morne Coubaril Estate and Diamond Botanical Gardens, are on the outskirts of town and can be visited in a couple of hours.

Although most visitors are day trippers on one of the many boat or land tours that take in Soufrière, much of what Soufrière has to offer, including its relaxed provincial character, is best appreciated by those who stay on. There are some interesting places to stay, ranging from affordable guesthouses to secluded top-end retreats.

Anse Chastanet

Soufrière's picturesque scenery is equally impressive beneath the water's surface. Anse Chastanet, a lovely sheltered bay a little over a mile north of Soufrière, has some of the finest nearshore snorkeling and

ST LUCIA

Caribbean house with gingerbread trim

diving on St Lucia. It also makes a fine choice if you're simply up for a swim.

At the beach is a hotel, a dive shop that rents snorkeling equipment (EC$12 an hour), a bar and a restaurant that serves both simple snacks and full meals. On foot, Anse Chastanet is about a 35-minute walk from Soufrière along the coastal road that skirts the north side of Soufrière Bay. If you're not up for a walk, you can usually arrange a water taxi from the village.

Sulphur Springs

Sulphur Springs is a barren and somewhat moonscapish terrain pocked with pools of boiling mud and steaming vents. The vents release great quantities of sulphuric gases, which are responsible for the yellow mineral deposits blanketing the area. The putrid smell, resembling rotten eggs, is hydrogen sulphide.

Visitors used to walk up close to the vents and peer directly into the mud ponds until a local guide leading a group of German tourists stepped through the soft earth and plunged waist-deep into the boiling mud. He lived to tell the story, but everything is now viewed from the safety of overlooks.

Despite the fact that this area is promoted as a 'drive-in volcano,' those expecting to peer down into a volcanic crater will be disappointed. The crater walls eroded away eons ago, and now the volcanic activity is along the side of a hill.

Sulphur Springs is open from 9 am to 5 pm daily and admission is EC$3. Having a guide walk through with you is compulsory; although the price of the guide is theoretically included in the entrance fee, a tip will be expected.

To get there from Soufrière, go south on the Vieux Fort road, which winds uphill as it leaves town. About a five-minute drive out of Soufrière take the downhill fork to the left at the Sulphur Springs sign, from where it's a half-mile farther to the park entrance. En route be sure not to miss the small pull-off, just south of Soufrière, which offers a picturesque view of the town.

Morne Coubaril Estate

Morne Coubaril Estate, on the Vieux Fort road about a half-mile north of Sulphur

Springs, is a working cocoa and coconut plantation that has been set up to give visitors a sense of life on the farm. There are displays on the processing of copra, cocoa and manioc, traditional buildings, and the ruins of a water and sugar mill. The EC$15 admission price includes an informative 35-minute guided tour. It's open daily from 9 am to 5 pm.

Diamond Botanical Gardens

The Diamond Estate's botanical gardens, waterfall and mineral baths are all at the same site and have an entrance fee of EC$7 for adults, EC$3.50 for children under 12.

Paths wind through the gardens, which are planted with tropical flowers and trees, including numerous heliconia and ginger specimens. At the back of the gardens a small waterfall drops down a rock face that is stained a rich orange from the warm mineral waters. The waterfall featured briefly in the movie *Superman II* as the site from which Superman plucked an orchid for Lois Lane.

The mineral baths date from 1784 when they were built atop hot springs so that the troops of King Louis XVI of France could take advantage of their therapeutic effects. The baths were largely destroyed during the French Revolution, but in recent times a few have been restored and are open to visitors for an additional EC$6.50 (communal use) or EC$10 (private bath).

The Diamond Estate is 1 mile east of Soufrière center, via Sir Arthur Lewis St, and the way is signposted. The grounds are open from 10 am to 5 pm Monday to Saturday and from 10 am to 3 pm on Sunday and holidays. There's an inexpensive snack bar.

South of Soufrière

A 20-minute walk along the dirt coastal road south of town leads to a quiet, undeveloped beach and to a mineral waterfall at Malgretout. Not only does this most unfrequented waterfall have a beautiful Eden-like setting, but visitors are allowed to shower in its warm volcanic waters – a situation that is not allowed at the more touristed waterfall at Diamond Botanical Gardens. To get to the falls continue along the coastal dirt road until you reach the pensioners home, then follow the steep road uphill for about 200 yards – a sign marks the way. Admission is EC$2.50.

Places to Stay

Home Hotel (☎ 459-7318), Bridge St, Soufrière, in the town center, has a friendly manager and seven simple but inviting rooms with fans and shared baths costing US$20/30 for singles/doubles. Guests have use of a kitchen and a common sitting area – whittle the day away watching the action on the central square from the veranda.

Mrs Camilla at *Camilla's Restaurant* (☎ 459-5379), 7 Bridge St, Soufrière, rents out a couple of comfortable rooms, with a kitchen, in the town center opposite the hospital. The rates, which vary a bit with the season and how long you stay, are around US$30/55 for singles/doubles.

Khayere Pann Inn (☎ 459-7441), PO Box 245, Soufrière, is a somewhat upscale B&B on the Castries Road at the north side of town. It has a splendid hillside view of the bay and Pitons and is only a 10-minute walk to town. The rooms have private baths and begin at US$45/55 for singles/doubles, breakfast included.

Hummingbird Beach Resort (☎ 459-7232), PO Box 280, Soufrière, on the north side of the harbor, has 10 rooms, a pool and a view across the bay to the Pitons. Rooms are pleasantly rustic with lots of wood, two with four-poster beds. From April to mid-December standard rooms with shared baths cost US$30/40 for singles/doubles, while fancier rooms with private baths start at US$70/80; in winter there's a mandatory breakfast and dinner plan that adds about US$50 per person to the rates.

Anse Chastanet Hotel (☎ 459-7000, fax 459-7700; in the USA ☎ 800-223-1108), PO Box 7000, Soufrière, on the beach at Anse Chastanet, is an appealing hideaway hotel with 48 rooms, some on the beach and others terraced up the hillside. All of them have a refrigerator, coffeemaker, ceiling fan and hardwood floors; many also

ST LUCIA

have open-beam ceilings and fine views of the Pitons. There's a scuba facility, tennis court and various water sports. Singles/doubles start at US$285/385 in winter, including breakfast and dinner; in summer the rates are US$120/166 without meals.

The *Ladera Resort* (☎ 459-7323, fax 459-5156; in the USA and Canada ☎ 800-841-4145), PO Box 225, Soufrière, is an exclusive resort with a stunning hillside setting. There are 19 suites and villas; most have private plunge pools and all have canopy beds with mosquito nets. The west side of every unit is wall-less, open to direct views of the nearby Pitons. Rates begin at US$195/330 in summer/winter, including breakfast and airport transfer. The resort is on the Vieux Fort road south of Soufrière.

Places to Eat

There are a handful of local restaurants offering good food at reasonable prices near the central square that borders Church, Sir Arthur Lewis and Bridge Sts. At the *New Venture* on Church St you can get a decent Creole meal for EC$15. *Camilla's* on Bridge St has good rotis and sandwiches at reasonable prices, as well as a variety of Creole seafood and meat dishes from EC$25 to EC$70. Below Camilla's is *Puto's*, a small bakery with fresh bread, while opposite is *Jacquot's*, which has hearty local meals costing EC$18 to EC$30.

Most tourists on a day visit pack in at the *Hummingbird*, a waterfront restaurant with a fine view of the Pitons. It features French and Creole dishes such as freshwater crayfish, shrimp coquilles St Jacques and Châteaubriand. Main courses range from EC$30 to EC$90 but there are also cheaper sandwiches and salads.

For those continuing south, an interesting option is *The Barbican*, on the Vieux Fort road between Soufrière and Etangs. Run by a friendly St Lucian couple with British ties, it serves up homegrown organic produce and juices. The menu includes pumpkin or callaloo soup (EC$6),

salt fish rotis (EC$11) and lambi (EC$25); it's closed on Monday.

VIEUX FORT

Vieux Fort, St Lucia's southernmost town, would be beyond the itinerary of most visitors if it weren't the site of the island's international airport, which is just north of the town center. The town has a mix of older wooden buildings and newer structures as well as the island's second-largest port. If you're overnighting here before a flight, there are white-sand beaches at the east side of town.

There's a lighthouse atop a 730-foot hill on Moule à Chique, the island's southernmost point, which offers a view of the Maria Islands, St Lucia's interior mountains and, if the weather's clear, the island of St Vincent to the south.

Places to Stay

St Martin's Guesthouse (☎ /fax 454-6674), on Clarke St in the town center, has small, simple rooms with shared bath. The elderly woman who runs the guesthouse, Mrs Romain, keeps the place tidy and clean; the cost is US$20.

The new *Juliette's Lodge* (☎ 454-5300, fax 454-5305), PO Box 482, Beanefield, Vieux Fort, has 17 cushy rooms with aircon, TV, bathtubs and balconies for US$50. It's about a 10-minute walk northeast of the airport. There's a pool and a moderately priced restaurant.

More expensive but slightly closer to the airport is *Skyway Inn* (☎ 454-6670, fax 454-7116), PO Box 353, Vieux Fort, which has 39 air-conditioned rooms starting at US$75/85 for singles/doubles; rates are US$10 cheaper in summer.

Places to Eat

Clarke St, Vieux Fort's main road, has grocery stores, a bakery and some inexpensive eateries. There's a *KFC* at the airport road rotary. *Chak Chak*, not far from the airport, has an unbeatable beachside setting, inexpensive sandwiches, fish & chips and reasonably priced Creole-style seafood dishes.

EAST COAST

The road up the east coast from Vieux Fort is relatively straight and uneventful, passing through a few local villages and numerous banana plantations before turning inland at the town of Dennery and making a scenic, winding cut across the mountainous rainforest to Castries.

There are two nature sanctuaries off the east coast. The Maria Islands Nature Reserve, east of Vieux Fort, is the only habitat of the kouwes snake, one of the world's rarest grass snakes, and the Maria Islands ground lizard. Because it's a sanctuary for terns, noddies and other sea birds, this two-island reserve is not accessible during the summer nesting season, but can be visited at other times of the year on tours arranged by the St Lucia National Trust (☎ 452-5005).

The Frigate Islands Nature Reserve encompasses two small rocky nearshore islands that are a summer nesting site for frigatebirds. The area is also a habitat for several types of herons, a couple of the island's indigenous rare birds (the Ramier pigeon and the St Lucian oriole), boa constrictors and the more dangerous fer-de-lance. There's a small interpretation center on the north side of Praslin Bay and tours of the area can be arranged through local tour agencies or the St Lucia National Trust.

Places to Stay

For those who want to be near the jungle interior *The Fox Grove Inn* (☎ /fax 455-3271), Mon Repos, is a pleasant off-the-beaten-path option. This European-managed inn offers nature trails, horseback riding and a hike to a secluded beach. The 11 rooms, which have ceiling fans and private baths, cost US$45/55 for singles/doubles, breakfast included. There's a pool, restaurant, bar and pool table. French and German are spoken. The inn is about a mile inland of the highway. The Vieux Fort bus (EC$4.50 from Castries) can drop you at the highway; call ahead and the manager will pick you up from there.

ST LUCIA

St Martin

St Martin is one of the Eastern Caribbean's most touristed islands. It boasts lovely white-sand beaches, a wide range of places to stay, good restaurants and two quite distinct sides, one administered by the French and the other by the Dutch.

The French side is developed on a smaller scale and has a decidedly French influence in language, food and culture. The Dutch side is more commercial, with large resorts, casinos and fast-food chains – and precious little that's solidly Dutch. Both sides are duty free and the two island capitals, Philipsburg and Marigot, are chock-a-block with fashionable shops.

The island is the world's smallest land area to be shared by two countries. Despite its dual nationality, the border crossings are marked only with inconspicuous signs and there are no stops or other formalities when passing between the two sides.

While the island is rather small and quite overdeveloped in places, there are still quiet niches to explore. Its beaches are surprisingly diverse, ranging from secluded coves and naturist retreats to busy resort-front strands.

St Martin is a prime jumping-off point for trips to neighboring islands – it's inexpensive and easy to get to Anguilla, Saba and St Eustatius, some of the Eastern Caribbean's most rural and least developed destinations.

Note that the Dutch side of the island is spelled Sint Maarten and the French side is spelled St Martin, a practice followed in this chapter when referring to the different sides. When referring to the island as a whole we use the spelling St Martin.

HIGHLIGHTS

- Sunbathing at clothing-optional Orient Beach
- Marigot, with its French-designer clothing boutiques and archeological museum
- A night of fine dining at Grand Case, St Martin's 'gourmet capital'
- Philipsburg's Frontstreet, with its duty-free jewelry and electronic shops
- Snorkeling the offshore islands of Îlet Pinel and Green Cay

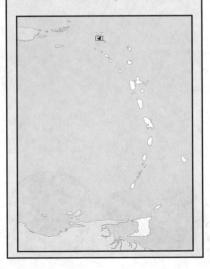

Facts about St Martin

HISTORY

Because of its many salt ponds, Amerindians called this island Soualiga, meaning 'Land of Salt.' According to popular belief, Columbus 'discovered' the island on November 11, 1493, and named it in honor of Bishop St Martin of Tours. However, some historians now think the island Columbus chanced upon that day was the more southerly Nevis and that he never actually sighted St Martin. At any rate, it wasn't until 1631 that the first

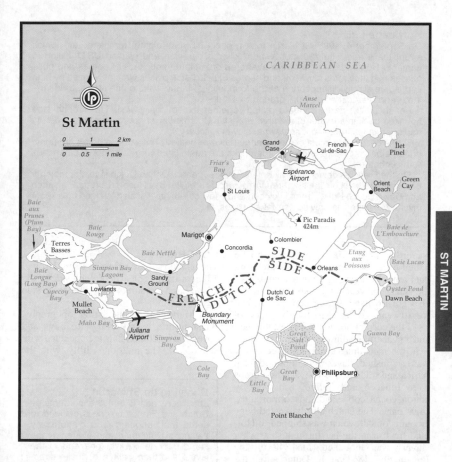

ST MARTIN

attempts at colonization were made, with the Dutch settling at Little Bay and the French in the Orleans area.

In 1633 the Spanish (who had claimed but not colonized the island) invaded St Martin, deporting all 128 inhabitants. The Spanish reinforced a fort that the Dutch had started and then built a second fort. In 1644 an attempt to retake the island was led by the renowned Dutch colonizer Peter Stuyvesant, who lost a leg to a cannonball in the fighting. Although the Dutch assault was unsuccessful, four years later the Spanish

reassessed their interests in the Eastern Caribbean and simply left on their own.

Both the Dutch and French hastily moved back and agreed to share the island, signing a partition agreement in 1648 that was to be repeatedly violated. During the period from 1670 to 1702 the French controlled the entire island. In 1703 the Dutch invaded from St Eustatius and then deported any French settlers who refused to leave the island.

On April 11, 1713, the Utrecht Peace Treaty returned half of the island to France.

Hurricane Luis

On September 4, 1995, St Martin took a direct hit from mighty Hurricane Luis, which swept the island with 130 mph winds, killed six people and caused US$1 billion in damage. Hundreds of boats were shattered onto piers, thousands of homes and businesses had their roofs blown off and scores of beachside places were pulverized by high surf, some simply disappearing at the foundations. In the wake of the storm, tourism – the island's largest employer – ground to a halt.

For the most part, islanders pulled together exceptionally well. The French side bounced back in a matter of months, while the Dutch side, where much of the property had been uninsured, had a somewhat slower recovery.

To the casual eye, most of the damage has now healed. The wooded areas are again green, albeit with fewer tall trees; the docks are again lined with sailboats, the beaches with sunbathers.

On the French side, virtually all hotels have reopened. On the Dutch side, the majority of places are back on line but three large resorts – Mullet Bay Resort, Port de Plaisance and Dawn Beach Hotel – remain closed and a few others have scaled back on their room inventory, reopening only some of their wings. ■

Nevertheless, St Martin continued to be batted back and forth, with the Dutch and the French each having complete control of the island for years at a time. The English also got involved, taking control in 1784 for 10 years and in 1810 for six years. In 1817 the current boundary was established and a peaceful resolution found.

In the meantime, a plantation economy was established, slaves were imported from Africa and trade flourished. The first crops were tobacco and indigo, followed by cotton, cocoa, coffee and, most importantly, sugar cane. The Dutch also harvested huge amounts of salt which was shipped to Holland for use in the herring industry. After slavery was abolished (in 1848 on the French side, 1863 on the Dutch side), the plantations declined and the island slipped into a subsistence economy.

When the Netherlands fell to the Nazis in 1940, the French took 'protective control' of the Dutch side of the island, but within two weeks France itself was under German control. An Allied occupation of the island followed and in 1943 the USA built a military airfield, now Juliana Airport. After the war the new airport, the region's largest, spurred the island's growth as a regional hub and brought on an early advent of tourism.

GEOGRAPHY

The island is 15km across at its widest and 13km at its longest. The French side of the island has 54 sq km of land, the Dutch side has 34 sq km.

St Martin has an interesting topography. Its shoreline is indented with bays and coves and its coastal flats are pocketed with salt ponds. The interior is hilly, with the

Divvying up St Martin

Local lore has it that the contentious Dutch and French colonists decided to settle their ongoing land disputes by having a Dutchman and a Frenchman stand back to back at one end of the island and then walk in opposite directions around the coastline. The island's boundary line would be established at the end of the day at whatever spot they finally met. As it turned out, the Frenchman walked much faster than the Dutchman and consequently the French side of St Martin ended up larger than the Dutch side.

It's said the Frenchman quenched his thirst along the way with French wine, while the Dutchman quenched his with more potent Dutch gin, thus accounting for the latter's slower pace! ■

highest point, Pic Paradis, rising 424 meters from the center of French St Martin.

The west side of the island is more water than land, dominated by the expansive Simpson Bay Lagoon, which is one of the largest landlocked bodies of water in the Caribbean.

CLIMATE

In January the average daily high temperature is 28°C (83°F) while the low averages 22°C (72°F). In July the average daily high is 30°C (86°F) while the low averages 24°C (76°F).

The average annual rainfall is 1029 mm (40 inches). The heaviest rainfall is from August to November, the lightest from February to April.

FLORA & FAUNA

The terrain is largely green but dry, with more palms, hibiscus and cacti than ferns or forests, although there are a few thickly vegetated areas in the interior.

Herons, egrets, stilts, pelicans, laughing gulls and other shorebirds are plentiful in the island's brackish ponds. Frigatebirds can be spotted along the coastline, hummingbirds and bright yellow-bellied bananaquits are common in gardens and there are colorful woodland birds in the hills. Lizards are abundant and can be seen scurrying about on walkways and other sunny areas.

GOVERNMENT & POLITICS

The northern part of St Martin is a sub-prefecture of Guadeloupe, which is an overseas department of France. Local control is in the hands of a sub-prefect appointed by the French government and a locally elected mayor and town council.

The southern section of the island belongs to the Netherlands Antilles, which is part of the Kingdom of the Netherlands. Regional control of the Netherlands Antilles is based in the southern Caribbean island of Curaçao, but Sint Maarten has its own lieutenant governor who, in conjunction with an elected island council and an appointed executive council is responsible for local affairs.

ECONOMY

The island's economy has long been fueled by tourism, a situation that has turned St Martin into one of the most heavily developed islands in the region. In part because of a glut in room inventory, some resorts on the Dutch side of the island never reopened after Hurricane Luis and an estimated 1000 hotel employees still remain out of work.

The whole island is one big duty-free shop and while many of the goods are geared for vacationing tourists, islanders from throughout the Caribbean also come here to buy electronics and other high-priced items.

POPULATION & PEOPLE

The official population is approximately 27,000 on the French side, 32,000 on the Dutch side, although it's estimated that an additional 16,000 to 20,000 illegal aliens also reside on the island, many from Haiti and the Dominican Republic.

The tourist boom of the past few decades has resulted in such an influx of job-seekers from elsewhere in the Caribbean that only about 20% of all residents were born on the island. Many of the people operating small hotels, restaurants and shops on the French side are from mainland France.

ST MARTIN

SOCIETY & CONDUCT

The island culture has its roots largely in African, French and Dutch influences, though scores of more recent immigrants have added their own elements to this multicultural society.

Dos & Don'ts

Topless sunbathing is customary on both sides of the island and nude bathing is officially sanctioned at Orient Beach on the northeast side of French St Martin.

RELIGION

The French side of the island is predominantly Catholic, while the Dutch side is more varied, with Anglican, Baptist, Jehovah's Witness, Methodist and Seventh Day Adventist churches.

LANGUAGE

French is the official language of French St Martin but English is also widely understood. Dutch is the official language of Dutch Sint Maarten, although in practice English is the first language spoken on that side, Dutch the second.

On both sides, most island-born people are multilingual and can speak English, French and Creole. There's also a sizable Spanish-speaking immigrant community, mainly from the Dominican Republic.

Facts for the Visitor

ORIENTATION

Marigot and Philipsburg are each about a 15-minute drive from Juliana Airport, although if you happen to hit heavy traffic the trip can easily take twice as long. Because of the way traffic funnels into the capitals, both Marigot and Philipsburg can get heavily congested, with the worst traffic jams typically occurring in late afternoon.

Driving around the island is fairly simple, because essentially one road loops around the western side of the island and another around the main eastern part of the island.

Side roads leading to beaches and resorts are generally marked.

Maps

There are a number of simple island maps that can be picked up at tourist offices and hotels; these will probably suffice for most exploration. Otherwise, the Institut Géographique National's 4608-G Série Bleue (1:25,000) map that covers both St Martin and St Barts is a detailed topographical map and the best road map of the island – it can be picked up at bookstores or newspaper stands around the island for about 50F.

TOURIST OFFICES
Local Tourist Offices

Several free tourist publications with information on sights, activities, restaurants and shopping are available at tourist offices.

On the Dutch side, the tourist office has information booths at Juliana Airport and at Wathey Square in Philipsburg. When requesting information by mail, write to: Sint Maarten Tourist Bureau (☎ 22337, fax 22734), Imperial Building, 23 Walter Nisbeth Rd, Philipsburg, Sint Maarten, Netherlands Antilles.

On the French side, the tourist office is at Marigot's harborfront. The mailing address is: St Martin Tourist Office (☎ 87 57 21, fax 87 56 43, sxmto@aol.com), Port de Marigot, 97150 Marigot, St Martin, French West Indies.

Tourist Offices Abroad

Overseas tourist offices for the French West Indies are listed under Tourist Offices in the Facts for the Visitor section of the Guadeloupe chapter. The overseas tourist offices for Dutch Sint Maarten are:

Canada
    Sint Maarten Information Center,
    243 Ellerslie Ave, Willowdale,
    Ontario, Canada M2N 1Y5
    (☎ 416-223-3501, fax 416-223-6887)
Netherlands
    Minister Plenipotentiary of the Netherlands
    Antilles, Badhuisweg 173-175,
    2597 JP, 'S-Gravenhage
    (☎ 070-351-2811, fax 070-351-2722)

USA
  Sint Maarten Tourist Office, 675 Third Ave,
  Suite 1806, New York, NY 10017
  (☎ 212-953-2084, 800-786-2278;
  fax 212-953-2145)

VISAS & DOCUMENTS

US and Canadian citizens arriving at Juliana Airport on the Dutch side can stay up to three months with proof of citizenship. Acceptable ID includes a birth certificate with a raised seal, plus a government-approved photo ID such as a driver's license, or a passport that is not more than five years past its expiration date. Citizens of other countries entering the island on the Dutch side require a valid passport.

If entering the island on the French side, US and Canadian citizens are allowed entry for stays of up to three weeks without a passport if they have the same type of documentation listed for the Dutch side. Citizens of the EU need an official identity card, valid passport or French *carte de séjour*. Citizens of most other foreign countries, including Australia, need both a valid passport and a visa for France if entering the island on the French side.

A roundtrip or onward ticket is officially required of all visitors to St Martin, regardless of whether entry is made on the French or Dutch side.

While documents are checked upon arrival, beyond that immigration controls are quite lax, a situation that is partially the result of unrestricted movement between the two sides of the island.

CUSTOMS

Although the police make occasional spot checks when suspicious, there are otherwise no customs checks coming into Juliana Airport – there's not even a counter for inspecting luggage.

MONEY

The French franc is the official legal tender on the French side and the Netherlands Antilles guilder on the Dutch side, but on both sides US dollars are widely used as well. This makes the US dollar the most convenient currency to carry as it's the only one readily accepted on both sides of the island.

On the French side, restaurants and hotels are split between posting prices in French francs or US dollars, while on the Dutch side they're virtually always posted in US dollars.

On both sides grocery stores mark goods in the local currency but generally have cash registers equipped with a key that can automatically convert the total to US dollars. Larger grocery stores, such as Match in Marigot and Food Center on the Dutch side, accept US dollar traveler's checks like cash and generally offer the full market rate – so you'll do better cashing your traveler's checks on food purchases than you would exchanging at a bank.

We find it useful to carry some francs for those times when a French business gives a bad exchange rate, but most places calculate at a fair rate and it generally works out fine to simply pay in dollars.

MasterCard and Visa credit cards are widely, though not universally, accepted around the island. ATMs that accept major credit cards and Cirrus and Plus bank cards can be found at some banks.

For details on the two island currencies, including exchange rates, see Money in the introductory Facts for the Visitor chapter.

POST & COMMUNICATIONS
Post

The main post offices are in Philipsburg and Marigot. When writing to the French side, end the address with '97150 St Martin, French West Indies.' When writing to the Dutch side, end the address with 'Sint Maarten, Netherlands Antilles.'

From the Dutch side, it costs Fls 0.90 to mail a postcard and Fls 1.75 to mail a 10-gram letter within the Caribbean; Fls 1.10 for a postcard and Fls 2.25 for a letter to the USA, Canada, UK or Europe; and Fls 1.30 for a postcard and Fls 3.25 for a letter to Australia, Asia or Africa.

From the French side, it costs 3F to send a postcard to France, 3.80F to the Caribbean or the USA, 4.40F to other parts of the

Americas and 5.20F to the rest of the world. This rate also covers letters up to 20 grams.

Telephone
Local numbers have five digits on the Dutch side, six digits on the French side. Calls between the two sides are charged as long distance.

To phone the Dutch side from the French side, dial 005995 before the local number. To call the French side from the Dutch side dial 00590 before the local number.

When calling the island from overseas, you must prefix local numbers with area code 590 for the French side, 5995 for the Dutch side.

On the French side virtually all pay phones are the card phone type, while on the Dutch side card phones predominate but there are some coin phones that take US quarters as well as Netherlands Antilles guilders.

For more details on phonecards, see Post & Communications in the introductory Facts for the Visitor chapter.

The area code for French St Martin is 590; for Dutch Sint Maarten it's 5995.

NEWSPAPERS & MAGAZINES
The Dutch side's three daily newspapers, *The Daily Herald*, *The Chronicle* and *The Guardian*, are printed in English. The French side has two weekly papers, *l'Hebdo* and *St Martin's Week*, both in French. Two useful free visitor magazines available at hotels and tourist offices are *Discover Saint Martin/Sint Maarten* and *Sint Maarten Events*.

The *International Herald-Tribune*, *New York Times*, *USA Today*, *Le Monde*, *Die Welt* and other foreign publications are available at larger grocery stores and newsstands around the island.

RADIO & TV
There are a handful of radio stations, including The Voice of Sint Maarten at

102.7 FM and 1300 AM, which broadcasts news at 1 and 6 pm and has talk shows in English. For European news in French, there's RFO at 88.9 FM.

Cable TV on the Dutch side carries a full range of North American network programs and movie channels. The English-language Leeward Broadcasting Corporation, on channel 7, has island news as well as CNN broadcasts.

On the French side TV is usually limited to three French language channels, CNN news and a couple of US movie channels.

ELECTRICITY
On the French side the voltage is 220 AC, 60 cycles, and plugs have two round prongs. On the Dutch side it's 110 volts AC, 60 cycles, and plugs have two flat prongs. Many hotels provide dual-voltage plugs for electric shavers.

WEIGHTS & MEASURES
Islanders use the metric system.

HEALTH
There are hospitals in Marigot (☎ 29 57 57) near Fort Louis and east of Philipsburg (☎ 31111) in the Cay Hill area.

DANGERS & ANNOYANCES
Normal safety precautions apply. Women should be cautious walking alone on deserted beaches and if hitching. Don't leave valuables in your car as break-ins, especially in remote spots, can be a problem.

EMERGENCIES
On the Dutch side, dial ☎ 22222 for police emergencies, ☎ 22111 for an ambulance. On the French side, dial ☎ 87 50 14 for the police, ☎ 87 86 25 for an ambulance.

BUSINESS HOURS
Shop hours in Philipsburg are generally from 8 am to noon and 2 to 6 pm Monday to Saturday. In Marigot, business hours vary but are typically from about 9 am to 12:30 pm and 3 to 7 pm Monday to Saturday. In Philipsburg, some shops open on Sunday if cruise ships are in port.

PUBLIC HOLIDAYS
& SPECIAL EVENTS

Public holidays on the island are:

New Year's Day	January 1
Good Friday	late March/early April
Easter Sunday	late March/early April
Easter Monday	late March/early April
Queen's Day (Dutch side)	April 30
Labor Day	May 1
Government Holiday (Dutch)	the day after the last Carnival parade, about a month after Easter
Ascension Thursday	40th day after Easter
Pentecost Monday (French side)	eighth Monday after Easter
Bastille Day (French)	July 14
Assumption Day (French)	August 15
Sint Maarten Day/ Concordia Day	November 11
Christmas Day	December 25
Boxing Day (Dutch)	December 26

On the French side, Carnival celebrations are held during the traditional five-day Mardi Gras period that ends on Ash Wednesday. It features the selection of a Carnival Queen, costume parades, dancing and music.

On the Dutch side, which has the larger Carnival, activities usually begin the second week after Easter and last for two weeks, with steel band competitions, jump-ups, calypso concerts, beauty contests and

costume parades. Events are centered at Carnival Village on the north side of Philipsburg.

Bastille Day, France's national holiday, is celebrated with a parade, sporting events and fireworks.

The November 11 holiday, called Sint Maarten Day by the Dutch and Concordia Day by the French, is marked by a ceremony at the Boundary Monument obelisk that notes the amicable coexistence of the two countries.

For sailors, the annual Heineken Regatta, held the first weekend in March, features competitions for racing yachts, large sailboats and small multihulls. For fishers, there's the Marlin Open de St Martin invitational tournament held in June.

ACTIVITIES
Beaches & Swimming

The island has beautiful white-sand beaches, ranging from crowded resort strands to long secluded sweeps. Most of the best and least developed beaches are on the French side. The clothing-optional Orient Beach is a lovely beach though it attracts a crowd. Long Beach is great for seclusion, while Baie Rouge, Dawn Beach and the islets off the northeast coast are good places for both snorkeling and swimming. All beaches are public, although around some of the Dutch resorts access is marked with the tiniest of signs.

Diving

The most popular diving is at Proselyte Reef, a few kilometers south of Philipsburg, where in 1802 the British frigate HMS *Proselyte* sank in 15 meters of water. In addition to the remains of the ship, there are 10 dive sites in that area, including coral reefs with caverns.

Dive Shops The following dive shops are full-service facilities. Prices are competitive. On average, single dives cost around US$45, while multi-dive packages lower the price to around US$35 per dive. Most of the shops also conduct open-water certification courses for around US$350 and accept referred students for about US$200. Some also offer half-day 'discover scuba' resort courses for beginners, including a little beach dive, for US$50 to US$75.

Blue Ocean Dive Center,
Royal Food Store center, Baie Nettlé
(☎ 87 89 73, fax 87 26 36)
Octoplus Dive Center, Grand Case
(☎ 87 20 62, fax 87 20 63)
Pelican Watersports, Pelican Marina,
Simpson Bay (☎ 42640, fax 42476)
Scuba Fun Dive Center, Marina, Anse Marcel
(☎ 87 36 13, fax 87 36 52)
Sea Dolphin Dive Center, Le Flamboyant hotel,
Baie Nettlé (☎ 87 60 72, fax 87 60 73)
Sea Horse Diving, Marine Hotel, Baie Nettlé
(☎ 87 84 15, fax 87 84 74)
Trade Winds Dive Center, Great Bay Marina,
Philipsburg (☎ 75176)

Snorkeling
There's decent snorkeling at a number of places, including Baie Rouge, Dawn Beach and the islands of Green Cay and Îlet Pinel off the northeast coast.

You can rent snorkeling gear at most dive shops and hotel beach huts; the going rate is about US$10 a day. Many of the dive shops offer snorkeling tours for around US$25.

A few boats offer day trips to the more pristine waters around Anguilla, with the greatest frequency of cruises in the winter season. One company, SeaHawk Cruises (☎ 71359 or 87 59 49), sails year-round and charges US$66, including a barbecue lunch, open bar and use of snorkeling gear.

Hiking
The island's most popular hike is up to Pic Paradis, St Martin's highest point. Not only will this hike reward you with great views, but Pic Paradis also serves as a take-off point for a few longer hikes that reach down to the coast. For details, see the Pic Paradis heading later in this chapter.

If you don't want to trek off on your own, guided hikes are offered by St Martin Action Nature (☎ 87 97 87), an organization that helps keep the island trails clear, and Sint Maarten's Heritage Foundation

(☎ 23379), which is affiliated with the Philipsburg museum.

Horseback Riding
Horseback riding is available from Bayside Riding Club (☎ 87 36 64) near Orient Beach, the OK Corral (☎ 87 40 72) at Baie Lucas and Caïd & Isa (☎ 87 45 70) at Anse Marcel. The cost for a two-hour beach ride is typically US$40 to US$50. Bayside also has one-hour sunset rides for US$45.

Golf
The island's only golf course is the 18-hole Mullet Bay Golf (☎ 52801), which has green fees that are US$109, cart included.

Windsurfing
Two of the island's top windsurfing spots are at Orient Bay and at the north end of Baie de l'Embouchure.

At Orient Beach, the Windsurfing Club (☎ 87 48 16), run by French windsurfing champion Nathalie Simon, rents boards from US$15 an hour or US$30 for three hours, has a course for beginners for US$140 (three 1½-hour sessions) and offers one-hour private lessons for US$55. The shop also rents surfboards and body-boards for US$12 to US$15 per half day.

At Baie de l'Embouchure, Tropical Wave (☎ 87 37 25) and Windy Reef (☎ 87 08 37) rent windsurfing equipment at comparable rates.

The St Martin Windsurfing Association (☎ 87 93 24) has information on races and tournaments.

Other Activities

Sunfish sailboats can be rented at some resort-area beaches and sailing cruises, deep-sea fishing and yacht charters can be arranged through the marinas. When the swell picks up, Mullet Bay and Orient Bay can be good for bodyboarding.

Information on cycling is under Bicycle in the Getting Around section.

ACCOMMODATIONS

Almost all of the Dutch side accommodations are between Philipsburg and Mullet Bay, with the majority of rooms being in large resorts. On the French side there's a resort cluster at Baie Nettlé but beyond that things are fairly widely dispersed with the majority of rooms in small-scale hotels and villa-style places. Accordingly, the places on the French side tend to be more personal and friendly.

At first glance rates may appear cheaper on the Dutch side. However, the Dutch add on to their quoted rates a 5% room tax and usually a 10% to 15% service charge – and a few of them pad the bill with an additional 5% 'energy charge'! On the French side some hotels have begun charging the 5% room tax on top of the bill, but service charges are usually included in the quoted room rates.

FOOD

There are numerous quality French restaurants on the island with prices that are quite moderate by Caribbean standards. Many people, regardless of where they're staying, drive to Grand Case for dinner, because it has one of the best concentrations of good eating spots of anywhere on the island. Marigot also has a number of good dining options, with the largest selection at the Port La Royale Marina.

On the Dutch side, Philipsburg has an abundance of restaurants. Fast-food eateries are plentiful along the road to the airport.

As for grocery stores, the ones on the French side are predominantely stocked with European foods, while the ones on the Dutch side are heavily stocked with American foods. The biggest grocery stores in St Martin, if not the entire Eastern Caribbean, are the two Food Centers, one on Bush Rd west of Philipsburg and the other on Union Rd just south of the boundary monument.

Note that some restaurants include a 15% service charge in their prices and at others you are expected to tip.

DRINKS

There are water desalination plants on the island, but because of the high water prices many places still use catchments. The desalinated water is fine to drink from the tap, but catchment water varies in quality and should generally be treated first. Reasonably priced bottled water is readily available at grocery stores.

Inexpensive Caribbean rums and French wines are plentiful and can be purchased at any grocery store. You might want to sample the local guavaberry liqueur, a sweet rum-based drink flavored with a small cranberry-like berry, *Eugenia floribunda*, which grows on the island's hills.

ENTERTAINMENT

The entertainment scene is centered at the Dutchside resorts and casinos, particularly in the Maho Bay area. The minimum gambling and drinking age is 18. There are a couple of cinemas in Philipsburg showing first-run movies in English.

The French side tends to be pretty low key, but there are a number of bars with entertainment in Marigot.

THINGS TO BUY

St Martin is the Eastern Caribbean's top duty-free shopping spot. Philipsburg's Frontstreet is the island's most commercial strip and has the largest selection of camera and electronics shops. In both Philipsburg and Marigot, shoppers will find chic boutiques, jewelers and perfume stores carrying top-name European products. In Marigot there's a concentration of shops at the north side of Port La Royale Marina and along the adjacent Rue du Général de Gaulle. For something more local, Marigot's harborfront market has handicrafts, T-shirts, pareos and the like.

If you're interested in art, you can help support the St Martin Archeological Museum by buying from its gallery, which sells watercolors, oils and prints of island scenes at reasonable prices.

Duty-free alcohol is a bargain. You can pick up a bottle of rum at shops around the island for around US$5.

Getting There & Away

AIR

All international flights arrive at Juliana Airport, on the Dutch side of the island. Espérance Airport, on the French side, has an airstrip only large enough to handle prop planes from nearby islands.

The following are the local reservation numbers for airlines that have scheduled flights to Juliana Airport:

Air Caraïbes	☎ 54234
Air France	☎ 54212
Air Guadeloupe	☎ 54212 or 87 53 74
Air Martinique	☎ 54212
Air Saint-Barts	☎ 53151 or 87 73 46
ALM	☎ 54240
American Airlines	☎ 52040
AOM	☎ 54344
BWIA	☎ 54646
Continental Airlines	☎ 52444
Corsair	☎ 87 94 07
KLM	☎ 52101
LIAT	☎ 54203
Winair	☎ 54230

USA & Canada

Continental and American Airlines have daily nonstop flights to St Martin from New York. American also has direct flights from Miami and connecting flights to numerous US cities via San Juan, Puerto Rico. There are occasional discounted fares as cheap as US$300 roundtrip, though the more typical excursion fare is about double that from the east coast.

Europe

There are a few flights offered weekly from Paris to St Martin by Air France and from Amsterdam to St Martin by KLM. Full-fare excursion tickets cost about US$1400, but travel agents can discount these fares substantially.

Within the Caribbean

American Airlines has four flights daily to St Martin from Puerto Rico; the one-way fare is US$138, the excursion fare US$187.

You can fly to St Martin from any of LIAT's Caribbean destinations, in most cases with same-day connections via Antigua. LIAT flights from Antigua to St Martin cost US$86 one way, US$123 for a same-day return and US$156 for a 30-day excursion with a stopover in St Kitts allowed.

Air Guadeloupe, Air Caraïbes and Air St Martin all offer daily flights between Guadeloupe and St Martin from around US$100 one way; Air Caraïbes currently has the lowest priced excursion, a 'super-promo' fare of US$137, but the other airlines also have attractive discount schemes on roundtrip tickets.

Air Martinique flies on weekdays between Martinique and St Martin, with Monday and Thursday flights into Espérance, other days into Juliana; the cost is US$188 one way and from US$211 roundtrip.

Airport Information

Juliana Airport The island's main airport is Juliana Airport on the Dutch side. The tourist information booth, near the arrivals exit, is not terribly helpful with hands-on information, but nearby there's a rack of useful tourist publications and a direct-line courtesy phone to a couple of hotels. There's a taxi stand just outside the arrivals exit and a line of car rental booths nearby.

Outside the departure lounge is a bank, a newsstand with international newspapers and magazines and duty-free shops selling liquor, jewelry, perfume, etc. There's a 2nd-floor restaurant open from noon to midnight and a more reasonably priced ground-level booth with pastries, sandwiches and drinks.

Both card phones and phones that accept US quarters are spread around the airport. Netherlands Antilles phonecards are sold at the airport post office. There's an ATM in the departure lounge.

Espérance Airport This small airport, in Grand Case in French St Martin, handles flights to St Barts, Guadeloupe and Martinique. The airport has card phones, car rentals and a snack bar.

SEA
Inter-Island Ferry
From St Martin, there are numerous daily ferries to and from Anguilla; daily catamarans to and from St Barts; and a ferry several times a week to and from Saba. Full details are in the Getting There & Away sections of the Anguilla, St Barts and Saba chapters.

Yacht
Yachts can clear immigration at Philipsburg and Marigot. There are marinas at Philipsburg, Marigot, Simpson Bay Lagoon, Oyster Pond and Anse Marcel.

Landlocked Simpson Bay Lagoon is one of the most protected anchorages in the Eastern Caribbean. There are two drawbridge entrances to it that open on set schedules: at 11 am and 6 pm weekdays and 4 and 6 pm weekends at Simpson Bay on the Dutch side, and at 9 am, 2 and 5:30 pm daily (no 2 pm opening on Sunday) at Sandy Ground on the French side.

Cruise Ship
St Martin is a popular cruise ship destination, largely because of the duty-free shopping there. Cruise ships land passengers in Philipsburg and Marigot.

LEAVING ST MARTIN
From Juliana Airport, there's a departure tax of US$12 for international departures and US$6 for flights to destinations in the Netherlands Antilles. There's no departure tax for children aged two and under, or for anyone who has been on St Martin for less than 24 hours. There are no departure taxes at all from Espérance Airport.

Note that Juliana is a sluggish and ill-planned airport, so don't cut anything close. Certainly give yourself extra time if you're flying out with LIAT, as tickets are sold at the check-in counter and at times lines can move tediously slow.

Getting Around

THE AIRPORTS
From Juliana Airport taxis charge US$10 to either Marigot or Philipsburg, US$16 to Grand Case and US$20 to Orient Bay.

A couple of taxis meet each flight arriving at Espérance Airport; if you miss them, security can call one for you. From Espérance Airport, taxis cost US$10 to either Marigot or Orient Beach.

BUS
There are two kinds of buses: larger public buses, which make Philipsburg-Marigot and Marigot-Grand Case runs and charge US$1.50, and more frequent private minivans that charge according to distance, from US$1 to US$3.

Buses have their starting and ending points marked on them, usually on the front window. The Marigot-Philipsburg buses have the longest operating hours, generally from 6 am to midnight; on most other routes buses are hard to get after 8 pm. In addition to the main Philipsburg-Marigot-Grand Case routes, there are less frequent buses to Mullet Bay, Simpson Bay and Orleans. Beyond that bus service is sketchy so touring the whole island by bus is not practical.

Although there are no airport buses per se, if you're traveling light, you can try catching one of the Philipsburg-Mullet Bay buses, which pass right by the airport.

In the capitals you have to stand at bus stops, which are found along Backstreet in Philipsburg and on Rue de Hollande in

ST MARTIN

Marigot. In rural areas you can flag down buses anywhere along the route.

TAXI

Taxi fares are set by the government. The minimum fare is US$5. From Marigot it costs US$10 to Philipsburg, Grand Case or the airports. Taxis from Philipsburg charge US$10 to Mullet Bay or Juliana Airport. Add US$2 for each additional passenger beyond two. There's a surcharge of 25% on fares between 10 pm and midnight and 50% from midnight to 6 am. There are taxi stands at the airports, Wathey Square in Philipsburg and the public market in Marigot.

CAR & MOTORCYCLE
Road Rules

Driving is on the right side of the road on both sides of the island, and your home driver's license is valid. Road signs and most car odometers are in kilometers. The speed limit in built-up areas varies from 20 to 40 km/h, while outside residential areas it's 60 km/h unless otherwise posted.

Rental

Car There are scores of car rental companies on the island, with the greatest abundance at Juliana Airport. If you don't have a reservation you can stroll the row of booths just outside the airport arrival lounge and compare prices. It's a competitive market and when things are slow, as is common in the off season, you can often find someone willing to drop rates to around US$20 a day. At busier times the going rate is closer to US$35. Rates include unlimited kilometers; optional CDW (collision damage waiver) costs about US$10 a day extra.

Sanaco Car Rental (☎ 87 14 93) and Esperanza Car Rental (☎ 87 88 57) have offices at Espérance Airport in Grand Case.

The following companies have offices at or near Juliana Airport:

Avis	☎ 53959
Budget	☎ 54030
Hertz	☎ 54314
National/Europcar	☎ 42168
Paradise Island	☎ 52361
Sunshine	☎ 52685

Motorcycle Motorcycles are available from Rent A Scoot (☎ 87 20 59) opposite the Hotel Laguna Beach in Baie Nettlé and Eugene Moto Scooter Rental (☎ 87 13 97) next to the museum in Marigot. Daily rates, including helmet and lock, are around US$22 for a 50cc scooter (no license required), US$28 for an 80cc scooter (driver's license required) and US$65 for a 650cc motorcycle (motorcycle license required).

BICYCLE

Frogs Legs Cyclery (☎ 87 05 11), next to Match supermarket in Marigot, rents mountain bikes from US$15 a day and organizes island cycling tours for US$20. BN Food Store (☎ 87 97 47) at the side of the Marine Hotel in Baie Nettlé has a few mountain bikes for US$10 a day.

HITCHHIKING

It's fairly easy to hitch rides on the island – indeed, many islanders do so. All of the usual safety precautions apply.

ORGANIZED TOURS

Taxi tours of the island that last about 2½ hours cost US$40 for one or two people. There's an additional fee of US$8 for each extra passenger.

St Martin Archaeological Museum in Marigot offers a morning bus tour of St Martin with an emphasis on island history. It lasts two hours and costs US$30; for reservations call ☎ 29 22 84.

Marigot

Marigot   the capital of French St Martin. It has some good restaurants and a couple of worthy sights.

Although it is not a large town, Marigot has two commercial centers. One of them, the area around the harbor front, has the public market with food vendors and souvenir stalls. The tourist office and the dock for boats to Anguilla and St Barts are also there. The other center encompasses the

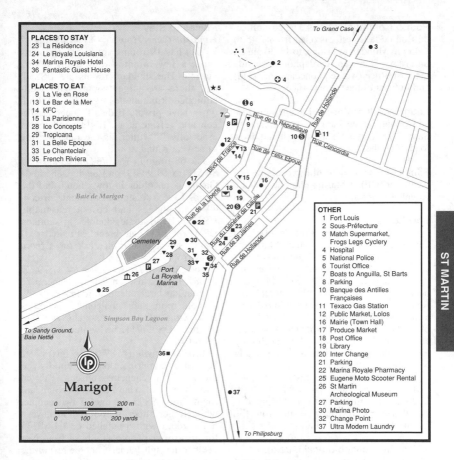

PLACES TO STAY
23 La Résidence
24 Le Royale Louisiana
34 Marina Royale Hotel
36 Fantastic Guest House

PLACES TO EAT
9 La Vie en Rose
13 Le Bar de la Mer
14 KFC
15 La Parisienne
28 Ice Concepts
29 Tropicana
31 La Belle Epoque
33 Le Chanteclair
35 French Riviera

OTHER
1 Fort Louis
2 Sous-Préfecture
3 Match Supermarket, Frogs Legs Cyclery
4 Hospital
5 National Police
6 Tourist Office
7 Boats to Anguilla, St Barts
8 Parking
10 Banque des Antilles Françaises
11 Texaco Gas Station
12 Public Market, Lolos
16 Mairie (Town Hall)
17 Produce Market
18 Post Office
19 Library
20 Inter Change
21 Parking
22 Marina Royale Pharmacy
25 Eugene Moto Scooter Rental
26 St Martin Archeological Museum
27 Parking
30 Marina Photo
32 Change Point
37 Ultra Modern Laundry

Marigot

To Grand Case
To Sandy Ground, Baie Nettlé
Simpson Bay Lagoon
Baie de Marigot
Cemetery
Port La Royale Marina
To Philipsburg

ST MARTIN

Port La Royale Marina, which is surrounded by a cluster of restaurants and boutiques that spill out onto bustling Rue du Général de Gaulle.

Marigot is a historic town in flux. There are still a number of older West Indian style buildings with fancy fretwork and second-floor balconies, but many other such buildings have made way for more modern structures. A new land reclamation project has just been completed along the harborfront, modernizing that section of town and turning much of it into a parking lot.

Information

Tourist Office The tourist office, on the north side of the harbor, is open from 8:30 am to 1 pm and 2:30 to 5:30 pm on weekdays, 8 am to noon on Saturday.

Money You can avoid transaction fees and long waits by bypassing the banks and instead changing money at the storefront currency exchange booths. Inter Change on Rue du Général de Gaulle is open from 8 am to 6:30 pm. Change Point, near the marina, is open from 7:30 am to 7 pm. Both are closed on Sunday.

Post & Communications The post office, on Rue de la Liberté, is open from 7:45 to 4:45 pm Monday to Friday, to 11:30 am on Saturday. There are card phones outside the post office (where phonecards are sold) and in front of the tourist office.

Laundry Ultra Modern Laundry on Rue de Hollande, open 7 am to 7 pm Monday to Saturday, charges US$8 to wash and dry a load of clothes.

Film There's one-hour film processing (24 prints for 97F) at Marina Photo at Port La Royale Marina.

Fort Louis

Fort Louis (also called Fort de Marigot) was built in 1789 to protect Marigot's warehouses from the frequent raids being staged by British privateers based on nearby Anguilla. After French and English hostilities ended in the 19th century, the fort was abandoned and slipped into decay. Today not much remains of Fort Louis other than some partially intact stone walls and a couple of cannons, but the hilltop locale offers a fine view of Marigot and Simpson Bay Lagoon.

To get there, drive up past the hospital and park at the large cross where you'll find steps leading up to the fort – just two minutes away. If you walk up from the harbor it takes about 15 minutes.

St Martin Archaeological Museum

This worthwhile little museum, on the road to Sandy Ground, is nicely presented with a focus on the Arawak Period. Shell amulets, bone artifacts, arrow points and bits of pottery help illustrate the culture of the island's early Amerindian inhabitants. There are also presentations on flora and fauna, period photos of Marigot and historical displays on the French/Dutch divide and St Martin's plantation era of sugar and salt production. There are detailed interpretive plaques in both French and English.

Hours are 9 am to 1 pm and 3 to 6 pm Monday to Saturday. Admission is US$5 for adults and US$2 for children under 12.

Places to Stay

Fantastic Guest House (☎ 87 71 09, fax 87 73 51) has 19 rooms above an auto parts shop, a few minutes walk south of the marina. The standard rooms are US$50, and there are larger rooms with well-equipped kitchenettes for US$75; both types have private baths, TV, phone, aircon and refrigerators. It's a good value, especially in winter, as the rates are the same year round.

The 68-room *Le Royale Louisiana* (☎ 87 86 51, fax 87 96 49) on Rue du Général de Gaulle is an older in-town hotel, but the rooms have a fresh coat of paint, air-con, TV and phones and cost a reasonable US$52/71 for singles/doubles in summer, US$66/88 in winter, breakfast included. If you're sensitive to noise ask for a room away from the street.

The 21-room *La Résidence* (☎ 87 70 37, fax 87 90 44), also on Rue du Général de Gaulle, has large adequate rooms with TV, air-con, room safes, balconies and minibars. Singles/doubles cost US$74/92 in summer, US$96/112 in winter, breakfast included.

Marina Royale (☎ 87 52 46, fax 87 92 88), at the marina, has 62 good-sized rooms with kitchenettes, air-con, TV and phones; most also have balconies. Standard rooms are US$95 for one or two people, while larger superior rooms that have a living room with a sofabed cost US$135 for up to four people. It's busy from November through January, but the rest of the year you can often negotiate a handsome discount. There are also monthly rentals from around US$700.

Places to Eat

Marina Port La Royale Marina has a waterfront lined with restaurants offering everything from pizza and burgers to seafood and nouvelle cuisine. There's fierce competition, with some of the island's lowest menu prices and lots of chalkboard specials. The best bet is to just wander around and see what catches your fancy.

The harborside *La Belle Epoque* is large and popular, serving standard fare that includes seafood, pasta and pizza, beginning around 45F. For more creative dishes with tantalizing sauces there's the streetside *French Riviera*, a small owner-run operation on the eastern edge of the marina that serves French bistro fare such as filet mignon, salmon carpaccio and good salads – all priced between 35F and 60F. Both places are open for lunch and dinner.

For dessert, don't miss *Ice Concepts*, which has homemade Italian ice creams and sorbets in tasty tropical flavors for just 10F.

A top choice for fine dining is the little family-run *Le Chanteclair* (☎ 87 94 60), where a full-course dinner costs around 140F, with a wide range of standard French starters and main dishes.

Another good intimate dinner option is *Tropicana* (☎ 87 79 07), which has classic French fare and usually offers a salad-to-dessert meal du jour for US$25; otherwise, expect dinner for two with wine to run closer to US$100.

Around Town There's a new complex at the public market with a dozen bars and *lolos* (barbecue stands) selling burgers, hot dogs and barbecued meals. Their chalkboard menus include lots of chicken and fish dishes served with plantain, peas and rice for around 40F and island favorites like bull-foot and pigtail soups. For ordinary fast food, there's a *KFC* on the opposite side of the street.

La Parisienne is a good bakery café with sidewalk tables, fresh salads, generous baguette sandwiches, quiche and lasagna, all at reasonable prices. It's open from 6 am to 8 pm Monday to Saturday, and to 12:30 pm on Sunday.

Geraldo Pizza Truck, which parks opposite Le Royale Louisiana hotel from 6 to 10 pm every day but Monday, has excellent take-away pizza priced from 35F to 50F. This little mobile pizza wagon actually has a wood-fired oven stoked up inside!

Le Bar de la Mer, near the harbor, draws a predominantly French-speaking crowd and is a popular spot to have a drink. It also has pizzas and salads from about 50F as well as fish and meat dishes for around 80F.

La Vie en Rose is a fashionable French restaurant with a choice location opposite the harbor. At lunch there's a sidewalk café with fish and meat dishes in the 70F to 100F range. Dinner is served in a more formal upstairs dining room. The à la carte menu features a dozen main courses, including the likes of lobster medallions and duck in raspberry sauce, all priced from 170F to 195F. It's open daily for dinner and for breakfast and lunch daily except Sunday.

Match, on the north side of Marigot, is a large, modern supermarket with pretty good deli and wine selections. It's open from 9 am to noon on Sunday, to 8 pm other days.

The produce market on Marigot's waterfront has tropical fruit such as passion fruit and bananas as well as local root vegetables, but the prices – especially for tourists – can be nearly as high as at grocery stores. There's usually someone selling drinking coconuts for US$2. It's open Wednesday to Saturday from sunrise to around 2 pm.

Around French St Martin

SANDY GROUND & BAIE NETTLÉ

Sandy Ground is the long, narrow, curving strip of land that extends west from Marigot, with Baie Nettlé (Nettle Bay) on one side of the road and Simpson Bay Lagoon on the other. The first hotel went up just a decade ago, but these days there's a strip of hotels, restaurants and small shopping centers one after the other.

In itself, Sandy Ground is not a place of any great interest – the ocean beach is marginal with a rocky shoreline shelf and the lagoon side is a bit mucky for swimming – but it can be a convenient base if you get a good hotel deal, and some of St Martin's finest beaches are just down the road.

The Royal Food Store shopping center, within walking distance of the Baie Nettlé hotels, has scooter and car rentals, a dive shop, a newsstand and a post office. There's a coin laundry at Laguna Beach Hotel.

Places to Stay

Hotel Royal Beach (☎ 29 12 12, fax 29 12 04) is an older 113-room hotel on the bay side. Although it's not as spiffy as its more upmarket neighbors, the rooms are certainly suitable for the price and have a two-burner hot plate, refrigerator, air-con, phone and TV. There's a pool. Singles/doubles start at US$57/76 and are usually the same price year round.

Laguna Beach Hotel (☎ 87 91 75, fax 87 81 65; in the USA ☎ 800-333-1970) has 62 pleasant units, all with balconies, two twin beds, air-con, phone and TV. Best value are the commodious one-bedroom apartments, which are split level with a kitchenette and living room downstairs and the bedroom upstairs, and cost from US$112/154 in summer/winter. Smaller studios, some with kitchenettes, start at US$96/128. The hotel has a pool.

The 175-room *Marine Hôtel* (☎ 87 54 54, fax 87 92 11) is a relatively large package-tour hotel with modern if nondescript rooms. Each has a ceiling fan, air-con, TV, phone, kitchenette and large balcony, some with a view across Simpson Bay Lagoon. There's a pool, tennis courts and a dive shop. Rates include a buffet breakfast. Standard rooms cost US$92/110 for singles/doubles in summer, US$146/159 in winter. Reservations can be made internationally through Resinter (☎ 0181-748-34-33 in the UK, ☎ 800-221-4542 in the USA and Canada).

Nettlé Bay Beach Club (☎ 87 68 68, fax 87 21 51) has some 40 triplex villas spread out along the edge of the bay. Hotel-style 2nd-story loft rooms with a queen-size bed, sun deck, and in some cases a kitchenette, cost US$125/185 in summer/winter. One-bedroom apartments, which have a separate living room and kitchen, as well as an ocean-facing terrace, cost US$160/275. All units have ceiling fans, thermostatic air-con, TV, phones and a pleasant decor. The

complex has four large pools, two restaurants and a water sports center.

Places to Eat

Royal Food Store, open daily from 7:30 am to 8:30 pm, is a small grocery with deli items, Häagen-Dazs bars, fresh baguettes and a good wine selection. In the same center is *Chez Swann*, where you can get continental breakfast or lunchtime sandwiches for 30F, dinner salads or pasta dishes from 40F to 50F.

Jardin Tropical, a pizzeria on the lagoon side of the road, has reasonable pizzas from 30F and spaghetti or salads for around 40F. It's open daily from 10 am to 10 pm.

Mac Abane Café, a popular beachside bar at Hotel Laguna Beach, has a tapas menu between 5:30 and 9 pm with a variety of inexpensive snack foods from simple tortillas to crab farci. They also offer affordable main courses, ranging from 40F for pastas to 70F for steak. It's open for lunch and dinner.

BAIE ROUGE

Baie Rouge, a kilometer west of Sandy Ground, is a long beautiful sandy strand with good swimming, though if you have children be aware that it drops off quickly to overhead depths. Although this golden-sand beach is just 150 meters from the main road it retains an inviting natural setting. For the best snorkeling swim to the right in the direction of the rocky outcrop and arch.

The dirt drive leading to the beach is at a 90° turn on the road from Sandy Ground to Mullet Bay – as you have to virtually stop to negotiate the turn, it's easy to find. There are a couple of beach shacks that sell drinks and barbecued foods and rent umbrellas, lounge chairs and snorkel gear, but the beach is delightfully free of jet skis and other motorized toys.

BAIE AUX PRUNES (PLUM BAY)

The remote and unspoiled Baie aux Prunes is a gently curving bay with polished shell-like grains of golden sand. The beach is popular for swimming and sunbathing and is backed by a little woods of white cedar trees with pink blossoms that attract hummingbirds.

It can be reached by turning right 1.3km south of Baie Rouge and immediately taking the signposted left fork. After 2km you'll come to a junction; veer right and continue for another 300 meters, where there's a parking area and a short walkway to the beach.

BAIE LONGUE (LONG BAY)

Long Beach, at Baie Longue, embraces two splendid kilometers of seemingly endless white sand. The only commercial development along the shoreline is La Samanna hotel, down at at the very southern tip. The beach is very big and well off the beaten path – a great place for long strolls and quiet sunsets.

You can get to Long Beach by continuing south from Baie aux Prunes or by taking the La Samanna turn-off from the main road and continuing past the hotel for 800 meters. There's a parking area in front of a chain-link fence and a short footpath leading to the beach.

Places to Stay

A favorite of the rich and famous is *La Samanna* (☎ 87 51 22, fax 87 87 86; in the USA ☎ 800-854-2252), a low-profile, exclusive beachside hotel with 80 rooms, each with air-con, a ceiling fan, minibar and ocean-fronting balcony. There's a pool, tennis courts and complimentary water sports. Rates start at US$325/575 in summer/winter and go up to US$1550 for a multi-terraced one-bedroom suite.

FRIAR'S BAY

Friar's Bay, 2km north of Marigot center, is a pretty cove with a broad sandy beach. This popular local swimming spot is just beyond the residential neighborhood of St Louis and the road in is signposted. There are a couple of beach huts selling burgers, beer and grilled chicken.

COLOMBIER

For St Martin's version of a country drive, take the road that leads 2km inland to the hamlet of Colombier. This short, pleasant side trip offers a glimpse of a rural lifestyle that has long disappeared elsewhere on the island. The scenery along the way is bucolic with stone fences, big mango trees, an old coconut-palm plantation and hillside pastures with grazing cattle.

The road to Colombier begins 350 meters north of the turn-off to Friar's Bay.

PIC PARADIS (PARADISE PEAK)

The 424-meter Pic Paradis, the highest point on the island, offers fine vistas and good hiking opportunities. The peak is topped with a communications tower and has a rough maintenance road that doubles as a hiking track. You can drive as far as the last house and then walk the final kilometer to the top.

The mountain gets more rain than the rest of the island and the woods are thick with viny trees and colorful forest birds. Ten minutes up, just before the tower, a sign to the left points the way to the best viewpoint. Take this track for about 75 meters, then veer to the right where the path branches and you'll come to a cliff with a broad view of the island's east side. You can see Orient Salt Pond and the expansive Etang aux Poissons to the east, the village of Orleans at your feet and Philipsburg to the south.

For a good view of the west side of the island, go back to the main track and walk up past the communications tower. From the rocks directly beyond you can see Marigot, Simpson Bay Lagoon and Baie Nettlé.

If you want to do more serious hiking, a network of tracks leads from the Pic Paradis area to Orient Bay, Orleans and the Dutch side of the island. Flash Media's St Martin map, available free at the tourist office, shows the trails.

The road to Pic Paradis is 500 meters north of the road to Colombier. Take the road inland for 2km, turn left at the fork (signposted 'Sentier des Crêtes NE, Pic

ST MARTIN

Paradis') and continue 500 meters farther to the last house, where there's space to pull over and park.

GRAND CASE

The small beachside town of Grand Case has been dubbed 'the gourmet capital of St Martin.' The beachfront road is lined with an appealing range of places to eat, from local lolos (barbecue stalls) to top-notch French restaurants. Some of the places are open for lunch, but Grand Case is at its liveliest in the evening.

The town itself is half-local, half-touristy, and while there are a few colorful buildings, dining is the premier attraction. Espérance Airport, which is bordered by salt ponds that attract water birds, is at the east side of town.

As for the beach, Grand Case's long curving strand is fine if you're staying there but it's not a destination for day trippers who generally opt for less-developed northside beaches.

Places to Stay

Hévéa (☎ 87 56·85, fax 87 83 88), at the restaurant of the same name, has half a dozen good-value colonial-style rooms with air-con. In summer, singles/doubles cost from US$40/55 for standard rooms, US$73/88 for units with kitchenettes. Winter rates are about 50% higher.

The *Grand Case Beach Motel* (☎ 87 87 75) is an older hotel with a dated decor, but it's got a beachside location and the seven units have fans, air-con, kitchenettes and small seaside patios. Rates are US$40/80 in summer/winter, plus a 10% service charge and an additional US$10 charge to use the air-con.

Les Alizés Motel (☎ 87 95 38) is a bit unkempt, but its eight small studios are right on the beach and each has cooking facilities and air-con. The cost is US$50/75 in summer/winter for regular units, US$60/100 for ocean views.

Flamboyant Beach Villas (☎ 87 50 98, fax 87 81 04) is a small complex of one and two-story buildings on the beach next to Grand Case Beach Club. The units are simple but pleasant, with cottage-style

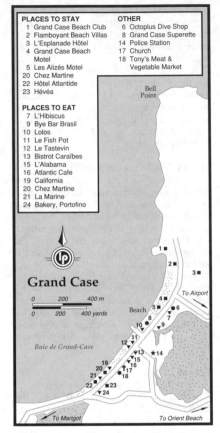

PLACES TO STAY	OTHER
1 Grand Case Beach Club	6 Octoplus Dive Shop
2 Flamboyant Beach Villas	8 Grand Case Superette
3 L'Esplanade Hôtel	14 Police Station
4 Grand Case Beach Motel	17 Church
5 Les Alizés Motel	18 Tony's Meat &
20 Chez Martine	Vegetable Market
22 Hôtel Atlantide	
23 Hévéa	

PLACES TO EAT
7 L'Hibiscus
9 Bye Bar Brasil
10 Lolos
11 Le Fish Pot
12 Le Tastevin
13 Bistrot Caraïbes
15 L'Alabama
16 Atlantic Cafe
19 California
20 Chez Martine
21 La Marine
24 Bakery, Portofino

Grand Case

0   200   400 m
0   200   400 yards

Bell Point

To Airport

Beach

Baie de Grand-Case

To Marigot

To Orient Beach

furnishings, one or two bedrooms and a combined kitchen, living room and dining room. There are ceiling fans and screened louvered windows on all sides to catch cross-breezes. Summer/winter rates are a reasonable US$60/96 for one-bedroom units, US$102/156 for two-bedroom units.

Chez Martine (☎ 87 51 59, fax 87 87 30) has five air-conditioned rooms with private baths at the side of its restaurant. The rates, which include breakfast for two, are US$80 in summer, US$114 in winter.

Hôtel Atlantide (☎ 87 09 80, fax 87 12 36) is a modern beachside complex with seven commodious apartments. The units are well equipped, each with a full kitchen, living room, a big ocean-fronting balcony that serves as a dining room, TV, phone, air-con, bathtub and marble floors. Rates begin at US$110/195 in summer/winter for one-bedroom units, while the fanciest two-bedroom units top off at US$240/325. If they're not full you can often negotiate a discount of about 25%.

Grand Case Beach Club (☎ 87 51 87, fax 87 59 93; in the USA ☎ 800-447-7462), on the quiet northeast end of the beach, has 74 pleasant condo-like units with air-con, full kitchen and balcony. Studios have two double beds and a small dining table, while the roomy one-bedroom units have a separate living room. Gardenview studios cost US$100 in summer, US$220 in winter and US$130 in spring and autumn. One-bedroom units are US$115/270 in summer/winter, US$170 in spring and autumn. There are also two-bedroom, two-bath units. Children aged 12 and under stay for free in all rooms other than the studios. There's a restaurant, pool and tennis court and rates include continental breakfast.

L'Esplanade Hôtel, (☎ 87 06 55, fax 87 29 15) is a newer hillside hotel on the northeast edge of town. There are 24 studios and one-bedroom suites, each with a kitchen, ceiling fan, air-con, TV, phone and ocean-view terrace. The one-bedroom units, which have a king bed and a living room with a sofabed, cost US$118/165 in summer for singles/doubles, US$159/235 in winter. Studios cost US$99/144 for singles/doubles in summer, US$198/278 in winter.

Places to Eat

Each evening, a ritual of sorts takes place on Grand Case's beachfront road, with restaurants placing their menus and chalkboard specials out front and would-be diners strolling along the strip until they find a place that strikes their fancy.

Hurricane Luis took a particularly heavy toll on the locally popular beachside barbecues, called lolos, found near the pier, but some are beginning to reopen. For under US$10 you can feast on johnnycakes, rice

and peas, chicken legs, spareribs and potato salad – all sold à la carte.

An affordable light-eats place is the simple *Atlantic Cafe* – it has no view or ambiance, but a continental breakfast with coffee costs 30F, crêpes are 12F to 25F and spaghetti, salads and burgers start around 40F.

For someplace more substantial, *California* (☎ 87 55 57) has pizzas, pastas and salads for 50F to 65F and a nice waterfront setting.

If you've come to Grand Case for fine dining, a fine option is *L'Hibiscus* (☎ 29 17 91), which combines classical French cuisine with tasty Creole spices. Main dishes range from 75F for such things as pan-fried snapper with yucca or boneless chicken with foie gras to 130F for the rum-flambéed lobster. Appetizers and desserts cost around 40F. It's open from 6:30 to 11 pm nightly.

Another decent choice is *Bistrot Caraïbes* (☎ 29 08 29), which has more traditional French fare – although, as with L'Hibiscus, there's no water view. Main dishes include the likes of roast duck, beef tenderloin or scallops with asparagus-basil sauce for around 100F. The conch stew appetizer (50F) is a house specialty. It's open from 6 to 10:30 pm nightly.

Four other reputable upscale French restaurants – all with ocean views – are *La Marine* (☎ 87 02 31), *Le Fish Pot* (☎ 87 50 88), *Chez Martine* (☎ 87 51 59) and *Le Tastevin* (☎ 87 55 45), the latter one of only a handful of top-end places open daily for lunch as well as dinner.

Other restaurants worth a look are *Bye Bar Brasil*, serving traditional Brazilian food; *Portofino*, good for reasonably priced pizza and Italian food, as well as live country-western music on Wednesdays; and *L'Alabama*, with moderately priced French-continental fare.

ANSE MARCEL

Secluded Anse Marcel is a deeply indented bay with calm protected waters and a long sandy beach that's backed by French St Martin's largest resort hotel.

Anse Marcel has a flashy marina that's home base to a couple of yacht charter companies, including Stardust and Nautor's Swan Charters. The marina has a few fashionable boutiques, a small convenience store that sells liquor and foreign newspapers, a dive shop, a laundry, Hertz and Sanaco car rentals, and a store that sells charts and basic yachting supplies. The port office will hold mail for boaters.

Places to Stay

The beachfront *Le Méridien* (☎ 87 67 00, fax 87 30 38; in the USA ☎ 800-543-4300) is a bustling 400-room hotel with full resort amenities and standard 1st-class rooms. Summer/winter rates begin at US$160/280.

Recommended is the nearby *Hôtel Privilège* (☎ 87 37 37, fax 87 33 75), which has friendly management and 16 roomy units located above the marina shops. Each has a pleasant wood interior, TV, bathtub, queen or king bed, air-con and a large balcony strung with a hammock. There's no pool, but guests can use the beach fronting Le Méridien. Studios cost US$100/120 for singles/doubles. Suites, which have a sofabed in the living room, cost US$150 for two people. A two-bedroom suite with a kitchenette costs US$180 for two people, US$220 for four. Rates are the same all year round except from December 15 to January 15 when they jump $40 to $80.

Places to Eat

The best affordable place to eat in Anse Marcel is the harborside *La Louisiane*, which is open from 7 am to about 10 pm daily. In addition to reasonably priced sandwiches, you can get salads, omelets and pasta dishes from about 40F and meat and fish dishes for about double that. The bar features a two-for-one happy hour from 6 to 7 pm.

The *Privilège Restaurant* (☎ 87 38 38) is Anse Marcel's favorite top-end choice, with a scenic hillside location and expensive French-Creole fare. There's a free shuttle to the restaurant from the marina.

FRENCH CUL-DE-SAC

French Cul-de-Sac is a small seaside community just north of Orient Bay. While there's no beach of note, local fishers run boats back and forth all day to the white sands of nearby Îlet Pinel.

Îlet Pinel

Pinel, the most visited of the area's offshore islands, is just a kilometer from French Cul-de-Sac. Totally undeveloped, Pinel is the domain of day trippers, who are deposited on the islet's calm west-facing beach where there's good swimming, a water sports hut (snorkel gear US$10) and a couple of lolos (barbecued chicken meals US$10).

The island is under the auspices of the national forest system and just a two-minute walk south of the swimming beach is a little roped-off area set aside for snorkelers. For the best coral and fish, head for the single white buoy in the center.

It's easy to get to Pinel – simply go to the dock at road's end in French Cul-de-Sac, where you can catch a small boat. The five-minute ride costs US$5 roundtrip. Boats also go to Pinel from Orient Beach.

Places to Stay

All of the following places to stay, except for Sunrise, which is in the village, are on the south side of French Cul-de-Sac and within walking distance of Orient Beach.

Jardins de Chevrise (☎ 87 37 79, fax 87 38 03) is not the newest or spiffiest of places, but the price is fair and it's about a 10-minute walk to the beach. This two-story complex, which is partly residential, has 29 apartment units and a pool. Rates start at US$75/90 in summer/winter.

Sunrise Hotel (☎ 29 57 00, fax 87 39 28) is a cozy 20-room hotel managed by a friendly young French couple. The rooms are modern and comfortable, each with fully equipped kitchen, air-con, TV, phone, room safe and private terrace. There's a small pool, an ice machine, a collection of French and English books and a storage room where you can leave gear between stays. The rates begin at

US$100/130 in summer/winter. Children under 12 are free.

Orient Bay Hotel (☎ 87 31 10, fax 87 37 66; in the USA ☎ 800-742-4276) is a pleasant 31-unit place with a tropical decor in a quiet location just outside the Hôtel Mont Vernon. Units each have a kitchen, living room, air-con, phone and at least one terrace or balcony. Summer/winter rates are US$105/135 for two people in one-bedroom units, US$139/185 for up to four people in two-bedroom units. There's a pool.

Hôtel Mont Vernon (☎ 87 62 00, fax 87 37 27) is a rambling 394-room hotel perched on a rise overlooking the northernmost end of Orient Bay. Catering to package tours, it has standard resort rooms, each with a balcony. Singles/doubles begin at US$120/170 in summer, US$215/235 in winter, breakfast included. You can usually get significantly cheaper rates if you book the hotel as part of a package tour. There's a large pool, tennis courts, a water sports center and a couple of restaurants.

Places to Eat
The following places are on the village's main road.

Konga's, run by an Aruban-Canadian couple, has good burgers and salads for around 30F and a variety of main dishes such as ginger or curried chicken for around 60F. It's open from noon to 3 pm and 6 to 10 pm except Saturday.

Le Piccolo Café (☎ 87 32 47) is an unpretentious place serving gourmet-quality food at café prices. Although there's no sign, this brightly painted little eatery is so popular that reservations are usually necessary. Piccolo is run by a classically trained French chef with a penchant for Creole spices. Instead of the clichéd red-snapper-with-lemon-butter, the snapper preparation here is enlivened with peanuts, cream and a little hot pepper. Most dishes cost just 50F to 75F. It's open from 6:30 to 10:30 pm nightly except Tuesday.

Also good but pricier is the nearby *Le Cotonnier* (☎ 87 44 56), where fish and meat main courses, including atypical options such as octopus stew or Creole black sausage, range from 70F to 90F. It's open for dinner nightly except Monday.

For Vietnamese food, there's *Hoa Mai*, which has beef, chicken and seafood main courses from 60F to 90F. The Texaco gas station has a mini-mart.

ORIENT BEACH
Orient Beach is a splendid, gently curving sweep of white sand and bright turquoise waters. Clothing is optional along the entire 2-km beach, although nudity is de rigueur only at the southern end where there's a naturist resort, Club Orient. A decade ago Club Orient was the only development in the area. In recent years a handful of villa-type places have been built near the center of the stretch but none are situated directly on the beach and all are relatively small scale.

The bay is an underwater nature reserve and the waters are usually calm and good for swimming. The bay is also an active spot for water sports, including windsurfing, Hobie-Cat sailing and jet skiing. The latter in particular warrants caution as amateur jet-skiers zip through the same waters swimmers use.

The easiest public beach access is adjacent to Pedro's beachside bar. Here you'll find a touristy scene with lines of lounge chairs and beached jet skis, and vendors selling T-shirts and batik pareos. During the height of the day this strip can take on a certain carnival atmosphere attracting a few voyeurs with cameras, but for the most part it's just a mixed bag of people enjoying the beach.

If you're into nude sunbathing, walk south to the Club Orient beach where there are like-minded souls. If you just want to avoid the crowds that pack the center of Orient Beach, especially on weekends, head for the quiet north end of Orient Bay.

Information
There are numerous water sports centers along Orient Beach, with the largest concentration at the north side of Club Orient. Robert's Watersports, next to Pedro's,

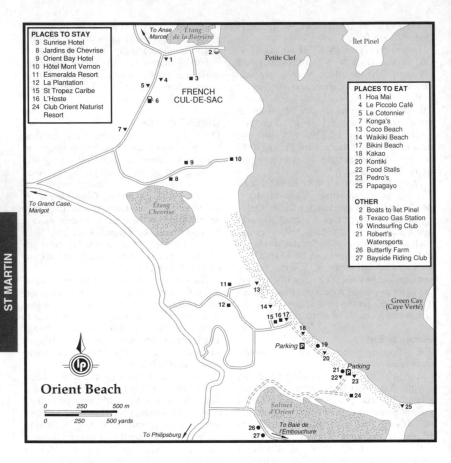

PLACES TO STAY
3 Sunrise Hotel
8 Jardins de Chevrise
9 Orient Bay Hotel
10 Hôtel Mont Vernon
11 Esmeralda Resort
12 La Plantation
15 St Tropez Caribe
16 L'Hoste
24 Club Orient Naturist
   Resort

PLACES TO EAT
1 Hoa Mai
4 Le Piccolo Café
5 Le Cotonnier
7 Konga's
13 Coco Beach
14 Waikiki Beach
17 Bikini Beach
18 Kakao
20 Kontiki
22 Food Stalls
23 Pedro's
25 Papagayo

OTHER
2 Boats to Îlet Pinel
6 Texaco Gas Station
19 Windsurfing Club
21 Robert's
   Watersports
26 Butterfly Farm
27 Bayside Riding Club

To Anse Marcel
Étang de la Barrière
Îlet Pinel
Petite Clef
FRENCH CUL-DE-SAC
To Grand Case, Marigot
Étang Chevrise
Green Cay (Caye Verte)
Orient Beach
Parking
Salines d'Orient
To Philipsburg
To Baie de l'Embouchure

0   250   500 m
0   250   500 yards

ST MARTIN

---

rents snorkel sets for US$10 a day, beach chairs or umbrellas for US$5, and makes speedboat runs to Green Cay (US$10 per person roundtrip) and Îlet Pinel (US$15).

Other water sports centers front each of the beachside restaurants. Papagayo Watersports, Bikini Watersports and Kontiki Watersports all rent snorkel sets and provide boat taxis to the offshore islands for the same price as Robert's. Papagayo also offers a nude snorkeling trip for US$15.

Behind Pedro's there are showers (US$1) and restrooms (US$0.50). Taxis can usually

be found nearby, charging US$15 (per taxi) to either Marigot or Philipsburg.

Green Cay (Caye Verte)

Green Cay is a small islet 500 meters off Orient Beach with a nice sandy spit at its southern end and reasonably good snorkeling in the surrounding waters. The water sports centers can shuttle you over by speedboat and pick you up at a prearranged time. There's no shade or facilities, so consider bringing along a beach umbrella and something to drink.

Don't try to grab shade or rain cover from the trees at the rocky end of the beach, as they're poisonous manchineel trees. The rocks are a habitat for numerous small *Anolis* lizards; the males put on an interesting show, puffing up orange sacs under their necks as a territorial warning.

Butterfly Farm

You can walk amidst 45 varieties of colorful butterflies imported mainly from the rainforests of Brazil and Indonesia at the Butterfly Farm, on the road south of Orient Beach. Admission includes an informative guided tour with a close-up view of butterflies in all stages, from foraging caterpillars and emerging pupae to adults on the wing. Although tickets may seem a bit steep at US$10 (US$5 for children) they allow multiple entries for the length of your vacation. It's open daily from 9 am to 4:30 pm.

Places to Stay

La Plantation (☎ 29 58 00, fax 29 58 08; in the USA ☎ 800-727-7388) is one of the area's better-value places to stay. There are 16 villas of plantation-house design, each with a one-bedroom suite and two studios. All units are large and pleasant with high-pitched ceilings, air-con, ceiling fans, TV, room safes, kitchens and private verandas facing the ocean. In summer, studios cost US$95/113 for singles/doubles. Suites, which have a separate living room, cost US$150 for doubles; add US$20 for each additional person. Winter rates are a bit complicated, varying by the month, with a studio for two people, for example, costing US$143 in January, US$165 in February and US$137 in March. Rates include a breakfast of fruit, yogurt and bread. There's a restaurant and pool; it's about a five-minute walk to the beach.

St Tropez Caribe (☎ 87 42 01, fax 87 41 69; in the USA ☎ 800-622-7836) is an 84-unit complex just inland from the beach. The rooms are in Mediterranean-style three-story buildings and have a sitting area, terrace or balcony, central air-con, TV, small refrigerator, room safe and phone. All have either a king bed or two twins. Rates

are US$120 to US$150 in summer, US$170 to US$225 in winter, with the lower rates for ground-floor rooms.

L'Hoste (☎ 87 42 08, fax 87 39 96; in the USA 800-742-4276) has 28 units identical to those in the adjacent St Tropez Caribe, but it's closer to the beach and has recently been renovated. Rates are US$120 to US$170 in summer, US$170 to US$210 in winter.

Club Orient Naturist Resort (☎ 87 33 85, fax 87 33 76, clubo@virtualaccess.net) is the Eastern Caribbean's only clothing-optional resort. All activities, including dining, water sports, tennis and sailing cruises, are au naturel. The accommodations, which were leveled by Hurricane Luis, have been completely rebuilt. There are now 136 units, most red-pine chalets with a queen bed, sofa, desk and chair, ceiling fan, bathroom, kitchen and an outdoor dining area with a picnic table. Most have air-con. Studios, which are in duplex chalets, cost US$135/198 for doubles in summer/winter. One-bedroom units occupy a whole chalet and cost from US$165/288. Single rates are about 15% cheaper.

The upscale *Esmeralda Resort* (☎ 87 36 36, fax 87 35 18) has 65 rooms and suites in 18 villa-style buildings. Rooms have cooking facilities, TV, phones, air-con, ceiling fans and room safes and start at US$180/275 in summer/winter. Suites, which have a separate living room and kitchen area, start at US$300/450. Each villa has its own pool.

Places to Eat

Near the parking lot at the southern end of the beach you'll find a couple of stalls selling cheap hot dogs and burgers, as well as *Pedro's*, a popular beachside bar with barbecued chicken for US$7 and fish for US$10. There are a handful of other beach bars nearby offering a similar menu.

In addition there are five simple open-air restaurants spread along the center of the beach that are primarily lunch spots, although a couple of them stay open late enough for an early dinner. You can get a meal at any of them for US$10 to US$25.

ST MARTIN

From south to north they are: *Kontiki*, which specializes in seafood; *Kakao*, with pizza and pastas; *Bikini Beach*, with a tapas-style menu; *Waikiki Beach*, which has a tank full of lobsters; and *Coco Beach* with French and Creole dishes.

The beachside *Papagayo* restaurant at clothing-optional Club Orient has omelets, salads, sandwiches and burgers in the US$8 to US$10 range and fish and meat dishes for around US$20. It's open daily for breakfast, lunch and dinner.

OYSTER POND

The Dutch/French border slices straight across Oyster Pond, a largely rural area with a number of small condominiums and other vacation rentals. A marina and most of the accommodations fall on the French side, while the area's finest beach (Dawn Beach) is on the Dutch side (see the end of this chapter).

Oyster Pond is not a pond, but a protected bay whose shape resembles an oyster. For a good vantage of Oyster Pond, there's a short path leading up the cactus-studded hill on the northeast side of the bay.

Captain Oliver's Marina has 100 slips, the standard marina services, a couple of places to eat, scuba gear rentals and a few shops and offices including those of The Moorings and Sun Yacht Charters companies.

Places to Stay

Captain Oliver's (☎ 87 40 26, fax 87 40 84), at the marina, has 36 standard hotel rooms with air-con, kitchenettes, phones, TV, room safes and balconies. There's a pool. Singles/doubles cost from US$72/120 in summer, US$105/175 in winter, buffet breakfast included.

Columbus Hotel (☎ 87 42 52, fax 87 39 85) is a newer complex with 29 condo-type units a few minutes walk from the marina. Each has a separate bedroom, TV, phone, kitchenette and a terrace or balcony. Rates begin at US$85/126 for singles/doubles, continental breakfast included.

The nearby *Blue Beach Hotel* (☎ 87 33 44, fax 87 42 13) has 42 small modern rooms with kitchenettes, air-con, phones,

TV and terraces. Some rooms have ocean views at no extra cost. Singles/doubles cost US$88/116 in summer, US$120/180 in winter. It's possible to rent a unit on a monthly basis for US$800 plus utilities. There's a pool and restaurant.

Places to Eat

Dinghy Dock Bar, a snack bar with picnic tables on the marina dock, serves up US$6 sandwiches, chili dogs, full meals and Foster's on tap. Next door is a small convenience store with groceries, alcohol and sundries.

Captain Oliver's, an open-air restaurant at the marina dock, has a daily US$10 breakfast buffet, burgers with fries for about the same price and seafood and meat dishes from US$15 to US$20. It's open daily from 7 am to 11 pm.

Frog's at the Blue Beach Hotel is a pleasantly informal roof-top French restaurant with a varied chalkboard menu and a bit of a sea view. House standards include frog legs, salmon and grilled meats for around US$12. It's open for dinner from 6 pm to about midnight daily except Tuesday.

Philipsburg

Philipsburg, Dutch Sint Maarten's main town, is centered on a long, narrow stretch of land that separates Great Salt Pond from Great Bay. There are some older buildings mixed among the new, but overall the town is far more commercial than quaint. Most of the action is along Frontstreet, the bayfront road, which is lined with boutiques, jewelry shops, restaurants, casinos and duty-free shops selling everything from Danish porcelain to Japanese cameras and electronics.

Wathey Square, the town center of sorts, has a tourist information booth, a wharf where cruise-ship tenders dock and an old courthouse that dates from 1793. On cruise ship days, vendors on the square sell drinking coconuts and souvenirs; more street vendors, selling T-shirts and wood

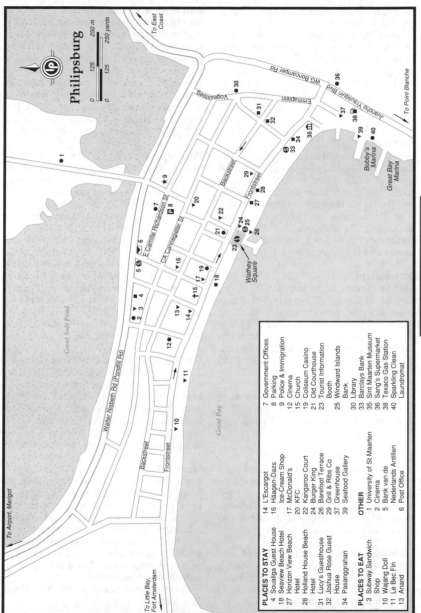

Philipsburg

PLACES TO STAY
4 Soualiga Guest House
18 Seaview Beach Hotel
27 Horizon View Beach
   Hotel
28 Holland House Beach
   Hotel
31 Lucy's Guesthouse
32 Joshua Rose Guest
   House
34 Pasangrahan

PLACES TO EAT
3 Subway Sandwich
   Shop
10 Wajang Doll
11 Le Bec Fin
13 Anand

14 L'Escargot
16 Häagen-Dazs
   Ice-Cream Shop
17 McDonald's
20 KFC
22 Kangaroo Court
24 Burger King
26 Barefoot Terrace
29 Grill & Ribs Co
37 Greenhouse
39 Seafood Gallery

OTHER
1 University of St Maarten
2 Cinema
5 Bank van de
   Nederlands Antillen
6 Post Office

7 Government Offices
8 Parking
9 Police & Immigration
12 Cinema
15 Church
19 Coliseum Casino
21 Old Courthouse
23 Tourist Information
   Booth
25 Windward Islands
   Bank
30 Library
33 Barclays Bank
35 Sint Maarten Museum
36 Sang's Supermarket
38 Texaco Gas Station
40 Sparkling Clean
   Laundromat

ST MARTIN

ST MARTIN

carvings, can be found at the north side of the courthouse.

Great Bay Beach borders the entire town of Philipsburg, but the buildings lining Frontstreet face inland and it's easy to walk along the street without noticing the beach at all. Although Great Bay is not one of Sint Maarten's more pristine beaches, the water is calm and some people do opt to swim there.

Orientation
Four streets run east to west and numerous narrow lanes (called *steegjes)* connect them north to south. Frontstreet has one-way traffic that moves in an easterly direction and Backstreet has one-way traffic heading west. Public buses can be picked up along Backstreet. The north side of Philipsburg is sometimes referred to as Pondfill, as much of this area is reclaimed land.

Information
Money There are a number of banks around Philipsburg, including Barclays Bank at Frontstreet 19, open 8:30 am to 3 pm weekdays, and Windward Islands Bank on Wathey Square, open 8:30 am to 3:30 pm weekdays. The latter has a 24-hour ATM that accepts Cirrus, Plus, MasterCard and Visa.

Post The post office, at the west end of E Camille Richardson Rd, is open from 7:30 am to 5 pm Monday to Thursday, to 4:30 pm on Friday.

Library The public library, on Vogesssteeg, carries the daily *New York Times* and has a good collection of English-language Caribbean books. It's open from 10 am to 1 pm on Saturday, 9 am to 12:30 pm Tuesday, Wednesday and Friday and also from 4 to at least 6:30 pm Monday to Friday.

Laundry At the Sparkling Clean Laundromat at Bobby's Marina you can leave a load of clothes to be washed, dried and folded for US$8. It's open from 8 am to 6 pm Monday to Saturday.

Sint Maarten Museum
This little but growing museum, in an alley at Frontstreet 7, has displays on island history, including Arawak pottery shards, plantation-era artifacts, period photos and a few items from the *HMS Proselyte*, the frigate that sank off Fort Amsterdam in 1801. There's also an interesting exhibit on the damage caused by Hurricane Luis. It's open from 10 am to 4 pm weekdays, 10 am to 2 pm on Saturday. Admission is US$1.

Fort Amsterdam
In 1631 the Dutch built their first Caribbean fort, Fort Amsterdam, on the peninsula separating Great Bay and Little Bay. It didn't withstand an invasion by the Spanish, who captured the fort two years later, expanding it and adding a small church.

Despite its historic significance the fort site is neglected with little remaining other than crumbling walls and a few rusting cannons. It does, however, offer a reasonably nice view across the bay to Philipsburg. To get there, drive to Little Bay and park near the Little Bay Beach Resort tennis courts. The fort is a 10-minute walk up the hill to the south.

Sint Maarten Zoo & Botanical Garden
This very small zoo, with some 35 reptile, bird and mammal species, is located beneath the hillside TV satellite dishes on Arch Rd, on the north side of Great Salt Pond. Admission is US$3 for adults, US$1 for kids. It's open from 9 am to 5 pm on weekdays, 10 am to 6 pm on weekends.

Marina Area
Great Bay Marina and adjoining Bobby's Marina on the southeast side of Philipsburg have a couple of restaurants, a small grocery store, car rental agencies, a dive shop, a laundry and several stores with marine supplies. For information on crews wanted, boats for sale etc, check the bulletin board next to Island Water World marine store (which also sells charts).

Boats going to St Barts leave from Great Bay Marina.

Places to Stay

Philipsburg's best low-end option is *Soualiga Guest House* (☎ 20077), Walter Nisbeth Rd 29A, which has six clean rooms with cable TV, ceiling fans and private baths. Singles/doubles cost US$35/45 in summer, US$45/55 in winter. As it's on a busy road, ask for a room as far back as possible if you're sensitive to traffic noise.

Lucy's Guesthouse (☎ 22995), Backstreet 10, is quite rudimentary with small bare rooms and is overpriced at US$40/55 for singles/doubles.

Joshua Rose Guest House (☎ 24317, fax 30080), Backstreet 7, has 14 straightforward rooms with private baths, air-con, phones, TV and mini-refrigerators. Standard rooms, which have one double and one twin bed, cost US$45/55 for singles/doubles in summer, US$55/71 in winter. Superiors, which are larger top-story rooms with high ceilings and two double beds, cost US$10 more.

A step up is the family-run *Seaview Beach Hotel* (☎ 22323, fax 24356), PO Box 65, Philipsburg, a two-story hotel on the beach above a casino. Most rooms are on the small size but they're adequate and have air-con, TV and private baths. Rates start at US$46/55 for singles/doubles in summer, US$79/99 in winter.

Pasanggrahan (☎ 23588, fax 22885; in the USA ☎ 800-223-9815), PO Box 151, Philipsburg, is a 30-room beachfront inn on Frontstreet. The restaurant and lobby are in a former governor's residence but most rooms are in less-distinguished side buildings. The standard rooms, which cost US$78/128 in summer/winter, are simple and small with a shared seaside balcony. The deluxe rooms are larger, fancier and have private balconies; they cost US$95/158. All rooms have ceiling fans, air-con and private baths.

Holland House Beach Hotel (☎ 22572, fax 24673; in the USA ☎ 800-223-9815), PO Box 393, Philipsburg, has a central beachfront location and 54 spacious rooms. Overall, they're Philipsburg's nicest, featuring hardwood floors, balconies, cable TV, phones, air-con and in most cases a kitchenette. Rates begin at US$74/89 for singles/doubles in summer, US$130/145 in winter.

Horizon View Beach Hotel (☎ 32120, fax 20705), PO Box 1054, Philipsburg, on Frontstreet, is a condo complex with 30 units. Studios, some with balcony, have a double bed and kitchenette for US$90/123 in summer/winter. The beachfront suites each have a separate bedroom, kitchen and large living room with plate-glass windows that provide a fine bay view and cost US$139/185. All units have air-con, cable TV and phones.

Places to Eat – budget

Barefoot Terrace, right on the waterfront at Wathey Square, has alfresco dining with breakfast omelets and lunchtime sandwiches or burgers costing around US$5, chicken or baby back ribs for US$10 and a full menu of local dishes, like goat stew, at reasonable prices. It's open from 7 am to 6:30 pm Monday to Saturday.

Kangaroo Court, at the east side of the courthouse, is a pleasant deli café with courtyard dining and an emphasis on light, healthy food. In addition to fresh-brewed espresso and cappuccino, there's homemade zucchini bread and carrot cake, fresh fruit plates, US$6 sandwiches and various pasta and salads for around US$8. It's open from 7 am to 7 pm Monday to Saturday.

Anand, on Hotelsteeg 5, is a popular little place serving cheap East Indian fare. A range of vegetable and chicken dishes cost around US$7, goat and beef dishes a tad more. It's open from noon to 3 pm Monday to Saturday and 6 to 10 pm nightly.

On Backstreet there's a *Häagen-Dazs* ice-cream shop with 30 flavors at US$2 a scoop, as well as ice-cream bars, sundaes, sodas and US$1.25 Heineken beers. It's open daily from 11 am to 11 pm.

Chain fast-food eateries include *Burger King* at Wathey Square, *McDonald's* on Frontstreet, *KFC* on CA Cannegieter St and *Subway Sandwich Shop* on Walter Nisbeth Rd.

ST MARTIN

Places to Eat – middle & top end

Grill & Ribs Co at the Old Street shopping center is a popular open-air 2nd-floor eatery featuring all-you-can-eat baby back ribs for US$15. The ribs are good but if you don't want to pig out on pork a better dish is the chicken fajita plate for US$12. Until 5 pm, you can get burgers and grilled chicken sandwiches served with fries for US$5.50. It's open from 11 am to 8 pm daily. No credit cards are accepted.

Greenhouse, at the north end of the marina, is a lively spot best known for its happy hour from 4:30 to 7 pm, which has two-for-one drinks and half-price snacks. It's open for food from 11 am to 10 pm daily. At lunch, there are burgers and sandwiches for around US$6, barbecued ribs or chicken for twice that. At dinner, meat and seafood dishes cost US$13 to US$19.

The *Seafood Galley*, on a pier at Bobby's Marina, has a nautical decor and a raw bar with oysters and clams on the half shell. From 11:30 am to 3 pm, you can get a Spanish omelet, fishburger or teriyaki chicken sandwich with fries for US$8, salads and seafood dishes for a few dollars more. Dinner, from 6 to 10 pm, ranges from local catch of the day for US$17 to lobster at market prices. While you're there, take a look at the giant mullet that swarm below the pier.

Pasanggrahan, at the Frontstreet inn of the same name, is an atmospheric place with a quiet garden courtyard. From noon to 3 pm, there's a range of lunch specials, including pasta and salads, for around US$10. Dinners are priced from US$17.

L'Escargot (☎ 22483), a French restaurant in a colorful 19th-century house, has light lunches such as seafood crêpes or quiche with salad for around US$9. Dinner features various escargot appetizers for under US$10 and main courses, such as crisp duck in pineapple and banana sauce, for around US$23.

The *Wajang Doll* (☎ 22687), Frontstreet 237, is well known for its rijsttafel, a traditional Indonesian buffet. It costs US$19 for 14 dishes, US$25 for 19 dishes. It's open from 6:45 to 10 pm Monday to Saturday.

Le Bec Fin (☎ 22976) is an upscale French restaurant with a good reputation and a fine sea view. Main courses range from US$16 for red snapper in lime sauce to US$31 for rum-flambéed lobster. There are also set three-course dinners for US$25 and US$35. There's a simpler and cheaper menu at lunch, which is served from noon to 3:30 pm Monday to Saturday. It's open for dinner from 6 to 10 pm nightly.

Around Dutch Sint Maarten

SIMPSON BAY

The Simpson Bay area is a narrow strip of land separating Simpson Bay from Simpson Bay Lagoon. A channel between the two bodies of water is spanned by a drawbridge that is raised twice a day to allow boats to pass from one side to the other.

West of the drawbridge there's a sandy beach with some moderately priced guesthouses, but it's an odd destination as the airport runway stretches the entire length, just a few hundred meters away. Despite the proximity to the airport, staying in this area is not a convenient way to avoid taxi fares or car rentals as you'd have to walk clear around the runway to get to the guesthouses, a good 20-minute haul along a busy road. On the other hand, airport noise shouldn't disturb early risers, as there are no scheduled flights between 9 pm and 7 am.

East of the drawbridge there are a couple of marinas, a clutter of bars and restaurants, and a few complexes with casinos and condos.

Places to Stay

The first three places can be reached by turning south on Houtman Rd at the east end of the airport runway. Just 100 meters down Houtman Rd is *Calypso Guest House* (☎ 54233, fax 52881), the cheapest and closest place to the airport. Rooms, which are on the 2nd floor above a Mexican restaurant, are not fancy but they're

Top Left: Grand Case, St Martin (Tony Wheeler)
Middle Left: Hats, Marigot market, St Martin (Ned Friary)

Top Right: Cyclist, St Martin (Ned Friary)
Bottom: L'Escargot restaurant, Philipsburg, St Martin (Glenda Bendure)

Top Left: Rum casks in archway, Kingstown, St Vincent (Ned Friary)

Middle: Admiralty Bay, Port Elizabeth, Bequia, St Vincent (Ned Friary)

Top Right: Police station, Kingstown, St Vincent (Ned Friary)

Bottom: Beach cricket, Villa Beach, St Vincent (Tony Wheeler)

large and have a kitchenette, table and chairs, air-con and TV. Summer rates begin at US$50/60 for singles/doubles, winter rates at US$60/80. It's a few minutes walk to the beach.

About 700 meters beyond is the beach-front *Mary's Boon* (☎ 54235, fax 53403; in the USA ☎ 800-696-8177), PO Box 2078, Simpson Bay, which has 14 large spiffy studios with kitchenettes and balconies. The friendly new Texan managers are upgrading the property, adding four-poster king beds, cable TV and air-con. Rates are US$90 in summer, US$125 in spring and autumn and US$150 in winter. There's a five-day minimum stay in winter.

La Chatelaine (☎ 54269, fax 53195), PO Box 2065, Simpson Bay, is a modern complex just before Mary's Boon. It has a pool, a beachside location and 17 units with kitchenettes and patios. Summer/winter rates begin at US$90/115 for studios, US$110/$150 for one-bedroom apartments and US$165/235 for two-bedroom apartments.

Pelican Resort & Casino (☎ 42503, fax 42133; in the USA ☎ 800-550-7088), PO Box 431, Simpson Bay, is on a beach at the east side of Simpson Bay. Although some of the buildings remain closed since the hurricane, this sprawling time-share complex has reopened 342 units, from studios to two-bedroom suites, all with kitchenettes, queen or king beds and the standard amenities. Studios cost US$95/114 in summer/winter, while one-bedroom units begin at US$170/204. There are pools, tennis courts, a casino, water sports, restaurants and a shopping arcade.

Places to Eat

A number of eateries line the airport road. A good place for a cheap bite is the *Bagel Factory*, next to Burger King, which has good New York style bagels and makes its own frozen yogurt.

Don Carlos, a moderately priced Mexican restaurant beneath Calypso Guest House, has tostadas or an enchilada with rice and beans for US$13 and standard breakfast fare for US$6 to US$8.

Directly opposite the airport terminal is a *Stop & Shop* grocery store with a deli inside and a lagoonview café out back. You can get salads, a cheeseburger or a boneless chicken roti for US$5 to US$7 and breakfast standards for about half that price. It's open daily from 7:30 am to 7:30 pm.

MAHO BAY & MULLET BAY

Maho Bay and Mullet Bay are adjacent resort areas along the southwest shore. Driving into the Maho Bay area is a bit like suddenly finding yourself on the central strip in Las Vegas. While little more than a block long, it's dense with multistory buildings housing exclusive jewelers, boutiques, art galleries, restaurants and a huge resort and casino. Parking street side is nearly impossible; it's best to pull into the Maho Beach complex where there's inexpensive indoor parking.

Maho Bay has a nice enough beach except that it's at the very end of the runway. The area is even marked with a sign warning beach goers that 'low flying and departing aircraft blast can cause physical injury'!

Mullet Bay, dominated by a single resort that's been closed since Hurricane Luis, has an operational golf course that fronts a fine white-sand beach. Although access to the north end of the beach is restricted by the resort, there's public parking at the south side of the golf course.

The island's main south-coast road runs straight across the golf course and consequently some killer speed bumps have been installed that are apt to bottom out many low-slung cars.

Places to Stay

Maho Beach Hotel (☎ 52115, fax 53180; in the USA ☎ 800-223-0757) has 600 air-conditioned rooms with private balconies that start at US$155/165 for singles/doubles in summer, US$215/235 in winter. One hotel wing faces Maho Beach, while another fronts Maho Bay's commercial strip. The hotel has pools, tennis courts and a casino.

Places to Eat

Cheri's Cafe, a large open-air restaurant and bar beside the Casino Royale, is one of the island's liveliest eat-and-meet spots. The varied menu includes salads, sandwiches and burgers for under US$7, grilled seafood dishes for about double that and kids' dishes for US$5. It's open daily from 11 am to midnight, with live music beginning at 8 pm. Credit cards are not accepted.

The *West Indies Yogurt Co*, next to Cheri's, has Häagen-Dazs ice cream and Colombo frozen yogurt.

Trattoria Pizzeria, a small unpretentious eatery in the alley behind Cheri's, has pastas and pizzas for US$10 as well as cheaper sandwiches.

Also in this area is *Fountain of Health Natural Foods*, which has packaged natural food items, dried fruits and vitamins.

CUPECOY BAY

If you're looking for a beach that's quiet but not totally secluded, Cupecoy is a good choice. This pleasant white-sand beach is backed by low sandstone cliffs which are eroded in such a way that they provide a run of small semiprivate coves. There's beach parking down an unmarked drive at the north side of the Ocean Club in Cupecoy.

DAWN BEACH

Dawn Beach, on the east coast near the French/Dutch border, is a lovely white-sand beach with clear turquoise waters. Swimming and snorkeling are good when the seas are calm. Although it's a bit silted, snorkelers can expect to find waving sea fans, soft corals and small tropical fish.

To get to Dawn Beach from French St Martin, follow the road around the south side of Oyster Pond. There's parking, a shower and snorkel gear rentals near Mr Busby's, at the north end of the beach.

Places to Eat

Mr Busby's, a likable open-air eatery right on the beach, has salads, sandwiches and mediocre burgers for US$7 and good grilled fish plates for US$10 to US$15. It's open daily from 11 am to 9 pm. There's a happy hour with half-price drinks weekdays from 5 to 6 pm.

St Vincent & the Grenadines

St Vincent & the Grenadines is a multi-island nation well known to wintering yachters but off the beaten path for most other visitors. The northernmost island, St Vincent, is the nation's commercial and political center and accounts for 90% of both the land area and population. The island is lush and green, with deep valleys cultivated with bananas, coconuts and arrowroot, and a mountainous interior that peaks at La Soufrière, a 4048-foot active volcano.

The island of St Vincent remains a backwater of sorts and doesn't really cater to tourists. There are no major resort hotels, the airport is only large enough to handle inter-island aircraft and St Vincent's beaches can't compete with those in the nation's more alluring half, the southerly Grenadines. While St Vincent disappoints some visitors, others find its raw edge and rugged natural qualities refreshing.

On the other hand, the Grenadines are one of the most popular cruising grounds in the Caribbean. These small islands, which reach like stepping stones between St Vincent and Grenada, are surrounded by coral reefs and clear blue waters ideal for diving, snorkeling and boating. The islands are lightly populated and the level of development remains pleasantly low key. Although some of the Grenadine islands such as Mustique and Palm Island cater to the rich and famous, others like Bequia and Union Island are yachting havens attracting an international crowd and offering some quite reasonable places to stay and eat.

Facts about St Vincent & the Grenadines

HISTORY

When Spanish explorers first sighted St Vincent, the island was thickly settled with Carib Indians, who had taken it by force from earlier Arawak settlers. Heavy Carib resistance kept European colonists at bay long after most other Caribbean islands had well-established European settlements.

One of the most significant events of early foreign influence occurred in 1675, when a Dutch slave ship went down in the channel between St Vincent and the neighboring

St Vincent & the Grenadines

0   5   10 km
0   3   6 miles

St Vincent Passage

Chateaubelair
Georgetown
Barrouallie
✪ Kingstown
St Vincent

CARIBBEAN SEA

Bequia

The Grenadines

Mustique

Canouan

Mayreau   Tobago Cays
Union Island   Palm Island

GRENADA

Carriacou   Petit St Vincent
Petit Martinique

ST VINCENT

grants, more objectionable than the French. The Caribs allowed the French to establish the first European settlement on the island in the early 1700s.

In 1783, after a century of contesting claims between the British and French, the Treaty of Paris placed St Vincent under British domain and a series of open rebellions followed. In 1795, under French instigation, Black and Yellow Caribs simultaneously swept the island, torching plantations and massacring English settlers. They joined forces on Dorsetshire Hill where Chief Chattawae of the Black Caribs, buoyed by the success of his raids, is said to have challenged the British commander Alexander Leith to a sword duel. To the dismay of his followers Chattawae quickly lost his life to Leith, an accomplished swordsman.

The following year a contingent of British troops was dispatched to the island to round up the insurgents who, with the exception of a few small bands hiding in the hills, were shipped to Roatan, an island off the coast of Honduras. In all, more than 5000 Caribs were forcefully repatriated. A small number of Yellow Caribs who were not involved in the uprising were relocated at Sandy Bay on the remote northeastern side of the island.

With the native opposition gone, the plantation owners briefly achieved the stability and success that had earlier eluded them. In 1812, however, a major eruption of La Soufrière volcano spewed a suffocating ash over northern St Vincent, destroying most of the coffee and cocoa trees. The eruption also took a heavy toll on the Carib reservation at Sandy Bay.

At around the same time the British abolitionist movement was gaining political and popular favor back in London. When slavery was abolished in 1834, the plantation owners were forced to free more than 18,000 slaves. As opportunities arose, the former slaves left the plantations, and planters began bringing in foreign laborers. The first to come were Portuguese from Madeira, followed later in the century by indentured servants from India.

island of Bequia. While none of the European crew survived, a fair number of Africans made it to shore. The shipwrecked slaves were accepted by the Caribs and allowed to marry with Carib women. Their offspring became known as Black Caribs, as distinct from the purely native Yellow Caribs. Tensions developed between the two groups, especially after the Black Caribs began to increase in number, and separate communities were eventually established.

The Caribs were generally hostile to all Europeans, but by and large they found the British, who claimed their land by royal

Natural disasters, such as a powerful 1898 hurricane that ravaged the cocoa trees and a 1902 eruption of La Soufrière that destroyed sugar cane fields, battered much of what remained of the plantation economy. For the remainder of the British colonial period the economy remained stagnant; plantations were eventually broken up and land redistributed to small-scale farmers.

In 1969 St Vincent became a self-governing state in association with the UK and on October 27, 1979, St Vincent & the Grenadines acquired full independence as a member of the Commonwealth.

GEOGRAPHY

St Vincent is a high island of volcanic origin; it's the northernmost point of the volcanic ridge that runs from Grenada in the south up through the Grenadine islands.

Of the 150 sq miles that comprise the national boundaries of St Vincent & the Grenadines, the island of St Vincent totals 133 sq miles. The other 17 sq miles are spread across some 30 odd islands and cays, fewer than a dozen of which are populated. The largest of these islands are Bequia, Canouan, Mustique, Mayreau and Union Island.

The highest peak on St Vincent is La Soufrière, an active volcano that reaches an elevation of 4048 feet. On May 7, 1902, the volcano erupted violently, wreaking havoc on the island's northern region and causing an estimated 2000 deaths. A more recent eruption, on April 13, 1979, spewed a blanket of ash over much of the island and forced 20,000 people to evacuate the northern villages. Although the crop damage was substantial, no lives were lost.

The larger of the Grenadine islands are hilly, but relatively low lying, and most have no source of fresh water other than rainfall. All have beautiful white-sand beaches.

CLIMATE

In January the average daily high temperature is 85°F (29°C) while the low averages 72°F (22°C). In July the average daily high is 86°F (30°C) while the low averages 76°F (24°C).

January to May are the driest months, with a mean relative humidity around 76%. During the rest of the year the humidity averages about 80%. In July, the wettest month, there's measurable rainfall for an average of 26 days, while April, the driest month, averages six days of measurable rainfall. All these statistics are for Kingstown; the Grenadine islands to the south are drier.

FLORA & FAUNA

The island of St Vincent has an interior of tropical rainforest and lowlands thick with coconut trees and banana estates. The Mesopotamia Valley, northeast of Kingstown, has some of the most fertile farmland and luxuriant landscapes.

The national bird is the endangered St Vincent parrot, a beautiful multi-hued Amazon parrot about 18 inches in length. The parrot lives in St Vincent's interior rainforest, as do numerous other tropical birds. The forest also provides a habitat for opossum (locally called manicou) and agouti, a short-haired rabbit-like rodent. The latter can readily be seen at Young Island, where they roam freely.

St Vincent has three species of snakes: the Congo snake, which coils itself around tree branches, and two terrestrial species, the black snake and the white snake. All three are harmless.

GOVERNMENT & POLITICS

St Vincent & the Grenadines is an independent nation within the Commonwealth. The British monarchy is represented by a Governor-General, but executive power is in the hands of the prime minister and cabinet. There is a unicameral legislature, which consists of 13 members, each elected for a five-year term. The present prime minister, James (Son) Mitchell, the leader of the majority New Democratic Party, has held the office for most of the period since independence.

ECONOMY

On St Vincent, agriculture remains the mainstay of the economy, accounting for

ST VINCENT

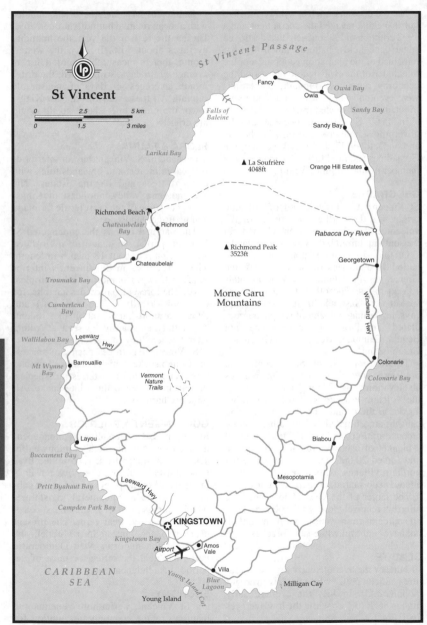

St Vincent Passage

Fancy

Owia

Owia Bay

Sandy Bay

Sandy Bay

Falls of Baleine

Larikai Bay

▲ La Soufrière
4048ft

Orange Hill Estates

Richmond Beach

Chateaubelair Bay

Richmond

Rabacca Dry River

▲ Richmond Peak
3523ft

Chateaubelair

Georgetown

Troumaka Bay

Morne Garu
Mountains

Cumberland Bay

Wallilabou Bay

Leeward   Hwy

Windward Hwy

Mt Wynne Bay

Barrouallie

Colonarie

Colonarie Bay

Vermont Nature Trails

Layou

Biabou

Buccament Bay

Petit Byahaut Bay

Leeward Hwy

Mesopotamia

Campden Park Bay

KINGSTOWN

Kingstown Bay

Airport

Amos Vale

Villa

Milligan Cay

CARIBBEAN SEA

Young Island Cut

Blue Lagoon

Young Island

St Vincent

0   2.5   5 km

0   1.5   3 miles

Arrowroot

St Vincent is the world's leading producer of arrowroot. The plant's name is derived from its former use as an antitoxin in the treatment of wounds from poison arrows. The rhizomes of the plant yield a nutritious and highly digestible starch that's used as a thickener in gravy and other food preparations. Although less-expensive cornstarch has largely replaced the use of arrowroot in the kitchen, arrowroot now has a new modern-day use as a coating on computer paper. ∎

more than half of all employment. Bananas are the leading export crop, followed by arrowroot, coconuts, cocoa and spices. The government is encouraging crop diversification. Attempts to revive the sugar industry in 1981, largely to provide a domestic source for rum production, were unsuccessful and abandoned a few years later. A budding cut-flower industry of anthuriums and heliconias and an increase in small-scale vegetable farming are meeting with more success, in part due to a government land reform program that has turned idle plantation lands into small family farms.

On the outer islands, tourism and fishing are the mainstays of the economy.

POPULATION & PEOPLE

St Vincent & the Grenadines has a population of 112,000. More than 90% live on St Vincent, with 30,000 of those in the Kingstown area. About 75% of all islanders are of pure African descent, while 15% are of mixed descent, including nearly a thousand Black Caribs. On Bequia and St Vincent there's a sizable population of Scottish descendants, many with a noticeable Scottish brogue. Others are of English, Irish, French and Asian descent.

SOCIETY & CULTURE

Reggae, calypso and steel band music are popular reflections of island culture. The main sports are cricket and European football. Some of the Grenadine islands, Bequia

in particular, have long been reliant upon the sea for a living; boat building, both full-scale and models, is an island art form.

Dos & Don'ts

Casual cotton clothing is suitable for almost any occasion, including dining at the more exclusive Grenadine resorts.

RELIGION

The majority of islanders are Protestant, with Anglicans representing the largest denomination. Other religions include Methodist, Seventh Day Adventist, Baptist, Streams of Power and Baha'i. About 20% of Vincentians are Roman Catholic.

LANGUAGE

English is the official language. Some islanders also speak a French patois.

Facts for the Visitor

ORIENTATION

St Vincent's airport is midway between Kingstown and the island's main resort area at Villa, about 1.5 miles from both. The Windward Highway runs all the way up the east coast to Fancy at the northernmost tip of the island but the Leeward Highway goes only three-quarters of the way up the west coast. If you want to tour both coasts, you have to backtrack through Kingstown.

The main Grenadine islands, with the exception of Mustique, are served by ferries from Kingstown. Bequia, Union Island, Canouan and Mustique have airports.

Maps

The Ordnance Survey 1:50,000 scale map of St Vincent is the most detailed map available. It can be purchased at the Wayfarer Book Store, on Upper Bay St, Kingstown, or at the airport sundry shop.

TOURIST OFFICES
Local Tourist Offices

The main office of the Department of Tourism for St Vincent & the Grenadines

ST VINCENT

(☎ 457-1502, fax 456-2610) is in Kingstown; the mailing address is PO Box 834, Kingstown, St Vincent, West Indies.

There's also a tourist information desk at St Vincent's ET Joshua Airport and branch tourist offices in Bequia and Union Island.

Tourist Offices Abroad

Overseas offices of the St Vincent & the Grenadines Department of Tourism are:

Canada
    32 Park Rd, Toronto, Ontario N4W 2N4
    (☎ 416-924-5796, fax 416-924-5844)
Germany
    c/o Mr Bruno Fink, Wurmberg Str 26,
    D-7032 Sindelfinger
    (☎ 70 31 80 10 33, fax 70 31 80 50 12)
UK
    10 Kensington Court,
    London W8 5DL, England
    (☎ 0171-937-6570, fax 0171-937-3611)
USA
    801 Second Ave, 21st Floor,
    New York, NY 10017 (☎ 212-687-4981 or
    800-729-1726, fax 212-949-5946)
    6505 Cove Creek Place, Dallas, TX 75240
    (☎ 972-239-6451, 800-235-3029)

VISAS & DOCUMENTS

Citizens of the USA, Canada and the UK can visit St Vincent & the Grenadines with proof of citizenship in the form of a birth certificate or voter's registration card, accompanied by an official photo ID, such as a driver's license. Citizens of other countries must be in possession of a valid passport. A roundtrip or onward ticket is officially required of all visitors.

CUSTOMS

Up to a quart of wine or spirits and 200 cigarettes may be brought into the country duty free.

MONEY

The Eastern Caribbean dollar (EC$) is the local currency; US$1=EC$2.70.

Major credit cards, while not as widely used as on other Caribbean islands, are accepted at most hotels, car rental agencies and dive shops.

A 10% service charge is added onto most restaurant bills, in which case no further tipping is necessary.

POST & COMMUNICATIONS
Post

The general post office is on Halifax St in Kingstown and there are branch post offices in larger towns and villages.

It costs EC$0.60 to mail postcards within the Caribbean, EC$0.70 to other destinations. A letter weighing up to half an ounce costs EC$0.70 within the Caribbean, EC$0.90 to the USA and Canada, EC$1.10 to the UK and Europe, and EC$1.40 to Australia or Asia.

International mail is routed through other Caribbean nations, so mail sent to the UK takes about a week, while mail sent to other international destinations, including the USA, can easily take double that.

To write to hotels or other businesses listed in this chapter, simply follow the business name with the village and/or island name. For example, the mailing address for Julie's Guest House is: Julie & Isola's Guest House, Port Elizabeth, Bequia, St Vincent & the Grenadines, West Indies.

Telephone

St Vincent phone numbers have seven digits. When calling from overseas add the area code 784.

Both coin and card phones can be found on the major islands. Phonecards can be purchased at Cable & Wireless offices or from vendors near the phones. It costs EC$0.25 cents to make a local call. For more information on card phones and making international calls see Post & Communications in the introductory Facts for the Visitor chapter.

The area code for St Vincent & the Grenadines is 784.

NEWSPAPERS & MAGAZINES

There are two small local newspapers, *The Vincentian* and *The News*, that focus on local issues; *The Herald* covers international news. All are weeklies that hit the streets on either Friday or Saturday and cost EC$1. You can buy *Time* and *Newsweek* magazines at the airport sundry shop.

There are two useful publications available for free through the tourist office and hotels. The *Escape Tourist Guide* is a 100-page glossy magazine with general tourist information, lists of places to stay and eat, ads and a few feature articles. *Discover St Vincent & the Grenadines* is pocket-sized with a similar content.

RADIO & TV
St Vincent has two island TV stations and one radio station (705 AM).

ELECTRICITY
The electric current is 220-240 volts, 50 cycles.

WEIGHTS & MEASURES
St Vincent & the Grenadines uses the imperial system.

HEALTH
The main hospital (☎ 456-1185), a 200-bed facility, is in Kingstown. There's also a hospital in Port Elizabeth on Bequia (☎ 458-3294), clinics throughout the islands and pharmacies in Kingstown and Port Elizabeth.

DANGERS & ANNOYANCES
Kingstown has its fair share of young men who can be a bit pesky about wanting to carry your bags from the ferry or to act as a tour guide. If you're not interested in their services, turn them down politely but firmly.

On the Grenadines, which are far more laid-back, hassles are rare.

EMERGENCIES
Dial ☎ 999 for fire, police and coast guard emergencies.

BUSINESS HOURS
Shops are generally open from 8 am to 4 pm Monday to Friday and to noon on Saturday, although supermarkets often have extended hours. Most government offices are open from 8 am to noon and from 1 to 4:15 pm Monday to Friday. Banks are generally open from 8 am to 1 pm Monday to Thursday, and from 8 am to 1 pm and 3 to 5 pm on Friday.

PUBLIC HOLIDAYS & SPECIAL EVENTS
Public holidays are as follows:

New Year's Day	January 1
St Vincent & the Grenadines Day	January 22
Good Friday	late March/early April
Easter Monday	late March/early April
Labour Day	first Monday in May
Whit Monday	eighth Monday after Easter
Caricom Day	second Monday in July
Carnival Tuesday	usually second Tuesday in mid-July
August Monday	first Monday in August
Independence Day	October 27
Christmas Day	December 25
Boxing Day	December 26

St Vincent's carnival, called Vincy Mas, is the main cultural event of the year. It usually takes place around the first two weeks of July, with a 12-day run of calypso and steel band music, colorful costume parades and lots of dancing and activities. Most of the action is centered in Kingstown.

On Bequia, there's a major regatta held over the Easter weekend.

ACTIVITIES
Beaches & Swimming
There are exceptional white-sand beaches on virtually all of the Grenadine islands and some tan and black-sand beaches on St Vincent. For details on specific beaches, see the individual island sections.

Diving
There are first-rate diving spots off virtually all the islands. The waters offer excellent visibility and extensive coral reefs. Divers will find colorful sponges, soft corals, great stands of elkhorn coral, branching gorgonian, black coral and a few sunken wrecks. There's a range of dives suitable for any level of experience, from calm, shallow

dives to wall dives and drift dives. Spear-fishing is prohibited.

Dive shops on four islands – Dive St Vincent, Dive Bequia, Dive Canouan and Grenadines Dive (on Union Island) – offer a 'pick-and-mix' 10-dive package for US$400 that allows divers to take their dives as they please from any of the four shops. Otherwise, the going rates are around US$50 for a single dive, US$90 for a two-tank dive and US$60 for a night dive. A 'resort course' for beginners that includes a couple of hours of instruction and a shallow dive are available for around US$70.

Many dive shops also offer complete certification courses. Dive St Vincent, one of the islands' best regarded shops, charges US$435 and offers PADI, NAUI or CMAS accreditation.

Dive Shops Dive shops in St Vincent & the Grenadines include:

Bequia Dive Resort, Bequia Beach Club,
    Friendship Bay, Bequia (☎ 458-3248)
Dive Bequia, PO Box 16, Bequia (☎ 458-3504,
    fax 458-3886, bobsax@caribsurf.com)
Dive Canouan, Tamarind Beach Hotel, Canouan
    (☎ 458-8044, fax 458-8875)
Dive St Vincent, PO Box 864, Young Island
    Dock, St Vincent (☎ 457-4714,
    fax 457-4948, bill2s@caribsurf.com)
Grenadines Dive, Sunny Grenadines Hotel,
    Union Island (☎ 458-8138, fax 458-8122)
Sunsports, PO Box 1, Bequia (☎ 458-3577, fax
    457-3031, sunsport@caribsurf.com)

Other Water Sports

Trade winds blow unimpeded across the Grenadines, creating some fine conditions for windsurfing. Many resorts offer guests free use of windsurfing gear and there are water sports huts on many of the more developed tourist beaches that rent windsurfing equipment.

Some of the huts also rent out snorkeling gear, Hobie Cats and Sunfish boats.

Hiking

Overall, hiking trails are not very well developed on St Vincent and access to them can be rough. The most popular walking

area is the Vermont Nature Trails, a series of short walking tracks 3.5 miles inland from the Leeward Highway. See Leeward Highway later in this chapter for details.

The most challenging hike on St Vincent is to La Soufrière volcano. The route passes through banana estates and rainforest, up past the tree line to the barren summit where, weather permitting, hikers are rewarded with views down into the crater and out over St Vincent. The easiest access is from the island's east side and even that is a hardy hike of about 7 miles roundtrip. As the trailhead is 1.5 miles west of the Windward Highway and the nearest bus drop, the easiest way to do the hike is to join a tour. See Organized Tours in the Getting Around section of this chapter.

ACCOMMODATIONS

There are a handful of exclusive resorts on St Vincent & the Grenadines; all of them are of the 'barefoot' variety, situated on remote beaches and completely casual in orientation. Hotels of all categories are small – only a handful have more than a couple of dozen rooms and none have more than 50 rooms.

In St Vincent, many hotels have the same rates all year round. The rates listed in this chapter do not include the 7% hotel tax or the 10% service charge.

There are no established campgrounds on St Vincent & the Grenadines and camping is not encouraged.

FOOD

St Vincent has rich volcanic soil and produces most of the fruits and vegetables sold throughout the Grenadines. The sweet and juicy St Vincent orange is ripe while still green, and sells for about two to the dollar. Produce markets are found in larger towns and are the best places to pick up fruits and vegetables. Seafood is abundant, with conch, fish, shrimp and lobster making an appearance on most menus.

Common West Indian foods include callaloo soup, pumpkin soup, salt fish, pig-foot souse and various breadfruit preparations. A popular St Vincent dish is bul jol, which is made of roasted breadfruit and

salt fish with tomatoes and onions, and can be found at local restaurants on Saturdays.

DRINKS
On St Vincent the tap water comes from mountain reserves and is chlorinated and generally safe to drink. On the Grenadines water comes from individual rain catchment systems and therefore should be boiled or treated before drinking. Bottled water is available on all the islands.

St Vincent Brewery in Kingstown not only makes the local brew, Hairoun lager, but also produces the region's Guinness stout.

ENTERTAINMENT
In Kingstown, *The Attic*, a pleasant 2nd-floor jazz club in an old stone building on Melville St, has live jazz a few nights a week and occasionally a soca band on Saturday. Music is from 9 pm to around 1 am; the cover charge ranges from EC$10 to EC$15.

In the Villa Beach area, the *Aquatic Club* at Young Island Cut, has live bands every Saturday and on alternate Fridays, usually a mix of calypso, reggae and soca, with a cover charge typically between EC$15 to EC$25.

Young Island Resort has a cocktail party at Fort Duvernette at 6:30 pm each Friday that's open to the public for EC$40.

THINGS TO BUY
In Kingstown, St Vincent Crafts near the university sells locally made straw bags, place mats, pottery, banana-leaf art and West Indian dolls. You'll also find attractive handicrafts and souvenirs at Noah's Arkade on Upper Bay St. You can buy colorful commemorative stamps at the Philatelic Bureau, also on Upper Bay St.

Bequia, Mustique and Union Island all have good boutiques and gift shops.

Getting There & Away

AIR
There are no direct flights to St Vincent & the Grenadines from outside the Caribbean. Hence, international passengers must first fly into a neighboring island and then switch to a prop plane for the final leg of their journey.

American Airlines (☎ 458-4380) flies a 46-passenger ATR plane once daily to St Vincent from San Juan, Puerto Rico, with connections to the US mainland. The fare between San Juan and St Vincent is US$201 one way and US$285 roundtrip. American's excursion fares from the US east coast to St Vincent are typically around US$500 in summer and US$650 in winter.

LIAT (☎ 457-1821 reservations, 458-4841 airport) flies direct to St Vincent from Barbados for US$95/144 one way/roundtrip, from St Lucia for US$51/102, and from Grenada for US$66/104. All of these LIAT routes have about five flights daily.

Two small Grenadine carriers, Airlines of Carriacou (☎ 457-1821) and Region Air Caribbean (☎ 458-8847), make island hopping flights a couple of times daily between Grenada and St Vincent. From Grenada it costs US$50/86 one way/roundtrip to Union Island and US$70/110 to Bequia or St Vincent. Between Carriacou and Union Island, fares begin at US$22 one way, US$44 roundtrip.

Mustique Airways (☎ 458-4380) has daily scheduled flights from Barbados to St Vincent (US$95), Mustique (US$98), Bequia

(US$95), Canouan (US$105) and Union Island (US$105). Roundtrip fares are double these one-way fares.

Grenadine Express (☎ 457-5777, email express@caribsurf.com) connects Barbados with Mustique, Canouan and Union Island. One-way/roundtrip fares from Barbados are US$120/200 to Mustique, US$125/210 to either Canouan or Union Island.

Air Martinique (☎ 458-4528) flies daily from Martinique to St Vincent for US$250 roundtrip.

For information on flights between islands in the Grenadines, see the Getting Around section of this chapter.

Airport Information

St Vincent's ET Joshua Airport in Arnos Vale is a modest facility with an exchange bureau open from 8 am to noon and 3 to 5 pm weekdays, a small bar, two gift shops, a duty-free liquor shop, and coin and card phones.

If your luggage is very light, it's possible to get a minibus to Kingstown or Villa Beach from the main road in front of the terminal. Otherwise, taxis meet the flights.

SEA

The passenger/cargo boat M/V *Windward* links St Vincent with Barbados, St Lucia, Trinidad and Venezuela. For details see Boat in the Getting Around chapter at the start of the book.

Information on boats between Carriacou (Grenada) and Union Island is in Getting There & Away in the Union Island section.

Yacht

On the island of St Vincent, yachts can clear immigration and customs at either Kingstown or Wallilabou Bay.

Wallilabou has a customs officer on duty from 4 to 6 pm daily, while outside these times it's possible to clear customs at the police station in the village of Barrouallie, immediately south of Wallilabou Bay. Many yachters prefer to clear customs here and avoid the hassles and long lines sometimes

encountered in Kingstown. Moorings, water, ice and showers are available at Wallilabou Anchorage (☎ 458-7270, VHF 68).

Other popular anchorages on St Vincent include remote Petit Byahaut to the north of Kingstown and the more frequented Young Island Cut and Blue Lagoon to the south. Blue Lagoon (☎ 458-4308) has a 20-berth marina with fuel, water, electricity, laundry and showers.

On the outer islands, there are customs and immigration offices at Bequia, Mustique and Union Island.

Cruise Ship

Cruise ships dock at the deep-water wharf in Kingstown Harbour, at the south side of the town center. Cruise ships also visit some of the Grenadine islands, with Bequia, Mayreau and Union Island being the most popular destinations.

LEAVING ST VINCENT

The departure tax is EC$20.

Getting Around

AIR

Mustique Airways (☎ 458-4380) has inter-island flights connecting various Grenadine islands with St Vincent. The one-way fare is US$17 between St Vincent and Bequia, US$23 between St Vincent and Canouan, US$26 between Bequia and Canouan. Fares between Union Island and either St Vincent, Bequia or Canouan are US$26. There's a discount of about 20% on roundtrip fares.

Grenadine Express (☎ 457-5777) connects Mustique, Canouan and Union Island. Fares to Mustique from either Canouan or Union Island are US$25 one way, US$40 roundtrip. You can also fly between Canouan and Union Island on Grenadine Express for the same fare.

Airlines of Carriacou (☎ 457-1821) flies between Union Island and Bequia or St Vincent for US$26 one way.

BUS

Buses on St Vincent are privately owned minivans that can cram in a good 20 people. The destinations are usually posted on the front windshield. There's a 'conductor' on board who arranges the seating order and collects fares; you pay as you get off. Many of the buses have sound systems that blast reggae music and as long as you're not claustrophobic the buses are a good opportunity to rub shoulders with locals as well as a cheap way to travel.

Kingstown's central bus station, next to Little Tokyo, the city fish market, is a busy but surprisingly orderly affair. The bus stands are clearly marked – either Leeward, Windward or Kingstown, depending on the destination – and getting the right bus is fairly straightforward.

Fares around Kingstown are EC$1. Fares from Kingstown are EC$1.50 to Villa, EC$2 to Layou, EC$3 to Barrouallie, EC$4 to Georgetown and EC$5 to Sandy Bay or Chateaubelair. The buses are most frequent in the morning and from mid to late afternoon when they load up with students and Kingstown commuters; however, getting a bus on a main route, such as between Villa and Kingstown, is fairly easy all day. As a general rule the farther from Kingstown you go the less frequent the buses.

There are also buses on Bequia and Union Island; see those island sections for details.

TAXI

On St Vincent, taxis are readily available at the airport and in the greater Kingstown area. You can also have your hotel call for one or flag one down along the street.

From the airport it costs EC$20 to either Kingstown or Villa Beach. From Kingstown, it's about EC$10 to Fort Charlotte, EC$25 to Villa Beach, EC$40 to Layou and EC$80 to Georgetown.

CAR
Road Rules

Driving is on the left. A local license must be obtained in order to drive on St Vincent;

the fee is a hefty EC$40. In Kingstown, licenses can be obtained at the Traffic & Transport office, inside the main police station, 24 hours a day.

St Vincent roads can be narrow and a bit potholed; generally, the main ones are in fairly good condition though as a rule the farther north you go the worse they become. Be cautious, as minibus drivers commonly switch to whichever side of the road is least potholed and a few drivers have a penchant for passing with the least clearance possible.

The northernmost gas stations on St Vincent are at Georgetown on the Windward Highway and Chateaubelair on the Leeward Highway.

Rental

At present there are no internationally affiliated car rental agencies on St Vincent. Two local companies near the airport are Sunshine Auto Rentals (☎ 456-5380) and Unico Rentals (☎ 456-5744); both will deliver cars to your hotel. Other companies include Star Garage (☎ 456-1743) and Kim's Rentals (☎ 456-1884), both on Grenville St in Kingstown.

Rentals typically begin at around US$50 a day for a car and US$60 for a 4WD vehicle. Around 75 free miles are commonly allowed and a fee of EC$1 for each additional mile driven. Note that collision damage insurance is not a common concept and if you get into an accident you're likely to be liable for damages.

On most of the Grenadine islands there are no car rentals at all – on some there are no roads!

BICYCLE

Sailor's Cycle Centre (☎ 457-1274), on Middle St in Kingstown, rents road bikes and mountain bikes for EC$25 per day.

BOAT

For information on the main ferry service that operates between Bequia and Kingstown, see Getting There & Away in the Bequia section.

ST VINCENT

The mail boat M/V *Barracuda* carries passengers and cargo three times weekly between St Vincent, Bequia, Canouan, Mayreau and Union Island. The boat leaves St Vincent at 10:30 am on Monday and Thursday and 10 am on Saturday, arriving in Union Island at around 4 pm. En route it stops at Bequia (bypassed on Saturday and occasionally on other days if there's no Bequia cargo), Canouan and Mayreau. On Tuesday and Friday the boat departs from Union Island at dawn, and makes the same stopovers on the northbound route back to St Vincent. On Saturday, the boat usually leaves Union Island around 5:30 pm and makes the return nonstop, arriving in St Vincent around 10:30 pm.

Fares from St Vincent are EC$15 to Bequia, EC$15 to Canouan, EC$20 to Mayreau and EC$25 to Union Island.

Although en route departure times vary depending on how long it takes to unload cargo, the sailing time between islands is one hour from St Vincent to Bequia, two hours from Bequia to Canouan, one hour from Canouan to Mayreau and 20 minutes from Mayreau to Union Island.

ORGANIZED TOURS

Sam's Taxi Tours (☎ 458-3686) arranges a variety of tours of St Vincent, with day tours that take in the sights on either the west coast or east coast for around US$100 for up to two people. Sam can also put together a hiking trip to La Soufrière volcano for US$100 for up to six people.

HazEco Tours (☎ /fax 457-8634) concentrates on St Vincent's natural scenery, with a half-day outing to the Vermont Nature Trails for US$25 per person, or a hiking trip to the summit of La Soufrière volcano for US$90 for up to two people. They also arrange sightseeing trips to either the west or east coast of St Vincent for US$35 per person.

For an interesting high-energy alternative, Sailor's Cycle Centre (☎ 457-1274, sailor@bsi-svg.com) offers various mountain bike outings for as little as US$15 per person, if at least four people sign up. The most demanding one combines mountain

biking with a hike to La Soufrière's summit for US$55 per person.

Fantasea Tours (☎ 457-4477) arranges sailing day tours from St Vincent to the Grenadine islands. One goes to Mustique and Bequia for US$60 and another takes in Canouan, Mayreau and the Tobago Cays for US$80.

For information on tours to the Falls of Baleine, see that section under Leeward Highway.

Kingstown

Kingstown, the capital and commercial center of St Vincent & the Grenadines, is a bustling city of 30,000 people.

The city center consists of a dozen blocks that can easily be explored in a few hours. There are some appealing old cobblestone streets, brick archways and stoneblock colonial buildings scattered around the center; worth a look are the buildings lining Melville St and the churches, courthouse and police station. Still, none of these buildings is grand and overall Kingstown is more interesting for its local character than for any particular sights. It's the islanders selling their produce along Bay and Bedford streets, the crowds at the fish market and the rum shops at the bus terminal that give the town its color.

Ferries from the Grenadines arrive at the jetty just south of the city center. On days when the banana boats are being loaded, the port is abuzz with activity as trucks packed with stalks of bananas line the streets to the dock.

Information

Tourist Office The tourist office (☎ 457-1502) is on the ground floor of the government building on Upper Bay St. It's open 8 am to noon and 1 to 4:15 pm Monday to Friday.

Money There's a Barclays Bank on Halifax St, opposite the LIAT office, and a Scotiabank a block west on Halifax St.

Kingstown

PLACES TO STAY
1 Bella Vista Inn
3 Haddon Hotel
29 Cobblestone Inn
36 Heron Hotel

PLACES TO EAT
10 Pick A Snack
12 KFC
13 Aggie's
14 Sardine's Bakery
26 Bounty
29 Basil's Bar &
   Restaurant
30 Chams
34 Chung Wua

OTHER
2 St Martin's School
4 Hospital
5 Texaco Gas Station
6 MagiKleen
7 Star Garage Car Rentals
8 Kim's Car Rentals
9 Methodist Church
11 The Attic
15 Royal Pharmacy
16 Courthouse
17 Bus Station

18 Little Tokyo Fish
   Market
19 Public Market
20 Cable & Wireless
21 Taxi Stand
22 Police, Immigration
23 Scotiabank
24 Tourist Office,
   Government Complex
25 Bonadie's Supermarket
27 General Post Office
28 Philatelic Bureau
31 LIAT
32 Barclays Bank
33 St Vincent Crafts
35 Noah's Arkade
37 Wayfarer Book Store
38 Sailor's Cycle Center
39 Port Authority, Customs

ST VINCENT

Both are open from 8 am to 3 pm Monday to Thursday, 8 am to 5 pm on Friday.

Post & Communications The general post office, on Halifax St, is open from 8:30 am to 3 pm weekdays, to 11:30 am on Saturday.

You can make phone calls and send faxes, telexes and telegrams at the Cable & Wireless office on Halifax St. It's open from 7 am to 7 pm Monday to Saturday, 8 to 10 am and 6 to 8 pm on Sunday.

Laundry For laundry and dry cleaning, there's MagiKleen on Lower Bay St, open

from 7:30 am to 5 pm weekdays, to 2 pm on Saturday. Drop your laundry early and you can pick it up later the same day. It costs EC$2.50 a pound to wash and dry.

Botanic Gardens

The St Vincent Botanic Gardens are the oldest botanical gardens in the West Indies. Originally established in 1765 to propagate spices and medicinal plants, the gardens now comprise a neatly landscaped 20-acre park with lots of flowering bushes and tall trees.

Inside the park you'll find a small **aviary** that is home to about 20 of the island's remaining 500 St Vincent parrots. Most of the birds were born there, as part of a breeding program that hopes to bring the parrot back from the brink of extinction.

Just 10 yards uphill from the aviary is a breadfruit tree that was grown from a sucker of one of the original saplings brought to the island from Tahiti in 1793 by Captain Bligh. The ill-fated captain introduced the tree, with its large starchy fruit, as an inexpensive food source for plantation slaves.

Also on the grounds is the **St Vincent National Museum**, which has numerous pre-Columbian stone carvings, clay works and shell tools created by the island's early Amerindian settlers. The curator, Dr Earle Kirby, is a veterinarian turned historian who spearheaded the founding of the museum in 1979. The museum is planning to eventually move to the old library on Granby St in central Kingstown.

The botanic gardens are a 10-minute walk north of the hospital, along the Leeward Highway. Although admission is free, expect to meet tour guides at the gate who will try to convince you to accept their services for US$3 per person. Although some of the guides are knowledgeable, the gardens are quite pleasant to stroll through quietly on your own.

Churches

There are three interesting churches in a row along Grenville St.

Worth a look for its eclectic design is **St Mary's Catholic Cathedral**. The original church dates from 1823, but most of the present structure was built in the 1930s by Dom Charles Verbeke, a Belgian priest. The gray-stone edifice boldly, and somewhat fancifully, incorporates a number of architectural styles, including Romanesque arches and columns, Gothic spires and an element of Moorish ornamentation.

St George's Anglican Cathedral, circa 1820, is of late Georgian architecture. The interior has the traditional altar and stained-glass windows of a typical Anglican church but the walls are brightly painted in yellow and turquoise. There are interesting marble

plaques. One inscribed stone in the center aisle beneath the chandelier venerates the British colonel Alexander Leith (1771-98), who took the life of Carib chief Chattawae, only to die of 'great fatigue' following the battle. You may not be able to see the inscription, however, as in recent times a carpet has been laid over it.

From the outside, the **Methodist Church** is a rather secular looking structure that could be mistaken for a warehouse. However, should you happen by when the doors are unlocked, the aqua blue interior, which is light and colorful, bears remarkably little resemblance to the exterior.

Fort Charlotte

Fort Charlotte, on a 660-foot ridge north of the city, is a rather modest fortification, but it does provide a good view of Kingstown and of the Grenadines to the south. You can also walk through the old officers' quarters, whose walls are lined with paintings depicting Black Carib history. Most of the rest of this 18th-century fort is off limits, and one area is used as a women's prison.

The fort is an hour's walk from the center of town. If you want to go by bus, look for the van marked 'Mad Dog' at the bus terminal; the driver can drop you off below the fort, from where it's a 10-minute uphill walk for EC$1, or take you right to the fort for EC$2.

Places to Stay

The *Bella Vista Inn* (☎ 457-2757), on a hill above the west side of town, offers a homey family scene in a private residence. There are seven simple guest rooms, most with two single beds and standing fans. Singles/doubles cost US$17/28 with shared bath, US$22/32 with a private bath. Breakfast (EC$10) and dinner (EC$15) can be arranged. Bring mosquito repellent. The guesthouse is about a 10-minute walk from the city center; take the steep footpath leading uphill opposite St Martin's School.

Haddon Hotel (☎ 456-1897, fax 456-2726), PO Box 144, Kingstown, is in a quiet location just north of the high school and only a few minutes walk from the bustling city center. The hotel has 18 simple, wear-worn rooms that vary in size, but have private baths. Rates are US$45/61 for singles/doubles with air-con, US$38/52 without. Across from the main hotel is a spiffy new tower wing with eight large, modern units – all with full kitchens, pleasant rattan furnishings, air-con and TV. Studios cost US$98, one-bedroom units US$115 and two-bedroom units US$140.

Cobblestone Inn (☎ 456-1937, fax 456-1938), PO Box 867, Kingstown, on Upper Bay St, is an atmospheric hotel in a renovated 1814 Georgian-style warehouse of cobblestone construction. The 19 rooms possess a pleasant old-world character, wooden floors, bathtub, air-con and cobblestone walls. The hotel, which is popular with business travelers, is both the most comfortable and most secure place to stay in the city center. The only drawback is that the stones hold moisture so the rooms can be a bit mildewy. Singles/doubles cost US$60/72.

Heron Hotel (☎ 457-1631, fax 457-1189), PO Box 226, Kingstown, on Upper Bay St a block south of Cobblestone Inn, has 15 basic rooms with private baths, air-con and phones. Avoid the streetside rooms, which can get a bit noisy. It's pricey for what you get, at US$45/59 for singles/doubles.

For a place to stay near the airport, *Adams Apartments* (☎ 458-4656), a two-minute walk from the terminal, is cheap and convenient with about a dozen run-down rooms for US$19 a day (US$22 with cooking facilities). Ask to see the room in advance as some lack fans and have broken windows.

Places to Eat

The *Bounty* on Egmont St is a friendly local place with a streetside balcony view. Rotis, omelets or macaroni cheese pie cost around EC$5, fish or chicken with chips EC$12. Order and pay at the register and then give your receipt to the counter clerk. It's open from 7:30 am to 5 pm Monday to Friday, to 1:30 pm on Saturday.

Chams, in a quiet courtyard off Halifax St, is an inviting lunch spot with good rotis for EC$6 or full chicken meals for double

that. It also serves breakfast – a bacon and eggs plate with coffee costs EC$10. It's open from 8 am to 5 pm Monday to Friday, 8 am to 2 pm on Saturday.

Aggie's, a 2nd-floor bar that's a hangout for expats, has good local food at reasonable prices. You can get a chicken roti for a mere EC$5 and a number of hot dishes, such as fish and rice for under EC$20. It's open from 9 am (noon on Sundays) until late at night.

Chung Wua, on Upper Bay St opposite the Cobblestone Inn, has average Chinese food. For the best value, skip the menu and ask about the EC$15 daily specials, which usually include a crispy sweet and sour chicken with fried rice. It's open daily for lunch and dinner.

Basil's Bar & Restaurant, on Upper Bay St beneath Cobblestone Inn, has a bit of colonial character and a central location. The most popular meal is the weekday (noon to 2 pm) lunch buffet, which features a couple of hot West Indian main dishes, pumpkin fritters, salad and desserts for EC$32.

The *Cobblestone Inn* also has a pleasant rooftop restaurant, featuring breakfast fare, sandwiches and fish & chips in the EC$5 to EC$15 range. It's open from 7:30 am to 3 pm daily.

There's a *KFC* on the corner of Melville and Grenville Sts, and another on the corner of Upper Bay and James Sts. Two pieces of chicken and a biscuit cost EC$8, or EC$11 with fries. They're open from at least 11 am to 10 pm daily.

Sardine's Bakery on Grenville St is a good place to pick up inexpensive bread and local pastries such as coconut rolls. It's open from 6 am to 5 pm weekdays, to 1 pm on Saturday. For fancier treats continue west a block to *Pick A Snack*, which specializes in cakes (EC$1.50 a slice), including a tasty orange version; it's open from 8 am to 9 pm Monday to Saturday.

There are a number of grocery stores in town; one of the most modern is *Bonadie's Supermarket* on Egmont St.

If you have cooking facilities you can buy fresh fish at the *Little Toyko Fish*

Market (open from 7 am Monday to Saturday) next to the bus terminal on Lower Bay St and pick up fresh produce from vendors at the nearby public market. At the bus terminal you'll also find rows of rum shops, popcorn stands and sidewalk vendors selling roasted corn on the cob and drinking coconuts for EC$1.

Around St Vincent

VILLA BEACH & INDIAN BAY
St Vincent's main 'resort' district is the Villa area, a couple of miles southeast of Kingstown. It begins at Villa Point and runs along Indian Bay and Villa Beach, where it takes in the Young Island Cut, a narrow channel that separates the St Vincent mainland from Young Island.

The Villa area is a relatively well-to-do seaside suburb with about a dozen small hotels and inns. While Villa might be a fine neighborhood to live in, it's not really the type of place most tourists would envision when thinking of a Caribbean vacation.

The area is fairly well populated and the beaches are not pristine. Indian Bay Beach, which has grainy golden sands, is generally clean enough, but Villa Beach has a couple of storm drains emptying across it and can get a bit trashed after heavy rains.

There's decent snorkeling around the rocky islet with the cross on top, but be careful of surges and spiny sea urchins. Those who want to stay closer to shore can snorkel at the south side of Indian Bay.

Eternal View
Between Indian Bay and Villa Beach are a couple of small rocky islets, one of which sports a large white cross. Beneath the cross in an upright position is the body of a local landowner who once owned much of Villa's shoreline property. He requested to be laid to rest in a standing position in order to watch the sun set each day. ■

Most services, including water taxis, land taxis and the largest concentration of places to eat are near the Young Island Cut.

Young Island
Young Island is a small privately operated island, about 200 yards off Villa Beach, which has been turned into an exclusive resort. Access is via a small blue and white ferry that the resort uses to shuttle guests and staff between Young Island and the Villa Beach dock.

There's a courtesy phone line direct to the resort at the Villa Beach dock that visitors can use to request the ferry. The resort shuttles diners across to eat at its restaurant and if they're not busy will sometimes let non-guests come over just to see what the island is like – but not always, and the decision seems to be made at whim.

Fort Duvernette
Immediately south of Young Island is a high, rocky, gumdrop islet that the British turned into a fortress following the Carib uprising of the late 1790s. Some 250 steps wind up from the landing to the summit of Fort Duvernette, where you'll find the old fort's cannons and a fine view of the Grenadines. The island is under the auspices of the St Vincent National Trust. Transportation to Fort Duvernette can be arranged with one of the water taxis at the dock fronting Young Island Cut for around EC$10.

Places to Stay – budget
Ocean View Inn (☎ 457-4332), PO Box 176, Villa Point, a minute's walk from the Grand View Beach Hotel, is a private home with five small rooms for US$35/45 for singles/ doubles, continental breakfast included.

Tranquillity Apartments (☎ 458-4021, fax 457-4792), PO Box 71, Indian Bay, has friendly family management and seven studios just above Indian Bay Beach. The rooms aren't fancy but they're perfectly adequate, each with a kitchenette, private bath and screened windows. They also have little balconies with fine views of Young Island and other nearshore islands.

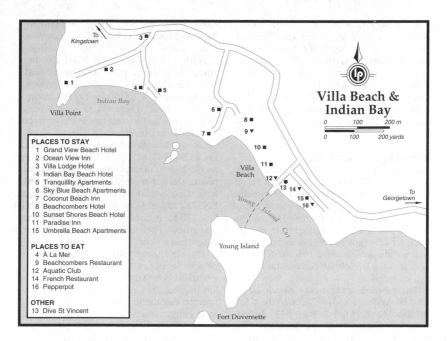

PLACES TO STAY
1 Grand View Beach Hotel
2 Ocean View Inn
3 Villa Lodge Hotel
4 Indian Bay Beach Hotel
5 Tranquillity Apartments
6 Sky Blue Beach Apartments
7 Coconut Beach Inn
8 Beachcombers Hotel
10 Sunset Shores Beach Hotel
11 Paradise Inn
15 Umbrella Beach Apartments

PLACES TO EAT
4 À La Mer
9 Beachcombers Restaurant
12 Aquatic Club
14 French Restaurant
16 Pepperpot

OTHER
13 Dive St Vincent

Villa Beach & Indian Bay

Singles/doubles cost US$40/50 in summer, US$45/55 in winter.

Umbrella Beach Apartments (☎ 458-4651, fax 457-4948), PO Box 530, Villa Beach, has nine simple but brightly painted rooms with ceiling fans, private baths and kitchens. Singles/doubles cost US$42/52. The apartments are adjacent to the French Restaurant, a good eatery that's under the same management.

The recommendable *Coconut Beach Inn* (☎ 457-4900), PO Box 355, Indian Bay, has a pleasant beachside location. A bit removed from other Indian Bay hotels, it's about a 10-minute walk from the main road or the Young Island Cut. The nine rooms are simple and clean with fans and private bath. Rates, which depend on the room size and the number of beds, range from US$36 to US$52 in summer and US$45 to US$65 in winter; two of the higher-priced rooms share a waterview balcony.

Sky Blue Beach Apartments (☎ 457-4394, fax 457-5232), PO Box 87, Indian Bay, is a top value with eight large new apartments, each with a full kitchen and TV, for just US$45/55 for singles/doubles. Summer rates are US$5 less and there are discounts for weekly stays. The complex is in a residential neighborhood that's only a couple of minutes walk from the beach.

The newly remodeled *Paradise Inn* (☎ 457-4795, fax 457-4221), PO Box 1286, Villa Beach, has eight inviting rooms with fans, thermostatic air-con, TV, phone and private bath. The winter rates are US$50 to US$60 for singles and US$60 to US$80 for doubles; the higher-priced units have refrigerators and seaside balconies. In the same price range you can also get a nicely furnished apartment with a full kitchen and a small living room that has an extra sofabed. All rates are US$10 cheaper in summer.

ST VINCENT

Sea Breeze Guest House (☎ 458-4969), Arnos Vale, is about a mile east of the airport, at a busy corner on the road between the airport and Villa Beach. While the location may not be ideal, the six simple guest rooms each have a private bath, rates are just US$20/30 for singles/doubles and it's right on the bus route. There are common kitchen facilities and they offer inexpensive island tours.

Places to Stay – middle

Beachcombers Hotel (☎ 458-4283, fax 458-4385), PO Box 126, Villa Beach, on the west side of Villa Beach, is a friendly family-run operation with a dozen straightforward but adequate rooms. The rooms vary in size and decor but all have private baths, ceiling fans and patios, and the hotel has a fine beachside location. Singles/doubles cost US$60/80, continental breakfast included.

The 12-room *Indian Bay Beach Hotel* (☎ 458-4001, fax 457-4777; from the USA ☎ 800-742-4276), PO Box 538, Indian Bay, has a good beachside location. The rooms are wear-worn but all have air-con and private baths. When making a reservation, specify that you want a kitchenette unit as there are a couple of smaller rooms without them for the same rate: US$55/65 for singles/doubles in summer, US$65/75 in winter. There are also a few roomy two-bedroom units that cost US$90 for up to four people.

Places to Stay – top end

Sunset Shores Beach Hotel (☎ 458-4411, fax 457-4800), PO Box 849, Villa Beach, has 32 ordinary rooms with air-con, TV and phones. There's a pool and restaurant. The place is OK but not special for the price: US$90/115 for singles/doubles in summer, US$120/140 in winter.

Villa Lodge Hotel (☎ 458-4641, fax 457-4468), PO Box 1191, Indian Bay, is popular with visiting Caribbean politicians and business travelers. There are 10 attractive rooms with TV, air-con, small refrigerators, phones and bathrooms with tubs;

some of the rooms (Nos 7 through 10) have gorgeous views as well. Singles/doubles cost US$95/105 in summer, US$105/115 in winter. The hotel also has attractive self-contained apartments with full amenities that cost US$120 for one-bedroom units, US$150 for two-bedroom, two-bath units. There's a pool, a breezy sitting room and a small moderately priced restaurant on site.

Grand View Beach Hotel (☎ 458-4811, fax 457-4174), PO Box 173, Villa Point, is an old hilltop plantation house on a scenic point. The 19 rooms are large and many have fine ocean views. Rates begin at US$210 a double for the older rooms and US$270 for refurbished room with modern amenities. There's a health club, tennis courts and a pool.

The exclusive *Young Island Resort* (☎ 458-4826, fax 457-4567), PO Box 211, occupies Young Island. Accommodations are in pleasantly rustic stone cottages that open to surrounding gardens. The cottages have simple amenities, louvered windows, patios, alfresco showers, ceiling fans and refrigerators; they're stocked daily with fresh fruit and flowers. Rates include breakfast and dinner, beginning at US$300/430 in the summer/winter for doubles. Singles are US$90 cheaper.

Places to Eat – budget

The oceanfront restaurant at *Coconut Beach Inn* is casual and friendly, with good inexpensive food and a view of Young Island. An egg breakfast with juice and coffee costs EC$15. At lunch, rotis or sandwiches are EC$8, while at dinner you can get a hearty meal for EC$25. Dinner requires advance reservations.

Pepperpot, an unpretentious seaside place at Villa Beach, specializes in West Indian food. At any time of the day you can get a chicken roti for EC$10. Other dishes include fish blaff or the local favorite bul jol for EC$30 and a tasty curried coconut shrimp for EC$35. There's live music a couple of nights a week; it's closed on Wednesday.

The *Aquatic Club* near the Young Island dock is best known as an entertainment spot, but also offers up lunch and dinner daily. At lunch, conch souse, rotis or burgers cost EC$8, fish & chips EC$15. Dinners range from EC$40 for chicken to EC$65 for Creole lobster.

The open-air *Beachcombers Restaurant*, above Villa Beach, has sandwiches and burgers for EC$12, pizza for EC$20 and chicken or fish dishes for EC$32.

The little restaurant at *Villa Lodge* has good fresh food at reasonable prices and is open for three meals a day. Creole chicken, catch of the day or Cajun fish are all priced between EC$30 and EC$35 and come with salad, rice and rolls.

The Indian Bay Beach Hotel has water-view dining at its *À La Mer* restaurant. At lunch, there are burgers or rotis for EC$10, fish & chips for EC$20. Full dinners, which range from EC$40 to EC$65, are not special enough to warrant the price.

Places to Eat – top end

The *French Restaurant* (☎ 458-4972) at Villa Beach serves up French food with a West Indian accent. At lunch, sandwiches cost EC$10, fish or chicken dishes double that. At dinner, starters include an excellent onion soup for EC$20, while main seafood and beef dishes average EC$55. It's closed on Sunday.

The *Grand View Restaurant* at the Grand View Beach Hotel at Villa Point offers continental breakfasts for EC$16 and full breakfasts for EC$26. At lunch there are sandwiches, salads and omelets, most in the EC$12 to EC$25 range. Dinner is a fixed-price meal, by reservation, with a choice of two main dishes (usually meat and fish), soup, dessert and coffee, all for EC$65.

For a different sort of dining experience, *Young Island Resort* (☎ 458-4826) has an EC$95 multi-course dinner from 7:30 to 9:30 pm. On Tuesday there's a nice barbecue lunch buffet for EC$54; on other days lunch is more ordinary and costs around EC$35. Some of the seating is outdoors under individual thatched huts, which

can be quite romantic. Reservations are required for all meals.

WINDWARD HIGHWAY

St Vincent's east coast, its windward side, is raw and rugged with a jungly interior and a surf-pounded shoreline. The Windward Highway winds up and down the east coast, passing black-sand beaches, roadside banana plantations and deep valleys thickly planted in coconut trees. Along the route are a number of small villages, an intermingling of old wooden shanties and simple cement homes.

The road is potholed here and there and is narrow in places, but by island standards it's in reasonably good condition. The final leg between Owia and Fancy is part cement and part dirt. If you're driving, allow at least an hour to get from Kingstown to Georgetown. To drive the entire 35 miles from Kingstown to the end of the road at Fancy would take a good two hours each way, not including time to stop and explore.

Buses from Kingstown to Georgetown are fairly regular (except on Sunday) and cost EC$4. Continuing north from Georgetown by bus can be a bit iffy, so it's a good idea to get information from the Kingstown bus terminal before heading off.

Georgetown

Georgetown is a fairly good-sized but rather poor town that was once the center of the island's sugar industry. Now just a shadow of its former self, its main street is lined with cobblestone sidewalks and two-story buildings with overhanging balconies. Once stylish, many of these buildings are now in various stages of disrepair, a few simply falling apart and abandoned.

Few tourists come this way and there really aren't any sights per se. The two churches, one Methodist and one Anglican, that sit side by side on the main street are in need of restoration, but are open to visitors.

Places to Eat The 2nd-story *Footsteps Restaurant & Bar* (☎ 458-6433) above the grocery store on the main road in the center

ST VINCENT

of town is a good place for a meal. You can get breakfast for about EC$10 and a good hearty West Indian lunch or dinner for EC$15 to EC$20. The accommodating owner, Ferdie Toney, sometimes has a couple of rooms for rent as well.

North of Georgetown

The farther north you go, the wilder the landscape gets; the valleys are deeper and the villages less developed. The active volcano La Soufrière looms inland as you continue along the road, adding a primeval element to the scenery.

About a mile north of Georgetown the road goes over a hardened lava flow known as the Rabacca Dry River, a former stream that filled with lava during La Soufrière's violent 1902 eruption. The river now flows through a gravel bed buried beneath the lava. During heavy rains, however, flash floods occasionally flow above the lava, making the road crossing hazardous or impossible.

North of the dry river, a 4WD road heads inland through coconut and banana plantations towards **La Soufrière** and the beginning of a 3.25-mile hiking trail that leads to the rim of the crater.

Continuing north, the Windward Highway passes through **Orange Hill Estates**, where a 3160-acre coconut estate, once the world's largest, has been divided up and parceled out to small farmers as part of a government land reform project. In addition to coconuts, Orange Hill produces bananas, limes, spices and vegetables.

A couple of miles farther is **Sandy Bay**, a sizable village that has the island's largest concentration of Black Caribs. A proud people with a turbulent history, they are distinguished from other Vincentians by their short, stocky builds and high cheekbones.

North of Sandy Bay is Owia Bay and the village of **Owia**. Turn east on the main village road at the police station to reach the coastal Owia Salt Pond. Here you'll find tidal pools protected from the crashing Atlantic by a massive stone shield. This is a popular swimming hole with crystal-clear waters; there are thatched shelters, picnic tables, restrooms and a view of St Lucia to

the north. Use caution during high tide or if the waves are breaking over the rocks and watch out for yellow sea anemones that can sting. Owia also has an arrowroot mill and a couple of churches that can be visited.

True diehards can go to **Fancy**, where the road ends at St Vincent's most remote village, a rather rudimentary settlement with no electricity or phones. There's an old arrowroot mill with a rusting mill wheel that now serves as the medical clinic, a school and a couple of simple shops selling groceries and provisions.

LEEWARD HIGHWAY

The Leeward Highway runs north from Kingstown along St Vincent's west coast for 25 miles, ending at Richmond Beach. The west coast offers some lovely scenery. Leaving Kingstown the road climbs into the mountains and then winds through the hillside and back down to deeply cut coastal valleys that open to coconut plantations, fishing villages and bays lined with black-sand beaches.

The drive from Kingstown to Richmond Beach takes about 1½ hours, not including stopping time. Just north of Kingstown, there are a few narrow sections where the shoulderless road is crumbly and a miscalculation could result in a tumble over the cliff. Otherwise, the road as far as Barrouallie is in good condition, albeit narrow and winding.

There are fairly frequent weekday buses from Kingstown to Barrouallie (45 minutes, EC$3). Buses generally don't run in the evening; plan on catching a return bus to Kingstown by 5 pm from Barrouallie to be safe. It's a 15-minute walk from the last Barrouallie bus stop to Wallilabou Bay, although the driver might be willing to take you directly to Wallilabou for a few dollars more. Generally, only four buses a day (two in the morning, two in the afternoon) continue north from Barrouallie to Richmond.

Vermont Nature Trails

About a 15-minute drive north of Kingstown is a sign along the Leeward Highway pointing east to the Vermont Nature Trails,

3.5 miles inland. Here you'll find the Parrot Lookout Trail, a 1.75-mile loop trail that passes through the southwestern tip of the St Vincent Parrot Reserve. The island forestry department, with assistance from the Worldwide Fund for Nature, established the reserve in 1987 to protect the endangered St Vincent parrot, which numbers only about 500 in the wild.

The Parrot Lookout Trail climbs 500 feet in elevation into a mixed tropical rainforest of towering native hardwood trees, lush ferns, bromeliads, heliconias, abandoned cocoa trees and introduced groves of eucalyptus. The hike takes about two hours; it can get slippery so hiking boots are recommended. Be prepared for wet conditions, as the forest averages some 200 inches of rain a year, and bring insect repellent. Hikers should wear long sleeves and pants as a precaution against chiggers, which can be quite pesky along this trail.

Near the trailhead you'll find a welcome board with background information and a map. Twenty interpretive signs posted along the trail, give brief descriptions of the flora and fauna encountered along the way.

The best times for parrot sightings are generally early morning and late afternoon; even if you don't spot the parrots there's a good chance you'll hear their loud squawks as they move from tree to tree. Other birds sometimes seen along the trail include the rare whistling warbler, a black and white bird with eye rings that is endemic to the island, as well as brightly colored hooded tanagers, hummingbirds, broad-winged hawks and common black hawks.

Layou

The Leeward Highway comes out to the coast for the first time at the black sands of Buccament Bay. Shortly after that, the road curves around the coastal mountains giving a fine bird's-eye view of the fishing village of Layou, before descending to Layou Bay. The village is colorful, a mix of simple old wooden structures and brightly painted concrete homes.

There are a scattering of petroglyphs on St Vincent's west coast. The best known

are in Layou, a short walk from the river near the Bible Camp on the main road at the north end of town. However, they're on private property and if you want to see them, you'll need to arrange it with the owner, Victor Hendrickson (☎ 458-7243), who charges visitors EC$5.

After Layou the road goes inland before coming back out to the coast at the north side of Mt Wynne Bay, a lovely black-sand beach backed by a broad sweep of coconut trees. Some of the tours to the Falls of Baleine stop at this undeveloped beach for picnics.

Barrouallie

Like Layou, Barrouallie is a typical St Vincent fishing village. Barrouallie villagers are perhaps best known for their hunting of pilot whales, which are referred to as blackfish on the island.

The village has some interesting older architecture with gingerbread trim and there are petroglyphs in the yard of the Barrouallie secondary school.

Wallilabou Bay & Falls

Wallilabou is a quiet little bay lined with a black-sand beach and surrounded by high cliffs, complete with a picturesque little rock arch at its northern end. The waters are usually quite calm and it's possible to snorkel at the southern end of the bay.

Wallilabou is a port of entry to the island and a small flotilla of young men offering to sell provisions and run errands often row out to the yachts as they pull into the bay.

A popular little side excursion is to the Wallilabou Falls, which are about 13 feet high and drop into a waist-deep bathing pool. The falls are near the inland side of the main road about a mile north of Wallilabou Bay; once you cross the Wallilabou River bridge, it's about a 10-minute walk.

Places to Stay & Eat *Wallilabou Anchorage* (☎ 458-7270, VHF 68), PO Box 851, Wallilabou, which runs the mooring facilities here, has a pleasant bayside restaurant and bar that's open for three meals daily. Sandwiches start at EC$8, and there are also hot dishes – the Creole fish for EC$20 at lunch (EC$30 at dinner) is a favorite. Adjacent to the restaurant is a small hotel with seafront rooms from US$50.

North of Wallilabou
North of Wallilabou, the next beach you come to is **Cumberland Bay**, a pretty little anchorage backed by coconut palms and lush green hills. On the north side of the bay is Stephen's Hideout, a restaurant with moderately priced West Indian seafood dishes.

The road passes a few settlements, including the town of **Chateaubelair**, before ending at **Richmond Beach**. This long black-sand beach has stands of tropical almond trees and is a popular swimming and picnicking spot. Avoid swimming near the river mouth at the north side of the beach, as it can have a strong undertow.

East of Richmond is the trailhead to **Trinity Falls**, a remote triple cascade with a 40-foot drop. The falls are about 3 miles inland on the road beginning at the old Richmond Vale Academy. The road is bad, but with a 4WD vehicle it's usually possible to drive about half of that distance and then continue to the falls on foot along a rugged hiking trail. There's a lot of loose gravel on the trail, so the walk itself can be an ankle-twister, though the rainforest is attractive. Note that although the pool beneath the falls is deep enough for a dip, swimming can be treacherous because of a strong churning current and the possibility of falling rocks.

Also from Richmond, it's possible to hike up to the crater rim of La Soufrière. However, this trail is rougher and less defined than the one on the windward side of the island and a local guide is necessary. The hike would take about five hours round trip.

FALLS OF BALEINE
The 60-foot Falls of Baleine, at the isolated northwestern tip of the island, is inaccessible by road but can be visited by boat from Kingstown. The scenic falls, which cascade down a fern-draped rock face into

a wide pool, are a few minutes walk from the beach where the boats anchor.

Hotels, guesthouses and dive shops can arrange tours to Baleine, most of which stop for snorkeling en route. Some tours use a speedboat, which zips to the falls in about an hour. Sailboats offer a more leisurely pace, usually taking a couple of hours each way, and offer better odds of spotting dolphins.

Sea Breeze Boat Service (☎ 458-4969) usually uses a 36-foot sloop and has the island's cheapest tour at US$30 (most companies charge US$40). Call ahead for reservations as this tour requires at least three people to go out. Sea Breeze leaves at 9 am and returns at around 5 pm, stopping for snorkeling en route. Bring your own lunch.

Bequia

Just an hour's sail south of St Vincent, Bequia is the northernmost, the largest (7 sq miles) and the most populated (5000 people) of St Vincent's Grenadine islands.

Bequia is a delightful place, neat, hilly and green, with lots of flowering bushes and some fine golden-sand beaches. It has a rich seafaring tradition that includes boat building, whaling and sailing. These days most of the boat building done on the island is on the scale of models, and more than 90% of the boats pulling into the harbor are visiting yachts. Bequia has become the main yachting haven in the Grenadines and at the height of the season Admiralty Bay, the deep protected bay fronting the town of Port Elizabeth, is chock-a-block with yachts.

THE GRENADINES

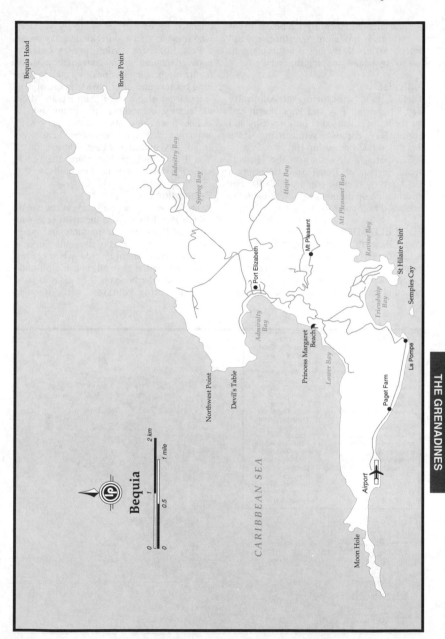

There are a number of good places to eat and several appealing guesthouses and hotels. All in all, Bequia is a fun place to add to any island-hopping itinerary.

Activities

There's good windsurfing at Admiralty Bay, Friendship Bay and Paget Farm and for the more advanced at Industry Bay and Spring Bay. Paradise Windsurfing has a rental booth at Friendship Bay.

Sunsports, a dive shop at the Gingerbread Restaurant, Port Elizabeth, offers a 1½-hour snorkeling trip for US$20. For information on diving, see Activities in the front of this chapter.

PORT ELIZABETH

Port Elizabeth, built along the curve of Admiralty Bay, is an appealing seaside community and the island's commercial center.

The town has an international flavor and a fair number of the restaurants and shops are operated by expatriates – mostly yachters who came to visit and decided to stay on.

Port Elizabeth strikes a nice balance between quaintness and convenience. Many of the waterfront businesses cater to visiting boaters and offer a wide range of services, from places to pick up ice and drop off laundry to good bars and dining spots.

The town has lots of boutiques with attractive batik and silk-screened clothing, frond baskets and other island crafts. You'll also find vendors along the beach selling T-shirts and handmade dolls.

Orientation

A narrow shoreline walkway at the south side of Port Elizabeth is the main access to many of the town's restaurants and other visitor businesses. Part of the route can be a bit precarious at high tide when waves splash up on the seawall, and it's hit-and-miss as to whether you'll be able to pass without getting your feet wet. Although

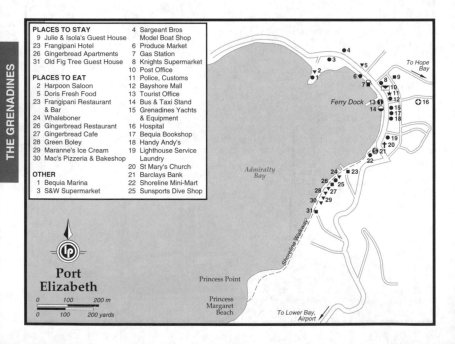

PLACES TO STAY
9 Julie & Isola's Guest House
23 Frangipani Hotel
26 Gingerbread Apartments
31 Old Fig Tree Guest House

PLACES TO EAT
2 Harpoon Saloon
5 Doris Fresh Food
23 Frangipani Restaurant
   & Bar
24 Whaleboner
26 Gingerbread Restaurant
27 Gingerbread Cafe
28 Green Boley
29 Maranne's Ice Cream
30 Mac's Pizzeria & Bakeshop

OTHER
1 Bequia Marina
3 S&W Supermarket
4 Sargeant Bros
   Model Boat Shop
6 Produce Market
7 Gas Station
8 Knights Supermarket
10 Post Office
11 Police, Customs
12 Bayshore Mall
13 Tourist Office
14 Bus & Taxi Stand
15 Grenadines Yachts
   & Equipment
16 Hospital
17 Bequia Bookshop
18 Handy Andy's
19 Lighthouse Service
   Laundry
20 St Mary's Church
21 Barclays Bank
22 Shoreline Mini-Mart
25 Sunsports Dive Shop

Port Elizabeth

0   100   200 m
0   100   200 yards

To Hope Bay

Ferry Dock

Admiralty Bay

Shoreline Walkway

Princess Point

Princess Margaret Beach

To Lower Bay, Airport

there's barely a beach here, this southerly section of Port Elizabeth is sometimes referred to as Belmont Beach.

Information

Tourist Office The Bequia Tourist Bureau (☎ 458-3286), at the ferry dock, is open from about 9 am to noon daily, as well as from 1:30 to 4 pm every day but Saturday.

Money Barclays Bank is at the north end of the shoreline walkway and the Caribbean Banking Corporation is at Bayshore Mall opposite the ferry dock. Both are open from 8 am to 1 pm Monday to Thursday and from 8 am to 1 pm and 3 to 5 pm on Friday.

Post & Communications The Port Elizabeth post office, opposite the ferry dock, is open from 9 am to noon and 1 to 3 pm on weekdays, 9 to 11:30 am on Saturday.

There are card and coin phones outside the tourist office.

Bookstore The Bequia Bookshop in Port Elizabeth is an excellent little bookstore that stocks everything from charts and survey maps to yachting books and guides on flora and fauna. It also has a small but select collection of West Indian literature.

Laundry The Lighthouse Service, behind St Mary's Church, will do your laundry for EC$20 per load.

Princess Margaret Beach

The nicest beach in the Port Elizabeth area is Princess Margaret Beach, a secluded golden-sand beach in an invitingly natural setting. To get there, take the shoreline walkway to its end; from there a dirt path climbs up over a coastal hill before ending at the beach, 10 minutes away. The path, which passes agave, yucca and air plants, is a bit steep but not too strenuous and offers some picturesque glimpses of Admiralty Bay.

Places to Stay

The aging *Old Fig Tree Guest House* (☎ 458-3201), on the waterfront, has six Spartan rooms above the restaurant of the same name. The rates are US$13/26 for singles/doubles with shared bath, US$32 for a double with private bath.

Model Boats

Bequia's shipbuilding heritage lives on through local artisans who build wooden scale models of traditional schooners and Bequian whaling boats. The boats are crafted to exact proportions, painted in traditional colors and outfitted with sails and rigging.

There are a couple of workshops opposite the waterfront on the north side of Port Elizabeth. The best known, Sargeant Bros Model Boat Shop, near the Bequia Marina, will let visitors into the workshop to watch the boats being built. The shop also does quite a brisk custom-order business, making replicas of visiting yachts for their owners. One of their best-known works was a model of the royal yacht, HMS *Britannia*, which was presented to Queen Elizabeth II during her 1985 visit.

While there are sometimes a few simpler models priced from US$100, most of the boats sell from US$400 to US$1000 and those with the finest detail cost up to US$2500. Many of the models are shipped off the island and sold to collectors. ■

Julie & Isola's Guest House (☎ 458-3304, fax 458-3812) is an old wooden boarding house that could have been torn from the pages of a Somerset Maugham novel. The 1st floor has a bar and restaurant, while the 2nd floor has simple, clean rooms with showers (cold water) and toilets that are separated from the sleeping area by a curtain. The thin wooden walls between the rooms offer no barrier to sound, so it's best to request a corner room, which has only one adjoining wall. The louvered windows have no screens, but there are mosquito nets over the beds. If you prefer comfort (hot showers) to character, Julie's also has rooms in a new cement building opposite the waterfront, just a couple of minutes walk away. Singles/doubles cost US$36/58, which includes breakfast and a three-course West Indian dinner.

The *Frangipani Hotel* (☎ 458-3255, fax 458-3824, frangi@caribsurf.com), PO Box 1, Port Elizabeth, is a delightful 15-room waterfront inn with its own dinghy dock. Owned by the family of the prime minister, who was born here in room No 1, this family home was converted into an atmospheric inn two decades ago. The 2nd floor of the old wooden main house has pleasantly simple rooms with mosquito nets, sinks and fans. Out back are some newer cottage-like 'garden units,' which have natural stone walls, king beds, private baths and sun decks. Rooms in the main house, with shared bath, cost US$30/40 singles/doubles in summer, US$35/55 in winter. The garden units cost US$100/120 in summer, US$130/150 in winter.

The *Gingerbread Apartments* (☎ 458-3800, fax 458-3907), PO Box 1, Port Elizabeth, consists of three older but tidy apartments, one beneath the Gingerbread Restaurant and two behind. The units vary, but each has cooking facilities, a bathroom and a porch. The largest unit, good for families, has a spacious living room, a main bedroom and a second smaller bedroom that's reached by walking through the first. Doubles cost US$65/90 in summer/winter. There are also six fancy new waterview

units with full kitchens and porches that begin at US$100/130.

Village Apartments offers weekly rentals in seven units on the Paget Farm road, a 10-minute uphill walk from the center of Port Elizabeth. These modern apartments have kitchenettes, fans, porches, red-tile floors and casual PVC pipe furniture; some also have air-con. There's a studio apartment for US$240/330 a week in summer/winter, one-bedroom apartments from US$300/400 a week and two-bedroom cottages going for US$400/560 a week. Reservations can be made by contacting Val or George Whitney (☎ /fax 458-3883, tvabqsvg@caribsurf.com; in the USA ☎ 800-265-3447), PO Box 1621, Kingstown.

Places to Eat
On the Walkway *Maranne's Ice Cream*, a little kiosk just north of Mac's Pizzeria & Bakeshop, has good homemade ice cream, sorbet and frozen yogurt (EC$2.50 a cone) in a variety of tropical flavors; it's open from 11 am to 6 pm daily. The *Green Boley*, in a beach shack north of Maranne's, has tasty inexpensive rotis and callaloo soup.

Mac's Pizzeria & Bakeshop has porchside dining with a view of Admiralty Bay. It's a popular spot with a full range of pizzas, from a nine-inch green olive version for EC$24 to a 15-inch lobster pizza for EC$80. You can also order a variety of whole wheat or pita bread sandwiches for EC$10 and an appetizer of Conch Mac-Nuggets for EC$15. Other items include quiche, lasagna and a recommendable rum-raisin banana bread. It's open from 11 am to 10 pm daily.

The waterfront *Frangipani Restaurant & Bar* is in the lower level of the old Mitchell house, which once served as a storeroom for the 130-foot *Gloria Colita*, the largest schooner ever built on Bequia. (Incidentally, the boat disappeared in 1940 and was found drifting in the Bermuda Triangle, with no trace of its crew!) Today the main anchorage for yachts fronts the Frangipani and its seaside bar is Bequia's foremost watering hole for sailors and expats. Until

5 pm there are sandwiches, burgers, salads and omelets from EC$10 to EC$20 or a fresh fish dish for EC$25. At dinner most main dishes are EC$35 to EC$60. It's open daily from 7:30 am to 9 pm.

The 2nd-floor *Gingerbread Restaurant* is a popular dining spot with high ceilings, gingerbread trim and a fine harbor view. At lunch there are sandwiches, omelets and pasta dishes from EC$10 to EC$20. Dinner features seafood dishes from EC$35 to EC$48 and on Wednesday and Sunday there's music by De Real Ting string band. At happy hour, from 5 to 6 pm weekdays, you can get two rum punches for the price of one. Breakfast is from 8 to 11 am, lunch from 11 am to 5 pm and dinner from 6:30 to 9 pm.

Gingerbread Cafe, at the south side of the restaurant, has cakes, ice cream, coffee and cappuccino. It's open from 7:30 am to 6:30 pm daily. There's also a daily lunch barbecue of grilled chicken, fish and burgers served outdoors from noon to 3 pm.

Vestiges of Bequia's whaling history can be found at the *Whaleboner*, where there's a bar framed with a huge piece of whalebone and bar stools that use whale vertebrae as their posts.

Elsewhere in Port Elizabeth The *Harpoon Saloon*, at Bequia Marina at the north side of the bay, is a large open-air restaurant and bar. At lunch there are burgers, sandwiches and smoked fish salads for EC$10 to EC$25; at dinner, rum chicken or catch of the day costs EC$35. There's a jump-up on Saturday from 9 pm, with a EC$10 cover charge (free to diners).

There's usually a vendor selling drinking coconuts (EC$1.50) near the ferry dock. The *produce market*, just west of the dock, is the place to pick up fresh fruit and vegetables. Simple pastries can be bought at the *Bread Basket* in the Bayshore Mall. For groceries, you'll find a handful of supermarkets on the waterfront road.

Doris Fresh Food, opposite the produce market, sells wine, cheese and fresh croissants, baguettes and whole-wheat bread.

LOWER BAY

Lower Bay is a quiet little beach community at the southern end of Admiralty Bay that's fronted by a pretty golden-sand beach and clear turquoise waters. It's one of the island's nicest beaches and has good swimming conditions.

Lower Bay has a few guesthouses, but it's a bit off the main tourist track, which adds to its appeal. This would be a fine place to hang out and play beach bum.

It's a 10- to 15-minute walk to Lower Bay from the Port Elizabeth-Paget Farm road, where you'll find the nearest bus stop. There's also a footpath leading from Princess Margaret Beach to Lower Bay.

Beware of manchineel trees that grow along some sections of Lower Bay Beach; they look like large inviting shade trees but the oils from their leaves can cause a serious rash.

Places to Stay

The 11-room *Keegan's Guest House* (☎ 458-3530) is right across from the beach at Lower Bay. Two nice rooms are Nos 8 and 9, which are big, well appointed and share a balcony with an ocean view. All rooms have private baths, fans and comfortable beds with mosquito nets. Rooms in the older wing are smaller, but even they are good value compared to most places at Port Elizabeth. Rates, which include breakfast and dinner, are from US$45/65 for singles/doubles.

Lower Bay Guest House (☎ 458-3675), a minute's walk up from the beach, has eight small, basic rooms with sink, louvered windows and shared bath. Singles/doubles cost US$26/40.

De Reef Apartments (☎ 458-3484) are five self-contained apartments, just inland of the beachside De Reef restaurant, that rent for US$300 weekly for a one-bedroom unit and US$430 weekly for a two-bedroom unit.

Places to Eat

Keegan's, opposite the beach at Lower Bay, serves breakfast (from 8 to 9:30 am), lunch (from 11 am to 2 pm) and dinner daily. At lunch you can order sandwiches for around EC$8 and chicken or fish & chips with salad for EC$22. Dinner is by reservation and usually features fresh seafood. There's a small bar.

For a local treat there's *Fernando's Hideaway*, in the village center, which serves reasonably priced West Indian dinners, including a traditional Saturday night goatwater.

At the east end of the beach is *Theresa's*, a simple little concrete hut with a handful of tables that offers moderately priced West Indian dinners, lunchtime sandwiches and burgers, and a popular Sunday afternoon jam session.

The brightly painted *Coco's Place*, on a hill at the south end of Lower Bay, is a very popular lunch and dinner spot with good, moderately priced seafood dishes. The bartender packs a mighty rum punch and when there's entertainment this is the place to be.

FRIENDSHIP BAY

Friendship Bay is a deep, beautiful bay with a nice golden-sand beach and good swimming and windsurfing. The area is quiet and caters to tourists, mostly European, rather than sailors. The waterfront is only a few minutes walk from the Port Elizabeth-Paget Farm road and it's easy to catch a shared 'dollar cab' from Port Elizabeth.

The uninhabited island of Petit Nevis, which lies about a mile south of Friendship Bay, is the site of a deserted whaling station, complete with piles of whale bones and a few rusting iron try-pots that were once used for rendering blubber. The island is a popular day anchorage with good snorkeling, though currents can be strong.

Places to Stay & Eat

Blue Tropic Hotel (☎ 458-3573, fax 457-3074), on the main road just above Friendship Bay, has 10 rather basic rooms with kitchenettes, showers, ceiling fans and balconies with partial views of the bay. Singles/doubles cost US$55/75 in summer, US$66/92 in winter.

Bequia Beach Club (☎ 458-3248, fax 458-3689), situated on Friendship Bay, has

eight attractive beachside apartments with ceiling fans, kitchens and one king or two double beds. Summer/winter rates are US$65/80.

Friendship Bay Hotel (☎ 458-3222, fax 458-3840), PO Box 9, Friendship Bay, is a pleasant 27-room beachfront hotel under Swedish management. Summer/winter rates begin at US$110/155. The hotel has a tennis court, a dive shop and a jetty. There's a beach hut and bar selling sandwiches, salads and chicken dishes for EC$16 to EC$30, and a more formal restaurant with a splendid water view and pricier fare.

GETTING THERE & AWAY
Air

Bequia's airport is near Paget Farm, at the southwest end of the island. Daily flights connect Bequia with St Vincent and the other Grenadine islands. For details see the Getting Around section at the beginning of this chapter.

Sea

Ferry The scheduled ferry between Bequia and St Vincent is not only cheaper than flying, but also usually more convenient. The docks are located in the center of Kingstown and Port Elizabeth, the ferries are generally punctual and the crossing takes only one hour.

Travelers prone to seasickness should be aware that the crossing between the islands often gets choppy midway; it's not too bad on a calm day but at other times you might want to avoid eating a large meal before hopping on the boat. Tickets are sold on board; the fare is EC$12 one way, EC$20 roundtrip.

Boats leave Bequia on weekdays at 6:30 am, 7:30 am, 2 pm and 5 pm; on Saturday at 6:30 am and 5 pm; and on Sunday at 7:30 am and 5 pm. Departures from St Vincent are at 9 am, 10:30 am, 12:30 pm, 4:30 pm and 7 pm on weekdays; 11:30 am, 12:30 pm and 7 pm on Saturday; and 9 am and 7 pm on Sunday.

For details on the cargo/passenger ferry *Barracuda*, which plies between St Vincent and Union Island, see the Getting Around section at the beginning of this chapter.

Yacht Port Elizabeth is a port of entry for St Vincent & the Grenadines. Customs and immigration, opposite the ferry dock, are open from 9 am to 3 pm. There are a couple of well-stocked chandleries in Port Elizabeth, and water, fuel, bottled gas, ice and nautical charts are readily available.

If you don't have a boat you might be able to find someone willing to take you on for shared expenses or for crew work. The Bequia Marina and the bar at Frangipani Hotel can be good spots to touch base with sailors. In addition, Mac's Pizzeria has a notice board that sometimes has a listing or two of people looking for passengers.

GETTING AROUND
The island is small and from Port Elizabeth a lot of places are accessible on foot. Three of the island's best beaches – Lower Bay, Friendship Bay and Hope Bay – are within 45 minutes walking distance.

Bus
Local transport is a system of private 'dollar cabs,' which are shared taxis that will take you on short trips for EC$1 and longer trips for EC$2. The busiest route is from Port Elizabeth to Paget Farm.

Taxi
Taxis are commonly open-air pick-up trucks with bench-type seats in the back. Taxis charge set fees and are generally distinguished from dollar cabs by a 'taxi service' sign. From Port Elizabeth it costs EC$15 to Lower Bay or Friendship Bay, and EC$25 to the airport. There are usually a couple of taxis at the airport when the flights come in.

Car, Motorcycle & Bicycle
Handy Andy's (☎ 458-3722), opposite the waterfront in Port Elizabeth, rents mountain bikes (US$15), motor scooters (US$25), Honda 250cc motorcycles (US$50) and Jeep Wranglers (US$70).

Organized Tours
There are a handful of boats that offer cruises throughout the Grenadine islands.

In addition to those in the following listing, you can usually find a few options posted on the notice board at Mac's Pizzeria or at the tourist office. Note that on all of the boats there's a bit of elasticity in the sailing schedules; boats generally don't sail if they fail to pull together enough passengers to make it worthwhile.

One of the more interesting boats is the 80-foot *Friendship Rose* (☎ 458-3202), a Bequian-built wooden schooner that once served as the mail boat between Bequia and St Vincent. The schedule varies according to demand, but each week there are typically day trips from Bequia to Mustique for US$60 and others to Canouan or the Tobago Cays for US$80. On-board lunch is included. Tours vary in length from 8½ to 11 hours.

The 60-foot catamaran *Passion* (☎ 458-3884) offers a day trip on Tuesday and Thursday to Mustique via Moonhole and Petit Nevis, with stops for snorkeling and a lunch stop at Basil's. The cost is US$60, not including lunch. On Wednesday and Sunday the boat usually makes an 11-hour trip to the Tobago Cays for US$75.

The S/Y *Pelangi* (☎ 458-3255), a 44-foot cutter with two double guest cabins, is available for private charters. Day trips cost US$50 per person, with a minimum of four people. A three-day, two-night charter costs US$800 for two people, US$1200 for four people, including meals and drinks.

Mustique

Mustique, lying 7 miles southeast of Bequia, is a privately owned island that has been developed into a haven for the rich and famous. Like the other Grenadines, this 5-mile-long island is dry and hilly. It has a population of about 800, most of whom work either directly or indirectly for those who vacation here.

Colin Tennant, a rather eccentric Scotsman, purchased the island in 1958. In the 1960s the island was planted with about 250 acres of sea island cotton but Tennant's

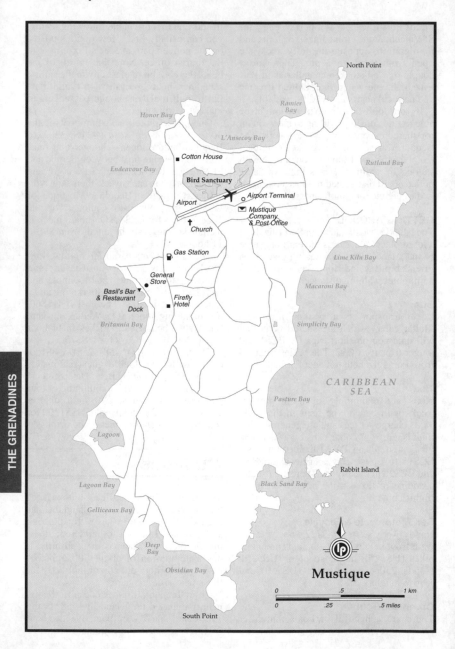

Mustique

real intent was to turn Mustique into a retreat that would appeal to his aristocratic friends. Tennant brought the island's free-roaming sheep and cattle under control and planted coconut palms and citrus trees. In 1960 he presented Princess Margaret with a wedding gift of a 10-acre house lot perched between Gelliceaux Bay and Deep Bay. Today there are 72 privately owned villas on the island belonging to people of wealth, including such celebrities as Mick Jagger and David Bowie.

Mustique has pretty much developed into the exclusive retreat that Tennant planned. The island is now under the management of the Mustique Company, which is responsible for everything from operating the medical clinic and desalination plant to providing accommodations for the Britannia Bay fishers who still live on Mustique.

The island has an irregular coastline that's richly indented with bays and coves, most of which harbor fine sandy beaches.

While there are no towns on the island, Britannia Bay is a center of sorts where Mustique's dock, general store and a handful of boutiques are located. The airport is about a mile northeast of the dock. The post office, telephone exchange and Mustique Company office are opposite the airport terminal.

There's good swimming and snorkeling along the west coast, including at Britannia Bay. Beware, however, of sharp sea urchins; they can be particularly thick on the reef running south of the dock. The Mustique Company can arrange diving and horseback riding.

Places to Stay

The *Firefly Hotel* (☎ 458-4621, fax 456-4499), PO Box 349, Mustique, sits on a cliffside overlooking Britannia Bay. Each of the four rooms has a private bath and ocean view. Once the only moderately priced guesthouse on the island, Firefly has been upgraded by new owners and the rooms now start at a more Mustique-typical US$200 a night, breakfast included. Firefly is a five-minute walk from Basil's Bar & Restaurant.

The *Cotton House* (☎ 456-4777, fax 456-5887; in the USA ☎ 800-826-2809), PO Box 349, Mustique, the island's only sizable hotel, is built around a renovated 18th-century stone and coral warehouse once used to store cotton. There's also an old stone sugar mill on the grounds and a collection of cottages. The hotel's 20 rooms have ceiling fans, verandas and pleasantly understated plantation decor. There are tennis courts and a pool and a sandy beach at Endeavour Bay is a few minutes walk away. Rates for doubles, which include breakfast, afternoon tea and dinner, begin at US$490 in summer and US$740 in winter.

The Mustique Company (☎ 458-4621; in the UK ☎ 0628-755-44, in the USA ☎ 800-225-4255), PO Box 349, Mustique, operates a rental pool that includes about 50 of Mustique's exclusive homes. As the houses are privately owned, the decor and amenities vary but each house comes with its own cook/housekeeper and most have private swimming pools. In winter, weekly rates range from US$4000 for a two-bedroom villa that can accommodate four people to US$18,000 for a lavish five-bedroom villa. In summer the prices drop by an average of 20%. Rates include the use of a jeep or similar vehicle.

Places to Eat

Basil's Bar & Restaurant (☎ 458-4621, VHF 68), a delightful open-air thatch and bamboo restaurant that extends out into Britannia Bay, is *the* place to eat (and drink) on Mustique. A more romantic setting is hard to imagine. Breakfast and lunch fare are moderately priced, while dinner features grilled fish (EC$65) and lobster (EC$85). On Wednesday night, Basil's has a lively jump-up with a steel band and barbecue buffet for EC$75.

You can pick up groceries at the general store near Basil's.

Getting There & Away
Britannia Bay is the port of entry and the only suitable anchorage for visiting yachts; immigration and customs can be cleared at the airport.

There is no scheduled passenger boat service to Mustique. There are scheduled flights from Barbados and other Grenadine islands; see Getting There & Away and Getting Around at the beginning of this chapter. For day tours to Mustique see the Bequia and Barbados sections.

Canouan

Canouan, midway in the Grenadine chain, has dry scrubby hills and near-deserted beaches. While it extends about 3.5 miles in length, in many places this anchor-shaped

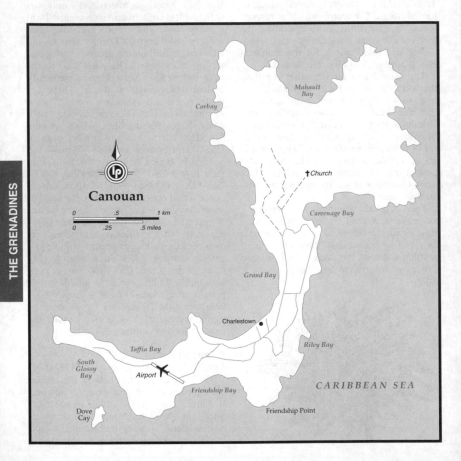

Top Left: Rastafarian woodcarver, Tobago (Ned Friary)
Bottom Left: Miss Esmie at her food stall, Store Bay, Tobago (Glenda Bendure)

Top Right: Trinidad punch (Tony Wheeler)
Middle Right: Parlatuvier Bay, Tobago (Ned Friary)
Bottom Right: Pitch Lake, Trinidad (Tony Wheeler)

Top Left: Coconut trees over the Manzanilla Mayaro Rd, Trinidad (Ned Friary)
Bottom: Snorkelers at Tobago Cays, Grenadines (Ned Friary)
Top Right: Coconuts for sale, Port of Spain, Trinidad (Ned Friary)
Middle Right: Kingstown market, St Vincent (Tony Wheeler)

island is so narrow that it can be walked across in a few minutes. There are about 700 people and at least as many goats. A large new resort development with an 18-hole golf course and luxury villas is under way at the north side of the island, so Canouan's quiet rural nature may be about to change.

Canouan's main attraction is its beautiful sandy beaches, several of them reef protected and good for swimming and snorkeling. Other than that, you can take long walks, including one to the old stone Anglican church which sits at the site of an abandoned village that was destroyed by a hurricane in 1921.

The main anchorage is in Grand Bay, where the jetty is located, while the airport is about a mile to the west. Diving can be arranged with Dive Canouan, which is based at the Tamarind Beach Hotel.

Places to Stay

The *Anchor Inn Guest House* (☎ 458-8568) at Grand Bay has three straightforward rooms in the two-story home of George and Yvonne de Roché. Singles/doubles cost US$65/95, breakfast and dinner included. It's only a few minutes walk to the beach.

The 43-room, French-owned *Canouan Beach Hotel* (☎ 458-8888, fax 458-8875), PO Box 530, Canouan, is on a nice sandy beach on South Glossy Bay. Rates, which include all meals and some water sports, cost US$135/270 for singles/doubles in summer, US$255/340 in winter. Rooms are cottage style, with air-con and patios.

The new *Tamarind Beach Hotel* (☎ 458-8044, fax 458-8851, cantbh@caribsurf .com; in the USA ☎ 800-223-1108, in the UK ☎ 1453-83-58-01) is right on the beach at Grand Bay. The 42 rooms, in three two-story buildings, have wicker furnishings, louvered doors and beachfront patios or balconies. Rates, which include breakfast and dinner, are US$180/240 in summer, US$240/300 in winter.

Places to Eat

The *Anchor Inn Guest House*, southeast of the pier at Grand Bay, offers a West Indian

dinner for EC$40 but you need to call ahead for reservations.

The *Canouan Beach Hotel* offers breakfast from 7:30 to 9 am, lunch from 12:30 to 2 pm and dinner from 7:30 to 10 pm. The French chef serves up continental and West Indian dishes with an emphasis on seafood. There are barbecues a few times a week; a band plays on Saturdays. At dinner, most meals, including lobster, are priced around EC$70, appetizer included. You'll find comparable prices at the Tamarind Beach Hotel's *Palapa Restaurant*, which serves Caribbean and Italian food.

Getting There & Away

A mail boat from St Vincent connects Canouan with the other Grenadine islands, and there are also prop-plane flights to Canouan. For information, see the Getting There & Away and the Getting Around sections at the beginning of this chapter.

Mayreau

Mayreau is a small island, 1.5 miles in length, with a population of 200. It has no airport and just one short road, which runs from the dock at Saline Bay, on the central west coast, up to the island's sole village.

Lying just west of the Tobago Cays, Mayreau is most commonly visited on sailing cruises that combine time at the cays with a sail into Salt Whistle Bay, a deep U-shaped bay at the island's northern tip.

Salt Whistle Bay is protected from rough Atlantic breakers by a long narrow arm, which in places is just a few yards in width. This gorgeous bay has clear waters, beautiful white sands, calm swimming conditions and a protected anchorage for visiting yachts. The Salt Whistle Bay Club resort, which is tucked back from the beach just beyond the palms, operates a beachside restaurant and bar open to day visitors. Beware of manchineel trees, especially near the southern end of the beach.

There are no roads from Salt Whistle Bay, but a track leads south to the village, a

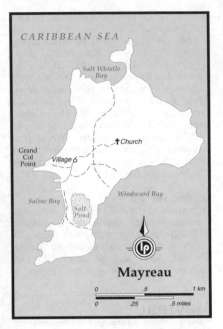

CARIBBEAN SEA

Salt Whistle
Bay

✝ Church

Grand
Col
Point

Village ⊙

Saline Bay

Windward Bay

Salt
Pond

Mayreau

0   .5   1 km

0   .25   .5 miles

20-minute walk away. The footpath begins through the gate at the southern end of the beach. The path is a bit eroded as it climbs uphill, but as long as it's dry it's easy to walk and simple to follow (if in doubt, bear to the right). The track passes cacti, is enhanced by bird song and offers some nice views near the crest. For a particularly good view, check out the hilltop stone church at the northern side of the village.

Saline Bay is where the mail boat, the M/V *Barracuda*, pulls in a few times a week. Cruise ships occasionally come into Saline Bay as well, discharging hundreds of passengers to picnic on the beach.

It's about a five-minute uphill walk from the dock to the village center. There's a sandy beach along Saline Bay and deserted beaches within easy walking distance on the east side of the island.

Places to Stay

Dennis' Hideaway (☎ /fax 458-8594, VHF 68), Saline Bay, has five rooms with private baths and oceanview balconies, above a grocery store in the village center. Singles/doubles cost US$50/70 in winter and US$35/50 in summer, breakfast included. Dennis is helpful and can arrange snorkeling tours and fishing trips.

The *Salt Whistle Bay Club* (☎ 458-8444, fax 458-8944, VHF 16/68) is a minimalist-style beachside resort with rather simple but spacious stone bungalows. The rooms vary, but all have ceiling fans and patios and most have king beds. The resort picks guests up at the airport in Union Island and shuttles them by boat to Mayreau, a 30-minute ride. Singles/doubles begin at US$200/300 in summer, US$300/450 in winter, including breakfast and dinner.

Places to Eat

The Rastafarian-run *Righteous & De Youths*, uphill in the village, is a good snack bar with pizza, rotis and West Indian food such as breadfruit and salt fish. You can eat well for around EC$20.

Dennis' Hideaway is open from 7 am for inexpensive breakfasts and lunchtime sandwiches from EC$10. Dinners served with soup cost EC$45 for conch or fish and EC$70 for lobster.

Island Paradise, run by the amiable James Alexander, is a popular eatery with good views, and homemade Creole food at prices similar to Dennis'. It's also the place to go for drinks, music and dancing.

On the other side of the island, the *Salt Whistle Bay Club*'s open-air restaurant offers a full breakfast from 8:30 to 10:30 am for EC$35. At lunch, from noon to 2:30 pm, sandwiches and salads are EC$15 to EC$35. At dinner, from 7 to 8:30 pm, a three-course meal with a choice of fish or meat main courses costs EC$75.

Getting There & Away

For information on the M/V *Barracuda*, the mail boat that connects Mayreau with the other Grenadine islands, see the Getting Around section at the beginning of this chapter.

The Captain Yannis catamaran tours from Union Island can drop passengers off at Mayreau one day and pick them up the next day at no charge other than the usual cost of the day tour. More information is under Union Island.

Union Island

Union Island, the southernmost port of entry in St Vincent & the Grenadines, is high, rocky and dry. About 3 miles in length and half that in width, the land is largely covered in thorny scrub and dotted with cacti, the consequence of decades of foraging by free-ranging goats. It has a population of 1900.

While the west side of the island reaches 1000 feet at Mt Tabor, the island's most distinguished landmark is The Pinnacle, a 738-foot plug-shaped rock face that rises abruptly in the interior of the island between Clifton and Ashton, the two main villages.

Although the terrain is mildly interesting and Union Island has a couple of reasonably nice beaches, most visitors don't come here to see Union. Instead, the island serves as a jumping-off point for cruising the uninhabited Tobago Cays and other nearby islands.

CLIFTON

Clifton is the commercial center of the island and the site of virtually all visitor-related facilities, including the marina, airport, shops and restaurants. The town is more functional than quaint.

Clifton is at the center of Union Island's thriving tour industry. Every morning, tour groups are flown in from Barbados, Martinique and other Caribbean islands, taken by bus to the dock in the center of town and then by catamaran to the Tobago Cays. In the late afternoon they sail back into the bay and are taken back to their chartered planes. While they see little of Clifton,

THE GRENADINES

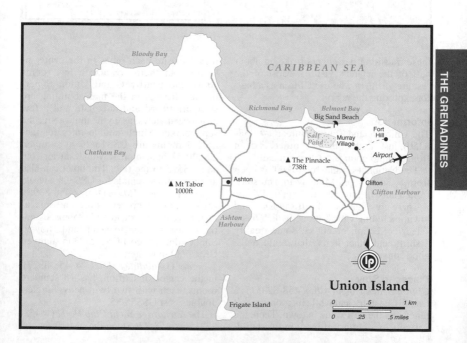

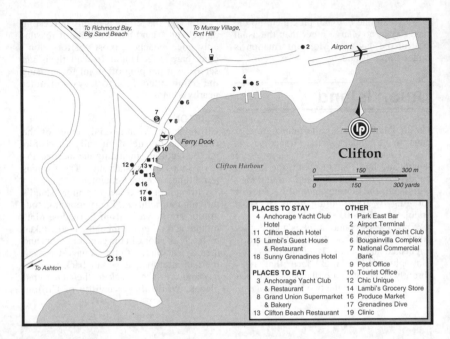

PLACES TO STAY
4 Anchorage Yacht Club
   Hotel
11 Clifton Beach Hotel
15 Lambi's Guest House
   & Restaurant
18 Sunny Grenadines Hotel

PLACES TO EAT
3 Anchorage Yacht Club
   & Restaurant
8 Grand Union Supermarket
   & Bakery
13 Clifton Beach Restaurant

OTHER
1 Park East Bar
2 Airport Terminal
5 Anchorage Yacht Club
6 Bougainvilla Complex
7 National Commercial
   Bank
9 Post Office
10 Tourist Office
12 Chic Unique
14 Lambi's Grocery Store
16 Produce Market
17 Grenadines Dive
19 Clinic

these transiting passengers make up about half of the island's visitors. Most of the rest are yachters who use Clifton as a base for exploring the region.

Information

The Union Island Tourist Bureau (☎ 458-8350), just south of the post office, is open from 9 am to noon and 1 to 4 pm daily.

The National Commercial Bank is open from 8 am to 1 pm Monday to Thursday, from 8 am to 1 pm and 3 to 5 pm on Friday.

There are a number of gift shops around town, including Chic Unique, which has a select collection of books, some quality T-shirts and other items that could make good souvenirs.

Places to Stay

Clifton Beach Hotel (☎ /fax 458-8235) is a friendly hostelry and while its rooms aren't fancy, it's the best value in town. There are 25 units in all, most of them in two build-

ings opposite each other in the center of Clifton but there are also a few rooms above the nearby Grand Union Supermarket. Rooms in the main building are straightforward and adequate and a few have ocean views, as do the units above the supermarket. Single/double rates for fan-cooled rooms are US$16/29 in summer, US$20/33 in winter. If you want air-con, add US$15 to the rate. The hotel can also arrange cottage rentals for US$300 a week.

Lambi's Guest House (☎ /fax 458-8395), above Lambi's grocery store and restaurant, has a dozen island-style rooms, essentially just a place to sleep and shower. Singles/doubles cost US$15/23 in summer, US$20/30 in winter.

Sunny Grenadines Hotel (☎ 458-8327), in the center of Clifton, has 18 standard rooms, each with two twin beds. Singles/doubles cost US$55/85.

The *Anchorage Yacht Club Hotel* (☎ 458-8221, fax 458-8365), on the waterfront and close to the airport, is Union Island's most upmarket option. The hotel caters to French tourists and visiting sailors. Rooms are comfortable with ocean-facing balconies, aircon and phones; rates are US$100/110 in the summer/winter. There are also rooms called 'cabanas' that are a bit bigger and nicer, and have similar amenities, for US$140/150. All rates include continental breakfast.

Places to Eat

The *bakery* in the back of the Grand Union Supermarket is a nice place to pick up a cheap breakfast of coconut buns and banana bread.

The *Clifton Beach Restaurant* makes a generous triple-decker club sandwich for EC$11 and serves good fresh fish and conch meals for EC$30 in an open-air setting behind the Clifton Beach Hotel, at the edge of the water.

Lambi's Restaurant, a large waterfront restaurant in the village center, is named after its friendly owner, Lambert Baptiste, as well as for the conch (lambi) shells that deck the walls. At lunch and dinner there are chicken, fresh fish and conch dishes from around EC$30.

The *Anchorage Yacht Club* has a pleasant open-air restaurant and bar on the waterfront. Appetizers cost from EC$12 for callaloo soup, while main courses range from grilled chicken for EC$36 to lobster for EC$75. During the afternoon the bar serves baguette sandwiches, pastries and croissants at reasonable prices and pizza to order. On Monday there's steel pan music and on weekends a reggae band plays.

Every third building in Clifton is a grocery store, painted in bright colors and posted with names like Kash & Karry, Pay & Take and Determination Bar & Grocery. Grand Union Supermarket and Lambi's are two of the biggest markets. Virtually all produce is imported from other islands, so prices are high.

The *Grenadines Vine Shop*, in the Bougainvillea complex, carries a good selection of imported wines, as well as other liquor and fruit juices.

ASHTON

Ashton is a quiet place that's backed by high hills and untouched by tourism. It can be worth a visit just to see what Union Island's more traditional West Indian half is like. There are a few older homes with weathered gingerbread trim and many brightly painted houses and shops, but no sights per se. In general people are friendlier and less hurried in Ashton than in Clifton.

If you want to do some exploring, there are a few hiking tracks leading into the hills above Ashton, with one of the smoother tracks beginning at the upper road on the northwest side of the village.

Places to Eat

There's a small family-run eatery in the home of Claire Adams, next to the Jehovah's Witnesses hall and post office. From Monday to Saturday she prepares a lunch of fish, baked chicken or mutton with rice, salad and provisions for EC$10 to EC$15 and on Friday and Saturday she does an evening barbecue served up with breadfruit salad for the same price.

There are also a few grocery stores around the village.

RICHMOND & BELMONT BAYS

There are two remote beaches on the undeveloped northern side of the island: Belmont Bay and Richmond Bay. The two bays are separated by a point and both have turquoise waters and powdery white sands.

Big Sand, the beach at Belmont Bay, has nice views of Mayreau and the Tobago Cays, a few cows lazing in the bush, and terns and pelicans feeding in the inshore waters. Richmond Beach, while not as scenic as Big Sand, is more protected and a better beach for swimming.

From Clifton, the walk to Richmond Beach takes about 25 minutes. Start at the road leading north from the bank; you'll pass the power plant after five minutes. About halfway the road skirts around a large salt pond that is rich in bird life. Continue along the western side of the pond and in about 10 minutes you'll spot Richmond

THE GRENADINES

Beach on the left. To get to Big Sand Beach, take the road that comes in at the right and continue for about five minutes. From Richmond Beach it's possible to continue walking along the coastal road southwesterly to Ashton, a walk of about 35 minutes.

GETTING THERE & AWAY
Air
Airlines of Carriacou, Grenadine Express, Region Air Caribbean and Mustique Airways have flights to Union Island. Details are in the Getting There & Away and Getting Around sections at the beginning of this chapter.

Sea
Details on the M/V *Barracuda*, which connects Union Island with St Vincent's other main islands, are in the Getting Around section at the beginning of this chapter.

Two very small wooden sailing boats, *Wisdom* and *Jasper*, run between Ashton and Hillsborough (Carriacou) on Monday and Thursday. The boats leave from the pier near Waterfront Trading in Ashton around 7:30 am, unload their cargo in Carriacou and then return around noon. Passengers can go along for EC$15 each way, but as you're crossing into another country you should check with immigration ahead of time. The crossing takes about two hours. Because the cargo is stored below, passengers typically sit up on deck – fun in the sun on a calm day, but keep rain gear handy to avoid getting soaked at other times.

Yacht The port of entry is in Clifton. Immigration is at the airport. Anchorage Yacht Club (VHF 16/68), midway between the airport and Clifton center, has stern-to berths for 15 boats, ice, water, fuel, showers and laundry facilities.

Other popular anchorages are Chatham Bay on Union Island's west coast and the west sides of Frigate Island and Palm Island.

GETTING AROUND
The island is small enough to explore on foot. It's less than 10 minutes' walk from the airport to the center of Clifton, and 30 minutes from Clifton to Ashton.

There are a few pick-up trucks with a double row of benches that serve as buses making runs between Clifton and Ashton for EC$2. Hotels will often pick you up at the airport if you have a reservation; otherwise, it costs EC$10 for a taxi from the airport to Clifton center.

Organized Tours
Captain Yannis (☎ 458-8513) operates three 60-foot sailboats, the catamarans *Cyclone*, *Typhoon* and *Tornado*, which account for most of the daytime sailing business from Union Island. The crews are friendly, there's a good buffet lunch and an open bar of rum punch and beer. The itinerary usually includes a stop on Palm Island, a few hours in the Tobago Cays for lunch and snorkeling and an hour or so on Mayreau, before returning to Union Island in the late afternoon. The boats generally leave Clifton around 9 am but the exact time depends on when the charter flights come in, as most passengers fly into Union Island to pick up the tour. The price is a bargain at EC$120.

Other Islands

TOBAGO CAYS
Many consider the Tobago Cays to be the crown jewels of the Grenadines. They comprise a number of small, deserted islands surrounded by coral reefs and splendidly clear turquoise waters. The islands, which are rocky and cactus studded, have tiny coves and beaches of powdery white sand.

The Tobago Cays have been set aside as a national park. Several measures have been taken to protect the area, including the installation of moorings and the enactment of prohibitions against the taking of marine life. Perhaps the biggest danger to the cays is their popularity, as the waters often get fairly crowded with visiting yachts.

The Tobago Cays have some very good snorkeling spots although the catamaran day tours don't always take in the best sites, opting instead to balance the wishes of snorkelers with those who just want to sit on the beach. There are also good breezes in the cays, making for some fine windsurfing conditions. See the preceding Union Island section for information on day trips to the Tobago Cays.

PALM ISLAND
Palm Island, a 10-minute boat ride southeast of Union Island, is a small whale-shaped island that's the domain of a private resort. The beach has long been a popular anchorage with yachters and is a stopover on many day tours between Union Island and the Tobago Cays.

Spread along the sandy fringe of this 130-acre island are two dozen cottages operated by Texan John Caldwell who took out a 99-year lease from the government back in the mid-1960s. Swamps were filled, palm trees were added to the shady casuarina trees that grow along the beach, and the island name was changed from Prune Island to the more alluring Palm Island.

At the western side of the island, where boats dock, is the picture-perfect Casuarina Beach, with sands composed of small bits of white shells and pink coral.

Places to Stay & Eat
The *Palm Island Beach Club* (☎ 458-8824, fax 458-8804) has 24 rooms in bungalows of wood and stone, each furnished with either two twins or a king bed, a private bath and a refrigerator. Rooms are airy with screened, louvered windows, a ceiling fan and sliding glass doors that open to a patio. Singles/doubles cost from US$235/350 in winter, US$165/245 in summer. Rates include meals and use of windsurfing gear and Sunfish boats. The resort also books a handful of villas and apartments.

For day trippers there's a beachside bar and restaurant with good mixed drinks and moderately priced sandwiches and burgers.

PETIT ST VINCENT
Often abbreviated to PSV, Petit St Vincent is the southernmost and smallest of the islands belonging to St Vincent & the Grenadines. This 113-acre island is fringed by white-sand beaches, coral reefs and clear waters.

The island has been developed into a single-resort 'hideaway' destination. As with Palm Island, guests must first get to Union Island. At the Union airport they're met by resort staff and taken over to PSV by motorboat, a 30-minute crossing.

While a few yachters anchor off PSV, day sails generally bypass the island and it sees less traffic than its neighbors to the north. Visiting yachts can anchor off the southwestern side of the island; there's a dinghy dock just below the restaurant.

Places to Stay
Petit St Vincent Resort (☎ 458-8801, fax 458-8428; in the USA ☎ 800-654-9326) has 22 suites in stone bungalows that are spread around the island to offer maximum privacy. The bungalows have a bedroom with two queen beds, paddle fans, a living room with tropical decor and pleasant sundecks. There are no TVs, air-con or other unharmonious 'conveniences.' In place of a phone, each cottage has a bamboo flagpole used to 'call' for room service. A creation of US expatriate Haze Richardson, the resort is considered the ultimate retreat among the Grenadine getaway islands and it has tariffs to match. Singles/doubles cost US$385/490 in summer, US$600/770 in winter, including meals and use of a tennis court, sailboards, glassbottom kayaks, Hobie Cats and Sunfish sailboats. The resort is closed in the months of September and October.

THE GRENADINES

Trinidad & Tobago

Trinidad and Tobago are the southernmost islands in the Caribbean, a mere 11km off the coast of Venezuela. Surprisingly, there's very little South American influence – instead the country draws most strongly from its British, African and East Indian heritage.

Trinidad, the dominant partner in the twin-island nation, is the Eastern Caribbean's largest and most heavily populated island. It has a mix of urban sprawl, rainforested mountains and small farming communities.

Despite its size, Trinidad is one of the least touristed islands in the Caribbean – it doesn't have the sort of beaches that attract vacationers and the capital city, Port of Spain, certainly has more bustle than charm. The island does, however, offer some of the Caribbean's finest bird watching, from flocks of scarlet ibis roosting in mangrove swamps to jungle interiors teeming with colorful forest birds. Trinidad also has the Caribbean's most festive Carnival, when Port of Spain turns into one huge street party that attracts thousands of revelers from around the world.

The 'little sister' island of Tobago, with just 4% of the country's population and 6% of its land area, stands in sharp contrast to Trinidad. There are claims that Daniel Defoe had Tobago in mind when he wrote *Robinson Crusoe*. Indeed, some visitors who trip upon Tobago these days think of it as the last undiscovered gem in the Caribbean. Tobago is pleasantly relaxed with good beaches, reef-protected waters and casual oceanside hotels. It too has rainforests with good bird watching opportunities, and in addition has excellent diving and snorkeling.

Trinidad & Tobago is often abbreviated T&T and Port of Spain is written POS for short – expect to see the latter on highway signs. 'Trini' is the common nickname for a native of Trinidad.

Facts about Trinidad & Tobago

HISTORY
Trinidad
Known to Amerindians as Lere, 'Land of the Hummingbirds,' Trinidad was sighted in 1498 by Columbus, who christened it La

---

HIGHLIGHTS

- A two-island slice of the Caribbean that's only lightly touristed
- Port of Spain's spectacular pre-Lenten Carnival festival
- Tobago's lovely white-sand beaches and affordable hotels
- Excellent birding, including brilliant flocks of scarlet ibis at Trinidad's Caroni Swamp
- Top-notch diving and snorkeling on Tobago

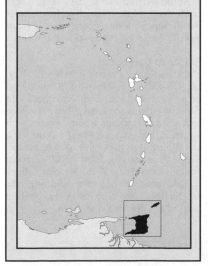

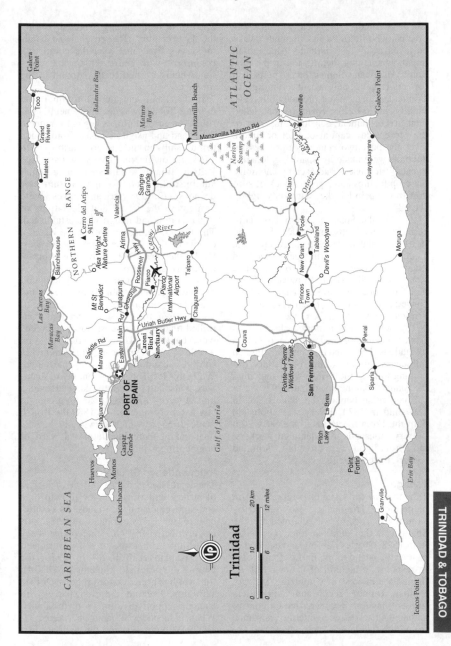

Trinidad

Isla de la Trinidad, for the Holy Trinity. The Spanish who followed in Columbus' wake enslaved many of Trinidad's Amerindian inhabitants, taking them to toil in the new South American colonies. Spain, in its rush for gold, gave only scant attention to Trinidad, which lacked precious minerals. Finally, in 1592, the Spanish established their first settlement, San Josef, just east of the present-day capital of Port of Spain. Over the next two centuries unsuccessful attempts were made by Spanish colonizers to establish tobacco and cacao plantations, but crop failures and a general lack of support from Spain left the island only lightly settled.

In 1783 the Spanish government, concerned that the British might take the island if it remained undeveloped, enacted the Cedula, a decree offering generous land grants and other incentives to encourage Roman Catholic settlers to move to Trinidad from other Caribbean islands. As a consequence, scores of settlers came to Trinidad, mostly from the French islands.

The new settlers imported slaves from Africa and established sugar and cotton plantations. The island took on many French influences but the influx of settlers did nothing to keep the British from snatching the islands from the Spanish in 1797.

The British banned the slave trade in 1807 and in 1834 slavery was abolished outright. From the 1830s to the early 20th century thousands of indentured workers, most from India, were brought to Trinidad to work the cane fields.

Tobago

Tobago's history stands separate from neighboring Trinidad's. Also sighted by Columbus, Tobago was claimed by the Spanish but they didn't attempt to colonize it. In 1628, Charles I of England decided to charter the island to the Earl of Pembroke. In response, a handful of nations took an immediate interest in colonizing Tobago. English, Dutch, French and Courlanders (present-day Latvians) wrestled for control among themselves, encountering resistance from both the native Amerindians and the Spanish on neighboring Trinidad. During the 17th century, Tobago changed hands numerous times between the competing colonizers, with entire settlements sometimes being burned to the ground in the process.

In 1704, in an attempt to quell the fighting, Tobago was declared a neutral territory. As a result pirates began to frequent the island and use it as a base from which to raid ships in the Eastern Caribbean. In 1763, following the Treaty of Paris, the British finally established a colonial administration on Tobago. Within two decades 10,000 African slaves were brought to the island and plantations of sugar, cotton and indigo were established. The French gained control of the island a couple of times in the following decades, but by the early 1800s Tobago was firmly under British control.

Tobago's plantation economy slid into decline after the abolition of slavery but sugar and rum production continued until 1884, when the London firm that controlled finances for the island's plantations went bankrupt. The plantation owners, unable to sell their sugar and rum, quickly sold or abandoned most of their land. While this left Tobago's economy in shambles, it also left most of the islanders with a plot of land – those who had no money to buy it simply squatted. In 1889 the British made Tobago, which previously had its own independent legislature, a ward of neighboring Trinidad.

Independence Struggles

The depression of the 1930s lead to a series of strikes and riots and the growth of a labor movement on the islands. As a consequence, the British granted universal suffrage, effective in 1946, and took measures to institute a measure of self-government for Trinidad & Tobago. In 1956, the People's National Movement (PNM), founded by former Oxford scholar Dr Eric Williams, became the first party with enough support to form its own cabinet. When independence came on August 31, 1962, Williams became the nation's first prime minister, a position he held until his death in 1981.

An oil boom in the late 1970s brought prosperity to the nation and helped buoy the PNM's grip on power, despite the party's growing reputation for corruption and its failure to appeal to the interests of the East Indian community. But in 1986, with the economy suffering, the PNM was defeated resoundingly by a coalition party, the National Alliance for Reconstruction (NAR). In 1989, following a period of division in the NAR, three East Indian cabinet ministers were dismissed, leading to accusations of racism in the NAR.

On July 27, 1990, members of the Jamaat al Muslimeen, a minority Muslim group led by Yasin Abu Bakr, attempted a coup. They stormed the parliament and took 45 hostages, including Prime Minister ANR Robinson, and seized the TV station and police headquarters. Bakr demanded that Robinson resign, new elections be held within 90 days and that the coup members be given amnesty.

The prime minister, who was shot in the leg after refusing to resign, was released on July 31 to receive medical attention. On August 1 the rebels surrendered after the president of the Senate, in his capacity as acting head of state, offered an amnesty to end the crisis. All in all, 30 people died and another 500 were injured in the coup attempt and during concurrent street riots that broke out in the capital.

The government immediately ruled the amnesty invalid on the grounds that it was offered under duress and announced its intention to try the 114 defendants involved in the coup. A long series of appeals, including those to the Privy Council in London and the Trinidad & Tobago High Court, ruled in favor of the amnesty and against the government.

GEOGRAPHY
Trinidad's land area is 4828 sq km and Tobago's is 300 sq km. Geographically, boot-shaped Trinidad was once part of the South American mainland. Over time a channel developed, separating Trinidad from Venezuela. The connection to South America is readily visible in Trinidad's lofty Northern Range, a continuation of the Andes, and in its abundant oil and gas reserves, which are concentrated on the southwestern side of the island facing oil-rich Venezuela.

The Northern Range spreads east to west, forming a scenic backdrop to Port of Spain. In the center of the range, above Arima, lies the 941-meter Cerro del Aripo, the country's highest peak. Much of the rest of the island is given to plains, undulating hills and mangrove swamps. Trinidad's numerous rivers include the Ortoire River, which runs 50km on its way to the southeast coast, and the 40-km Caroni River, which empties into the Caroni Swamp.

The island of Tobago, 20km northeast of Trinidad, has a central mountain range that reaches 620 meters at its highest point. Deep fertile valleys run from the ridge down towards the coast, which is indented with bays and sandy beaches.

CLIMATE
Because of Trinidad's southerly location, temperatures are equable year round. The average daily high temperature in Port of Spain is 31°C (88°F) in both January and July, while the low averages 22°C (72°F) in July and is only one degree cooler in January.

February to May are the driest months, with a mean relative humidity of 74%. The rest of the year the humidity ranges from 78% to 83%. June to August, the wettest months, average 260 mm (10 inches) of rain and 23 rainy days each month. In contrast March sees only 34 mm (one inch) of rain, with measurable precipitation on an average of nine days. These measurements are for Piarco Airport, near Port of Spain; the rainforests get significantly higher amounts of rainfall.

Trinidad and Tobago are outside the central hurricane belt and as a consequence generally don't experience the severe storms that hit the more northerly Caribbean islands.

TRINIDAD & TOBAGO

Leatherback Turtles

Leatherback turtles nest on some of Trinidad's northeast beaches and on Tobago's leeward beaches. Leatherbacks are the largest species of sea turtle. Some weigh more than a half-ton and reach up to two meters in length.

The nesting season runs roughly from March to August. Between nightfall and dawn, the female leatherback crawls up on the beach, uses her flippers to dig a hole, deposits 80 to 125 rubbery white eggs, covers the hole with sand and trudges back to the sea. After two months, the hatchlings emerge from the sand, make a mad dash for the ocean and swim away. Only a few will survive to maturity; however, the females that make it will eventually return to the same beach to lay their eggs.

During the nesting season, the Grafton Beach Resort and Turtle Beach Hotel in Tobago hold turtle watches on their beaches every night. The Pointe-à-Pierre Wildfowl Trust leads turtle-watching trips to beaches on Trinidad, and the main tour operator, Trinidad & Tobago Sightseeing Tours, offers an overnight turtle-watching outing on Trinidad's north coast.

As turtles are easily disturbed when nesting and may return to the sea prematurely if bothered, turtle watchers should remain at a distance of at least 15 meters until the turtle begins laying her eggs, be completely silent and avoid shining lights. The turtle, eggs and nest area should not be touched. ∎

Armadillo

FLORA & FAUNA

Because of its proximity to the South American continent, Trinidad & Tobago has the widest variety of plant and animal life in the Eastern Caribbean. There are more than 400 species of birds, 600 species of butterflies, 50 kinds of reptiles and 100 types of mammals, including red howler monkeys, anteaters, agouti and armadillos.

Tobago has fewer species than Trinidad but parrots and other bright tropical birds are nonetheless abundant in the mountainous interior. You can commonly spot pelicans, osprey and frigatebirds along Tobago's coast.

Plant life is equally diverse, with more than 700 orchid species and 1600 other types of flowering plants. Both islands have luxuriant rainforests and Trinidad also has elfin forests, savannahs and both freshwater and brackish mangrove swamps.

GOVERNMENT & POLITICS

Trinidad & Tobago is an independent republic within the Commonwealth. The nation is headed by a president, although political power is concentrated in the office of the prime minister. The legislature is comprised of a House of Representatives, whose 36 members are elected every five years by popular vote, and a Senate, whose 31 members are appointed by the president upon the advice of the prime minister and minority party leader.

Political parties are largely divided along ethnic lines, with the PNM being the predominant party of Afro-Trinidadians and the UNC party representing the interests of the East Indian community. The PNM, which has led the country in all but six of the past forty years, was defeated in November 1995 when it called a snap general election a year ahead of schedule. The current prime minister, Basdeo Panday of the UNC, is the country's first prime minister of East Indian descent.

Local government is divided into three municipalities, eight counties and the island of Tobago. Tobago has its own legislative assembly and since 1987 has exercised an extended measure of internal self-government in an effort to protect itself from becoming co-opted by more dominant political forces on Trinidad.

ECONOMY

Trinidad has sizable oil and gas reserves. Petroleum exports are the mainstay of the economy, accounting for nearly 50% of government revenue. Reliance upon world oil prices has led to uneven economic growth, however, and the government is attempting to diversify the economy.

Trinidad has deposits of asphalt, coal, iron ore and limestone. Industry includes the production of processed foods, fertilizers, cement, steel and electronics. The main agricultural products are sugar, rice, cocoa, citrus, coffee and tobacco.

The country is far less reliant on tourism than other Caribbean nations, although concerted efforts are being made to develop Tobago into a resort destination. Tourism, fishing and government-related work are the main sources of employment on Tobago. Unemployment is estimated at 18%.

POPULATION & PEOPLE

The population is 1,265,000, with just 51,000 people on Tobago and the rest on Trinidad. Trinidad has one of the most ethnically diverse populations in the Caribbean, a legacy of its colonial history. The majority are of African (43%) and East Indian (36%) ancestry. Most other islanders are of mixed ancestry, but there are also notable minorities of European, Chinese, Syrian and Lebanese people. In addition, a community of a few hundred native Caribs lives in the Arima area.

SOCIETY & CONDUCT

Carnival reaches its heights in Trinidad, which has the most elaborate costumes and festivities in all the Caribbean. Integral to Carnival is the music of the steel drum (pan), which was invented in Trinidad half a century ago using the hammered-out ends of discarded oil drums. Panyards, where steel drum bands practice in the evenings, are abundant around the capital and are particularly active in the weeks preceding Carnival.

Calypso, a medium for political and social satire, has roots on Trinidad, stemming back to the days when slaves would sing in patois mocking their colonial masters. The Mighty Sparrow, longtime king of calypso, is a Trinidadian native, as are many of the Caribbean's up-and-coming calypso stars.

Trinidad has a number of internationally known writers, including VS Naipaul, Samuel Selvon and CLR James. St Lucian native Derek Walcott, the 1992 Nobel Prize winner in Literature, lived in Trinidad for much of his adult life and is an active advocate for local theater projects.

Cricket is the most popular sport.

Dos & Don'ts

Dress is casual on both Tobago and Trinidad but skimpy clothing should be restricted to the beach.

RELIGION

Roughly a third of all islanders are Roman Catholic. Another 25% are Hindu, 15% Anglican, 13% various other Protestant denominations and 6% Muslim.

LANGUAGE

The official language is English. Also spoken in ethnic enclaves are Hindi, Creole and Spanish.

Facts for the Visitor

ORIENTATION

Trinidad is a large island but few visitors tour it all. Most of Trinidad's attractions – Port of Spain, the Northern Range and the

Caroni Bird Sanctuary – are in the north-west section of the island, all within an hour's drive of the airport.

Tobago's airport is in the midst of the central resort area at the southwest tip of the island and the rest of Tobago can be toured in a pleasant one-day drive.

Maps
The tourist office distributes free, reasonably good maps of both Trinidad and Tobago.

Still, if you're going to be doing a lot of exploring, the best road maps are the government Lands & Surveys Division maps of Tobago (TT$15), Trinidad (TT$23) and Port of Spain (TT$15), sold at the airport tourist office. You can also buy them in island bookstores but they're generally a couple of dollars more.

TOURIST OFFICES
Local Tourist Offices
There are tourist offices at the airports on Trinidad and Tobago, on Philipps St in Port of Spain and in Scarborough on Tobago. The airport offices tend to be the best stocked and most helpful.

When requesting information by mail, write to: Trinidad & Tobago Tourism Development Company (☎ 623-1932, fax 623-6022, tourism-info@tidco.co.tt), 10-14 Philipps St, Port of Spain, Trinidad & Tobago, West Indies. You can currently reach this office toll free by calling ☎ 888-595-4868 from the USA, 0800-960-057 from the UK, 0130-81-16-18 from Germany and 1-678-70272 from Italy.

Tourist Offices Abroad
Overseas offices of the Trinidad & Tobago Tourism Development Company are:

Canada
　　Taurus House, 512 Duplex Ave,
　　Toronto M4R 2E3, Ontario
　　(☎ 416-485-8724, fax 416-485-8256)
Germany
　　Ges Fur Tourismus und Dienstleistung
　　mbH, Am Scheleifweg 16, D-55128 Mainz,
　　(☎ 06131 73337, fax 06131 73307)
UK
　　Kevan International, 47 Chase Side,
　　Enfield, Middlesex EN2 6NB, England
　　(☎ 0181-367-3752, fax 0181-367-9949)
USA
　　247 Cedar Ave, Long Branch, NJ 07740
　　(☎ 732-728-9426 or 800-748-4224,
　　fax 732-728-9428)

VISAS & DOCUMENTS
All visitors must have a valid passport. Visas are not needed by citizens of the USA, Canada, UK or most European countries for stays of under three months.

Visas are required by citizens of Australia, New Zealand, India, Sri Lanka, Papua New Guinea, Nigeria, Tanzania and Uganda, but not of other Commonwealth countries. In most countries, visas are obtained through the British Embassy.

Foreign Embassies in Trinidad
The following countries have diplomatic representation on Trinidad & Tobago:

Canada
　　Canadian High Commission,
　　Huggins Building, 72-74 South Quay,
　　Port of Spain (☎ 623-7254)
France
　　Embassy of France, Tatil Building,
　　11 Maraval Rd, Port of Spain
　　(☎ 622-7446)
UK
　　British High Commission, 19 St Clair Ave,
　　Port of Spain (☎ 622-2748)
USA
　　US Embassy, 15 Queen's Park West,
　　Port of Spain (☎ 622-6371)
Venezuela
　　Venezuelan Embassy, 16 Victoria Ave,
　　Port of Spain (☎ 627-9821)

There are also embassies or consulates for Austria, Belgium, Brazil, China, Colombia, Denmark, Germany, India, Italy, Jamaica, Japan, Korea, the Netherlands, Norway, Panama, Sweden, Switzerland and Uruguay. The yellow pages of the phone book have addresses and phone numbers.

CUSTOMS
Visitors can bring in one quart of liquor, 200 cigarettes and gifts up to TT$1200 in value without paying duty.

MONEY
The Trinidad & Tobago dollar (TT$) is the official currency. Banks will exchange a number of foreign currencies, including British sterling, Canadian dollars, German marks and French francs, but you'll generally get slightly better rates for US dollars.

Visa and MasterCard can be used at most moderately priced restaurants, hotels and guesthouses. A few restaurants add a 10% service charge; for those that don't, a tip of 10% is standard.

Currency
One Trinidad & Tobago dollar equals 100 cents. Coins are in 1, 5, 25 and 50 cent denominations. Notes, which are colorfully adorned with birds, pan drums, oil rigs and the twin-tower Financial Complex, come in 1 (red), 5 (green), 10 (gray), 20 (purple) and 100 (blue) dollar denominations.

Exchange Rates
In 1993 the Trinidad & Tobago dollar, which had been long fixed at an exchange rate of TT$4.25=US$1, was floated on the world market. The exchange rate now fluctuates; the current rate can be found on page 4 of the *Daily Express*, the country's largest newspaper.

As we go to print, the current rate of exchange for the TT$ is:

Australia	A$1	=	TT$3.95
Canada	C$1	=	TT$4.53
France	FF1	=	TT$1.07
Germany	DM1	=	TT$3.61
UK	UK£1	=	TT$9.97
US	US$1	=	TT$6.20

POST & COMMUNICATIONS
Post
Postcards cost TT$1 to other Caribbean countries, TT$2 to North America, Europe, the UK and Australia. Letters up to 20 grams cost TT$1.25 to other Caribbean countries, TT$2.50 to the USA or Canada, TT$3 to the UK, Europe or Australia.

When addressing mail from overseas, follow the street or box number with the town and 'Trinidad & Tobago, West Indies.'

Telephone
The area code is 868, which is added in front of the seven-digit local number when calling from overseas.

There are both coin and card public phones. Phonecards are sold in TT$20, TT$60 and TT$100 denominations and can be purchased at airports, shopping malls and other public places.

More information on phonecards and making long distance calls is under Post & Communications in the introductory Facts for the Visitor chapter.

> **The area code for Trinidad & Tobago is 264.**

BOOKS
You can get a sense of the country's multiethnic culture by reading some of novelist VS Naipaul's books. Naipaul's *A House for Mr Biswas* creates a vivid portrait of life as an East Indian in Trinidad.

Former prime minister Eric Williams is author of *From Columbus to Castro*, one of the most authoritative histories of the Caribbean.

For bird watchers, in addition to the well-regarded *Birds of the West Indies* by James Bond, there's also Richard Ffrench's comprehensive *A Guide to the Birds of Trinidad and Tobago* and William L Murphy's 125-page *A Birder's Guide to Trinidad and Tobago*.

The Trinidad and Tobago Field Naturalists Club Trail Guide describes hiking trails on the islands, complete with sketch maps.

NEWSPAPERS & MAGAZINES

The *Daily Express* and the *Trinidad Guardian* are the main daily newspapers, both published in the morning. *Discover Trinidad & Tobago*, a handy full-color 100-plus-page magazine chock full of general tourist information and ads, can be picked up free at airport tourist offices.

RADIO & TV

The government-owned National Broadcasting Service (NBS) radio operates on 610 AM and 100 FM and there are a dozen independent radio stations.

There's a state-sponsored TV network (channels 2 and 13) that carries a variety of programming; AVM (channels 4 and 16), a private local network that carries US-based ABC newscasts; and CCN (channels 6 and 18), which carries CBS newscasts. All have a pretty heavy dose of US programming. Cable also carries movie channels such as HBO.

ELECTRICITY

Trinidad & Tobago has electric current of both 110 and 220 volt AC, 60 cycles. Check the voltage before plugging in anything.

WEIGHTS & MEASURES

Trinidad & Tobago has recently converted to the metric system. Highway signs and car odometers are in kilometers, but the small highway markers at the sides of some roads still measure miles and many people give directions in miles.

HEALTH

In recent years a South American cholera epidemic has spread into Venezuela, Trinidad's closest neighbor. Health officials, who believe it's possible that the disease will eventually cross into Trinidad, put the island on a health alert.

On Trinidad, the general hospital (☎ 623-2951) is at 169 Charlotte St in Port of Spain, but most expatriates prefer to use the St Clair Medical Centre (☎ 628-1451) at 18 Elizabeth St. There are smaller hospitals in San Fernando and Mt Hope, the latter near Tunapuna.

On Tobago, there's a 98-bed general hospital (☎ 639-2551) at Fort King George in Scarborough.

DANGERS & ANNOYANCES

Trinidad is not a well-regarded place for safety and visitors should be on guard. At night avoid walking around dark areas, particularly in Port of Spain. Note that the north coast of Trinidad has a reputation for smuggling and the road to Maracas Bay sometimes has armed military roadblocks and car searches.

Theft can be a problem on both Trinidad and Tobago, so be sure to keep an eye on your valuables.

There are poisonous manchineel trees at some beaches on Tobago. Trinidad has venomous bushmaster, fer-de-lance and coral snakes; however, snake bites are rare. There are no poisonous snakes on Tobago.

EMERGENCIES

Dial ☎ 999 for police, ☎ 990 for fire or ambulance emergencies.

BUSINESS HOURS

Government and business hours are generally from 8 am to noon and 1 to 4:30 pm Monday to Friday, while most shops are open from 8 am to 5 pm weekdays, from 8 am to noon on Saturday.

Most banks are open from 8 am to 2 pm Monday to Thursday and from 8 am to noon and 3 to 5 pm on Friday.

PUBLIC HOLIDAYS & SPECIAL EVENTS

Trinidad & Tobago has the following public holidays:

New Year's Day	January 1
Good Friday	late March/early April
Easter Monday	late March/early April
Whit Monday	eighth Monday after Easter
Corpus Christi	ninth Thursday after Easter
Indian Arrival Day	May 30
Labour Day	June 19
Emancipation Day	August 1
Independence Day	August 31
Christmas Day	December 25
Boxing Day	December 26

Carnival

The king of all Caribbean Carnivals is unmistakably Trinidad's. Many Trinidadians prepare for Carnival with a near-consuming devotion. From New Year's Day activities swing into full gear. The *mas camps* work late into the evenings creating costumes, the panyards are full of steel band performers tuning up their rhythms and calypso music blasts through the night at pre-Carnival jams. A week before Carnival, preliminary competitions for the King and Queen contenders get underway.

Carnival festivities begin on Monday morning, two days before Ash Wednesday, with the predawn J'Ouvert procession into the heart of the city. As the day proceeds, masquerade 'bands' hit the streets with members of each troupe wearing identical costumes. Tens of thousands of revellers parade and dance throughout the night and the event takes on the character of a massive street party. On Tuesday, the activities culminate with competitions for the Band of the Year and by midnight Carnival is officially over.

Most of the larger Carnival events take place at the Queen's Park Savannah in the center of Port of Spain, including the major steel band and calypso competitions.

Information on upcoming Carnivals is available from the National Carnival Commission (☎ 627-1530 or 627-5051), Queen's Park Savannah, Port of Spain. ■

Carnival Monday and Carnival Tuesday are also holidays in practice, with banks and most businesses closed.

Trinidad's main annual event is of course Carnival, which begins two days before Ash Wednesday, but there are a number of smaller festivals. The Pan Jazz Festival, held in November, brings together pan drummers and jazz musicians for three days of concerts.

Dates for East Indian festivals vary with the lunar calendar. The biggest Hindu festival is Divali (usually in November), followed by Phagwa (usually in March). Muslim festivals are Eid ul Fitr (usually in February or March) and Hosay (usually in June or July).

Tobago has its own lively Carnival, which runs simultaneously with the much larger festivities in Port of Spain. Tobago also has a Heritage Festival – two weeks of traditional-style festivities that begin in late July. For something quintessentially local, there's goat and crab racing in Tobago's Buccoo village on the Tuesday after Easter.

ACTIVITIES
Beaches & Swimming

Tobago has some fine strands on par with many of the Caribbean's better known destinations. There are attractive white-sand beaches at Store Bay and Pigeon Point and numerous protected bays around the island, some fronting small villages, others more secluded.

Trinidad is not known for its beaches. The island's singular favorite is Maracas Bay, a scenically set bay north of Port of Spain. There are also some undeveloped beaches along Trinidad's east coast but the shoreline is unprotected and water conditions are hazardous.

Diving

Tobago has extensive coral reefs, a great diversity of marine life and some top-notch diving. The largest concentration of dive sites is around the islets off Tobago's north coast. There are drift dives off the east side of Goat Island; rocky pinnacles and an underwater canyon off St Giles Island; and a manta ray feeding ground off Little Tobago. Elsewhere around Tobago, there's good diving at Arnos Vale, which has eels and rays, and at the Mt Irvine Wall, popular for night dives.

Tobago Dive Shops Tobago is a competitive market and you can usually find cut rates with start-up companies. Otherwise, the going rate for single dives averages US$50 with equipment included, US$40 if you bring your own gear. Multi-dive packages can lower the cost. PADI open-water certification courses are available from a number of dive shops for around US$375.

Dive companies include:

AquaMarine Dive at Blue Waters Inn in
    Speyside (☎ 660-4341, fax 639-4416,
    amdtobago@trinidad.net)
Dive Tobago, before the gate to Pigeon Point
    (☎ 639-0202, fax 639-2727)
Man Friday Diving, a Danish-run operation in
    Charlotteville (☎ /fax 660-4676)
Manta Dive, Crown Point
    (☎ 639-9209, fax 639-0414)
Tobago Dive Experience at Manta Lodge in
    Speyside (☎ 660-5268, fax 660-5030)
Wild Turtle Dive, at Pigeon Point
    (☎ 639-7936, fax 639-7232)

Snorkeling
In addition to the standard Buccoo Reef tour, you can find very good snorkeling in Tobago at Pirate's Bay on the north side of Charlotteville; at Angel Reef, off Goat Island; and in Arnos Vale Bay. Snorkel sets can be rented at various dive shops and at Pigeon Point for US$10 a day.

Windsurfing
There are spots around the southwestern end of Tobago with decent windsurfing conditions, including Pigeon Point. At the very tip of the point there's a shelter where you can rent standard windsurfing boards for US$15/40 an hour/day or high-performance boards for US$20/50. Windsurfing lessons can be arranged for US$25 an hour.

Hiking
There are several hikes on Trinidad, including trails to waterfalls, but robberies and attacks on hikers are not unknown. The trail to Blue Basin Waterfall in the Northern Range is one that should be considered unsafe unless you're on an escorted tour. One good place to get into the wilderness is at the Asa Wright Nature Centre (☎ 667-4655), which has a network of trails within its confines. Another relatively safe place to hike on Trinidad is behind Pax Guest House (☎ 662-4084) at Mt St Benedict in Tunapuna.

On Tobago, the Tobago Forest Reserve, in the north-central part of the island, has some short trails that you can do on your own and longer treks more suitable for walking with a guide. Two well-versed Tobagonian guides who lead nature walks are forestry ranger Renson Jack (☎ 660-5175) and ornithologist David Rooks (☎ 639-4276).

Bird Watching
Both Trinidad and Tobago have an abundance of bird life and superb bird watching opportunities. There are three main bird watching spots on Trinidad: Caroni Bird Sanctuary, Pointe-à-Pierre Wildfowl Trust and the Asa Wright Nature Centre. All are detailed in the Around Trinidad section of this chapter.

In Tobago, bird watching activities are concentrated in the northern part of the island where there are a couple of small resorts geared for bird watchers. Little Tobago, the island off Speyside, is the most visited bird sanctuary.

Tennis
There are tennis courts at some of the larger hotels, including the Hilton in Port of Spain and on Tobago at the Mt Irvine Bay Hotel and Blue Waters Inn.

Golf
There are 18-hole par 72 courses at the St Andrew's Golf Club (☎ 629-2314) in Maraval on Trinidad and the Mt Irvine Bay Golf Club (☎ 639-8871) on Tobago, both with golf pros, carts and club rentals. Also on Trinidad is the nine-hole Chaguaramas Public Golf Club (☎ 634-4349) in Chaguaramas and courses in Pointe-à-Pierre and La Brea.

Other Activities
In Trinidad, the Queen's Park Savannah in Port of Spain and the Arima Race Club have horse racing 28 days a year, with the main meets around New Year's and from April to June.

The main venue for cricket is the Queen's Park Oval, a few blocks west of the Queen's Park Savannah on St Clair Ave, Port of Spain.

ACCOMMODATIONS
Both Trinidad and Tobago have good-value guesthouses and small hotels. If you arrive without reservations, both islands have helpful airport tourist offices that can assist in booking rooms. Finding a room in Tobago is seldom a problem, but during Carnival season hotel reservations in Trinidad should be made far in advance.

There's a 15% value-added tax (VAT) tacked onto hotel rates and a 10% service charge. Guesthouses and apartments without housekeeping service generally do not add the service charge, although there's not 100% consistency on that. Many, but not all, hotels allow children under 12 to stay for free; if you're traveling with children, inquire when booking.

FOOD
Trinidad and Tobago have West Indian, Creole, Chinese and continental restaurants. East Indian influence prevails in the ubiquitous roti, a Trinidadian creation found throughout the Caribbean, and a similar fast food called doubles, a sandwich of curried chickpeas wrapped in a soft, flat bread. Curried meats and seafood are common local main dishes, often served with a side of pelau, a rice mixed with peas, meat and coconut.

Another popular Trinidadian fast food is shark & bake. This sandwich, made with a slab of fresh shark and deep-fried bread, is the standard at informal beachside eateries. Fried flying fish & chips is another inexpensive local favorite.

Between the large East Indian population and a sizable number of Seventh Day Adventists, vegetarian food is easy to come by on both Trinidad and Tobago.

DRINKS
Tap water is safe to drink on Trinidad and Tobago. The Eastern Caribbean's premium beer, Carib, hails from Trinidad and the island also produces a number of rums, including Vat 19 and Royal Oak.

ENTERTAINMENT
You can find steel pan music in Port of Spain year round at the Amoco Renegades Pan Theatre on Charlotte St, which has steel band performances at 6 pm on Friday. In addition, there's usually a steel band playing at one or more Port of Spain hotels on weekends. On Tobago you can catch a steel band performance a couple of nights a week at Bonkers pub in Crown Point.

Nightclubs have a quintessential local flavor; most play a combination of soca, calypso, reggae, American chart hits and a bit of Euro-techno. While the mix may be a strange one, locals find it ideal for wining, a favored dance in which men and women grind their bodies together in time to the music.

There are many clubs in Port of Spain, including *Mas Camp Pub* on Ariapita Ave, which has live entertainment most evenings, and *Club Coconuts* on St Ann's Road, near the Hilton, which attracts a college-age crowd. For a mellower scene, there's *Pelican Inn*, a cheery pub on the north side of the Hilton that's popular with expats.

There are numerous cinemas, including five in Port of Spain and one in Scarborough, Tobago. Hollywood movies are most popular, though Hong Kong kung fu and movies from India are also shown.

THINGS TO BUY
The central area of Port of Spain, especially around Independence Square, Queen St and Frederick St, is filled with malls and arcades, selling everything from spices to fabric by the yard. Some interesting locally made products that could make good souvenirs include hot pepper sauce, Trinidadian rum and Angostura bitters, the latter made from the bark of a citrus tree. A recording of steel band or calypso music makes a lightweight souvenir; you can pick up the latest tunes at Rhyner's Record Shop, which has branches at 54 Prince St in Port of Spain and at Piarco Airport.

Getting There & Away

Information on traveling between Trinidad and Tobago is in the following Getting Around section of this chapter.

AIR
Airlines
Many airlines have offices near Independence Square in Port of Spain. The LIAT and BWIA office is on Edward St, two blocks west of Woodford Square.

Airline reservation numbers in Trinidad & Tobago include:

Air Canada	☎ 664-4065
Air Caribbean	☎ 623-2500
ALM	☎ 625-1719
American Airlines	☎ 664-4661
British Airways	☎ 625-1811
BWIA	☎ 627-2942
LIAT	☎ 623-1837 on Trinidad
	☎ 639-0276 on Tobago

USA
American Airlines has daily flights to Trinidad direct from Miami and from New York via San Juan or Miami. The typical midweek excursion fare to Trinidad is around US$400 from Miami and US$500 from New York in the off season; fares are about US$150 more in the winter.

BWIA has direct flights daily to Trinidad from Miami and New York, with fares comparable to American Airlines. ALM offers a twice weekly service between Miami and Trinidad, which allows a free stopover in Curaçao, for US$400 in the low season and around US$600 in winter.

All these fares allow stays of 30 days.

Canada
Air Canada flies from Toronto to Trinidad twice weekly. The lowest midweek fare is C$614 in the low season, C$759 in the high season, for a 21-day excursion ticket.

BWIA flies from Toronto to Trinidad three times a week with fares that are comparable to Air Canada.

UK
British Airways flies to Trinidad from London every day except Friday, stopping en route in either Barbados or Antigua. An excursion ticket, allowing a stay of seven days to six months and requiring a 21-day advance purchase, costs UK£864. BWIA also has near-daily flights between London and Trinidad at comparable fares. Caledonian Airways, which has a reputation as a price cutter, flies twice weekly to Tobago from London and commonly offers discounted fares of around UK£325.

Europe
In winter BWIA has a once weekly flight from Frankfurt to Trinidad with a fare of DM2396 and a maximum stay of three months.

South America
BWIA flies daily from Georgetown, Guyana, to Trinidad for US$156 one way, US$190 for a 30-day excursion ticket.

Within the Caribbean
LIAT LIAT has nonstop flights between Tobago and Grenada and between Port of Spain and Grenada and St Lucia. In addition the airline has connecting flights via Grenada and St Lucia to the rest of its Caribbean network. The fare from Grenada to either Port of Spain or Tobago is US$93 one way, US$144 roundtrip. Between Trinidad and St Lucia it's US$142 one way and US$177 roundtrip. Note that if you're coming from or going to Port of Spain from another Caribbean country, Tobago can be included as a free stopover.

LIAT also offers good-value fares between Trinidad and some of the more distant Caribbean islands. For example you can fly roundtrip between Trinidad and St Martin on an excursion ticket allowing a seven-day stay for just US$231, about half the cost of the regular 30-day roundtrip ticket and less than the US$306 one-way fare.

BWIA BWIA has direct flights daily between Barbados and Trinidad with a one-way fare of US$121 and a roundtrip fare of

US$133 that allows a stay of up to 14 days. There are daily flights from Antigua to Trinidad for US$283 one way and US$423 for a 30-day excursion; flights four days a week from St Lucia to Trinidad for US$134 one way and US$169 for a 30-day excursion; and twice weekly flights from St Martin to Trinidad for US$274 one way and US$374 for a 30-day excursion. In addition, BWIA sometimes offers discounted seven-day roundtrip tickets for less than the one-way fare.

Airport Information
Trinidad Trinidad's only airport, the Piarco International Airport, is 23km east of Port of Spain. There's a tourist office; duty free shops selling alcohol, watches and perfume; car rental booths; and a money exchange office open from 6 am to 10 pm daily. Between immigration and customs there are courtesy phones with a direct line to a number of hotels and guesthouses. The airport has a simple café near the domestic departure gate and a more substantial restaurant at the international departure gate.

Tobago Tobago's Crown Point International Airport is a small airport with courtesy phones to hotels and car rental agents, a snack bar, a tourist information booth and a bank with limited hours.

SEA
Passenger/Cargo Boat
Windward Lines Limited has a reasonably priced passenger/cargo boat that connects Trinidad with St Lucia, Barbados, St Vincent and Venezuela. Information is in the introductory Getting Around chapter of this book.

Yacht
Trinidad and Tobago are beyond the main sweep of Caribbean islands frequented by most yachters, but there is a growing yachting industry. Chaguaramas Bay has the primary mooring and marina facilities as well as the immigration and customs office for yachters.

The Trinidad & Tobago Yacht Club (☎ 637-4260), Bayshore, has 50 berths, water, electricity, showers, laundry and a restaurant. Trinity Yacht Facilities (☎ 634-4303, fax 627-0391), PO Box 3163, Carenage, Chaguaramas Bay, has an outhaul and storage facility.

Cruise Ship
Cruise ships dock at the south side of Port of Spain, where there's a large cruise ship complex. It contains a customs hall, a few souvenir and clothing shops, car rental agencies, taxis, and a couple of local eateries. There's a smaller cruise ship facility in central Scarborough on Tobago.

LEAVING TRINIDAD & TOBAGO
There's a TT$75 departure tax and a TT$10 security fee, which must be paid in local currency. There's no departure tax when flying between Trinidad and Tobago.

Getting Around

Information on getting around Tobago is at the end of the Tobago section of this chapter.

AIR
Air Caribbean (☎ 669-2500 in Trinidad, ☎ 639-8238 in Tobago) is the main carrier between Tobago and Trinidad, with numerous daily flights making the 15-minute jaunt between the islands. The cost is US$20 each way.

BUS
Trinidad has two kinds of public buses. The ordinary service, which uses blue and white buses, is not terribly reliable and is most common in the mornings when it takes children to school and vendors to town.

The express buses, on the other hand, are quite reliable and offer a quick weekday service between Trinidad's largest cities in air-conditioned red, black and white buses. You must buy tickets before boarding from a kiosk or shop near the bus terminal. The main departure point in Port of Spain is the South Quay Bus Terminal.

From Port of Spain, express buses run to San Fernando (TT$6) via the highway and to Arima (TT$3) via the priority bus route; buy tickets at the kiosk on the north side of Bhagan's Drugs.

There's a very limited express bus between Port of Spain and the airport that's geared specifically for commuting airport workers, though travelers can take it if their schedule happens to coincide. It departs Port of Spain for the airport at 6:30 and 7 am only and returns from the airport at 4 and 5 pm only; the bus does not operate on weekends. The cost is TT$4.

If you need to know more about routes or schedules, the bus company maintains a 24-hour hot line at ☎ 623-7872.

TAXI
Regular Taxi
Regular taxis, locally called tourist taxis, are readily available at the airport, the cruise ship complex and hotels. Taxis are un-metered but rates are established by the government; hotel desks and the airport tourist office have a list of fares. Make sure you have established the rate before riding off. From the airport to Port of Spain the fare is US$20, to Maraval US$24 and to San Fernando US$31. There's a 50% surcharge after 10 pm. To call for a taxi dial ☎ 675-2424 or ☎ 669-1689 in Port of Spain.

Route Taxi
The predominant mode of transportation within Port of Spain is the route taxi. One type is a shared taxi that travels on a pre-scribed route around the city and charges TT$2 to TT$3 to drop you anywhere along the way.

The other and more common type of route taxi is the maxi-taxi, a minivan that operates a regular bus route within a spe-cific zone. Maxi-taxis operating within the Port of Spain district have yellow stripes. Those operating on the east coast have red stripes; on the south coast, green stripes; in the San Fernando area, brown stripes. Fees vary with the distance; from Port of Spain

it costs TT$1.50 to Maraval, TT$3 to Chaguaramas, Arima or Maracas Bay (the latter service is infrequent), TT$5 to San Fernando. If you're going to a Maraval guesthouse that's a little off the main road, maxi-taxis can usually drop you off at the door if you pay a double fare.

In Port of Spain, the main maxi-taxi ter-minal, known as City Gate, is on South Quay, adjacent to the public bus terminal. Route taxis to Maraval can be picked up on the corner of Duke and Henry Sts; those to St Ann's (Normandie hotel, Alicia's House, etc) leave from the south side of Woodford Square; and those to the west side of the city leave from the corner of Park and St Vincent Sts.

Outside the city center route taxis can be hailed down along the route. All taxis, including route taxis, can be identified by the 'H' on the license plate.

CAR & MOTORCYCLE
Road Rules
Driving is on the left. A home driver's license from the USA, Canada, UK, France or Germany or an International Driving Permit is valid on Trinidad & Tobago for stays of up to three months.

All gas stations are National (NP), a state-owned network. Gas is at a fixed price of TT$2.45 a liter throughout Trinidad & Tobago.

Rental
There are a number of small car rental companies on Trinidad. Prices are gener-ally high, averaging about US$60 a day with insurance and unlimited kilometers. If you're renting from an agency not located at the airport, office hours can be quite erratic even on weekdays.

AR Auto Rentals, which has offices at both the airport (☎ /fax 669-2277) and in Port of Spain in the Uptown Mall on Edward St (☎ 623-7368), has relatively good rates, beginning at around US$50 a day with insurance; weekly rates are six times the daily rate.

Other rental companies that have offices at the airport include Econo-Car Rentals

(☎ 669-2342, fax 622-8074), Singh's Auto Rentals (☎ 664-5417, fax 664-3860), Southern Sales & Service Co (☎ /fax 669-2424) and Thrifty (☎ /fax 669-0602).

HITCHHIKING

Hitchhiking is common among islanders, especially with children who hitch to and from school and with workers trying to get home at night. However, it is not necessarily a safe mode of transport for foreign visitors. Lonely Planet does not recommend hitchhiking.

As for picking up hitchhikers, be aware that young men will sometimes try to hitch a ride near major tourist sights, not so much for the ride as for the opportunity to tout their services as a guide. They can be a real pain to shake off once they've managed to hustle their way into your car.

BOAT

Ferries run daily between Port of Spain in Trinidad and Scarborough in Tobago. The journey takes about five hours and costs TT$30 one way, TT$60 roundtrip. Cabins are available for TT$80. If your travel date is near the weekend, it's wise to book as far in advance as possible.

The boat departs from Port of Spain at 2 pm Monday through Friday and at 11 am on Sunday. It departs from Scarborough for Port of Spain at 11 pm Sunday through Friday. There are generally no passenger ferries on Saturday, except in August, around Carnival and at Easter. Be sure to arrive at least two hours before sailing or your ticket can be resold.

For more information call the Port Authority (☎ 625-3055 or 625-4906 on Trinidad, ☎ 639-2417 on Tobago).

ORGANIZED TOURS
Sightseeing Tours

You can arrange island tours with individual taxi drivers. For an all-day round-the-island tour, drivers will generally ask about US$160, though you should be able to negotiate that down by about 25%.

Trinidad & Tobago Sightseeing Tours (☎ 628-1051), 12 Western Main Rd, St

James, Port of Spain, offers a variety of full-day tours, each for US$55. One is a circle-island tour that skirts the perimeter of Trinidad; a second combines Asa Wright Nature Centre and the north coast, taking in a couple of hours of bird watching and some of Trinidad's most dramatic scenery; and a third tour heads south, visiting Pitch Lake and the wildfowl trust in Pointe-à-Pierre. In addition, there are shorter tours, such as the Caroni Bird Sanctuary boat tour to see scarlet ibis (US$34) and a three-hour Port of Spain city tour (US$25). From March through midsummer, there's also an overnight 'turtle watching adventure' (US$135) to Grand Riviere, on Trinidad's north coast, which involves a stroll along the beach to search for nesting leatherback turtles.

Other tour companies in Port of Spain include Legacy Tours (☎ 623-0150), 7 Wrightson Rd, and The Travel Centre (☎ 625-1636), 44 Edward St.

Ecotourism

Those interested in piecing together an organized 'ecotour,' whether it be bird watching, rainforest tours or just general environmental and cultural appreciation outings, will find a number of recommendable tour guides on Trinidad and Tobago.

Perhaps the most renowned is David Rooks Nature Tours (☎ /fax 639-4276), PO Box 348, Scarborough, Tobago. Rooks is president of the Trinidad & Tobago Field Naturalist Club and has worked on BBC and PBS nature programs.

Other recommendable ecotourism operators on Tobago include: Pat Turpin (☎ 660-4327, fax 660-4328), Man-O-War Bay Cottages, Charlotteville Estate; and Hubert 'Renson' Jack (☎ 660-5175), c/o Division of Agriculture and Forestry, Scarborough.

On Trinidad, David Rooks' son, Courtenay Rooks (☎ 622-8826, fax 628-1525, rookstours@fm1.wow.net), 44 La Seiva Rd, Maraval, Trinidad, operates similarly minded ecotours. Other ecotourism operators on Trinidad include: Pax Nature Tours (☎ /fax 662-4084), Mount St Benedict,

Tunapuna; and South East Eco Tours (☎ 644-1072), Fuentes St, Rio Claro.

Port of Spain

Port of Spain, the country's capital and commercial center, is a bustling metropolitan hub of some 300,000 people. It's not a tourist city – the handful of hotels are geared for business travelers and the attractions are few in number.

The center has a mingling of modern office buildings, old corrugated tin stalls and 19th-century colonial buildings – some are worth a look, but few rate as must-see sights.

The south end of Frederick St is the central shopping area, vibrant and congested, with both labyrinthine pedestrian arcades and air-conditioned indoor malls. Along the street, vendors hawk fruit and jewelry between police patrols.

The pulse of the city is Independence Square – not really a square at all, but rather two long streets bordering a narrow pedestrian strip. At Independence Square you can pick up a taxi and find travel agents, banks and cheap eats.

Strolling around Port of Spain in the day you're apt to be approached by panhandlers, and at night it's simply not safe to walk in many areas. Still Port of Spain is not an unfriendly city and it can be interesting poking around.

Port of Spain is at its best and brightest during Carnival. If you happen to be in the city in the weeks preceding Carnival, be sure to take a look into some of the many mas camps where artists create colorful costumes and visit the panyards where local steel bands diligently practice their rhythms for the upcoming festivities.

Information

Tourist Office The tourist office (☎ 623-1932), 10-14 Philipps St, is open from 8 am to 4 pm Monday to Friday.

Money There are numerous banks on Independence Square. The Bank of Commerce is open from 8 am to 2 pm Monday to Thursday, from 8 am to 1 pm and 3 to 5 pm on Friday and has a 24-hour ATM.

Post The general post office, on Wrightson Rd opposite the Holiday Inn, is open Monday to Friday from 7 am to 5 pm.

Bookstores You can get maps and books on the region at Trinidad Book World, on Queen St opposite the cathedral, and at the nearby Metropolitan Book Suppliers, upstairs in the Colsort Mall on Frederick St.

Travel Agents There are a number of travel agents at the west end of Independence Square; Constellation Tours (☎ 623-9269), 1 Richmond St, has excursion deals to the neighboring islands. If you're taking the M/V *Windward* to Venezuela or Barbados, you can buy tickets at Global Steamship Agencies on Wrightson Road.

Pharmacy Bhagan's Drugs (☎ 627-5541) on Independence Square South is open daily until 11 pm (9 pm on Sunday).

National Museum & Art Gallery

The National Museum & Art Gallery is in a classic colonial building at the corner of Frederick and Keate Sts. There are simple displays on rocks, shells, colonial agriculture and oil exploration; a room full of Carnival costumes; and paintings by Trinidadian artists John Newel Lewis and Jackie Hinkson.

The presentation is a bit lacking, but the museum is free. It's open from 10 am to 6 pm Tuesday to Saturday and you'll have to check your bags and camera at the door.

Woodford Square

Woodford Square is a public park with benches, pigeons, gospel preachers and a fair number of people just hanging out. Surrounding the park are some interesting buildings, including **Red House**, the imposing red parliament building constructed in 1906 in Renaissance style; the contemporary steel-and-concrete **Hall of Justice**; and the public **library**, circa

1901. Behind Red House is the shell of the **police station** burned in the 1990 coup attempt; one little corner at the end of Hart St is still used by the police.

Holy Trinity Cathedral
This majestic Anglican church, at the south side of Woodford Square, dates from 1818, seats 1200 and has a Gothic design. Its impressive ceiling is supported by an elaborate system of mahogany beams, whose design is said to have been modeled on London's Westminster Hall. There are also stained glass windows that open to the breeze and a marble monument to Sir Ralph Woodford, the British governor responsible for the church's construction.

Queen's Park Savannah
The city is crowned by Queen's Park Savannah, once part of a sugar plantation and now a public park with a race track. Largely an expansive grassy field, the park itself is not particularly interesting but there are some sights along its perimeter. In the park's northwest corner there's a small rock garden with a lily pond and benches. The road circling the park has one-way traffic, flowing in a clockwise direction.

Magnificent Seven
Along the west side of the Queen's Park Savannah is the Magnificent Seven, a line of seven fancy colonial buildings constructed in the late 19th and early 20th centuries. From south to north, they are: the Queen's Royal College, of German Renaissance design; Hayes Court, the Anglican bishop's residence; two private homes; the Catholic archbishop's residence; stately White Hall, the prime minister's office; and Stollmeyer's Castle, built to resemble a Scottish castle complete with turrets.

Emperor Valley Zoo
Just north of Queen's Park Savannah is the Emperor Valley Zoo, which has some local creatures, including colorful tropic birds, ocelots, monkeys, scarlet ibis, red brocket deer and various snakes, as well as a few large exotics, such as tigers and lions. The

park is open from 9:30 am to 6 pm daily. Admission is TT$4 for adults, TT$2 for children ages three to 12.

Botanical Gardens
East of the zoo are the botanical gardens, which date from 1820 and have grand trees and attractive strolling paths (not safe after dark). The President's House, a mansion originally built as the governor's residence in 1875, is adjacent to the gardens, as is the prime minister's residence.

City Views
The Hilton hotel offers a rather good view of the city. If you want a higher perch you could drive up to Fort George, the site of a former British signal station, 4km northwest of the city at the end of Fort George Rd.

Places to Stay
While there are reasonable accommodation options in the heart of the city, many visitors to the capital stay at the quieter north end, where most of the hotels are located, or in Maraval, a rather cushy suburb a couple of kilometers farther north, which has some guesthouses.

Town Center The *YWCA* (☎ 627-6388), 8 Cipriani Blvd, a couple of blocks south of Queen's Park Savannah, is central and has simple double rooms for women only at US$15 per person.

Trinbago (☎ 627-7114), 37 Ariapita Ave, is a small guesthouse with six simple rooms. It's on a heavily trafficked street and there are open ventilation cuts on the upper walls so mosquitoes and noise could be an issue – but singles/doubles cost just US$14/22 with shared bath, while a double with a private bath costs US$28.

La Calypso (☎ 622-4077 or 622-6430, fax 622-6895), 46 French St, is a recommendable guesthouse for those on a budget. It has 18 freshly painted rooms, each with a phone and either a fan or air-con. The new management is helpful and friendly; breakfast is available for US$4 and there are good restaurants within walking distance. Singles/doubles cost US$16/25 with shared

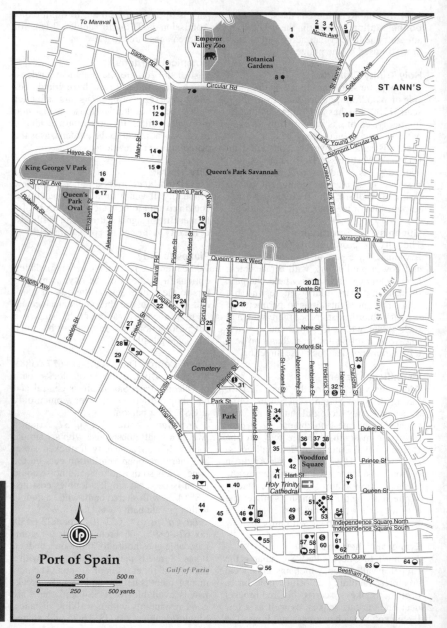

To Maraval
Saddle Rd
Emperor
Valley Zoo
Botanical
Gardens
Nook Ave
St Ann's Rd
Coblentz Ave
ST ANN'S
Circular Rd
Hayes St
Mary St
King George V Park
Queen's
Park
Oval
St Clair Ave
Roberts St
Elizabeth St
Alexandra St
Ariapita Ave
Gallus St
Luis St
French St
Maraval Rd
Tragarete Rd
Picton St
Woodford St
Cipriani Blvd
Queen's Park West
Queen's Park West
Queen's Park Savannah
Lady Young Rd
Belmont Circular Rd
Queen's Park East
Jerningham Ave
St Ann's River
Keate St
Gordon St
New St
Oxford St
St Vincent St
Abercromby St
Pembroke St
Frederick St
Henry St
Charlotte St
Colville St
Wrightson Rd
Cemetery
Phillips St
Victoria Ave
Park St
Park
Richmond St
Edward St
Duke St
Prince St
Woodford
Square
Hart St
Holy Trinity
Cathedral
Queen St
Independence Square North
Independence Square South
South Quay
Beetham Hwy
Gulf of Paria
Port of Spain
0   250   500 m
0   250   500 yards

TRINIDAD

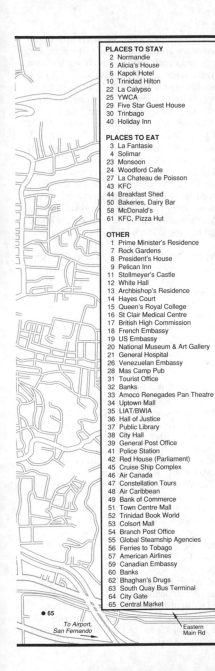

PLACES TO STAY
2 Normandie
5 Alicia's House
6 Kapok Hotel
10 Trinidad Hilton
22 La Calypso
25 YWCA
29 Five Star Guest House
30 Trinbago
40 Holiday Inn

PLACES TO EAT
3 La Fantasie
4 Solimar
23 Monsoon
24 Woodford Cafe
27 La Chateau de Poisson
43 KFC
44 Breakfast Shed
50 Bakeries, Dairy Bar
58 McDonald's
61 KFC, Pizza Hut

OTHER
1 Prime Minister's Residence
7 Rock Gardens
8 President's House
9 Pelican Inn
11 Stollmeyer's Castle
12 White Hall
13 Archbishop's Residence
14 Hayes Court
15 Queen's Royal College
16 St Clair Medical Centre
17 British High Commission
18 French Embassy
19 US Embassy
20 National Museum & Art Gallery
21 General Hospital
26 Venezuelan Embassy
28 Mas Camp Pub
31 Tourist Office
32 Banks
33 Amoco Renegades Pan Theatre
34 Uptown Mall
35 LIAT/BWIA
36 Hall of Justice
37 Public Library
38 City Hall
39 General Post Office
41 Police Station
42 Red House (Parliament)
45 Cruise Ship Complex
46 Air Canada
47 Constellation Tours
48 Air Caribbean
49 Bank of Commerce
51 Town Centre Mall
52 Trinidad Book World
53 Colsort Mall
54 Branch Post Office
55 Global Steamship Agencies
56 Ferries to Tobago
57 American Airlines
59 Canadian Embassy
60 Banks
62 Bhaghan's Drugs
63 South Quay Bus Terminal
64 City Gate
65 Central Market

● 65

To Airport,
San Fernando

Eastern
Main Rd

bath, US$25/30 with a private bath. Kitchenette units are available for a few dollars more.

The *Five Star Guest House* (☎ /fax 623-4006), 7 French St, has 16 basic but clean rooms, each with a sink; bathrooms are in the hall. Singles/doubles cost US$20/30.

Alicia's House (☎ 623-2802, fax 623-8560), 7 Coblentz Gardens, is a modern 14-room guesthouse in an upmarket residential neighborhood north of Queen's Park Savannah. Rooms have refrigerators, ceiling fans, private baths, phones, air-con and TV. There's a pool and jacuzzi out back and overall the place is quite nice, if not as personable as some of the smaller family-run guesthouses. Singles/doubles start from US$30/45; optional breakfast is US$8 per person more.

The *Kapok Hotel* (☎ 622-6441, fax 622-9677), 16 Cotton Hill, a popular business hotel at the south end of Saddle Rd, has 71 rooms with rattan furnishings, TV, phones and air-con. Singles/doubles cost US$76/89; add US$3 more if you want a kitchenette. There's a pool, restaurant and computer room.

The 54-room *Normandie* hotel (☎ 624-1181, fax 624-0108), 10 Nook Ave, has a relaxed, old-fashioned style. The rooms are pleasant, if a bit pricey, and most face a central courtyard and pool. Standard rooms have a double bed, air-con and phone, while superior rooms have two double beds and a bit more space. Singles/doubles cost US$62/72 for standard rooms, US$77/87 for superior rooms and US$87/97 for loft units with two bedrooms.

The *Holiday Inn* (☎ 625-3366, fax 625-4166; in the USA ☎ 800-465-4329) on Wrightson Rd has a central city location opposite the cruise ship complex. It has 235 large rooms with balconies and standard amenities. Some of the floors have been recently renovated and other are not as spiffy, so it's a good idea to see the room before settling on it. There's a pool, exercise room, a couple of on-site restaurants and free parking. Singles/doubles cost US$99/109 but there are often specials that include breakfast for a couple of dollars less.

The 394-room *Trinidad Hilton* (☎ 624-3211, fax 624-4485), PO Box 442, Lady Young Rd, is Trinidad's largest and most upscale hotel. It has a hillside location with a sweeping city view across Queen's Park Savannah. While not one of the more distinguished hotels in the Hilton chain, it does have a swank facade and large, modern rooms, most with balconies and good views. Rates begin at US$175. There are a couple of restaurants and a very large pool.

Maraval *Monique's Guest House* (☎ 628-3334, fax 622-3232), 114 Saddle Rd, Maraval, has two different setups. In the original guesthouse there are 10 pleasant rooms with two single or double beds, private baths, air-con, phones and TV. Singles or doubles cost US$45, triples US$50. In their new hillside building there are 10 large studio rooms that have two king beds and the addition of toaster ovens, hot plates, refrigerators and balconies. At just US$10 more these are a particularly good deal and close enough to the hills that you can sometimes spot parrots in the tree tops. At Carnival time, all units have a five-night rate of US$650. Monique's is on Saddle Rd, 3km north of Queen's Park Savannah.

Carnetta's House (☎ 628-2732, fax 628-7717), 28 Scotland Terrace, Maraval, also has two separate but neighboring buildings. In total there are 11 rooms; all are comfortable and have air-con, cable TV, phones and private baths. Five rooms are at the home of Winston and Carnetta Borrell, in a quiet neighborhood off Saddle Rd. Six new rooms, most of which have kitchenettes, are right on Saddle Rd, opposite Monique's. Rates in either building begin at US$45 for two people; add US$10 more for a room with a kitchenette. There are plans to open a riverside bar and provide simple Creole meals. Winston, a military reserve commander and former tourist board director, enjoys helping guests plan their daily outings.

The 14-room *Tropical Hotel* (☎ 622-5815), 6 Rookery Nook, Maraval, is a handsome colonial-style stone building in an upscale neighborhood, 1km north of the Savannah. Rooms are straightforward but large and comfortable enough, each with a private bath, air-con and phone. Singles/doubles cost US$50/60. The hotel has a pool and restaurant and is within walking distance of other places to eat.

The 68-unit *Royal Palm Suite Hotel* (☎ 628-5088, fax 628-6042), 7 Saddle Rd, Maraval, is at the rear of a shopping center, half a kilometer north of KFC. This is a modern, if somewhat impersonal, place, with large air-conditioned suites that have queen-size beds, kitchens and living rooms from US$100/110 for singles/doubles. There are also some smaller rooms without kitchens for US$65/75.

Airport Area If you have some dire need to be close to the airport, the overpriced 58-room *Bel Air International Airport Hotel* (☎ 664-4771, fax 664-4771) is half a kilometer from the terminal. Rooms are basic and not very cheery, but they do have air-con, phones and private baths. There's a restaurant, a pool and free transport to and from the airport. Singles/doubles begin at US$56/73.

Places to Eat – budget

Pick-up trucks piled high with chilled drinking coconuts (TT$2) can be found along the road that circles Queen's Park Savannah; after sunset they're joined by vendors selling raw oysters and other snacks. There's a supermarket south of Town Centre Mall in the city center.

For Western fast food there are a couple of *KFC* eateries in the city center, one on Henry St and another two blocks south on Independence Square South. The latter also doubles as a *Pizza Hut*; a personal pan pizza or two-piece chicken snack meal costs TT$13. There's a *McDonald's* a block to the west.

A better bet is to walk over to the other side of Independence Square, where you'll find a run of *bakeries* selling TT$5 take-out rotis, meat pies and various pastries. On the same block as the bakeries is the *Dairy Bar*, which has TT$5 ice cream cones.

A handy spot for a quick, cheap sit-down lunch is Town Centre Mall, 20 Frederick St, which has a tidy 2nd-floor food court with about a dozen fast-food stalls encircling a central dining area. *Carmen's Cuisine* has tasty Creole dishes and nice salads, while *Lisa's Indian Cuisine* cooks good Indian rotis to order. Other choices range from Chinese and Italian to burgers. You can easily get a hearty lunch for TT$15. The food court is open from 10 am to 5 pm weekdays, until 2 pm on Saturday. The basement of the nearby Colsort Mall also has some simple, inexpensive eateries.

The *Breakfast Shed*, literally a tin shed at the west side of the cruise ship complex, is a good place to rub shoulders with locals. Everything is made from scratch by island women who set up their cookstoves around the perimeter of the shed. A big meal of Trinidadian fare, including fish, dasheen, plantains and rice, costs TT$15 and is served from 10:30 am to about 3 pm – try to arrive before 2 pm as the food sometimes runs out early.

For a good-value meal, *Monsoon*, on the corner of Tragarete Rd and Picton St, has East Indian food that's served from steamer trays but kept fresh, particularly at mealtimes. Both the food and atmosphere are pleasant. The most common meal includes a choice of three vegetables plus curried chicken, either wrapped in a dhal roti or served on a plate with rice, for TT$16. There are also vegetarian and seafood options. It's open from 11 am to 10 pm Monday to Saturday. *Woodford Cafe*, a sister restaurant, on the same block at 62 Tragarete Rd, has good Caribbean food, the same hours and similar prices.

Places to Eat – top end

For an atmospheric treat, there's *La Chateau de Poisson*, 38 Ariapita Ave. This quality French-Creole restaurant has a charming setting in a gingerbread-trimmed colonial house. At lunch, weekdays from 11:30 am to 2:30 pm, there's a TT$50 buffet that includes soup, salad, seafood dishes, vegetables and desserts. At dinner, served from 6:30 pm daily except Sunday,

starters average TT$25, while main dishes include the likes of squid au gratin, crawfish gumbo or crab-stuffed snapper for around TT$70.

La Fantasie at the side of the Normandie hotel features 'nouvelle Creole' cuisine in its brightly painted dining room or alfresco on the terrace. There's a soup-to-dessert business lunch on weekdays for TT$55 and reasonably priced sandwiches, pasta and salads at the adjacent café. At dinner there's an à la carte menu with main dishes ranging from TT$40 for chicken to TT$100 for lobster thermidor. It's open from noon to 2 pm and from 6 to 10 pm.

Solimar (☎ 624-6267), 6 Nook Ave, near the Normandie hotel, is an innovative restaurant run by an Englishman, Joe Brown, a well-traveled former chef for the Hilton chain. Solimar features a changing menu of international dishes, priced from TT$65 to TT$150, which on any given night might include Asian, Indian and Italian food. It's open for dinner Tuesday to Saturday from 6:30 pm.

Around Trinidad

MARACAS BAY

Maracas Bay, Trinidad's most popular beach, makes a nice outing from Port of Spain. Not only is the beach quite lovely but the views along the way make for a very scenic drive, just 40 minutes from the capital. The North Coast Rd, which begins north of Maraval, climbs up over the mountains through a lush tropical forest of tall trees, ferns and bamboo. When you reach the north coast there's a stunning cliffside view before the road descends to the coast.

Maracas Bay has a broad sandy beach, a small fishing hamlet at one side and a backdrop of verdant mountains. The waters can be flat in the summer, but at other times the bay usually has good waves for bodysurfing. There's a lifeguard, changing rooms, showers, picnic shelters and huts selling inexpensive shark and bake sandwiches. On weekends the beach gets pretty crowded but the rest of the week it can feel almost deserted.

Tyrico Bay, just to the east of Maracas Bay, is quieter and less commercial. **Las Cuevas**, 8km east of Maracas Bay, is a pretty U-shaped bay with a nice brown-sand beach; there's surfing at its west end and calmer conditions at the center.

From Las Cuevas it's possible to continue over the mountains to Arima but it's a long, lonely road. You'd actually save time by going back to Port of Spain and taking the highway to Arima.

CHAGUARAMAS

Chaguaramas, on the northwestern end of the island, was the site of a major US military installation during WWII and now has a small golf course and a few other minor attractions. It's about a 30-minute drive from the capital.

Gasper Grande, an island at the south side of Chaguaramas Bay, has a cave with stalactites and stalagmites that can be toured from 9 am to 2:30 pm daily (TT$10). Boats to the island can be arranged at the Island Homeowners' jetty on the west side of Chaguaramas; expect to pay about TT$25 per person.

Places to Eat

A good place to have a drink or a reasonably priced seafood meal is *Anchorage* on Point Gorde Rd, which has a fine waterfront location.

MT ST BENEDICT

On the hillside north of Tunapuna there's a Benedictine monastery with a secluded guesthouse and a pleasant wooded setting. The monastery itself isn't a major sight; the area is of most interest to people who want to stay or eat at the guesthouse or hike into the rainforest.

The thickly wooded hills behind the monastery are habitat for hawks, owls and numerous colorful forest birds, as well as the occasional monkey. The area is considered one of the safest for hiking on Trinidad. A favorite track is the Donkey Trail, which offers good birding and takes just a couple of hours to walk roundtrip from the guesthouse.

To get there from Tunapuna, take St John's Rd north 3.3km from Eastern Main Rd. During the day there's a bus service to the monastery roughly every 30 minutes from the corner of Eastern Main Rd and St John's Rd.

Places to Stay & Eat

Pax Guest House (☎ /fax 662-4084), Tunapuna, is a restored colonial house owned by the monastery. This pleasantly relaxed place has long been a favored destination for bird watchers but it's a fine choice for anyone looking for a peaceful retreat. There are 18 rooms with teak floorboards, washbasins and fine views. Some have two twin beds, others have antique four-poster queen-size beds. Bathrooms are shared. Singles/doubles cost US$45/75, including breakfast and a multi-course dinner. The helpful management treats guests like family.

Non-guests can have a full breakfast for TT$15 or lunch for TT$30, or just come up for a delightful afternoon tea with scones or Trinidadian sweet bread for TT$15. Reservations are appreciated for the meals but are not necessary for tea, which is served from 3 to 6 pm.

ASA WRIGHT NATURE CENTRE

The Asa Wright Nature Centre is a former cocoa and coffee plantation that has been turned into an 80-hectare nature reserve. Located amidst the rainforest in the Northern Range, the center has attracted naturalists from around the world since it was founded in 1967. There's a lodge catering to birding tour groups, a research station for biologists and a series of hiking trails on the property.

A wide range of bird species inhabit the area, including blue-crowned motmots, chestnut woodpeckers, palm tanagers, channel-billed toucans, blue-headed parrots, 10 species of hummingbirds and numerous raptors. The sanctuary encompasses Dunston Cave, which is home to a breeding colony of the elusive nocturnal guacharo, or oilbird.

The trail network starts at the main house and branches out through the property. The Bellbird Trail is a recommended lightly trodden path with rewarding sightings that might include the bearded bellbird, ochre-bellied flycatcher and red-crowned ant tanger. Day visitors can join guided walks along the center's trails for US$6; reservations should be made at least 24 hours in advance. A variety of seminars and field trips are also offered, most geared for people staying at the center's lodge.

Asa Wright Nature Centre is about a 1½-hour drive from Port of Spain. At Arima, head north on Blanchisseuse Rd for 12km, turning left into the center after the 7½ mile marker.

Places to Stay & Eat

Asa Wright Nature Centre and Lodge (☎ 667-4655, in the USA ☎ 800-426-7781), PO Box 4710, Arima, has 24 rooms, some in the weathered main house and others in nearby cottages, all quite simple but with private baths. Singles/doubles cost US$107/162 in summer, US$139/210 in winter, including three ample meals a day, tax and service charge. Airport transfers can be arranged for US$40 per person roundtrip.

Non-guests can eat at the lodge, but reservations need to be made 48 hours in advance.

EAST COAST

Trinidad's east coast is wild and rural, a mix of lonely beaches with rough Atlantic waters, mangrove swamps and coconut plantations. The east coast is most logically included in a circle-island drive, a pleasant enough day outing but certainly not a must-do excursion – in fact, you may not encounter another tourist along the entire route.

To get to the east coast from Port of Spain, head east on the Churchill Roosevelt Highway (avoid the Eastern Main Rd between Port of Spain and Arima, a horribly congested route). At Waller Field the highway will merge with the Eastern Main

Rd and highway signs will guide you through the town of Sangre Grande and south to Manzanilla.

The Manzanilla Mayaro Rd, which runs along the east coast, is narrow but only carries light traffic. Except for the occasional pothole and some precarious-looking wooden bridges, the road is in reasonably good condition. There are free-roaming cows and water buffaloes and you can easily spot vultures, egrets and herons along the way. In places, coconut palms and orange heliconia line the roadside.

The main east-coast beach, **Manzanilla Beach**, has brown sand, palm trees and white beach morning glory. The winds are often strong and the waters tempestuous.

The road continues south, skirting a freshwater swamp much of the way, and crosses the meandering **Nariva River** a couple of times.

After crossing the **Ortoire River**, Trinidad's longest river, there are a couple of small settlements with simple wooden houses on stilts and then you'll reach the town of **Pierreville**, where a sign points west to San Fernando, 56km away.

SOUTH-CENTRAL TRINIDAD

The south-central part of Trinidad is heavily populated, largely by the descendants of East Indians brought to the island to work the plantations after the abolition of slavery. In time the laborers came to own much of the land. The towns now have a decidedly East Indian appearance, from the style of the homes to the roadside temples and mosques.

The countryside is tame with undulating hills and is planted with citrus, coffee, cocoa and bananas. In **Rio Claro**, there's a Muslim mosque, a couple of bakeries, a central produce market and a Hindu temple along the main road.

If you're curious you can check out **Devil's Woodyard**, one of the island's dozen 'mud volcano' sites where small mounds of mud have built up as a result of gases released from the earth. Hindustan Rd, a narrow cane road, leads 3.5km south from the highway to Devil's Woodyard;

TRINIDAD

the turn-off is signposted about 1.5km west of New Grant.

The highway continues to **Princes Town**, a large town in the center of sugar cane country. Traffic in the town can be a bit confusing but as long as you end up continuing west on either the northerly Naparima Rd or the southerly Manahambre Rd, you'll get to San Fernando.

SAN FERNANDO
San Fernando, Trinidad's second-largest city, is the center of the island's gas and oil industries. The center of town is dominated by San Fernando Hill, a spot once sacred to Amerindians. The hill is oddly shaped, a consequence of earlier excavations that have now been halted.

There is a golf course west of the city, but San Fernando has little of interest for tourists and most of those who see the city are just passing through on their way to Pitch Lake, 15km to the south.

PITCH LAKE
Pitch Lake is perhaps Trinidad's greatest oddity. This 40-hectare lake of tar is 90 meters deep at its center, where hot bitumen is continually replenished from a subterranean fault. The lake is the world's single largest supply of natural bitumen and as much as 300 tons is extracted daily.

The surface of Pitch Lake has a wrinkled elephant-like skin that is hard enough to

---

Pitch Lake

According to legend, Pitch Lake was once the site of a wealthy Chiman Indian village. The village was surrounded by gardens and orchards that attracted flocks of birds. The Chiman angered the gods by capturing the sacred hummingbirds that flew into the gardens. One night, as the Chiman slept, the gods took their revenge – the villagers' homes sank beneath the earth and in their place a barren sea of tar appeared. The resulting Pitch Lake became known to Amerindians as the entrance to the underworld. ■

---

walk across in many places. However, as the site is essentially a huge field of tar, resembling a parking lot, many people find it anticlimactic after the two-hour drive from Port of Spain.

Pitch Lake is on the west side of the highway, just south of La Brea. It's possible to get an express bus or maxi-taxi from Port of Spain to San Fernando and from there a maxi-taxi onward to Pitch Lake.

Expect to be met by young men who will want to be your guide. They can be a bit gruff and tend to hustle you, but most are competent; Benjamin Fletcher is one who's recommended. The tourist office once tried to organize the guides and set fees but it was unsuccessful, so you'll have to negotiate on your own – TT$20 to TT$25 is average; be sure to agree on the price before starting out.

CARONI BIRD SANCTUARY
Caroni Bird Sanctuary is the roosting site for thousands of scarlet ibis, the national bird of Trinidad & Tobago. At sunset the birds fly in to roost in the swamp's mangroves, giving the trees the appearance of being abloom with brilliant scarlet blossoms. Even if you're not an avid bird watcher, the sight of the ibis flying over the swamp, glowing an almost fluorescent red in the final rays of the evening sun, is a treat not to be missed.

Long, flat-bottomed motorboats that can hold about 30 passengers pass slowly through the swamp's channels. En route the guide points out various flora and fauna – commonly seen are a two-toed sloth, a boa constrictor sleeping on a tree branch and mudskipper fish that cruise alligator-like with their beady eyes above the water. The boat then stops deep in the midst of the swamp for a good vantage point under the flight path of the ibis.

To avoid disturbing the birds, the boats keep a fair distance from the roosting sites, so a pair of binoculars is recommended although you can still see the birds with your naked eye. You can also expect to see lots of herons and egrets, predominant among the swamp's 150 bird species.

Note that ibis roosting at Caroni is seasonal and during the summer months very few ibis are sighted.

The main swamp tour companies are David Ramsahai (☎ 663-4767), Nanan Tours (☎ 645-1305) and James Madoo Tours (☎ 662-7356). All offer tours from 4 to 6:30 pm daily. Reservations are recommended but if you just show up you'll probably be able to find space on one of the boats. David Ramsahai charges TT$35 per person, James Madoo TT$40 and Nanan Tours TT$60.

The sanctuary is off the Uriah Butler Highway, 14km south of Port of Spain. Turn at the highway sign for Caroni Bird Sanctuary and park near the old LPG gas plant opposite the boat dock. If you don't have your own vehicle, tour companies such as Trinidad & Tobago Sightseeing Tours (☎ 628-1051) combine bus transportation from Port of Spain with the swamp tour for US$34. Although it's possible to get dropped off by a southbound maxi-taxi, it would be problematic on the return as you'd have to walk out to the highway and try to wave down a fast-moving vehicle in the dark – you'd certainly be better off arranging in advance for a taxi.

If your main interest is photography, the light is more favorable in the morning. Morning tours, which leave at 4:30 am, can be arranged through David Ramsahai.

POINTE-À-PIERRE WILDFOWL TRUST
The Pointe-à-Pierre Wildfowl Trust (☎ 637-5145) is a special place. Despite being in the midst of the island's sprawling oil refinery, a few kilometers north of San Fernando, this wetland sanctuary has a rich abundance of bird life in a highly concentrated (26-hectare) area. There are about 90 species of birds, both wild and in cages, including endangered waterfowl, colorful songbirds and ibis, heron and other wading birds. Trails edge a lake and lead into the woods and in a 20-minute stroll around the grounds you can easily spot a few dozen bird species.

A non-profit organization, the trust is a center for breeding endangered species and has programs in environmental education. The visitors' center has small exhibits and a gift shop.

To visit, you should make reservations a couple of days in advance, as the staff likes to stagger the number of visitors. There are a number of entrances into the surrounding PetroTrin oil refinery and gate access to the sanctuary occasionally changes, so get directions when you make reservations. Hours are 10 am to 5 pm Monday to Friday, with shorter weekend hours.

Tobago

Tobago is a delightfully relaxed island with much to offer travelers. There are good beaches, pristine snorkeling and diving spots, excellent bird watching opportunities and just enough tourism to make visiting Tobago easy, yet not so much that the island feels overrun. Although it's no longer the sleeper it was just a few years ago, Tobago is still one of the most overlooked and best-value destinations in the Caribbean.

Most of the white-sand beaches and tourist activities are centered at the southwestern side of Tobago, starting in Crown Point at the tip of the island and running along a string of bays up to Arnos Vale. The lowlands that predominate in the southwest extend to Tobago's only large town, Scarborough.

The coast beyond Scarborough is dotted with small fishing villages, while the interior is ruggedly mountainous with thick rainforest. This area is a habitat for parrots and other tropical birds and is being promoted for ecotourism, with most activities centered in the easternmost villages of Speyside and Charlotteville. The nearby uninhabited islets of Little Tobago, Goat Island and St Giles Island are nature reserves abundant in both bird and marine life.

For information on diving and other water sports see Activities in the Facts for the Visitor section of this chapter.

TOBAGO

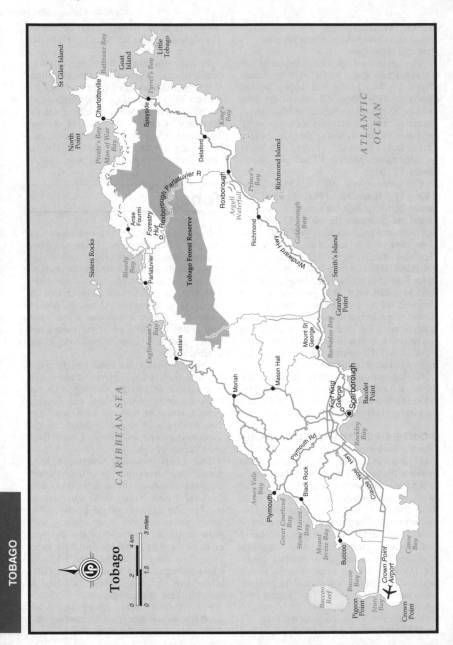

CROWN POINT

Tobago's Crown Point Airport is literally in the middle of the island's main resort area – hotels, restaurants and the beach are all within a few minutes walk of the terminal.

Crown Point has a good range of reasonably priced accommodations and attracts a younger crowd than most Caribbean destinations, with foreign visitors fairly evenly divided between Europeans and North Americans.

Store Bay, the body of water at the west side of Crown Point, has white sands, a lifeguard and good year-round swimming. Store Bay is a center of activity of sorts – there are vendors selling souvenirs and hawkers pushing glass-bottom boat tours of Buccoo Reef, but otherwise the scene is low-key.

The remains of the small coastal **Fort Milford**, built by the British in 1777, is along Store Bay Rd, a five-minute walk southwest of Store Bay. The area has been turned into a small park and there's still a bit of the old fort walls and half a dozen cannons.

Pigeon Point, 1.5km north of Store Bay, is a lovely palm-fringed beach with powdery white sands and clear aqua water. The entrance is on Milford Rd Extension. The admission of TT$10 (TT$5 for children) allows access to the facilities, which include changing rooms, showers and thatched shelters. The complex has a dive shop, an outdoor bar and a snack shop that sells reasonably priced burgers, hot dogs and fish & chips. Windsurfing gear can be rented at the northernmost end of Pigeon Point.

Information

Tourist Office The tourist office (☎ 639-0509) at the airport is normally open daily from 6 am to 10 pm. The staff can give you brochures, answer general questions and help book rooms.

Money Republic Bank at the Crown Point Airport is open from 8 to 2 pm Monday to Thursday, from 8 am to noon and 3 to 5 pm on Friday.

Places to Stay – budget

With more family-run guesthouses going up every year, there are plenty of good-value options in Crown Point, and it's unlikely you'll have trouble finding a reasonably priced place to stay.

Sandy's Guest House (☎ 639-9221), on Store Bay Rd next to Bonkers is a clean friendly place that charges just US$12 per room. There are four rooms, each with a double and twin bed, portable fan and shared bath. Guests have access to a kitchen and a new 2nd-floor addition is in the making.

The four-room *Jeffrey's House* (☎ 639-0617), on Milford Rd, is another good budget option, this one charging US$18/24 for singles/doubles, for a room with a bed, fan and private bath. Guests have access to a kitchen, TV and videos.

If you don't mind being a few minutes walk from the main road, then *Coral Inn Guesthouse* (☎ 639-0967) on John Gorman Trace is a choice low-end option. There are four apartments with kitchens, baths and two bedrooms; each bedroom has a double bed, mosquito netting and fan. The cost is US$15 for one person, US$30 for two, US$35 for three and US$45 for four. Rates are negotiable on longer stays.

House of Pancakes (☎ 639-9866), on Milford Rd, is the home of a friendly couple who operate an informal restaurant and rent out four rooms. Either a compact one-person room or a room squeezed with two double beds and a twin bed cost US$15 per person. If you need more space there's a nice air-conditioned room with shared bath for US$25 single or double and a room with TV and a private bath for US$35. Breakfast of pancakes and fruit is available for TT$36, a home-cooked Creole dinner for about double that.

Next door are the *Douglas Apartments* (☎ 639-7723), which has seven apartments with kitchens, air-con, TV and separate dining areas for US$35 to US$40. The higher rates are for the 3rd-floor units, which are the nicest. Rates are US$5 cheaper in summer and negotiable on longer stays.

TOBAGO

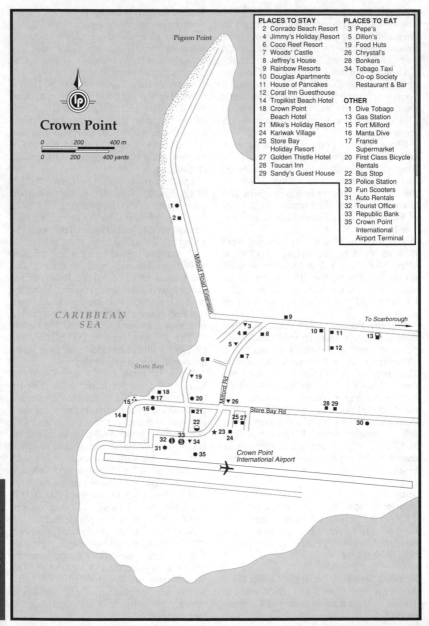

Crown Point

Pigeon Point

CARIBBEAN
SEA

Store Bay

Milford Road Extension

Milford Rd

Store Bay Rd

To Scarborough

Crown Point
International Airport

PLACES TO STAY
2 Conrado Beach Resort
4 Jimmy's Holiday Resort
6 Coco Reef Resort
7 Woods' Castle
8 Jeffrey's House
9 Rainbow Resorts
10 Douglas Apartments
11 House of Pancakes
12 Coral Inn Guesthouse
14 Tropikist Beach Hotel
18 Crown Point
    Beach Hotel
21 Mike's Holiday Resort
24 Kariwak Village
25 Store Bay
    Holiday Resort
27 Golden Thistle Hotel
28 Toucan Inn
29 Sandy's Guest House

PLACES TO EAT
3 Pepe's
5 Dillon's
19 Food Huts
26 Chrystal's
28 Bonkers
34 Tobago Taxi
    Co-op Society
    Restaurant & Bar

OTHER
1 Dive Tobago
13 Gas Station
15 Fort Milford
16 Manta Dive
17 Francis
    Supermarket
20 First Class Bicycle
    Rentals
22 Bus Stop
23 Police Station
30 Fun Scooters
31 Auto Rentals
32 Tourist Office
33 Republic Bank
35 Crown Point
    International
    Airport Terminal

Woods' Castle (☎ 639-0803), a restaurant and bar on Milford Rd, has nine clean, simple rooms with ceiling fans, air-con, TV and good firm mattresses. Singles/doubles cost US$25/30.

Places to Stay – middle

Mike's Holiday Resort (☎ 639-8050), a two-minute walk north of the airport, has 12 straightforward apartments with kitchens for US$32 for a one-bedroom unit and US$48 for a two-bedroom unit. Each bedroom has one double bed. Most units have air-con and a few have TV.

Store Bay Holiday Resort (☎ 639-8810, fax 639-9733), a five-minute walk east of the airport, is a recommendable family-run place with 25 self-contained units. Most are studio and one-bedroom apartments that rent for US$33 to US$38, but there are also a few larger units at higher prices. All have TV, most have air-con; there's a small pool.

Golden Thistle Hotel (☎ /fax 639-8521), off Store Bay Rd, is a low-key place with 36 straightforward studio units, each with full cooking facilities, air-con and TV; many have king beds. There's a pool and a small restaurant and bar. Singles/doubles cost US$45/60 in winter, US$40/50 in summer.

Jimmy's Holiday Resort (☎ 639-8292, fax 639-3100), on Milford Rd, has 18 simple two-bedroom apartments with air-con, TV, phone and a large combo kitchen/dining room with seating for six. Upstairs units have small balconies. If you're traveling with a family or group, Jimmy's is good value as the rate of US$55 is the same for up to six people. They can also block off one bedroom and rent the unit for US$30/40 for singles/doubles.

The two-story *Rainbow Resorts* (☎ 639-8271, fax 639-9940), on Milford Rd, is a pleasant place consisting of a dozen new apartments that are spotlessly clean and well equipped. Each has a full kitchen, a separate bedroom with two comfortable queen beds, thermostatic air-con and a private balcony overlooking the pool. The management is helpful and can usually provide free airport transfers. A couple of rooms are wheelchair accessible. Rates can be a bit flexible but are generally US$40/50 for singles/doubles.

Toucan Inn (☎ 639-7173, fax 639-8933, bonkers@trinidad.net), Store Bay Rd, has 10 rooms in duplex bungalows adjacent to Bonkers bar and restaurant. While suitably simple, they have comfortable beds, air-con and natural teak-wood furnishings. There's a small pool. Rates are US$45/55 in summer/winter.

Places to Stay – top end

The *Conrado Beach Resort* (☎ 639-0145, fax 639-0755), Milford Rd Extension, is on a narrow white-sand beach a five-minute walk from Pigeon Point. This older family-run hotel has 31 rooms that vary quite a bit in size but have air-con, fans, TV and phones. Winter rates begin at US$65 for a room facing inland, though it's well worth the extra US$10 for one of the oceanfront rooms that sport a sun deck overlooking the beach. Rates are US$20 cheaper in summer.

Kariwak Village (☎ 639-8442, fax 639-8441), off Store Bay Rd, has a pleasant atmosphere and two dozen air-conditioned rooms in duplex cabanas. There's a pool and a good restaurant. Rates are US$60/90 in summer/winter.

Tropikist Beach Hotel (☎ 639-8512, fax 639-1110), about a 10-minute walk west of the airport, is a modern seaside hotel with 33 comfortable rooms. Each has air-con, a phone, a balcony and a small refrigerator but no cooking facilities. Singles/doubles cost US$65/90.

Although it's seen better days the *Crown Point Beach Hotel* (☎ 639-8781, fax 639-8731) has a good location on a jut of land at the south end of Store Bay. There are 77 self-catering rooms, a pool and tennis courts. Summer/winter rates for two people are US$53/64 in a small studio, US$63/74 in a cabana and US$69/79 in a one-bedroom apartment.

Tobago's largest hotel is the swank new *Coco Reef Resort* (☎ 639-8571, fax 639-2717; in the USA ☎ 800-221-1294), whose 135-room sprawl would be right at home in

TOBAGO

tony Bermuda, but seems out of place in laid-back Crown Point. Summer/winter rates start at US$154/198.

Places to Eat – budget

A row of food huts opposite the beach at Store Bay offer rotis, shark & bake, crab & dumplings and simple plate lunches for TT$8 to TT$25. *Miss Jean's* stall is a favorite. Wash it all down with a drinking coconut (TT$2) that you can pick up from beachside vendors.

The *Tobago Taxi Co-op Society Restaurant & Bar* at the Crown Point terminal has inexpensive fast food, including rotis, burgers and chicken – all better than one might expect for an airport snack bar.

A popular place for cheap local food is *Chrystal's* on the corner of Store Bay and Milford Rd. It has fruit juices, shark & bake and flying fish dishes; hours are from 7:30 am to 11 pm.

The *Conrado Beach Resort*, on the road to Pigeon Point, has a lovely beachside setting and outdoor patio dining. You can get a continental breakfast, or lunchtime sandwiches with salad and fries, for TT$22.

Another restaurant with good reasonably priced food is *Pepe's*, just before the Milford Rd Extension, which has a varied menu, large servings and friendly service. They serve everything from pizza and burgers to hearty TT$70 seafood meals that include soup, salad and dessert. It's open for dinner nightly from 6:30 to 10:30 pm.

A favorite liming spot is *Bonkers* on Store Bay Rd. Run by two English expatriates, this bustling restaurant and bar has a pleasant open-air setting. Breakfast, sandwiches, salads and fish & chips cost around TT$30. Dinner main courses, including fish, pork, lamb and shrimp, average TT$75. Food is available from 7 am to 8 pm and the bar stays open to around midnight. There's music nightly from 8 to 10 pm, with steel pan on Sunday and Wednesday.

There's a small, reasonably priced minimart open from 7 am to 11 pm daily at Jimmy's Holiday Resort. Although the hours are shorter, *Francis Supermarket*, at

the side of the Crown Point Beach Hotel, has a wider grocery selection.

Places to Eat – top end

Although the setting is a bit of a dud, *Dillon's* (☎ 639-8765), on Milford Rd is a popular dinner restaurant featuring good seafood dishes. The best deals are the specials: fish for TT$85 or mixed seafood for TT$100, each with callaloo soup and salad. It's open from 6 pm nightly.

A top choice for fine dining is *Kariwak Village* hotel, whose alfresco restaurant has a romantic atmosphere and consistently good food – they grow many of their own herbs and vegetables on site. On weekdays, dinner is a TT$100 four-course meal that changes nightly; a typical menu is pumpkin soup, sesame salad, Creole fish and banana cream pie. Service can be slow, so come prepared for a relaxed evening. Friday and Saturday nights feature a TT$120 Creole buffet and a steel pan band.

The *Shirvan Watermill* (☎ 639-0000) on Shirvan Rd, between Crown Point and

Buccoo Bay, is pricier, but it has some of the island's best food. Located beside the mill of a former sugar estate, this dinner restaurant has pleasant gazebo dining. Gazpacho, salads and appetizers begin around TT$20, while entrees range from chicken Creole for TT$75 to lobster for TT$180.

BUCCOO

Buccoo is a small village that's only lightly touristed. The narrow brown-sand beach at Buccoo Bay doesn't compete with the generous white sands at Store Bay, but Buccoo's offshore waters are lovely.

Buccoo Reef Tours

A handful of glassbottom boats provide tours of the extensive fringing reef between Buccoo and Pigeon Point. The boats pass over the reef, much of which is just a meter or two beneath the surface, stop for snorkeling and end with a swim in the Nylon Pool, a calm shallow area with a sandy bottom and clear turquoise waters.

Johnson & Sons (☎ 639-8519) does a nice tour. Unlike most boats that go out at 11 am every day, Johnson goes out when the tide is low (and the snorkeling best), leaving between 9 am and 2 pm. Meet at the end of the pier at Buccoo Beach. If you're an avid snorkeler, let Johnson know beforehand and he can stop at some deeper spots with pristine coral, otherwise the tours generally stick to shallower waters. Tours last about 2½ hours and cost TT$60.

There are also boats to Buccoo Reef leaving from Store Bay and Pigeon Point for around the same price.

Places to Stay

Miller's Guesthouse (☎ 639-0534), on the waterfront directly above the glassbottom boat pier, is a casual place with 12 simple rooms, most with shared baths, from TT$55 per person. Expect late-night partying.

For a quieter scene, there's *St Anthony's Holiday Home* (☎ 639-0081) on Battery St, a few minutes inland from the beach, which is run by an elderly woman. Basic rooms, some with kitchenettes and private baths, cost TT$55 per person.

Places to Eat

There are a few food huts near the beach serving cheap, simple fare. Opposite the beach, you'll find the *Sandwich Bar*, selling fish or chicken & chips for TT$18.

There's good pizza and a friendly atmosphere at *Teaside Pizza*, on Battery St, 200 meters north of the beach. Prices start at TT$30 for a small pizza with up to seven toppings; you can order meat or vegetarian, whole-wheat or white crust. Teaside also has fruit juices and desserts. It's open from 3 to 10 pm daily except Tuesday.

For something fancier, *La Tartaruga*, opposite the beach, has authentic Italian food.

MT IRVINE TO GREAT COURLAND BAY

The stretch of coastline from Mt Irvine to Great Courland Bay is a rather exclusive area with the island's only golf course and three resort hotels, each on a separate bay: Mt Irvine Bay Hotel on Mt Irvine Bay, Grafton Beach Resort on Stone Haven Bay and Turtle Beach Hotel on Great Courland Bay.

There's a roadside public beach, **Mt Irvine Beach**, 200 meters north of the Mt Irvine Bay Hotel, with sheltered picnic tables and a beach bar selling rotis, bake & fish and sandwiches. The beach can have some good surfing conditions over a mix of sand and rocks.

On a rocky hill at the north side of Stone Haven Bay is **Fort Bennett**. Little remains of the fort other than a couple of cannons, but there's a good view of the coast from this site. The turnoff is marked and the fort is only about 500 meters west of the main road.

Places to Stay

The *Old Grange Inn* (☎ /fax 639-9395), PO Box 297, Scarborough, is less than a kilometer east of Buccoo, opposite the south end of the golf course. This small 18-unit lodge is a bit off the road and beyond the sound of traffic. Rooms are large with high wooden ceilings, air-con, ceiling fans and private baths and cost US$35/50 in summer, US$50/70 in winter. There's a pool.

TOBAGO

At the Buccoo Junction, adjacent to the Old Grange Inn, is *Golf View Apartments* (☎ 639-0979), PO Box 354, Scarborough, which has a dozen good-value apartments with cable TV, air-con and kitchens for US$50/65 in summer/winter. It has a quiet setting and a pool.

The *Mount Irvine Bay Hotel* (☎ 639-8871, fax 639-8800; in the USA ☎ 800-448-8355), PO Box 222, Scarborough, is a 105-room resort between Mt Irvine Bay and the hotel's 18-hole golf course. Hotel rooms in the two-story main building have air-con, a balcony and standard resort amenities. Rooms cost from US$165/235 in summer/winter. The resort has tennis courts and a pool.

The *Grafton Beach Resort* (☎ 639-0191, fax 639-0030; in the USA ☎ 800-223-6510), Black Rock, is a modern upscale hotel with a pleasant beachside location. The 112 rooms have air-con, ceiling fans, TV, minibars, a patio or balcony and, in most cases, two queen beds. There are squash courts, a pool and complimentary use of water sports gear. The standard rate is US$162/225 in summer/winter, however, the hotel sometimes lures local visitors with rates that are less than half that.

The *Turtle Beach Hotel* (☎ 639-2851, fax 639-1495; in the USA ☎ 800-448-8355), PO Box 201, Scarborough, is the area's largest hotel with 125 rooms in two and three-story buildings along a long curving beach. The rooms are not as upmarket as the area's other two resorts, but they have ocean-fronting balconies, air-con, phones and radios. Rooms cost US$110 in summer and rise to nearly double that in the height of winter.

Places to Eat

Papillon Restaurant (☎ 639-0275) at the Old Grange Inn, owned and operated by Swiss chef Jakob Straessle, has food that's both better and cheaper than at neighboring resort restaurants. There's a complete set dinner of the day, from soup to dessert, that can range from TT$60 for chicken to TT$110 for lobster. On the regular menu, main courses include a vegetarian platter or

a recommendable baby shark marinated in lime and rum for TT$55 and lobster thermidor or boeuf Chez Jacques for TT$130, all with soup, rice and salad.

The restaurant at the *Turtle Beach Hotel* has burgers at lunch for TT$55. On Saturday evenings there's a steel band and barbecue buffet for TT$210. Most other nights, meat and seafood main courses are priced from TT$100.

The *Grafton Beach Resort* has a beach bar that sells snacks, a moderately priced seafood restaurant and an expensive ocean-view dinner restaurant.

PLYMOUTH

Plymouth, the largest town on the west coast, is not a major destination but does have a few sights clustered along its west side. Just opposite the tourist information booth on Shelbourne St is the **Mystery Tombstone** of Betty Stiven, who died in 1783, presumably during childbirth. Her tombstone reads rather cryptically: 'She was a mother without knowing it, and a wife, without letting her husband know it, except by her kind indulgences to him.'

Fort James, 200 meters west of the tourist booth, is a small hilltop coastal fort overlooking Great Courland Bay. This British-built fortification, erected in 1811, remains largely intact, with four of its cannons still mounted.

Coming back from Fort James, turn right after the tourist booth and continue 150 meters to reach the **Great Courland Bay Monument**, an odd concrete creation honoring the early Courlander colonists who settled the area in the 17th century.

Places to Stay & Eat

Bailey's Guest House (☎ 639-2797), on the corner of Great and Shelbourne Sts, is a funky old house with basic but clean rooms for just TT$35 per person. It's casual, friendly and a good way to immerse oneself in an island family scene.

King Solomon Mine (☎ 639-2545) is at the end of George St, a block east of Cocrico Inn. The congenial owner, Leroy Solomon, has six pleasant units at bargain prices. All have kitchen access; those with the kitchen outside the room are US$10/20 for singles/doubles, while apartments with their own kitchens, including a very nice upstairs 'executive suite,' are US$20/40.

Cocrico Inn (☎ 639-2961, fax 639-6565), PO Box 287, on Commissioner St in the center of Plymouth, has 16 straightforward rooms with private baths and aircon or fans. There's a little pool on the grounds. Singles/doubles cost US$40/50 in summer, US$55/65 in winter. It's within walking distance of the beach and a 10-minute drive to Mt Irvine or Buccoo Bay.

Cocrico Inn has a reasonably priced restaurant open for three meals a day. A full breakfast, or a lunch of flying fish & chips or crab & dumplings costs around TT$35. At dinner fresh fish of the day costs TT$65.

SCARBOROUGH

Scarborough, the island's administrative center, is a bustling little city with one-way streets and congested traffic. There are some simple wooden homes on stilts along the side streets and a few older buildings in the center but the town's character is largely commercial. Other than visiting Fort King George on the east side of town, which is quite interesting, there's not much else to see or do.

Scarborough's botanical gardens, between the highway and town center, are little more than a public park with a few identified trees. They are only worth a stop if you're passing by. The sign 'Botanic Gardens Layby' marks the turn-off at the side of the highway.

Docks for cruise ships, the Trinidad ferries and visiting yachts are in a row, along with the customs office, in the town center. The public market is a few minutes walk to the north, up Wilson Rd. The bus terminal is immediately northeast of the market, at the corner of Post Office St and Greenside Rd.

Information

Tobago's central post office is north of the market on Post Office St. The tourist office (☎ 639-2125), open weekdays 8 am to 4 pm, is in the NIB Mall, near the post office.

Five of the six banks in Trinidad are in Scarborough, most of them near the waterfront just east of the docks. Republic Bank on Castries St has an ATM that accepts Visa and MasterCard as well as Cirrus and Plus system cards.

Fort King George

Fort King George sits on a hill at the end of Fort St, a kilometer from Main St, immediately beyond the hospital. This British-built fort, which is the only substantial colonial fortification remaining in Tobago, is well worth a visit both for its historic significance and its fine coastal view. There's no admission charge to enter the fort grounds.

Cannons line the fort's old stone walls and a number of the period buildings have been restored. The old hospital building now contains a fine arts center with changing exhibits of island art. Another building contains a small museum (TT$5) with displays on Amerindian artifacts and Tobago's colonial history; it's open weekdays from 9 am to 5 pm. A shop in the old powder magazine sells locally made handicrafts.

The lighthouse at the fort has a lead crystal Fresnel lens that can throw a beam 50km out to sea using just a 3000-watt light. If you have a keen interest in these impressive prismatic lenses that have been

---

A Distant Revolution

In 1781, two years after the construction of Fort King George, the French captured Tobago and held it until 1793, when the British finally retook the island. One might expect destructive battle scars during the fighting between rival French and British forces, but in fact the most damaging blow to occur during this period took place when French domestic unrest spilled over to this sleepy island outpost. In 1790, in the midst of the French Revolution, the French soldiers stationed at this fort mutinied, killing their officers. In the melee that followed, Scarborough, known to the French as Port Louis, was burned to the ground. ∎

decommissioned just about everywhere else in the world, the friendly lighthouse keeper will probably be willing to give you a quick tour.

Places to Stay

If you need to stay in Scarborough center, there are a couple of cheap guesthouses about a five-minute walk inland from the waterfront. *Jacob's Guest House* (☎ 639-2271), 49 Carrington St, has six simple clean rooms, three with shared baths, three with private baths, most with fans, and all at TT$50/100 for singles/doubles. Breakfast is available for TT$15.

If no one's home, try *Federal Villa Guest House* (☎ 639-3926), which is just around the bend from Jacob's, and has five basic rooms at slightly higher prices.

Still, the best budget option is *Hope Cottage* (☎ 639-2179) near Fort King George on Calder Hall Rd, about a 15-minute walk uphill from the dock. Located in the former home of a 19th-century governor (James Henry Keens, who's buried in the backyard), it's a great place to stay if you want to hang out awhile or meet other foreign travelers. There are a variety of rooms, including some atmospheric ones in the main house with private baths for TT$80 a double, and others with shared bath for TT$70. Smaller rooms in adjacent cottages cost TT$45/70 for singles/doubles. There's a big group kitchen, a couple of hammocks and helpful management.

Sandy's Bed & Breakfast (☎ 639-2737), at the back of the Blue Crab Restaurant, Robinson St, consists of two rooms in the home of Ken and Alison Sardinha. The rooms are set off a bit for privacy and are pleasantly simple like those of an old-fashioned inn, with pine-wood floors, ceiling fans and private baths. It's within walking distance of the bus terminal. Singles/doubles cost US$25/50, breakfast included.

Places to Eat

Near the marketplace are a couple of inexpensive shops selling rotis and there's a *KFC* with the usual fried chicken options opposite the ferry terminal.

East Ocean Restaurant, on Milford Rd 1km west of the cruise ship dock, is a small, unpretentious restaurant with a full menu of inexpensive Chinese dishes. There are also combination plates for TT$22.

Blue Crab Restaurant, at the east side of town on the corner of Main and Robinson streets, is a family-run restaurant with a pleasant alfresco setting and good West Indian food. At lunch, from noon to 3 pm on weekdays, there's a choice of a few main dishes such as Creole chicken or flying fish served with rice and vegetables for TT$40. Dinner is much pricier and by reservation.

WINDWARD RD

Just east of Scarborough, the landscape turns mountainous and rural. The Windward Rd, which connects Scarborough with Speyside, winds in and out from the coast, passing scattered villages, jungly valleys and the occasional brown-sand beach. The farther east you go the more ruggedly beautiful the scenery becomes. Although much of the road is quite narrow and curving, it's easily driveable in a standard vehicle. If you were to drive straight through from Scarborough to Speyside it would take about 1½ hours.

Eight km east of Scarborough is Granby Point, a jut of land separating Barbados Bay from Pinfold Bay. In 1764 the British established a temporary capital on the east side of Barbados Bay and built **Fort Granby** at the tip of the point. It's only a couple of minutes walk from the parking lot to the old fort site, but little remains other than the gravestone of James Clark, a soldier who died in 1772. There are a couple of hilltop picnic tables, a nice view of nearby Smith's Island, a brown-sand beach, changing rooms and the Dry Dock restaurant, which has inexpensive eats.

The **Argyll Waterfall**, an attractive triple-tiered falls on the Argyll River, is at the north side of the Windward Rd just west of Roxborough. There's a TT$25 admission fee plus a charge of TT$15 for a guide who will lead visitors to the falls, which are about a 20-minute hike away.

Roxborough itself is a sizable village with a post office, a gas station and a few stores where you can pick up snacks.

Five km east of Roxborough is **King's Bay**, a deep, pretty bay with powdery dark sands and beach facilities. After King's Bay the road winds and twists its way over the mountains to Speyside.

Places to Stay & Eat

Richmond Great House (☎ 660-4467), Belle Garden, is a small inn occupying a restored plantation house at the edge of the rainforest. The inn has simply furnished rooms with private baths for US$70/100 for singles/doubles in summer, US$80/120 in winter, breakfast included. There's a pool and hilltop views. The owner, Hollis Lynch, is an African history teacher at New York's Colombia University and some of the common rooms are decorated with African crafts.

Non-guests can come up to the house for breakfast (TT$50), lunch (TT$55) or dinner (TT$110) – all full-course meals. Reservations are required for dinner. The inn is 150 meters north of the main road, 750 meters after entering the village of Richmond; the turn-off is marked.

SPEYSIDE

Speyside is a small fishing village fronting Tyrrel's Bay and the jumping-off point for excursions to the uninhabited island of Little Tobago, a bird sanctuary 2km offshore. There are facilities at the south end of the beach where the Windward Rd makes its first contact with the bay.

Tyrrel's Bay has protected inshore waters, but for the best snorkeling consider taking one of the glass-bottom boats (see Little Tobago) or arranging with a fisherman to take you out to the reefs; either way the cost is TT$50. Be particularly careful if swimming around the offshore islands as there is a ferocious current between Goat Island and Little Tobago.

Places to Stay

Donna Yawching, a journalist from Canada, operates the seven-room *Speyside Inn* (☎ /fax 660-4852), Windward Rd, opposite Jemma's restaurant. The four upstairs rooms are particularly pleasant with high ceilings, red-tile floors and private baths; French doors lead to small balconies with nice breezes and a good sea view across Goat Island to Little Tobago. Singles/doubles with breakfast cost from US$65/80 in winter and US$50/65 in summer.

Manta Lodge (☎ 660-5268, fax 660-5030; in the USA ☎ 800-544-7631), PO Box 433, Scarborough, is a modern new hotel geared for divers fronting the beach in Speyside. There are 22 comfortable rooms with oceanview balconies, private baths and either air-con or ceiling fans. Singles/doubles cost US$65/75 in summer and US$85/95 in winter. There's a pool, bar, restaurant and dive shop on site.

The *Blue Waters Inn* (☎ 660-4341, fax 660-5195; in the USA ☎ 800-742-4276), Batteaux Bay, caters largely to bird watchers and divers. The 35-room hotel is secluded on a little brown-sand cove about a kilometer north of Speyside. You can take walks into the rainforest behind the hotel and there's a dive operation and tennis court. Rooms are in contemporary cottages and small two-story buildings, have ceiling fans and either one king or two double beds. Singles/doubles cost US$75/85 in summer, US$108/128 in winter.

Places to Eat

Jemma's (☎ 660-4066), along Tyrrel's Bay on Windward Rd, is a simple seaside restaurant with an interesting tree-house setting and good local food. Fish, chicken and shrimp dishes are priced from around TT$50. It's open daily from 9 am to 4 pm and every evening except Friday from 6:30 to 9 pm. Jemma's also has a small fruit and vegetable stand.

The beachfront restaurant at *Blue Waters Inn* offers a buffet breakfast for TT$65. At lunch there are simple eats like sandwiches, burgers and a fruit plate from TT$20 to TT$50. A complete dinner, with a choice of a few main dishes that usually includes fresh fish, costs TT$124, while a vegetarian meal costs TT$65.

LITTLE TOBAGO

Little Tobago, also known as Bird of Paradise Island, has an interesting history. In 1909 Englishman Sir William Ingram imported 50 greater birds of paradise from the Aru Islands, off New Guinea, and established a sanctuary on Little Tobago to protect the bird, which was in danger of becoming extinct. In 1963 Hurricane Flora devastated the habitat and decimated the flock; the bird of paradise hasn't been sighted on Little Tobago since 1981.

Little Tobago, now managed by the government, remains an important sea bird sanctuary nonetheless. Red-billed tropicbirds, red-footed boobies, brown boobies, Audubon shearwaters, brown noddies and sooty terns are some of the species found on the island.

This hilly, arid island, which averages just 1.5km in width, has a couple of short trails. Be sure to bring something to drink as there are no facilities and it can get very hot.

There are three glassbottom boats that take passengers over to the island, a crossing that takes about 15 minutes. The rate, which includes a land tour of the island, is TT$70 per person.

Fear Not leaves from in front of Jemma's (ask for Mr Roberts), the other two boats depart from Blue Waters Inn. The schedules can vary a bit. Frank's Glass Bottom Boat, for example, typically makes two trips a day from Blue Waters, once at 10 am and again at 2 pm. Most people go for either the morning or the afternoon but you could also arrange to stay for the whole day.

The boats usually make a stop for snorkeling on the way back but you should bring along your own gear. You can also take the boats solely for snorkeling, in which case the charge is TT$50.

Serious birders who want to get a more in-depth tour can do so by making advance arrangements with one of three naturalist guides who are very knowledgeable about island ecology: Renson Jack (☎ 660-5175), Pat Turpin (☎ 660-4327) and David Rooks (☎ 639-4276).

CHARLOTTEVILLE

It's four scenic, winding kilometers over the mountains from Speyside to Charlotteville. At the summit, before the road snakes down to Charlotteville, a marked gravel road leads north to Flagstaff Hill. Taking this rough side road for just a few hundred meters will provide some fine jungle views and a chance of seeing, or at least hearing, a flock of parrots.

Charlotteville is a delightful little fishing village. Sleepy, secluded and with an earthy simplicity, it has the appearance of some long forgotten outpost. In the winter, the hillsides behind the village are bright with the orange blossoms of immortelle trees, which were introduced from Martinique in colonial times to shade cocoa plantations.

Man of War Bay, the large horseshoe-shaped bay that fronts the village, is lined with a palm-studded brown-sand beach and offers good swimming. When it's calm, there's excellent snorkeling at Pirate's Bay, a 15-minute walk across the point at the north side of Charlotteville, and good snorkeling around Booby Island just south of the village.

Pirate's Bay

Pirate's Bay derives its name from the secluded haven it provided to marauding buccaneers who established a base here three centuries ago. The island proved ripe grounds for piracy after rival colonial powers, tired of battling over Tobago, declared it a 'no-man's land.' As a consequence, Tobago became a staging grounds for pirate attacks on both treasure-laden Spanish ships sailing from South America and British cargo ships in the Grenadines. It's rumored that there's still buried treasure around Pirate's Bay.

Today this lovely, deserted bay is a feeding grounds for the frigatebird, a sort of pirate in its own right – the frigatebird feeds itself by attacking terns and gulls in mid-air and snatching their food. ∎

If you're up for more exploring, take a walk to the site of the old Fort Campbelton, on the west side of the bay, which offers a good coastal view, or take a more substantial hike up Flagstaff Hill.

Places to Stay

There are a number of small unofficial guesthouses in Charlotteville, most found by word of mouth, and there's seldom a problem getting a room.

There are also some self-catering flats, including *Cholson Chalets* (☎ 639-8553), a clean, friendly place right on the beach next to the village rum shop. It has six two-bedroom apartments with kitchens and private baths. The cost for one or two people ranges from US$28 to US$50. The higher rates apply to the larger upstairs units. Add US$11 to the price of the room for each additional person.

Man-O-War Bay Cottages (☎ 660-4327, fax 660-4328), Charlotteville Estate, is on the beach about a five-minute walk south of the village. The grounds are like a little botanical garden with lots of tropical trees, ferns and flowering plants. There are six simple cottages with private baths, kitchens and screened louvered windows that open to the breeze and the sound of the surf. Rates for two people in a smaller cottage are US$60/80 in summer/winter. The cottages are owned by Pat Turpin, who leads naturalist tours around Tobago.

Places to Eat

There are a handful of small family-run restaurants in Charlotteville offering good homemade food at honest prices. *Pheb's Ville View Restaurant*, opposite the old library, has an excellent cook who makes inexpensive West Indian dishes, including fish and vegetarian meals.

Also recommended is *Jane's Quality Kitchen*, which is right on the water under the shade of an almond tree. It's run by an amiable couple, Jane and Charles, who make fresh rotis for TT$8 and, with advance notice, can cook up a full soup-to-dessert fish dinner for around TT$30.

There are also small stores in town where you can pick up provisions.

TOBAGO FOREST RESERVE

The Roxborough Parlatuvier Rd, which crosses the island from Roxborough to Bloody Bay, is a bit narrow and curving but it is paved and rates as one of the best roads on the island. It's a nice 30-minute jungle drive, completely undeveloped, with pretty valley and mountain views.

The road passes through the Tobago Forest Reserve, which was established in 1765, making it the oldest forest reserve in the Caribbean. There are a number of trailheads leading off the main road where you could make a jaunt into the rainforest.

There's excellent bird watching in this area and it's not uncommon to hear squawking parrots and see hummingbirds, cocricos, woodpeckers, hawks and blue-crowned motmots.

Three-quarters of the way across is a roadside forestry hut with a scenic view of Bloody Bay and the offshore Sisters Rocks. From there it's just a five-minute ride down to Bloody Bay, which takes its name from a fierce battle that occurred here between the Dutch, French and British in the 1600s.

Once you reach Bloody Bay it's about an hour's drive south to Plymouth. There are a couple of nice beaches and villages along the way, unhurried places with kids playing cricket in the road. Just west of Bloody Bay is Parlatuvier, a tiny fishing village on a strikingly beautiful circular bay. Castara, farther south, is a pleasant bayside village with a good beach right in town.

GETTING THERE & AWAY

There are ferry and air services between Tobago and Port of Spain. Information on both is under the Getting Around section at the beginning of this chapter.

GETTING AROUND
Bus

There are two main public bus routes on Tobago: one from Crown Point to Scarborough, the other from Scarborough to Plymouth via Buccoo and Mt Irvine. The buses run from about dawn till 8 pm. Departures average every half-hour on weekdays, about half as frequently on weekends.

All bus fares are TT$2; tickets are purchased in advance. In Crown Point, buy tickets at Jetway Holiday Resort (east of the airport terminal) and wait for the bus at the shed outside the hotel. In Scarborough, tickets are sold at the bus terminal.

Route Taxi In addition to buses there are also privately run route taxis, identified by the letter 'H' on their license plates. They don't run on strict schedules, but they do cover more distant parts of the island and have fixed fares. The rate is TT$5 from Crown Point to Scarborough, TT$4 from Scarborough to Plymouth, TT$7 from Scarborough to Roxborough and TT$12 from Scarborough to Charlotteville.

Taxi
Taxis are available at Crown Point Airport and charge about TT$25 to hotels around Crown Point, TT$30 to Pigeon Point, TT$50 to Scarborough, TT$60 to Mt Irvine or Buccoo and TT$220 to Charlotteville.

Car & Motorcycle
There are a few scattered gas stations around the island, but it's wisest to fill up before doing extensive touring, as hours can be random and stations occasionally run out of gas.

There are two car rental companies at the side of the Crown Point airport: AR Auto Rentals (☎ 639-0644) and Hillcrest Car Rental (☎ /fax 639-5208) both rent small cars such as a Nissan Sentra for around TT$230, tax and CDW (collision damage waiver) insurance included.

You can also rent cars from Singh's Auto Rentals (☎ 639-0191) at the Grafton Beach Resort, from Jordan's Car Rental (☎ 639-1032) and through most hotels and guesthouses.

Fun Scooters (☎ 639-9579) in Crown Point rents 125cc motorcycles for TT$120 a day, plus a TT$200 deposit.

Bicycle
First Class Bicycle Rentals rents out mountain bikes on a corner lot a block north of the airport in Crown Point. The cost is TT$10 an hour, TT$40 for 24 hours, with discounts for longer periods. Child seats are available and guided cycle tours can be arranged.

Glossary

accras – Creole-style cod or vegetable fritters

agouti – a short-haired rabbit-like rodent with short ears, which has a fondness for sugar cane and looks like a guinea pig with elevated feet

bake – a sandwich made with fried bread and usually filled with shark or other fish

biguine – also spelt beguine, this Afro-French dance music with a bolero rhythm originated in Martinique in the 1930s

blaff – a seafood preparation poached in a spicy broth

breadfruit – an introduced tree whose round, green fruit are prepared like potatoes throughout the Caribbean

bul jol – roasted breadfruit and salt fish made with tomatoes and onions

callaloo soup – a soup made with dasheen leaves, resembling a creamy spinach soup

calypso – a popular Caribbean music that's essential to Carnival

Carnival – the major Caribbean festival that originated as a pre-Lenten festivity but is now observed at various times throughout the year on different islands

chattel houses – a type of simple wooden dwelling placed upon cement or stone blocks so it can be easily moved; often erected on rented land

christophene – a common pear-shaped vegetable eaten raw in salads or cooked like a squash

colombo – a spicy, East Indian-influenced dish that resembles curry

conkies – a mixture of cornmeal, coconut, pumpkin, sweet potatoes, raisins and spice, steamed in a plantain leaf

cou-cou – a creamy cornmeal and okra mash, commonly served with salt fish

crabes farcis – spicy stuffed land crabs

Creole – in terms of people, Creole refers to a person of mixed black and European ancestry; in terms of language, Creole refers to local pidgin that's predominantly a combination of French and African; in terms of food, Creole is characterized by spicy, full-flavored sauces and a heavy use of green peppers and onions

cutter – a salt-bread roll used to make meat and fish sandwiches, or the name of such a sandwich

dasheen – a type of taro; the leaves are known as callaloo and cooked much like spinach or turnip leaves, the starchy tuberous root is boiled and eaten like a potato

dolphin – both a marine mammal found in Caribbean waters and name given to a common type of white-meat fish (also called mahimahi); the two are not related and 'dolphin' on any menu always refers to the fish

flying fish – a gray-meat fish named for its ability to skim above the water

frangipani – a low tree with fragrant pink or white flowers; also known as plumeria

goat water – a spicy goat meat stew often flavored with cloves and rum

gommier – a large native gum tree found in Caribbean rainforests

Ital – a natural style of vegetarian cooking practiced by Rastafarians

jambalaya – a Creole dish usually consisting of rice cooked with meat or shellfish, tomatoes, onions and peppers

johnnycake – a cornflour griddle cake

jug-jug – a mixture of Guinea cornmeal, green peas and salted meat

jump-ups – a type of night-time street party that usually involves dancing and plenty of rum drinking

lambi – Caribbean name for conch, a large mollusk whose flesh is a common food

lime or **limin'** – to hang out, relax

lolo – a sidewalk barbecue stand where meat is grilled and sold

mahimahi – see dolphin

mairie – the name for town hall in the French West Indies

manchineel – a common tree on Eastern Caribbean beaches whose sap can cause a skin rash

manicou – the opossum, a small marsupial

mas camps – 'mas' as in masquerade, these are the workshops where artists create Carnival costumes

mauby – a bittersweet drink made from the bark of the mauby tree, sweetened with sugar and spices

mountain chicken – the legs of the *crapaud*, a type of frog

obeah – a belief system related to black magic

oil down – a food dish made of breadfruit, pork, callaloo and coconut milk

panyards – the places where steel pan bands practice their music in the months leading up to Carnival

pareo – a type of wrap skirt that's commonly sold on beaches in the Caribbean

paw paw – common Caribbean name for papaya

pepperpot – a spicy stew made with various meats, accompanied by peppers and cassareep

pigeon peas – brown, pea-like seeds of a tropical shrub that are cooked like peas and served mixed with rice

pitt – in the French West Indies, an arena where cockfights take place

plantain – a starchy fruit of the banana family that is usually fried or grilled like a vegetable

Planters punch or **Planteur punch** – a punch mixing rum and fruit juice

roti – West Indian fast food of curry filling, commonly potatoes and chicken, rolled inside a tortilla-like flat bread

sorrel juice – a lightly tart, bright-red drink rich in vitamin C that's made from the flowers of the sorrel plant

souse – a dish made out of a pickled pig's head and belly, spices and a few vegetables

steel pan – also called steel drum, it refers both to the instrument made from oil drums and to the music it produces

tamarind – the legume-like pod of a large tropical tree, or the juice made from the seeds

zouk – popular French West Indies music that draws from the biguine, bebop-like cadence and other French Caribbean folk forms

Internet Resources

GENERAL EASTERN CARIBBEAN INFORMATION

www.caribbean-on-line.com
www.geographia.com/index.html
www.cpscaribnet.com

TRANSPORTATION

Airlines

Air Canada
www.aircanada.ca

Air France
www.airfrance.fr/en/copyright.html

American Airlines
www.amrcorp.com

British Airways
www.british-airways.com

Continental Airlines
www.flycontinental.com

KLM
www.klm.nl/home.htm

Tour Companies

Bare Necessities
www.bare-necessities.com

Caligo Tours
www.caligo.com

Go Classy Tours
www.gonude.com/welcome.com

Landfall Productions
www.ecotravel.com/landfall

PADI Dive Centers
www.padi.com

Scuba Voyages
www.scubavoyages.com

Smithsonian Institution
www.si.edu/tsa/sst

Car Rental Agencies

Avis – www.avis.com
Dollar – www.dollarcar.com
Hertz – www.hertz.com
National – www.nationalcar.com

Yacht Charters

The Moorings – www.moorings.com
Sunsail – www.sunsail.com

ANGUILLA

General Information

Anguilla Local News
www.news.ai

Anguilla Tourist Board
www.candw.com.ai/~atbtour

What We Do in Anguilla
www.anguillatourguide.com

Places to Stay

Anguilla Great House
www.erols.com/gafaxa/aghbr.html

ANTIGUA & BARBUDA

General Information

Antigua & Barbuda Department of Tourism
www.interknowledge.com/antigua-barbuda

BARBADOS

General Information

Barbados Tourism Authority
http://barbados.org

Ins & Outs of Barbados
www.fleethouse.com/barbados

Places to Stay

Edgewater Inn
www.edgewaterinn.com

Sea Breeze Beach Hotel
www.sea-breeze.com

DOMINICA

General Information

Delphis – A Virtual Dominica
www.delphis.dm/home.htm

Activities

Dive Dominica – www.divedominica.com

Places to Stay

D'Auchamps Cottages
www.delphis.dm/champs.htm

Evergreen Hotel
www.delphis.dm/evergreen.htm

Garraway Hotel
home.sprynet.com/sprynet/inglisp

Petit Coulibri Guest Cottages
www.wp.com/dolphinsoft/petit.htm

Springfield Plantation Guest House
www.tod.dm/dolphinsoft/sceptre

Sutton Place Hotel
www.delphis.dm/sutton.htm

GRENADA

General Information

Grenada Board of Tourism
www.interknowledge.com/grenada

Activities

Dive Grenada
www.divegrenada.com

Tanki's Watersport
www.cacounet.com/paradise-inn-resort

Places to Stay

Blue Horizons Cottage Hotel
www.cpscaribnet.com/ads/blue/blue.html

Cinnamon Hill & Beach Club
www.cpscaribnet.com/ads/cinhill/cinhill.html

Flamboyant Hotel
www.cpscaribnet.com/ads/flambo

Paradise Inn
www.cacounet.com/paradise-inn-resort

Siesta Hotel
www.cpscaribnet.com/ads/siesta/siesta.html

GUADELOUPE

General Information

Civilized Explorer – www.cieux.com

MARTINIQUE

General Information

Martinique Promotion Bureau
www.nyo.com/martinique

MONTSERRAT

General Information

Government of Montserrat and the Montserrat Volcano Observatory
www.geo.mtu.edu/volcanoes/west.indies/soufriere/govt

Montserrat Photos, Maps & Links
www.clark.net/pub/innanen/montserrat

Montserrat Tourist Board
www.clark.net/pub/innanen/montserrat/touristboard/index.html

Sustainable Ecosystems Institute
www.sei.org/montserrat.html

SABA

General Information

Saba Tourist Bureau
www.turq.com/saba

Activities

Dive Saba Travel
www.ghgcorp.com/divesaba

Saba Deep
www.sabadeep.com/~diving

Saba Reef Divers
www.empg.com/sabadive

Sea Saba
www.3route.com/scuba/seasaba.htm

Places to Stay

Captain's Quarters
http://saba-online.com

The Cottage Club
www.turq.com/cottage-club

The Gate House
http://members.aol.com/travelsaba

ST BARTS

General Information

St Barths Online
www.st-barths.com

Sibarth/Wimco Villas
www.well.com/~wimco

ST EUSTATIUS

General Information

St Eustatius Tourist Office
www.turq.com/statia

Activities

Dive Statia
www.island.net/divestatia

Golden Rock Dive Center
www.divetrip.com/goldenrock

ST KITTS & NEVIS

General Information

St Christopher Heritage Society
www.islandimage.com/schs/home.htm

St Kitts & Nevis Department of Tourism
www.stkitts-nevis.com

Nevis Express Air
www.nevisexpress.com

Places to Stay

Fort Thomas Hotel
www.mangomaxx.com

Gateway Inn
www.ubnetwork.com/gateway/index.html

Montpelier Plantation Inn
www.stkitts-nevis.com/montpelier

Mount Nevis Hotel
www.mountnevishotel.com

Old Manor Estate
www.cpscaribnet.com/oldmanor

Oualie Beach Hotel
www.oualie.com

ST LUCIA

General Information

St Lucia Tourist Board
www.interknowledge.com/st-lucia

ST MARTIN

General Information

Dutch St Maarten Tourist Office
www.st-maarten.com

French St Martin Tourist Office
www.interknowledge.com/st-martin

ST VINCENT & THE GRENADINES

General Information

St Vincent & the Grenadines Tourist Office
http://vincy.com/svg

Activities

Dive Bequia
www.empg.com/dive-bequia

Sailor's Cycling Tours
http://vincy.com/sailor's.htm

Places to Stay

Palm Island Beach Club
www.cpscaribnet.com/ads/palmisl

Sunset Shores Beach Hotel
www.cpscaribnet.com/ads/sunset

Village Apartments, Bequia
www.grenadines.net/bequia/
villageapartments.htm

TRINIDAD & TOBAGO

General Information

Trinidad & Tobago Tourism Development Company
www.visittnt.com

Trinidad Business Information
http://tradepoint.tidco.co.tt

Activities

AquaMarine Dive
www.trinidad.net/bwi-tobago

Mas Bands, Performances
www.callaloo.co.tt

Tobago Dive Experience
www.trinidad.net/tobagodive

Trinidad & Tobago Field Naturalists' Club
www.wow.net/ttfnc

Trinidad & Tobago Sightseeing Tours
www.wp.com/trinbago

Index

534

538   Index

SIDEBARS

LONELY PLANET

Guides by Region

Lonely Planet is known worldwide for publishing practical, reliable and no-nonsense travel information in our guides and on our Web site. The Lonely Planet list covers just about every accessible part of the world. Currently there are 16 series: Travel guides, Shoestring guides, Condensed guides, Phrasebooks, Read This First, Healthy Travel, Walking guides, Cycling guides, Watching Wildlife guides, Pisces Diving & Snorkeling guides, City Maps, Road Atlases, Out to Eat, World Food, Journeys travel literature and Pictorials.

AFRICA Africa on a shoestring • Cairo • Cairo City Map • Cape Town • Cape Town City Map • East Africa • Egypt • Egyptian Arabic phrasebook • Ethiopia, Eritrea & Djibouti • Ethiopian (Amharic) phrasebook • The Gambia & Senegal • Healthy Travel Africa • Kenya • Malawi • Morocco • Moroccan Arabic phrasebook • Mozambique • Read This First: Africa • South Africa, Lesotho & Swaziland • Southern Africa • Southern Africa Road Atlas • Swahili phrasebook • Tanzania, Zanzibar & Pemba • Trekking in East Africa • Tunisia • Watching Wildlife East Africa • Watching Wildlife Southern Africa • West Africa • World Food Morocco • Zimbabwe, Botswana & Namibia
Travel Literature: Mali Blues: Traveling to an African Beat • The Rainbird: A Central African Journey • Songs to an African Sunset: A Zimbabwean Story

AUSTRALIA & THE PACIFIC Auckland • Australia • Australian phrasebook • Australia Road Atlas • Bush-walking in Australia •Cycling New Zealand • Fiji • Fijian phrasebook • Healthy Travel Australia, NZ and the Pacific • Islands of Australia's Great Barrier Reef • Melbourne • Melbourne City Map • Micronesia • New Caledonia • New South Wales & the ACT • New Zealand • Northern Territory • Outback Australia • Out to Eat – Melbourne • Out to Eat – Sydney • Papua New Guinea • Pidgin phrasebook • Queensland • Rarotonga & the Cook Islands • Samoa • Solomon Islands • South Australia • South Pacific • South Pacific phrasebook • Sydney • Sydney City Map • Sydney Condensed • Tahiti & French Polynesia • Tasmania • Tonga • Tramping in New Zealand • Vanuatu • Victoria • Walking in Australia • Watching Wildlife Australia • Western Australia
Travel Literature: Islands in the Clouds: Travels in the Highlands of New Guinea • Kiwi Tracks: A New Zealand Journey • Sean & David's Long Drive

CENTRAL AMERICA & THE CARIBBEAN Bahamas, Turks & Caicos • Baja California • Bermuda • Central America on a shoestring • Costa Rica • Costa Rica Spanish phrasebook • Cuba • Dominican Republic & Haiti • Eastern Caribbean • Guatemala • Guatemala, Belize & Yucatán: La Ruta Maya • Healthy Travel Central & South America • Jamaica • Mexico • Mexico City • Panama • Puerto Rico • Read This First: Central & South America • World Food Mexico • Yucatán
Travel Literature: Green Dreams: Travels in Central America

EUROPE Amsterdam • Amsterdam City Map • Amsterdam Condensed • Andalucía • Austria • Baltic States phrasebook • Barcelona • Barcelona City Map • Berlin • Berlin City Map • Britain • British phrasebook • Brussels, Bruges & Antwerp • Brussels City Map • Budapest • Budapest City Map • Canary Islands • Central Europe • Central Europe phrasebook • Corfu & the Ionians • Corsica • Crete • Crete Condensed • Croatia • Cycling Britain • Cycling France • Cyprus • Czech & Slovak Republics • Denmark • Dublin • Dublin City Map • Eastern Europe • Eastern Europe phrasebook • Edinburgh • Estonia, Latvia & Lithuania • Europe on a shoestring • Finland • Florence • France • Frankfurt Condensed • French phrasebook • Georgia, Armenia & Azerbaijan • Germany • German phrasebook • Greece • Greek Islands • Greek phrasebook • Hungary • Iceland, Greenland & the Faroe Islands • Ireland • Istanbul • Italian phrasebook • Italy • Krakow • Lisbon • The Loire • London • London City Map • London Condensed • Madrid • Malta • Mediterranean Europe • Mediterranean Europe phrasebook • Moscow • Mozambique • Munich • the Netherlands • Norway • Out to Eat – London • Paris • Paris City Map • Paris Condensed • Poland • Portugal • Portuguese phrasebook • Prague • Prague City Map • Provence & the Côte d'Azur • Read This First: Europe • Romania & Moldova • Rome • Rome City Map • Russia, Ukraine & Belarus • Russian phrasebook • Scandinavian & Baltic Europe • Scandinavian Europe phrasebook • Scotland • Sicily • Slovenia • South-West France • Spain • Spanish phrasebook • St Petersburg • St Petersburg City Map • Sweden • Switzerland • Trekking in Spain • Tuscany • Ukrainian phrasebook • Venice • Vienna • Walking in Britain • Walking in France • Walking in Ireland • Walking in Italy • Walking in Spain • Walking in Switzerland • Western Europe • Western Europe phrasebook • World Food France • World Food Ireland • World Food Italy • World Food Spain
Travel Literature: Love and War in the Apennines • The Olive Grove: Travels in Greece • On the Shores of the Mediterranean • Round Ireland in Low Gear • A Small Place in Italy • After Yugoslavia

LONELY PLANET

Mail Order

Lonely Planet products are distributed worldwide. They are also available by mail order from Lonely Planet, so if you have difficulty finding a title please write to us. North and South American residents should write to 150 Linden St, Oakland, CA 94607, USA; European and African residents should write to 10a Spring Place, London NW5 3BH, UK; and residents of other countries to Locked Bag 1, Footscray, Victoria 3011, Australia.

INDIAN SUBCONTINENT Bangladesh • Bengali phrasebook • Bhutan • Delhi • Goa • Healthy Travel Asia & India • Hindi & Urdu phrasebook • India • Indian Himalaya • Karakoram Highway • Kerala • Mumbai (Bombay) • Nepal • Nepali phrasebook • Pakistan • Rajasthan • Read This First: Asia & India • South India • Sri Lanka • Sri Lanka phrasebook • Tibet • Tibetan phrasebook • Trekking in the Indian Himalaya • Trekking in the Karakoram & Hindukush • Trekking in the Nepal Himalaya
Travel Literature: The Age of Kali: Indian Travels and Encounters • Hello Goodnight: A Life of Goa • In Rajasthan • A Season in Heaven: True Tales from the Road to Kathmandu • Shopping for Buddhas • A Short Walk in the Hindu Kush • Slowly Down the Ganges

ISLANDS OF THE INDIAN OCEAN Madagascar & Comoros • Maldives • Mauritius, Réunion & Seychelles

MIDDLE EAST & CENTRAL ASIA Bahrain, Kuwait & Qatar • Central Asia • Central Asia phrasebook • Dubai • Hebrew phrasebook • Iran • Israel & the Palestinian Territories • Istanbul • Istanbul City Map • Istanbul to Cairo on a shoestring • Jerusalem • Jerusalem City Map • Jordan • Lebanon • Middle East • Oman & the United Arab Emirates • Syria • Turkey • Turkish phrasebook • World Food Turkey • Yemen
Travel Literature: Black on Black: Iran Revisited • The Gates of Damascus • Kingdom of the Film Stars: Journey into Jordan

NORTH AMERICA Alaska • Boston • Boston City Map • California & Nevada • California Condensed • Canada • Chicago • Chicago City Map • Deep South • Florida • Great Lakes • Hawaii • Hiking in Alaska • Hiking in the USA • Honolulu • Las Vegas • Los Angeles • Los Angeles City Map • Louisiana & The Deep South • Miami • Miami City Map • New England • New Orleans • New York City • New York City City Map • New York City Condensed • New York, New Jersey & Pennsylvania • Oahu • Out to Eat – San Francisco • Pacific Northwest • Puerto Rico • Rocky Mountains • San Francisco • San Francisco City Map • Seattle • Southwest • Texas • USA • USA phrasebook • Vancouver • Virginia & the Capital Region • Washington DC • Washington, DC City Map • World Food Deep South, USA • World Food New Orleans
Travel Literature: Caught Inside: A Surfer's Year on the California Coast • Drive Thru America

NORTH-EAST ASIA Beijing • Beijing City Map • Cantonese phrasebook • China • Hiking in Japan • Hong Kong • Hong Kong City Map • Hong Kong Condensed • Hong Kong, Macau & Guangzhou • Japan • Japanese phrasebook • Korea • Korean phrasebook • Kyoto • Mandarin phrasebook • Mongolia • Mongolian phrasebook • Seoul • Shanghai • South-West China • Taiwan • Tokyo
Travel Literature: In Xanadu: A Quest • Lost Japan

SOUTH AMERICA Argentina, Uruguay & Paraguay • Bolivia • Brazil • Brazilian phrasebook • Buenos Aires • Chile & Easter Island • Colombia • Ecuador & the Galapagos Islands • Healthy Travel Central & South America • Latin American Spanish phrasebook • Peru • Quechua phrasebook • Read This First: Central & South America • Rio de Janeiro • Rio de Janeiro City Map • Santiago • South America on a shoestring • Santiago • Trekking in the Patagonian Andes • Venezuela
Travel Literature: Full Circle: A South American Journey

SOUTH-EAST ASIA Bali & Lombok • Bangkok • Bangkok City Map • Burmese phrasebook • Cambodia • Hanoi • Healthy Travel Asia & India • Hill Tribes phrasebook • Ho Chi Minh City • Indonesia • Indonesian phrasebook • Indonesia's Eastern Islands • Jakarta • Java • Lao phrasebook • Laos • Malay phrasebook • Malaysia, Singapore & Brunei • Myanmar (Burma) • Philippines • Pilipino (Tagalog) phrasebook • Read This First: Asia & India • Singapore • Singapore City Map • South-East Asia on a shoestring • South-East Asia phrasebook • Thailand • Thailand's Islands & Beaches • Thailand, Vietnam, Laos & Cambodia Road Atlas • Thai phrasebook • Vietnam • Vietnamese phrasebook • World Food Thailand • World Food Vietnam

ALSO AVAILABLE: Antarctica • The Arctic • The Blue Man: Tales of Travel, Love and Coffee • Brief Encounters: Stories of Love, Sex & Travel • Chasing Rickshaws • The Last Grain Race • Lonely Planet Unpacked • Not the Only Planet: Science Fiction Travel Stories • Lonely Planet On the Edge • Sacred India • Travel with Children • Travel Photography: A Guide to Taking Better Pictures

The Lonely Planet Story

L onely Planet published its first book in 1973 in response to the numerous 'How did you do it?' questions Maureen and Tony Wheeler were asked after driving, bussing, hitching, sailing and railing their way from England to Australia.

Written at a kitchen table and hand collated, trimmed and stapled, *Across Asia on the Cheap* became an instant local bestseller, inspiring thoughts of another book.

Eighteen months in South-East Asia resulted in their second guide, *South-East Asia on a shoestring*, which they put together in a backstreet Chinese hotel in Singapore in 1975. The 'yellow bible', as it quickly became known to backpackers around the world, soon became *the* guide to the region. It has sold well over half a million copies and is now in its 9th edition, still retaining its familiar yellow cover.

Today there are over 350 titles, including travel guides, walking guides, language kits & phrasebooks, travel atlases, diving guides and travel literature. The company is the largest independent travel publisher in the world. Although Lonely Planet initially specialised in guides to Asia, today there are few corners of the globe that have not been covered.

The emphasis continues to be on travel for independent travellers. Tony and Maureen still travel for several months of each year and play an active part in the writing, updating and quality control of Lonely Planet's guides.

They have been joined by over 120 authors and 280 staff at our offices in Melbourne (Australia), Oakland (USA), London (UK) and Paris (France). Travellers themselves also make a valuable contribution to the guides through the feedback we receive in thousands of letters each year and on our web site.

The people at Lonely Planet strongly believe that travellers can make a positive contribution to the countries they visit, both through their appreciation of the countries' culture, wildlife and natural features, and through the money they spend. In addition, the company makes a direct contribution to the countries and regions it covers. Since 1986 a percentage of the income from each book has been donated to ventures such as famine relief in Africa; aid projects in India; agricultural projects in Central America; Greenpeace's efforts to halt French nuclear testing in the Pacific; and Amnesty International.

LONELY PLANET OFFICES

Australia
PO Box 617, Hawthorn, Victoria 3122
☎ 03 9819 1877 fax 03 9819 6459
email: talk2us@lonelyplanet.com.au

UK
10a Spring Place, London NW5 3BH
☎ 020 7428 4800 fax 020 7428 4828
email: go@lonelyplanet.co.uk

USA
150 Linden St, Oakland, CA 94607
☎ 510 893 8555 TOLL FREE: 800 275 8555
fax 510 893 8572
email: info@lonelyplanet.com

France
1 rue du Dahomey, 75011 Paris
☎ 01 55 25 33 00 fax 01 55 25 33 01
email: bip@lonelyplanet.fr

World Wide Web: www.lonelyplanet.com *or* **AOL keyword: lp**
Lonely Planet Images: lpi@lonelyplanet.com.au